"Johannes Brahms"

A BIOGRAPHY

JAN SWAFFORD

Alfred A. Knopf New York 1997

THIS IS A BORZOI BOOK
PUBLISHED BY ALFRED A. KNOPF, INC.

http://www.randomhouse.com/

Owing to limitations of space, all acknowledgments of
permission to use previously published or unpublished material
will be found following the index.

Library of Congress Cataloging-in-Publication Data
Swafford, Jan.
Johannes Brahms: a biography / by Jan Swafford.
p.   cm.
Includes bibliographical references (p.   ) and index.
ISBN 0-679-42261-7 (alk. paper)
1. Brahms, Johannes, 1833–1897.
2. Composers—Germany—Biography.
I. Title.
ML410.B8S93   1997
780'.92 — dc21   97-29308 CIP
[B]   MN

Manufactured in the United States of America
First Edition

For my brother, Charles Johnson—

with thanks, among other things,
for all the laughs and all the patience

Contents

*Inserts of illustrations of 8 pages each will be found
following pages 134 and 390 respectively*

Introduction

A HUNDRED YEARS AGO as of this writing, on April 3, 1897, Johannes
Brahms died in Vienna. The city gave him one of the grandest funerals
ever seen in a place that loves extravagant funerals. Brahms was a prophet
very much honored in his adopted country and even, belatedly, in his
own. When he died the flags in the harbor of his native Hamburg flew at
half-mast. It was an uncommon tribute from a mercantile, matter-of-fact
town to an elusive master of an elusive art. North German Hamburg, and
Vienna, which is like nothing but Vienna—the two cities marked the
poles of his life and career.

"My God, what do you want?" Brahms exclaimed in later years to a
friend who had tried to call him underappreciated. "I've gotten far
enough!" Soon after, at the inauguration of a new concert hall in Zürich,
he looked up to the ceiling to find likenesses of Bach, Beethoven, and
Brahms. Two decades before that, in the wake of his First Symphony, one
of the leading conductors in Europe had proclaimed the formula "the
three great B's of music," the others being his companions on the ceiling
in Zürich. If Brahms was not the equal of Bach and Beethoven and knew
it, he was the only composer of his generation writing chamber and symphonic music at their level of ambition, craft, and originality, and he
knew that too.

Among his prophecies was that in those respects he was the end of the
line. Once again, in his terms, he was correct. Gustav Mahler, the
prophetic genius of the next generation whose early symphonies Brahms
knew, could only say of his own achievement, "My time is yet to come."
He meant, "when I am dead." In one way or another, most composers
since Mahler have said the same. As far as Brahms was concerned, the

heyday of his music was his own lifetime. His ultimate fear was that when his milieu fell apart, as was happening before his eyes, so would his audience. But still he knew that he had triumphed as few composers have ever done in their own era, and had done it under incredible conditions: introduced to the world at age twenty as the heir of Beethoven and the Messiah of music, having to grow to maturity with that sword hanging over him.

It is perhaps an inevitable human consequence and balancing-out that none of it made him happy. Given his personality, at once blustery and withdrawn, it is also inevitable that as the withering glare of renown turned on him, Brahms would retreat into himself, revealing less and less, placing the finely wrought mask of his music between himself and the world. Near the end of his life he exploded to old friends: "I have no friends!"

The world that he wanted to keep at bay included the necessary evil of biography. Early in his career he wrote Clara Schumann: "What would become of all historical research and biographies if undertaken with an eye to the susceptibilities of the subject?" In later years, he lectured a potential biographer in the opposite doctrine: "The chief consideration, in the selection of material for a biography of an artist or author, should be whether the facts in question were of a nature to make the artist, whom we love and honor in his art, also win our esteem as a man." Material contrary to the honor of a great man, he had concluded, must be obliterated. So he destroyed by fire and water much of the record of his life that he could get his hands on.

Did he hope to avoid the predations of biography entirely? No, he was too realistic for that. If his work had any chance of survival, biography was part of the game. Did he have something terrible to hide? Perhaps terrible to him, perhaps not so unusual from the perspective of our time, perhaps nothing so terrible in any case. His craving for prostitutes, the only major peccadillo we know of in his adulthood, was nothing remarkable for a bachelor in his day in Germany and Austria.

Still, whatever his reasons for hiding from history, and however incompletely he succeeded, his attempt had its effects. The triumph of his music, contrary to his fears, did not begin to slacken from the day of his death but persisted through the Modernist century. Yet during that period, as millions took up his music, Brahms remained an oddly isolated figure, appearing irrelevant not only to Modernism but to his own time—especially in comparison to his mentor Schumann and his rivals Liszt and Wagner. In contrast to those three, Brahms destroyed many of his personal records and never wrote a word of aesthetics or criticism or direct comment on his own or anyone else's music. His first foray into public musical politics, one embarrassing page in length, was also his last. Thereafter he wielded his influence behind the scenes, letting others fight it out onstage.

As a result, his story has remained shrouded, his art hard to place, his influence ambiguous, his person indistinct. At the same time his music, which unites magisterial perfection with lyrical warmth, a monumental style with whispering intimacy, lay in the hearts of listeners everywhere. Beyond the overwhelming presence of his music in the repertoire, his reputation has largely run in the course critics laid out in his own life-time: Brahms the conservative, the abstractionist, the great unifier of Classical and Romantic streams. Beyond that have been the millions who love his music, and the musicians who admire it the way a bricklayer admires a straight, sturdy wall.

It is important to realize that Brahms has existed that way in history because he wanted to. Rather than avoiding biography, he attempted to keep his future biographers on a short leash. From an early period in his fame he realized that strangers might be interested in what he wrote in a letter, so he guarded his pen. Most of his personal papers, unpublished manuscripts, musical sketches, receipts, musings, juvenilia, everything in reach, he either tossed out or burned or committed to the nearest river. His maid was required to leave the lid of his wastebasket open at all times; it was his most important item of furniture.

It was not because he cared nothing for history that Brahms attempted to obliterate the record of his life. It was very much the reverse: he was in awe of history. To a degree perhaps beyond any composer up to his time—and like most to come—he was obsessed by the past. He was personally involved with the development of musicology in his era, and counted among his friends several of the figures who shaped that new discipline. He owned an important private collection of composers' manuscripts, including their sketches and letters. Which is all to say: this eager student of history did everything he could to eradicate his own.

Yet he failed. Through carelessness, accident, perhaps here and there by design, a significant number of letters and a few sketches and juvenilia escaped annihilation. He failed also because one cannot put words together, no matter how discreetly, without revealing something to somebody who can read between the lines, especially when those lines are held up against the background of events. And he failed because now and then alcohol loosened his tongue, and in the decades of his fame there were people waiting to write down everything he said.

As a biographer, I can only be happy that Brahms failed in his efforts to restrain biographers. At the same time, as a composer myself, I have to admire him for the attempt. Brahms wanted the story of his music to be the story of his life. He did his best to live the same way, struggling relentlessly to escape the consequences of life and love. He wanted his biography to be the shining edifice of his music, and beyond that a brief and edifying story of exemplary service to art.

But biographers are devious, and sooner or later the attempt to hide behind his music in his life and in history becomes, of course, a theme of his biography. If in part that struggle was idealistic and exemplary, it was also temperamental. Brahms lived behind barricades of silence, jokes, sarcasm, flight, anger, and music. He hid also behind the flowing beard, the forget-me-not eyes, even behind the genius and generosity and fame. He studied Beethoven's sketches and letters and burned his own because he saw what history had made of Beethoven's letters, and was afraid his own music might not survive the operation. Well and good: his life must not sully his music. Beyond that it was his nature to hide, and at least some of what he was hiding can be discerned. That is a story beginning in the proverbial reticence of the North German, amplified to unshakable aloofness in the brothels of Hamburg, continuing through his troubled relations with men and especially with women, at once his *bêtes noires* and his indispensable muses.

Over the course of the century since he died, however, Brahms's attempts to manipulate history, though they tend to dissolve under close scrutiny, have indeed resulted in the kind of portrait he would have liked. On the whole, scholars have left him the lofty Master on the pedestal. Most of the important studies—including those of Karl Geiringer and Walter Niemann, and the recent one by Malcolm MacDonald—are divided between a brisk survey of his life and a lengthy examination of his work. Their assumption seems to be that there are not enough sources available for an intimate look at Brahms the man. And perhaps scholars have been a little overawed by the figure on the pedestal, and thus reluctant to read between the lines or illuminate the shadows.

In other words, biographers on the whole have left Brahms the privacy he wanted, have not attempted to draw him in light and shade, and have left the details to two exhaustive early works: the four volumes of *Johannes Brahms*, published in German over the years 1912–21 by his friend Max Kalbeck, and the two-volume *Life of Brahms* in English from 1905, by his piano student Florence May. Between those two writers the available facts are largely parceled out. Both authors knew Brahms close up, in the constrained way he allowed anyone to know him. Yet while both authors cover his life more dutifully than any later ones, neither study is satisfactory for a modern reader. Kalbeck's is voluminous but inchoate, the details crowding out the big picture and the story. (Mainly for that reason, his volumes have never appeared in English.) Florence May, for all her labors and her insider's understanding of the musician's life, did not attempt to probe beneath the formidable veneer of her hero.

Meanwhile, as far as we have discovered in a hundred years, there are in the story none of what we Americans call "smoking guns"—no dramatic, revealing developments. Kalbeck remains the essential source, fleshed out largely by May, a row of personal memoirs, and the volumes of surviving letters. At the same time, this century has turned up no serious and sustained attempts to understand Brahms as a person, in the context of his art and his age.

My book is that attempt. On the hundredth anniversary of his death, as a testament from the New World to the Old, I have set out to paint the fullest portrait possible with the material Brahms and his observers left us, to place him in the context of his place and time, to relate his life to his music to the degree that the two can confidently be said to relate. I do that as Brahms's music enters the period on the other side of the era we still call Modernist.

FOR MYSELF, only half-jokingly, I've called my project *Brahms ohne Bart,* "Brahms without beard." In that respect I am building on current scholarship. Years ago I was startled to come across a portrait of the composer in his handsome, thin, smooth-cheeked thirties. Only later did Brahms become the familiar bearded bear. And only in the last decade or so have we begun to realize to what degree his music grew out of his life and feelings—especially his experiences in the years *Vorbart,* before beard. In the process, the once-common wisdom of Brahms the abstractionist has faded. As with most common wisdom, there is something to that, but it is only part of the picture.

If our age has begun to understand the searing experiences that lie beneath the magisterial surface of Brahms's music, it becomes necessary to reexamine what we know of his life. It has been my intention to take him off the pedestal and put him back in the world of the living, with his feet on the ground. I have told the story largely in sequence, to convey his life as it was lived, his music as it was created. To show Brahms amid the quotidian is not to diminish him but to see his genius, his courage, and his achievement more clearly, eye to eye with those of us who have less genius, but do possess at least the perspective of time. (Time is the only real advantage a biographer has, and not one to be abused by imposing on the past the assumptions of the present.)

While avoiding unsupported speculation or psychologizing, I have tried to show the human reality behind Brahms's music—not only the individual reality of my subject, but the reality of being a musician at the summit of his trade in the nineteenth century, in a time of relative peace in Europe, of middle-class prosperity and concomitant passion for music, in a time when music was called, in Walter Pater's celebrated phrase, "the art to which all other arts aspire." That encapsulated the nineteenth century's view of tonal art, which was only natural given the unprecedented power of the work that had emerged, much of it from Vienna, during the previous century and a half.

Brahms composed for himself first, for a few close friends second, and for the bourgeois audience third. This was his approach in assessing his work: What do *I* think? What will *he* think? What will *she* think? What will *they* think? So in writing I asked, What did it mean to be a musician in nineteenth-century Europe? What were the struggles, the pressures, the expectations of musicians? What were the *terms* in which Brahms thought about his own and other music? What were the terms of his friends, who included some of the finest performers and most sophisticated amateurs of the day? What were the terms of his critics and of the music-loving, middle-class public? How did those terms intersect and diverge? How did these various groups talk about music, when music was in its prime?

In many ways the process of becoming a first-rank musician then was much the same as in any other age, a matter of unrelenting discipline, of ambitious parents and teachers working with an extraordinary talent, of endless hours in lonely rooms while the world outside pursues the normal course of life. What does that do to one's psyche, and to one's relations with the world outside music? How is that inflected by growing up when music, for the first time, was dominated by the looming presence of almost mythical creative giants: Bach, Haydn, Mozart, Beethoven, Schubert? Added to those inspirations and intimidations, what happens to a hypersensitive prepubescent boy who is required to play the piano all night in cheap brothels?

To get behind the beard I've had to read between my subject's words and deeds, to hold them up to the story and the other characters. In a much-cited letter Brahms wrote his great muse: "Passions are not natural to mankind, they are always exceptions or excrescences. . . . The ideal and the genuine man is calm both in his joy and in his sorrow. Passions must quickly pass or else they must be hunted out." This has always been called the credo of a reticent North German who indeed tried (only sometimes successfully) to hunt out his passions and destroy them. That is, however, only one dimension of Brahms's words. Also crucial is that they were written to a woman of genius who was in fact prone to hysteria, and one, moreover, whom he had in effect just thrown over. For a full understanding of what this famous letter reveals about both characters, we need to examine all these facets. Likewise it is only between the lines of letters and diaries, wisps of reminiscence, intersections of places, events, and compositions, that we can trace the long, sad passion of the aging Brahms for a young woman, and how it affected his relationship with her mother.

Naturally the story of an artist includes the story of the work, but the relation between the two is not simple. An artist's life and work run not together but in parallel streams, touching here and diverging there. Musical traditions have abstractions and kinds of logic and rules of craft peculiar to them, which occupy one profoundly whether one is a German *Kapellmeister* or the director of a Balinese gamelan. In that sense a composer's music has its own logic and development, a life parallel to its creator's, the two lives connecting in unpredictable ways. At the same time one's art is inevitably of a time and a place and a person. The work comes from everything one has seen, heard, experienced, every shaping event and circumstance and force of logic.

In other words, an artist's work distills everything an artist *is*, interacting with the nature of the art as guided and interpreted by the culture. The particular traditions are mutable, cultural; the nature of the interaction is universal. Thus the significance in the arts, tangential but persistent, of biography. The art is the vital thing. Everything else—biography, technical analysis, theory, psychology—is a prism that can turn up matters of value, but cannot encompass the art.

THE FAMILIAR PORTRAIT of Brahms has been of a creator whose work stands on its own abstract integrity. In contrast, everyone who knew him understood that his earlier music used hidden symbols to represent his life and the people in it, and that throughout his life he turned his sorrows and joys into music. Clara Schumann wrote of one work: "This piece seems to me neither more nor less than the expression of his own heart's anguish. If only he would for once speak as tenderly!" Max Kalbeck exclaimed over the ebullient opening of the G Major Quintet, "Brahms in the Prater!" and Brahms replied, "You've got it!"

Still, during the last decades as the personal experiences adumbrated in Brahms's music have been rediscovered, some writing on the arts has swung toward a position that can distort the nature and purpose of art. To put it in the context of my subject: A common illusion of the past was that Brahms epitomized the "purity" of music, an abstract perfection nearly free of personality, biography, and setting. A common illusion of the present is that art is little *but* setting, autobiography, hormones. This is the post-Marxian, deconstructed, pop-psychology version of the artist, whose archetype is Andy Warhol: an art pursued for the purpose of getting rich and powerful and famous, and so mainly of interest in what it tells us about this celebrity who so seduces and deceives us.

As I hope to show, Brahms refutes those assumptions, the clichés both of his own time and of ours. Out of the highest idealism, and at the same time hardheadedly and without illusions, he created a body of work at once remote and personal, atavistic and of an age and prophetic. In the process he employed his own life and feelings, without depending on them any more than on his superb craftsmanship. Much current biography looks at art for what it tells us about the artist, which is to say: about the Celebrity. From my own experience as an artist, I say that while doing art may help put its creator's feelings to rest, when it comes to the work those feelings are one tool among others.

In other words, I don't believe the meaning of art lies in autobiography. Autobiography is the part of the artist's tool-chest that grounds the work in the reality of life and feeling—something necessary and incapable of being faked. Autobiography is the foundation in breathing life that every art requires. But it is only a foundation, not the purpose or point. A great work is great in large part because of what it tells us not about the artist but about ourselves and the world we inhabit, including the world of sounds. The more an art speaks to our selves whoever we are, and our world wherever we are, the more "universal" it is. Accordingly, I will be concerned here not so much with what Brahms's art tells us about his life and times, as what his life and times tell us about his art, which is as nearly universal as anything Western tradition has produced.

So while this is primarily a life of Brahms and the focus is on my man, his music lies at its center. Without the music, no point to the story. All the same, unlike many Brahms biographers I haven't tried to include every piece he composed, and a biography is no place for ambitious new theories of the work. Rather, I examine all the major pieces and selected others, with the overriding goal of limning the biography of his art and its most salient *terms*—the terms in which Brahms thought about music, gleaned from the evidence of the music itself, from his surviving sketches, his words, and the responses of friends and critics. We shall see that thematic development, counterpoint, and form were the dominant technical terms in which Brahms and his age thought about music. I note that he had unique ideas about rhythm and meter and phrasing, which is something that entirely escaped the attention of his time. My musical examples are chosen mainly to illustrate particular aspects of his craft. Since the analytical literature on his music is extensive and I am writing for the listening public as well as for the profession, I have generally avoided technical language. There will be the occasional paragraph that is tricky for a nonmusician—I ask for a paragraph's indulgence, now and then.

The personal echoes—the tool of feeling that worked together with the tools of thematic and contrapuntal and formal mastery—appear to come and go in his work. For someone so reserved, Brahms could be surprisingly forthcoming about the autobiographical elements. Eventually, though, he decided that the personal aspect excused nothing in the music; from then on he largely stopped talking about it. The point at which he seems to have reached that conclusion, paradoxically around the time of the profoundly autobiographical G Major Sextet, is as good a place as any to date the beginning of his full maturity. His songs, which he composed steadily from his teens onward, functioned at times (as with most composers) like a diary. That does not mean that every song is a diary entry. Whenever I examine the personal dimension of a piece, it is because Brahms left clues to that effect or the connection is inescapable. Just as often, especially in his maturity, he needed little more than the excitement of an idea, or of a particular performer, to inspire him. Un-Romantic, unpostmodern, but true.

I should mention that I began the book intending to explore the idea of Brahmsian lyricism as revealing the "feminine" side of a composer who on the surface, at least in his bearded age, was a cigar-smoking, salty-talking old bachelor and man's man, egregiously if inconsistently misogynistic. (In fact a good deal of his life and work revolved around women, both his muses and probably the larger part of his audience.) During the writing, however, I found that having undergone a decade of obsession over gender in books and magazines and academic discourse—scholarly exegeses of "gay" and "straight" cadences in music, and theories of men and women speaking different languages and coming from different planets—I no longer have any sensible idea at all of what constitutes "male" and "female." Are lyric melody and falling-away cadences feminine, and *forte* dotted figures and downbeat cadences masculine? Shameful stereotypes, surely! The future can deal with the "feminine" in

Brahms, if the future is up to it. Besides, I'm more interested in the sexes in their messy relations than in their noble isolation.

THIS IS QUITE A DIFFERENT BOOK than my last, about composer Charles Ives. In large part, that is because as a historian I submit as humbly as possible to my subject and the nature of my material. I viewed Ives through an Ivesian prism, Brahms through a Brahmsian. One man was archetypically American, the other North German with a weakness for decadent Vienna. Besides being an idiosyncratic composer who constituted a kind of one-man milieu, Ives was a businessman and occasional philosopher, he rarely threw away anything, and his music demands much explanation and, in some degree, justification. Brahms never tried to be anything but a composer and performer, was a creature of the Austro-German musical mainstream, threw away much, and wrote music that, while it welcomes analysis, demands relatively little explanation. Brahms's work, among the most widely beloved bodies of music ever composed, has stood every conceivable test of time (which is not to say it is beyond criticism, only that it does not need justification). It is Brahms the man and his context—especially in relation to Germany in the Romantic period, to Vienna as it approached the fin de siècle, and to his rival Richard Wagner—that have never been adequately examined.

As with all Brahms scholars, my mainstays have been Max Kalbeck and the volumes of the *Briefwechsel*, the surviving correspondence. I've made occasional but critical use of *The Schumanns and Johannes Brahms* by Eugenie Schumann, daughter of Robert and Clara, who observed the entire course of the relationship between Brahms and Clara Schumann and provides, in her discreet way, not only information but insight. Some of my sources have been translated into English, some not. When good translations were available for quotes, I used them (sometimes with revisions), otherwise I translated for myself. May's *Life of Brahms*, nearly as thorough as Kalbeck's but less intimate, was done independently and adds details that Kalbeck overlooked. Of modern biographies the classic is Karl Geiringer's, first published in 1947, written from his experience as librarian of the Gesellschaft der Musikfreunde and thus overseer of the largest collection of Brahms manuscripts and letters.

While one can't commend the psychological insight of any of these three—Kalbeck is the only one who creates a figure who casts a shadow—they have long been fundamental to research and thinking about Brahms and likely always will be. For that reason none of the three is cited in the endnotes, except when a substantive quote is involved. From a basis in Kalbeck, the essential tales of Brahms's life have been told many, many times. It is the implications and the setting that I have undertaken to fill in. There are in the endnotes occasional mini-essays on technical or other matters that did not fit in the text. These notes are meant to be browsed.

There are more of Brahms's own words here than in any other study. I have tried to translate him, or revised previous translations, into more modern and idiomatic English. Most previous translations of his letters and words sound stiffer and more archaic than the German originals. To convey his oblique and ironical voice, I have used contemporary phrasing, contractions, and the like. This is especially important when Brahms is joking, as he often is, and often with a subtle grace and wit. The book is also full of letters and recollections of Brahms's compatriots—among others, Josef Joachim, his oldest friend and collaborator, Clara Schumann, his great love and first of his muses, the legendary surgeon and musical amateur Theodor Billroth, and Elisabet von Herzogenberg, who for nearly a decade may have been the person Brahms most trusted for criticism (she has gotten grievously short shrift in previous biographies). I've made more use than any other biographer of the memoirs of composer, critic, and Brahms friend Richard Heuberger, in which we find the clearest record of Brahms's preoccupation with Wagner and his despair over the state of music. The words of these and other figures form the dialogue of the story, a colloquy on art and life that went on for decades among those who were intimately involved with Brahms and his music.

My method as a biographer is to weave together the best and most relevant existing scholarship with my own research and conclusions. I hope this book will stand as an echo of Kalbeck's and May's early biographies, from a perspective on the other side of Modernism. I hope also to complement recent surveys of the music, especially Michael Musgrave's *The Music of Brahms*, Malcolm MacDonald's in *Brahms*, and Reinhold Brinkmann's admirable book on the Second Symphony, *Late Idyll*. Still in print is one of my touchstones, Hans Gal's slim but irreplaceable study from 1963, *Johannes Brahms*.

MY OWN CONNECTION to Brahms has much to do with my having stumbled into music in the first place. Perhaps the story is worth telling, because it could stand for the way many innocents around the world come to love a figure from another time and another country. It begins when I was a teenager in Chattanooga, Tennessee, playing trombone in the junior high band and having as my main ambition in life: to get on the football team.

The first thing I ever did of any account came that year, when I won first chair in an all-district band. Among the pieces we played was a number with a vaguely uplifting title, something like "The Song of Freedom." As I listened to the piece during rehearsals (trombones have interminable rests), its theme filled my heart as no music ever had. As usual, I paid no attention to the composer; it appeared to be the sort of generic school-band piece we always played. Yet for months afterward I'd run through the melody in my mind because it gave me a piercing sensation in the pit of my stomach, an unfamiliar yearning poised somewhere between happy and sad. (This time was, of course, coincident with puberty.) Then, one day, I discovered that "The Song of Freedom" had vanished from my head. Losing that bittersweet feeling was a little like losing a girlfriend, or a familiar consolation. Over the next months I kept thinking about the tune, struggling to find it again.

One night, as part of her ongoing attempts to inject some culture into her son, my mother took me to a concert unusual for Chattanooga: the New York Philharmonic under Leonard Bernstein, somebody you actually saw on television from New York, unutterably glamorous. I had rarely heard classical music outside of Bernstein's *Young People's Concerts* on TV, and never a full program by a big-city orchestra. The concert began with Bernstein's own overture to *Candide*, which seemed marvelous, then Aaron Copland's *El Salón México*, even more so.

The second half of the concert was taken up by another work and composer I'd never heard before: the First Symphony of Brahms. As the music unfolded, I experienced what many listeners did in the nineteenth century on hearing Brahms for the first time—transported by the mingled warmth and boldness of his voice, at the same time befuddled by the complexities of his melodic and tonal language. I sat in the balcony of the cavernous hall straining to keep my mind on the music but mainly waiting for Bernstein to jump up in the air again.

Finally, in the last movement came something to get hold of, a soaring theme for French horn. A flute picked up the tune while strings shimmered beneath. After a solemn chorale for trombones—at last, trombones—from out of nowhere the violins took up a full-throated melody that made my jaw drop and brought tears to my eyes. Of all things, it was "The Song of Freedom," the tune I'd played in the band months before, that I'd lost and now found again. The piece had been a band arrangement of the main theme from Brahms's finale.

After that concert I became not only a devotee of Bernstein and Copland and Brahms, I also discovered what it means to be in love with music. Music and I have had a stormy and frustrating union since, but the love endures. From that night I became a musician, and before long a composer. The wistful, piercing melancholy that overwhelmed me when I listened to Brahms and a good deal of other classical music—a depth of feeling pop music has never approached—only abated a little when I began writing music. In part, that feeling had been a longing to plunge deeper into music than listening and playing could take me, to create it for myself. The essence of that revelation I owe to Johannes Brahms. I count the night when Leonard Bernstein led the orchestra into the main theme of the First Symphony as my initiation into the most magnificent, demanding, absurd, and hopeless endeavor on this earth. Brahms, I'm convinced, felt much the same way about it.

I imagine that moment of mine as something like what Robert and Clara Schumann felt when a boyish blond stranger sat down at their piano and launched into the astounding C Major Sonata that became his Opus 1, and what Josef Joachim experienced when he first heard "Liebestreu," and likewise millions since who have in a few dazzling moments taken Brahms into their hearts. In the book I call it the Brahms epiphany. I have had it many times with him since that first time, in my forty-year journey with one of the greatest and most elusive creators in our tradition.

If there are two composers most responsible for first drawing me into music, they are Brahms and Copland. Near the end of Copland's life I was able to thank him in person. (He threw his head back and chortled, "Don't stop! Don't stop!") Among other things, this book is my thanks to Brahms for his part of the same great and ambiguous gift.

OF THOSE TO WHOM I OWE thanks for their help with the book, I begin with the readers who added to it their sensitivity and expertise: musicologist and pianist Ira Braus, Raphael Atlas of Smith College, friend and composer Steven Gerber, and Terry Desser, all of whom read the whole manuscript and made dozens of suggestions that I happily adopted. Peter Burkholder and Veronica Jochum made some incisive corrections. Thanks to the Fulbright Foundation for sponsoring my research in Vienna and at the Gesellschaft der Musikfreunde. Thanks to my editor at Knopf, Robin Desser, who once again provided the kind of insightful counsel that I thought had disappeared from the writing trade. What shortcomings that remain are entirely my own. Finally, thanks to Gilles from Chamonix, a stranger who materialized to prevent me from falling off an Alp while this book was in the works. As I said that day in my toast to Gilles: *À la vie!*

Johannes Brahms

Prologue

THE MINOR CHORDS that drive the symphony to its end reeled to their final E minor shout, and the Viennese leaped to their feet. From audience and orchestra together a hysterical bellowing and clapping erupted, an ovation like none ever heard before in the Golden Hall. Hundreds of eyes rose past the golden caryatids to the balcony where the little figure stood in the director's box. They cried out as if they could thus bring him back to life, revive him and what he embodied, to them and to the world.

Everyone in town had heard the rumor, but for most of the audience it was the first confirmation. Brahms was dying, they could see it all over him. He had risen to acknowledge the applause after each movement of this his last symphony, and everyone had looked up with a shudder, and the grieving had built through the course of the stark, sorrowful work until this explosion at the end. Brahms stood in the box leaning on the balustrade with tears pouring down his face. For once he did not try to hide them.

The sight of him was terrible, unbelievable to the Viennese. The little husky figure had bustled through the streets of the city for as long as most of this audience could remember, had stood before them in countless performances. When he was not onstage, they would catch sight of the unmistakable florid face in the audience before concert or play or opera, leaning over the balustrade to search the crowd with his opera glasses, chuckling to himself. Even the old ones may have forgotten what Brahms looked like when he first came to the city in 1862, his music unknown there but his name already legendary. In those days his beautiful North German face was beardless and fresh as a boy's. Since then the magisterial beard had become part of the city's landscape like a monument, his quips repeated in cafés, his approvals and disapprovals the stuff of daily gossip, and so for years the Viennese had hardly given him a glance and only the tourists stared. Now he stood before the tumultuous crowd at the Musikverein shrunken and trembling, the hair and famous beard stringy, eyes yellow, face sickly brown and gaunt under the sheen of tears.

The ovation roared on and on until it became almost unbearable, for the audience and for Brahms. Some of them must have been thinking: this wild hurrah for the Fourth Symphony of all things, which had always been too gloomy and austere for the Viennese. After its first performance in the city in 1886, a local wit had set words to the lilting minor-key thirds of the opening: *Es fiel . . . ihm wie . . . dermal . . . nichts ein,* "yet again he had no ideas." The city had presented Brahms the back of its collective hand often enough, but that only made the cheers sweeter when it chose to give them to him. On this night it was not for this symphony they shouted. They cried out for all the music and for the man, for Brahms who was dying, and with him an age.

He had vanished from the streets months earlier, now and then struggling out to a concert or a dinner with one of the eminent families that had adopted him. Now he spent much of his time sitting at home by the window, looking out to the looming dome of the Karlskirche across the street and beyond it to the gaslit park and the River Wien and to this hall, the Musikverein, where for twenty-five years he had seen failures and triumphs in succession, and had loved it all and loved the fickle, cynical, inexplicable people who had made music the town's glory, and its music the glory of the world.

Finally, exhausted, the crowd stuttered to silence and hundreds of eyes turned away in sorrow. Brahms still stood uncertainly in the director's box. Someone handed him his coat and bowler hat, wary of his bark if they offered to take his arm and help him down the stairs. He made his way backstage to thank the director and players, then accepted a carriage home. A year before, he would have scorned such laziness. After so many concerts he had walked home alone, across the Elizabeth Bridge and the Resselpark, past the Karlskirche to his three plain rooms with rented furniture. Now, leaving the carriage and solicitous friends with a gruff *ade,* he pulled himself up the three flights of stairs. Maybe once more before bed, as Frau Truxa helped him with his coat, he glanced through the big windows to the silhouette of the great cathedral he had seen most days for twenty-four years, all the while calling himself a vagabond in the wilderness of the world.

. . .

THE KARLSKIRCHE that lay before Brahms's window was finished in 1739, erected from the vow of Emperor Charles VI to his namesake Saint Charles Borromeo, to honor the saint and the Austrian Empire, and to reward God for taking only ten thousand souls in the plague of 1713. Once the cathedral had loomed over the vineyards that surrounded the old walled city. Like the polyglot empire it celebrated, the Karlskirche's exterior subsumes an extraordinary mélange of elements from other times and places: reminiscences of the Pantheon of Rome, the Invalides in Paris, the imagined Temple of Jerusalem. For further touches of Viennese extravagance and incongruity, the stately Classical portico is flanked by two spiral columns modeled after Trajan's in Rome and topped by Eastern-style minarets, and the wings have pagoda roofs.

The maker of the Karlskirche, Johann Fischer von Erlach, was a historian of architecture as well as a visionary practitioner. If, for all its amalgam of historical elements, the exterior of the cathedral is still a splendid and harmonious exercise in public architecture, to enter the sanctuary is to be drawn into the mystery of faith. In the interior, Fischer von Erlach fashioned cold stone into an uncanny evocation of the immaterial. As with most cathedrals, the interior concerns itself with light as quality and symbol, but few have exploited light like this one. A worshipper first sees the veined marble of the walls, the sunburst altarpiece with floating cherubs and the saint in glory. Then the eye and the spirit are drawn upward, seeking the light. From any point in the sanctuary most windows are hidden in deep galleries or recessed in the cupola. You move to find one window and others disappear. Wherever you stand, light floods in from mysterious springs, a radiance whose source, like the divine radiance, is hidden from us.

Fischer von Erlach's sermon in stone was created to make tangible the invisible, unknowable presence at the center of existence. As such it is not only a symbol of divine mystery but a prophecy of the German Romantic spirit that a century later, Johannes Brahms inherited. Like E. T. A. Hoffmann's stories, Schubert's last songs, the poems of Heine and Eichendorff and their settings by Robert Schumann, the cathedral is haunted by the Unseen.

But as Hoffmann's ghostly and vertiginous tales reveal, for artists of the nineteenth century that mystery had come to appear as much demonic as divine, as much menace as salvation: the sublime emanating not pure radiance as in the Karlskirche, but an ambiguous twilight before a night threatening despair. The German Romantic era of magical poetry and triumphant music was also an age of madness and suicide. Likewise the architectural themes from across centuries and cultures that Fischer von Erlach integrated so masterfully in the Karlskirche, the highest monument of the city's Baroque glory, had become in the crumbling empire of late-nineteenth-century Vienna the kitsch eclecticism of the Ringstrasse.

Brahms was born into the atmosphere of German Romanticism and, laboring in a long period of sporadically interrupted but still unprecedented peace and prosperity across Europe, turned that spirit to his own eclectic and history-haunted purposes—his singular integration of conservative and progressive, Classical and Romantic, atavistic and prophetic. By the night of his last concert in the Musikverein, history appeared already to have rushed past Brahms and left him at once victorious and irrelevant, stranded on his lonely promontory. In that year approaching the last turn of century before the millennium, Europe was falling toward unimaginable catastrophe, and the arts toward the corollary of Romanticism: the ferment and fever called Modernism.

Brahms saw it coming. And he could not believe that the triumphs he had experienced in his lifetime could endure, that his work could find a place in a such a world. He feared that the future would sweep away his public and his art, leaving him little more than a footnote in history. Perhaps that too lay behind his tears at the Musikverein on March 7, 1897, when with the Fourth Symphony—his last testament to the highest level of idealism and craft, and to something in the direction of despair—Brahms heard his music played in public for the last time.

CHAPTER ONE

Homeland

IN 1826 JOHANN JAKOB BRAHMS, aged nineteen, his gray eyes full of hope and good humor, arrived in the port city of Hamburg carrying musical instruments and a Certificate of Apprenticeship. He intended to make his fortune in music, which appeared to him the grandest of professions. Through the course of a long career, Johann Jakob was to discover that in fact there was no fortune to be found in that trade, at least not for a man more zealous than talented, more dogged than resourceful, with a flair for fruitless schemes. He was prepared to work his way up from the bottom, and so he would. In due course his son Johannes, who managed to be born with a talent of historic dimensions, would be expected to earn his first talers in Hamburg the same way his father had, in the same squalor. Yet for both men a childhood passion for music would survive a life of toil and care—one toiling in obscurity, the other in the unforgiving glare of renown.

Johann Jakob's people were small-town bourgeois. The family name, indifferently spelled *Brahms* or *Brahmst* or *Brams*, identified them as Lower Saxon, speakers of Plattdeutsch, the Low German drawl. Their name comes from the broom plant, *Planta genista*, called *Bram*, common as dust but sturdy and useful, whose yellow flowers cover the sandy heathland and dunes of the Ditmarsh region on the edge of the North Sea. In France, Johann Jakob might therefore have been a Plantagenet, but in Germany he was plain Brahms: child of the broom, son of the heath. In his dingy Hamburg quarters Johann Jakob would display, framed over the sofa, what he called the family coat of arms—three brambles, a wheel in a shield, a helmet, and so on. Everyone knew what that amounted to, an attempt at respectability whipped up, for a fee, by a local genealogist. In the Brahms chronicles there had been no great deeds, no shield and helm. The first history knows of them is three generations back from Johann Jakob's son, who would make the family name illustrious after all.

Around the middle of the eighteenth century the first-recorded of the clan, carpenter and wheelwright Peter Brahms, labored his way from Hanover northward until he settled in the seaport hamlet of Brunsbüttel, in fen country north of the Elbe. There Peter married and in 1769 fathered a son named Johann, grandfather of Johannes the composer. Like his father, this Johann drifted north in search of work. He took up innkeeping and selling groceries, married a country girl named Christiana Asmus, and settled in Heide, which means heath: town of Heide, area of Ditmarsh, state of Holstein, North Germany—when there was no country of Germany at all, rather a loose confederation of kingdoms and duchies and principalities and free cities. Although Heide is a little way from the coast, it has the North Sea weather of looming clouds and sudden squalls. Old Peter Brahms finally joined his son there, to spend his dotage sitting in front of Johann's inn puffing a pipe and hailing passersby. One of those passing was a schoolboy named Klaus Groth, who would grow up to put Ditmarsh and its people and dialect into the poems of his *Quickborn*, and track the generations of the Brahms family down to his friend Johannes.

Johann and Christiana Brahms had two boys, Peter Hinrich and, fourteen years later, Johann Jakob. These sons were expected to take up the family trade of innkeeping. Peter Hinrich was agreeable to that; he married at twenty and succeeded his father at the inn. He had five children and many descendants, the only branch of the family to flourish. To innkeeping he added a pawnshop, which burgeoned into a house overflowing with antiques. Klaus Groth relates that in his old age a lame Peter Hinrich spent his days in an armchair inside the door of his antique shop, pointing out favorite pieces to visitors with a stick—here a suit of armor, there a fine pot—but he could not easily be persuaded to sell any of them. Such a preference for aesthetic over financial concerns would also characterize his brother Johann Jakob (disastrously) and his nephew Johannes (triumphantly).

Johann Jakob Brahms was born in 1806. If we did not know what he grew up to be, we might call him a dreamer. As a boy he was given to wandering out on the heath, his head full of tunes. Neither school nor innkeeping interested him. What did seize Johann Jakob's attention were the bands of musicians who accompanied the eating and drinking and dancing in the family place as in most inns, who enlivened town holidays and harvest festivals and weddings. Johann Jakob was a sociable and amusing sort, dazzled by music and the laughing, skillful figures of the players. To become one of them seemed to him thrilling. When, however, Johann Jakob begged his father to let him study an instrument, Johann senior refused, in the way of parents everywhere who look on the trade of music with dismay: music is a fine thing, a fine hobby, but a treacherous profession.

But Johann Jakob would not give it up. As a teenager he began playing hooky from school once a week to take music lessons. One day his father, on a visit to a nearby village, was shocked to find his son sawing at a viola among the musicians at a dance. There was a scene and his father forbade the foolishness, whereupon Johann Jakob ran away from home to continue his studies with one Theodor Müller, a local leader of the old *Stadtpfeifer* guild.[1] In a sort of medieval-style apprenticeship, the teenager lived with Müller's family, worked in house and garden for his keep, and was taught his notes. After a while he had learned a little violin, viola, cello, flute, and French horn. When he was able enough, he began playing for his master in the town band.[2]

Twice the prodigal son returned to the inn, hoping his father would consider his career as settled. But Johann Brahms disdained the idea as much as ever, and Johann Jakob bolted again. (These escapades were noted by Klaus Groth, who learned them from Johannes Brahms, who observed in the telling: "I can't give such proof of *my* devotion to music!"[3]) At last Johann Jakob's father wearily gave in: his son was not destined for the respectable trade of innkeeper, but would be a mere horn-blower and fiddle-scraper.

On December 16, 1825, the boy of nineteen received his signed and sealed Certificate of Apprenticeship:

> I Theodor Müller, privileged and invested *Musicus* of Weslingburen in the region of Northern Dithmarsch attest herewith, that Johann Brahmst of Heide has studied three years with the *Stadt-Musicus* in Heide and two years with me in order to learn instrumental music. Now, as during his apprenticeship the aforementioned Johann Brahmst has proved himself conscientious, thirsty for knowledge, diligent and obedient towards myself, I declare herewith his apprenticeship to be over and done.[4]

Now Johann Jakob was prepared to mount the most splendid stage he could imagine: Hamburg. He parted with blessings and bedding from his parents, along with his instruments, probably a horn and flute and fiddle, maybe a contrabass on his back. He headed for the Free and Hanseatic City—proud, rich, and not as welcoming of musicians as Johann Jakob Brahms imagined, or as his son Johannes would bitterly wish.

THOUGH IT LAY SIXTY-FIVE miles from the North Sea, for centuries Hamburg had been one of the primary gateways in and out of German lands. The reason was the River Elbe, its channels spreading miles wide below the city and opening to the sea. The city's harbor brought Hamburg prosperity even before the Middle Ages, when it joined the fabled Hanseatic League of North German trading cities. Hamburg had never concerned itself as much with empire or religion as with profit. Its stock exchange, the first in Germany, was organized in 1558. It invented convoy protection for its ships in 1662, and in the seventeenth century it rode out the Thirty Years War relatively untroubled while most of Germany was left a ruin. When Johann Jakob arrived in 1826, Hamburg had some 200,000 souls and was rising toward its greatest years, in the decades around the turn of the twentieth century. The city's fleets were the largest and some of the fastest in the world, making it one of Europe's primary departure points for sending goods and immigrants and refugees to the Americas. In the second half of the nineteenth century, much of the city's wealth flowed back across the Atlantic from the United States via the Hamburg-American Line. By the 1860s the port was the largest in the German states.

In Johann Jakob's time the old city was still enclosed within the defensive walls built during the Thirty Years War to keep out the armies of Sweden and Denmark. At sunset the city still locked the gates. Five Protestant cathedrals raised their steeples; returning sailors looked for the columned tower of St. Michael's to tell them they were home. Temperate overall in weather, Hamburg was also perennially rainy, foggy, muddy, and sooty: "on the whole somewhat raw," wrote a visitor in 1783, "damp and cold most days of the year, just like most of the people."[5]

In 1826 the city roared and teemed mostly along close streets and labyrinthine alleys. The broad artificial lake called the Alster in the middle of the city connected to the harbor on the Elbe with a network of canals crossed by hundreds of bridges, the effect reminiscent of Amsterdam or Venice. Unlike Venice, Hamburg existed for business, not as a showpiece for empire or an intellectual center. There was no university until 1919, mainly because the merchants did not want professors and intellectuals meddling in their business. The medieval houses of the old town and the merchants' elegant new residences along the Alster were counterpointed by the sordid alleys and pubs of St. Pauli, where sailors and the poor lived and amused themselves. Still, everyone could enjoy the tall beeches along the Sachsenwald, the section of the Elbe called "piece of Italy," and the woods and fields and classical buildings of next-door Altona. On summer nights the Alster was filled with lighted boats and swans and music.[6]

In the way of North Germans, Hamburgers were proverbially taciturn, tight with money and with words, conservative, at the same time hardworking, unpretentious, good-hearted, ready to enjoy themselves in the traditional modes: goose at Christmas, carp on New Year's Eve, eggnog at celebrations, and a healthy allotment of beer to get you through the day. If these were the qualities of a Hamburg citizen, Johannes Brahms would run true to type.

As with all cities, music was required everywhere. The wealthy bourgeois of Hamburg wanted waltzes and polkas and mazurkas to grace their promenades and pavilions and cafés. Every theater employed musicians, and the first opera house dated from 1678. At the other end of the social scale, sailors lurching from ships into waterfront dives needed fiddlers and pianists to accompany their debauches. The city possessed an orchestra, the Hamburg Philharmonic, but it had never attained the polish of orchestras in smaller, less prosperous, but more musical places like Leipzig—once J. S. Bach's home, where later Felix Mendelssohn blazed at the summit of his short life.

Hamburg's musical glory days had been in the eighteenth century. In 1772, when historian Charles Burney visited to interview Carl Philipp Emanuel Bach, this eminent son of J. S. Bach observed to the Englishman, "You should have come fifty years ago!" In that time G. P. Telemann, J. S. Bach's more successful rival, was preeminent among musicians in the city. Hardly less important in that era was the composer, singer, music theorist, and historian Johann Mattheson. Working at the Opera, Mattheson became friends with a young violinist named Georg Friedrich Händel, and nearly ended Händel's career when he came within an inch—or rather the width of a waistcoat-button—of stabbing him in a duel. The two made up and Händel wrote his first operas in the city before moving on to find his glory as George Frederick Handel, in Britain. Staying put, Mattheson among other herculean labors wrote the first biography of Handel. In the next century the Mendelssohn family also left Hamburg for greener pastures, taking two-year-old Felix with them. By the early nineteenth century the city's lack of interest in the creative arts was so much a byword that a journalist from Leipzig entitled his observations "Musical Doings from the Unmusical City."[7]

In Hamburg, music existed as an amusement incidental to real life. For most of the orchestral musicians and the few composers, music was a job like any other. As a young man, Johannes Brahms knew all about that: "Everybody always has business on his mind," he complained. He would be the only first-rate composer actually reared in Hamburg, and the city shrugged him off. Yet for all his artistic idealism, inexplicable for a native of that place, Brahms would love Hamburg to the end of his life, in rosy exile in Vienna.

ALONG THE BANKS of the Alster the rich merchants' houses stood gleaming and straight, and the Stock Market and other marble trading edifices of the city grand and solid. This was the world of the North German well-to-do that Thomas Mann captured in *Buddenbrooks*:

> Say what you will, it is pleasant to awake every morning in a large, gaily tapestried bed-chamber, and with one's first movements to feel the soft satin of the coverlet under one's hand; to take early breakfast in the balcony room, with the sweet fresh air coming up from the garden through the open glass door; to drink, instead of coffee, a cup of chocolate handed one on a tray.

St. Pauli and the Gängeviertel, where Johann Jakob Brahms lived during his early years in Hamburg, were a warren of reeking canals and dirty passages only as wide as a wagon, stuffed with high-gabled, many-windowed, half-timbered houses that doddered in long rows down alleys, leaning like drunken sailors. When Johann Jakob arrived in the city in 1826, he began playing on the streets and in waterfront dives for small change and grog, and sleeping in squalid rooms next to the dives. He became a familiar figure in the little bands of players standing here and there, indoors and out, sawing away in the gray out-of-tune whine of musicians who play much of the day for an audience that is hardly listening. The German term, derisive but accurate, is *Bierfiedler*, beer-fiddler.

Garrulous and good-looking, Johann Jakob made friends easily. Nobody ever accused him of great intellect, but various stories recall a droll peasant wit. There was the time in his later years when a conductor declared his bass-playing out of tune and Johann Jakob rejoined, "Maestro, any decent sound from a contrabass is purely accidental." Friends knew Johann Jakob as a reliable player on several instruments, no less a reliable drinking companion, a *Bierfiedler* par excellence, a joker, a buffoon.[8]

Slowly, he got ahead. He practiced, took every job he could manage, learned the stacks of music he needed to have at his fingertips. He began to focus on the contrabass, a good practical instrument because most groups needed one. The bulky wooden box shared his narrow quarters like a wife. In May 1830, Johann Jakob petitioned successfully to be made a *Bürger* of Hamburg, testifying before Almighty God that he would honor and decently represent the city.[9] Thus he became a certified wage-earning citizen, even if his wages were fickle and he roomed in slums.

And so Johann Jakob's great plan went forward. As a necessary part of his ascent to the position of proper *Bürger*, he began courting a prospective bride. The object of his affections, Johanna Henrike Christiane Nissen, seems a curious choice as an inamorata. She was sister to Frau Christina Detmering, in whose house on Ulrikusstrasse Christiane lived when Johann Jakob came there to room, early in 1830. Christiane was small, sickly, gimpy from a short leg, plain of face though she had enchanting blue eyes (they reappeared in her son Johannes), and a complainer. When twenty-four-year-old Johann Jakob became smitten with her, she was a spinster of forty-one.

Christiane came from a line of town-councillors, pastors, and teachers, her family manifestly more respectable than her suitor's. Though her father had been a tailor, she could claim a real coat of arms, tracing her mother's side of the family back to illustrious names in the fourteenth century. But Christiane had grown up frail and plain and found no husband, and had done small handiwork from the age of thirteen. In those years, after a day's labor at sewing outside the house she would often come home and help her mother sew until midnight. At nineteen she became a household servant and remained one for ten years; then there was more sewing, for eight years at a Hamburg firm. Legend calls Christiane an exquisitely skilled seamstress. Nothing remains of her life's labor, but she had to be skilled, to live. After her sister married longshoreman Johann Detmering, Christiane moved in with them and they opened a shop, "Nissen Sisters—Dutch Wares," which meant sewing articles and other small goods.[10]

When Johann Jakob Brahms began courting Christiane a week after he took up residence in Ulrikusstrasse, she thought he had to be joking; it was unbelievable. After all, though poor he was a fine-looking figure of a man, with a handsome forthright face and flowing brown hair; and his dark gray eyes were roguish and merry. Surely he could find a younger and prettier wife. But Johann Jakob proposed, and appeared to be earnest about it, and Christiane's brother-in-law Detmering persuaded her that she should accept: it was her last chance for home, children, happiness. "And so," Christiane was to write her son Johannes shortly before she died, "I considered it Destiny."[11] Christiane and Johann Jakob were married on June 9, 1830.[12]

There is no indication of why Johann Jakob chose Christiane, but a likely reason in his mind was that, having become a *Bürger*, he intended to be a proper one, and that meant having a wife and children, and the sooner the better. If the reasoning sounds elementary, his son Johannes would share more or less the same North German bourgeois ideal. Besides, Christiane was a fine seamstress and her experience as a servant made her a splendid cook and housekeeper. Friends described her eggnog and bilberry fritters as "famous." Her son would become a connoisseur of fritters and of Germanic cooking generally.

In her later years a family friend called Christiane, approvingly, "a little withered mother who busied herself unobtrusively with her own affairs, and was unknown outside the house."[13] Few noticed her intelligence, her plainspoken wit and articulateness. Though her husband would not have cared, she seems to have been well read. (Biographer Max Kalbeck's idea that Christiane Brahms could quote all of Schiller by heart is an embellishment[14]—an attempt to conjure up some explanation for the unaccountable sensibilities of her son.) Christiane's letters to Johannes reveal her as reasonably literate, archetypically motherly, shrewd in understanding his needs and gifts.

As far as Johann Jakob was concerned, Christiane would be a fastidious *Hausfrau*, perhaps grateful for his saving her from spinsterhood. He probably aspired to no more complicated a household. He had married up in the social scale; her life may have been easier after she joined him. Apparently their first years together were relatively happy, however shabby their setting. It would be only after some three decades under the same roof that their incompatibility, and the cumulative effects of their seventeen-year difference in age, overwhelmed them.

The Brahmses changed houses nine times in their three decades together,[15] much of the moving due to Johann Jakob's restlessness and his financial mishaps. In February 1831, daughter Elisabeth, called Elise, was born. Soon afterward, Johann Jakob joined the Hamburger Musikverein, a sort of trade union that he hoped would improve his prospects. If it did, the trend was slow to develop. Johann Jakob spent much of his time at the Musikverein's clubhouse, where jobs were posted and there was a pub on the premises.[16] In 1833 he moved the family to a ramshackle half-timbered house on Specksgang—"Bacon Lane"—in the Gängeviertel, the "Lane Quarter."

At that point and for a long time after, the Brahmses were nobodies living nowhere. The Gängeviertel was an area of dark streets and passages, infested with sailor's dancehalls that doubled as brothels—hence the familiar Hamburg name for the place: "Adulterer's Walk." As late as 1892 a sanitation inspector said of the Gängeviertel that he "had never seen such unhealthy places, pest-houses and breeding-places for every infection. . . . I forget that I am in Europe."

The house on Specksgang fronted not on anything so respectable as a lane but on a narrow alley. Christiane and Johann Jakob probably lived on the first floor in two tiny, low-ceilinged rooms, a kitchen/entrance and a sitting room with sleeping closet. Unlike most of the houses in the Gängeviertel, this one was set back from the street by a small littered court, and on that account given the hopeful name Schlutershof, "Schluter's Court."

They lived there only two years, but that was enough to make the house live in history. It vanished, along with most of Hamburg, in the Second World War. Photographs show a five-storied front like hundreds of others in the city, covered with windows hanging crookedly from their frames, out of true like the whole place. From these windows wives leaned out to shout at their husbands and their urchins, the din of shouts and rough laughter echoing up and down the squalid alley in a suffocating human symphony all day long and into the night. Inside was the smell of smoked meat and cabbage and herring and unwashed tenants. The scene was brutal, the kind of thing of which Dickens made a dark poetry. This is the world Johannes Brahms awoke to. He was born in Specksgang on May 7, 1833.

JOHANN JAKOB laid out some of his scarce funds to announce in the *Weekly News* that he had produced a son.[17] The baby was named for his grandfather and father: Johannes, son of Johann. When he was a child, the family called him "Hannes" and "Jehann." When he was grown and famous, his father would start signing himself "Johann" instead of Jakob[18]—the son re-creating the father. At the new baby's christening at St. Michael's on May 26, 1833, his grandfather Johann Brahms came down from Heide to stand as godfather along with Uncle Philip Detmering. Apparently, in his childhood Johannes would be taken on a visit to Heide only once, and old Johann died when the boy was six.

In 1833, the year Johannes was born, other figures and factors destined to appear in his chronicle had milestones large and small. The scattered German states took a step toward the old dream of unity by creating the Zollverein, the Customs Union (without Holstein and Hamburg, who were prideful of their freedom). Since the wars of the

Napoleonic years and their negation in the 1814–15 Congress of Vienna, Europe had been generally peaceful; but it was an enforced peace, with great repressions and ensuing resentments simmering under the placid surface of what, in Germany and Austria, would be named the Biedermeier Era.

By the time of Brahms's birth, music was becoming king of the arts, the position it would occupy for the rest of the century. That resulted above all from three generations of composers who had worked in Vienna—Josef Haydn, W. A. Mozart, Ludwig van Beethoven, and Franz Schubert. In 1833 Beethoven had been dead only six years, but his memory loomed over living composers like an awesome ancestral presence. Schubert had died in Vienna a year after Beethoven, with his full stature yet to be understood.

Elsewhere in Europe in 1833, French composer Hector Berlioz was thirty and notorious, Frédéric Chopin twenty-three and finding his way in Paris, Franz Liszt twenty-two and worshipped, Gioacchino Rossini forty-one and retired, and Felix Mendelssohn twenty-four with some of his best work behind him. Meanwhile, Anton Bruckner was nine, Johann Strauss, Jr., eight, Josef Joachim two. Richard Wagner and Giuseppe Verdi were both twenty, Verdi wondering if he was talented enough to write operas, Wagner convinced of his genius but not quite decided what to be a genius at. Clara Wieck of Leipzig was a famous piano prodigy at fourteen, shortly to become a sensation. Her future husband, Robert Schumann, was twenty-three, recently a piano student of Clara's father, and had composed his astonishing first opuses for the piano. In 1834, Schumann would found the *Neue Zeitschrift für Musik* and make it the most important journal in Europe promoting progressive composers.

The Brahmses' second son and the last of three children was born in February 1835 and christened Friedrich, called Fritz. Apparently, that year Johann Jakob secured his first steady job; he began playing keyed bugle in the brass band of the Second Jäger-Bataillon of the Hamburg Bürgerwehr, the town militia. (The Free City had its own post office, diplomatic service, and military.) Johann Jakob prized his green uniform with the embroidered collar and high pompom. From the job and the uniform he acquired a small steady paycheck and a little respectability. Fortunately the Bürgerwehr required no actual military discipline and occupied much of its time with splendid parades. Johann Jakob had only to show up for a half dozen "watches" in the winter, and in summer a few exercises before the city gate, which were followed by crowds of children.[19] He would keep his place in the band for thirty-two years, until the militia was dissolved.

From 1831, Johann Jakob had been a substitute at a better job, with a sextet that played daily from noon to midnight at the Alster Pavilion. The café lay on the promenade of the Jungfernstieg, on the southern edge of the Inner Alster. There the fashionable families of Hamburg liked to stroll and drive along the rows of lindens, looking out to the swans on the water and the little boats passing under low bridges, in and out of the canals. Besides wealthy *Bürgers* of the town, patrons of the Pavilion included tourists, literati, and artists. Eduard Marxsen, Hamburg's leading piano teacher and composer, took his coffee there, enjoying the music dispensed by the sextet.[20]

The group consisted of two violins, viola, contrabass, flute, clarinet, plus whatever instruments the members could double. They played overtures, operatic arrangements, the latest waltzes from Vienna, and the like. For nine years, Johann Jakob substituted at the lowest rung of the sextet, mostly playing horn and handing round the plate.[21] That may be how he met Eduard Marxsen and others on the higher levels of the *Bürgertum:* with begging bowl in hand.

Finally in 1840 the bass player of the Alster Pavilion sextet was so good as to die, and Johann Jakob took his place as a regular. The militia and the sextet would be his slim staples for many years. In the 1840s he also found work playing bass in town theaters. Years after, his persistence would secure Johann Jakob a job in the bass section of the Hamburg Philharmonic; even in old age he kept up his other instruments and apparently was a capable flutist. All the same, typical of the meager and backhanded progress that characterized his life, there was no pay for the Philharmonic rehearsals so he had to keep taking jobs in theaters and cafés and beer gardens.[22] Until Johann Jakob retired on a pension from his famous son, a *Bierfiedler* he remained.

As the years went by, the family at least felt a sense, or an illusion, of improvement however halting. Whenever there was a little money to spare, though, Johann Jakob was apt to become ambitious to bad effect. He lost a good deal of the family savings playing the lottery, and tried raising chickens, rabbits, and pigeons, all with unfortunate results. When Hannes was three they moved from Ulrikusstrasse to marginally larger quarters at Erichstrasse, in grimy, crime-ridden St. Pauli, and two years later back to another place on Ulrikusstrasse.

In 1839, Hannes began attending a private school on the Dammthorwall; at eleven he was placed in a school run by a Johann Friedrich Hoffmann on A-B-C Strasse. This school was progressive, with a strong course in mathematics and natural history, a gymnasium, and an atmosphere less tyrannical than that of most schools of the day. There, besides his usual lessons, the boy would acquire a fair reading knowledge of French and English, useful to citizens of a seafaring town. In 1846, Hannes wrote extended Christmas greetings *"à mes chers parens . . . par leur fils Johannes Brahms."*

Johannes grew up surrounded by water, the immense expanses of harbors and the canals lapping at the feet of ramshackle houses, and everyplace littered with boats, from the fishing smacks and skiffs that moored in the canal at the foot of Fuhlentwiete to the great fleets of sailing ships, the forests of high masts and furled sails that stretched numberless along the docks on the sea-restless Elbe. Like all Hamburg children, he spent years exploring the dockside and the warehouses and granaries and butcher shops there, and he dreamed of ports in America and the East. Yet though he prowled the byways of the old city throughout his youth, the slums and where the tumbledown edged into antique charm, though he knew the docks as well as he knew Scripture, Brahms would never happily set foot on a ship in his life, and never board an oceangoing one at all. He had an instinctive fear of sailing, one more thing that made him a peculiar native of Hamburg. He would travel much, by preference on solid land. Sailing measureless seas was not his style. The Eisenbahn, the iron road, would be his vessel.

From early on, what fascinated Hannes, far more than the romance of an old harbor town, was music and musical notation, the arcane language of dots and flags hanging from lines. At age six, not quite clear that there already was such a thing, he invented his own method of writing down music.[23] Johann Jakob was delighted to discover that his boy had perfect pitch—not a guarantee of talent, but a good sign. Even better, Hannes loved to play "Katz und Maus" and the other children's games that were always accompanied by song; even when he was tiny he could sing any number of tunes for you in his piping voice. When Johann Jakob practiced at home, the boy would leave his toy soldiers and come listen, then sing back what he had heard.[24]

Johann Jakob took it as a matter of course that his son would take up his trade. He would start the boy in music himself, then turn him over to teachers who would make him into an orchestral player, the highest level of success Johann Jakob himself aspired to. To that end, Hannes would work his way up in the musical world just as his father had, such as it was, playing fiddle or cello or horn, and perhaps someday end up in the Hamburg Philharmonic. That would be a banner day, a proud achievement, when Hannes did that.

All this was the style of the time: one found a niche and stuck to it. After the early Napoleonic wars, the nineteenth century was an era of unprecedented social and economic stability in Europe. Wars flared only briefly, and ran their course with far less destruction than in the past (or the future). During this century the middle class triumphed not only economically but in its influence on social and artistic life. Three decades of relative peace and conformity followed the aristocratic restorations of the 1815 Congress of Vienna, which as far as possible turned the clock back before Napoleon. The time is captured in the term *Biedermeier,* with its implications of bourgeois domesticity, cozy interiors, sentimentality, philistinism, and kitsch. The characteristic design elements of the era were the household chair and the chest of drawers.[25] The operative tone was *Gemütlichkeit,* meaning something on the order of cozy, sanguine, wine-enhanced good cheer. *Nur immer gemütlich!* went the saying: Take it easy, don't get excited.

Prosperous, bustling, conservative Hamburg suited the era and its style. In the Biedermeier, between 1815 and 1848, life seemed good and getting better for those, like the Brahmses, who did not stop to notice how fragile and police-enforced the *Gemütlichkeit* was. Across Europe the complacency would shatter with the barricades and cannons of 1848. But outside that flare of revolution, quickly suppressed, no extended wars or social upheavals troubled the course of Johannes Brahms's life, and he left the scene before European peace of mind departed for good. In those decades, writes Brahmsian Hans Gal, "The course of a successful man's life . . . was of almost trivial uniformity; it could be practically reconstructed from a set of surveyable given conditions.[26] Whatever imagination, genius, innovation, touches of nonconformity Brahms grew up to, he would never entirely outgrow that style, those North German bourgeois and Biedermeierish ideals: loving wife, cozy kitchen and parlor, laughing children, and a respectable position.

WHEN HANNES WAS ABOUT FOUR, Johann Jakob began teaching him the useful instruments violin and cello and the valveless *Waldhorn.* Thus he would find a trade and a place in the world. Hannes became good enough on cello to manage the Romberg Concerto. But the boy unaccountably demanded to learn the piano. Where did he get such ideas? There was not even a piano in the house. Johann Jakob resisted his son's demand for three years—there was no place for a pianist, he reminded Hannes, in the Hamburg Philharmonic. Finally, perhaps remembering his own childhood obstinacy, he gave in.[27]

In 1840, Johann Jakob took his seven-year-old to the home of Hamburg piano teacher Otto Friedrich Willibald Cossel and drawled, "My Hannes should learn as much as you know, Herr Cossel, then he'll know enough. He dearly wants to be a piano player." The studies began, and Cossel took to the boy. Delicate and blond, with his mother's forget-me-not eyes, Hannes would show up for lessons sometimes barefoot, sometimes in clattering wooden shoes. He would sit his tiny form down before the big keyboard and attack it with a large determination. His progress was remarkable, but once again the strange obstinacy turned up, as though the child had some vision before his eyes that only he could see. Now he insisted to Cossel that he wanted to learn how to compose music, not just play it. But that would be another struggle, in due time: if the piano seemed impractical to Johann Jakob, composing was an absurd indulgence for anybody expecting to make a living at music.

When he began teaching Brahms, Otto Cossel was twenty-eight. By then, defeated by a weak heart, he had given up his own hopes of becoming a keyboard virtuoso.[28] He was still an able pianist who had studied with Eduard Marxsen, Hamburg's leading light. Cossel tended to teach the children of less well-to-do families and gave them all the time he had, so he lived not much better than the Brahmses. Devoted and meticulous, he kept the boy at his scales and exercises and sonatas, his Czerny and Cramer and Clementi.[29]

Johannes would never quite become a virtuoso either, but from Cossel he picked up a solid foundation on the keyboard. Besides the technical and analytical part of playing, his first master taught Hannes that music was more than an ordinary job. The fingers "should be able to express what the heart feels." That was the meaning of technique, not virtuosity for its own sake.[30] So Hannes learned something he would not forget: musical skill, whether of the fingers or the composer's craft, is inextricably connected to the heart.

For his lessons with Cossel, whom he began seeing nearly every day to practice and study and talk about music, Johannes was at first forced to walk a considerable distance between school, home, and teacher. In 1842 the Brahmses' boarder on Ulrikusstrasse left to marry and Johann Jakob moved the family to a smaller place nearby, at No. 29 Dammthorwall. The flat was tiny for four people. Johannes practiced when he had to on a shabby upright piano that Johann Jakob installed in the parlor, with family and friends chattering noisily around him. Whenever possible Hannes practiced outside of the house, at his teacher's or at local piano stores. Meanwhile, Cossel brought his own family to the Brahmses' previous place, to be closer to his pupil.

In other words, Cossel was now organizing his and his family's life around his student. By the age of eight this little boy from the slums had acquired the aura of the extraordinary that would surround him for the rest of his life. Already Johannes commanded not only respect but devotion from older musicians, without his asking or expecting it—and sometimes with his snarling resistance. Even Cossel's other students recognized the primacy of this one. At home it was the same; Hannes was his mother's golden child and would remain that to her last day.

So Brahms grew up a favored son and behaved like one, with an air of privilege. At the same time he could hardly be called pampered. The family was too poor for that, and the job of becoming a soloist too exacting. To Johann Jakob this son was a mystery and in some ways a disappointment. Years later Brahms said to a friend, with a bitterness unusual when he spoke of his family: "If my father were still alive and I were sitting in the orchestra in the first chair of the second violins, then at least I could say to him that I had accomplished something."[31] All the same, Johann Jakob knew musical talent when he saw it. He cannot be said to have stinted on his son's education, even if prodding from his wife probably had much to do with it. Johannes got the best teachers Hamburg had.

The other children got what was left over. Elise would always be a burden, afflicted with chronic migraine headaches that could keep her in bed for weeks. (Johannes had migraines too in his childhood, but outgrew them.) Elise looked a good deal like her brother but without the aura, the penetrating intelligence in the eyes, or the sheer attractiveness. Because of her health Elise could learn little; she would live at home, collecting her one-taler-a-week allowance, until her mother died. She seemed content to play her role as semi-invalid and patient virgin, and to help keep house as best she could. She adored flowers and birds, shiny floors and tidiness, entertaining friends. Ostensibly with affection, Christiane Brahms called her daughter the *dicke dumme Deern*, the "fat dumb peasant."[32] Always the two women of the house teamed up against Johann Jakob's foolishness and impracticality.

Brother Fritz, not afflicted like their sister, reasonably bright and talented but only so much, had the more difficult task psychologically: to live in the shadow of the golden child. Like Johannes, he resisted his father's attempts to make him an orchestral player and took up the piano, following his brother with the same teachers but to less effect. If he took on music as a profession, he did it in his negligent fashion, without Johannes's drive or his ruthlessness. The brothers never exactly feuded, but were never close. Most of the time Johannes simply ignored Fritz. Great talents, geniuses, may sometimes illuminate those around them, but not always, and in any case a favored child goes hard on the others. Considering what he had to work with, maybe Fritz did all right for someone who came of age known around town as "the wrong Brahms."

In 1841, Uncle Philip Detmering died and the Brahmses borrowed three hundred marks of his estate from his widow, Christiane's sister, to set up another Dutch Wares shop, with frilly curtains and embroidery in the windows, at the house on the Dammthorwall.³³ Hannes was still progressing marvelously on piano; to Otto Cossel he seemed a phenomenon, a prodigy. What had begun as Johann Jakob's idea of a practical education on the keyboard had slipped into something of another order—an intense and disciplined training toward a career as a virtuoso. That may well have happened without Johann Jakob's even being aware of it.

Still, Johannes did not have the relentless education in music that some suffer, among them Beethoven. It was not all piano and study. At home he spent hours on the floor arranging toy soldiers in parades and battle formations, the martial music and the fury of battle roaring in his mind, sighting the cannons, laying out his rifle battalions as later he arranged the forms and forces of his music. (Perhaps the bright-painted lead figures reminded him of his father, parading with the militia in his Jäger-Bataillon uniform.)

In May 1842 a fire broke out in Hamburg, spreading from the medieval Deichstrasse to roar through the city for four days, one of them Hannes's ninth birthday. The boy watched the terrifying glow in the sky, the roiling smoke and flames approaching the house. The police appeared to tell the neighborhood to pack up and get out. Then, like a miracle, the wind shifted and the house stood. When the inferno had run its course, a third of the inner city was consumed and a tenth of the population homeless. The elegant Jungfernstieg lay in shambles, though the Alster Pavilion survived.

After this historic disaster Hamburg rebuilt with little effect on its prosperity. That same year the Hamburg-Bergedorf section of the Berlin railroad opened, bringing the city's first experience of a staggering new speed in moving goods and people. From the small two-track station you set out in the spindly cars that looked like conjoined post-coaches, behind a little smoke-belching locomotive whose engineers stood on an open platform at the back. For Brahms the line presaged a life dependent on railroads for his career as well as his vacations. Like many working

Hamburgers, his family used the new line to go out to Bergedorf and relax at the inn Zur Schönen Aussicht (At the Beautiful Prospect).[34]

Still, while the city rebuilt from the fire there was less time or money for music. For a while Johann Jakob had no work at the Alster Pavilion.[35] That threatened the always shaky family finances. Johann Jakob probably concluded that if the boy could play the piano nicely now, he was going to have to earn his keep with it. In 1843 Hannes survived a wagon running over his chest; he recovered after six weeks in bed, with no lasting effects. Convalescence from the accident may have kept him from hard labor for a time, but he would not long be spared a dismal initiation into the profession of music.

In 1843, Johann Jakob pulled together something of a formal debut for his son. It was a private benefit concert to raise money for Hannes's studies, and to show off to the paying public the ten-year-old who played the piano like a grown-up. The program included a Mozart piano quartet, a Beethoven quintet for piano and winds, and a virtuosic étude by Henry Herz. Johann Jakob contributed his bass-playing to the occasion. His son's performance seems to have done credit to his family and his teacher Cossel.

But the results of the concert were too dramatic for Cossel's taste. An impresario who had been in the audience took Johann Jakob by the arm and offered to take the boy—why, the whole family—across the ocean to the United States: this blue-eyed prodigy could make heaps of money on those golden shores. Perhaps the scenario the promoter had in mind was to present tiny Johannes as younger than he was, a wunderkind like Mozart.

Johann Jakob was naturally bedazzled by the scheme, but this time so was Christiane. To the teacher's wife she declared, "Look here, Frau Cossel, if we go to America and Johannes plays there, we can live in hotels and I won't have to do any more scrubbing."[36] In short order the Dutch Wares shop was sold, at a loss, to collect funds for the trip. (Widow Detmering would not get back a groschen of the money she had loaned the Brahmses until a decade later, when she received it from Johannes.) Glorious strategies were spun out in the parlor. Our Hannes is going to be another Mozart! In America!

Otto Cossel was horrified. He knew that prodigies are fragile creatures; the great majority of them crash and become nothing. This uprooting and sailing and American show business he could only see as a disaster for a student just ten years old, far from what he could become if he kept on track. How, Cossel reflected in desperation, could he convince the parents to give up this idiotic scheme? He had given Johannes a fine foundation in music, but this teacher's true service to art, and his immortality, lie in this: he had the courage and the insight to let go of what he recognized as an extraordinary talent.

It would not be easy to do. Cossel brought Johannes to his one-time teacher Eduard Marxsen and asked him to take on the boy. In three years, Cossel told Marxsen, he had taught the child everything he knew about the piano. If Johannes was to develop properly, he needed Herr Marxsen's superior gifts as a teacher and musician. Besides, the boy wanted to compose and Cossel could not help him with that. (He had tried, without success, to discourage composing as a distraction from practice.) Presumably Cossel added in his proposition to Marxsen a more pressing reason to get a more advanced teacher: the parents needed something as impressive as Marxsen's opinion to get them to give up this mirage of Hannes making them rich in America.

Then in his late thirties, Eduard Marxsen was more experienced than Cossel, had seen more and better students come and go.[37] Upon hearing this ten-year-old play, he was impressed but not overwhelmed. As he probably sized up Johannes, here was a child obviously gifted and diligent, but one who took to the keyboard more as to a duty than as a fish to water. That is how great pianists take to the piano, even before they become great. Johannes might become a fine player, even a soloist, but he did not seem likely to develop into a true virtuoso. Something held him back. He hadn't the fire in the belly.

Marxsen told Cossel he was crazy to give up this student. The boy was doing perfectly well under his tutelage and he should stay there. But Cossel would not retreat. Day after day he appeared at Marxsen's door to renew his plea. A few months later, Johann Jakob also showed up, entreating the Herr Doktor to teach his son.

Under this assault Marxsen finally gave in, to the extent of agreeing to give one lesson a week; the boy should also continue with Cossel as before. Somewhere in these maneuvers the American boondoggle was dropped. So one more of Johann Jakob's schemes came tumbling, leaving the family worse off. After some months of sharing Johannes, Cossel once more declared that he could not trust himself with this kind of talent. Only then did Marxsen agree to become the boy's sole teacher.[38]

If Eduard Marxsen assessed Johannes as having no great promise as a virtuoso, he was an earnest child and his progress at the piano continued steadily. But with that curious persistence for one so frail and dutiful, the boy kept prodding Marxsen to help him with composing. He was already doing it on the side, in fact by age eleven had composed a piano sonata that he played for a young musician named Luise Japha, whom he had met at a piano store where he practiced. Luise, seven years older, thought the sonata quite a feat for his age.

Marxsen tried to keep his student's mind on his work: You can compose all in good time, my boy, now do your scales. But Johannes would not be put off. So once again Marxsen relented. He began looking at his pupil's little songs and piano pieces, initiating him into the arcana of musical theory and the forms of music as perfected by the masters of the past. Very soon it became clear to Marxsen what had been holding back this student. Here was the real thing, the fire in the belly.

YEARS LATER, Eduard Marxsen recalled the period when he first discovered Johannes Brahms's gift.

> When I started teaching him composition, he exhibited a rare acuteness of mind which enchanted me, and, insignificant though his first attempts at original creation turned out to be, I was bound to recognize in them an intelligence which convinced me that an exceptional, great, and peculiarly profound talent was dormant in him. I therefore shrank from no effort or work in order to awaken and form it, that I might one day rear a priest of art, who should preach in new accents what was sublime, true, and eternally incorruptible in art.[39]

At the time, Marxsen was probably less lofty in his attitude. He had always been more a practical composer than priest of the sublime. A compact man with plump cheeks and a sardonic glint in his eye, Eduard Marxsen was Hamburg's most prominent musician in those days—well read, well dressed, a notable pianist and prolific composer. His music was Mendelssohnian in style, and included many fashionable "homage" pieces for piano, the honorees including Jenny Lind and Clara Schumann.[40] Still, his most celebrated effort was an 1835 arrangement for orchestra of Beethoven's *Kreutzer Sonata*, the sort of thing that later in the century would be understood as an aberration.

Where Otto Cossel had been earnest and in awe of Johannes, Marxsen was flinty and worldly, with a hardheaded perspective on the profession. In his fashion, though, he was also a generous and idealistic artist. "I'll never forget," Brahms recalled, "how he refused to accept the heavy moneybag that my father had saved up for the lessons: he wouldn't take it, yet I was to come four times a week and it would be a pleasure for him to teach me."[41] Marxsen would rear this pupil as an idealist and no less a shrewd professional.

Johannes still did much of his practicing at Otto Cossel's house and in piano showrooms. (He stayed close to his first teacher; as late as 1857, Brahms stood as godfather to one of Cossel's daughters.) Although Marxsen continued to teach the boy piano, as Johannes moved into his teens composition and theory took precedence. The training was based on the towering Germanic musical tradition that had been created mostly by artists of living memory. Marxsen had studied in Vienna with men who had personally known Mozart, Haydn, Beethoven, and Schubert. Those composers were Marxsen's touchstones, as well as J. S. Bach, whose work had been nearly forgotten and was only now being explored, like a vast half-known territory. The forms, craft, and principles of these demigods defined what Marxsen meant by the "sublime, true, and eternally incorruptible in art."

Marxsen made sure Johannes knew these composers exhaustively and founded everything he composed on their example. At the same time the boy was allowed room to find his own voice, what Marxsen called "new accents" on the eternal patterns of musical language. By age eighteen, with the first works he allowed to survive, Brahms possessed something that cannot be taught: a musical voice audibly grounded in tradition and at the same time unlike any other ever heard. In his recollections Marxsen took some of the credit for that, and he deserved it. In more than one sense, he had reared a priest of art.

The great Viennese had been the composers most responsible for raising Western music to the peak of its influence, "the art to which all other arts aspire." That would not have been said in any earlier age. The overwhelming presence of Haydn, Mozart, and Beethoven—later joined by Schubert and Schumann—would make the past increasingly present in the musical repertoire, as it had not been in the time of Bach and Mozart, when most music heard had been new music.

In the course of the nineteenth century, the discipline of music history first flourished and the concert hall became a museum as well as a proving ground for the latest music. Increasingly, listeners no longer wanted to hear new work for its own sake; they wanted to hear certified Masterpieces. In Brahms's training in the 1840s we see that process already at work. Marxsen gave his student mostly those masterpieces, and very little music by living composers—perhaps a hint of Chopin, not all that much Schubert, the occasional piece of Marxsen's own.[42] It would be Luise Japha, years later, who first told Johannes about Robert Schumann.

As the months went forward, Marxsen found composition opening the boy's intellectual curiosity to an extraordinary depth and breadth. In and out of music, Johannes leaped at everything given him, took it in and made it his own. Along with the lessons Marxsen gave him books, and the boy devoured them too. Though he was to be a freethinker in religion, Johannes pored over the Bible beyond the requirements for his Protestant confirmation.

His teacher had never seen a talent like this, and he was willing to stake his reputation on it. In 1847, when Felix Mendelssohn died and Johannes was fourteen, Marxsen declared to friends, "A great master of the musical art has gone hence, but an even greater one will bloom for us in Brahms."[43]

At the same time, Marxsen had to have wondered where it came from. A little towheaded slum child like this, son of that blockhead Johann Jakob and a simple goodwife like Christiane, with a weak-minded sister and a brother of no great gifts—how could he have acquired this depth of talent and intelligence, this idealism and ambition, this endless curiosity, this thirst not only for skill and knowledge but also for wisdom? How could he have known so unerringly, from the beginning, where he wanted to go?

NONE OF THOSE MYSTERIES can be answered—not what lay behind those bright blue eyes, what was going on in the child's head as he gravely lined up his toy soldiers, why the passion for books and Scripture and everything to do with music. Neither then nor later, through years of talking about his life, did Brahms really reveal himself. Nor from moment to moment could you tell what would come out of him, or why. From his childhood on, sometimes what came was kindness, sociability, volubility. At other times it was slashing sarcasm, an imperious indifference to everyone and everything except his own concerns.

Later, when he and Luise Japha became friends, she admired the younger musician greatly but did not really like him. When she knew him, Luise said, Johannes was *sehr herbe im Wesen:* very harsh, bitter, acrid in nature. Eventually, when he had money and power in abundance, he showed enormous generosity. Nearly everyone close to Johannes Brahms understood that underneath it all he had a great heart. But in dealing with him face to face you rarely got beyond the surface, and much of the time that surface was *sehr herbe im Wesen.* So, like Luise, all his friends were wary of him. He could bite as well as bark, and he had wounded them all.

Why were there doors inside Brahms that he never opened for anyone? Never opened in his golden-boy childhood, nor in his gruff maturity? It is one of the great questions of his life. Only some of it can be accounted for. But clearly in his youth there were dark counterweights to his brilliance and eagerness, his sunny virtues.

As with every child raised in an exacting discipline, with long hours in lonely rooms, the rest of life and education took second place. That is the only way to train a virtuoso. Most of Brahms's closest friends in later life had gone through something comparable as children. The eternal problem is that such an upbringing teaches you how to make music but not how to be a friend or a lover or husband or wife: how to *live*. To the degree at least that Hannes still spent time with his parents, he absorbed from them something of life's pleasures and values—Johann Jakob's waggery and garrulousness, Christiane's generosity and her love of books. Brahms would say that some of the happiest hours in his life were spent by the fireside talking with his mother. When it came time, he launched into adulthood with extraordinary poise and fine North German common sense.

Yet his maturity remained incomplete, his socialization crippled in startling and frustrating ways. Despite his sociability, much of the time Brahms seemed to have something better to do than be with a friend or a lover, and he could express it with wounding heedlessness. He shared that self-absorption with the virtuosos he called friends. A good deal of the time, for all the mutual love and admiration, they could hardly endure him or he them.

Besides the repercussions of a virtuoso's education, humiliating experiences weighed on him. They came from the time of his first paying jobs, which rose from his family's poverty, compounded by an all-but-fatal ignorance.

As soon as Hannes was able, Johann Jakob took it as a matter of course that he must start playing for money. There is no record that Christiane objected. Eduard Marxsen may never have known about it. They were a poor family and, with Elise incapable, it was the boys who had to bring in money. That meant starting in St. Pauli near the docks, playing piano in dives.

The waterfront places in Hamburg were known as *Animierlokale*, roughly "stimulation pubs." For their clients fresh from sailing ships the *Lokale* handily integrated the services of dancehall, bar, café, and whorehouse, integrated them also in the persons of the "Singing Girls" who served the food and drink, sang and danced with the customers, and took them upstairs for more intimate services. The St. Pauli girls hung around in a flock by the door, their low-cut dresses catching the attention of passing gents. Inside, the dancing was continuous. The house pianist sat at a clangy, out-of-tune piano playing songs and dances all night long, the traditional pay *twee Dahler un duhn*, two talers and all you can drink.

Johannes began playing in the *Lokale* of St. Pauli in 1846, before he turned thirteen. Often he went to bed at home only to be dragged up by his father at midnight and sent down the street to play until dawn. After a few months of it he was weak, anemic, tormented by migraines. But he was kept at the jobs until better came along, off and on through that year and maybe longer.

His months in the *Animierlokale* do not seem to have interfered with his studies or his intellectual growth. Once Johannes's fingers had learned the requisite waltzes, polkas, mazurkas, and such, he would place on the piano rack a novel or a volume of poetry and read the night away as he played, leaning into the book nearsightedly, the revels going on behind him. It sounds almost charming. But the effects of the *Lokale* on him were deep and indelible. For the rest of his life, with friends or in his cups, Brahms would recall those nights as dark and shameful. No one has had a harder time of it than I have, he would say, and narrate the shocking details. He told one beloved that "he saw things and received impressions which left a deep shadow on his mind."[44]

It had not been all polkas and poetry. Johannes was surrounded by the stench of beer and unwashed sailors and bad food, the din of rough laughter and drunkenness and raving obscenity. He had to accompany the bawdy songs, he had to turn around and look sometimes at the drunken sailors fondling the half-naked Singing Girls, and he had to participate sometimes too. Between dances the women would sit the prepubescent teenager on their laps and pour beer into him, and pull down his pants and hand him around to be played with, to general hilarity. There may have been worse from the sailors. Johannes was as fair and pretty as a girl.

Many years later, in Vienna, the old Brahms got drunk and broke up a birthday dinner by branding all women with a word that nobody would repeat. Later that night, walking it off with a friend, he spoke disjointedly of what he had seen and suffered in those places. In a seizure of anguish and rage he cried out: "You tell me I should have the same respect, the same exalted homage for women that you have! You expect that of a man cursed with a childhood like mine!"[45]

Everything that happens plays a part in an artist's life. What elevates one and not another to the level of genius is not only talent and ambition and luck, but a gift for turning everything to the purpose. Many first-rank creators have had traumas in their lives—Beethoven's drunken father and his chronic illness and deafness, Robert Schumann's mental decline, Bartók's sickly childhood. With Brahms, it was first of all the lowlife of Hamburg. The Singing Girls shaped him along with the training in music, the novels and poetry. The brutal dichotomy between the squalor of his home and the *Lokale* with his playing jobs in bourgeois theaters and restaurants, and with the idealistic intensity of his studies and his reading—all that is one with the story of his music.

As he approached puberty, Brahms was steeped in an atmosphere where the deepest intimacies between men and women were a matter of ceaseless and shameful transaction. That sense of human relations haunted him for life. He felt intimacy as a threat, female sexuality as a threat. To preserve yourself, look away, get away! Even before puberty his relations with women were subverted: "You expect *me* to honor them as you do!" All his life Brahms would sustain a taste for whores and a deep-lying misogyny.

True, this attitude only exaggerated norms of his time and culture. Hamburgers like most North Germans were proverbially taciturn and reserved. In the terms of a later era, all Germany was misogynistic, the role of women relentlessly circumscribed by *Kinder, Kirche, und Küche* (kids, church, and kitchen). Only women of unusual talent and courage could break through those boundaries. Many unmarried men resorted to prostitutes in an era of repressed sexuality, which was constrained further by the scarcity of birth control, the ubiquitous threat of syphilis, and a prudery that left sexual matters unmentionable in polite society.

Brahms was driven beyond those dismal norms. As a grown man, he suffered from what Freud would name "degradation in erotic life": he had difficulty sleeping with women he loved, had difficulty loving women he slept with.[46] In his relations with women he was possessed by the old, poisonous dichotomy of virgin and whore.

Even so, his fear and hatred of female sexuality was only part of the equation. In regard to women too he turned away from corruption toward the ideal: the poetry on the whorehouse piano. His need for women contended incessantly with his scorn. Starting with his mother, a few women would play an irreplaceable role in his life and music. He admired those women extravagantly and depended on them and fell in love with them, all without giving up a contempt for their sex that now and then boiled to the surface, sometimes in jokes, sometimes in wrath. In his mind the women he loved must be talented, and must be eternal virgins. And he must not soil them with his lust.

The sharp dichotomies of experience in his teens played other roles too, however hard to pin down. Johannes lived amid irreconcilable

worlds: the elegant pavilion and the whorehouse, the ideal and the degraded. His teacher Cossel told Brahms to make his fingers express his
heart; Marxsen taught him to submit passion to relentless craftsmanship.
In his maturity, his art would be marked by a reconciliation of elements
that would seem irreconcilable had he not resolved them so magnificently, so nearly seamlessly.

These conflicting elements have been given names such as Classical
and Romantic, Apollonian and Dionysian. In his maturity, Brahms's music amounted to this: passion constrained within abstraction, personal
anguish dissolved in impersonal form. Before that, the whorehouses
taught him something in the direction of the same lesson, in a more soul-
searing way: Hide! He would live as a revered master with something to
hide. In and out of music, he would become adept at masking his feelings,
his identity.[47]

Which is to say, in the meanness and corruption of brothels something
was crushed in the young Brahms, and at the same time something lib-
erated—if he could survive the experience. Perhaps that is a common element in the story of genius: beyond talent and ambition and luck, in
some degree you have to be forcibly booted out of everyday life and
everyday goals.

In any case, it was like that with Brahms. The fulfillment of love was
denied him so that other things might take wing. In degraded places he
formed an implacable compulsion to follow his course whatever the obstacles. For all his delicacy of build and romantic exuberance, he reached
adulthood tough as nails, without illusions about himself or about humanity. What tortured him was that he understood what he had gained
and what he had lost, and he could never stop grieving for what he had
lost.

So in his teens Brahms played tunes in places mean and gradually better, and he read books, and with the guidance of teachers he made himself a very fine pianist and a creative genius of the highest rank. The
abuse he suffered in dives was a kind of tragedy; it created a dangerous
fissure in his psyche. Yet he not only survived that shame but exploited
it, turning the random events of his life to the purpose—as genuine creators must. In later years, Brahms spoke of the *Lokale* with as much pride
as bitterness: "I would not on any account have missed this period of
hardship in my life, for I am convinced that it did me good."[48] Other
times there was anguish, but never real regret. He never blamed his parents for subjecting him to the experience (though others did). The *Lokale*
steeled him. He felt the shadow lingering on his soul, and he prospered
in it.

At the same time, these experiences left him with an impetus to hide, to shroud himself, to escape—into his own, and into loneliness. Whether the dark side of life that Brahms endured early had a direct or indirect or symbolic relation to his music, its joining of irreconcilables, may be left to conjecture. In ways both clear and unsearchable, the Singing Girls marked and molded what he became, and so molded his art. Not least, they left him with a simple but compelling ambition: to get out of there. Yet all his life Brahms would return to places like the *Animierlokale* and over and over revisit the scenes of his degradation, and also re-enact his escape, his victory.

CHAPTER TWO

Kreisleriana

BY THE SUMMER OF 1847, Christiane and Johann Jakob Brahms could no longer ignore the plight of their son. By day Hannes was the precocious high-minded music student, by night a piano-tinkler in brothels. Headaches tortured him; he had become anemic and overwrought. Likely in the *Animierlokale* he dosed himself with the unlimited supply of drink to ease the oppressiveness of the places. Sometimes in the mornings he could only make it home by staggering from tree to tree. He was fourteen years old.

His father had gotten Hannes into that predicament; now his father got him out of it. Playing at the Alster Pavilion, Johann Jakob made the acquaintance of an amateur musician named Adolph Giesemann, who owned a paper mill and farm in Winsen-an-der-Luhe, a hamlet south of Hamburg on the Lüneburger Heath. Giesemann was an aficionado of Johann Jakob's Pavilion sextet, and also enjoyed listening to the gabby bass player go on about his talented sons Hannes and Fritz. In the spring of 1847 the talk turned to the older boy's health. Johann Jakob made a proposal: let Hannes come out to Winsen for a few weeks to live with the Giesemanns, get some sun on his pale skin, and teach piano to daughter Lieschen. At the end of his next visit to Hamburg, Giesemann took the boy home with him.

Johannes had never been out of the city for any length of time, but he took to the country as if born to it. In Winsen during this and the next summer he found a love of forests and hills that never left him. Here was presaged the Brahmsian seasonal rhythm of city man in winter and spring, outdoorsman in summer and fall. From that point too, his works would mostly be conceived during walks in woods and countryside. And the cure worked spectacularly. After weeks of drinking milk and wandering in the woods and swimming in the river, Brahms turned a corner into a lifetime of robust health.

As in his later career, these two Winsen summers were working vacations. He brought with him a silent practice keyboard and every week took a steamer to Hamburg for a lesson with Eduard Marxsen. He got in the habit of rising at the farmer's hour of five a.m. to have a swim in the river. After breakfast and piano practice, Frau Giesemann would send him into the fields with his keyboard and notebook, with orders not to come back until dinner.

From the dirt and inglorious dives of Hamburg, Johannes had been transported into an Edenic idyll, with a little sister to share it. His pupil Lieschen Giesemann, one year younger, accompanied him on treks around Winsen. Besides her lessons and her pleasure in music, Lieschen shared Johannes's passion for books. They roamed the heath looking for flowers, sat in the shade reading. A local boy they befriended, Aaron Löwenherz, was willing for a small fee to sneak books for them from his mother's lending library. One of them was a play called *The Robbers*, by Schiller. Johannes had never heard of this author but thought him quite fine. More compelling to the friends, though, was the medieval romance *The Beautiful Magelone and the Knight Peter with the Silver Keys.* Johannes and Lieschen sat in the fields reading aloud that tale of a knight inspired by a minstrel to go adventuring, who finds and loses and regains an eternal love.

With the serendipitous good fortune that marked his early life, practical experience fell into his lap. The Giesemanns liked to spend Sunday afternoons after church in a pub at the nearby village of Hoopte. As the grown-ups talked, Johannes would sit at the piano and run through his repertoire of dance tunes. That led to an offer to try his hand at conducting the local men's chorus.

It probably seemed like a joke at first, the slight, girlish boy leading a group of men. But the men of the chorus were charmed by this teenager's aplomb, his knowledge, his forceful if childish time-beating. Unanimously, they declared Johannes their conductor. The twelve members practiced in a schoolroom or around a billiard table in a Winsen bar; now the practices were called to order by the soprano voice of their blond maestro. That summer Johannes wrote two pieces for his men's choir— an "ABC" song, consisting of the alphabet in four-part harmony, and a "Postilion's Morning Song."[1] The next summer he would arrange a couple of German songs for them, the first record of a lifetime's concern with folk music.

None of Brahms's Winsen music survives. In later life he obliterated those pieces along with his other juvenilia, demanded the return of his letters and musical manuscripts from the Giesemanns, and despite his old benefactors' tears destroyed them too (some of that music was dedicated to the family).[2] With a ruthless instinct for recognizing and seizing what he required, Brahms drew from the experience of Winsen what it could teach him, how it could save him, then covered his tracks. He did not want history nosing too much into what the German language calls his *Bildung*—his growth in knowledge and wisdom, his creative and sentimental education.

In Winsen the teenager continued to inspire people to do things for him without his seeming to ask, or even to notice. As his teachers had discovered, there was an aura around him. A town official, Amtsvogt (Bailiff) Blume, offered his piano for practice and spent hours with Johannes playing Beethoven in four-hand arrangements—the way much orchestral and chamber music was heard in the nineteenth century. Johannes became friendly with choir member and music teacher Alwin Schröder of Hoopte, who made himself available for questions of music theory. One day Schröder delivered his young friend late to the worried Giesemanns, telling them that Johannes had gotten lost and simply gone to sleep out on the heath, his keyboard and notebook by his side.

Lieschen Giesemann remembered another day, when the fourteen-year-old had just arrived from Hamburg, pale and frail, and ran afoul of some older rowdies at the river. She found little Hannes, his long hair bedraggled, stripped of his notebook and everything else in his pockets, crying on the riverbank. Since the culprits were still playing in the water, a wrathful Lieschen went down and demanded her friend's things back, and got them.

After the piano and his compositions, that notebook was the most important thing in Johannes's creative life. Probably it was an early stage of the collection he would name "Des jungen Kreislers Schatzkästlein" (The Young Kreisler's Treasure Chest). In it, he was copying down quotations from books he had read. The Young Kreisler of the title is Johannes himself, in his alter ego.

FROM HIS TEENAGE YEARS, when he became attached to literature and history and Scripture, Brahms looked to books for knowledge and wisdom. As someone who thought in tones and felt clumsy with language, he was willing throughout his life to let writers articulate ideas for him. Thus the quotes of "Des jungen Kreislers Schatzkästlein" that filled several notebooks from his teens and twenties. After a lapse of decades he would put down the final entries, in a shaking hand, in the last months of his life.[3]

The "Schatzkästlein" is the record of Brahms's *Bildung*—the part of it he allowed to survive. Like a diary in other people's words, the notebooks sketch out a conception of music and art that he shared with his age. Its title and the figure of the half-mad composer Kreisler he gleaned from E. T. A. Hoffmann, who with his stories and criticism initiated the high noon of musical Romanticism. The title "Young Kreisler" also echoes one of the iconic books of that era, Goethe's *Sorrows of Young Werther*, the story of a poet who kills himself over a frustrated passion for the betrothed of a friend.

Brahms took the quotes and aphorisms of "Des jungen Kreislers Schatzkästlein" largely from German Romantic writers. Carl Dahlhaus dates the musical part of Romanticism between Viennese landmarks: from Beethoven's late works and Schubert's early lieder around 1814, to the combination of Arnold Schoenberg's "emancipation of the dissonance" and Richard Strauss's backward-looking opera *Der Rosenkavalier* in 1914.[4] Like all periods, the Romantic is a vast, cloudy, and self-contradictory affair, different in each country and in each medium, yet the zeitgeist was pervasive and powerful.

Literary and philosophical ideas defined the era. When Johannes read *The Beautiful Magelone* he unknowingly steeped himself in a founding element. Romanticism is named for the medieval prose narrative called the romance, one example of which is *Schöne Magelone*—not the real medieval but the Romantic-medieval, a fairy-tale world of gallant knights and minstrels and fair maidens and sorcerers. That in turn suggests one of the foundations of Romanticism, a turning away from the Classical notions of beauty and logic that dominated the eighteenth century, and an embrace of the boundless territory of creative fantasy. As a product of fantasy, art could conjure a world beyond this one, a place infinite and mysterious. And art was the only thing that could bring us to that territory. (Already a doctrine like that implies the course of Romanticism through the century: art merging with religion, eventually taking over religion, finally *becoming* religion, and artists priests in that religion.)

Through the course of the century the corollaries of these intuitions played out in myriad ways, but for all the contradictions some essentials are plain to see and hear. In the nineteenth century there rose a craving to shatter boundaries, leave old forms behind, throw over tired notions of beauty and taste. What we call the Classical period of the eighteenth century exalted the lucid, objective, unpretentious, universal, and finished. Its defining figures include the rationalist philosophers of the Enlightenment and the composers Haydn and Mozart. The Romantic period of the nineteenth century preferred the subjective and emotional, the characteristic and idiosyncratic and fantastic, the nationalistic, the grand and terrible, the quality of *the sublime* that passes human understanding. Its figures include the philosophers Herder and Schopenhauer, the writers Hoffmann, Novalis, Eichendorff, and Heine, the composers Schubert, Schumann, and Berlioz.

In Germany, the heart of the Romantic movement, Goethe spanned Classical and Romantic in literature as Beethoven did in music (music generally following in the wake of literature). Above all, Beethoven expressed for the first time in music the overwhelming force of an individual personality. His music seems to take each of us by the shoulders and shake us, speaking person to person, saying: *I am telling you something of supreme importance.* Still, during the nineteenth century, which saw the ascendancy of the middle class across Europe, all those cloudy intuitions were counterbalanced by a rejection of anarchy as such, and in practical terms by the pressures of the marketplace—artists had to live largely by selling their wares to the bourgeoisie. The marketplace and the holding back before the specter of anarchy served as brakes on the boundless creative imagination of the era.

The Classical era admired restraint, practicality, the practical present; the Romantics exalted the emotional, the idealistic, the mysteries of past and future. The eighteenth century exalted Greek architecture and formal gardens and ironic detachment; the nineteenth preferred savage forests, castles in ruins, and a different kind of irony. The philosopher Schlegel defined Romantic irony as the creator's freedom to shatter his own illusions on the page, to break his own mirrors: the creator refusing to submit even to his own creation. A characteristic musical product of the Classical era was *sonata form*, a musical grammar and syntax that unfolded with great freedom, yet as logically as a well-wrought essay. The characteristic Romantic product was a fragment: the art song, the little character piece for piano, the prelude that is a prelude to nothing in particular.

As part of the Romantic fascination with the past came a new discipline in studying it. During the nineteenth century, history, musicology, and ethnology flourished. In the process the past became even more enchanted as more of it was revealed—still Romantic because distant and unattainable. Meanwhile, obsessed with history and with art and artists, the Romantic era raised creators to the status of pedestaled demigods.

Now began the cult of Genius. Accordingly, the art of the past began to accumulate in books and museums and concert halls, piling up to burden the artists of the present.

If the age exalted both passion and scholarship, no less did it honor simplicity and directness in authentic forms, or forms masquerading as authentic. In his 1778–9 collection *Stimmen der Völker (Voices of the People)*, the philosopher Herder declared folk poetry the wellspring of all poetry, a spontaneous and ingenuous outpouring of a people's soul. Goethe sponsored the epochal collection of German folk poetry called *Des Knaben Wunderhorn* (The Youth's Magic Horn). Assembled by Achim von Arnim and Clemens Brentano in 1805–8, the *Wunderhorn* became a resource and inspiration for generations of poets and composers.

Yet much of the work in those collections turned out to be ersatz. A great deal of what passed for "folk" music and poetry had been written by professionals, sometimes working anonymously, sometimes under pseudonyms. After the *Wunderhorn*, creating verse and music in folk style became a commonplace. (One day Brahms would play that game himself, in some of his Hungarian Dances.) In the hands of Franz Schubert the German art song, called lied, became a sublimation of folk song into sophisticated forms. (Brahms was to make folk song the model for many of his lieder.) At the end of the century, Gustav Mahler achieved in his *Wunderhorn* settings an uncanny evocation of the atmosphere of folk poetry and fairy tale.

Another collection championed by Herder and used by countless composers from Schubert on, including Brahms, was Scottish poet James Macpherson's "translations from the ancient Gaelic" of fragmentary epics by the bard Ossian—books in fact largely penned by Macpherson himself. This kind of pseudo-mythology, admitted or covert, is manifest in the vogue for building "ruined" castles from the ground up, and in the fake-medieval citadels erected by King Ludwig of Bavaria. Some young Romantics dressed in yellow waistcoats like Goethe's young Werther and cultivated Romantic yearning, and sometimes followed their hero to the end of the story as suicides. Many Romantic touchstones (folk music and poetry, perhaps nationalism itself) proved like "Ossian" a delusion or a pose or a beautiful fraud.

The obsession with the past in both scholarly and imaginative dimensions, the myth of "authentic" folk art as the soul of a people and a nation, the exaltation of yearning and the supernatural—these hungers and hazy imaginings lay behind the language and metaphor of the age, and its characteristic blurring of boundaries in the arts. Novalis turned from philosophy and declared poetry the ultimate reality: "The more poetic, the more true."⁵ Robert Schumann, torn in his youth between poetry and music, determined to compose poetic music and declared that novelist Jean Paul, "with a poetic companion-piece, can perhaps contribute more to the understanding of a symphony or fantasy by Beethoven" than a critic or theorist.⁶

Beside Schumann the rhapsodic critic and poetic musician, some Romantic composers turned more forcefully to words to inspire and justify their notes. In 1830, Hector Berlioz composed his *Symphonie fantastique* on a program of an artist's opium dreams; thereby he sparked the great age of Romantic program music. In voluminous writings, Franz Liszt and Richard Wagner enlarged on the position that music could no longer properly exist at all without a literary or dramatic foundation. Their "Artwork of the Future," whether written for stage or concert hall, was music built over a gigantic apparatus of words, of poetry, myth, philosophy, feuilleton, screed, and rant.

The age's interpretation and interpenetration of history and poetry and music and myth and philosophy evidenced an unprecedented self-consciousness. The Romantic era was the first to name itself. Obsessed by the past, the age obsessively attempted to define its own zeitgeist. "Romanticism," wrote Jean Paul, "is beauty without bounds—the beautiful infinite."⁷ Walter Pater wrote that the essence of Romanticism is "the addition of strangeness to beauty." Every artist painted himself into history, amid the intimidating company of pedestaled Geniuses. Brahms became an archetype of this pattern, in thrall to the past and what he called "the tramp of giants" behind him.

The literary-based creed of Liszt and Wagner was in part a revolt against earlier Romanticism, which upheld the primacy of instrumental music over vocal. (That would remain Brahms's Romanticism, despite all his vocal music.) In that aesthetic, music without words was called superior *because* it has no defined subject but is rather absolute form, expressive in the abstract, pure suggestion. Possessed by history, nineteenth-century theorists codified and deified the "abstract" instrumental forms perfected by Haydn, Mozart, and Beethoven—above all the principal named "sonata form."

If Classical-era grammar and syntax brought nonreferential instrumental music, and its abstract formal devices such as sonata form, to a point of superiority over vocal music and word-setting, it was exactly that achievement that Liszt and Wagner were accused of betraying: music, having divested itself of subservience to the word, was once again to be harnessed to words even when the orchestra played alone. Wagner rejoined: Music, in whatever partnership, will always be the superior art.

In the 1840s, when Brahms was receiving his education in Romanticism, a historic battle loomed around these questions.

Inevitably in an age when artists exulted in the unattainable and irrational, there was inherent in Romanticism a neurotic frustration and a taste for the bizarre. In his fatal passion for a friend's betrothed, Goethe's Young Werther suffers not only literally but symbolically from what he cannot attain; he leaves himself with nowhere to go but the dark portal of death. Artists and thinkers and aesthetes of the early nineteenth century took up Werther as a symbol of the age. In midcentury, Wagner revived the old romance of Tristan and Isolde as another image of the zeitgeist: a love-death is the only transcendence possible for his lovers. Which is to say, a tendency to despair—whether interpreted negatively by Goethe or positively by Schopenhauer and Wagner—was inherent in Romanticism's yearning for the infinite. Over time, that despair infected both individuals and the spirit of the age.

Meanwhile the novelist Jean Paul established the literary motif of the *Doppelgänger*, the terrifying mirror of oneself walking in the world. Franz Schubert caught the weirdness of that image in setting verses of Heinrich Heine: the poet sees a figure standing in despair before the house of an old love, discovers it is his double, and cries out: "Pale companion, why do you ape the torments of love I suffered in this place, so many nights, so long ago?" Ludwig Tieck wrote a play called *Puss in Boots* that satirized philistines and Enlightenment rationality. The main character is a tomcat, and the piece constantly comments on its own existence as a play, breaking out of the dramatic frame like a series of mirrors. In literature, Doppelgängers and mirrors proliferated, representing the endless mystery of reality and identity.

These were the kind of intoxicating intimations among which young Brahms, who came to call himself Young Kreisler, formed his own shadowy identity during his teens when, as he was to write his closest friend, "chaotic emotions seethed in me."[8]

THE FIRST ENTRY in Johannes's "Des jungen Kreislers Schatzkästlein" comes from the mystical philosopher-poet Novalis, the second from Jean Paul (the most quoted writer in the "Schatzkästlein"), whose rhapsodic novels as much created as embodied the Romantic spirit. The opening citations in the "Schatzkästlein" are abstract, philosophical. Novalis: "Hypotheses are nets, and only he who throws them out catches something; was not America itself discovered through hypotheses?" And the second citation, from Jean Paul: "Many blooms open themselves to the sun; only one perpetually follows the sun. My heart, be like the sunflower; be not only open to God, but also obey Him." And then Shakespeare, the Romantics' preferred dramatist, from *The Merchant of Venice:* "Bring the musicians out. How sweetly the moonlight sleeps on the hills!"[9]

Rocked by events and feelings and ambitions he could not yet grasp, the aspiring artist seized on Jean Paul's raptures to speak for his own:

O Music! Echo of a distant harmonious world! Sighs of the angel within us! When the word is speechless, and when the embrace, and the weeping eye, and our voiceless hearts lie lonely in our breasts: O, then only through you may men call to one another in their dungeons, and their faint sighs unite in the wilderness![10]

The book is diary, aesthetics, and prophecy of what was to become of Young Kreisler after a marvelous and grueling education in sentiment and in life. Johannes quotes Herder: "Loneliness is to the unfortunate one as a peaceful harbor, outside which the sorrows of other men storm, without disturbing its waters."[11]

The ecstatic images of Novalis turn up again and again: "Our life is no dream, but ought to be and perhaps will become one."[12] Novalis writes as if in anticipation of Brahms's mature music: "Lucid intellect coupled with warm fantasy is the true, healthy food of the soul."[13] And again, foreshadowing the Alto Rhapsody, "Every sickness is a musical problem, its healing a harmonic resolution."[14]

Yet even if less quoted in the "Schatzkästlein," E. T. A. Hoffmann is the presence behind it. The title of Johannes's notebook came from Hoffmann, and so did his alter ego.

In the beginning of the nineteenth century the Romantic spirit turned up the fantastic figure of Hoffmann as symptom and archetype. Among other endeavors, he wrote fantastic fiction, poetry, music, and music criticism. More than any other single figure he created the Romantic agenda as it applied to music, both as spiritual force and as architecture: he was the first to write about the "structure" of music. Across Europe, Hoffmann helped establish music as the most Romantic of arts in an era when the arts as a whole were regarded (by artists certainly, but often by the middle-class public as well) as the most important intellectual and spiritual endeavor of the human race. He claimed Haydn and Mozart for the Romantic movement, especially the demonic Mozart of *Don Giovanni.*

The third initial in Hoffmann's name stands for Amadeus, a name he gave himself in honor of Mozart. His gaze stretched back into what at the time was considered the distant past in music, to the sixteenth century and Palestrina. His magic opera *Undine* of 1816 was the first German Romantic opera, the beginning of a line that led to Carl Maria von Weber and Richard Wagner. His stories, meanwhile, helped establish themes and standards for fantastic and supernatural fiction. Jacques Offenbach's fantasy oper *Tales of Hoffmann* was a natural subject for its era.

The first important music critic in a century when the critic would become a ubiquitous adjunct to the concert hall, Hoffmann was mainly responsible for elevating Beethoven to the status of demigod. He did that above all in his 1813 review "Beethoven's Instrumental Music"; those pages, Carl Dahlhaus writes, "set the tone of musical discourse for an entire century."[15] Like most of his musical generation and the ones before and after, the young Johannes Brahms read in Hoffmann's Beethoven article:

> [Music] is the most romantic of all the arts—one might also say, the only genuinely romantic one—for its sole subject is the infinite . . . music discloses to man an unknown realm . . . a world in which he leaves behind him all definite feelings to surrender himself to an inexpressible longing.

Inexpressible longing, Johannes read, sitting beneath a tree in a Winsen glade, or beside the harbor in Hamburg. And this:

> Every passion—love, hatred, anger, despair and so forth . . . is clothed by music with the purple luster of romanticism, and even what we have undergone in life guides us out of life into the realm of the infinite.

Life, the teenaged Brahms read there, one's own life, all human life and emotion, can be encompassed in music that intimates a world apart and better. Music evokes an existence beyond this one, toward which the soul inexpressibly yearns. *Music is the voice of the inexpressible.* So, in the heart of his essay, Hoffmann writes,

> Beethoven's music sets in motion the mechanism of fear, of awe, of horror, of suffering, and wakens just that infinite longing which is the essence of Romanticism.[16]

That infinite longing, Johannes read, *which is the essence of Romanticism.* Hoffmann took these dazzling and cryptic metaphors further. In the Beethoven essay, with a characteristic turn of mirrors, the true author vanishes. It turns out that the one supposedly writing all this is not Hoffmann at all, but his alter ego: "The gifted lady who indeed honored me, Kapellmeister Kreisler, by today playing the first trio. . . ." Hoffmann placed the article in a series of writings and stories called *Kreisleriana,* circling around the fictional half-mad Kapellmeister Johannes Kreisler. His name is taken from *Kreis,* "circle," and thus signifies "Circler."

For the teenaged Johannes Brahms, the mirroring of the name Johannes, the fact that Hoffmann/Kreisler was a composer like himself[17]— these were reasons the dreamy young artist refracted his identity between mirrors he called Brahms and Young Kreisler, and why Kreisler became his Doppelgänger, shared with Hoffmann: an alter ego of an alter ego.

One of the most enigmatic stories in the *Kreisleriana* cycle is called "Johannes Kreisler's Certificate of Apprenticeship." For the boy Johannes Brahms, this story begins as if directly addressed to him, and to his yearnings: "Now that you, my dear Johannes, really want to escape from your apprenticeship and seek your own fortunes in the wide world, it is only fair that I, your master, should stuff a certificate into your pouch so that you have a passport to show to all musical guilds." It had been with just such a Certificate of Apprenticeship that Johann Jakob Brahms had come to Hamburg. To his son, perhaps, Hoffmann's story amounted to a similar but secret and mystical credential, no less personal to him: "Ah, my dear Johannes, who knows you better than I do, who has so deeply looked into you, nay, has looked out from inside you?"

In Hoffmann's "Apprenticeship," the music master/narrator tells a story of a "quiet, friendly youth, whom we call Chrysostomus." (A clue there: in Hoffmann's unfinished novel *Kater Mürr,* Kapellmeister Kreisler is born on St. John Chrysostom's Day.[18]) This youth tells a story-within-the-story, actually related to him by his father (another level of story), about a stranger who appears at a castle and bewitches the nobleman's daughter with fables and songs—something like Count Peter in the *Magelone,* Brahms would have noted. But the tale takes a malignant turn. After learning the art of music from the mysterious stranger, the maiden elopes with him; when her father rides out to search for her, he finds his daughter murdered in the forest, her body lying beneath a stone.

Upon hearing the tale, Chrysostomus is drawn with strange fascination to the fatal stone. After his father teaches him music, the youth conceives an uncanny project: to re-create the songs of the murdered girl, hinted at in a wild notation in the mossy designs of the rock where she was killed. The story-within-story-within-story concludes with her enchanted melodies singing in his mind as Chrysostomus lies dreaming on the stone: "Its veins blossomed into dark carnations whose fragrance rose almost visibly in bright, sounding rays. The rays condensed, as the long crescendo of the nightingale sounded, into the figure of a beautiful woman, but the form was again one of divine, delightful music."[19]

"As you can see, my dear Johannes," the music master concludes to his apprentice Kreisler, "the story of our Chrysostomus is most educational." The tales within tales, the young man dreaming the song of a murdered maiden from the notation of mosses on a stone, the dream figure of a woman who is also flower and fragrance and bird and light and music, is a parable of what to Kreisler, to Hoffmann, and to a great degree to Brahms and the Romantic century, *music is*, as it floods our senses and our spirits with visions fantastic and ungraspable. As the music master explains to his pupil Kreisler in the "Certificate":

> Our realm is not of this world . . . for where in nature can we find, as painters and sculptors do, the prototypes of our art? . . . But then, does not the spirit of music, even as the spirit of sound, pervade all nature too? . . . Music . . . is the universal language of nature, speaking to us in beautiful, mysterious sounds, and we wrestle in vain trying to confine these in symbols, those artificial notes no more than hints of what we have heard.

Having poetically intimated nature as the fount of music to Johannes reading in Winsen's woods and fields, at the end Hoffmann the magician creates one of his most dizzying shifts of identity: "This cross will . . . serve as seal to this Certificate of Apprenticeship, and thus I sign my name—which is also yours: Johannes Kreisler." Thus Kreisler, who is Hoffmann, confers his seal of mastery on himself. What could be more Hoffmannesque, more Kreisleresque, more Brahmsian, than this self-created circle of personas?

As a teenager contending with chaotic emotions, Johannes Brahms lived in Hoffmann's hall of mirrors that seemed to spread in every direction and to whisper directly to him: "Johannes . . . your music has really moved the beloved's heart," says a character in *Kreisleriana*.[20] So perhaps did Young Kreisler dream. In another story, Kreisler sits at the piano playing one chord after another, in turbulent modulations, rhapsodizing between: "They carry me to the land of eternal yearning, but as they take hold of me, pain awakens and attempts to tear out of my breast."[21] There music sings directly from a suffering heart. And indeed, in *Kater Mürr* Hoffmann encourages others to enter his hall of mirrors: "I will never be convinced that the bizarre name Kreisler was not smuggled in and substituted for a quite different family name."[22] That other, secret name, Johannes thought, could be his own.

In that labyrinth of identities lay a seductive retreat for Brahms in his teenage years, when his life was wrenched between the ideals of art and the degradation of brothels. Heaped on that came the necessity not only to master two crafts as pianist and composer, but the far more difficult and elusive drive to find his creative soul. These struggles already set him apart from business-obsessed Hamburg, and from most of its musicians as well. Under it all lay the torments of puberty and the anxiety of delayed or somehow incomplete development—Johannes's voice had not significantly changed by twenty, and he tried then without success to grow a beard.[23] No surprise that in his seething imagination the teenager needed to dream of other worlds, to find a more Romantic disguise than Johannes Brahms—son of a *Bierfiedler*, obscure music student, pianist in dives. Johannes escaped the *Animierlokale*, but in his mind and his sexual identity he never left them. As with the poetry on the whorehouse piano, he needed to create refuges in his mind. So he withdrew into a hall of mirrors where he could refract his identity.

The paradox is that in his art no composer ever had a more consistent and audible stylistic signature than Johannes Brahms, and he had it in some degree from the first works he allowed to survive. From early on he knew where he was going, and stayed on his path with an unrelenting discipline, day after day, year after year. Elsewhere in Germany in the same period, these games of identity, equally Hoffmann-inspired, perhaps contributed to Robert Schumann's ruin, overwhelmed by divine and demonic music roaring in his mind. Brahms, more stable as man and artist, would survive in his hall of mirrors and prosper. The game of identities would help make his mature music possible; it equipped him for a time in history where one could not work in a natural style, without a lacerating self-consciousness, without the looming presence of history. At the same time, his game of identities could not make Brahms happy, nor help in his always problematical dealings with the concrete and social world. He was all too adept at escape.

Brahms maintained his alter ego for a decade or more. A few of the pieces written in his first flush of public creative activity he actually signed "Johannes Kreisler, Junior." Amid the frustration and exaltation of love, he would start and abandon a piano quartet in C♯ minor, just as in a story Kapellmeister Kreisler starts and abandons a trio in that key. (Kreisler speaks of the trio in the context of a night on which "I was given a different name."[24]) In the 1870s, when Brahms proposed the Italian fantasist Gozzi's plays for opera librettos, he echoed Hoffmann/Kreisler's love of Gozzi.[25] In other words Brahms never left Kreisler Junior entirely behind him. His Doppelgänger, and Hoffmann's extravagant conception of music, only retired underground, singing in the lyrical transports of his grown-up music, emerging in his grown-up tears.

Yet for all his Romantic *Bildung*, in the end Brahms did not turn out a high-Romantic composer in the image, say, of Robert Schumann, even though Schumann himself was to help complete Brahms's *Bildung*. Brahms was too much an individualist to fall totally under the sway of any time, any personality. Besides, his musical loyalties stretched backward far beyond the Romantic age.

Romanticism remained a galvanizing force in Brahms's personal and creative consciousness, but not the boundless, infinite, form-shattering side of it. In his maturity he would put away that part. Against the chaos of life, especially the chaos of emotional life, Brahms would create something as classically perfect as humanly conceivable, that both captured and restrained the chaos of emotion. By that means, he erected walls around darkness and imperfection, contained the minotaur in a labyrinth of exquisite form. Work at it over and over again, ran his famous formula, until "there is not a note too much or too little, not a bar you could improve on. Whether it is also *beautiful* is an entirely different matter, but perfect it *must* be."[26] That *must* was the essence of Brahms as man and artist, the unforgiving credo of his religion.

JOHANNES RETURNED HOME from Winsen in autumn 1847 tanned and hale. Perhaps he still had to put in time in Hamburg *Lokale*, but now he began to acquire his own piano students to bring in money, and to find jobs in respectable restaurants and theaters. So far his teacher Eduard Marxsen, cautious as always in managing this talent, had not encouraged Johannes to play in public even though the boy was ready for it. Other prodigies of the era—Franz Liszt, Clara Wieck, violinist Josef Joachim— had been famous by age fourteen. As of autumn 1847, though, Marxsen agreed to his charge's making an official debut (his concert at age ten had been by invitation). So Brahms's introduction to the public as a soloist fell on November 20, 1847, in Hamburg's Apollo Concert Room.

This was not the modern notion of a "recital," involving a single artist and a single medium for a whole concert. That kind of program was still novel. Franz Liszt had introduced the idea and the poetic term *recital* in 1840. Chamber-music programs of the 1840s and 50s still tended to mix ensembles, to break up multimovement pieces with interpolated works, even to present single movements of longer works. Brahms's concert of November 1847 was such an event, a benefit sponsored by Hamburg violinist Karl Birgfeld involving several players and singers. Brahms's contribution, in sixth place on the program, was the virtuosic Fantasy on Themes from Bellini's *Norma* by then-celebrated pianist and composer Sigismund Thalberg.

A few days later came a pleasant notice in the Hamburg paper *Freischütz:* "A very special impression was made by the performance of one of Thalberg's fantasias by a little virtuoso called J. Brahms, who not only showed great facility, precision, clarity, power, and certainty, but occasioned general surprise and obtained unanimous applause by the intelligence of his interpretation." In fact the notice was written anonymously by Eduard Marxsen, as a pat on the head for his pupil. The occasion brought no further comment. A week later, Johannes appeared in another concert, playing the fantasy again and a Thalberg duet with Frau Meyer-David, with a similar review and the same outcome.[27]

Hamburg "the Unmusical City" in fact had an increasingly active musical scene, even if not of the caliber of Leipzig and Berlin. Friedrich Wilhelm Gund conducted the Philharmonic and a *Singakademie* he had founded. There were concerts by the orchestral Musikalische Gesellschaft and choral Cäcilienverein. If these groups tended to the second-rate, one could still hear good chamber music and visiting artists of stature, among them Hector Berlioz (he conducted his mammoth *Requiem* in Hamburg), Liszt, Thalberg, and soprano Jenny Lind.[28] In March 1848, Johannes, then fourteen, heard sixteen-year-old prodigy Josef Joachim play the Beethoven Violin Concerto with the Philharmonic. Seven years later, Brahms would write Joachim that in his innocence "I reckoned the concerto to be your own. . . . I was certainly your most enraptured listener."

Already a constant reader, Johannes was becoming a bibliophile and collector, haunter of second-hand bookshops in search of rarities. Prowling bookstalls that year, he found a 1743 treatise on figured bass. Bound in the back of it was another old tome on keyboard playing by Johann Mattheson, biographer and friend of Handel from their Hamburg days. Brahms not only collected old volumes and music and manuscripts, he also studied them as living texts. As he was someday to inform Richard Wagner: "I do not collect 'curiosities.' "

In spring of 1848, around the time he turned fifteen, Brahms returned to "Uncle" and "Auntie" Giesemann and to conducting the men's choir. (His second departure to Winsen marks the end of his formal schooling.) On this visit there were further evenings of piano duets with Amtsvogt Blume. Since Lieschen Giesemann had given up the piano, they had no more lessons, but she remained a music fancier. Lieschen and Johannes had one more memorable time together when Adolf Giesemann sent them to Hamburg to take in Mozart's *Marriage of Figaro*. It was Johannes's first experience with opera. "Lieschen, Lieschen," he whispered when the whirling, whispering overture began, "Listen to the music! There never was anything like it!"

That summer, at the last meeting of the men's choir, he recited a poem of farewell, and there were tears. One of the men picked up little Johannes and carried him around the room piggyback to the sound of singing and hurrahs. In his life Brahms would leave many situations with tears and ceremonies, and rarely returned to any of them. He always had somewhere else to go, something else to do than what anyone expected of him. But he would visit Winsen and the Giesemanns for the rest of his time in Hamburg.

DURING JOHANNES's gemütlich sojourn in the country that summer, revolution simmered and boiled all over Europe. In February 1848, Marx and Engels published the *Communist Manifesto* and a popular revolt overthrew King Louis Philippe in Paris. Beginning in March the French uprising touched off a wave of revolution. All the uprisings were liberal-democratic to socialist in politics and, in occupied lands like Hungary, nationalist in import. Soon the ferment spread to Vienna, which drove out the autocratic Prince Metternich in March, and erupted again in October to send the emperor running to Innsbrück. After a third revolution in Vienna, Emperor Ferdinand abdicated and his nephew Franz Josef took the throne, to remain on it for sixty-eight years. With and without gunfire, with initial success in some places but in the end unavailing everywhere, there were insurrections in Germany, Hungary, Italy, and Czechoslovakia.

Bursts of fighting continued into the next year. Lajos Kossuth led Hungary in proclaiming independence from Austria, but in August 1849, Austria reclaimed Hungary by force at Vilagos. In May of that year, Richard Wagner, Kapellmeister of the court of Dresden, ascended a church steeple to direct rebel forces against Prussian troops, and watched his opera house burn down during the fighting. Within days the Prussians had suppressed the Dresden rebellion; Wagner fled an arrest warrant to live in exile from Germany for eleven years.[29] Also in Dresden that month, Clara and Robert Schumann were driven from their back door with their oldest child by fighting in the streets. Clara, seven months pregnant, returned through the fields in the middle of the night to face down armed men and lead her other children to safety.[30]

Progressive forces lost out everywhere in that flare of revolution, yet after the explosions the pieces came down in quite different configurations. In German lands the time before the March revolutions would be given its own name: *Vormärz*, Before March. With the end of that gemütlich era (only later called the Biedermeier) also ended Metternich's regime that had made Austria into a police state, with a full complement of censors and spies. The next decades would see the rise to power of Austrian liberalism by means of parliamentary rule. Across Europe the period after 1849 would be marked by lingering unrest but also by prosperity and relative peace around Europe—the Age of Speculators, it has been called, in Germany the *Gründerzeit*, and in Vienna the Ringstrasse Era. For the moment, Realpolitik and bourgeois prosperity triumphed over ideology. The situation would suit music, and Brahms, very well.

The revolutions of 1848–49 stayed distant from Hamburg, in its far corner of Germany. Citizens went about their business and kept going to concerts. One of the less noticed programs came on September 21, 1848, the first recital with Johannes Brahms as principal. He shared the program with a local soprano, violinist, cellist, and clarinetist, whom he accompanied. His solo pieces, mostly conventionalities of the time, included a virtuosic fantasy on themes from Rossini's *William Tell* by Döhler and a Marxsen serenade for the left hand, but also a Bach fugue—the last generally perceived as too intellectual for a normal program.

He gave a second recital on April 14, 1849, this time advertised in the paper with apparently good results in attendance. The program was a potpourri similar to the last, but in addition to the requisite virtuoso piece—Thalberg's *Don Juan* Fantasy—Johannes played Beethoven's fiery and difficult *Waldstein* Sonata. And there was a novelty, "Fantasia for Piano on a Favorite Waltz, composed and performed by the concert-giver." Thus Brahms made his debut as a composer, with a little salon piece. Later—history, biography, and sentimentality notwithstanding—he exterminated it.

His teacher Marxsen wrote another anonymous polite review for the paper. Then, gauging the results of these two efforts, Marxsen discouraged more recitals. In a memoir he wrote that his student's time "seemed to me too precious, as interludes of this kind often upset a man's studies

very considerably. At any rate, the press always spoke of these first attempts with great appreciation."³¹ He was joking with the last, because
most of the appreciation had come from himself.

In fact the programs generated no particular enthusiasm. Brahms had
tested the waters as a virtuoso, and he would never really try it again.
Marxsen was resigned now to his student being composer first, pianist
second. That in itself would make 1849–52 a watershed in Brahms's life.
Nothing dramatic happened, but in his work creative powers gathered
that were to burst across Europe with extraordinary effect.

BY AGE SIXTEEN, Johannes was earning his keep mainly by giving cut-
rate piano lessons to talentless students—probably the overflow from
Cossel and Marxsen—and playing incidental music in various venues.
Over the years these included Sundays at the Bergedorf inn Zur Schönen
Aussicht (for three marks and free food) and manning piano and harmonium behind the scenes of plays at the Thalia Theater. Here and there
jobs turned up accompanying virtuosos who were passing through town.
Probably he arranged and composed little pieces for his father's sextet at
the Alster Pavilion. It was the way any number of musicians lived, in
Hamburg and everywhere else. His piano career appeared to be settling
into the position of workaday accompanist, something Brahms was
suited for technically but not temperamentally. He was composing more
serious pieces now, and would say that some of his best lieder melodies
came to him as he polished his boots at dawn for another day's work.

Johannes often practiced at the firm of Baumgarten and Heinz, and
there in 1849 he again ran into Luise Japha. With this older student he
formed one of the few close friendships of those years—a strained friendship, like all of them. Despite his boyish high spirits, Johannes lived too
much in his own thoughts and labors to adapt to the demands of friendship. Earlier he had spent much time in Bergedorf playing duets with a
young admirer named Christian Miller. This pianist recalled that when
they were together away from the piano Johannes usually ignored him,
walking hat in hand humming to himself.

One night a friend of Luise Japha, impressed with his music, escorted
Brahms home but could not get a single word out of him. Later Johannes
explained to Luise, "One is not always inclined to talk . . . and then it is
best to be silent. You understand that, don't you?" She did not.³² Luise
was not particularly keen on his "harsh, acid" personality. Tempered by a
genuine compassion and need for companionship, Brahms's social skills

would eventually improve in some degree, but he remained maladroit and unpredictable even with close friends.

Luise, seven years older than Johannes, was herself exceptional as a pianist and song composer, and headed for a notable performing career. For all the harshness of Brahms's manner, she found much remarkable about him. Once he brought her a counterpoint exercise Marxsen had assigned him and told her that doing it had given him a terrible headache, but "that's always when it works best for me." His students were stupid, he said, and the ones who appreciated him the least paid him the least. He did not, Luise recalled, talk to her about playing dances in bars, or how poor his parents were.

They got along, in the distant and sometimes abrasive way one got along with Brahms. They played duets together, talked technique, discussed books, critiqued each other's music. Once they played through a long piano duet that Johannes finally admitted was his own. Luise praised it, but when he dismissed one of the themes as routine she agreed. Suddenly indignant, he barked, "Why didn't you say so? Why did I have to ask you?"[33] She could tell that Johannes had picked up his teacher's deification of Bach and Beethoven, and was suspicious of newer music. Already a Schumann devotee, Luise showed Johannes an aria from Schumann's oratorio *Paradise and the Peri*. He condemned it for beginning with a seventh chord, an unprepared dissonance forbidden in the theory books. (Presumably he forgot that Beethoven's First Symphony begins likewise.)

His conservative reaction to Schumann says something about Marxsen's training. Brahms's subsequent development says more. In the first of his surviving pieces, songs and piano music written from ages eighteen and nineteen, Brahms already possessed an urgent youthful expressiveness. For a young man that is not surprising. Beyond that, in his earliest surviving works there is a precociously sophisticated sense of form and melodic development—some of the most difficult things to master.

From Marxsen, Johannes seems to have learned to derive the melodic material of a piece from pregnant short patterns called *motives*, the germs of melody. This was a relatively new technique. Where earlier Classical composers tended to base their work on clear-cut melodic themes, reworked and disassembled and reassembled in the course of a movement, Beethoven in his later music sank the basic material of a piece deep in the texture, until the discourse was carried on less in the overt themes than in the subthemes: the subliminal logic of forging melodic germs into melodies.³⁴ Brahms would carry that motivic technique further; he began doing it in his earliest surviving works.

Marxsen also taught his pupil to revere and exploit the musical forms that theorists had abstracted and codified from the music of the masters. These went under such names as *sonata form, theme-and-variations, rondo, fugue,* and *canon.* In previous centuries such formal designs had guided much of the music written, and in the process had brought Western music to its highest development.

By the nineteenth century, these patterns had taken on the aura of the geniuses who had used them. To honor Beethoven and Bach and Mozart, Johannes was taught, one must honor their designs. In the first movement of a sonata or symphony, for example, one presents a first theme, a transition, and a second theme in a related key, and then repeats that *exposition;* then comes the *development,* a play of keys and thematic fragmentation and dramatic contrast, which leads back to the *recapitulation* that revisits the exposition but resolves the harmonic tensions into a single key. On that basic "sonata form" (as it was dubbed in the mid-nineteenth century) one can develop many variants under the influence of the material at hand, but the essential design must remain as a foundation or the music falls into confusion.

Marxsen called the procedures of the masters "eternally incorruptible." He infused Brahms with that sense of traditional form, part technique and part religion. Brahms never strayed from that spirit, no matter how creatively he varied the details of the old designs. From his apprenticeship on, all else but allegiance to the past and its procedures appeared to him as chaos. There was a danger lurking in this faith, which Brahms also understood and escaped, but which snared many composers: these formal abstractions tended to harden into dogma, time-hallowed patterns into which composers poured notes (which is exactly what Bach, Mozart, and Beethoven did not do). As time would prove, more than any other composer of his time, Brahms demonstrated that it remained possible for a true creator to revitalize the old forms. Even Richard Wagner would have to concede that.

Meanwhile, it would be exactly those forms that Liszt, Wagner, and their New German School rejected—or rather, the aura of dogma and phony holiness the forms had acquired. Dahlhaus writes that in the Romantic period, form "as a rough categorization, either . . . was schematic or it was disintegrated."³⁵ In other words, the central musical debate of the later nineteenth century would line up in terms of traditional form versus free, which usually meant "absolute music" versus "program music." Eventually, all these abstractions would be contained in tangible dichotomies: Leipzig versus Weimar, Brahms versus Liszt and Wagner.

That Brahms lined up on the conservative half of this divide was clearly a matter of temperament and aesthetics as much as training. In his first pieces, we can see that Marxsen taught his student melodic development and a traditional approach to form remarkably thoroughly. Probably he kept Johannes at writing theme-and-variations pieces as well. The idea of theme-and-variations is to present a musical statement (the theme) and then transform it into a series of contrasting statements (the variations), each in some way derived from the original statement—ornamenting its melody, improvising on its harmonies or its bass line. The theme-and-variations genre is an idea at the heart of musical form: making many things out of one.

In some elements of musical craft, Marxsen skimped Johannes, or his pupil concluded he did. Brahms reached adulthood so inexperienced at handling instruments that in his first attempts with the orchestra he was practically at a loss. With the help of friends, over a period of years, he would have to teach himself orchestration. It would be some time, however, in larger works, before he could break entirely from his own instrument, the piano. In maturity, his handling of instrumentation, though hardly weak, was all the same his weakest suit, the one matter of craftsmanship in which he felt chronically unsure of himself. That recalls the more conservative, characteristically North German attitudes of the time. Walter Niemann writes of "the austere North German conception of . . . music, a conception concerned with form rather than color, contrapuntal . . . rather than homophonic.[36] In the 1870s, British composition student Ethel Smyth found the circle of composers around Brahms largely indifferent to the coloristic use of instruments, the stunning new art of orchestration developed by Berlioz and Wagner.[37] They seemed to look at scoring as merely the efficient presentation of ideas. To Smyth's taste the results were gray and awkward.

Brahms did not assume that conservative posture in practice; eventually he developed a distinctive voice with the orchestra. Yet something in his artistic conscience seemed to whisper that instrumental color, the mere sensuous clothing of an idea, was suspicious, beside the point. In the history of music, Germany had long been associated more with counterpoint and form than with color, lightness, charm, melodiousness—the latter, traditionally, were the provenance of the French and the Italians. (Mozart specialized in unifying German and Italian qualities.) Brahms grew up believing that the point of composition was the perfection and expressiveness of the notes, of the organic logic, counterpoint, and form: the high-German qualities that Marxsen and his culture taught him.

As Luise Japha recalled, with his teacher Brahms studied the intricate craft of interweaving melodic lines that is called counterpoint. J. S. Bach, who called music "an art and a science," had been the consummate master of counterpoint and its complex exigencies of craft and taste. Counterpoint is the joining of disciplined science with expressive art: to superimpose beautiful and logical melodies whose combination also, magically, creates beautiful and logical harmonic progressions. With that, as musicians put it, a composer unifies the "horizontal"/melodic dimension of music with the "vertical"/harmonic. Yet for all his studies with Marxsen, at a time when he had already become famous Brahms concluded that he had not yet mastered counterpoint. He would spend years making up the deficiency, or what he perceived as one.

If Marxsen fell short in teaching Brahms some things, to his glory he did give his student free rein to develop his own voice, and that rein was all Brahms needed. From his time with Marxsen onward, he relied on others for ideas, stimulation, criticism. Yet he was never compromised by anyone or anything, was never other than his own man.

In practice, Brahms would honor his teacher, for decades sending him work for comment. Yet in adulthood he once growled to a friend about Marxsen's lessons that "I faithfully attended, but I learned absolutely nothing."[38] He was lying then, either to his listener or to himself. He liked to portray himself as entirely his own creation. Besides that, though, for all his gratitude Brahms could never entirely forgive his teacher for what he had failed to teach, and the years it cost to make that up.

JOHANNES SPENT 1849 with little to mark his doings. He studied and he did his playing jobs. That year he picked up some hackwork writing pieces and arrangements for a Hamburg publisher under the pseudonym "G. W. Marks." It appears that this prolific creator of light music was actually a blanket name for a number of anonymous journeymen composers, among them Eduard Marxsen—who probably got his pupil the job.[39] The music was intended to fill the piano benches of bourgeois parlors, and the pay was not bad.

Despite Brahms's later efforts to suppress everything he turned out under aliases, one of these "Marks" potboilers appears to have survived: *Souvenir de la Russie*, a fantasy/suite of Russian tunes. The piece is entirely self-possessed for its genre, as prettily innocuous as it was paid to be.[40] If the work is in fact by Brahms, it displays in some pages his early interest in the "Hungarian" style. In any case, his labor as one of "G. W. Marks'" incarnations steeped Brahms in the popular music of the time—a higher level of it than the dances he played in the *Lokale*—and that would serve him well as he attempted to make a living selling his notes. So by the first two years of the new decade Brahms had become, in addition to a competent professional pianist and piano teacher, a workaday composer like his teacher. He never considered remaining that.

Elsewhere the progressive musical world went its way, Brahms and Hamburg largely oblivious. In Weimar in 1850, Franz Liszt unveiled the first of a new kind of work he invented and championed, a "symphonic poem" called *Bergsymphonie*, based on an ode by Victor Hugo. That year Robert Schumann completed his last and finest symphony, if still a flawed entry in the genre—the grand and lyrical *Rhenish*. That year too, writing in exile in Zürich, Richard Wagner decreed in his treatise "The Artwork of the Future" that Beethoven was the last symphonist and the symphony was dead. Except for the unsteady example of Schumann, the symphonies turned out in the 1850s and '60s by men like Gade, Raff, and Rubinstein yielded little to contradict Wagner's requiem for the genre.

Toward the end of 1849 a dramatic concert was given at Hamburg's municipal theater by a violinist named Eduard Hoffmann. Born to a Jewish family, out of Hungarian patriotism he had restyled himself Eduard Reményi. When Austria and Russia put down the Hungarian revolt in 1848, Reményi had been one of hundreds of political refugees who fled prison or the noose, many of them heading for Hamburg, often on their way to America. A sizable Hungarian community collected in Brahms's city.

Reményi's "farewell concert" in Hamburg featured, as always with him, a collection of "national dances," characterized as Magyar and *Zigeuner*—Hungarian and/or gypsy folk music. (The terms were fluid.) Partly from the efforts of Reményi and his compatriots Liszt and Joachim, and later of Brahms, this driving, soulful style found a vogue as one of the more exotic nationalistic repertoires. In reality its folk origins were as dubious as any. As Bartók and Kodály were to discover in the next century, this "Hungarian" style arose not as the spontaneous outpouring of peasants, but instead as an urban popular music played mostly by gypsy bands in streets and cafés, the bands often consisting of two violins, cimbalom (a Hungarian dulcimer), and bass. The authentic peasant music, unfettered in mode and rhythm, lay undiscovered in the Hungarian countryside, beyond the musical horizon of the nineteenth century.

The familiar "gypsy" and "Hungarian" styles were a distant commercial echo of the real thing, faux-exotic but wildly popular.

Brahms may or may not have attended Reményi's Hamburg farewell, but he certainly heard about this virtuoso who had made a sensation in the city with his perfervid playing of both the standard and nationalistic repertoires. Meanwhile, Reményi stayed on and concertized for some time after his "farewell." In August 1850, Brahms got to know him when the violinist asked him to accompany a private concert at the house of a local merchant. That was an honor for Brahms; if this virtuoso was not world-renowned yet, he seemed likely to be—he had the thirst for it.

Brahms and Reményi began playing and socializing with the violinist's circle of Hungarian exiles. There were trips to Winsen for pleasant evenings of playing at the Giesemanns'. Already a devotee of folk music in general, Brahms responded enthusiastically to the *czardas* and other styles that made up the *alla Zingarese* (in the gypsy style) repertoire. Still, there was little more to their relations than playing chamber music, a few shared interests, some sociable times in city and country. At that point, Reményi was likely just another contact for Johannes, who had no discernible plans for his career and little time for friends. The fun ended in early 1851, when rumors of an arrest warrant put Reményi on a boat to America.

In March 1850, there was a ripple of excitement in Hamburg when composer Robert Schumann arrived for concerts with his wife, Clara Schumann née Wieck (as she took pains to note on her programs). Since Clara was far more celebrated than her husband the excitement had largely to do with her presence, especially since Madame Schumann gave two concerts with adored soprano Jenny Lind, "the Swedish nightingale." Robert Schumann conducted the Philharmonic in the overture to his opera *Genoveva*, about to be premiered in Leipzig; on the concert his wife soloed in his A Minor Piano Concerto. Applause was scant for his pieces, but Schumann was used to that.[41]

Brahms may have skipped the concerts, but prodded by Luise Japha he bundled up some of his compositions and sent them to Schumann at the hotel, hoping for comment and a meeting. Schumann, busy with his concert and with the question of whether to accept a position as music director in Düsseldorf, did not have time to examine a parcel of music from an unknown youth. Brahms was disgusted to receive the package back unopened. The resentment he felt toward Schumann over that rebuff must have increased when in the autumn of 1852 Luise, the closest of his few friends, told him that she was moving to Düsseldorf to study with the

Schumanns—piano with Clara, composition with Robert. "Don't go!" Brahms entreated Luise. "You're the only one here who takes any interest in me!"[42]

There is no record of what music Brahms sent Schumann. He had been writing no one knows how many pieces, in no one knows what genres. Rumors survive of sonatas for one and two pianos, string quartets, fantasias and variations, dozens of songs. A few of his instrumental pieces he aired under the name Karl Würth, yet another pseudonym. Finally in 1851 he produced the first two works he would be willing to preserve and to publish with his name on them—the demonic E♭ Minor Scherzo and a short song on Uhland's "Heimkehr." The latter is marked *Allegro agitato*; its wandering tempos and breathless dynamics lead to a final overwrought peroration on "World, don't perish; sky, don't fall, until I'm with the girl I love!" The E♭ Minor Scherzo and a few other piano pieces and songs were soon to drop the jaws of leading musicians in Europe. Brahms played the scherzo privately in February 1851, for visiting composer Henri Charles Litolff.[43] (Next year, probably for the money, Brahms arranged a Litolff overture for piano and "Physharmonica," a predecessor to the modern harmonium.[44])

Everything was scattered, inconclusive. The month after Litolff heard the E♭ Minor Scherzo, Brahms briefly visited the Giesemanns and wrote a "Farewell to Winsen" for the men's choir, another piece later suppressed. In July there was a bit of glory when he appeared with Danish composer Niels Gade, an old friend of Robert Schumann's (who wrote a piece whose theme begins with the notes G-A-D-E). To this private concert Brahms contributed two of his "Karl Würth" pieces, a piano trio and a cello and piano duo, both later destroyed. By then he had built up a small but significant collection of masks, named Young Kreisler, G. W. Marks, Karl Würth. After that would come another: Werther.

IF THE STORY of Brahms's life around the beginning of the new decade seems shadowy and aimless, surely that is how he perceived it himself as he approached adulthood. His artistic work was pulling together remarkably well, but otherwise he had no very good idea how he was going to earn a living. Doing it with composition was of course unimaginable, except maybe by means of the "G. W. Marks" species of parlor music. Few composers outside Beethoven, Rossini, and a few others had survived entirely on the proceeds of serious composing. At the same time Johannes was not interested in making a name as a virtuoso, and conversely could not have wanted to stay at the kind of hackwork he

had been composing. Full-time piano teaching would surely have horrified him as well.

So he lived an aimless and in many ways shabby existence, with his
family in the slums. Around 1852 the situation appeared on the verge of
becoming even shabbier. After long and anxious hesitation, his mother
revealed to Johannes that Johann Jakob had gotten fed up with the
women in his family and was thinking of moving out of the house. When
his mother told him, Johannes burst into tears.[45] Probably owing in part
to his entreaties the crisis receded, but the wretched possibility of a broken family lay on his mind from then on. If it happened, there would be
no question of Johannes's siding exclusively with his mother and sister.
Among his driving motivations had become his desire to show his father
that he could amount to something—on his own terms. But what were
his terms?

Otherwise, on the surface 1852 continued about the same as the previous year, but Brahms's creative work was burgeoning. That year he
completed more songs that would appear in his first collections of lieder.
(Opus 6, mostly from 1852, is dedicated to Luise Japha and her artist sister Minna.) In February came the poignant variations on the folk song
"Verstohlen geht der Mond auf" that would serve as the slow movement
of Opus 1, the C Major Piano Sonata. In November, he completed the
first sonata he would publish under his own name, the F♯ Minor, Opus 2.

In January 1853, Brahms composed the haunting, impetuous song
"Liebestreu," placed first in his published lieder and one of the most
striking of his life. The ideas were coming fast now, all of them emotionally heated, Romantic, but he made them tight in the telling. Brahms
had already achieved a music singular in personality, yet different from
what he would be writing a decade later, when life had beaten the youth
and impetuousness out of him. Around March 1853 came the remaining
movements of the C Major Piano Sonata and the second and fourth of
the rhapsodic F Minor Piano Sonata, Opus 5. Both manuscripts are
signed "Joh. Kreisler, Junior." By then he had written the bulk of the
works that were to become perhaps the most astonishing first six opus
numbers in the history of Western music.

Back from America and Paris, Eduard Reményi showed up in Hamburg again in December 1852, ready to present more concerts. He and
Brahms picked up their playing and their friendship (friendships with
Brahms were generally carried on in large part by music-making). At
some point it was suggested that they do a concert in Winsen, where they
had often visited Hungarian friends and the Giesemanns. The concert
came off on April 20, the program Beethoven's C Minor Violin Sonata,

a virtuosic Vieuxtemps Violin Concerto in piano-violin arrangement, and a group of Reményi's trademark Hungarian melodies. Sitting proudly in the audience for the concert were the Giesemanns and their friends. The duo played again next day in Hoopte, in the schoolroom of Brahms's old mentor Alwin Schröder. Though it all went well, for Johannes the performances seemed no more auspicious than earlier ones, none of which had caused much stir outside the circle of his friends and family.

At some point Brahms and Reményi decided to keep going, to make a little tour of it. Why not? Biographer Max Kalbeck surmises that "spring and Wanderlust" inspired the two, which is as likely as anything.[46] Probably for Reményi it was something to kill time, fish for contacts; they could visit Reményi's school friend and fellow Hungarian patriot Josef Joachim in Hanover. For Johannes, it was some excitement, a chance to go south and see a bit of Germany for the first time—the Black Forest, real mountains.

When it came to touring, in those days concert managers hardly existed; soloists and their friends did the planning, arranging, and legwork themselves. Brahms's Winsen admirer Amtsvogt Blume found them engagements through contacts in Lüneburg and Celle, the latter conveniently close to Hanover and Joachim. Their repertoire for the tour would include the Beethoven sonata, the Vieuxtemps, the show-stopping *alla Zingarese* tunes, plus Johannes's A Minor Violin Sonata and E♭ Minor Scherzo.

They left Hamburg with blessings from Johannes's parents, who agreed that it was time for the boy to try his hand in the larger world. No doubt Johann Jakob remembered his journey to Hamburg at the same age, nineteen. Mother and son vowed to write regularly. A half hour after the duo left Hamburg, police showed up at the Brahms house looking for Reményi on suspicion of subversion.[47]

Two musicians, a semi-famous violinist and his obscure accompanist, set out on a small-time concert tour. That day an uninterrupted trajectory of growth and fame and triumph was set in motion that continues to the present day, and bids to continue until the last days of music.

CHAPTER THREE

Two Journeys

IT WAS A MISMATCHED DUO that set out on their concert tour in April 1853: violinist Eduard Reményi twenty-three, choleric and swaggering, ever impersonating the great virtuoso; his accompanist unassuming, quiet, watchful behind flashing blue eyes. Although Brahms turned twenty that May, the face under the long blond hair was still girlishly pretty—virginal and innocent, people were apt to infer, before they knew him. From walking and gymnastic exercises he had made himself wiry and athletic, for all the slightness. Graceful he was not. A Hamburg acquaintance described him in his teens as "shy, awkward, and constrained." Eugenie Schumann remembered a lumbering gait and wobbly tall hat.[1] There had been no teenage growth surge and Brahms's voice remained high as a boy's. He was trying to cover his baby fat with a beard when he left Hamburg with Reményi, but it was not working.

When he sat at the piano, however, Brahms suddenly assumed maturity and authority. He aimed his playing toward musicians, who understood his subtleties, in contrast to virtuosos like Liszt who seized the public by the throat. Still, sometimes nerves inhibited Brahms's performances, especially in his own work. Even when he did well, some critics would not like his playing, but few missed the ferocious intelligence that informed everything he did.

Following the Winsen concerts that hatched the tour, in the first half of May the duo gave two concerts each in Lüneburg and Celle playing Beethoven, Brahms, Vieuxtemps, and the Hungarian melodies. Besides the friends of his Winsen patron who had helped arrange the tour, a newspaper notice in each town served to bring in listeners. Brahms seems to have played the repertoire out of his head. He had an extraordinary memory for music, as for everything else good and bad.

At their Celle concert on May 2 he accomplished a coup that became legendary. They found the piano tuned nearly a half tone flat. Rather than ask Reményi to retune his violin so radically, in the performance Brahms transposed the whole accompaniment of Beethoven's C Minor Sonata to C♯, and apparently did it without the music in front of him.[2] At the end the violinist announced the feat to the audience and it caused a sensation.[3] Brahms probably shrugged—Eduard Marxsen had taught him to transpose as a matter of course.

Offstage the duo did not get along; rehearsals were punctuated by shouts. One problem was that both of them inclined to rhapsodic tempos and it is hard to rhapsodize together, especially when the accompanist does not have the temperament to follow anybody.[4] To the end of his life Brahms tended to play chamber music as if he were alone.

The emotional peak of each program came when Reményi, his fiddle sobbing with nationalistic zeal, dispensed his Magyar and *Zigeuner* tunes. Brahms worked out his own accompaniments for the pieces and probably never wrote them down. This repertoire would be of great consequence to him. From Reményi and later from Joachim, he absorbed not only the style but the spirit of "Hungarian" folk music. Unlike these two colleagues, however, Brahms took no interest in the Hungarian nationalism that underlay their devotion to the music. There is no record of his saying anything about Hungary's struggle to free itself of Austria. He seems to have been indifferent to other cultures and to Romantic nationalism generally (as distinct from German patriotism). Likely Brahms shared that indifference with many enthusiasts of the gypsy style: he simply liked the music.

In those days people sat in smoky cafés and listened to tawny and exotic gypsy bands in much the same spirit with which another generation would sit in clubs listening to black men playing jazz. In fact, the entire tradition of a lower-caste popular music percolating into more "sophisticated" styles began with gypsy music.[5] As jazz would give later concert composers fresh ideas, so did gypsy music inspire composers from Haydn and Schubert to Brahms and Joachim with new tonal colors, new kinds of expression with kaleidoscopic shifts from slow and soulful to fast and fiery, and an emancipation from the rhythmic tyranny of unbending beat and bar line. In his *Zigeuner* music and out of it, Brahms would make steady use of lessons he learned from the style. His experience with it helped counter his conventional training and conservative instincts.

So with Reményi as tutor, Brahms learned the "Hungarian" style and a number of melodies that may or may not have been common property. Later, more than anything else it would be his own volumes of Hungarian Dances that enabled him to become that rarity, a more or less freelance composer who ate well. (Reményi always claimed that Brahms stole some tunes that the violinist had composed himself and passed off as folk music.[6])

If fractious and indifferently successful for a while, their tour was still entertaining enough for the duo, especially for Johannes, who had never been far from home, never played regularly onstage, never been so completely on his own. Years afterward he recalled a couple of concerts in the town of Hildesheim south of Hanover. The first evening was hastily arranged and the audience tiny. At a restaurant afterward, the performers made merry with the patrons, who after dinner followed Reményi like the Pied Piper down the street to the house of an aristocratic lady who had sponsored the concert. They serenaded her with song and Reményi's improvised fantasia on Bellini's *I Puritani*, and the attention all this garnered in a small town brought in a full house for the next concert.[7]

Of course, Reményi had said at the outset, while we're in the area we should try for an engagement in Hanover and call on my old schoolmate Josef Joachim. The two virtuosos had studied together in Vienna, both were Hungarian/Jewish in background, and they shared nationalistic enthusiasms. Brahms had an indelible memory of Joachim's Hamburg performance of the Beethoven Violin Concerto five years before, when the violinist was seventeen. Maybe rumors had reached Brahms and Reményi that at the Lower Rhine Music Festival that month, Joachim had caused a furor with the same work. Brahms also remembered his frustration with approaching the famous—when Schumann returned his package in Hamburg. But some concerts might turn up, so why not? They boarded the train for Hanover.

IN MAY 1853 Josef Joachim was about to turn twenty-two and for nearly ten years had been among the preeminent musicians of the age. After studies in Budapest and Vienna he became, at twelve, a protégé of Mendelssohn in Leipzig. Joachim made his first sensation the next year, playing the Beethoven Violin Concerto in London under Mendelssohn's baton. That greatest of violin concertos had been neglected until Joachim made it unforgettable. He did the same with the Bach unaccompanied sonatas and partitas. In his younger years, he was as much conductor and composer as violinist, still unsure of where to place his focus. His playing was transcendent in technique, French in inspiration, pure and antivirtuosic. As Viennese critic Eduard Hanslick noted on his first hearing, Joachim did not play the crowd but searched deep in the music for structure and meaning.[8]

At seventeen Joachim had become professor of violin at the Leipzig Conservatory, then two years later accepted a call to be concertmaster of Franz Liszt's court orchestra in Weimar. It amounted to joining the most exciting musical laboratory in Europe. Liszt devoted his orchestra to spreading his musical revolution, what would eventually be called the New German School. But despite the adulation Joachim received in Weimar, and the Hungarian patriotism he shared with this mentor, he had felt uncomfortable there, with the orchestra spending much of the time reading over Liszt's trial sketches.[9] For all his admiration for an incomparable pianist and generous friend, Joachim could not escape his growing disillusion with Liszt's music, could not endure the circle of sycophants or Liszt's shameless grandstanding in performance—the grimacing and fainting, the suffering-Christ act. By 1852, when Joachim left Weimar and went to work as concertmaster and soloist for the Hanover court orchestra, he was divorcing Liszt and his revolution, even if he did not yet admit it.

Part of the process of divorce would involve finding alternative visions of the future to which Joachim could commit himself. The first alternative proved to be Schumann. The enthusiasm Joachim's Beethoven performance aroused at the 1853 Lower Rhine Festival led to a close connection with Robert and Clara Schumann. Even critics were beside themselves; one reported: "We will not attempt to describe his success; there was French frenzy, Italian fanaticism, in a German audience."[10] Robert, then town music director in Düsseldorf, found the performance a revelation not only of Beethoven but of violin-playing. Schumann's D Minor Symphony and A Minor Piano Concerto had been aired at the festival, the latter naturally with Clara soloing. Caught up in the music of a composer he had admired only from a distance, Joachim eagerly returned the friendship offered by the Schumanns.

After leaving Düsseldorf and the ovations of the festival, Joachim had an uneasy week's visit with Liszt in Weimar, then returned to Hanover to prepare for summer courses in philosophy and history at the University of Göttingen. At the end of May, Joachim was pleasantly interrupted by a visit from his old schoolmate Reményi, who had brought along his shy blond accompanist. Brahms was a composer, was he? Well then, they should hear something.

The youth played. Fifty years later Joachim was to recall, "Never in the course of my artist's life have I been more completely overwhelmed." Some of it was Brahms's manner, "noble and inspired."[11] Joachim found the music blindingly strong and fresh. Beyond that, perhaps Joachim already sensed that here in this youth, in the first flush of his genius, lay the alternative to Liszt.

Besides some music later discarded, Brahms played Joachim the Sonatas in C Major and F♯ Minor, the E♭ Minor Scherzo, and the song "Liebestreu" ("Fidelity"). The song begins, "Oh sink your sorrow, my child, in the deep sea!" The expression is Romantically urgent, the technique masterful and original; the piano's bass line seems to create the voice's melody as an echo, making the music a duo between a singer and her shadowy double. Like some of Schubert's youthful lieder, "Liebestreu" is the kind of song that takes the world by the ear. Joachim described it as a revelation.[12]

Nor had he ever heard anything like the sonatas. To Joachim, who was young and fiercely earnest and looking for new heroes, these pieces flashed from Brahms's hands like a bolt of lightning. If the violinist was still half-consciously fleeing the Weimar progressives back to a familiar world of formalism and continuity with the past, the hair must have raised on his neck when he heard the impetuous opening of the C Major Sonata, with its echoes of Beethoven's *Hammerklavier* transformed into the voice of Johannes Brahms.

The music went by Joachim, movement after movement, all of it too new and marvelous to grasp. One could only say that it was marvelous and wait to hear it again. For Joachim, as for others to come, all of it worked together like an epiphany: this delicate-looking figure appearing out of nowhere and playing unheard-of music with heavenly grace on the keyboard. Within days the two musicians had formed a bond of affection and shared ideals that would endure for life.

If the affectionate part of their friendship was to be like a stormy marriage, with terrible arguments and long separations, that is only to say that this was for both men like most of their relationships. Brahms and Joachim had both been reared as virtuosos, and in that consuming discipline their social instincts, the skills of friendship and love, had been forced to the side. Joachim tried to remedy the narrowness of his education by studying history and philosophy; he would become a friend of poets and philosophers, and in his personal relations he often revealed a clear-headed perception of people and events. But he lacked wisdom in knowing how to live, never learned to handle a brooding and vindictive streak that drove him over and over to turn on his loved ones.

On their first meeting, Joachim did more than listen to Brahms and express his pleasure. At twenty-two the violinist was an old pro and knew how to promote an artist. He also happened to be one of those who admired Johannes's playing. For his employer, George V, King of Hanover, he arranged a private soiree to show off Brahms and Reményi. To his friend the court pianist Joachim wrote, "Brahms has a quite exceptional talent for composition and a nature that could have been developed in its integrity only in the strictest retirement—pure as the diamond, tender as the snow." Perhaps later he would wish to amend the adjectives—say, "hard as the diamond, cold as the snow"—but Joachim had astutely noted the effect of seclusion on his friend. He wrote the Countess Bernstorff at court that Johannes possessed "that concentrated fire, what I may call that fatalistic energy and precision of rhythm, which prophesy the artist, and his compositions already contain much that is significant, such as I have not hitherto met with in a youth of his age."[13]

At the court of Hanover on June 8, 1853, Brahms played his E♭ Minor Scherzo. The blind king, a knowledgeable musical amateur, dubbed the youth "little Beethoven."[14] In one form or another, that name would come up for the rest of Brahms's life—the comparison all young composers wanted to earn, as in an earlier time they aspired to be "another Mozart." (Those acquiring such a tag would spend their careers, as Brahms did, trying to escape it.) Reményi also played in the king's soiree. Had he noticed yet that his accompanist was stealing his thunder?

There were a few more pleasant days in Hanover before the chief of police heard of this Hungarian revolutionary who had played at court. Reményi was hauled in to be grilled by the police, and barely escaped being escorted across the border; it was time for the duo to get out of town. For his friends, the old one and the new, Joachim did the best favor he could think of: he dispatched them with his blessings to Weimar and Liszt, sending a letter of introduction ahead. Privately, he told Johannes that if things did not work out with Reményi—and if he knew Reményi they would not—Johannes must come to stay with him in Göttingen.

FRANZ LISZT held at Weimar the post of court Kapellmeister, and lived in the mansion and on the manna of his mistress, polemicist, and ghostwriter Princess Carolyne von Sayn-Wittgenstein. Wherever he went, the virtuoso maintained something like the style of an Oriental potentate, with a court of acolytes singing his praises. Hungarian-born (in 1811) and another fiery nationalist, Liszt had nonetheless been a citizen of Europe since childhood and barely spoke his native language. He had long been adored for his beauty as much as his talent, and both qualities attracted legions of female devotees. (In Weimar a lady at court wore always at her breast, in a golden locket, one of Liszt's cigar butts.) Yet despite the wild adulation he had aroused since his teens, in the first of several retirements from the world the young Liszt, inspired by the uncanny virtuosity of the violinist Paganini, had secluded himself with the intention of making himself the greatest pianist who ever lived. By all accounts, he succeeded. Even Brahms would say with genuine admiration: "Whoever has not heard Liszt cannot even speak of piano playing."[15]

In accepting a position as Kapellmeister of the provincial court of Saxe-Weimar in 1848, Liszt curtailed his stupendous career as a recitalist. He gave himself completely to composing, conducting, and proselytizing for his New German School. From the title of a famous essay by Liszt's colleague Richard Wagner, the Wagnerian branch of the movement would be associated with the tag "The Artwork of the Future." For both Liszt and Wagner, the underlying doctrine was *the unity of the arts*— literary, visual, musical. For Wagner that meant making his operas into *music drama* and his theater productions into a *Gesamtkunstwerk*, a "total work of art" uniting music, poetry, drama, and the visual arts. Liszt's path was to base his instrumental music on literary or visual-art foundations, with the cross-fertilization of arts creating freer forms, fresh harmonies, new kinds of musical organization. Thus Liszt's invention of the *symphonic poem*, with its literary or pictorial underpinning, called a "program." (Unlike many who followed him, Liszt cited evocative ideas for his programs rather than dramatic scenarios.)

A prime inspiration for the new movement was Hector Berlioz, whose *Symphonie fantastique* and its program of an artist's opium dreams, its melodic idée fixe recurring in new guises in every movement, had marked the high noon of Romanticism in orchestral music. Now the aging Berlioz served as godfather to the revolution of Liszt and Wagner.

No doubt by 1853 Liszt suspected that his former concertmaster Joachim was turning against him. But he still admired the violinist, and when Joachim's letter arrived announcing the approach of Brahms (Liszt already knew Reményi), word went out to the faithful to assemble at the princess's mansion, the Altenburg, to behold this new star.

Brahms and Reményi arrived at the mansion on June 12, 1853, and stood chatting with guests as Liszteans Peter Cornelius, Joachim Raff, and the American William Mason perused manuscripts Brahms had deposited on the piano. Finally, Liszt made his entrance and his usual gracious introductions. Gesturing to the piano, he asked the young man to play. Brahms declined; as sometimes happened in those days, he was paralyzed with nervousness. "Well then," said Liszt, picking up the E♭ Minor Scherzo with its barely decipherable handwriting, "I shall have to play."[16]

This was Brahms's first experience of Liszt at the keyboard, and it must have been a revelation—not only hearing his own music from an incomparable virtuoso, but witnessing a tour de force that few have duplicated and Liszt accomplished time and again: to put on the piano rack any piece, of any difficulty and medium, and sight-read it brilliantly in notes and expression, accompanied by a running commentary. In this case the commentary was highly pleased.

Brahms's E♭ Minor Scherzo, written when he was eighteen, is demonic in tone and relentless in rhythmic drive, with two lyrical trios as contrast. Even if he did not sign it Kreisler Junior, it has the Kreisler voice. The main melodic idea, which seems to arise from fragments accumulating and dissolving, is the first surviving example of the distinctive Brahmsian minor theme. Its relations appear mainly in his later works evoking death: the *Begräbnisgesang* (*Funeral Song*) of 1858, the "All flesh is grass" movement of *Ein deutsches Requiem*, the song "For it goes with man as with the beast" from the last year of his life. These melodies, their hollow and archaic minor, are the Brahmsian equivalent of the old Gregorian funeral chant—the *Dies Irae*, Day of Wrath, whose tones evoked death for many composers of the Romantic century, including Berlioz and Liszt.

So Brahms's E♭ Minor Scherzo was Liszt's kind of music, gleefully demonic, the piano sound big and colorful, almost orchestral. And Liszt was a generous person and always on the lookout for disciples. For a few minutes at least, Brahms looked like a prospect for the cause. Liszt praised the scherzo effusively. Raff observed that its beginning recalled Chopin's B♭ Minor Scherzo. Brahms denied he had ever heard any Chopin, but he was probably fibbing, and Raff probably right.[17] After more pleasant talk, Liszt played over some of the C Major Sonata.

Eventually somebody took his cue and asked Liszt to play something of his own. He picked a new work he knew stood near the summit of his keyboard music, the B Minor Sonata, eventually dedicated to Robert

Schumann and one of the towering sonatas of the era. The piece is a dense, one-movement study in the technique of thematic integration and transformation that Liszt pioneered—technique not far, in fact, from the sort Brahms was to perfect: a basic motive pervades the texture and generates the entire melodic discourse.[18] But Liszt's B Minor, even if it subsumes echoes of traditional sonata form and has contrasts in tempo, is no sonata at all as Brahms understood the term, a multi-movement work using familiar formal patterns.

The B Minor Sonata also features, of course, the Lisztean voice—passionate and compelling if one is moved by it, garish and overripe if one is not. Brahms was not. He appreciated Liszt's cordiality and he was surely stunned by the playing. But he despised the music. When he came to know the aesthetics of the New German School—especially the idea of unifying the arts—he would disdain that as well. Brahms could put aesthetics aside if he liked a composer's notes; he did just that with Wagner. But Liszt's work Brahms probably found shaky in form, thin in substance, overwrought in emotion. His eventual term for the whole New German School, Wagner always excepted, was "swindle."[19]

Besides, when Brahms first met Liszt he was equally disgusted by the Altenburg. Biographer Max Kalbeck reports that the Princess's mansion combined "the church with the boudoir, the state hall with the library, the hotel with the residence, the cabinet of curiosities with the workplace." Liszt did his composing in the Blue Room, a priceless engraving of Dürer's *Melancholia* on the wall to provide atmosphere. The opulence, the court of acolytes, the theater of the place, turned the stomach of plain North German Johannes Brahms.

Reményi reported that, as Liszt often did, at a particularly affecting moment in the sonata he looked over his audience to gauge the effect, and discovered Brahms asleep in the chair. Liszt kept playing, but at the end he brusquely rose from the keyboard and left the room.

Reményi, it should be kept in mind, was as given to improvisation in his recollections as in his playing. But that incident or something like it seems to have alerted Liszt that Brahms was not seduced by his music and not likely to serve the revolution. There was nothing new in that for Liszt; it had happened before and was happening now with Joachim. On the surface the virtuoso remained warm, and his cordiality would persist through all the dissonance of the coming years. When Brahms left Weimar, Liszt presented him with a keepsake in the form of a cigar box engraved "Brams." All the same, Liszt was never to play or conduct a single Brahms work in public.

For his part, however disgusted by Liszt and his milieu, Brahms lingered in Weimar for nearly three weeks. He and Reményi occupied rooms just vacated by pianist, conductor, and New German apostle Hans von Bülow.[20] In those rooms Reményi no doubt listened to his companion run down their host day after day, and no doubt Reményi persistently responded that they had better pay court to someone as powerful as Liszt. It was bound to happen anyway, but mainly over this dispute the duo split apart. Reményi knew what side his bread was buttered on and he was not going to let this damned accompanist get in the way of his career.

On June 9, Brahms wrote in fury to Joachim in Göttingen: "If I were not named 'Kreisler' I should now have well-founded reasons to be somewhat dispirited, to curse my art and my enthusiasm, and to retire as a [clerk] into solitude . . . Reményi is leaving Weimar without me."[21] He added that he cannot return to Hamburg with so little tangible to show, but if there he "should feel happiest with my heart tuned in C-G sharp." (The Key of C♯ minor is Kreisler's.) In the letter Brahms asked to visit Joachim in Göttingen and was happily accepted. Meanwhile, Reményi made haste to write Liszt with nationalistic ardor as "Admirable Compatriot!" "Conceive the immense joy," he continued. "Your favor is my talisman!" Et cetera. At the bottom of the page Reményi added a curt postscript: "Brahms has left for Göttingen."[22]

That June of 1853, Brahms's mother, having received reports from Johannes about his friendship with the famous Josef Joachim, wrote him a prophetic reply:

Happy Johannes, and we his happy parents. . . . Now, Johannes dear, your life really begins, now you will reap what you have sown with toil and diligence here. Your great hour has come. You must thank Divine Providence which sent an angel to lead you out of the darkness into the world where there are human beings who appreciate your worth and the value of what you have learned. How much we should love to be with you a few hours, to see your happy face.[23]

In Göttingen in July and August, sharing small quarters as Joachim attended his university lectures, Brahms and Joachim began using with each other the familiar *du*, "thou," which signifies deepest affection. Johannes called Joachim by his nickname, Jussuf. They played together constantly, their own music and the masters', and talked art and religion and philosophy late into the night. Brahms began to study Joachim's

music, convincing himself that this friend had greater talent for composing than his own. History would fail to find a distinctive voice in
Joachim's work, but he knew the orchestra inside out; soon Brahms
would need that knowledge. The violinist was working then on a couple
of overtures; without telling Joachim, Brahms made piano arrangements
of them. Their music copying began to look remarkably similar. Meanwhile Johannes sampled the jolly undergraduate life of the *Sachsen*, the
student clubs whose songs he would draw on decades later for the Academic Festival Overture.

Around that time in "Des jungen Kreislers Schatzkästlein," then over
two hundred entries long, aphorisms begin to appear with an attribution
of three musical notes drawn on a staff: F-A-E. With Johannes's encouragement, Joachim had written these entries into the notebook. The
pitches serving as signature were the violinist's motto, perhaps arising
from his ongoing lovesickness over Gisela von Arnim, daughter of the famous Achim and Bettina. For Joachim the notes F-A-E signified *frei aber
einsam*, "free but lonely."

In the "Schatzkästlein" Joachim wrote, "Artists should not be servants,
but priests of the public." "Write down everything that you feel, so that
it becomes part of you, as if it were a reminiscence."[24] In response to
these, Johannes added a fragment of dialogue from Goethe that was
prophetic for both friends:

A: It's said you're a misanthrope.
B: I don't hate men, thank God.
    But hatred of mankind, that blew over me like a cold wind,
    And I've responded in kind.
A: So what came of it?
B: I've resolved to live a solo-fiddler.[25]

For Johannes, that first visit with Joachim in Göttingen seems to have
been for the most part blithe and sociable. During the summer he produced several songs, including the two versions of "Liebe und Frühling,"
the folklike and gently lilting "Wie die Wolke nach der Sonne," and
"Nachtigallen schwingen," with its vivacious rhythm and rich harmony.
Love and spring, clouds in the sun, nightingales in flowers: the camer-
aderie of those weeks infected his songs, most of their texts full of youth
and hope. (In that they are uncommon for Brahms.) For his friend's
twenty-second birthday in July, Brahms produced the joking "Hymn for
the Glorification of the Great Joachim," for two violins and contrabass
(suppressed—he did not let his jokes survive either).

On July 10, his mother wrote expressing surprise and concern over the break with Reményi: "I hope you parted friends." But what was he doing for money? Fritz offered to send his savings, or maybe Christiane offered for him.[26] Johannes declined the gift, insisting he needed nothing. His mother doggedly responded: "Even if you have free lodging, food, and drink, you must have clean linen, your boots wear out, and, after all, how can you live away from home without money? If you have to get every little thing from Joachim, you will be under too great an obligation. . . . You understand people too little and trust them too much." Then and for years after, his parents worried that he was oblivious to practical matters, living on air—which he more or less was. To get by, Johannes would take on concerts and pupils, grudgingly, here and there, and depend on friends for funds and lodging.

Sister Elise appended to a letter that Herr Marxsen would like his student back but, "We think it's best for you to try your luck in foreign parts, even though we'd love to have you home. . . . How is the young girl who always brings you your coffee, is she pretty and not as fat as me?"[27]

In an effort to ease parental anxieties, Joachim took it upon himself to write them:

> Allow me . . . to write and tell you how infinitely blessed I feel in the companionship of your Johannes. . . . Johannes has stimulated my work as an artist to an extent beyond my hopes. To strive with him for a mutual goal is a fresh spur for me on the thorny path that we musicians have to tread through life. His purity, his independence, young though he is, and the singular wealth of his heart and intellect find sympathetic utterance in his music, just as his whole nature will bring joy to all who come into spiritual contact with him. How splendid it will be when his artistic powers are revealed in a work accessible to all! And with his ardent desire for perfection nothing else is possible. You will understand my wish to have him near me as long as his presence does not interfere with his duty to himself.[28]

Christiane Brahms replied to this rhapsodic testimonial—shaped for the purpose, but genuine—as best she could. Even Johann Jakob penned a few words to Joachim, adding his stolid blessing to this son who seemed to be impressing all sorts of famous people: "I hold it for a particularly favorable sign from heaven and it allows me to look to the future with high hopes and confidence." Maybe, in other words, the boy will actually make a living. Still, they would be wondering around the dinner table in Hamburg, how can he earn any real money without Reményi?

At the end of July, Christiane tried again to get a handle on the situation: Invite Joachim to come to Hamburg and visit with us, we'll make you chocolate and get theater tickets, whip up a bowl of egg punch and your favorite pastries. . . . "Ach, this is all silly. You can see your way better than I can."[29] For all the motherly worrying and advice, Christiane Brahms's letters reveal an extraordinary confidence in the judgment of her shining boy. She had observed the child take one decisive step after another from the beginning of his studies, and she sensed there was some pattern in it visible only to him. Joachim and other friends had recognized that, but it is remarkable for a parent to see it.

Johannes had a more immediate plan that he was ready to put in motion. He and Joachim gave a concert in Göttingen and Brahms devoted the proceeds to a long-anticipated hiking tour of the Rhine, the spiritual heartland of Germany. On August 26, he arrived in Mainz for the beginning of the trip, staff in hand and pack on his back. His mother wrote: "Such steep rocks! How easily you could fall! . . . Nestler's daughter died of a hemorrhage after such a hike! Malwine Erk was killed in Helgoland by lightning! Oh, enough of this, buy a winter coat, write if you need money."[30]

Before Brahms left Joachim said: you must introduce yourself to Robert and Clara Schumann in Düsseldorf, which after all is on the way. Brahms replied, not after that experience with the unopened parcel in Hamburg. Forget that, Joachim said: ring the doorbell. There the matter rested. As Brahms left they agreed to meet in Hanover in October, when Joachim had returned to work at court.

Brahms's Rhine journey, intended only to explore that most Romantic of rivers, would be one more instance when serendipity shaped momentous things.

IN THE LAST DAYS OF AUGUST, Brahms hiked along the lower Rhine Valley, exulting in the medieval villages, the Lorelei cliffs, the hillsides covered in vineyards and watched from the heights by ruined castles. Excited by the scenery so long anticipated, electrified by the events of the past weeks, in a few days he covered over a hundred kilometers to Bonn. His family wrote regularly. On September 3 Fritz wrote to say that he wished he were going along. Christiane wrote telling Johannes not to put ideas in Fritz's head. Elise wrote that they had shown the letters about Joachim to Uncle and Aunt Giesemann, who wept as they read them.[31] Joachim also wrote to the Giesemanns.

In Bonn, Brahms presented one of Joachim's greeting cards, signed on the back "Joh. Kreisler, Jun.," to J. W. von Wasielewski. A violinist and composer serving as a town choir director, Wasielewski had recently been concertmaster of Robert Schumann's orchestra in Düsseldorf. As was becoming the pattern now, this older musician was charmed by Johannes's looks, his air of authority, his unaffected manner, but was impressed most of all when he sat down at the piano. Wasielewski recalled only one piece in particular, an arrangement of the popular Hungarian piece *Rakóczy March* that Brahms gave a bravura treatment. According to pattern too, Wasielewski insisted that Brahms must stop off in Düsseldorf and visit the Schumanns. Once more Brahms rehearsed the story of the returned manuscripts, but he was wavering. Wasielewski sent him on his way with a letter of introduction to Schumann and one to the Deichmann family, in Mehlem across the river.

Deichmann, a financier and arts patron, opened his house to the wandering musician. Brahms wrote Joachim about the "splendid people" and "heavenly visit."[32] He explored more of the Rhine and its tributaries with Deichmann's three sons, and got to know musical friends of the family, including composer/conductor Franz Wüllner, who was to play a large role in the careers of both Brahms and Wagner. With Brahms, Wüllner later recalled, "We young musicians were immediately delighted and carried away."[33] Some of his teenage awkwardness and shyness had receded. Despite the distractions of the journey, Brahms started a piece in F minor, destined to be his last and finest piano sonata, and a new book of quotes he called "Schöne Gedanken über Musik" ("Beautiful Thoughts on Music.")

Like nearly everyone else Brahms had met lately, the Deichmanns were Schumann devotees. During his visit he began going through their collection of the composer's work, perhaps the first time he had seen any of it beyond the little Luise Japha had shown him. In Mehlem, playing through piece after piece of Schumann's, he found himself overwhelmed by the poetic voice of a composer he had once deplored to Luise. There came the spine-tingling moment when Young Kreisler first opened Schumann's rhapsodic set of piano pieces after E. T. A. Hoffmann, called *Kreisleriana*. Perhaps it was that moment when Brahms knew he must visit Schumann: once again fate seemed to be addressing him directly, through the agency of Hoffmann. So Brahms said his farewells to the Deichmanns and headed along the river toward Düsseldorf.

On the way he stopped off at Cologne, where he met composer/conductor Ferdinand Hiller—Schumann's predecessor as music director in

Düsseldorf—and Carl Reinecke, who in the next decade became conductor of the Leipzig Gewandhaus. Then Brahms took a train north. Around noon on September 30, he stood before the arched doorway of the Schumanns' modest two-story house, his pack stuffed with music, trying to subdue his nerves as he looked at the iron bellpull.

His life had been incredible that year. It had been like one of those puzzles of little steel balls that have to go into holes: sometimes you set things in motion and before your eyes every ball falls into place, one after another. It is a haunting experience, because you know things like that have more to do with luck than volition, and they never happen again. For Brahms the last part of the puzzle was about to fall into place.

He rang the bell.

CHAPTER FOUR

The Eagle's Wings

AROUND NOON on September 30, 1853, on Belkerstrasse in Düsseldorf, Robert and Clara Schumann's daughter Marie ran to answer the bell. She opened the door to find a young man with long blond hair, staff in hand and pack on his back. Despite his travel-weary air and worn alpaca jacket, Marie found him handsome as a picture. He said his name was Brahms and he would like to see Herr Schumann. Poppa and Mamma are out, Marie said.[1] Brahms hesitated—he had planned to stay in town only the day—but then asked if he could come back tomorrow. Marie told him to ring at eleven: they always go out at noon. He agreed and turned away. When her parents got home Marie reported the visit, and that night Robert Schumann noted in his diary, "Herr Brahms from Hamburg." He had been expecting the call. Joachim had come through Düsseldorf at the end of August and preached the gospel of Johannes.[2]

Brahms rang the bell next morning and the door was opened by Robert Schumann, in dressing gown and slippers. Shyly, diffidently, the young man introduced himself. Awkward moments followed, the youth tongue-tied and Schumann mumbling. As most people had been that summer, the older man was enchanted by Brahms at first sight. He was so appealing to look at; there was something burning in his eyes that belied the delicate features and the shyness.

Schumann roused himself to be hospitable. He was forty-three then, music director in Düsseldorf. Even as he held that public post, for some time he had been lapsing inward, glazing over, sitting in company with lips pursed as if whistling silently while people waited for him to say something. Well, if conversation was hard with this stranger who came so well recommended, music could speak. Schumann invited Brahms into the narrow parlor where the Graf piano waited, and asked him to play.

Brahms sat down and struck into a piece he thought might make a good impression, the C Major Piano Sonata. Schumann listened to the Beethovenian opening, reminiscent of the *Hammerklavier* Sonata, quickly modulating down a step like the *Waldstein*. Schumann would have noted these echoes of Beethoven, not mistakable for their models but rather a meditation on the past as a new starting point. With rising excitement he heard the brash theme of the beginning break up into ingenious contrapuntal elaboration, every idea growing organically from the opening measures.

Brahms felt Schumann's touch on his shoulder. "Please wait a moment. I must call my wife." Schumann rushed from the room as Brahms sat staring at the keyboard, his heart pounding. He may never have heard Clara Schumann play, but he knew about her. Clara had performed only sporadically since her marriage in 1840, but her teenage years were still spoken of with awe. When the two Schumanns entered the room, Brahms must have risen to greet her struggling with the kind of anxiety that had made it impossible for him to play at Liszt's. This was not the palatial Altenburg, though, but a cozy bourgeois parlor, and Clara greeted him with a smile that lit up her dark-blue eyes.

"Here, dear Clara," Schumann said, "you shall hear music such as you have never heard before. Now begin your sonata again, young man."[3]

Brahms played, with more fire and confidence this time. If not a full-blown virtuoso, he was still a superb pianist in those days. He played his work as composers do when they are able performers: from the inside, from a penetrating understanding of every gesture and its meaning to the form and expressive shape. The Beethovenian first movement gave way to tender, introspective variations on a folk song—classical in technique, Romantic in inspiration, unique in sound. As the music unfolded the youth bent intensely over the keyboard, sometimes unconsciously humming along with the melody.[4] An electrifying scherzo broke out, with a songful trio for contrast. Then a finale headlong and scherzo-like, with startling shifts of accent that must have appealed to Schumann—he had done things like that with rhythm. If in principle the finale too much resembled the third movement in rhythm and texture, the material was too breathtaking to leave room for complaint.

The Schumanns heard a work that from beginning to end combined youthful extravagance of invention with a precocious sense of form and continuity. And they saw a boyish-looking artist who already possessed the capacity to shape a long piece with the most rigorous logic, yet with the freedom of an improvisation. It is a skill training can refine but in the end is a gift, a supremely rare one. (Did Schumann understand that he never quite possessed the gift himself?) The Schumanns also saw that the sonata strained the limits of the piano and ten fingers. This music yearned for an orchestra.

The sonata pounded to a close with double handfuls of staccato chords. Then came the paralyzing moment of waiting for a response. Schumann only said they would like to hear more, anything he wanted to show them. So Brahms went on, playing piece after piece, the repertoire that had dazzled musicians in the last weeks—the F♯ Minor Sonata, the E♭ Minor Scherzo, other works of which nothing survives. Would the music persuade these two? Apparently Robert and Clara said little, just listened.

It was well past noon when Brahms had displayed all the wares he cared to. Schumann rose, patted him on the shoulder, and said, "You and I understand each other." What did he mean by that? Brahms wondered.[5] Still uncertain over the impression he had made, the visitor was ushered to the door with an invitation to lunch next day.

Marie Schumann came home from school to find her parents at the table talking rapturously about nothing but Brahms. Clara wrote first impressions in her journal:

> Here again is one who comes as if sent from God! He played us sonatas and scherzos of his own, all of them rich in fantasy, depth of feeling and mastery of form. Robert could see no reason to suggest any changes. It is truly moving to behold him at the piano, his interesting young face transfigured by the music, his fine hands which easily overcome the greatest difficulties (his things are very difficult), and above all his marvelous works. . . . A great future lies before him, for when he comes to the point of writing for orchestra, then he will have found the true medium for his imagination.[6]

Schumann's diary note that night is laconic, but no less significant: "Visit from Brahms (a genius)."

NEXT DAY BRAHMS DITHERED, too nervous to set off for his lunch invitation. When he failed to turn up, Robert dispatched Clara to track him down. She walked through Düsseldorf peering into one cheap inn after another until she found the youth and towed him back to the house with her.[7] That day Brahms began to realize the impression he had made. It seemed unbelievable, but Schumann the great and still neglected creator, and his wife the legendary pianist, admired him and offered their friendship. Brahms wrote Joachim:

> What shall I write you about Schumann; shall I break out into encomiums of his genius and character, or shall I lament that people still sin grievously in misjudging and so little honoring a good man and divine artist? And I myself, how long did I sin likewise?[8]

The Schumanns persuaded Brahms—his incredulity still made him shy—to stay on in Düsseldorf until Joachim showed up for some performances at the end of October; then the two could return together to Hanover. Brahms finally accepted the eager hospitality of the couple.

The month that followed was as magical as living out a fairy tale. There were walks and evenings of music, Brahms and Clara alternating at the keyboard, playing his work along with Robert's and older masters'. There were endless hours of high grand talk, Brahms dazzled by Schumann's flights of imagination. Clara's journal recalls those days: "Robert says there is nothing to wish except that heaven may preserve [Brahms's] health. . . . In the afternoon Brahms came in, and played us some of his things, which made a deep impression on all of us (I invited some of my pupils and Fr. Leser). . . . After dinner Brahms played us several very curious Hungarian folksongs."[9]

In hours away from the piano Robert taught his new friend chess and table-turning. (Schumann had become obsessed with the parlor game of séances.) Brahms also had a reunion with his Hamburg friends Luise and Minna Japha. Luise had been working nominally with both Schumanns, studying piano and composition, but had hardly set eyes on the taciturn, reclusive Robert.[10] Johannes asked Luise what she thought Schumann had meant by "We understand each other." She had no idea. Before long, the entire musical world would find out.

Schumann opened his extensive library to Johannes, who shared it with the Japha sisters. He spent evenings reading aloud to Luise, especially from Schumann's volumes of E. T. A. Hoffmann. He showed her a letter from his mother, who had promised to write three pages a week and kept to it, even if she had to flesh out the pages with items copied from newspapers. "What's she supposed to do when she has no more news?" Johannes told Luise with ironical affection. "She can't write a philosophical treatise, but she always sends me three whole pages.[11]

For all the placid hours of reading and games and sharing music, events ripened fast. Robert contacted his publishers Breitkopf & Härtel and asked them to publish music by his discovery. Just over a week after their meeting, Schumann was already thinking of saying something in print about Brahms. He wrote Joachim in his most flowery mode:

> If I were younger, I might write a few rhapsodies on the young eagle who swooped down so suddenly on Düsseldorf from the Alps, or, to use another metaphor, the magnificent torrent which is at its best when, like Niagara, it dashes down as a cascade from the heights . . . while its shores are haunted by the butterfly and nightingale. I believe Johannes is another John the Baptist, whose revelations will puzzle many of the Pharisees, and every one else, for centuries. Only the other apostles will understand his message, including possibly Judas Iscariot. . . . All this is for the Apostle Joseph alone.[12]

Schumann's sense wanders in the letter, but he knew Joachim would understand whom he meant by Judas Iscariot: Liszt, the betrayer of music. Even though Joachim still nominally belonged to the Weimar circle, still exchanged friendly letters with his old mentor, he did not protest the word *Judas*. Schumann also wrote of Brahms: "This is he that should come,"[13] implying that somehow Johannes was Messiah to his own John the Baptist. (Or more likely: Schumann was losing his way in thickets of metaphor.)

Brahms wrote Joachim asking for advice on what pieces he should show Breitkopf & Härtel, and in what order—Schumann had suggested a list, but Brahms wanted another opinion. Two of the pieces in these discussions, a fantasy for piano trio and a violin sonata, never saw light. To his friend's query, Joachim replied with Romantic ardor: "You ask me to tell you in what order you should let your music cry out to the world the fact of which you have long been joyfully conscious: *I am!* I am unspeakably touched by this." Joachim proposed an order close to what in fact appeared, but it was characteristic of Brahms to solicit opinions and then make his own decisions. It would be Opus 1, the C Major Sonata; Opus 2, the F♯ Minor Sonata; Opus 3, Six Songs (starting with "Liebestreu"); and Opus 4, the E♭ Minor Scherzo. When Luise Japha asked Johannes why he started with the C Major rather than the flashier and more rhythmical scherzo, he told her, "When one first shows oneself, it is to the head and not the heels that one wants to draw attention."[14]

With October's furor of activity and excitement, musical ideas came to Brahms so fast and strong that he did not have time to write them down.

He worked out the first, third, and fifth movements of the F Minor Sonata during the month, to add to the two movements composed earlier. During a day of sociable music-making on the twelfth, he played, mostly from his head, a provisional version of the new sonata for the Schumanns. As Opus 5, the F Minor would be the crown of his early keyboard music. It was the only work of Brahms on which Robert Schumann commented in progress.

At the same time, Brahms began to practice the piano intensively, with coaching from Clara.[15] She had taken to calling him "Robert's Johannes."[16] For all her own enthusiasm, neither then nor later did Clara turn off her critical intelligence. After he had played the trio fantasia and the E♭ Minor Scherzo she noted in her journal, "Here and there the sound of the instruments was not suitable to their characters, but these are trifles in comparison with his rich imagination and feeling." Once she came indoors thinking someone was playing four-hand duets and discovered Brahms alone at the piano, his hands flashing all over the keyboard. He loved drawing great handfuls of sound from the instrument.

Naturally, Schumann broadcast the news around his circle in Düsseldorf. At a rehearsal of the town choral society he introduced Brahms to composer Albert Dietrich, and they immediately struck up a friendship, once more owing to Brahms's person and personality as much as his music. Brahms and Dietrich took to breakfasting together in the Hofgarten, and Dietrich sent out word to acquaintances. Kreisler—so Dietrich and others called him—radiated a talent and boyish impetuousness that seemed to intensify under the adulation of the Schumanns. In those days, you could almost see the halo around his head. Dietrich wrote, "I was particularly struck by the characteristic energy of the mouth, and the serious depths in his blue eyes." He cherished Kreisler's athleticism, his boyish pranks, his ability to drop off to sleep in a second, the way he would dash upstairs and drum on your door with both fists and burst into the room. In private moments over a glass of beer, Brahms whispered to Dietrich about the shadows in his life—the poverty, the *Animierlokale*.[17] He also made the acquaintance of painters in Düsseldorf; the beauty of the city full of gardens had drawn many visual artists there.[18] Always scouting for ideas and stimulation; Brahms added painting to literature as a catalyst for his work.

Friendship itself was a discovery for him, a new inspiration. Other than his teachers, in Hamburg it had been mostly Luise Japha and Eduard Reményi who were interested in him, and in fact neither ended up liking him particularly. Eduard Marxsen had kept Brahms so wrapped up in his studies that it had been as if the teacher were reserving this student for himself. Then Brahms had gone out into the world and immediately gained the attention and affection of musicians numbered among the finest in Europe. He fell into that new life as if born to it, born to be a genius among geniuses—or failing that, a misfit.

In October Robert Schumann had a visit from an admirer, painter Jean-Joseph Laurens. The Frenchman made portraits of Schumann and his protégé. Laurens's two drawings of Brahms—delicate profile and long curling hair, lost in thought—are the images that best evoke him in those years: dreaming Kreisler of the maidenly features. That force of insight carries over into Laurens's portrait of Schumann, which shows a face weary and haunted. Laurens told Clara that the pupils of Schumann's eyes were oddly dilated. She admitted that her husband had not been well.[19]

Yet in those days Schumann seemed elated and full of energy. His output of music had been prodigious in Düsseldorf, but now amid other projects he omitted nothing in his efforts to spread the word about Johannes. On October 13, Schumann wrote Joachim, "I have begun to collect and arrange my ideas on the young eagle. Much as I should like to assist him in his first public flight, I fear that my personal attachment is too great to admit of an impartial consideration of the lights and shadows of his plumage." Next day, Schumann finished an essay on Brahms[20]—one hardly impartial, in fact incredible. Schumann notified Breitkopf & Härtel to watch for the article, which he intended to publish in the *Neue Zeitschrift für Musik.*

The day the article came out and before Brahms knew of it, Joachim made a surprise visit to the Schumanns'. The violinist had just performed in a festival in Karlsruhe and visited Liszt and his circle there, and afterward went with Liszt to meet Richard Wagner in Basel. Perhaps after those days among the revolutionaries, Joachim fled to the Schumanns and Brahms as an antidote. He felt painfully torn between his old mentors and his new. (Once Schumann and Liszt had been close, but in 1848 they broke over an incident when Liszt shrugged off Schumann's Piano Quintet and slighted the late Mendelssohn, at which Schumann became enraged. They never reconciled, though Liszt remained openhanded toward both Schumanns.)[21]

After Joachim's brief surprise visit, Robert proposed a surprise of his own: a sonata in the violinist's honor to be composed jointly by himself, Albert Dietrich, and Brahms. They would present it as a gift on Joachim's return for his appearance with Schumann's orchestra. With his old taste for cabalistic codes in notes, Schumann proposed for the work's title and idée fixe the notes F-A-E, Joachim's "free-but-lonely" motto: *frei aber einsam.*

By the time Joachim reappeared in Düsseldorf at the end of October, the *F A E* Sonata was ready. The unveiling was set for the day after his performance with the orchestra. Among invited guests for the occasion were Gisela von Arnim, from whom Joachim had recently become free but lonely, and her celebrated mother, Bettina—writer, friend of Beethoven and Goethe, widow of Achim von Arnim the collector of *Des Knaben Wunderhorn.* Dressed in peasant costume, Gisela began the evening by presenting the sonata to Joachim hidden in a basket of flowers. For him that must have been a wrenching moment. But he went through the ceremony, expressing delight when he found the piece amid the flowers. He was asked to play it through with Clara, to see if he could identify the composers. Joachim named them off easily: Dietrich the opening, Schumann the intermezzo, and the last movement, a driving and brilliant scherzo, Brahms.

During the previous days, Joachim's rehearsals with Schumann and the orchestra had been an agony. The program consisted of his signature work, the Beethoven Violin Concerto, plus Schumann's Fantasy for Violin and Orchestra, and Joachim's own *Hamlet* Overture. Schumann, as municipal director of music in Düsseldorf and conductor of the orchestra and choral society, had never been comfortable on the podium and lately had fallen into bizarre behavior—constantly letting the baton go flying, sometimes becoming so engrossed in the music that he forgot to conduct. In rehearsal with Joachim, Schumann plowed straight through Joachim's overture, let mistakes go by, never noticed that the horn player missed a solo. Finally, desperate, Joachim took the podium and ran through the piece himself, with good results. But when the orchestral committee begged him to conduct the performance, Joachim refused because of the insult it would represent to Schumann.

The concert was the expected fiasco. Immediately the committee tried, as gently as possible, to remove Schumann from the conductorship, though not from his post as town music director. Outraged, Clara insisted that he fight back against this "infamous intrigue."[22] Schumann was in no shape for fighting, but humiliating confrontations and forced compromises continued into December. He never conducted again. In the end, the matter would be settled not by negotiations but by fate.

·   ·   ·

BY THEN, Schumann's article on the young eagle, the Niagara cataract, Young Kreisler, prophet and savior, had appeared in the *Neue Zeitschrift für Musik*. Schumann had founded the journal himself in 1834. In his first New Year's editorial, he had issued a statement of goals:

> To be remindful of older times and their works and to emphasize that only from such a pure source can new artistic beauties be fostered; at the same time to oppose the trends of the more recent past, proceeding from mere virtuosity, and, finally, to prepare the way for, and to hasten, the acceptance of a new poetic era.[23]

At that point Robert Schumann was a friend of Liszt, both of them searching for a "new poetic era" in music. They would divide bitterly over the direction of that search, Schumann on the path of tradition, Liszt of revolution. After a historic decade of promoting progressive composers and flaying philistines, Schumann sold the *Neue Zeitschrift* to Franz Brendel. During his long tenure as editor, Brendel turned the journal into a propaganda organ for Liszt and the New Germans—in other words, into a standard-bearer for ideals Schumann hated. (It was Brendel who coined the term "New German School" for Liszt and his followers.)

So while Schumann had begun as a firebrand and champion of revolutionaries like Chopin and Berlioz, by 1850 he had become disillusioned with the progressive faction. He wanted nothing to do with the Artwork of the Future. His loyalty was to the past, the line of Beethoven and Felix Mendelssohn. Over and over, Schumann and Joachim and their circle called Brahms, approvingly, "a real *Beethovener.*"

Schumann's "rhapsody" appeared in the *Neue Zeitschrift* on October 28, 1853, and fixed that date to the wall of history. He called it "Neue Bahnen," "New Paths":

> Years have passed—almost as many in number as those dedicated by me to the previous editorship of this journal, namely, ten—since I appeared on this scene so rich to me in remembrances. Often, in spite of arduous productive activity, I have felt tempted; many new and considerable talents have appeared, a fresh musical energy has seemed to announce itself through many of the earnest artists of the present time, even though their works are, for the most part, known only to a limited circle. [In a footnote, Schumann cites these composers, including Joachim, Clara's half-brother Woldemar Bargiel, Theodor Kirchner, and Albert Dietrich.] I have thought, watching the path of these

chosen ones with the greatest sympathy, that after such a preparation someone must and would suddenly appear, destined to give ideal presentation to the highest expression of the time, who would bring us his mastership not in process of development, but springing forth like Minerva fully armed from the head of Jove. And he is come, a young blood by whose cradle graces and heroes kept watch. He is called Johannes Brahms. . . . He bore all the outward signs that proclaim to us, "This is one of the elect." Sitting at the piano, he proceeded to reveal to us wondrous regions. We were drawn into circles of ever deeper enchantment. His playing, too, was full of genius, and transformed the piano into an orchestra of wailing and jubilant voices. There were sonatas, rather veiled symphonies—songs, whose poetry one would understand without knowing the words . . . single pianoforte pieces, partly demoniacal, of the most graceful form—then sonatas for violin and piano—quartets for strings [Brahms would suppress the latter pieces]—and every one so different from the rest that each seemed to flow from a separate source. And then it was as though he, like a tumultuous stream, united all into a waterfall, bearing a peaceful rainbow over the rushing waves, met on the shore by butterflies' fluttering, and accompanied by nightingales' voices.

If he will sink his magic staff in the region where the capacity of masses in chorus and orchestra can lend him its powers, still more wonderful glimpses into the mysteries of the spirit-world will be before us . . . his companions greet him on his first course through the world, where, perhaps, wounds may await him, but laurels and palms also. . . .

There is in all times a secret union of kindred spirits. Bind closer the circle, ye who belong to it, that the truth of art may shine ever clearer, spreading joy and blessing through the world.[24]

As everyone understood, the figure Schumann here unveils, with graces and heroes at his cradle and a god for a father and a mystical order of spirits around him, is a Messiah destined to bring a new age of joy and blessing to the art of music. Never has a composer debuted on the world's stage with an introduction like that.

Yet little of Schumann's astonishing prophecy is what it seems. The metaphors of "Neue Bahnen" are incoherent, its prophecies flawed. Johannes had not appeared as a fully formed offspring of the gods but had a long struggle ahead of him to find his way. Schumann had told Johannes at the outset, "We understand each other," but they did not. Schumann wanted his chosen one to stay with the early pieces' subjective high-Romantic ardor, reined in by a solid grasp of form—in other words, to inhabit the same territory of poetic Romanticism Schumann had, but with more discipline in the larger genres. But in the end Brahms would not take the New Paths Schumann prophesied. He was constitutionally incapable of following any path but his own.

Certainly time proved Schumann correct in two of his predictions—the laurels and palms, and the wounds. He was also right to call the piano pieces "veiled symphonies," straining toward orchestral expression. In the article and in person, Schumann urged Brahms to take up orchestral music, to write real symphonies and concertos—as Schumann had done himself, with prodding from his wife and with ambiguous success in comparison to his songs and piano miniatures. That call to compose grand works Brahms would obey, for a while, then abandon.

Besides the misconceptions, Schumann's article has more on its agenda than the apparent one of hailing a young genius. "Neue Bahnen" was a calculated insult that probably raised editor Brendel's hackles, and was intended to. It would have a similar effect all over musical Europe. Near the beginning, Schumann cites his list of "earnest artists of the present time." All are friends and disciples of his own. Pointedly omitted from his "union of kindred spirits" are Berlioz, Liszt, and Wagner—onetime friends now in the enemy camp. The article aims, in other words, to position Brahms alongside Schumann as a *Beethovener*, in opposition to Liszt's New German School and Wagner's Artwork of the Future.

Which is all to say that "Neue Bahnen" reflected Schumann's own purposes and patterns and fantasies more than it did the reality of twenty-year-old Johannes Brahms. For himself as a composer Schumann knew what he had accomplished, probably had a good idea of both his achievements and his limitations in shaping large-scale forms. Maybe he also suspected that his vein was nearly exhausted, despite the stacks of music he had composed in Düsseldorf.

In fact, for a long time Schumann had been waiting for a savior to carry his vision of music beyond what he could manage himself. Now he wanted Brahms to realize his own frustrated ambitions—to become the new, perfected Robert Schumann. Maybe in some unarticulated way Schumann had been awaiting a personal redeemer too. Brahms was not the first of his elect, his "secret union of kindred spirits." In an 1834 issue of the *Neue Zeitschrift für Musik*, Schumann published an article including this prophecy:

One winter night a year ago a young man joined our group. . . . Every eye was focused upon him. Some were reminded of a John the Baptist figure . . . the eyes aglow with enthusiasm . . . the luxuriant head of tumbling curls, and beneath it all a lithe, slim torso. . . . I heard a voice within me saying: "He it is whom you are seeking."[25]

These words introduced composer Ludwig Schunke, Schumann's beloved companion and first John the Baptist, who died soon after the article appeared. Other shining youths followed, notably British composer William Sterndale Bennett. Everyone familiar with Schumann's writings knew about his history with handsome young composers. Famously, none of them had achieved the stature he predicted.

Thus to a modern reader another question lingers in the background of "Neue Bahnen": To what degree was Schumann's interest more than political and abstractly musical? Was the older man attracted to Brahms? Was he bisexual? Schumann's teenaged diaries hint at "Greek" episodes with men.[26] Throughout his life and his affairs with women and his passionate connection to Clara, he was still attracted to handsome and talented youths. Johannes the Fair was the last of them—perhaps the most beautiful, certainly the most gifted.

Did Johannes see the manic quality in Schumann's response to him? Did he know about the enthusiasm for young men? Did he suspect darker currents in Robert's mind, secrets he was not party to? Brahms was away from home for the first time in his life, and for all his struggles he remained new to adulthood and its sorrows. As he was to find in terrible days to come, the Schumanns had more than ordinary sorrows besetting them.

Among the hundreds of Europe's leading musicians who read "Neue Bahnen" was Hans von Bülow, who testily wrote Liszt, "It doesn't trouble my sleep in the least. . . . Fifteen years ago Schumann said exactly the same thing about the 'genius' of William Sterndale 'Benêt'" (the pun meaning "blockhead"). Wagner and the New Germans began referring to Brahms sarcastically as "heiligen Johannes," "Saint John."[27] All the same, if the revolutionaries resented Schumann's calculated insult, conservatives in Leipzig were no happier. Schumann had also slighted the city's god and savior, Mendelssohn.[28] (That was unintended—Schumann and Mendelssohn had been close friends.) Conservative Leipzig's contempt for Brahms as rival Messiah was to simmer through the coming years.

Brahms went to Hanover on November 4, for a visit with Joachim. There he read "Neue Bahnen" for the first time—surely with disbelief, and many times. Schumann's prophecy broke over him like thunder. The tour with Reményi so casually arranged, the meeting with Joachim almost by chance, the encounters with influential musicians in Weimar and along the Rhine, the extraordinary reception the Schumanns had given him—all of it amounted to a stupendous run of good fortune, with its climax in Düsseldorf. Yet his luck this year had run to the point where luck becomes almost too much to bear.

Schumann had been struck with admiration for Brahms's works, and in that he was like nearly everyone else. But Brahms had also rung other chords: Schumann's attraction to beautiful youths, his frustrated desire to write confidently in large forms, his search for a Messiah for German music, which is to say: for all music. "Neue Bahnen" flowed from all these forces within Robert Schumann, all these seductions of the fair young genius.

When he walked through the Schumanns' door in Düsseldorf, Brahms had stepped unknowingly into a whirlwind that caught him up and deposited him in a place he never expected, never asked for, could not have wanted. He had set out from Hamburg in the spring of 1853 utterly unknown. Six months later, before he had done anything before the public to earn it, his name was on music lovers' lips all over Europe. Even at twenty, Brahms understood what a terrifying election it is, to be pronounced Messiah. He knew his scripture: Christ had gotten palms too, shortly before the Crucifixion.

But he would not pass the cup handed him. If he had been nominated for Messiah, he would give everything he had to fulfill the prophecy. He could not have known how much that would cost him, how almost monastic a withdrawal from the course of life would be required of him. Neither he nor anyone else could know if he had the talent, the intelligence, poise, wisdom, courage, and luck to survive it. He would require every one of those qualities, the courage and luck most of all.

After "Neue Bahnen" the musical world awaited his next steps. Brahms and Joachim knew that many hoped he would fall on his face.

Soon after the article appeared, Schumann sent a copy to Johannes's parents in Hamburg with a note: "We have come to feel great affection for your son Johannes, and his musical genius has given us richly joyful hours. . . . I send you these pages and think they will bring your fatherly heart a little joy. You may look forward with complete confidence to the future of this darling of the Muses."[29] Brandishing Schumann's letter, Johann Jakob Brahms charged into the house of a musician friend shouting, "You, Fritz, now what d'you say to this? Schumann declares my Hannes a great, important artist and he'll be a second Beethoven!" Fritz bellowed back, "That stupid, tow-headed little urchin is to be a Beethoven? Are you crazy?" And so it went, back and forth, before Johann Jakob retreated with a parting shot: "But *Schumann says so!*"[30]

In Hanover, Brahms let it all stew for three weeks, sitting with Joachim talking late into the night, before he wrote Schumann these circumspect thanks for a great and terrible gift.

> Honored Master,
>   You have made me so immensely happy that I cannot attempt to thank you in words. God grant that my works may soon prove to you how much your affection and kindness have encouraged and stimulated me. The public praise you have bestowed on me will have fastened general expectation so exceptionally upon my performances that I do not know how I shall be able to do some measure of justice to it. Above all it obliges me to take the greatest care in the selection of what is to be published . . .
>   Further I wish to tell you that I have copied out my F Minor Sonata, and made considerable alterations in the finale. . . . I should like also to thank you a thousand times for the dear portrait of yourself that you have sent me as well as for the letter you have written to my father. By it you have made a pair of good people happy, and for life Your
>
> > > > Brahms[31]

Putting the music in print was the next step. Schumann had continued to prod Breitkopf & Härtel and urged Brahms to visit the publisher in person. He wrote Joachim, "He must go to Leipzig; persuade him to do this, or they will get a wrong idea of his works; he must play them himself.[32] After some resistance, Johannes gave in. He arrived in Leipzig, city of J. S. Bach and Mendelssohn, Goethe and Lessing, on November 17, 1853.

His welcome in Germany's musical center proved warmer than expected, given the jealousy and resentment that must have been seething in town after the article. Heinrich von Sahr, Albert Dietrich's friend, introduced Brahms to Dr. Härtel the publisher and to leading Leipzig musicians, among them Clara Schumann's father Friedrich Wieck, the celebrated Beethoven pupil Ignaz Moscheles, and Gewandhaus concertmaster Ferdinand David. Once a teacher of Joachim's, and the man for whom Mendelssohn wrote the Violin Concerto, David asked Brahms to join him in a chamber music program at the Gewandhaus.

Sahr wrote to Dietrich in Düsseldorf: "He is perfect, the days since he has been here are amongst the most delightful in my recollection. He answers so exactly to my idea of an artist. And as a man!"[33] Countess Ida von Hohenthal invited Brahms to her estate near the city for a few days; he wangled a piano-teaching position there for his brother Fritz.[34] For her kindness the countess would receive the dedication of the F Minor Piano Sonata, but Fritz soon bungled the job and returned dejected to Hamburg.[35]

Another new Leipzig acquaintance, composer and conductor Julius Otto Grimm, kept pace with Brahms as a brash young artist discovering his powers. From Düsseldorf, Grimm wrote Joachim the following spring, "Kreisler is the most marvelous person . . . he wants to go to Grafenberg, so that we can lie in the moonlight in the woods. He is as mad as he can be—as the artistic genius of Düsseldorf he has adorned his room with . . . [pictures] of Madonnas and brats—so as to have something worthy of his contemplation while he is at work."[36]

After Brahms had played his works for Härtel in Leipzig, the publisher agreed to pay fifty gold pieces for the Sonatas in C Major (dedicated to Joachim) and F♯ Minor (dedicated to Clara Schumann), Six Songs (dedicated to Bettina von Arnim), and the E♭ Minor Scherzo. None of these early opuses is dedicated to Robert Schumann; Brahms considered none of them worthy of it.

Despite the excitement and the new acquaintances in Leipzig, Brahms felt restless and anxious to work. He went to Hanover for a few days to consult with Joachim over last revisions for the publications, and pounded away at the F Minor Sonata. Already he had his lifelong habit of showing new pieces to trusted friends, soliciting critiques that he only occasionally accepted. Yet Brahms needed the feedback as a touchstone, a sign of his connection to musicians and to listeners. The process also had the useful effect of keeping influential people involved in his work, feeling almost party to its creation. At least Brahms allowed them to feel that, even though it would rarely be true—except in some of the earlier works, when he needed all the advice he could get from more experienced orchestral composers like Joachim and Grimm.

That November, Josef Joachim lingered in the aftershock of his failed romance with Gisela von Arnim, and brooded over his connection to Liszt. After years of friendship and collaboration, Liszt had recently asked Joachim to use the familiar *du*, "thou." In a letter Liszt wrote, "Wagner had the most friendly feelings for you," pointedly complimented Schumann's new Violin Sonata, politely inquired after Brahms.[37]

Meanwhile, having heard a mistaken report that Joachim and Gisela were to be married, Schumann wrote Joachim playfully proposing to write a Wedding Symphony. He concluded, "I should like to write much more. But I have fallen into a merry mood and cannot get out of it. So good-bye, dear bridegroom." Joachim replied gloomily, enclosing a new piece of his own with the notes F-A-E circled. The notes have, he wrote Schumann, "not only an artistic but a human significance for me: their meaning is *'frei aber einsam.' I am not engaged.*"[38]

Yet Joachim and his lost love stayed close, and in letters to her the virtuoso poured out his feelings and frustrations. On November 27, he wrote Gisela as Brahms dozed on the sofa after a day of work:

> Brahms has been here since Friday, when, on coming back from a late walk, I found the young green and gold tiger lying in wait for me, greener than ever by reason of his laurels and newly gilt by publishers who are printing all his things. He was in splendid spirits and talked far into the night of old friends in the town of booksellers [Leipzig]. You have really seen deep into his nature—he is egotistic and always on the lookout for something to his advantage—but at any rate he is sincere . . . with none of the false sentimentality with which others of his kind like to deceive themselves.[39]

It appears that Gisela von Arnim never liked Brahms. She saw the calculation, the egotism and solipsism. Joachim saw them too, but understood and tried to forgive. Yet Brahms's self-absorption weighed on his best friend, as it sooner or later weighed on everyone who knew him. Brahms had made the first close friends of his life, but he was better at making friends than keeping them happy, or keeping them at all. His mind was closed to giving anything of himself beyond time and money—in those he was lavish. But no one must ask for anything deeper.

So there were struggles. Time and again Joachim would come and sit on Johannes's bed and beg abjectly to be reassured that Johannes loved him. "Certainly I explained to him that we were just as before," Brahms recalled, "but those kinds of questions were completely unbearable."[40] Despite the adulation of thousands, Joachim could never find enough affection, or at least not the kind he craved. And being made that way, he was thrown in with a man like Brahms for whom any expression of affection was rare and difficult. That crack in the foundation of their relationship foreshadowed its course for over forty years: a friendship and collaboration incomparably rich in artistic fruits, but emotionally frustrating, neurotic, and ill-defined.

In 1853, however, Johannes was still, for Joachim and others, the golden boy, the young eagle, the green and gold tiger, the fervid Young Kreisler dragging friends out to bask in the moonlight.

DURING NOVEMBER the Schumanns made a tour of Holland that turned out an artistic triumph, but no respite from the troubles overtaking them. On their return they had a letter from Brahms addressed "Mynheer Domine" in honor of the Holland visit, and continuing, "Forgive this playful form of address on the part of one whom you have made infinitely happy and joyful. . . . Härtels have told me that they are ready to print my first attempts." At that point, whatever burdens Schumann's article had placed on him, Brahms felt ready to take them up, with apprehension but also in the highest spirits of his life: *infinitely happy and joyful.*

After a brief stay in Hanover, Brahms took the train to Leipzig for more socializing and career-building. At a fashionable party a young lady observed Schumann's chosen one with a mixture of insight and wrong guesses as "fair, delicate-looking, with clear-cut features free from all passion. Purity, innocence, naturalness, power and depth. . . . And yet . . . a thin boy's voice which has not yet changed! And a child's countenance that any girl might kiss without blushing." They spoke of Jean Paul, Eichendorff, and Schiller; Brahms urged her to read E. T. A. Hoffmann and boasted, "I spend all my money on books; books are my greatest pleasure. I have read as much as I possibly could since I was quite little, and have made my way without guidance from the worst to the best."[41]

In Leipzig, Brahms dutifully visited Liszt and in his company made the acquaintance of the Parisian Hector Berlioz, spiritual father of the New Germans, in town for a program of his work. Once again Liszt received Brahms graciously. Brahms in turn was untypically careful not to offend him, and found he genuinely liked New German disciple Peter Cornelius. Making a reciprocal call on the young hero with his retinue, Liszt issued an ironical invitation, with one eye on his audience: "I hope that before too much time has passed, your 'New Paths' will bring you again to Weimar."[42] Then at the Berlioz concert in the Gewandhaus, Brahms sat looking with disgust on Liszt and his row of grinning apostles, among them his one-time partner Eduard Reményi.

In those years, with the instinctive knowledge and poise that accompanied him all his life, Brahms seemed to understand how to promote himself. He was no opportunist but rather a brilliant careerist—in the strategies of finding a reputation and power, if not always in the person-to-person part of it. With both enemies and friends he could be curt, sarcastic, graceless, and insulting as readily as he could be kind, helpful, and entertaining. Nobody ever knew which Brahms was going to turn up, or why.

Through this visit to Leipzig, however, he remained on his best behavior. As he wrote Joachim, he had been making the rounds he should make, courting the people he needed to court:

> Liszt also called upon me, with Cornelius and others. On Friday I went to see David, as well as Liszt, Berlioz, etc. On Sunday I even went to see [*Neue Zeitschrift* editor] Brendel . . . [after an ensuing salon performance arranged by Brendel[43]] Berlioz praised me with such infinite warmth and cordiality that the others humbly followed suit . . . On Monday Liszt is coming here again (very much to the disadvantage of Berlioz).[44]

In fact, Hector Berlioz had embraced Brahms after the performance and compared his profile to Schiller's.[45] Soon Joachim received another report from Leipzig, this time from Berlioz:

> Brams [sic] has had a great success here. He made a deep impression on me the other day at Brindel's [sic] with his scherzo and his adagio [from the F Minor Sonata]. I am grateful to you for having let me make the acquaintance of this diffident, audacious young man who has taken into his head to make a new music. He will suffer greatly.[46]

Exhausted and near the end of a career making new music and being more often pilloried than acclaimed for it, Berlioz was not phrasemaking when he wrote to Joachim of suffering for art.

Letters between the friends tracked back and forth, each with exciting news. Brahms wrote that Liszt wanted Joachim to send the *Hamlet* Overture for a performance.[47] The sage of Weimar continued to try everything he could think of to keep his violinist in the flock, but Joachim was inching away from him. Nor, for all the pleasantries and his attempts to court the powerful, could Brahms see Liszt's music and ideals as anything but a fraud. Over the years, that shared enmity was to be one of the things that held Brahms and Joachim together. The violinist required a hero, a cause, and now that wedded him to Johannes. Brahms understood that, counted on it, and over the years took ruthless advantage of it.

On the earlier Leipzig stay, Brahms had played his A Minor Violin Sonata in a private concert with Ferdinand David. It was the last time that work was heard of. Liszt borrowed and perhaps lost the sonata or, more likely, Brahms got it back and destroyed it. (The publisher Senff, to whom it had been offered, received the F Minor Piano Sonata instead.[48]) On December 17, Brahms made his public debut in Leipzig, playing the C Major Sonata and E♭ Minor Scherzo at a concert of the David Quartet, in the Gewandhaus. The reception was mixed, but the *Neue Zeitschrift* critic ringingly concluded that Brahms "will, advancing steadfastly and safely along his 'new paths,' someday become what Schumann has predicted of him, an epoch-making figure in the history of art."[49] Brahms had gotten through his first trial as Messiah in one piece.

In Leipzig, however, the pleasant words did him little good. In addition to the radical Weimar/conservative Leipzig dichotomy, a liberal-conservative split had developed within the city itself. These factions divided over Brahms only a little less bitterly than over Liszt and Berlioz. Brahms was willing to court powerful individuals if he respected them, but declined to align himself with any party. With one disastrous exception, he would always stand apart from factional confrontation in public. So in the political ferment Brahms was left outside: if he detested everything to do with Weimar, he still never really reached out to the logical alternative, the Leipzig conservatives. In any case, they hated him. (A group sympathetic to Brahms did accumulate in Leipzig, but for years remained marginal.) Through it all, *Neue Zeitscrift* editor Franz Brendel, for all his New German sympathies, struggled to build bridges between the parties and in the process would do Brahms several good turns.

Yet ultimately Brahms remained solitary. As man and artist, his own company suited him best. Naturally there were costs to pay for that. When the time came, Leipzig's conservatives would strike back, devastatingly.

Brahms had been reporting the excitement of the last seven months to his parents in Hamburg. As the Christmas season approached, homesickness overtook him in Leipzig. To Schumann he wrote, "I shall probably get copies of my first works before Christmas. Imagine what my feelings will be when I see my parents again after almost a year's absence. I cannot describe the feeling in my heart when I think of it."[50]

Brahms took the train from Leipzig on December 20 in the company of new confederate Julius Otto Grimm, to whom he gave the manuscript of the Opus 6 Lieder with the inscription "In remembrance of Kreisler." Grimm, wry and spirited if something of a pedant as composer and teacher, was perhaps the friend who most enjoyed the Kreisler side of Johannes—more than did the melancholic Joachim. Leaving Grimm in Hanover, Brahms arrived in the Hamburg station that night. Johannes the Fair had returned home in triumph.

.   .   .

HE BROUGHT HOME WITH HIM new printed copies of the C Major
Sonata and Opus 3 Lieder. Music engraving moved fast in those days;
having accepting the works in November, Breitkopf & Härtel issued the
first four opus numbers around the end of the year. After years of seeing
his work only in his own handwriting, a composer contemplates the first
engravings with awe, like watching a dream acted out in public. At the
end of the year, Brahms sent copies to Schumann with a poetical note:
"Herewith I take the liberty of sending you your first foster children
(who owe to you their citizenship of the world). . . . In their new garb
they seem to me too prim and embarrassed—almost philistine. I still cannot accustom myself to seeing these guileless children of nature in their
smart new clothes."[51]

Each of the early piano works, including the F Minor Sonata published in 1854, strikes a similar tone of Romantic drama, even melodrama: portentous thundering octave figures contrast with tender
moments. There are songful slow movements, impetuous fast ones. Each
successive sonata shows an unmistakable advance on the last. Together,
even at this youthful stage, they reveal Brahms transforming traditional
developmental technique, in which themes are dissolved into their constituent motives during the development section, toward the pervasive
thematic transformation characteristic of late Beethoven—and of Liszt.[52]
The result, in mature Brahms, would be the protean motivic technique
Arnold Schoenberg named "developing variation."

In its tone the rhapsodic F♯ Minor Piano Sonata, Opus 2 but the first
written, is the most Young Kreisler of the three. Its expressive world recalls the Sturm und Drang movement, the form-shattering "storm and
stress" emotionalism of Goethe's Young Werther and of middle-period
Haydn. In keeping with that tone, in the finale Brahms tries an experiment: an introduction like an improvisation on the main theme, which
repeatedly dissolves into quiet, rushing figuration; after the intense and
often marcato movement proper, the finale ends with the texture of the
introduction and trails off into ambiguous filigree, with two loud chords
for a deliberately unfulfilled finish. It all makes for a hazy, Kreislerian beginning and end—the kind of Romantic self-indulgence Brahms would
rarely allow himself again. (In the First Symphony, though, he would return to the idea of a slow introduction to the finale.)

Even at his most rhapsodic, in the F♯ Minor Sonata Brahms still pursues large-scale thematic integration. The rushing main theme of the

scherzo, for example (EX. 1C.), begins with a transformation of the delicately songful melody of the andante (1B.), both of them a transformation of the sonata's opening theme (1A.).

EX. I

A. **Allegro non troppo ma energico**

B. **Andante con espressione**

Scherzo
C. **Allegro**

The C Major Sonata, called Opus 1 but composed second, seems intended as a contrast to the F♯ Minor, beginning with its muscular major theme based on Beethoven's *Hammerklavier*. In further contrast to the rhapsodic F♯ Minor, Brahms made the C Major tight and economical. All the same, he had begun to rethink the formal models he inherited from Mozart and Beethoven—say, the transition from development to recapitulation in sonata form, usually dramatic and decisive. Instead, in the first movement's recapitulation Brahms makes the tonic C-major chord ambiguous by adding a dissonant seventh, sending the music into restless tonal peregrinations, but ones that still unfold without calling attention to themselves.[53] (Even at this stage, Brahms's harmonic audacity rivaled Wagner's. The difference is that Brahms did not care to show off his audacities; usually they are integrated into the voice leading and structure,

EX. 2

A. Allegro

Finale
B. Allegro con fuoco

there to find for those who know where to look. Wagner placed his novelties to give the galleries goose bumps.)

In the C Major, Brahms once again carefully shapes the relations of his themes. The breathless beginning of the finale, which launches as if already in mid-flight (EX. 2B.), is made from the same motive as the vigorous *Beethovener* opening of the sonata (EX. 2A.), and both of them make the same quick deflection to G major.

Likely Robert Schumann would have been shocked to know that the massive, five-movement F Minor was to be Brahms's last piano sonata. For all Brahms's youth—twenty when he composed it—the piece has a seasoned maturity beyond the earlier pieces. There is less virtuosity for its own sake, less reliance on mechanical harmonic sequences to whip up excitement, more expressive depth and ambiguity. The F Minor seems almost like a summary and compendium of its predecessors: portentous and virtuosic first movement like the F♯ Minor, but tightly made like the C Major, with all the melodic material derived from transformations of a single theme;[54] brash scherzo, rhythmically dazzling like its predecessors, but the placid trio more contrasting than usual; another songful movement, mostly quiet and inward, the most touching of these interludes in the sonatas (Brahms sometimes played it alone in recitals, and it resembles his later freestanding piano pieces). The finale approximates rondo form (traditionally A B A C A, etc., but here varied) and is perhaps the most expressively complex movement he had written—the almost

playful beginning grows into expansive and intense sections, these resolve into an ingenuous chorale theme, and all finally comes to a crashing, two-fisted coda. There is a formal experiment, more convincing
than earlier ones: a brief intermezzo titled "Rückblick" (Reminiscence),
between movements three and five. It amounts to a recall of the second-
movement andante, but now with an air of fatality and imitations of
pounding kettledrums, strings, winds, and blaring brasses.

For all their differences, common elements unite the three sonatas.
One is their massive, orchestral approach to the piano—the reason
Robert Schumann called them "veiled symphonies." Another element, a
telling one for Brahms's future, is the connection of several movements
to song. The *Andante con espressione* of the F♯ Minor is a set of variations
on the old Minnesinger melody "Mir ist leide" ("It saddens me that winter has bared the wood and heath"); the andante of the C Major varies the
German song "Verstohlen geht der Mond auf" ("Furtively, the moon
rises"—Brahms had the words printed under the melody), and pictures
the text verse by verse;[55] the *Andante espressivo* of the F Minor is not an
old tune but rather a song without words, whose text by Sternau Brahms
cites at the head of the movement: "The twilight falls, the moonlight
gleams, two hearts in love unite, embraced in rapture."[56] Brahms told Albert Dietrich that he associated the racing finale of the C Major with
Robert Burns's folk song "My Heart's in the Highlands."[57]

These connections to song in general and, in the sonatas' first two
slow movements, German song in particular, manifest Brahms's Romantic and nationalistic devotion to folk music and to the idea of songfulness,
of lyric melody in instrumental music. If he had not quite found the
Brahmsian lyric voice of his later music, he was near it—especially in the
lovely andante of the F Minor, with its succession of singing themes.
(They begin with a chain of thirds, a Brahms thumbprint all the way to
the Fourth Symphony.)

The song-based sonata movements adumbrate another, more subtle
prophecy of his coming work: a sense of meanings beneath the surface,
secrets hidden within the abstract forms of instrumental music. Soon
Brahms would go beyond just suggesting song texts. As he worked on the
F Minor Sonata in Düsseldorf, he picked up from Schumann and from
Joachim a more esoteric means of symbolizing feelings, ideas, and people by means of musical pitches: an explosion of F major near the beginning of the F Minor Sonata finale proclaims Joachim's F-A-E theme,
the idée fixe of the *F-A-E* Sonata.[58] Schumann had written pieces
with themes whose notes came from the names of his friends Abegg and
Gade; more covertly, he created themes to represent Clara in his music.

A cabala in pitches and unsung texts suited Brahms as well as it had Robert Schumann. It would be a means of capturing his own life and suffering, burying them in notes that had no words to betray the chaos of feelings that he was determined to hide, but could not avoid expressing. Thus the paradox of Brahms's music in the 1850s and 60s: at the same time that he turned away from the Romantic subjectivity of his youthful, Kreisleresque piano music and in the direction of neoclassic objectivity, his work simultaneously became, for a time, not less but more personal and lyrically expressive. Still later, he would veil his life and feelings behind a mask of impeccable form.

FROM HAMBURG, after a delightful Christmas with his family and with Eduard Marxsen at the end of that phenomenal year, Brahms wrote Joachim, "As happy as if in heaven are my parents, my teacher, and I."[59] It was a happiness incomparable—the kind of happiness the world cannot sustain, that fate crushes with the promise: *you have flown so high, so low you must fall.* And with that, fate ensured that Brahms would never trust happiness again.

On January 3, he returned to Hanover for a long stay with Joachim. There he began the first chamber work he would allow to survive, and the first written with Schumann's prophecy hanging over him—the B Major Piano Trio. He would not feel reassured by what the piece told him about his command of large forms in chamber music. The year of endless good news was over. As he composed now Brahms had to confront, in the spotlight, rudiments of craftsmanship that he had not yet mastered. In that confrontation some of his chief assets, beyond tenacity, were that he never let praise reassure him, never flagged in a relentless and unforgiving self-criticism. Over and over it would be said by those who knew Brahms that for all the manifest arrogance and self-absorption, he was one of the most modest of artists.

In this Hanover trip he met New German disciple Hans von Bülow, who had been visiting Joachim over Christmas, perhaps as emissary from Liszt. This splendid conductor and pianist had greeted "Neue Bahnen" with the same groans and sarcasm as had all his circle, but on meeting "heiligen Johannes" Bülow was honest enough to be intrigued. He wrote his mother, "I have got to know Robert Schumann's young prophet Brahms fairly intimately; he has been here two days and is always with us. A very charming, candid nature, with really quite a touch of divine grace about his talent." That March, Bülow played the first movement of the C Major Sonata in Hamburg—the first public Brahms performance by anyone other than the composer (thereby foreshadowing an association that in later days would save Bülow's life).

Brahms, Grimm, and Joachim formed a threesome they called the *Kaffernbund*, the League of Silly Asses.[60] Brahms, who chain-smoked cigarettes and cigars, initiated Joachim into the vice.[61] The three friends' days, convivially seasoned with wine and tobacco, were all gaiety and charm and happiness and hope. For all Joachim's gloom and suspiciousness, he knew how to have a jolly time.

More pleasures turned up at the end of January when Robert and Clara Schumann arrived in Hanover for a concert to be conducted by Joachim. Schumann's admiration for Brahms had not diminished, even if he had developed doubts about what he wrote in "Neue Bahnen" (he left the article out of his collected writings). Just before he came to Hanover, Schumann wrote the violinist, "Now where is Johannes? . . . Is he flying high—or only amongst flowers? Is he setting drums and trumpets to work yet? He must call to mind the beginnings of the Beethoven symphonies; he must try to do something of the same kind."[62]

The Hanover concert, featuring Schumann's Fourth Symphony, his Fantasy for Violin and Orchestra with Joachim soloing, and the Beethoven *Emperor* Concerto with Clara soloing, found a good response. King George of Hanover received the Schumanns graciously; Clara played twice at court. Each evening the Schumanns and their protégés made music together and ended the night enlivening the café of the train station with laughter and stories. But Brahms struck an odd note; Clara found him muttering and withdrawn.[63] Was it that Robert was unduly excited, or not making sense? Was it something about Clara? Somehow the situation seemed more complicated. Things were not being said.

Still, the visit left a pleasant afterglow, especially from the last evening when for the assembled friends Clara played Johannes's F♯ Minor Sonata and with Joachim the Schumann D Minor Violin Sonata. Next day, Brahms, Joachim, and Julius Grimm saw the Schumanns off at the train station.[64] To Albert Dietrich in Düsseldorf Brahms wrote, "What festive times we have had, thanks to the Schumanns! . . . Since then everything here seems to me thoroughly alive."[65]

Schumann soon wrote Joachim this letter dated February 6—understandably elated, unaccountably strange:

> We have been gone a week, and we have not yet sent a word to you and your comrade! But I have often written to you with invisible ink, and there is a secret writing between these lines which will come to light later on.

And I have dreamed of you, dear Joachim . . . you had heron's feathers in your hands from which flowed champagne—how prosaic! But how true!—

We have often thought of the days we spent with you; may there soon be more like them! The kindly royal family, the excellent orchestra, and the two young demons in the midst of it all—we shall never forget it. . . .

Music is silent at present—externally at any rate. . . .

I'm enjoying the cigars very much. They seem to have a Brahmsian tang, as usual very strong but good! Now I can see him smiling.

I'll stop now. It's getting dark.[66]

The young demons received no more such letters from Düsseldorf. Their next communication was from Albert Dietrich to Joachim, with the news that changed their lives. "Dear Friend," it began, "I have terribly sad news for you and Johannes."[67]

There had been other demons inhabiting Robert Schumann's mind. They had been whispering and singing to him for a long time, a chorus of wailing and jubilant voices. They had sentenced him to make an end to the evil charade of his life. On February 27, Schumann eluded his watching family and jumped into the Rhine. He had been pulled alive from the water, but his mind seemed horribly, perhaps irretrievably, shattered.

CHAPTER FIVE

Waiting

BEFORE ROBERT SCHUMANN threw himself in the Rhine, Brahms knew
him as an underappreciated composer, an important critic, part of an extraordinary husband-and-wife collaboration, a generous friend and mentor. Certainly Brahms had heard that Schumann could be erratic, and he
knew firsthand of the older man's inclination to extremes—one example
of it was "Neue Bahnen." But in the background of that suicide attempt
lay a story Brahms could not have known, of an artist wasted by years of
battle with demons at once creative and destructive. The satisfactions of
a family and creative life had only kept at bay the ruinous visions that beset Robert Schumann for over twenty years. For the length of their marriage, Clara had been the main bulwark between her husband and the
abyss.

On September 30, 1853, the same day Brahms first rang the Schumanns' doorbell in Düsseldorf, Clara wrote in her journal: "My last good
years are passing, my strength too. . . . I am more discouraged than I can
possibly say." She had discovered that she was pregnant for perhaps the
tenth time since her marriage in 1840. One or two pregnancies had
ended in miscarriage and one child died in infancy. Now, with another
baby on the way, she had to give up an already long postponed concert
tour to England.[1] Despite her loyalty to Robert and her children, performing before an audience was woven too much into Clara's identity to
give up. Unlike her husband, she had heard ovations most of her life, and
she thrived on them.

Beyond the immediate frustration, surely Clara felt more anxious than
usual about Robert. With the Düsseldorf orchestra his conducting had
gone from precarious to helpless; he was obsessed by spiritualism and

séances[2]; he felt chronically weak, at times could barely talk, complained of tones ringing incessantly in his ears. Always a composer who depended on inspiration more than craft, he had been working at a manic pace in Düsseldorf, but Clara knew that the music was not as fresh and confident as it had been a decade before. Worst of all, he had become irritable with her, and sometimes bitterly disparaged her playing. To Clara Schumann, rejecting her playing was the same as rejecting her, body and soul.[3] It was almost more than she could bear from the man who had been the only love of her life, whom she admired above all the celebrated men and women she had known.

When Clara was born in Leipzig in September 1819, her father, Friedrich Wieck, had already decided to make his daughter a great pianist. With ruthless dedication and a remarkable gift for teaching, Friedrich shaped Clara to his blueprint, in the process divorcing her mother and brutalizing her brothers and repudiating anything else that threatened his design. Clara did not merely submit to her father's manipulation, she blossomed in it. She grew up with Friedrich Wieck's single-minded tenacity, if without his ruthlessness and cynicism. The father ran on ambition and envy and money and malice, the daughter on a religious devotion to music, driven competitiveness, an appetite for performing that she called "the very breath of my nostrils." In her childhood, the worst of her father's intricate punishments had been to forbid Clara to play the piano. He also expected her to compose, telling her she could do that or anything else as well as a man. In her teens, Clara wrote a piano concerto and a number of other pieces, and publishers battled for her work.

She debuted at the Leipzig Gewandhaus at age nine and at eleven performed her first solo concert there. Her first tour to Vienna at age eighteen set off a frenzy, with Grillparzer writing poetry to her and police having to prevent ticket-seekers from storming the box office.[4] In Vienna the emperor named her Royal and Imperial Chamber Virtuosa—the first time that exalted title had been given to a foreigner, a Protestant, a teenager, or a woman.[5]

For all its excitement, no one escapes the effects of a childhood as unforgiving as Clara's. By the time of her Viennese sensation, she was already showing the melancholy and hysteria that would mark her life, alongside the profound musical understanding, the impeccable technique, the relentless self-discipline. When she was a teenager one saw the sadness shadowing her face and her great dark-blue eyes. One observer said, "Poor child! She has a look of unhappiness and of suffering . . . but she owes perhaps a part of her fine talent to this inclination to melan-

The Karlskirche in Vienna.

Brahms's mother, Christiane, in 1 [...]
three years before she died.

Robert and Clara
Schumann about the
time they met
Brahms.

ms at twenty in 1853, by Laurens: Young Kreisler of the maidenly features. (Note the error in the inscription, presumably Laurens's—"Joseph Brahms.") Robert Schumann commented: "He is truly one of the handsomest of young men, and one of the greatest geniuses."

Laurens's companion drawing of Schumann in 1853. The artist could see his subject was ill, but could not know that he was making a portrait of incipient madness.

Josef Joachim in his dashing youth.

Joachim and Clara Schumann in a recital of December 1854, drawn by Adolph von Menzel.

Two views of Brahms in his beardless thirties: the features still fair,
but now an aggressive underlip and a magisterial gaze.

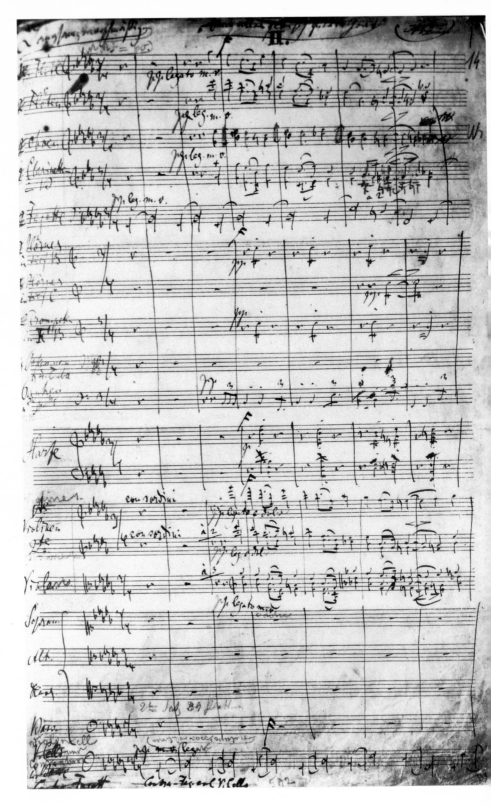

The beginning of "All flesh is grass" from Ein deutsches Requiem.
Brahms's hand was fast and inelegant, but decisive.

choly." Another, who may have been the poet Heinrich Heine, wrote, "It seems as though the child could tell a long story, a story woven out of joy and pain—and yet—what does she know? Music."[6]

By eighteen Clara had fallen in love with the extraordinary figure who replaced her father as the brilliant and volatile man in her life. Born in Zwickau in 1810, Robert Schumann came to live and study with Friedrich Wieck when he was twenty and Clara eleven. By then he had begun to compose and showed a flair for rhapsodic improvisations at the keyboard, but he mainly dreamed of becoming a piano virtuoso.

By then, the other compelling force in Robert Schumann's life had also announced itself: his first psychotic episode struck just before age eighteen, as he read a Jean Paul novel in a park outside Leipzig.[7] During the next years violent fantasies, heavy drinking, hallucinations, fervid and possibly homosexual alliances with youths, and creative transports kept Schumann ricocheting between euphoria and suicidal depression.[8] In 1830, he wrote in his journal after a period of manic debauchery, "I'm terrified and disgusting—drunk because of boredom—very high—my longing to throw myself into the Rhine."[9] From his demon-haunted teens onward, the waters of the Rhine lay in his imagination as an escape, or an inescapable fate.

A promise he had made his late father to study law intensified all this Romantic malaise. In autumn of 1830, Schumann fled law studies to Friedrich Wieck, with the hope that this famous teacher could reassure his mother that he had potential as a virtuoso. Wieck declared to Madame Schumann, "I give my pledge to make your son . . . into one of the greatest living pianists within three years." The mother relented, and Schumann plunged into piano studies with the same frenzy as he had his debauches. His life calmed somewhat, but soon new trouble appeared. He started an affair with a servant girl; he tried desultorily to write a novel, a play, a "poetic biography" of E. T. A. Hoffmann.[10] And he became disenchanted with Wieck, who cared little for any student other than his daughter, who treated his sons contemptibly and dictated Clara's life every minute of the day.

At the same time as the excesses and uproars, Schumann turned to the private world of composing with more and more exhilaration. After a few attempts at composition, at age twenty-two he completed the brilliant set of piano pieces called *Papillons*, which began a decade of heated creativity that finally accounted for much of his finest and most original work, including the piano collections *Carnaval*, *Kreisleriana*, and *Kinderszenen*, dozens of songs, and the first movement of the A Minor Piano Concerto. In pieces of this era, Schumann epitomized the poetically lyrical strain of

Romantic music, found fresh ways of writing for the piano, and made himself the finest composer of German lieder since Schubert.

In 1831, trying to write his novel in the direction of E. T. A. Hoffmann's Kreisler stories and their mirrored identities, Schumann discovered his own alter egos, avatars of a fragmented consciousness: impulsive Florestan, poetic and scholarly Eusebius, plus the classicist Master Raro in the image of Friedrich Wieck, and Cilia who was also Clara.[11] Schumann made use of his personas when he began his career as a music critic. In his first article, Eusebius sweeps into the room and cries to his comrades, "Hats off, gentlemen, a genius!" and opens the score of Chopin's Opus 2. Eventually in his writings Schumann's fictitious band became the Davidsbündler, the little League of David fighting the giants of empty virtuosity and philistinism. In the ten years from 1834 that Schumann founded and ran his journal Neue Zeitschrift für Musik, he used his imaginary voices to promote progressive composers from the distinguished to the disappointing. History has mainly remembered the times Schumann was right—notably about Chopin, Berlioz, and Mendelssohn. The last-named became Schumann's friend and lifelong hero.

Even in his most productive periods Schumann's infirmity lingered, manifesting as hypochondria, hallucinatory episodes, fantasies of suicide, periods of outright breakdown. A mechanical device he invented to strengthen his hands for the keyboard crippled the middle finger of his right hand and destroyed any hope of a piano career.[12] His obsession with young men continued. His relations with Friedrich Wieck and his composition teachers were fractious and unsatisfying. And gradually, as the years went by, Schumann found himself falling in love with his teacher's prodigy daughter, Clara.

CLARA AND ROBERT always had a teasing relationship, but during her teens the games and jokes took on more significance. Yet at the same time as their attraction heated up, Schumann began an affair with a teenager named Ernestine von Fricken. The main consequence of that romance, other than a period of estrangement from Clara, was the virtuosic piano pieces called Carnaval, whose twenty movements are unified by the melodic motive A-S-C-H. That is the name of Ernestine's hometown, in German musical terms the notes A-E♭-C-B; in the piece they are sometimes reformed into E♭-C-B-A (S-C-H-A) and A♭C-B (As-C-H). Schumann felt a mystical correspondence in the fact that S-C-H also began his own name.

Besides those cabalistic games with musical letters, the movements of

Carnaval have portraits of Eusebius, Florestan, Chopin, Paganini, Ernestine/Estrella, and Chiarina (another name for Clara). In 1835, when Clara was nearly sixteen, Schumann broke with Ernestine. Soon after, he wrote in his journal, "beautiful hours in [Clara's] arms."[13]

Friedrich Wieck, outraged at this challenge to his authority, and probably aware of Schumann's precarious condition mental and fiscal, began a campaign to crush the romance that went as far as threats to murder Robert. The lovers became adept at clandestine meetings and exchanges of letters. One of Clara's notes to Robert in that period read: "Be at our window at *exactly* 9. If I signal with a white cloth, walk slowly toward the old Neumarkt. I will follow soon after . . . since I have to fetch Mother at her mother's. *If I don't signal, it means she hasn't gone.*"[14]

Clara discovered a depth of passion in herself that kept pace with Robert's. She became the last and most profound of Schumann's muses; he was the only man she ever wanted unreservedly. Already they felt like soul mates, not only in love but in music. Robert wrote her in 1839, "Each of your [musical] ideas comes from my own soul, just as I must thank you for all the music I write." Finally, having created several piano works inspired by Clara and intended for her to play, just before her eighteenth birthday Schumann formally asked for her hand. Friedrich Wieck wrathfully forbade the marriage.

Desperate, Schumann filed a legal complaint, beginning a court case that dragged on for nine wretched and humiliating months. In depositions her father viciously libeled both Robert and his own daughter, demanding payment for Clara's entire training even though she had been the main family breadwinner for years. During the grueling months while they waited for the court's decision, Schumann in one of his creative transports wrote 128 lieder, some of them the finest since Schubert's, including the cycles *Myrthen*, *Dichterliebe* (*Poet's Love*, on Heine lyrics), the *Liederkreis* after Eichendorff, and his testament to Clara, *Frauenliebe und -leben* (*A Woman's Love and Life*).

Finally, Wieck's accusations were dismissed and Clara was free of him. She and Robert married in September 1840, the day before her twenty-first birthday. In her journal she called it "the fairest and most momentous day of my life."

Yet despite everything Friedrich Wieck had done to keep her from her beloved, Clara Schumann never repudiated her father. Music was not only her greatest joy but her means of escaping his domination; yet nothing could shake her gratitude for his part in making her one of the towering pianists of her time, which was an extraordinary time for the piano. Between Friedrich Wieck and Robert Schumann, Clara came of age knowing how to cope with brilliant and difficult men, adapt to them while preserving herself, and love what was fine in them.

Every man in her life, including her own sons, would be damaged and damaging in some way, yet despite frightful emotional costs Clara remained loyal to them. She felt that in marrying Robert she was not only following her passion, but joining her life to history. Her devotion to him stretched long beyond his death to her own.

If Clara and Robert did not live happily ever after, they still shared a tremendous love and a musical partnership unlike any before or since. Years after he died, a friend observed: "You can imagine Clara without Robert, but not Robert without Clara." He might have preferred his wife to stay home and play and compose and take care of the family, but he did not seriously stand in the way of her performing career. For her part, Clara talked the conventional, submissive daughter and wife, but in practice she had a will of steel and did exactly what she wanted—though that included a responsibility to her family that circumscribed her performing.

Determined that Robert must find the kind of acclaim and income she had, Clara prodded him to look for conducting work and to write symphonies and concertos and oratorios instead of the miniatures he had excelled at. "It would be best if he composed for orchestra," she wrote in her journal, "his imagination cannot find sufficient scope on the piano. . . . My highest wish is that he should compose for orchestra—that is his field! May I succeed in bringing him to it."[15] He gave in to her campaign and began to compose large works—with ambiguous success in comparison to his piano music.

After a joint Russian tour in 1844, Clara the main attraction as usual, Robert suffered one of his worst breakdowns, trembling and weeping for days, so weak he could barely walk.[16] In search of peace and recovery, they moved from Leipzig to beautiful Dresden. There, despite the birth of four children in five years, the revolutions of 1848 across Europe, and steady emotional turmoil, Schumann completed a stack of works including his Second Symphony, the Piano Concerto, and the oratorio *Paradise and the Peri*. Clara also composed some of her best work in Dresden, notably the Piano Trio. In 1850, with her encouragement, Robert accepted the post of town music director in Düsseldorf, which entailed conducting an orchestra and chorus. Over his three years there, as his mind tilted toward crisis, he composed a third of his life's work. But little of it counts among his most enduring music.

During their marriage, pregnant most of the time, with her children and fragile husband dependent on her, Clara gave around 150 public concerts between 1840 and 1854,[17] sometimes playing days before or after giving birth or suffering a miscarriage.[18] Always she pushed aside her fears about Robert's health even as she kept him afloat, but she understood exactly how important an artist he was. Slowly, her efforts as a performer spread her husband's work even as he himself became more and more brittle.

One would assume that Clara Schumann survived the tragedies of her life by means of an aloof and composed temper. In fact, she was the opposite. She was perpetually alive to everything and everybody, to every piece she played or heard. Brahms could retreat behind his wall of indifference and mockery. Clara was sober unto humorless, self-righteous, literalistic, a maker of meticulous lists, indifferent to nothing.[19] Her feelings slid easily into floods of tears and from there into hysteria. That she survived the inexorable ordeals of her life and her own lacerated sensibility testifies to a phenomenal resilience and strength of will.

Her daughter Eugenie remembered her mother in company, emotions washing over her face from moment to moment like cloud shadows. The pervading look, that shows in all Clara's photos, was the profound melancholy. But Clara also had a beautiful smile that transformed her solemn features. Her husband and her children would do a great deal to earn that smile. If over the years of her relationship with Brahms Clara was perennially baffled and outraged by his teasing, and if she always felt unattractive and uneducated alongside the extraordinary artists who were her friends, still Clara was part of every dialogue, and the dialogue usually brilliant in her house.

WHEN JOHANNES BRAHMS first swept into the Schumanns' life in September 1853, he saw only the bright, hopeful, public side of the famous couple. It was intoxicating to be around people like that, who had imagination and presence far beyond anyone he had known. For a while, Young Kreisler seemed to rejuvenate both of them. Robert became voluble, Clara's mournful eyes glowed.

But beneath the sociable veneer, madness gained on Robert. Most nights for some time Clara had escorted him to the door of a coffeehouse and picked him up at the end of the evening—she could not count on him to find his way home. He told her that after working at his desk his tongue felt so lame he could hardly speak.[20] One day a visitor, trying to get information from him, could only rouse Schumann to ask, "Do you smoke?" three times, with long silences between. He seemed perpetually stunned, listening to things only he could hear, his mouth puckered in an endless silent whistle. Obsessively he turned to séances and table-turning, as if they could draw him closer to the unseen world that had always called to Romantics, and whose spirits now called to him by name.

Toward the middle of February 1854, insidious auditory hallucinations attacked him. For days on end Schumann heard the same note maddeningly repeated; the note became harmonies; then every noise he heard turned into exquisite, unearthly music. Finally a superhuman orchestra roared day and night in his head.

On the seventeenth of the month, Robert rose from bed and wrote down a theme he told Clara an angel had sung to him. That night he lay beside her, eyes wide, telling her that he was looking into heaven and angels were circling above them and singing. By the next morning the angels had turned to hideous choruses wailing that they would take him to hell. To friends he hinted that the voices were ordering him to do something frightful. In less frenzied moments he began composing a set of variations on the angels' theme. Then, on February 26, he announced that he must go to an asylum, and carefully laid out his things. When Clara tried to comfort him, Robert shrank back, crying, "Ah, Clara, I am not worthy of your love!"[21] The doctors had nothing to say. All Clara had was her tears.

The climax was dreadful, grotesque. Clara had been sitting with Robert around the clock for days as he alternately lost himself in mirages and worked on the variations. Finally, exhausted, she asked daughter Marie to watch him while she consulted with a doctor. Marie opened the door to find her father standing in the middle of the room, deathly pale in a long dressing gown. When he saw her he hid his face with his hands and groaned "Oh God!" and stumbled through the door. For a moment Marie was too shocked to follow. When she looked into the next room her father had slipped from the house.

Schumann fled through the streets of Düsseldorf, toward the river. He had written a note to his wife that she would not find until long after: "Dear Clara, I am going to throw my wedding-ring into the Rhine, do the same with yours, and then the two rings will be united." There was a carnival in progress, the streets filled with costumed throngs and wild music. In dressing gown and slippers Schumann stumbled through the nightmare spectacle, a madman in the middle of a masquerade like something from one of Hoffmann's tales. He came to a bridge over the river. When a guard demanded the toll, Schumann shoved a silk scarf into the man's hand and pushed past. For so many years he had foreseen this moment. Masked revelers watched him run to the middle of the bridge, mount the railing, and throw himself into the water. As he floundered, some fishermen raced to pull him up, subduing him when he struggled to jump out of the boat. His wedding ring was missing. When they got to shore someone said, astonished: "This is Herr Musikdirektor Schumann."[22]

Daughter Marie, sent by a frantic Clara to look for him at a neighbor's, saw a crowd of people approaching on the street. In the middle was her father held up by two men, dripping wet and his hands over his face. Clara caught only a glimpse of him before the doctor ordered her away.[23]

Two DAYS LATER Dietrich's report reached Brahms and Joachim in Hanover.[24] Now Johannes's life intersected with Schumann's madness and Clara's prostration. The moment of Robert's leap would resound through the rest of their lives. Brahms rushed to Düsseldorf, arriving on March 3; Joachim would follow in a few days. As Schumann had requested himself, he was to be taken to an asylum at Endenich near Bonn. The doctors would not allow Clara to see her husband, insisting it would agitate him. As she waited in agony at her neighbor Fräulein Leser's, on March 4 Schumann was helped into a carriage with a doctor and two attendants. His children watched from an upper window. When he was seated in the carriage the doctor handed him a bouquet from his wife. Schumann did not seem to notice, then during the trip he smelled the flowers and smiled and presented one to each of his companions. The doctor gave his flower to Clara, who preserved it to the end of her life.[25]

Brahms took up residence on Schadowplatz, offering to console her with music, to stay with her until her child was born and her husband recovered, to devote himself to Schumann during his convalescence. As he tried to comfort the distraught Clara, Brahms also composed furiously, page after page of agitated music in D minor for two pianos. The doctors continued to keep her away from Robert. At the asylum he did not ask for her, never spoke her name.

Joachim arrived in Düsseldorf along with Clara's mother, Julius Grimm, and Albert Dietrich. Newspaper reports of the disaster brought floods of letters and further visits.[26] But most friends could stay only so long, their kind words go only so far. Now the old melancholy in Clara's eyes deepened to the anguished and haunted cast that resided in them from then on. She wrote in her journal, "Either I cannot sleep at all, or else I lie half-asleep and horrible pictures hover before my eyes—I constantly see and hear him."[27] It was as if Robert's sleeplessness, his madness, had invaded her. She was five months pregnant. Music and work would be her only solace—and her only income, with Robert gone. Two days after her husband was taken away, Clara began seeing piano students again.[28]

The friends who had gathered around her made music together, going over Johannes's and Joachim's work and Robert's. Everyone speculated about treatments for the sick man, fashionable ones of the time: the magnetic powers of a Parisian count, a water cure. The house and its contents remained open to friends and neighbors. Reading in the couple's diaries, Joachim found a chilling observation Robert had written years before: "The artist should beware of losing touch with society; otherwise he will be wrecked, as I am."[29] Clara wrote in her journal of playing her husband's music in the weeks after his collapse: "I lose myself in it; it moves my whole heart. . . . But when I finish playing my anguish is redoubled."

There were long evenings in the candlelit parlor with Clara and Brahms alternating at the piano before a quiet circle of listeners. He played the draft of his new B Major Trio, which struck her as fine if at times puzzling. Whatever her misery, her critical intelligence persisted: "I cannot quite get used to the constant change of tempo in his works, and he plays them so entirely according to his own fancy that today . . . I could not follow him, and it was very difficult for his fellow-players to keep their places. . . . Brahms was not very polite; it seems to me that he will be spoiled by the tremendous idolatry with which he is treated by the younger generation."[30] (Probably she meant Grimm and Dietrich.) Later in her journal Clara groused again, "It is not easy to play with Brahms; he plays too arbitrarily, and cares nothing for a beat more or less."[31]

Yet of the circle of friends surrounding her in her sorrow, it was Johannes who reached Clara most, as the rankling uncertainty stretched on and her pregnancy came to term. "That good Brahms always shows himself a most sympathetic friend. He does not say much, but one can see in his face, in his speaking eye, how he grieves with me. . . . Besides, he is so kind in seizing every opportunity of cheering me by means of anything musical."[32] Brahms could not speak his feelings, not yet at least, and never easily, but he could let music speak.

One day in mid-April, when news from Endenich seemed hopeful, Clara played over the trio twice with Joachim and Grimm. "Now everything in it is clear to me," she told her journal. She saw the digressiveness of the long opening movement and the other structural uncertainties (though the scherzo is another of Brahms's confident and vivacious ones), but she also saw much that was superb. In the first measures comes a fresh kind of singing melody: the lyrical Young Kreisler voice that would be always with him, growing in subtlety but holding a melting Romantic sweetness and yearning. She wrote her and Robert's publisher Breitkopf & Härtel, asking them to take the trio. They would publish it that year as Opus 8.

Despite the distress and distraction of those weeks, Brahms worked away. Perhaps that spring he composed the piano miniatures that became the Opus 10 Ballades. More ambitious, though it never appeared publicly in its original form, was a sonata in D minor for two pianos, whose catastrophic opening seemed to emerge from the nightmare events of February. On March 9, five days after Schumann was taken to the asylum, Brahms played three freshly composed movements for Grimm, who was enthralled. Another veiled symphony shoehorned into the keyboard, this music soon found its place in the orchestra, but that would not be the end of its journey.

Everything lay in the shadow of Schumann's illness. His hospital at Endenich was progressive for the time; he had a suite of rooms with a piano, and constant supervision. Reports from the doctors seemed to alternate randomly, hopeful for a while and then discouraging, and no one could say how long it might go on. Already Clara had asked herself, What if he never returns? There was no bearable answer to that question.

By the spring Robert was taking long walks and appeared better.[33] Then, at the end of April, Clara was alarmed by reports that he had been hearing voices again, seemed unable to remember things. The doctors said there was no immediate prospect for improvement.[34] A visitor to the house in May found Clara looking gaunt and aged, sobbing, "If I didn't have the firm hope that my husband would be better soon, I wouldn't want to live any more. I cannot live without him. The worst is that I may not be with him and he has not yet asked for me, not even once." Minutes later the visitor noticed that as they listened to Brahms play, she smiled and suddenly appeared younger.[35]

More and more she was taken by Johannes, his laughter and boyish energy, his blushing pleasure at her praise. Her burgeoning tenderness can be traced in journal entries, some of the few moments of pleasure in those mournful pages:

> He played a great deal. I always listen to him with fresh admiration. . . . I like to watch him while he plays. His face always has a noble expression, but when he plays it becomes even more rapt . . . his movements are always beautiful, not like Liszt's and others. He played Schubert's

A minor sonata, Weber's rondo . . . and a movement of Clementi's—all by heart. I am filled more and more with admiration for the great spirit which inhabits so small a body. . . . Brahms . . . played his F minor sonata. I do not quite clearly understand the last movement, but the other seems to me magnificent, except for a few roughnesses here and there. . . . Brahms and Grimm . . . can be merry as children.[36]

When Brahms first rushed to Düsseldorf his mother had been sympathetic: "That Schumann is so sick makes us endlessly sad. You did well to go there." With that letter Christiane enclosed twenty-five marks.[37] But as his stay stretched on with no indication of any plans, his parents worried that once again their son was drifting, living on air. At the end of April Christiane wrote, "You don't have any money? Without it you're a beggar in the world. . . . [If you come home] Herr Marxsen told Father that he could arrange concerts for you, with your compositions, and you could earn a lot." Fritz had recently returned home after losing the job Johannes had got for him in Leipzig. "Poor Fritz can't help it that he hasn't learned anything," Christiane moaned. "Father often said that I treated him as a stepmother would. Oh, what Fritz could learn from you if you really behaved like brothers!"[38] With Fritz as another flashpoint, the friction between Christiane and Johann Jakob continued unrelenting.

Brahms found a few piano students in Düsseldorf and halfheartedly applied for Schumann's position as town music director, but it came to nothing.[39] Clara pressed him to tour as a soloist; he resisted that as long as he could. He got by mainly on money borrowed from Grimm and Joachim and maybe other new friends. In the spring, he formed a lifelong bond with tall, slow-speaking Julius Allgeyer, then studying engraving in Düsseldorf, later biographer of the painter Anselm Feuerbach. Allgeyer wrote to a friend of Brahms's "bad manners of a frolicsome child and the understanding of a man." Early in their relationship he got Brahms to read Herder's *Stimmen der Völker* (Voices of the People); it included the Scottish ballad "Edward," of which Brahms soon made use.

One day in May Clara played for him her variations on a theme from Robert's *Bunte Blätter* (Mottled Leaves), written the year before as a gift for his birthday. Immediately he began writing his own set of variations on the theme, bringing each draft to Clara for comment as he finished it. There would be sixteen variations finally, published as Opus 9. Brahms wrote all but two of them between May 24 and June 15.[40] Though they have echoes of Robert's music and of Clara's variations, he still shows considerable independence from his mentors—nor for all his historical borrowings would he ever sound like anyone but himself. Julius Otto Grimm, who was very close to Johannes in those days, christened the Schumann Variations "Trost-Einsamkeit," "Consolation and Loneliness." In mid-August he would add two final ones, numbered 10 and 11.

On the manuscript he signed some of these variations *B* for Brahms, some *Kr* for Kreisler. This was an echo of Schumann, who attributed parts of his *Davidsbündlertänze—Dances of the League of David*—to his alter egos Eusebius and Florestan. Brahms seemed to associate his own name with Schumann's austere scholar Eusebius, Young Kreisler with Romantic and impulsive Florestan. For Brahms as for Schumann the name Florestan had another resonance as well: it was the name of Beethoven's hero in his opera *Fidelio*, chained in a dungeon and rescued by a heroic wife.[41] It had happened with Schumann and now with Brahms more than ever; alter egos flourished and contended, as in Hoffmann's stories. Schumann's imaginary circle had been symbol and symptom of his fragmenting consciousness. Who were Brahms and Young Kreisler now, as he spent every day with Clara? What were his alter egos thinking?

At the end of May the friends waited for Clara's lying-in, trying to keep the house calm. Several times in those spring days Clara and Brahms read through his D minor two-piano sonata, and she and Dietrich played it over so he could listen. (Like many composers, Brahms needed to hear new pieces run through others' fingers and ears to find some perspective after the inward process of composing.) Clara wrote in her journal of the sonata in progress, "This again seemed to me very powerful, quite original, on a grand scale, and at the same time clearer than the earlier things." A few days later, Johannes played her more of his Hungarian folk songs. At the same time he announced that he was completely broke, but that he always felt in good spirits when he had no money.

Every day they waited for word from Endenich. In the first week of June came news that Robert had begun to remember things. He remained quiet and the doctor's reports were guarded, but for the moment there were no outbursts or hallucinations.[42] On June 9, the day after what must have been a bleak commemoration of Robert's birthday, Clara wrote Joachim,

> I am learning to understand [Johannes's] rare and beautiful character better every day. There is something so fresh and so soothing about him; he is often so childlike and then again so full of the finest feelings. . . . And as a musician he is still more wonderful. He gives me as

much pleasure as he possibly can . . . and he does this with a perseverance which is really touching . . . The reports [of Robert] vary greatly,
but on the whole they point to a gradual improvement. I am swayed
continually by hopes and fears, and at the bottom of my heart I suffer
more than I can possibly describe.[43]

Two days later, Clara gave birth to her seventh surviving child and
third boy. She wanted to name him Felix, for their late friend and champion Mendelssohn, but she put off the christening until Robert could
make his own suggestion. The new baby consoled her as a token of connection to her husband, but at the same time created another obstruction
to her touring as a soloist. Nor were the older children any help: "The
children, instead of being a comfort to me, only agitate me the more, for
I keep thinking: 'What a father the poor children had! and now they have
lost him, perhaps forever.'"[44] As she recovered from childbirth, Brahms
handed her a manuscript of his own Schumann Variations, inscribed
"Short Variations on a Theme by Him. Dedicated to Her." She wrote in
her journal, "He sought to comfort me, he composed variations on that
wonderfully heartfelt theme that means so much to me, just as last year
when I composed variations for my beloved Robert."[45]

In July Brahms wrote Joachim a long letter of news and ideas musical
and otherwise. He had gotten 200 louis d'or from Breitkopf & Härtel but
owed a lot of it to Grimm, so he asked Joachim to wait for money owed
him. Brahms enclosed for Joachim's comment a series of little piano
pieces he proposed to call "Pages from the Diary of a Musician/edited by
the young Kreisler." He explained about this collection, which included
six neo-Baroque sarabandes, gigues, and gavottes, "The things should
not carry the anonymous title in order to be permitted to be worse than
my earlier stuff, but only for the sake of a joke, and because they're occasional pieces." These studies in archaic genres were hardly a diary of
emotional matters, but rather the diary of a young musician steeped in
study of the past, in Robert Schumann's library.

    With the letter to Joachim Brahms also enclosed the Schumann Vari-
ations with the observation that they are "perhaps indeed too little and
insignificant? One hardly needs more of such juvenilia."[46] Characteristically, he belittled the piece exactly because it meant a great deal to him.
Eduard Marxsen, to whom Brahms had sent the new pieces, responded
with detailed suggestions for the B Major Trio. Joachim replied enthusiastically about the variations but coolly to the Kreisler pieces and to the
pseudonym. That would be the end of any idea of publishing "Pages
from the Diary of a Musician," and the last to be seen of most of the

pieces—though eventually Brahms would make use of some of the material. It was also the end of the name Kreisler appearing on manuscripts. In the letter to Joachim, Brahms mentioned that he was leaving aside the D minor sonata for the moment: "Actually I've never been satisfied with two pianos."[47]

Amid these workmanly queries and comments Brahms made a stunning aside to Joachim, maybe more of a confession than he intended, maybe more than his friend could understand or accept. It was about Clara.

> I believe that I do not have more concern and admiration for her than I love her and am under her spell. I often have to restrain myself forcibly from just quietly putting my arms around her and even—I don't know, it seems to me so natural that she could not misunderstand.
>
> I think I can no longer love an unmarried girl—at least, I have quite forgotten about them. They only promise heaven while Clara shows it revealed to us.[48]

The relatively calm tone of these words does not reflect what Brahms felt. Something great and terrible had happened to him in the months since Schumann's collapse. Johannes felt like Goethe's Young Werther, living in an agony of frustrated desire. He wanted Schumann to get well; he wanted him to die. He wanted to soar in clouds and he wanted to put a gun to his head. He had fallen helplessly in love with Clara Schumann.

Though Johannes had not spoken his feelings, surely Clara knew and did not want to know. In the uncertainties of what was happening and likely to happen to her husband, Clara could not contemplate the reality that Johannes had fallen in love with her, or she with him. She could not wrestle with the implications of that now, only rationalize them. Anyway, to both of them a romance could only have seemed an outrage, a betrayal in a time when she had just borne her husband's child, when it still seemed possible that Robert could recover, when it was inconceivable for both of them not to hope for his recovery. And Clara was thirty-four, Johannes recently twenty-one.

But for Johannes there it was, resounding like a great bell in his mind: love, gnawing and inescapable, unlike anything he had experienced. When to Joachim he imagined embracing her, he pictured it a sign of his sympathy: "I often have to restrain myself forcibly from just quietly putting my arms around her . . . It seems so natural." In letters later destroyed and in conversations, Joachim must have replied: Beware, Johannes, beware.

Still, their words in that period, in her journals and in their letters and avowals to friends, are passionate but not as unequivocal as they look to a later time. As a celebrated pianist, after all, Clara was used to devotion. It was an age of emotional extremes, when ardent words between friends, even a man and a woman, did not necessarily entail bed, an affair. And for a while their words were restrained, at least in the letters that escaped destruction. Surely there was growing gossip about Clara and Johannes. But still it was possible to speak passionately and be respectable, to protest innocence honestly. In any case, with them that summer the ardent words did not mean anything physical. It is possible they never did.

Yet there was an irresistible vibration between them. It was a matter of mutual admiration and shared creativity and joy and sorrow, but amorous too in some enigmatic way. Except for her smile and in the dark-blue depths of her eyes, Clara was not beautiful. Since her flirtatious teens her personality had settled into somberness and tenseness, even if she had a warmly sociable side. Likely, all that meant little to Johannes. As with many musicians his musical and sexual responses were part of the same impulse (though the musical was respectable, nominally innocent: safe). Clara was a great pianist and a great woman; by those means, he wrote Joachim, she revealed heaven to him.

To all three of them music was language and religion and emotion and intellect at their highest, and music the most profound consolation. With Clara and others to come in Brahms's life, a gift for music made a woman beautiful. So no one would ever be as beautiful to him as Clara Schumann, because she was the greatest musician of any woman he ever knew. And despite the failings in their personalities and in their dealings with people, both had a noble and generous spirit and each recognized that in the other.

That summer of 1854 such understanding lay in the future. That summer Johannes seethed in his passion. His emotions had become like a harmonic suspension in music, when the composer allows a tone from a previous chord to linger piercingly into a new harmony, and the music cannot find rest until that dissonance is resolved. To Johannes, his love felt like an endless, unbearable suspension.

IN THE MIDDLE OF JULY came a vertiginous moment: a bouquet arrived at the house, sent to Clara by her husband. Robert still had not spoken her name, but he had picked the flowers himself and responded gaily to his attendant's question of where to send them with, "Oh, you know quite well!" The bouquet was an ambiguous token, but Brahms watched Clara dance around the room for joy over it, happier than he had ever seen her. His own feelings, as he reported the news to Joachim, appear as elated as hers.

He waited. Certainly there was plenty to occupy him. Clara had asked Johannes to organize Robert's library and papers, and he read and studied continually while he was doing it. He began reworking his D minor two-piano sonata into a symphony, the one Robert and Clara had pushed him to write. (All these efforts are lost.) As to the orchestration, he wrote Joachim, "I owe anything good there may be in it to Grimm, who helped me with sound advice. . . . I must just add that I want to let the low D predominate at the beginning, and that is why the F-B♭ in the clarinets and bassoons is so weak. . . . Will you encourage me to go on with the other movements? I feel like such an imbecile."[49]

He had already sketched out three movements of the sonata that now was becoming a symphony, and for all the misgivings he continued to labor doggedly over the orchestration of the first movement. When Joachim returned favorable comment on it Brahms only replied, "As usual you have regarded the movement of my Symphony through a rose-colored glass. I must alter and improve it all through. There is a good deal wrong even in the composition, and as to the instrumentation, I do not understand as much about it as it appears in the movement."[50] The symphony was destined to take still another turn, and the orchestration of the beginning never did settle down satisfactorily. The gestation of this music was going to be long and frustrating.

He waited, and his life turned around Clara. On August 10, she went to Ostend for a cure of sea-bathing, with a few concerts on the side. She was about to start touring again, ostensibly because her family needed the money. She refused to dip into Robert's investments that had helped keep them going, and rejected every offer of help from friends and admirers.[51]

While she was at Ostend, Johannes and friend Julius Grimm set out on a tour of Swabia, a vacation Clara had suggested. As soon as they left, Johannes discovered that for the moment nature had turned pale in his eyes. Within three days, after seeing the old university town of Heidelberg and making it as far south as Heilbron, he wrote Clara, "Honored Lady! Not once on my whole journey have I been as light-hearted and cheerful as is necessary on a walking tour, and as I usually am in any case. . . . The exhilarating and uplifting experience of being with you and having music together . . . how can I do without these things?"

He was at once lovesick and alarmed: "I often have struggles with myself, that is to say, Kreisler and Brahms struggle together. . . . This time . . . they were both quite confused, neither knew what he wanted and it was most comical to watch them. Incidentally tears almost stood in my eyes . . . I often have to lay down my pen because my thoughts overcome me."[52] Perhaps Clara did not perceive the obsession and fear in Johannes's words, did not ask questions about the tears, or what he meant by "Brahms" and "Kreisler." For the former, say: Brahms the son of Hamburg, the North German bourgeois, the scholar, the craftsman, the classicist. For Kreisler, say: the dreamer, the lyrical and passionate youth, the Romantic, the lover: Werther. And as they had in his Schumann Variations, both of them sang in his music from then on.

Next day he wrote Clara from Ulm, "I can't stand it any longer; I'm coming back today . . . so dull and colorless does everything seem to me." Now being by her side meant more to Johannes than nature, more even than freedom.

From Ulm, just before going back to Düsseldorf, he wrote his old Winsen friend Amsvogt Blume a poetic diagnosis of Schumann: "I consider the best description of him is to be found in some of the works of E. T. A. Hoffmann (. . . especially the splendid Kreisler, etc.). He has only stripped off his body too soon."[53] On the way to Düsseldorf, Brahms stopped off at Endenich. The doctors allowed him to conceal himself behind a window and observe the patient. Brahms trembled as he watched: Schumann came into the garden to enjoy the sunny weather, he smoked his pipe and smiled, he walked and talked and looked at the flowers like a sensible man. Nearly every day Schumann had been going to Bonn with an attendant, to visit the Beethoven memorial. Even though he had recently experienced some aural mirages, his condition allowed hope.[54] Maybe he could be brought back from whatever wilderness his mind had retreated to. And then what?

Brahms arrived back at the Schumann house before Clara returned from Ostend. He wrote her, "Will you be away much longer? I have a terrible longing to see you again, dearest lady."[55] Cutting short her cure, Clara returned home in time for her fourteenth wedding anniversary on September 12, and her thirty-fifth birthday the next day. Johannes reported to her what he had seen at Endenich. To her delight, for a birthday present he gave her a keyboard arrangement of Robert's Piano Quintet, and he had taught daughters Marie and Elise to play some of Robert's *Pictures from the East*.[56] Clara listened with tears as her girls dutifully threaded their way through their father's music.

Suddenly word came that Robert had spoken her name, even if in a foreboding way: he declared to the doctors that his wife must be dead, since he had not heard from her. At the doctors' suggestion she guardedly wrote to him. On the fifteenth, Brahms handed Clara an envelope from Endenich. He watched her open it and stammer, "A letter from my husband."

Robert had sent Clara love and memories: "Oh, if I could have a sight of you, a word with you all! But the distance is too great." He asked for news of family and friends, his books and publications, her performing: "How I wish I could listen to your beautiful playing again! . . . Was it all a dream—our tour in Holland last winter . . . ? You played . . . in such glorious fashion." The letter seemed straightforward, almost childlike, strange only in its tendency minutely to cite memories. Apparently he wanted to reassure Clara, and himself, that he was capable of remembering.[57] As she read her husband's letter Brahms watched Clara's face transform into a radiant expression that reminded him of the music of unspeakable joy at the end of Beethoven's *Fidelio*, when Leonore has saved Florestan from the dungeon and oblivion. Despite everything, it was an exalted moment for Brahms as well. He concluded his report to Joachim: "Rejoice with me, beloved, there can be no more doubts now?"[58]

Clara replied to Robert, only now telling him of the birth of their baby and other news. Another page came from Endenich: "What joyful news . . . that Brahms, to whom you will give my kind and admiring greetings, has come to live in Düsseldorf; what friendship! If you wish to consult with me in the matter of a name, you will easily guess my choice—the name of the unforgettable one!" He meant, as Clara realized with tears, that the baby should be named Felix, after Mendelssohn—the same name she had chosen. She wrote to Joachim:

> A joy has come to me for which I hardly dared to hope a fortnight ago, and yet . . . I must control the mighty beating of my heart and suppress so much! He says nothing about my going to him at present. . . . My old friend, my piano, must help me in this! Oh, dear Joachim, I thought I knew what a splendid thing it is to be an artist, but I only realize it for the first time now that I can turn all my suffering and joy into divine music, so that I often feel quite happy![59]

Of course Brahms celebrated with her. As yet his love for Clara was directionless; it was impossible to think around the barrier of Schumann, whom he loved as well. There was only the endless suspension, and surely fantasies taking now one tack, now another, fervent and unreal. He wrote Clara in October, "All my thoughts and dreams are of the glorious time when I shall be able to live with you two. I think of the present as the road which leads to the chosen land." And in December, "I wish the doctor would install me as nurse and attendant at Christmas. . . . I would write to you about him every day, and all day long I would talk to him of you."[60]

But what if Schumann could never hear those words of consolation? What if he could never find his way home?

DESPITE THE ELEVATED and suffocating emotions swirling in his mind, Brahms continued to pound away at the D minor music, once a sonata and now a symphony, and the piano Ballades. The symphony resisted pulling together, demanding a maturity with the orchestra and with large forms that he did not yet possess.

Alone and with Clara, Brahms continued to study the music in Schumann's library: Bach, Beethoven, Mozart, Mendelssohn, Chopin, Schumann, and other contemporaries including Liszt, who had recently dedicated the B Minor Sonata to Schumann and sent it with other music to Clara. (Brahms played over Liszt's offerings for her so they could revel in how much they detested it.)[61] In Robert's library he sought out music beyond Bach and Handel to masters of the early Baroque and Renaissance. He read prose as eagerly, now both in Schumann's library and his own growing collection of volumes, recently richer by authors including Aeschylus, Shakespeare, Goethe, Hoffmann, and Robert Schumann.

From the library and his own acquisitions Brahms added to the quotes in his notebook "Des jungen Kreislers Schatzkästlein." He copied down more aphorisms from Jean Paul, some of them conveying his frame of mind like a diary:

> And why does the dictionary of pain have so many alphabets, and that of delight and love so few pages? Only a tear, a pressing hand and a singing voice did the spirit of love and delight give us, and say: "Speak with these!"[62]

He wrote down words of Zacharias Werner, "Truly for us, when some try to make a sensation, it troubles us in a time like this, when everything in the world only crawls and sneaks." Next to that entry Brahms wrote the names *Liszt, Berlioz.* (Later, maybe years later with history weighing on him, he struck out the names.)[63] From Friedrich Schlegel he copied this verse,

> *Music is the art of love,*
> *conceived in the depths of the soul*

out of inflamed yearning
with the humility of holy compulsions.[64]

To his favored sages Brahms added new voices, completing his connection to the founders of musical Romanticism. There are long quotes
from W. H. Wackenroder and from Herder, and a series of aphorisms
from Schumann, among them:

"It has pleased, or it has not pleased," people say. As if there were nothing better than to please people.

To send light into the depths of the human heart—that is the artist's
calling![65]

At the same time, in his notebooks Brahms copied down ideas less lyrical, more caustic, in the form of misogynistic sermons. The longest is
from Friedrich Sallet's *Contrasts and Paradoxes*:

Perhaps a primary reason that women are so often shallow and sense-
less is exactly their superior talent for the external, which shows itself
in their earliest childhood ability quickly and sharply to grasp and imitate things. One sees with what comical verisimilitude little girls play
brides, wives, and mothers. . . . But it is a pity that most of them
thereby let things go . . . [and] hardly trouble themselves over the core
and deeper meaning of things. . . . Many grown women experience romance and carry it off with a convincing show of sincerity, but in fact
it is nothing more than a reiteration of their children's games . . . until
in their imaginations it is as if they really felt passion . . . without their
deeper being having the slightest conception of it. If however this su-
perficial performance gets to be an accustomed game and a need, then
it becomes coqueterie, and many a goodhearted woman in this way, little by little . . . becomes a treacherous harlot, without her even being
aware of it. . . . A[n individual] woman may be worthy of admiration,
but a group of women is worthy only of disdain and ridicule, something unpalatable to anyone with the least appetite for thought.[66]

Notations of that drift continue. A collection of German proverbs
begun in the following year includes, "No dress is more becoming to
a woman than silence."[67] Still later, in his copy of the Koran, Brahms
carefully underlined passages chastening and reproving women. That
hostility, bequeathed Brahms by German culture and distilled in
Hamburg's whorehouses, endured even as he idolized Clara Schumann,

and persisted through his lifelong devotion to women who had talent and ideas and realized them forcefully, and whom he honored and supported. His relations with women would be the great paradox of Brahms's life.

Beyond this paradox so dismal and inexplicable to a later time, his misogyny surely amounted to something else too: a refuge from women, especially a refuge from the feelings they aroused in him—the sexual, but also the tender and devoted. *Degradation in erotic life.* In Brahms's instincts women were corrupted by the sins of the brothel and its dark carnality. To preserve himself, he had to escape. The only way he could salvage some women, some of the time, from the taint was to keep his hands off them. At least then, for him, they could be eternally chaste. Brahms had written Joachim, "I think I can no longer love an unmarried girl." Thus, impasse: he would not sleep with a married one either. When lust called, there were always whores to whom lust belonged, and in return for their favors they demanded of him only a few talers.

Respectable women were the siren call of romantic love, and to that the persona he called "Kreisler" hearkened. Self-protection and devotion to art were another and contrary call, and misogyny one of the things that allowed him—name this side "Brahms"—to heed that call. At the same time, he felt an unquenchable craving for the security and certainty of home and children. Friedrich Nietzsche was not entirely wrong to declare Brahms "the musician of the unsatisfied."

Mixed into all this were the agonies of the Werther years, 1854 and 1855, when Brahms and Kreisler wrestled for his soul.

As THE END OF 1854 APPROACHED, Johannes felt uncertain of everything: his future, his burgeoning feelings for Clara, his music. He wrote Joachim, "I can't understand how you can take any interest in my things, in little Variations and Sonatas like mine!" In an era of revolutionary tone poems by Liszt and *Gesamtkunstwerke*, "total works of art," by Wagner, he felt the absurdity of writing old-fashioned pieces that verged on *Hausmusik*, music for the parlor.

"I always see you before me so vividly," he continued to Joachim, "when I play your things, deeply moved and exalted. . . . Frau Schumann . . . plays with all her old power . . . yesterday she played me my F Minor Sonata, just as I had imagined it, but with more nobility, more tranquil enthusiasm and with such a pure, clear rendering and such a magnificent tone in the stronger passages." He mentions the Schumann Quintet that he arranged; "I have been immersing myself in it deeper and deeper, as in a pair of dark blue eyes." Those eyes had their effect on the Schumann Variations as well. He had made "two new additions, in one of which *Clara speaks!*"[68]

Brahms was talking, obliquely, about the end of the tenth variation, the first of the new ones he wrote in August.[69] This is the most lyrical of the Schumann Variations, which are the first truly masterful set of his life. At the head of the manuscript of no. 10 stands (like something Schumann would write, therefore unlike Brahms) the Romantic subtitle "Fragrance of Rose and Heliotrope." That heading disappeared in the published version. Poignantly at the end of that rose and heliotrope variation, veiled in a middle voice, Clara speaks by way of a theme she had originally written for her *Romance*, Opus 3, composed when she was eleven. Robert had picked it up as the basis of his Opus 5 Impromptus:

The personal references in this musical ménage go beyond a theme of Clara's picked up in turn by her husband and Brahms. By that time Brahms probably understood that Robert Schumann's plaintively poetic theme on which he based the variations, and on which Clara had written her own set the year before, had a symbolic significance:

Thema
Ziemlich langsam

This melody is a variant of what Eric Sams has called Schumann's "Clara theme," found in works including the C Minor Piano Quartet and the D Minor Symphony.[70] Schumann used the notes C-B-A-G♯-A (often transposed) to outline the musical letters of Clara's name: C l A r A (B standing in for l, G♯ for r). For Brahms, Clara spoke in those notes too, even in his Schumann Variations where the C♮ is replaced by a C♯. The Clara theme is repeated like a mantra throughout the piece, now in the treble, now in the bass, now in canonic form.

Such musical cabala was not invented by Schumann or Brahms or the Romantic century, but rather goes back to the early age of polyphonic music in the West. In the fifteenth century Josquin des Prés used the musical letters of his employer's name in a work, to flatter the Duke of Ferrara. Three hundred years later J. S. Bach worked elaborate numerological and proportional symbolism into his music and, in his last fugue, introduced a countersubject on the letters of his own name: B♭-A-C-B♮, which in German notation spells B A C H. Before he met Schumann, Brahms certainly knew about these musical games; another example was his teacher Marxsen's piece about his favorite drink, its main theme the notes C-A-F-F-E-E. And there was the *F-A-E* Sonata based on Joachim's motto.

For Schumann as for Brahms, these connections in music, however private in import, were more serious than playful. Bach had used the connection of number and word and musical pitch to imply the mystical oneness of things. For Schumann, it was a way of suggesting unseen mysteries beneath the surface of his art; he sometimes pointed out the letters in his titles. For Brahms, however, these devices would be not a way of revealing secrets but of hiding them—his own feelings, his life, hidden behind his music.

So Schumann and Brahms, each on his own track, used symbolism to shadow forth his life and feelings in "abstract" music, and sometimes used music to help put those feelings to rest. Through such cabala, instrumental music can tell stories, manifest or implied, public or private, and among those can be the story of the composer's life. And for both men, music could be "poetic" because spoken and musical languages overlap. (More than either of them would have admitted, these intuitions brought them close to the New German School.)

At the same time, Schumann and Brahms aspired to telling their stories in tight-knit forms, as in traditional absolute music, whether or not a given piece used one of the traditional formal patterns like sonata or variations. Often the personal and the formal sat uncomfortably together. In relation to Schumann's *Carnaval,* which is pervaded by such symbolism, Charles Rosen writes of "eccentricity . . . tempered in the large-scale harmony by a conservative classicism often at odds with the small details."[71]

Yet for both Schumann and Brahms, the personal implications buried in their work did not govern its logic. There lies the divide between Schumann and Brahms on one hand, and on the other the New Germans, who expected their literary models to create novel patterns and perhaps to exonerate wandering forms. Still, while Brahms embraced traditional patterns in theory, in his early music—especially the D minor sonata/symphony/concerto—he would find great difficulty reconciling the demands of personal expression and absolute form. It would be some time before Brahms resolved that dilemma. George S. Bozarth writes, "To the degree that these works lack subtlety because of too direct . . . a reliance upon their poetic models, they must be considered immature."[72]

Besides the Schumann Variations, Brahmsian symbolism can be seen in the first number of his other important work of 1854, the Four Ballades, published two years later as Opus 10 and dedicated to Julius Otto Grimm. From now on his published piano music would mainly be in the form of variations, popularistic items, or freestanding Romantic character pieces with names like intermezzo, capriccio, romance, rhapsody, and ballade.

The name *ballade* implies a story, like a sung ballad, the music free of traditional formal patterns (though in such pieces Brahms tends to some kind of A B A outline). The first of the four Opus 10 pieces is a brooding song without words in D minor, the melody implying the first two verses of the Scottish ballad "Edward." Brahms had read the ballad, in German translation, in Herder's *Stimmen der Völker* that Julius Allgeyer had recommended to him:

> *Why does your sword so drip with blood, Edward, Edward?*
> *And why so sad are ye?*
> *"Oh, I have killed my hawk so fine . . ."*

But it is his father Edward has killed, not his hawk. In the first ballade the symbolism is not contained in the names of the notes; instead, the music sets the text of the ballad, like the implied songs of Brahms's sonata slow movements (Or might there be in "Edward" an ominous personal resonance? Johannes is responding to a story of a son killing his father at the urging of his mother.[73])

In any case, with the "Edward" ballade Brahms once more wrote music implying something beyond the notes. This piece is as close to Lisztean program music as he would ever approach. We sense that not only in the implied text, but in the sound of the music that seems to conjure a darkling landscape, returning over and over to primeval open fifths and octaves—as striking a piece of musical scene-painting as, say, Mendelssohn's *Fingal's Cave*. Through the years Brahms would turn for inspiration to bardic tales in Ossian and in Irish and Scottish folk music.

Which is all to say: the "Edward" ballade is the debut of the Brahmsian *bardic tone*. Later, he would set "Edward" for voices in Opus 75; the tone is also manifest in the Opus 17 Ossian setting for womens' voices, harp, and horns.

Each of the Opus 10 Ballades tells its own "story," concrete or abstract, each a striking piece, each something of a stylistic experiment. The allegro in no. 2 perhaps recalls the dancing course of some Schubert impromptus, no. 3 the earlier Brahmsian scherzos. No. 4 is the most expressively intricate, beginning with an almost Chopinesque grace but contrasting that with a brooding middle section, a quiet lento marked "with intimate sentiment." This music babbles on as if the fingers were drifting into its subtle tonal colors, the veiled murmuring melodic line at moments pulling yearningly away from the harmony.

IN THEIR STYLE, and in being short, separate character pieces, the Four Ballades set Brahms's future course as a piano composer. But he did not know that in 1854. Then, as far as he could see, he was drifting, overwhelmed with feelings for Clara and with the burden of Schumann's prophecy. The situation would drag on for years, Brahms remaining laconic unto silent as a composer while the world waited for him to fulfill the prophecy, or to make a fool of himself.

At the same time, a mainspring of his maturity began to manifest in 1854, in the intricate canons found in several of the Schumann Variations. In fact, the most elaborate of the canonic episodes is in the lyrical, Clara-dominated tenth variation, which begins with a melody taken from the bass line of the main theme. That melody appears in the treble while its mirror image (called *inversion*) forms the bass, and the lilting voices in between are a speeded-up rendering of Schumann's theme (called *diminution of the theme*, in contrapuntal technique). Then the opening soprano and bass become a canon by inversion at the distance of a measure. When Clara "speaks" at the end, Brahms works in her melody as counterpoint to his own—the former bass line. Thus he fashions a contrapuntal tour de force: the theme he extracted from the original bass line works as counterpoint to a diminution of the main Schumann theme, works both in simultaneous mirror with itself and also as a canon in inversion, and can be superimposed on Clara's melody. All of that must be made to work by strenuous thought and patient craft.

The tenth variation and the other canons in the set reveal that however overgrown his creative path at the end of 1854, Brahms had begun to show a regard for counterpoint that would preoccupy him for years.

On September 26, his third letter of that month, Robert Schumann wrote Clara from Endenich, "I am surprised that Brahms is working at counterpoint, which does not seem like him."[74] Plunging into dry technical study did not match what Schumann expected from his protégé—but that shows again how little Schumann really understood him. Johannes had begun a slow metamorphosis, during which he would grow out of the rhapsodic Kreisler and emerge from the chrysalis as Herr Doktor Brahms, who preached that craft counted more than inspiration.

As the winter of 1854 approached, Brahms sat with Clara and told her of his childhood, its joys and its shadows, the labyrinthine streets and canals of old Hamburg, the months in the *Animierlokale*. She wrote in her journal, "He told me much about himself, which half fills me with admiration for him, half troubles me. . . . Will not those who understand him be few in number? I believe it will be so, but the few will understand and love him, as my dear Robert did at once. Brahms has had a splendid idea, a surprise for you, my Robert. He has interwoven my old theme with yours—already I can see you smile."[75]

Robert did smile, it seems, when he received Brahms's variations on his theme at Endenich. At first, Schumann wrote a letter responding to each variation in detail, and with pleasure. But for some reason he discarded that draft and in November sent one toned down in enthusiasm and more general: "How I long to see you, dear friend, and hear your lovely Variations played either by you or by Clara. . . . There is an exquisite coherence about the whole work, a wealth of fantastic glamor peculiarly your own. . . . Thank you, too, my dear Johannes, for all your kindness to my Clara. She speaks of it constantly in her letters."[76]

CHAPTER SIX

Words Spoken and Unspoken

In October 1854, Clara Schumann and Brahms traveled together from Düsseldorf to visit Josef Joachim, and so united once more the trio of friends who had consoled each other, and kept Clara alive, when madness overtook her husband. After giving a concert with Joachim in Hanover, she went on alone to Leipzig to resume her career as a full-time virtuoso after a hiatus of some fifteen years. Between October 16 and December 21, Clara gave twenty-two concerts in twelve North German cities.[1]

She started her tour with a pair of programs at the Leipzig Gewandhaus, where in 1832 she had made her solo debut at age eleven. Through her teens Clara Wieck had appeared regularly in the old hall, playing Beethoven and Schubert and Mendelssohn and other masters of the recent past. Now her repertoire featured her husband's work, chipping away at the resistance his music had met all his life. Her Gewandhaus programs also included the andante and scherzo from Brahms's F Minor Sonata. Here began her lifelong commitment to the music of the second genius who loved her.

Leipzig embraced Clara as if she were a long-lost daughter. But for her and Johannes the tour was an ordeal, the first long separation since he had come to live in Düsseldorf. Like Robert Schumann, Brahms felt torn about Clara's touring—because she was a woman and mother, because he hated the separation, because he had little enthusiasm for performing himself so could not understand hers. He wrote Clara in August, "I think of you as going to the concert hall like a priestess to the altar. This, of course, is just as it should be. But I have never had that feeling, as I only know the public from a distance. I shun its proximity."[2]

From Leipzig Clara continued on to Weimar, playing with Liszt's orchestra there, then she had two engagements in Frankfurt where she again presented the Brahms sonata movements. In Weimar there had been the usual situation with Liszt, he friendly and flattering, she tight-lipped and hostile. Later that year he published an article on her in the *Neue Zeitschrift für Musik.* "A short time ago a charming playfellow of the Muses," he wrote, now Clara is "a consecrated, faithful, stern priestess whose eyes look upon men with a sad, penetrating gaze." Though the article was extravagantly laudatory, Clara never said a word to Liszt about it.[3] The portrait he painted there came to be the way the world, including Brahms, saw Clara Schumann: the tragic high priestess of the piano.

Afraid it would upset Robert, Clara did not tell him about this first tour. For years she had played mainly for his ears and approval. Now she anguished in her journal that Robert's "spirit does not go with me, when I go into a concert I do not feel that he is wishing me success. Then my heart sinks, and only one thing comforts and strengthens me when my courage threatens to give way, the thought that he, Johannes, dearest and best of friends, thinks of me and sends his good wishes."[4]

Clara's burdens accompanied her to every city and every hall. Stagehands would watch as she bowed decorously and swept off the platform in waves of applause, then sank into a chair backstage and burst into wracking sobs. Then she would dry her tears and arrange her gown and go out and play the next piece. It was a microcosm of her life—relentless determination, relentless misery.

As she toured, Brahms returned to his parents' at Hamburg, from where he wrote her: "We enjoyed a few more pleasant days [in Hanover]. Joachim and Grimm used to lie on the sofa at twilight while I played to them in the next room."[5] At the same time Joachim wrote Gisela von Arnim: "As for Brahms, who put up here on the black sofa for a few days, I did not really feel at ease with him. . . . Brahms is egoism incarnate, *without himself being aware of it.*"[6] Joachim had wearied of Young Kreisler's obliviousness to any feelings or opinions but his own, his inability to express affection, his withering sarcasm that boiled over into disdain: "He knows the weaknesses of the people around him, and he makes use of them, and then does not hesitate to show (to their faces, I admit) that he is crowing over them."[7]

Johannes could not help prodding and provoking even those he loved. He was egoism incarnate but also shy, generous but rarely capable of expressing it. Joachim's resentment was a theme to be replayed many times, with variations, by friends of Brahms. Yet there was also the blazing talent and the wisdom in managing it. Joachim continued to Gisela:

The way in which he wards off all the morbid emotions and imaginary troubles of others is really delightful. He is absolutely sound in that, just as his complete indifference to the means of existence is beautiful, indeed magnificent. He will not make the smallest sacrifice of his intellectual inclinations—he will not play in public because of his contempt for the public, and because it irks him—although he plays divinely. I have never heard piano playing (except perhaps Liszt's) which gave me so much satisfaction—so light and clear, so cold and indifferent to passion. His compositions, too. . . . I have never come across a talent like his before. He is miles ahead of me.[8]

It is surprising in the Romantic century to find a celebrated soloist praising the "cold and indifferent." But Joachim, like Clara Schumann, pursued an ideal contrary to that emotionally extravagant age. Their style was restrained, pure, antivirtuosic, expressing the music rather than the performer. Both of them admired the same qualities in Johannes's playing. His abiding problem was that when he went before the public his technique sometimes failed to gain the upper hand over his nerves.

Back home in Hamburg, in a cramped two-room flat on Lilienstrasse with his parents and sister and brother and a steady traffic of family friends, Brahms felt the things that had changed and not changed. Now his parents seemed to regard him with awe, as some incomprehensible creature they had engendered by some unaccountable decree of the gods. At the same time there was the old discord, Johann Jakob bustling out to work or carouse with friends, fleeing the house and its women. By then the senior Brahms had made himself one of the better bass players in town, a regular in theater orchestra pits. He still donned his green uniform, however, to play bugle in the Hamburg Bürgerwehr band.

Brahms wrote Clara from Lilienstrasse, "I cannot understand the life I used to lead." Still, he had another happy reunion with his teacher Eduard Marxsen, for whom he played Clara's variations and his own recent work. Johannes wrote her that Marxsen "is extremely pleased with the improvement in my playing. That too I have to thank you for. . . . Indeed, if anything passably good is in me, or ever likely to come out of me, have I not to thank you two and your great love?"[9] (Early in their romance, Robert Schumann had written Clara in nearly the same terms: "I must thank you for all the music I write.")

At home, Brahms did not fall back into his old life. Never again in Hamburg would he be so cloistered as in his teens. The year before, he had left his hometown nearly unknown; now he returned as Schumann's Messiah-designate. Despite the inevitable jealousy and spite around town, Brahms was welcomed by musicians who had not been so warm before. They included Theodor Avé-Lallemant, a bearded, garrulous old music teacher who sat on the Philharmonic committee and had a great deal of say over what transpired musically in town. Avé may have been put off by Brahms's imperious personality, but he still admired Schumann's young genius, and they shared a fancy for old music and books. The two would have a long acquaintance, strained at times as was axiomatic with Brahms, and in the end it would be Avé who more disappointed the younger man. More useful friendships formed with Karl Grädener, who conducted a women's chorus in Hamburg, and with Georg Dietrich Otten, director of the Musikverein concert series.

Johannes revisited his few acquaintances, once more prowled the docks and byways of the old city, at night watched the lighted boats bobbing on the Alster. What really kept him in Hamburg that autumn, though, was not the town or its people but waiting for Clara. In early November she arrived for three concerts with the Philharmonic. Johannes went out to meet her at Harburg and proudly escorted her through the city gates.

Clara was charmed by the Brahms family—Johann Jakob the affable peasant, Christiane now a toothless crone of sixty-five, but boundlessly kind: "His mother is splendid! She gives what she has, with agreeable simplicity, without fuss and talk, and that endears her to me." Clara formed an enduring bond of sympathy with Elise Brahms, and Johannes's housebound sister was dazzled by the attentions of the famous artist.

The public received Clara's concerts with the Philharmonic coolly, but that did not surprise her or sully the visit. She slept in a hotel and took meals with the Brahmses. Johannes's friend Julius Otto Grimm, visiting for Clara's concerts, stayed in the family flat. For his friends Johannes played the eager host, showing off his parents and his hometown, his desk and ranks of toy soldiers. They toured the harbor, walked between the lindens of the Jungfernstieg to the Pavilion where his father played. (Did he show them the *Animierlokale* where he used to sit all night at the piano?) Observing the simple home and simple people of Johannes's family, Clara wondered in her journal "how it was possible for Johannes to develop into·what he is, amidst such surroundings." Where had mad, dashing Young Kreisler come from?

She was puzzled to find that for all Johannes's reverence for his mother, he seemed to dote even more on Johann Jakob, to take pride even in his father's clownishness. For a long time he had brought people to the house to meet his father and listen to his yarns, told in priceless Plattdeutsch. A friend recalled that once when Johannes got paid by a publisher he lined up gold coins along the piano like soldiers and crowed, "This is for my beloved father in Hamburg!"[10]

Brahms's feelings toward his father may also have formed out of democratic sentiment on one hand, boastfulness on the other. He did not look down on his father but enjoyed what Johann Jakob amounted to— a peasant raconteur, a *Bierfiedler*. At the same time, maybe there was the opposite implication: This buffoon did not make me what I am, I did it myself. And it is I, who am incomprehensible to my family, who will redeem my family's name.

THE VISIT TO HAMBURG gave Clara more understanding of Johannes, and a greater tenderness. "Often I thank God for this friend," she wrote, "who has been sent to me in this time of bitterest trial, like a veritable angel of comfort." She added about Christiane, "I could not help wondering how long this good woman still has to live. Perhaps someday it will fall to me to take her place as mother to him." Clara and Johannes were trying on roles. Mother? Sister? For now the fantasy of substitute mother was the only one Clara allowed herself.[11]

On November 20, she left for her next engagements—twelve concerts in five weeks, ending in Berlin with a series in conjunction with Joachim.[12] After she left Hamburg, Julius Grimm wrote Joachim from Hamburg, "Our blond friend is blissful and droll."[13] Clara had agreed to Johannes's plea that in her letters she use the familiar *du*, "thou." To accept this usage is a charged event between friends, more so between a man and woman—a talisman of intimacy. Rapturous at seeing the word in her handwriting, Brahms acceded to Clara's demand that he continue to address her with the formal and respectful *Sie*. Before long, though, Johannes could hardly bear to apply the formal second person to Clara; *du* crept more and more into his letters.

For a while he lingered in Hamburg, restless and lovesick. He felt a stranger in his family, exasperated at the incessant chatter and bickering. To Clara he complained, "How little peace I am given here . . . if I ever have free time I have to have four at a time in one room, with continual running in and out. . . . Until now I was writing while five people had a lively conversation about my new coat."[14] He had been spending enough time out drinking to alarm her, so reassured her like a child: "Since you have gone I have not been in a single pub, so you can set your mind to rest on that score."[15] He wanted to be good for his Clara.

His passion was getting harder for her to receive in a motherly or sisterly way, but she offered no more than token resistance. She needed love as much as Johannes did; she did not have the will to push him away. Yet they could say little. On both sides there were pressures of love and need that could not be resolved because they could not be spoken, not yet.

Then Johannes pushed at the edge of the permissible again, writing her a letter that veiled his feelings thinly behind a screen of banter and fairy tale. After several rambling pages he burst out, "I have written you a dreadful letter. I can see that. So I shall write you a second one from out of the Thousand and One Nights. It describes my condition exactly although its writer was a prince and I am a composer." There follows the story of Prince Camaralzaman and Princess Badoura. He ends the letter ambiguously, as if he were still in the story, signing it CAMARALZAMAN EBN. BRAH. In fact, he is transparently speaking words from his own heart: "Would to God that I were allowed this day instead of writing this letter to you to repeat to you with my own lips that I am dying of love for you. Tears prevent me from saying more."[16]

IN THE ASYLUM AT ENDENICH, Robert Schumann had been calm in the last weeks, playing piano and writing letters to family and friends. Though everyone tried to stay cautious about his prospects, he evidently had gained ground. There were no voices in his mind, no supernatural orchestras. At her husband's request, Clara sent him one of the Laurens silverpoints of Johannes. Robert wrote its subject: "My dear wife has sent me your portrait, your familiar features, and I know its place in my room very well, very well—under the mirror. I continue to feel uplifted by your variations. I should like to hear many of them performed by you and Clara. . . . Clara wrote to me that on page fourteen the music recalls something. What is it?"[17] He had forgotten his wife's melody, that he used in his own Impromptus. In December the doctors told Clara that she could not hope to see her husband for some time still. Once again her heart fell.

She arrived back in Düsseldorf just before Christmas with Brahms and Joachim in tow. In her journal she confessed that by the end of her concert tour, "I had been simply longing for Johannes. To him alone can I utter all that is in my heart. Joachim, too, is a dear and faithful friend, but Johannes is even more to me."[18] During their decades-long friendship and musical collaboration, Clara and Joachim would never use *du*.

The day before Christmas Joachim traveled to Endenich, where he was allowed to see Schumann. It was the first time doctors had allowed a visitor in the ten months the sick man had lived there. Joachim returned to Düsseldorf with encouraging reports, and a letter for Johannes in which Schumann for the first time wrote *du*.[19] On Christmas Day, the first Brahms had spent away from home, the friends permitted themselves hope. Marie Schumann accompanied Joachim in her father's violin sonata; Elise performed a little play. Clara presented Johannes with the complete works of his favorite, Jean Paul.

Just after the holidays Clara began with Johannes's help to sort through Robert's letters, burning the ones that seemed too personal to leave to history. She noticed that Johannes's eyes shone with pleasure as he watched names and intimate words curl up and vanish in the fire.[20] He would preserve that pleasure, adding to it the satisfaction of seeing his own correspondence torn up and floating away on a river, the past drifting into oblivion.

Responding in kind to Schumann's warm letter, Brahms reported that after their visit Joachim "talked to us the whole evening about you, and your wife wept silently. We were all filled with the joyful hope of seeing you again soon." Of Clara, he added:

> How long the separation from your wife seemed to me! I had grown so used to her uplifting presence and had spent such a magnificent summer with her. I had grown to admire and love her so much that everything else seemed empty to me and I could only long to see her again. . . . I have to thank you above all for the beautiful word in your last letter—for the affectionate "*du*." Your kind wife has also gladdened my heart now by using this beautiful and intimate word to me.[21]

It may be that in this letter Johannes showed more innocence than was healthy, was more candid than he should have been. He wrote as if to a friend and confidant, as if to a well man, as if to someone other than the husband of the woman he wrote so rapturously about. They had all been sending restrained and guarded letters to Endenich during Robert's convalescence, so as not to upset him. Maybe this unconstrained letter was less than helpful to Schumann.

The belated and cheerless christening ceremony for the baby Felix came on New Year's Day 1855. Brahms stood in the church as one of three godparents, the others being family friends. Clara wanted Joachim as a godparent too, but the authorities proscribed that because he was Jewish. (He converted to Christianity later that year, with a fierce repudiation of the religion of his birth.) Soon after the christening, Clara and Johannes surprised Joachim by arranging a rehearsal in Hanover of his *Henry IV* Overture.[22] The violinist still composed actively and Johannes encouraged him with steady praise, but that was not to last for either of them.

On January 8 a letter arrived for Clara from her husband. She had sent him one of Brahms's sonatas and the Ballades, and Robert responded lucidly to them. He concluded, "Now on to overtures and symphonies! . . . A symphony or opera, which arouses enthusiasm and makes a great sensation, brings everything else more quickly forward. He must."[23] It was what Clara had once preached to Robert. Brahms wrote back to Schumann that he had indeed spent last summer "trying to write a symphony."[24] He did not mention that for the moment it had trickled out.

Then, with a welter of feelings, on January 11 Brahms made the journey to Endenich. There for the first time in nearly a year he sat face to face with the man to whom he owed his fame and his burden. Schumann was alert and sociable. The two chatted through the afternoon about times old and new. They tried some piano duets. Brahms played his Schumann Variations and Four Ballades for the smiling master. After a visit of several hours they walked to Bonn, where Schumann clung to Johannes nearly enough to make him miss his train.

Johannes returned to Clara with a hopeful report, just before she left for a tour of the Netherlands. In fact, he hid from her a feeling of foreboding over Schumann's condition[25]; her husband had been calm but still vague and childlike. Brahms accompanied Clara and her companion, Fräulein Schönerstedt, as far as Emmerich and then turned back. Then in Düsseldorf he found he could not endure the separation. Two days later he surprised Clara in Rotterdam, having spent most of his money for the ticket. Finally tearing himself back to Düsseldorf, he wrote her with naked desperation, "I can do nothing but think of you and gaze constantly at your dear letter and portrait. What have you done to me? Can't you remove the spell you have cast over me?"[26]

EVEN IF CLARA'S PLAYING found a good response in Holland, she felt ill and depressed and missed Johannes. Then came a devastating letter from Robert on January 26: "My Clara, I feel as if I were facing some terrible calamity. How dreadful if I should never see you and the children again!"[27] This after the promising signs of December, the too-candid letter from Johannes, the seemingly encouraging visits by Joachim and Brahms. In the two weeks since he had seen Johannes, Schumann had turned a corner. Before him he saw a dark road growing darker. And meanwhile, Johannes burned for Clara.

Here the story becomes obscure. There are letters destroyed, agonized private conversations, unspoken feelings. We do not know exactly, medically, what was wrong with Robert Schumann, or why he experienced an evil presentiment in the winter of 1855. But by the time of that letter to Clara he seems to have made a decision, or believed it had been made for him.

It appears that the voices were speaking to him again, more insistently than ever. They had sentenced him to death before and he had botched the execution. This time he must not fail. Now Schumann decided to make good his plunge into the Rhine by a surer means of killing himself: the slow but certain route of starvation.[28]

There was more to his despair now than the random attacks of madness he had suffered since his youth. It was what madness had done to him and his family. In the last decade, inspiration had given Schumann less than it had when he was younger. His energy had not declined—if anything he had worked himself into collapse—but the old boldness of thought had deserted him. Alfred Einstein wrote, "Had Schumann never passed his thirty-fifth birthday, he would have been the Shelley of music, the star of youth most resplendently gleaming."[29] In those words lies a certain regret that Schumann survived after his inspiration ran short. As of 1855, he was forty-five, and after decades of wrestling with his demons he felt sick and weary unto death. Doctors offered no explanation for his years of suffering, no assurance of relief. Beyond that, if he had outlived his inspiration and knew it, he had experienced one of the worst nightmares that can assail an artist still relatively young. Then, even if Clara his muse still lived, she would be no creative use to him any more, or he to her.

Another and more shadowy element might account for Schumann's decision to starve, if decision it was. After Brahms's December letter, Robert could see well enough what was happening in his house. From Johannes's letter and visit, Robert must have suspected that this protégé loved his wife, and maybe he suspected Clara's feelings for Johannes. She and Robert were soul mates; even at a distance he could feel what she was feeling—her anguish over him, her burgeoning love for a younger and healthier man. Perhaps Robert did not doubt Clara's loyalty if he were alive and well. But what if he were not well, or not alive? Who would take care of her?

Who else but Johannes?[30] On the face of it, Schumann still had reasons to fight off his demons and live—if not for his art, then for his family. But if he gave in to the weariness and the dark demands of his voices, there would still be Johannes to watch over Clara and the children. She could be muse to this young genius as she had been for Robert in his great years. The fact that Johannes had used Clara's melody, as once Robert had, was a talisman of a new and equally beautiful partnership.

Which is to say: Robert Schumann may have decided to stop fighting the voices because he believed he was leaving his wife and children in stronger hands. Once Schumann had proclaimed Johannes the Fair his successor in music. Now perhaps he retired from the scene to let the younger man be successor in his home and his bed.

None of this can be said for certain. This can: In Schumann's letters and actions there is no hint of jealousy regarding Johannes and his wife, but the opposite. As Schumann took his downward turn in the middle of 1855, he became even warmer toward the young eagle he had announced to the world. In March he wrote Joachim, "I am getting deeper into Johannes's music. The First Sonata was quite without precedent for a first published piece."[31] And to Brahms, after going over Opus 2, he wrote, "I live in your music. . . . There has never been anything like it before. . . . Without further ado, a crown of laurels to this Johannes who hails from regions so strange. And how I like your songs."[32] Maybe Schumann was not being figurative in the phrase "I live in your music."

Just in that period, as Robert's decline encouraged their unspoken connection, Clara and Johannes had their first touch of friction. In a letter Brahms tried cavalierly to brush away the seriousness of Robert's words about the "calamity." Clara knew enough to be terrified by them. Her response to Brahms's letter does not survive, but on receiving it he wrote her with brusque irony:

> Fair and Haughty Dame! What crime can I have committed to deserve so distressing a letter as your last? As far as I can remember all I did was to write curtly, but my intention was not disrespectful. If only, my dear Frau Clara, you would never be angry with me about my writing! Have I not often told you how seldom I succeed in getting my thoughts out of my heart and onto paper? It is exactly the same with my composing. . . . It simply won't flow from my heart.

He ends, "I can make canons in all possible artistic forms. I am wondering how I shall be able to get on with fugues."[33] Clara responded affectionately to his letter, he reciprocated, the tension receded. The next doctor's report said Robert was hearing music in his head again.[34]

They went on waiting. It was altogether strange, the Schumann household, in that year. The husband was ill and far away, no one knew for how long. When visitors came they found a noisy collection of seven children, ages two to twelve, seen after mostly by servants. Much of the time their mother, who existed in some limbo between wife and widow, was away on tour. Supposedly sleeping in a room upstairs but spending his time downstairs was the handsome blond youth, his name known to everybody but his music unknown. He would always be there in the house, working at the piano or reading in the library or playing with the children. He had no position or apparent income at all. He was athletic and boyish but revealed nothing. Surely rumors about his relations with the famous woman hovered around Düsseldorf, and probably the whole German musical community. No one can know what Robert Schumann thought.

EVEN THOUGH ROBERT'S SALARY as town music director continued to the end of 1855, Clara had been anxious to start touring for reasons not only financial but personal: she needed to play, it was her consolation and joy. For much of her career from now on, the need for money was as much excuse as explanation. For the first time since her teens, Clara settled into the virtuoso life, traveling city to city with a maid or a companion (women did not travel alone in that time), alternating hours of musical exhilaration and audience adulation with days of loneliness and anxiety and exhaustion. Recital earnings were slim. It took many soirees to feed and clothe seven children.

As Clara traveled, Johannes kept her posted on the household and himself.

> Eugenie has evidently caught a cold, she has no appetite, her face is flushed. . . . The boys are very well, even Felix. The alphabet doesn't seem to make much progress, in spite of large quantities of sugar loaf.

> Last Sunday I went with Bertha [the maid] and Marie and Elise to the Grafenberg. . . . We were all very lively, galloped about, and tore through the thickest bushes. . . . Last night—what do you think?— Ludwig slept in my bed; I put him to bed and showed him your picture to give him pleasant dreams. I didn't get much sleep, but did my dreaming awake. The little one woke up very early indeed, and then we had a good tussle together.[35]

In a letter of early February, Brahms told Clara that in a dream he had found himself performing his "unfortunate symphony" as a piano concerto, and as both soloist and audience he was "completely enraptured" by it.[36] Inspired by the dream, he decided to rework the D minor two-piano sonata/symphony into a concerto. In the process he would keep only the first movement, retooling it as necessary, hold back the original minor-key scherzo (it would be recycled in *Ein deutsches Requiem*), and compose a new finale. For a year now he had been pounding away at this intractable mass of material. Making a completed piano concerto out of it took three years more.

At the beginning of 1855 he started a brooding piano quartet in the key of C♯ minor—the key cited by Kapellmeister Kreisler—and perhaps sketched a first movement for another symphony. Something was to come of both ideas, but only decades later. He wrote Clara, "There are frightfully many notes buzzing in my head and around the paper, if I only had tranquility! But everything stays at the beginning stage, I can't finish anything."[37] Even though he worked steadily, after the previous year's modest outpouring of the Four Ballades and the B Major Trio, a creative block of alarming magnitude had set in.

Much of his difficulty may have been that in the work of this period—the D Minor Concerto, the piano quartet, and possibly a symphony movement—Brahms was writing too close to his emotions. And, as he told Clara, he wanted to write more from the heart. The musical demands stumbled over the personal, the tumult of his feelings coming out in passionate but inchoate form. All that is familiar to artists mining their own experience for creative ore. The problem is never how to get the anguish on paper; that comes out amply on its own. The problem is how to sort it out, to find the distance to shape and control and judge the results.

When after years of struggle Brahms did find the balance of expression and form to contain the chaos of emotion, and finished the pieces he started in the middle 1850s, he would be candid about the intimate references. Twenty years later, when some of the C♯ minor material had become the C Minor Piano Quartet, Brahms wrote his publisher an apparently joking conceit that recalls an excruciatingly actual state of mind two decades before:

> On the cover you must have a picture, namely a head with a pistol to it. Now you can form some conception of the music! I'll send you my photograph for the purpose. Since you seem to like color printing, you can use blue coat, yellow breeches and top-boots.[38]

Anyone of his era would understand the reference to the man in the blue coat and yellow breeches and boots: Young Werther, who wore that costume when he killed himself over another man's beloved. And in the opening of the Quartet, Brahms names the object of his despair by means of Robert Schumann's Clara theme—C–B–A–G♯–A—disguised in another key.

He would call these his Werther years. He floundered in a storm of unfamiliar and unwanted feelings. He wanted to get out of it all, to shoot himself, to find oblivion. The days empty of Clara he filled with his battle to discover his way as a composer, teaching a few students, reading, longing. The hyperbolic daydreams of lovesickness, the rankling hollowness in the pit of the stomach, accompanied his days.

He tried to keep himself occupied with reading and his old self-improvement projects, adding to "Des jungen Kreislers Schatzkästlein." From March 1855 dates the notebook devoted to German proverbs: "Speak little, but true; too much talk is dangerous." "Youth, waste not; poverty in old age is painful." "He who stays on the plain will not fall far." Beside the last he jotted, "Quite so." For himself in a vehement time, Brahms craved the emotional plain, however flat and lonely that landscape. For the notebook he collected over a hundred proverbs, prefaced by an injunction to himself: "Good maxims, wise lessons one must practice, not just hear."[39]

Clara came home for ten days in the middle of February, between tours again. Some of her upcoming programs would involve Joachim, some her old partner Jenny Lind. The new tour began with a visit to those performing partners in Hanover, where Lind resisted Clara's attempts to beguile her with the Schumann Variations and waxed indignant over "mistaken tendencies" in Brahms's music.[40] Clara's championing of Johannes came close to breaking up that friendship. She found resistance to Johannes's music disheartening, but she still urged his work on musicians everywhere she went. Just as she had done with Robert's music, she took spreading Johannes's work as a sacred calling.

As CLARA CONCERTIZED with Joachim in Berlin, Brahms returned to Endenich for an afternoon's visit. Schumann looked wan and vacant, but once again welcomed Johannes with an attempt at cheer. He asked after Clara's tour, where she was staying, what she was performing. Johannes gave Robert a portrait of her for his room; the sick man looked at it for a long time, his eyes filling with tears. At moments Schumann seemed his old self. He told Johannes he had been composing fugues, though they were not ready to show yet. He laughed over stories of the children and Felix's first tooth, reminisced about old times on the road with Clara, especially their last tour in Holland when he had heard ovations for his music like none before.

Other moments were distressing. An air of unreality pervaded everything. Brahms handed Schumann pen and paper and encouraged him to write a note to Clara. Schumann could only stare helplessly at the paper and finally said he was too excited; he would try again tomorrow. They sat down at the piano and played through a duet arrangement of Schumann's *Cäsar* Overture, but its composer could not keep the time and his piano was badly out of tune. Finally they walked to Bonn, an attendant trailing them watchfully. As they took in the cathedral, Schumann kept up with Brahms's bustling pace. Naturally they stopped at the Beethoven statue that Schumann had been visiting nearly every day; the monument was his church and his altar.[41]

When it came time for Johannes to go, they embraced and kissed. Then Brahms got on the train and sank into gloom as it pulled out of the station. It had been a visit with the disturbing sensation of a pleasant social call in the middle of a catastrophe. When he wrote Clara about it he filtered his impressions, as always. The only sour note he mentioned was that Robert seemed tired of the hospital. That became explicit when a letter came from Endenich: "I want to get out of here! . . . For more than a year, it's been exactly the same way of living, and the same view of Bonn. Where else can I go?"[42] Schumann meant what other hospital. There was no question of going home again, and the Endenich hospital was the best available. They ignored the plea.

In April Clara met Johannes in Hamburg, and this time stayed in the Brahms household. She had not come to perform but to hear the Philharmonic play Robert's *Bride of Messina Overture* and his overture and incidental music to Byron's *Manfred*. As she and Johannes listened to the music take wing in the hall, it seemed to them an overpowering token of Schumann's genius, and his tragedy.

Clara felt comfortable staying in the tiny family flat, but noted her concerns: Johannes's "mother and sister have some dim idea that there is something out of the ordinary in him, but his father and brother do not even go so far as this." Eduard Marxsen disappointed her; she found Johannes's teacher "looks upon an artist's life only in material terms."[43] All of it reinforced her dominant impression of Hamburg and its citizens, the philistine trading city Johannes inexplicably loved.

Once more they returned together to Düsseldorf. Joachim had taken rooms in town for a long stay, and on May 7 joined them for Johannes's twenty-second birthday. As a birthday gift Robert sent the manuscript of

The Bride of Messina, with greetings for Johannes. From Brahms's parents came a portrait of his mother and sister. Julius Otto Grimm, not able to be with them, sent a cake in his stead. Joachim contributed Liszt's two-piano arrangement of Beethoven's Ninth Symphony; it would occupy Brahms and Clara for many hours at the keyboard. There were volumes of Dante and Ariosto, a photograph of Robert. Friends joined in with music and dancing and laughter, even catching up Clara in the spirit: "I too seemed to grow younger, for he whirled me along with him and I have not spent so cheerful a day since Robert fell ill."[44]

Most touching of Brahms's birthday gifts that year was the A Minor Romance that Clara had composed for him. "Its tone is sad," she told her journal, "but I was sad when I wrote it." The piece marks nearly the end of her composing.[45] It shows her state of mind that the Romance was dedicated "to my dear friend Johannes" on the first copy. When she re-copied it for Robert's forty-fifth birthday, she inscribed it "to my beloved husband."[46]

Then she received a frightful note from Robert: "I sent you a spring message on May 1st. The following days were very unquiet; you will learn more from the letter which you will receive the day after tomorrow. A shadow flickers across it, but the rest of its contents will please you, my darling."[47] The second letter never arrived. If he wrote it, perhaps the doctors intercepted it. Those were the last words she ever received from her husband. Did he deliberately pick for his foreboding announcement the day of Johannes's birthday?

Now Robert's return, the return of their old life, was no longer a viable dream. When that had sunk in, the question remained: What did it mean for her and Johannes?

THE LOWER RHINE MUSIC FESTIVAL came around again in Düsseldorf at the end of May 1855. As a forum for large orchestral and choral works the event had seen much excitement in the last years, including Joachim's performances and some of the Schumanns' greatest triumphs. This year the luminaries included Liszt and Jenny Lind. Even if there was bad blood between them over Johannes's music, Clara was transported by Lind's performance in the title role of Robert's oratorio *Paradise and the Peri*.[48]

At the festival Lind and her husband, Otto Goldschmidt, met Johannes for the first time. His discomfort with them and with the situation joined with his gracelessness to make a wretched impression. The couple did not laugh at the jokes he cracked in his high voice. He struck them as impertinent and offensive. Clara went through the festival with her accustomed mixture of elation and revulsion. At a gathering in her house during the festival, Liszt insisted on playing the overture to Robert's *Genoveva* four hands with her. She snarled in her journal, "It was so dreadful that I could only find relief in tears. How he banged the piano. . . . I was beside myself at hearing His work so desecrated."[49]

During the festivities Brahms first made the acquaintance of the eminent Viennese critic Eduard Hanslick. The older man recalled his first sight of Brahms as "a young ideal hero of Jean Paul, with his forget-me-not eyes and his long fair hair."[50] Other new acquaintances included musicologist Otto Jahn, soon to begin the epochal biography of Mozart that absorbed Brahms and his time.

Also during the festival three princesses from Lippe-Detmold visited Clara and invited her to their court. Johannes was to receive considerable benefit from that connection. After the festival Clara went on to Detmold to spend several weeks giving lessons to Princess Friederike and performing, some of it with Joachim. During that visit she once more left Johannes at home with the children and with his waiting. When she sent him greetings and a nosegay from Detmold, he replied impetuously, "I always kiss [the boys] from you, but I would very much like to give you the kisses back again." He reported that he'd been practicing his running and jumping and could leap further than ever.[51] He had taught the children to turn somersaults, and performed acrobatics for their amusement. One of daughter Eugenie's early memories was of the children watching open-mouthed as little wiry Johannes performed a handstand on the hall banisters with his legs in the air, and ended with a reckless leap to the floor.[52] Such shenanigans would give way to age and girth, but the vigor remained.

The games and athletics only marked time. "I can no longer exist without you," Johannes wrote Clara in the perennial terms of forlorn lovers. "I want so much to be able to hold your hand again and to sit beside you." At the end of that letter he used *du*, "thou," for the first time: "Please go on loving me as I shall go on loving you always and for ever. Wholly yours, Johannes."[53] For a while in the letters that followed he backtracked to the respectful pronoun *Sie*, but then the intimate word crept back in. As he had pleaded, in her letters to him Clara wrote *du*.

She arrived home at the beginning of July to prepare for a concert in Bad Ems with Jenny Lind. The soprano had donated her services as a favor, but felt obliged to write advising Clara for her part of the program "to choose simple things which can be understood by people who love beauty." She did not elaborate, but the obvious point was: no Brahms.

Clara replied, with equal parts firmness and restraint, "I will yield to the public taste only insofar as it does not run counter to my convictions."[54] But she did not play Brahms on the program.

The experience in Ems proved dismal. Preparations had been rushed, with the result that Lind's husband, Herr Goldschmidt, had to do a lot of last-minute preparation besides playing his wife's accompaniments. He got no help from Johannes, who arrived with Clara, snubbed both Goldschmidts, and quickly headed off on a hiking trip.[55] Among other reasons for his chilliness, Brahms probably had a good idea of what Clara's friends thought of him and his music. In the concert, meanwhile, with the overflowing audience full of grandees from the Detmold court, Jenny Lind got most of the applause. Clara was livid:

> How degraded I felt by an audience which could not understand one of my pieces, and did not attempt to, but which cared for nothing but Jenny Lind. The whole of last winter, with all its torments, did not exact such a sacrifice as this evening when I was forced to humiliate myself from a sense of duty. . . . I cried bitterly when I got home—if only Johannes had been with me, he would have provided some comfort.[56]

Even if the proceeds of the concert turned out well enough to pay Clara's bills for the summer and finance a vacation, that was not enough to assuage her anger and resentment. This journal entry says a great deal about Clara Schumann: at least in the moment she wrote it, her husband's madness did not feel as dreadful to her as being upstaged by Jenny Lind.

AFTER THE DISTRESS of the concert, Clara and Johannes set out on a trip along the Rhine. It was their first vacation together, though they were not alone—for the sake of propriety, Clara's maid Fräulein Bertha attended them. In five days they made their way along the river on foot over a hundred miles, going on to the Neckar Valley and Heidelberg, and ending with a visit to Frankfurt. For all the gloom that perennially hung around Clara, it was a beautiful interlude for both of them—romantic, if any of their times together can be called that. Carrying their supplies in his knapsack, Johannes guided her through the resplendent Rhine landscape resonant with German history and folktale. Together they climbed the Loreley cliff, walked through the old gate of St. Goarshausen with the "Katz" Castle looming above, and walked down medieval streets lined with half-timbered houses. He made her laugh and forget; she basked in his youth. "He draws in great breaths of nature," she wrote, "and one grows young with him." Johannes clambered into trees to survey their route and pulled Clara up hills to admire ruined castles and hillsides covered with vineyards. She sat in the shade in the summer breeze, eating fruit and listening as he babbled away.[57] "I always like to see Brahms's radiant face. . . . Johannes very happy again. The old days ought to come back for him, his fresh, vigorous nature would suit them."[58]

During that idyll on the Rhine, something new entered their relations, or rather entered Brahms's side of them. Even if they never said it aloud, they knew now that Robert was not going to get well. If Clara and Johannes were ever physically lovers, it probably began during this trip. It is just as likely that they were not. In fact, whatever happened between them on the Rhine did not bring them closer at all. As far as Clara appears to have noticed, Johannes was simply happy, more than he had been in a long time. So they were happy together and did not dwell on what might come. But throughout the trip Brahms was thinking, looking into the morass of his feelings for something solid that could tell him what to do.

When they returned to Düsseldorf, they moved the family to a sunnier house on Poststrasse, where Johannes installed himself in a room on the first floor. Then Clara went to Kiel for another sea-bathing cure, gathering her strength and playing his music privately for friends. One of them, soprano Livia Frege, began to appreciate Brahms's Ballades after several hearings, but Clara was not encouraged: "I see . . . how difficult it will be for Johannes's works to be understood. . . . Robert's music . . . is always soft and melodious and sweet, which is not always the case with Johannes. . . . As with the man himself, the roughest husk conceals the sweetest kernel, but not every commonplace person is able to discover it."[59]

Back in Düsseldorf Brahms began to see his way, his situation becoming clearer in his mind. The change shows in what he wrote Clara, and in what he did not write. In August:

> I am always thinking of you. . . . Many a young man probably wishes he had the wings of an eagle, and may even imagine that he has them. Then he falls among books and music and soon sticks in the mire and forgets how to fly. . . . I frequently feel sad that I no longer seem to know how to compose. . . . Bertha [the maid] is a bit too much of a good thing with her lovesickness. . . . This love business is a funny thing. I am again confirming my old observations. It alters people so,

often for the worse. When they begin by being so happy in their love and regard it as the most important thing of all, for which alone the world exists, I can't stand it.[60]

He was turning away from love. His pages to Clara are still affectionate, but the ardor cooled in that autumn of 1855. He felt trapped, and not only in his practical situation: trapped by love. He did not know why he could not compose, but he suspected that Clara and her house and children were part of what held him down. He wanted to fly, to be a young eagle again, and he could not do it in that house. The year before he had written Clara, "I am dying of love." Now he wrote, "I feel ever more happy and peaceful in my love for you. Every time I miss you more but I long for you almost with joy."[61]

He was beginning to replace the actuality of Clara with longing for her. After the trip on the Rhine the spell of lovesickness broke like a fever. He awoke in what seemed to him the clear light of freedom, duty, possibility—alone. He still loved Clara deeply, but no longer helplessly. It was exactly the helplessness of love he could not endure. Mixed into it all was the inner voice from his childhood that forbade him to taint a respectable, beloved woman with the sordidness of sexuality. Even in their old age he would say of Clara: she is as virginal as ever. He was ready to substitute an archetypal, and unilateral, Brahmsian bargain: to live with yearning rather than fulfillment.

Nonetheless, Clara still relied on him utterly, and for the moment he stayed by her. His feelings had not settled out yet. To push away love, even a love frustrating and agonizing, is to give up passion for emptiness, something for nothing. Brahms could not make himself do that yet. Clara needed him. He had no money, no career, no public. What did he have at that point but love and an unfulfilled talent and her need? He made no final decisions in the autumn of 1855. He and Clara remained affectionate, occasionally wrangled, waited. The question that most troubled them remained unspeakable.

CHAPTER SEVEN

Resolution in a Minor Key

As CLARA'S THIRTY-SIXTH BIRTHDAY approached in September 1855, Brahms sent her a despondent greeting: "As I have written myself dry, aye and already getting along in years, I find I cannot compose, but I have written something for your birthday or for your return all the same."[1] It was a prelude and aria, the final movements of a Bach-inspired A minor suite that Brahms had been working on, based on old sketches.[2] He and Clara performed some of the movements in public in the next months, but most of the suite ended up in the stove. Whatever might be the solution to Brahms's creative block, little neo-Baroque gigues and gavottes were not going to cure it (though the surviving numbers proved useful in a more productive time). For months he had been living more or less on nothing, staying at Clara's, teaching a few students, borrowing from friends. For want of anything better to do, he accumulated practical experience wherever he could find it—grist for an idle mill.

That summer Joachim, still staying in Düsseldorf, got some associates together for a regime of reading chamber music twice a week, three or four pieces at a time. Outside, townspeople would gather to listen to the music drifting through the windows. Clara and Johannes attended the evenings regularly. Generally he claimed a corner sofa and sat listening, hand over his eyes. Before this period Brahms had usually heard chamber works in keyboard arrangements; now he had regular contact with the live article, and sometimes it overpowered him. One night during a Mozart adagio he leaped up from the sofa and stalked from the room, slamming the door behind him. Later he apologized to Joachim, explaining he had felt so full of the music that it was like being seasick and he could not bear another note. In sessions when Joachim wanted to try a piece with piano, Brahms usually took the part. Clara did not like to play with Johannes around because, she explained, "his criticisms are too sharp; and unfortunately he's always right."[3]

The year before, Clara's friend Fräulein Leser had scolded her for submitting to him, cheapening herself before this callow youth. Since then, others had made the same objection to an artist of her caliber putting up with his arrogance and imperiousness. "I am convinced that Brahms knows exactly what I am worth," she explained in her journal. "But it seems to me that an artist . . . is not to be judged by age but by intellect, and when I am with Brahms I never think of his youth, I only feel myself wonderfully stirred by his power, and often instructed."[4] It was like Clara to disguise—to herself—her attraction for a man behind a screen of giving sympathy or receiving wisdom. She had always considered herself too plain to appeal to men in the usual ways. In later, more hard-bitten years, Brahms expressed his own view of that period, maybe with Fräulein Leser in mind: "I believe that she would have gone mad if I, little man that I was, had not been near her, the only man among all those females to talk the nonsense out of her."[5]

Into the quiet but unsettled interlude of that time intruded terrible news from Endenich. On September 10 the doctors, though they still had little idea what was wrong with Schumann, declared that he could never completely recover. He was becoming incoherent, hearing voices. They did not mention that he was weak from refusing to eat.[6] "Can I wish him back to me in this state?" Clara groaned in her journal. "And yet can I help longing to have him back in *any* condition? . . . I have thought it all over a thousand times, and it is always terrible."[7]

In that limbo she went on living and working, incapable of deciding anything, Johannes her mainstay. But neither then nor in the decades after did Clara ever really know what he was thinking.

WHATEVER HIS PERSONAL and creative dilemmas, Brahms had finally conceded that he must play piano for his bread. In October he began practicing for a tour, protesting the whole time. He knew he would never find the acclaim Liszt and Joachim and Clara had, and he hardly cared. Never comfortable in front of an audience, he had long since given up any plans to become a virtuoso. He played best in private, among friends. But there appeared no other way for him to get by outside of concertizing. Neither Brahms nor his parents had ever imagined one could make a living purely as a composer. After all, most of the great masters had gone before the public as keyboard soloists; the endless list includes

Bach, Mozart, Beethoven, Mendelssohn, and Chopin. Some who performed less regularly, including Schumann and Berlioz (as conductors), had been forced to turn out journalism. Schumann's family had scraped by on his composing and criticism, a small inheritance, and Clara's performing.

At the end of October Brahms arrived in Hamburg to finish preparations to restart his playing career after a hiatus of two years. Earlier he had mainly appeared as an accompanist; now he proposed to play in chamber and orchestral concerts. He wrote Clara, "I shall certainly not be such a success as pianist; you will see that I shall fail."[8]

His boyish spirits had not failed, though. The letter also mentions that he had not been able to resist a set of toy soldiers in a shop window, when he was scouting Christmas presents for the Schumann boys. "Now I have the most delightful battle piece I ever saw. . . . At Christmas in Düsseldorf I will parade all my troops."[9] In Hamburg he spent his spare time and his little money in second-hand bookshops, ferreting out old scores and theoretical works. His acquisitions included dusty treatises on fugue and double counterpoint.[10] He not only wanted to study counterpoint, he wanted to learn it from the same sources as had Baroque Kapellmeisters.

Picking up Joachim in Berlin, Brahms went on to Danzig, where they took part in two of Clara's soirees. The programs included a sarabande and gavotte of his and the C Major Sonata, and Brahms and Clara played Schumann's two-piano variations. Nerves tripped his fingers, as often happened when Brahms went before the public. His confidence did not rise when his piano broke down during the second program and he had to change instruments in the middle of a piece.[11] During this time in Danzig, pianist Anton Door, a friend of Joachim and later of Brahms, first encountered the composer—which is not to say they met. On a visit to Joachim, Door noticed a diminutive blond youth pacing back and forth in the shadows, nervously smoking one cigar after another. Over the course of an hour or so, Brahms never acknowledged the presence of a stranger in the room. "I was empty air to him," Door recalled.[12]

Despite the nerve-wracking Danzig performances, Brahms was not about to renege on his engagements. Plodding on through his anxiety and disgust, he went to Bremen for his first appearance with an orchestra, playing the Beethoven G Major Concerto and Schumann's Opus 17 Fantasia. This time he received a warm response from the audience.[13] Hamburg went still better. In a concert with G. D. Otten's Akademie orchestra, Brahms played Beethoven's *Emperor* Concerto and solos by Schumann and Schubert. To Clara he reported "great applause, quite enthusiastic for Hamburg. I really did play with both fire and restraint."[14]

A local critic noticed more of the latter: "He carried his reserve too far. He might . . . have displayed rather more virtuosity."[15] During this visit he received, as a gift from Theodor Avé-Lallemant, another item of what would become an important private manuscript collection—a copy of Beethoven's A♭ Major Piano Sonata, with corrections in the composer's hand.[16]

As Brahms busied himself practicing and traveling and concertizing, his letters to Clara became newsy and practical, with little talk of love. Even when he warmed up, he hedged: "I regret every word I write to you which does not speak of love. You have taught me and are every day teaching me ever more to recognize . . . what love, attachment and self-denial are. . . . I wish I could always write to you from my heart to tell you how deeply I love you, and can only beg you to believe it without further proof."[17] Which is to say: there was going to be more self-denial, and fewer proofs.

As Robert Schumann grew weaker and relations between Brahms and Clara steadily more ambiguous, Joachim's feelings about Liszt came to a head. After hearing him conduct a performance of his symphonic poems and choral music, Joachim wrote Gisela von Arnim of his contempt for

> a man whom I had often called friend, in whom I had gladly pardoned colossal follies out of respect for his powers. I had to admit that a more vulgar misuse of sacred forms, a more repulsive coquetting with the noblest feelings for the sake of effect, had never been attempted. At the conductors' desk Liszt makes a parade of the moods of despair and the stirrings of contrition with which the really pious man turns in solitude to God, and mingles with them the most sickly sentimentality, and such a martyr-like air, that one can hear the lies in every note.[18]

No doubt Joachim growled likewise to Johannes. At some point Brahms browsed through some of the propaganda with which Liszt buttressed his revolution. The tracts appealed to him even less than the music. He and Joachim found the whole notion of propping up notes with words fraudulent. That included program music, for which Brahms developed a particular distaste—though in practice, if he liked a piece he was willing to forgive a program.

In the middle of December Johannes returned to Düsseldorf carrying Christmas presents for Clara and the children, and his new toy soldiers to parade for them all.[19] That month Richard Pohl, who wrote as "Hoplit" for the *Neue Zeitschrift für Musik*, completed a series of three articles on Brahms, critical but respectful. Among other things Pohl made a point of Brahms's individuality: even if inevitably aligned with the Schumannites, "Brahms is . . . no imitator of Schumann." Brahms could hardly quarrel with the critic's conclusion that he "should have been regarded as an artist not yet mature." He had been saying the same thing to Clara for a long time; contra Schumann, his *Bildung* was incomplete.[20]

For two years Brahms had lived with that realization. Schumann had nominated him for Messiah, but no one could advise him how to do the job. Of his living peers, Schumann was incapacitated and the others—mainly Wagner and Liszt and Berlioz—were of an older generation and resided in the enemy camp. Brahms felt baffled by the question of where to turn. As he stewed over that cloudy question, he decided that a still more intensive study of counterpoint, with its intricate demands and rules for corraling notes, could stand in for composing and teach him something of use, if he could only figure out how to use it.

On Christmas Day 1855, it was once again Brahms and Joachim with Clara and the children. She gave him the first volume of the complete Bach Gesellschaft edition, which Robert had helped instigate. The most monumental scholarly project in the history of music, the Gesellschaft issued sixty volumes between 1851 and 1900, and Brahms subscribed to the entire series. In the course of those fifty years those volumes inspired and transformed him, along with the whole of Western music. Joachim's gift that Christmas was didactic and antiquarian, a 1739 copy of Handel's Hamburg compatriot Johann Mattheson's *Der Vollkommene Kapellmeister,* "The Complete Music-Director."[21] Joachim knew that Johannes had been searching for the book, and not just as an item for his collection. Like a Baroque apprentice, Brahms aspired to make himself a Complete Music Director—in the image of J. S. Bach on the one hand, Kapellmeister Kreisler on the other.

AFTER THE HOLIDAYS Clara left for Vienna to present her first concerts there in nine years. They generated something like the furor she had experienced in her teens. At the first of her six appearances the audience recalled her fifteen times.[22] Just as gratifying for her, the Viennese showed themselves at last prepared to applaud her husband's music.

Eduard Hanslick, the city's most powerful critic, admired the purity of Clara's playing, her indifference to virtuoso fireworks, her grasp of contrasting styles. On her programs she included Brahms's C Major Sonata, two sarabandes and a gavotte from his never-published suite in A minor, and much work of Robert's. During her time in the city she visited the tombs of Beethoven and Schubert, sending Brahms leaves gathered from the graves. (The graves were not yet in their final location in the Central Cemetery.) At a fancy Vienna soiree Clara encountered Liszt, who, seeing her disgust at not being center stage, ironically suggested, "Why not play a couple of bad pieces by Liszt? That would be appropriate here." Oblivious to irony as always, Clara snapped, "You're right, but I can't do that."[23]

As 1856 arrived, Brahms surely felt something had to happen for him. So it would, mostly for the worse. Elsewhere this year Heinrich Heine died and Freud was born, Wagner wrote *Die Walküre* and Liszt the *Dante* Symphony. The world would not see much new and significant from Johannes Brahms. His beautiful but laconic Four Ballades, written in 1854, would be published this year, then nothing more until 1860. Starting in January, he continued his reluctant impersonation of a virtuoso, playing Beethoven's G Major Concerto at the Leipzig Gewandhaus, with his own cadenzas (he worked the B-A-C-H motive—B♭-A-C-B♮—into the first movement cadenza).[24]

Afterward, on a stopover in Hanover, he first met pianist and composer Anton Rubinstein, who in 1854 had emerged from Russia to create a sensation across Europe. Now Rubinstein was in town for a concert of his music with Joachim and the Hanover court orchestra. He and Brahms grated on each other. Rubinstein reported to Liszt, "I hardly know how to describe the impression he made on me. He is not graceful enough for the drawing-room, not fiery enough for the concert-room, not simple enough for the country, and not general enough for the town. I have but little faith in such natures."[25] At times over the years, the two men would approach cordial relations, but never based on admiration for each other's creative work. Rubinstein found his competitor's music dry and unmusical; Brahms considered the other a remarkable pianist, but his enormous compositional output facile and slipshod—which more or less matches history's conclusion.

Back home in Hamburg, having met Eduard Hanslick at the Lower Rhine Music Festival, Brahms attempted to read the critic's famous booklet on aesthetics, *On Beauty in Music*. He wrote Clara that in it he "found such a number of stupid things on first glance that I gave it up."[26]

He also reported to her a soiree at the house of her friend, the soprano Livia Frege. He had played works of Woldemar Bargiel—Clara's half-brother—and Joachim, with responses from the guests ranging from ennui to outrage. "Frau Frege had already sung both my songs and yours. I am only very moderately interested in singing. . . . She did not sing my best ["Liebestreu"] particularly well, and as for the others they interested me only remotely." Altogether Brahms found the pieces he inflicted on the party "a subtle revenge for so many boring hours in L[eipzig]."[27] Going on to a concert in Kiel, he first performed his B Major Trio in public, then at Hamburg played Mozart's D Minor Concerto with his cadenzas. Like it or not, he had a solo career now that brought in a little income. Certainly he noticed that for the single Mozart performance in Hamburg he received the equivalent of 160 marks, while Boosey & Hawkes had paid him 136 to publish the Four Ballades.[28]

THE REST OF THAT WINTER and spring, as Clara traveled and Johannes languished between playing jobs, he stayed on with his family in Hamburg, taught the occasional student, and contemplated his creative impasse. The effects of "Neue Bahnen" had sunk in; the paralysis afflicting him was becoming clearer. In February 1856, he wrote Clara one of the most revealing letters of his life.

> It always saddens me to think that after all I am not yet a proper musician; but I have more aptitude for the calling than probably many of the younger generation have as a rule. It gets knocked out of you. Boys should be allowed to indulge themselves in jolly music; the serious kind comes of its own accord, although the lovesick does not. How lucky is the man who, like Mozart and others, goes to the tavern of an evening and writes some fresh music. For he lives while he is creating.

He concluded jokingly, "What a Man!" and crushed his quill pen onto the page.[29] In fact, he was fighting despair.

It appears that Brahms had begun to discern the road he felt compelled to take. It was not one of Schumann's new paths, and the journey was not a cheering prospect. Schumann's article had inflicted on Brahms an unforgiving responsibility, crushing any hope of a natural, youthful development. Brahms had immense talent, enough in itself to achieve a great deal, but he was not to be allowed, or allow himself, to rest on that gift. Beyond the burden of Schumann's article, his and his time's fixation with the past and its pedestaled masters made the situation of a composer unprecedentedly difficult. It was no longer possible just to *compose*, unself-consciously, as Mozart and his generation had done. Mozart's lightness of spirit came in part from not being burdened with the past, or with the future. In Brahms's more ambitious works, at least, lightness was no longer possible, in his music or in his spirit.

After the ingenuous brilliance of his early piano music "Neue Bahnen" had stopped him in his tracks with no notion of where he was headed. At the same time as he worried over his technical uncertainties, he wrote Clara that he felt unable to connect his music to his heart, maybe to a degree because his heart was too wrought up in feelings he could neither understand nor control. In any case, heart-on-sleeve music was not his style. Given his temperament, he had to master his feelings in order to go on.

He began to discern, and hint to Clara, the implications of that for his external life. Mozart could *live* while he was creating, go to the tavern and write jolly music if he felt like it, collect his pay and go on to the next job, which might be something light or serious, inspired or not. For Brahms, composing in a spotlight, the signs at the crossroad said: life in one direction, music in another. He would not be permitted to embrace both. Robert Schumann and the burden of history had denied that to him.

The dilemmas multiplied. To earn his keep Brahms saw as yet no way around the life of an itinerant musician, but he also knew that he would never be a world-class pianist. It appeared that he had no reliable way to support a family at all, unless he could find some sort of position as a Kapellmeister—and for that he needed experience as a conductor. At the same time, if he were going to compose as he felt he had to, with absolute seriousness, he could not uncomplicatedly enjoy himself and laugh with friends in the tavern and go home to wife and children like Mozart or a good North German *Bürger*. To accomplish anything, he had to scrape together some kind of living and save himself for his work. He must write what he wanted, as he wanted—once he figured out what he wanted. (In fact Brahms never accepted a musical commission in his adult life, something that would have been incomprehensible to Mozart's generation.)

In short, he faced the frightening prospect that in order to fulfill Schumann's prophecy he would have to become in earnest what his teacher Marxsen would call "a priest of art," to live something like a monastic existence. He must choose music instead of life.

These imperatives came over him slowly, but inexorably. Aided by his ingrained drive to freedom and his temperamental solipsism, perversely abetted by his misogyny, Brahms gradually and reluctantly chose the path of denial. Everything and everybody, including his own desires, must be subordinated to perfecting his art. In practice, the heartlessness of that conviction would be tempered by a need for companionship and a fundamental decency of spirit. Yet through the decades to come and despite the accolades he earned in them, Brahms could never fully accept his path. He never stopped hearing the call to plain life and love, never felt happy in his isolation no matter how ruthlessly he enforced it.

By the end of 1856 the contention of *Kreisler* and *Brahms* would largely be decided. Brahms had won. As token of that, during 1856 he let go, for the time being, of the lovesick piano quartet in Kreisler's key of C♯ minor. If the Brahms side was the bourgeois family man as well as the ruthless craftsman, he would have to live with that dissonance. Kreisler's dreamy, lyrical Romanticism receded into the interior of his consciousness and his music, there to be shackled to the exigencies of craft and form that history calls Classical.

IN EARLY 1856, composing still seemed like a quagmire to him as he continued his campaign to make himself a "proper musician," a Complete Kapellmeister. Still tinkering with the C♯ Minor Quartet and trying to gear up for the D Minor Piano Concerto, Brahms meanwhile studied the contrapuntal art of Palestrina and other Renaissance masters. (He may have drafted an A major piano trio in this period, but even if the surviving copyist's score is authentic he suppressed the piece, probably after a tryout.)[30]

At the end of February he wrote Joachim, beginning like a good house-husband and continuing with his present preoccupation: "I am to remind you that tomorrow afternoon . . . the [Schumann] children are passing through Hanover. We are loading them up with bread and butter and oranges here; you are to see to the coffee. And then I want to remind you of what we have so often discussed . . . to send one another exercises in counterpoint."[31] Joachim agreed to Brahms's proposal to trade exercises by mail and correct each other's work.

The way Brahms phrased the proposal reveals an odd sidelight. In suggesting a fine for missed assignments, he echoes an old entry found in one of the Schumanns' marriage diaries, where Robert and Clara agreed to trade the duty of keeping the diary and failure to do so adequately "shall receive some sort of punishment, which we will have to figure out." (The "punishment" is amorous in implication.) Using terms close to the Schumanns', Brahms suggests to Joachim that the fine for failure to do their weekly counterpoint exercise will be used for buying books.[32] The words in which he expresses the terms suggest that Brahms had been reading Robert and Clara's diaries, which among other things had a special sign for each occasion they made love (it approached daily at times, after more than a decade of marriage). Whether or not Clara knew Johannes was perusing the marriage diaries, she did not try to hide these intimate records from him.

Naturally the counterpoint exchange between Brahms and Joachim turned out less systematic than planned, starting up slowly and trickling out at the end of the summer, and sporadically revived until as late as 1861. It still produced a good deal of work from the two, the results momentous for Brahms both directly and indirectly.

In spring and summer of 1856 the friends traded canons and fugues by mail, critiquing each other's work with due raillery and severity. The studies show that both of them had absorbed Schumann's use of musical cabala. Among his efforts Joachim produced canonic studies based on two motives pregnant for him—his F-A-E / *frei aber einsam* motto, and the pattern G♯-E-A. In German the latter figure is called Gis-E-La, thereby naming Joachim's lost love, Gisela von Arnim. (The intervals of the two motives are mirror inversions of each other, a coincidence Schumann would have found poignant and mystical.) In the last of Joachim's F-A-E / Gis-E-La studies a seven-voice double canon simultaneously links and superimposes both motives in the bass. He gave the piece the joking title *Schulfuchserei!*—Pedantry.[33] Brahms, of course, understood the motivic codes: "Much is implied there," he wrote Joachim.

Brahms's contributions included several movements of a canonic mass in more or less Renaissance/Palestrina style. Eventually he destroyed it, but sections survive in the motet *Warum ist das Licht gegeben?*, Opus 75, and more in copies made by Julius Otto Grimm for a proposed performance. While other canonic exercises were discarded in later years, some ended up in published pieces—a five-voice augmentation canon in the second Opus 29 motet, and two others, it appears, in the Opus 37 *Drei geistliche Chöre*.

For Brahms, moving to his maturity would have much to do with counterpoint, the least forgiving of musical disciplines, and its procedures such as canon: a grown-up version of a children's round, in which a composer fashions a melody and its echo in other voices to form effective harmony. That old contrapuntal game, at which Bach was a supreme master, is hard enough in itself; still harder is to make a canon not just technically perfect but beautiful—as are the canons of the Schumann Variations. Yet the real goal of studying counterpoint is not to write canons and fugues all the time, but rather to gain ultimate mastery of notes, to seize control of every part of the musical fabric, to be capable of composing with discipline and expressiveness in any formal design. Brahms felt driven to make his art unassailable, and to that end his technique must be unassailable. And he succeeded: he would arrive at his maturity a superb musical craftsman, as fine a one as ever lived.

Brahms's more substantial contrapuntal studies from April 1856 survived in forms that he published later and diffidently, but which stand as telling works—an A Minor Prelude and Fugue for organ and the A♭ Minor Fugue for Organ, both in Baroque style, and the *Geistliches Lied* (*Spiritual Song*) for choir and organ (built on a double canon at the ninth). Of the A♭ Minor Fugue Joachim wrote Brahms, "From beginning to end it is wonderfully deep; I know few pieces that have made such an impression of unity, beauty, and blissful peace on me." And of the *Geistliches Lied*, "On the whole very beautiful . . . the organ point must make a holy, devout effect. But there are many harsh places!"[34] His essential accusation here is that Brahms is more interested in counterpoint than in beauty—a charge Brahms could live with. All the same, on reflection he took several of Joachim's suggestions for the A♭ Minor Fugue.

If Joachim symbolized his own romantic life in his contrapuntal studies, Brahms naturally did the same, in forms he knew both Joachim and Clara would understand. He based the A Minor Prelude and Fugue on Robert's Clara theme of C-B-A-G♯-A. The fugue subject itself is formed from a variant and at the climax the complete theme thunders in the bass. In the A♭ Minor Fugue, marked on the manuscript "Slowly (despondently)," he uses themes from Schumann's *Manfred* music,[35] which had powerfully moved Brahms and Clara when they heard it in Hamburg the year before. Brahms presented this fugue to her in honor of Robert's birthday in June 1856, inscribed "quite particularly for my Clara."

Most subtle of all the intimate references is found in the *Geistliches Lied*. It seems to go back to a fantasy of Clara's during her husband's illness: to study organ secretly, then lure Robert unsuspecting into a church where he would find her playing his music on the instrument. Brahms's organ introduction to the *Geistliches Lied* may portray that fantasy like a program piece: threads of melody accumulate as if in the quietness of a church, then the choir enters. A peculiar task, to write a heartfelt song to paint a fantasy of one's beloved about her husband. But if Clara had imagined her surprise for Robert as a joyful and healing gesture, the tone of Brahms's music is lamenting, the choral text consoling the sorrowful with submission to fate: "Let naught afflict thee with grief; be calm, as God ordains. . . . Only be in all thy doings unchanging, steadfast. What God decrees is for the best." Fate was already one of Brahms's imperative themes, and it would remain so for the next forty years.

IN APRIL 1856 came the penultimate blow. Schumann's doctors pronounced him incurable. The conclusion was based on his declining strength, not on a real diagnosis—there had never been one. Clara got the news from Johannes soon after she reached London, where she had finally traveled for a tour after years of frustrated plans to go there. When she received the letter she wrote in her journal, "I could do nothing but weep aloud from morning till night, and then . . . I went to the concert. Heaven was gracious, it all went very well." In her three months in England, Clara wept endlessly but never canceled a concert. Her repertoire included a Brahms sarabande and gavotte; these light and later suppressed exercises in atavism comprised his English debut.

After the doctors' report that April, Brahms visited Endenich to see Schumann for himself. He found a shocking disintegration. Schumann blabbered on unintelligibly, one of the greatest minds of his time reduced to baby talk: *bababa, dadada*. Here and there Brahms could make out a few names—the children Marie and Julie, Berlin, Vienna, England. In Schumann's music the letters of names had figured as cabalistic tokens; now some consuming inner agenda around letters and places possessed him. All day long he pored over atlases, covering sheets of paper with names of cities and rivers arranged in alphabetical order, as if to impose some rationality on the unbearable tumult of existence. There was a harrowing debility of body as well as mind, which probably included severe starvation. The doctors said there would be, at best, no improvement.[36]

With that specter hanging over him, Brahms returned to Düsseldorf and to his preludes and fugues and *Spiritual Song*. A month later, he celebrated his twenty-third birthday alone. Clara was away, his friend Julius Otto Grimm lived in Göttingen now and Albert Dietrich in Bonn. A birthday greeting arrived from his mother: "This morning I woke up at the exact hour when you saw the light of day for the first time. . . . Half an hour later I held you in my arms, against my heart. —And now you are so far away. . . . We drank the health of all of you, especially of the poor sick man."[37]

At the Lower Rhine Festival a few days later, everyone was talking about Schumann. At the festival Brahms got to know Ditmarsh poet Klaus Groth, with his recollections of the Brahms family going back three generations. Another long-time association from this time was Theodor Kirchner, then a popular composer of Schumannesque piano miniatures, eventually a faithful Brahmsian in Switzerland, and a constant concern of Clara Schumann.

And Brahms made a connection with the superlative recital-and-oratorio baritone Julius Stockhausen. By the end of the month Brahms and Stockhausen had begun an important collaboration, presenting concerts in Cologne and Bonn. On those programs Brahms played Beethoven, Schubert, Bach, the A Minor Romance Clara had written for him, and nothing of his own. Together they performed lieder including Schubert's cycle *Die schöne Müllerin*. During those years the full scope of Schubert's songs was finally being revealed, mainly through the relatively new medium of the lieder recital. Brahms's collaboration with Stockhausen contributed to that history. At the same time, it helped galvanize a lifelong passion for Schubert that would be a prime source of Brahms's mature lyrical voice, not only in song but in instrumental music. Shortly before their first concert, Brahms had written Clara, "I am only very moderately interested in singing." Stockhausen and Schubert changed that. After the concert Brahms wrote her, "I don't think I have ever enjoyed singing as much as I did yesterday evening."[38]

Around that time Clara and Johannes, both of them exhaustively busy, both grieving over Robert's condition, fell into another skirmish in their correspondence. Apparently Brahms had been using the familiar *du* and now had stopped. Clara noticed his new restraint and responded with a burst of hysteria. He made a peremptory reply to her complaint: "My idea was that I could not avail myself immediately of your kindness and love as you might regret it later on. That is why I always continued to write to you in the [formal] second person. . . . I take it then that all these tactics of siege and assault had some connection with the unanswered question?"[39]

Perhaps Clara had only needed to know that the question was still pending. What would their relationship be when Robert was gone? She responded gently and once again he did the same, writing her in an echo of the old tone:

> I wish I could write to you as tenderly as I love you and tell you all the good things that I wish you. You are so infinitely dear to me, dearer than I can say. . . . If things go on much longer as they are at present I shall have sometime to put you under glass or to have you set in gold. If only I could live in the same town with you and my parents. . . . Do write me a nice letter soon. Your letters are like kisses.[40]

For all the extravagant language—which sounds like a true lover's in all senses—the distance still lingers between the lines: *set you in gold, live in the same town with you and my parents.* To set one's lover in gold in the presence of one's parents is not a prospective husband's fantasy. It means: I want to admire you, be near you, but stay with my own and not touch you.

On June 8, 1856, Schumann's birthday, Brahms returned to Endenich carrying a large atlas, for which the sick man had begged.[41] With Brahms came musicologist Otto Jahn, Klaus Groth, Albert Dietrich, and Brahms's new friend music critic Hermann Deiters. Brahms left them to go inside the hospital. He returned looking grim. Schumann had recognized him and thanked him for the present, then hardly raised his watery eyes from the new atlas.[42] At the beginning of July, Brahms went to meet Clara at Antwerp on her return from England. If he did not reveal the full horror, Clara still understood that a crisis had come.

Robert Schumann slipped away the way one often dies in a hospital—inch by inch, attended by the veiled hints of doctors, the family unprepared, everything dreamlike and confused. The doctors had forbidden Clara to see him since the day he left home in February 1854. For all her strength of will, Clara had submitted to that male authority. In the middle of June she went to Bonn to consult with the doctors, who told her they could not promise Robert would last out the year. It was the first time she realized that her husband was dying.

Little over a week later, as Clara struggled with that, word arrived that she must come to Endenich at once if she wished to see Robert alive. But when she got to the hospital on July 23 the doctors announced that the immediate danger was past and she should not go in to see him; the shock would be too great for both of them. Clara returned home, devastated. Then on the evening of July 27 she came back with Johannes and demanded to be taken to her husband. Only then did the doctors let them into the room.

Robert Schumann opened his eyes to find his wife kneeling by his bed. They had not seen each other since his nights of euphoria and terror over two years before. He struggled to sit up, awkwardly put his arm around her, smiled. The only thing he had left to give her was that sad mute acknowledgment. Clara wrote, "Not all the treasures in the world could equal this embrace." He sank back to the bed, mumbling incoherently as the moments struggled by. It seemed to Clara that Robert was communing with his spirits. He could hear only them, only they understood him. Now and then his eyes fell on her tenderly and he tried to form words: "*My . . . I know . . .* " She understood; he was trying to say *My Clara, I know you.*[43]

Next day she and Johannes watched over him as he lay shuddering and raving on the bed. Clara was allowed to feed him. For some time he had taken only wine and jellied consommé; now she dipped her finger in wine and he sucked at it like a baby. Johannes stood quietly aside, watching

Schumann's life and his own youth draining away together. The next day, July 29, he and Clara went to the train station to pick up Joachim. When they returned to the hospital, Schumann was dead. "I stood at the body of my passionately loved husband and was calm," she told her journal. "All my feelings were of thankfulness to God that he was finally free . . . oh—if he had only taken me with him! I saw him for the last time today— I laid some flowers on his head."⁴⁴

They gathered his effects, the pictures of Clara and Johannes and the children, the letters from Clara bound in a pink ribbon, musical sketches and studies, meticulous drafts of every letter he had written from the hospital. At the funeral in Bonn two days later, Brahms, Joachim, and Dietrich walked behind the coffin carrying laurel wreaths as Schumann was borne from Endenich by musicians from Düsseldorf. In the city a throng of musicians and music lovers joined the mourners; a brass band played chorales. Clara stayed behind in the chapel praying as the procession arrived at the grave surrounded by newly planted trees. After Brahms laid Clara's wreath on the coffin there was a short sermon from the pastor, a chorus and hymn, words from Schumann's friend Ferdinand Hiller, and the coffin descended. The friends threw in their ceremonial handfuls of earth and said farewell. In her journal Clara wrote, "All my happiness is over. A new life is beginning."⁴⁵

As Brahms and Clara picked up the tatters of their lives, the unanswered question loomed between them. Time, which had been contracting toward the single point of Schumann's crisis, rebounded frighteningly into the future: after a tragedy foreseen, the question of what to do, to fill the endless empty days. Joachim, staying with them in Düsseldorf, admired Johannes's strength of mind and wrote Liszt of "the noble lady, who appears to me, in her deep grief, a lofty example of God-given strength."⁴⁶ Brahms took over lessons Clara had scheduled with the Detmold royalty and got to know a court official named Karl von Meysenbug. Soon that would produce an invitation from the little principality.

Brahms and Clara decided on a vacation to Switzerland, to find out if there they could see anything clearly. It would still be improper for them to travel alone, so they brought along Clara's sons, Ferdinand and Ludwig, and Johannes's sister, Elise, who had never traveled far from home. Despite her grief, Clara wrote characteristically meticulous advice to Christiane Brahms, sinking with relief into the quotidian:

Do not let [Elise] take too many things. If she needs two chemises a week, let her bring six chemises. If she is used to wearing only one, about four will be sufficient. Stockings, six pairs. She only needs two changes of dress; keep the nice blue one at home; it would be a pity if it were spoiled in the packing. If she has a black petticoat, this would be best for traveling, and then she will only want one white underskirt in case she sometimes wears a light dress.

The letter continues through matters of hats and shawls and gloves. Clara ends, "You know how heavy my heart is. I don't want to talk of it; my heart bleeds at once. Johannes is my sure friend and protector—what a blessing I have him!"[47] Did she have him, and in what way? In the middle of August, when Johannes came to Hamburg to pick up his sister for the vacation, his mother found him anxious and miserable.

The party began their vacation with a visit to Schumann's grave in Bonn. Then, after stopovers including days with Joachim at Heidelberg, they spent two weeks in Gersau at the foot of the Rigi, walking and boating on the lake in the mild weather, and making music. For Elise Brahms the mountains and glaciers of Switzerland were like a fantastic dream; she bubbled over the trip for the rest of her life, cloistered in Hamburg. Clara had bought a Memory Book for Johannes, in which they pressed flowers and leaves, with labels: "Picked for Johannes in the woods," "Rapturous morning stroll with Johannes."[48] After the tragedy of the last two years the days seemed an idyll. The vacation ended with another wreath laid on Schumann's grave.

In the course of it, within the distractions and constraints of family, Clara and Johannes reached their answer. His letters through the past months reveal that he had already been moving toward his part of it. As for Clara, surely she had not sorted out her feelings. For her there had been too many feelings in too many directions—inexpressible sorrow, romance, inspiration, sexual yearning. The Memory Book shows her exaltation at the beginning of the trip. History will never know what was finally spoken between the two of them in Switzerland, or not spoken. We can only imagine the look in Clara's eyes, the shock and disbelief and fear, when she finally realized what Johannes had been trying for months to tell her: after all the misery and joy they had shared over the last two years, and the overpowering love that rose out of it, there would be no marriage.

"He broke away ruthlessly," daughter Eugenie was to write. "My mother had suffered all the more as she could not understand the change in him."[49] Some of his reasons seem discernible. Given the sentiments of his age, which were his own when it came to families, Brahms would have required himself to support Clara and her seven children—but he still had little idea of how he was going to support himself alone. Maybe that contributed to the deeper concern that he had hinted at to Clara: to write music as he must, he had to shut away life, deny himself a family, deny even a beloved woman who wanted and needed him. If he was far from resigned to that, the onus of his task still weighed inescapably on him.

He also had to deny Robert Schumann, who may have ended his life assuming that Johannes would take care of Clara. If that is true and Johannes suspected it, that would have been a terrible burden: he would have spurned two people he loved, who had done more for him than anyone. Whomever he betrayed and to whatever degree, Brahms felt the guilt from then on: "He had never gotten over the self-reproach of having wounded my mother's feelings," Eugenie wrote.[50]

Clara may have had her own misgivings about marrying someone as young, inexperienced, and egocentric as Brahms. That summer of 1856 she was thirty-six, he twenty-three. She wanted to be done with child-bearing and was determined to perform full-time. Yet it is inescapable that Clara did want him, for the same reason she had wanted Robert, however unrealistic that had been. She loved and admired Johannes, and for all her gravity Clara respected passion and had always followed hers, purely and directly. Eugenie wrote: "Her own mind and heart were laid down on such clear and simple lines that she could not enter into the more complex processes of the human soul. She remained towards Brahms what she had always been; she loved him truly and wholeheartedly. . . . The admiration she felt for the artist was also bestowed on the man." Eugenie added, "If only she had been able to understand the man as well as the artist!"[51] At the same time, Clara was too proud and too recently bereaved, and maybe in some ways too conventional, to make demands on Johannes. It was the man's part to decide, hers to submit. So he took this, his first and last opportunity to escape her.

No details of how it transpired survive in their letters or in Clara's accounts. In 1856, she wrote down what she wanted her children, and history, to know about the relations between herself and Brahms. Her journal, written for the record as much as for herself, did not note unseemly intimacies. She wrote a testament transparently idealized and evasive, perhaps self-deluding, extraordinarily forgiving.

He came as a true friend, to share with me all my sorrow; he strengthened my heart as it was about to break, he lifted my thoughts, lightened, when it was possible, my spirits. In short, he was my friend in the fullest sense of the word.

I can truly say, my children, that I have never loved a friend as I loved him; it is the most beautiful mutual understanding of two souls. I do not love him for his youthfulness, nor probably for any reason of flattered vanity. It is rather his elasticity of spirit, his fine gifted nature, his noble heart that I love. . . . Joachim, too, as you know, was a true friend to me, but . . . it was really Johannes who bore me up. . . . Believe all that I, your mother, have told you, and do not heed those small and envious souls who make light of my love and friendship, trying to bring up for question our beautiful relationship, which they neither fully understand nor ever could.[52]

Clara's feelings at the time of the break may have been closer to a terse entry she made just after the trip to Switzerland: "I am very worried to know how I ought to provide for the boys' future, for on the journey I saw clearly that they must have a man's hand over them or they will never turn out well."[53] A week later she noted, "Johannes has composed an excellent first movement for a concerto. I am delighted with its greatness of conception and the tenderness of its melodies."[54]

As it had been with her brilliant, obdurate father and with her husband, Clara Schumann sustained her loyalty to people who hurt her, if they had also inspired and loved her. It was that simple, though the suffering it caused her was not. Neither then nor in her rancorous quarrels with Brahms over the coming years did she waver in her faith in his music or in his essential goodness. A year after they parted, Clara wrote Joachim, "I suffer indescribably in being separated from Johannes. . . . And yet is it not most natural that I should love and esteem Johannes so much, after such a long and intimate relationship with him, during which I have learned to know fully the riches of his heart and mind?"[55]

Once when Eugenie took his part in a quarrel, Clara told her daughter wearily, "You don't know what he was like before, so full of tender and delicate feeling, an ideal person."[56] That was how she saw Johannes in his Young Kreisler years. But when they parted in 1856, he was no longer the same boy who had first knocked on their door. He had become harder, more ruthless, no less loving but more the master of his feelings. Now he left Düsseldorf for good, arriving home in Hamburg on October 21, 1856. Clara put him on the train. "I felt as if I were returning from a funeral,"[57] she wrote of the walk home. It felt to her like the second funeral in three months, and losing both the men she loved.

Brahms of course never wrote of his feelings like that—not in words, at least. Before long he would fall in love again and come close to marriage, maybe even closer than with Clara, and with a woman of his own age. But in turning away from Clara he committed a betrayal and a kind of suicide. If Kreisler had absorbed Romantic yearning from books, now Brahms knew the rankling misery and guilt of the real thing. The impetuous and moonstruck personality that Clara and others loved had been beaten out of him. At length it was replaced by Brahms the gruff and indifferent—though there would always be the touch of boyishness. If he loved his freedom, that did not erase what he had lost, or what he had done to Clara. As he came to understand with agonizing clarity, freedom was his curse and his blessing, his disease and his cure.

Yet if Brahms denied Clara as a wife, in his heart he could never desert her. To the end of his life he loved Clara Schumann to the extent of his crippled capacity to love. But always he placed that in some other time, some other world. She was the virginal priestess, going to the stage as to the altar. So in his mind and in his music only the past would seem truly alive—Young Kreisler's past. Maybe for that reason, some of the warmest and most haunting moments in his music seem to voice a lyrical Romantic evocation of what was or could have been: the lost idyll, the unattainable lightness of life.

CHAPTER EIGHT

Premiere and Postlude

BRAHMS RETURNED FROM DÜSSELDORF in late October 1856 to pick
up his life in Hamburg, to carry on the Sisyphean labor of his D Minor
Piano Concerto, and maybe somewhere in it all to confront his conscience after leaving Clara Schumann to her desolation. Clara wrote
Joachim: "When Johannes left me in the morning, my heart bled. On
that day and the days that followed, I lived through those three years of
suffering again."[1] There were other places Brahms might have gone,
Göttingen where Julius Otto Grimm lived, or Hanover with Joachim.
He chose to stay in his hometown, which remained his base through the
next years of wandering—like a vagabond, he would say, bitterly.

His mother found him *"brummig"*—grumpy—around the house.[2] Her
son had come back looking as boyish as he left, but not the same inside.
This new Johannes was subdued, chronically grumpy. Young Kreisler no
longer dragged friends out at midnight to bathe in the light of the moon.
Johann Jakob, rarely in the house anyway, would have greeted the boy
and left him alone, hardly noticing the change that Christiane saw without understanding it.

On October 25, Brahms soloed in Beethoven's G Major Concerto
with G. D. Otten's Akademie orchestra, and he appears to have been inspired by that magnificent, introspective, antivirtuosic concerto. His
playing found a poetic intensity that people still spoke of years later. He
could not duplicate that success the next month, when he played Schumann's A Minor Concerto with the Philharmonic to little effect; at the
same concert Joachim made a sensation with his trademark Bach Chaconne for Solo Violin and the Schumann Fantasia.[3]

By then, drafts of the piano concerto were traveling regularly among Brahms and Julius Grimm and Joachim, a thicket of scribbles and strike-outs accumulating on the pages, the friends supplying the orchestral proficiency that still eluded the composer. (When Joachim first saw the draft of the Concerto he burst out laughing at the first page.[4]) Much of his time in Hamburg Brahms spent socializing with musical acquaintances, especially music teacher Theodor Avé-Lallemant and conductor Karl Grädener, both influential men in town. Brahms retained the gift of befriending the right people to help him on his way. At the same time, he retained his propensity for treating friends cavalierly while depending on his talent and occasional charm to keep them on his side. Usually it worked, as witness Clara and Joachim.

There were other Hamburg acquaintances too, in the end perhaps more useful to Brahms than the leading musicians in town. As often with him, the immediate stimulation came from women. In this case they were not virtuosos like Clara but a collection of young amateurs who loved to sing. It began with Friedchen Wagner, daughter of a well-to-do family Brahms had gotten to know. The Wagners were of the German music-fancying middle class, and Friedchen was twenty, bright-eyed and effervescent, a good enough pianist to get Brahms's attention. In 1855 she had met him at Otten's house and, as he walked her home after some duets, convinced him to give her piano lessons. Friedchen remembered many duets with the two of them seated side by side, and playing Bach's Triple Concerto with Johannes and brother Fritz.

Friedchen liked to spend her evenings singing with her sisters Olga and Thusnelda. Maybe it was in the autumn of 1856, after Brahms returned from Düsseldorf, that she made another request of him. It must have been made charmingly, because Brahms agreed to arrange some German folk songs for the sisters, gratis of course. He was already working on a set for solo voice and piano that became the *28 Deutsche Volkslieder*, from which he probably adapted ten songs for the Wagner girls. They were duly thrilled, and friends began showing up at their house to sing these and other pieces. Finally the group had become a small chorus, who naturally invited Brahms to visit their meetings, and naturally he accepted now and then. What could be more agreeable than evenings of hearing his music, basking in the admiration of young ladies, while they enjoyed the attentions of this imposing musician who happened to be heartbreakingly handsome?[5]

Photos suggest that Brahms was at the peak of his good looks then, in his mid-twenties. A new element had entered people's descriptions of him, which also shows up in pictures: the aggressive forward thrust of his lower lip. Brahms was wiry and strong now, no longer girlish, and more than ever he emanated command and a certain imperious distance, for all his diminutive size and high, unchanged voice. Victims found it very unpleasant to face the disdain of that outthrust lip and the blue eyes drilling into them. The singing girls of Hamburg did not have to suffer that. For them his eyes shone with their full forget-me-not radiance, and they never did forget.

In the middle of 1856, Brahms was mainly occupied with hammering away at the Piano Concerto, almost in despair about it but unwilling to let it go. (Toward the end of the year he wrote the robust Variations on a Hungarian Song for Piano, to be paired with next year's more introspective Variations on an Original Theme.[6]) The D minor music had flared up as a sonata for two pianos in the wake of Schumann's suicide attempt three years before, had turned into a symphony, and had metamorphosed again after Schumann's death. By now the gargantuan first movement was the only music left from the original effort, retooled considerably in the change from symphony to concerto; inevitably, the retooling was something of a patchwork. Besides Joachim, Brahms naturally sent it to Clara for comment. She seems in a lost letter to have criticized his relying so much on others' opinions. Brahms was not about to stand for that. He considered it his friends' duty to support and critique his work. In one of his first letters to Clara since leaving Düsseldorf, he made a blunt reply to that missing letter of hers:

> My Clara, Your remarks about the value which I attach to your own and J.'s applause are amateurish. You know perfectly well how pleased I am if my things please my friends, and you also know whose praise I value most. . . . Joachim philosophizes and thinks a good deal about music . . . and because I think some of his ideas so splendid . . . I am always encouraged if my things come up to his standard. . . . The highest tribunal of all, however, is your loving nature and its yea.[7]

At the end, Brahms softened his bluntness with affection—as he usually did with Clara, sooner or later. He spent that Christmas in Düsseldorf with her and the children. On December 30, back in Hamburg, he wrote her, "I am painting a gentle portrait of you which will be the Adagio."[8] So the concerto struggled on. After three years of frustrating work on the successive versions, by May 1857 he had drafts of three movements substantially orchestrated, but he continued darning and patching all the way to the premiere nearly two years after that. Why was he so obsessed by the piece?

THE D MINOR PIANO CONCERTO begins with a shout of unrest, alarm, calamity: a low D in timpani and strings and snarling horns, that tonal anchor immediately undercut by a harmony of B♭, peculiarly dissonant in effect for a major chord that sends the introduction reeling into a harmonic instability that does not resolve into D minor until the twenty-fifth measure. Even then the harmony is unanchored, the tonic note weak in the bass. Introducing this harmonic flux, a pounding, declamatory line rises into chains of trills—not the delicate trills of Mozart, but wild chromatic shiverings. Over and over in the first measures the melodic line stresses the out-of-key note A♭, forming with the bass D the interval of a tritone that old theorists named *diabolus in musica*, the devil in music.[9]

The effect of this opening may be the most turbulent in the repertoire to that time—not the gleeful demonism of Liszt and early Brahms, or the dramatic flash of dissonance that opens the last movement of Beethoven's Ninth, but something darker and more savage. The opening and the ensuing first movement, one of the longest of all concerto movements, are as dramatic as Beethoven's Ninth and on a comparable scale of weight and time. But in contrast to Beethoven, Brahm's introduction is indifferent to conventional symphonic or concerto-like brilliance, almost indifferent to musicality.[10] The orchestra strains to bear the weight of expression demanded of it.

There is a sensation of immediacy, of *realism*, in this music that Brahms never attempted again. The explanation for it appears to be that in his mind the beginning of the Concerto evoked the tragedy that preceded its inspiration by a few days: Robert Schumann's leap into the Rhine.[11] Like the "Edward" ballade of the same year, this is Brahmsian program music, the tragedy this time not literary but real. If the vertiginous opening moments of the concerto are applied to the image of a desperate man leaping into the water, they become almost cinematically, kinetically apt.

In that connection we also find, perhaps, one of the reasons Brahms could not let go of this movement: its turmoil was too compelling to him, too close not only to Schumann's fall but to his own chaotic feelings in the aftermath. The primal gestures of the movement obsessed him. As Hans Gal has written, it "lay before him like an erratic boulder, huge and mysterious."[12] There was perhaps another reason: Brahms pounded away at the intractable mass out of loyalty and obligation, because this was the symphonic music that Robert and Clara Schumann had demanded of him.

Beyond all that, certainly Brahms felt obligated to stick with it because the ideas were too powerful to give up. For all the pain of its gestation and the shortcomings lingering in the final version, Brahms understood that in the first movement he had found ideas of Beethovenian scope and drama, one of the most electrifying and original concerto movements of the century. The material lay beyond his capacity to master, just as the expressive weight of the opening was beyond his or his advisors' skill with the orchestra, perhaps beyond orchestral means entirely. Yet whatever the obstacles, Brahms doggedly saw it through because he knew the results could be worth it.

If there is a programmatic story behind the movement as a whole, it was known only to Brahms. He was not about to follow the Liszt faction into self-proclaimed musical illustration. More likely, after the inspiration of the opening, the other material of the movement fell into place not in programmatic but "abstract" terms. It unfolds in a free version of the usual first-movement concerto layout, adapted from sonata form, even if its succession of themes (organically but not transparently related) and their incessant restless development obscures the familiar Classical outlines: orchestral exposition, second exposition with soloist (usually with two major themes, here at least six), development, and recapitulation. Perhaps partly because of the first movement's symphonic origin, there is no cadenza from the soloist to mark the beginning of the coda. (The other movements have cadenzas, if not the usual virtuosic ones.)

The first movement's second theme, lyrical and hymnlike in contrast to the stark opening, and in the expected F major, is the first extended solo; in fact, the piano tends to have the more gentle material until its pounding octaves during the development.[13] For the duration of the movement the solo part manages to be at once antivirtuosic and two-fistedly difficult, some of that due to sheer awkwardness. Given its difficulty and general indifference to practicality and popularity, the music ensured that for a long time, few soloists other than Brahms and Clara would be willing to take it on.

The second movement, the "tender portrait" of Clara that he promised her, likely came together more easily. Malcolm MacDonald writes that the slow movement has "something almost numbed about its lyricism, as if the experience of the first movement had left it in shock."[14] The tone of the music—gently spiritual, hymnlike—conjures the idealized Clara to whom Young Kreisler wrote early in his infatuation: "I think of you as going to the concert hall like a priestess to the altar." The descending scalewise lines of the main theme, subtly derived from the opening theme of the first movement, feature the characteristic Brahmsian chains of parallel thirds (as does much of the piano writing in the first movement). The middle section heightens the intensity, but in this music there is none of the anguish of the opening movement, nor any reflection of the suffering Clara. Only the vestal, pure and chaste. At the beginning of the manuscript, not for publication, Brahms placed a phrase from the Latin mass—*Benedictus qui venit in nomine Domine* (blessed is he that cometh in the name of the Lord). The phrase remains cryptic but suggestive: of the religious tone of the movement; of Robert Schumann whom Brahms jokingly called *Mynheer Domine* after his Dutch tour; of Clara herself, the high priestess of her husband's music.[15]

When he came to the last movement Brahms faced a quandary. He had been experiencing chronic finale problems. Since the B Major Trio in 1854 he had written none—the D minor symphony and C♯ minor piano quartet both collapsed when he got to the last movement. That he could not finish those pieces may have been partly because in those years his sense of the tone, tempo, and purpose of a finale was in flux. The last movements of piano concertos were traditionally light, brilliant, vivacious. Eventually most of Brahms's orchestral finales, and some of his chamber ones as well, were to be serious and monumental, as in Beethoven's Ninth. But Brahms had not yet arrived at that conception. Meanwhile, as of 1856, if he still did not know what to do when he got to the end, he was also grimly determined not to drop the piece. Now he got out of his quandary by cribbing: for the finale he stole from someone else's concerto—not unscrupulously but creatively, as true artists steal.

First, he followed a traditional form to the letters—the A B A C A B A of many rondo finales—and incorporated the driving rhythm characteristic of the genre. More specifically, he modeled the movement almost phrase by phrase, and even some of the gestures, on Beethoven's C Minor Piano Concerto. "The two finales," Charles Rosen writes, "may be described and analyzed to a great extent as if they were the same piece."[16] This borrowing solved for the moment his last-movement block and, perhaps most importantly, finished a piece that had become a gorilla on his back. Certainly the result is a fine, enjoyable, vivacious minor-key movement. It is also arguable that it fails to bring to resolution the expressive scope and intensity of the first movement, as Beethoven had accomplished in the Ninth. Hans Gal writes: "The Titanic struggle unleashed in the first movement does not in the [finale] lead to anything more than a devil-may-care, now-let-us-live attitude."[17]

Brahms would have put the inadequacies of the concerto in his own way, but he knew them and they tormented him. Surely he realized that he had created an extraordinary work; but it was not unassailable, not *perfect*, and moreover he found he could not resolve all the insufficiencies mocking him. That gnawed at his pride and his confidence—there are few things more unpleasant for an ambitious craftsman than to discover glaring holes in his technique. We see Brahms's uncertainty in his tinkering through 1857–8, and in his letters. As late as the end of 1858, shortly before the premiere, he was writing Joachim, "I'm still far too ignorant about it and don't know how to help myself. I've even gotten confused by the horns. Does it have to be deep B[♭] horns [at the beginning] . . . and perhaps at the end use D-horns?"[18]

He had stumbled into excruciating scoring demands in the first movement, especially for a composer still finding his way with the orchestra. Each of the half-dozen or more themes demanded a characteristic orchestral texture and color, to help guide the listener through the maze of material unfolding over a long time. (This sort of predicament a composer often discovers too late, well into the work.) Then the two succeeding movements turned up further scoring snags to beleaguer him.

Was it only when the D Minor Concerto was finished that Brahms finally realized what he had attempted? He had started his career as an orchestral composer with a work of the scale and ambition of the Ninth Symphony, which *ended* Beethoven's career. At least, though, afterward Brahms had a far better idea how much he needed to learn about the orchestra and about large-scale form. Though he soon produced more orchestral music, he would not put before the public another work of comparable scope until he was certain he was ready. Not for another fifteen years did he feel ready. He never sailed blind again.

AT THE END OF MAY 1857, having finished a draft of the Concerto, Brahms traveled to the small principality of Detmold to see what might come of a royal invitation he had received. The connection had begun with Clara's giving lessons to Princess Frederike and visiting the music-mad court of Leopold II. After Robert died, she handed over the lessons to Johannes, and thus the invitation. Detmold lay forty miles southwest of Hanover, on the edge of the Teutoburger Wald. There was no train there; one went by post-coach. For Brahms the legendary forest, where once Teutons and Romans had battled, was a large part of the attraction.

Royalty was not his style, even if this court maintained a good orchestra and chorus and had a number of pianists able to pay royally for lessons.

Brahms had gotten to know the Hofmarschall's young son Karl von Meysenbug, who met him at the coach when he arrived. Brahms was silent and awkward in the ornate drawing room of the castle but warmed up when he played for Karl's father. Then in a court concert he ran through the Beethoven G Major Concerto with the orchestra and joined in Schubert's *Trout* Quintet.

Afterward, happy with the results, Brahms caroused late into the night with the musicians. If his wit suited the younger crowd, it failed to make a distinguished impression on the dour Kapellmeister August Kiel, conductor of the orchestra. As he and Brahms chatted after the concert, Kiel remarked that he had been setting biblical Psalms and was puzzled by the phrase "to the chief musician on the Gittith." What, pray tell, said Kiel, the court's chief musician, is this *Gittith* that the chief musician is supposed to be *on*? "Probably a pretty Jewish girl," Brahms suggested straight-faced. The joke was not appreciated.[19]

The evening ended with Brahms and Karl, who had sneaked out of the house, climbing a hill to watch the sunrise. As they stumbled back into town looking as disreputable as they felt, the two ran into Karl's righteous auntie taking her morning constitutional. Despite some embarrassing repercussions over that, Brahms was offered the hoped-for position as pianist and chorus director for a three-month season at the end of the year. The salary was 556 talers plus lodging and board, enough to last him nearly a year in Hamburg. Given the musical enthusiasm of Prince Leopold's court, Brahms had found himself a gracious and profitable little sinecure, if he could stand it. He stood it for three seasons, three months at a time—as it turned out, one of the longest-term jobs of his life.

From Detmold, Brahms traveled to Bonn to make arrangements for the new headstone over Robert Schumann's grave (Clara was concertizing in England).[20] This year Liszt and his music were featured at the Lower Rhine Music Festival. For the first time since he began attending, Brahms skipped it, instead making another walking tour of the Rhineland. His absence from the festival would be suitably conspicuous.

Meeting Clara on her return from England, he settled down with her and the younger Schumann children for July and August on the Rhine, at Oberwesel and St. Goarshausen. With his functional bachelorhood returned, Brahms here began in earnest his pattern of summer working vacations in the country. In late July, Joachim appeared for a long visit, and there were shorter ones from Grimm, Otten, and other friends. After

Joachim departed in mid-August, Clara wrote him, "Johannes sank back into his former seriousness after you left us."[21]

Joachim must have been in a vindictive mood himself. No doubt with Johannes's encouragement, he had at last decided to finalize his break with Liszt. With his characteristic mixture of high-mindedness and venom, Joachim wrote his old mentor:

> The continued goodness and confidence which you show me, great and courageous spirit . . . gives me a sense of shame for the lack of candor I have shown up to the present. . . . So I shall remain silent no longer on a subject which, I confess to you, your manly spirit had the right to demand to know long before. Your music is entirely antagonistic to me; it contradicts everything with which the spirits of our great ones have nourished my mind from my earliest youth. If it were thinkable that I could ever be deprived of . . . their creations, all that I feel music to be, your strains would not fill one corner of the vast waste of nothingness.[22]

The letter continues in this vein, acknowledging Joachim's debt to Liszt while venting a barely veiled contempt. Liszt and his disciples declined to strike back. Before long, Brahms and Joachim would provide the New Germans with a bigger score to settle than Joachim's letter, which only spelled out in chapter and verse what everyone already knew. Unlike his colleague Wagner, Liszt was not vindictive in print or in person. Nearly thirty years later, when he and Joachim finally met again and moved toward reconciliation, Liszt only said mildly, "As you do not like my music, dear Joachim, I feel that I must admire yours in double measure."[23]

In September Clara moved from Düsseldorf to Berlin, mainly to be near family—her mother who was long since remarried to Adolf Bargiel, her half-brother Woldemar Bargiel, and half-sister Marie. Brahms, who had no affection for that city, visited her less there. Clara's brooding only intensified after the move; to Joachim she wrote, "I arrived in Berlin shattered in body and soul."[24]

The same week, Brahms wrote her an astonishing and eventually famous letter.

> My dear Clara, you really must try hard to keep your melancholy within bounds and see that it does not last too long. Life is precious and moods like the one you are in consume us body and soul. Do not imag-

ine that life has little more in store for you. It is not true. . . . Body and soul are ruined by persisting in melancholy. . . . The more you endeavor to go through times of sorrow calmly . . . the more you will enjoy the happier times that are sure to follow. . . . Passions are not natural to mankind, they are always exceptions or excrescences. The man in whom they overstep the limits should regard himself as an invalid and seek medicine for his life and for his health. The ideal and genuine man is calm both in his joy and in his sorrow. Passions must quickly pass or else they must be hunted out. Consider yourself for the moment, my dear Clara, as a serious invalid and without necessarily being anxious, but on the contrary, with calm and perseverance, try to look after yourself.[25]

These calm paternal words speak much, in several dimensions. To a degree they are practical advice to a friend with an inclination to gloom and hysteria and overwork. No doubt they express Brahms's own convictions and practice; he had instituted a stern emotional censor over himself in order to get through the experiences of the last three years. He had copied down in his collection of German proverbs "He who stays on the plain will not fall far," and in front of the collection wrote, "wise lessons one must practice."

In these respects Johannes's letter to Clara is judicious, well-meant, even kindly. But it is more than that. He counsels a kind of detachment that borders on indifference, and his tone patronizes an older woman who has been through a great deal more than he has. The subtext of the letter is beyond cold; it is cruel, addressed as it is to the loved one whom Brahms had not long before deserted in a time of anguish. In essence he says: get over the fact that I deserted you and go on with your job—for example, taking care of your children and playing my music.

Despite the letter's peremptory sermonizing, Clara did not turn away from him. She had heard that sort of thing from him before. Besides, she had never known intimately any other kind of man than those brilliant, erratic, manipulative, and sometimes cruel. In ways at once admirable and perverse, Clara and Johannes suited each other. Their lives together and apart would be mingled in a creative and spiritual communion of a high order, and at the same time in a continual swing between mutual affection and mutual torture.

Brahms's sermon about "the ideal and genuine man," of course, did Clara no good. Soon her inward distress over losing her husband and then Johannes turned outward. In November she had an attack of neuralgia she described "as if the bones were being torn out of my arms, neck, and breast with red-hot irons."[26] The doctor gave her opium, which did more than her friends could, or would, for the pain.

FOR HIS PART IN THOSE MONTHS, Brahms had a jolly time in his first season at the court of Detmold. There was an atavistic charm about these provincial courts, relics of medieval Germany when princes and barons of patchwork fiefdoms slaughtered one another for land and precedence. His duties were to conduct the Singverein (the mixed chorus), perform chamber and solo works for the court on piano, and give lessons to Princess Frederike and other aristocratic amateurs.

The old castle had a looming tower from its days as a fortress, and an expansive plaza in front. To his relief, Brahms did not have to stay in a dusty castle apartment or in the newer princely residence, but received cozy bourgeois lodgings opposite the castle gate at the Gasthof Zur Stadt Frankfurt. His room was equipped with an old grand piano courtesy of the Frau Hofmarschall. Nobody at court cared about his compositions, but that hardly bothered him. Another matter annoyed him more: even if now and then Kapellmeister Kiel allowed him to rehearse the orchestra, that experience and his duties with the Singverein did not satisfy Brahms's new craving for the podium. F. W. Grund, long-time conductor of the Hamburg Philharmonic, was getting on in years and Brahms had begun to imagine himself as head of his hometown orchestra.

Besides friend Karl von Meysenbug and his younger brother, Brahms fell in with orchestra concertmaster Karl Bargheer (a student of Joachim) and other congenial commoners. He had mornings for work and usually lunched with Bargheer at the Stadt Frankfurt, followed by a tramp in the arch-Romantic gloom of the Teutoburger Wald. Lessons with his titled students began in mid-afternoon. In the evenings came keyboard performances and weekly rehearsals with the Singverein. On Sundays there were day-long picnics; by scrimping on his daily wine allowance, Brahms was able to buy a bottle of Malvoisier, whose exemplary effects were amplified by sun and breeze in forest glades. A Detmold friend remembered, "He was happy as a king at these times, he loved nature so much."[27]

In court concerts Brahms cast off his usual performance anxiety and enjoyed himself. Playing Mozart violin sonatas with Bargheer, he might launch into the piece in the wrong key, both as a practical joke and as a test of the violinist's transposing skills. In the same way, Brahms enjoyed reading through local composers' keyboard pieces, not only playing them at sight but transposing them to any requested key. Chamber-music soirees covered the repertoire from Bach, Mozart, and Haydn through Beethoven and Schubert to Schumann. To those names Brahms added his own, playing his B Major Trio and later the G Minor Piano Quartet, to scant applause. In December 1857, he joined in the Beethoven Triple Concerto with the orchestra, but his efforts mainly produced more squabbles with Kapellmeister Kiel. Brahms was not cut out to function cheerfully under anyone's direction.

After work there were pleasant hours at the Stadt Frankfurt with a collection of new friends. On the whole, the Detmold job was Ge-mütlichkeit itself, a retreat from the world in sumptuous surroundings, with plenty of money, merry company, and good wine on hand. Being Brahms, he appreciated it all, but it was only a matter of time before the situation grated on him. It was not in him to smile at bores merely because they happened to pay his rent. As he wrote Clara later, looking back on it,

> How attractive is a post at one of these little Courts. One gets plenty of time to play to oneself, but unfortunately one cannot always feel happy at heart, for, after all, one would become nauseated by the faces one sees there, they are enough to make anyone a misanthrope. One can enjoy the beauties of nature in solitude, but when playing music in the drawing-room before people, one does not wish to be alone.[28]

As always, nothing impeded his creative work, whatever trouble it gave him in those days, or his counterpoint study or other self-improvement schemes. He made good use of the Mozart and Haydn scores in the castle library. Meanwhile he decided to lower his embarrassingly high voice by doing vocal exercises of his own devising, and to strengthen the vocal apparatus by the method of shouting above the din at his Singverein rehearsals. The result of this regimen, besides annoying his singers, was to give himself a voice permanently hoarse and barking, while still rather high. The good singing voice he had once possessed was ruined. From then on, in heated moments his voice would break like a pubescent teenager's. Given his disappointing vocal endowment and physical size, Brahms would be forced to rely on cigars, alcohol, gruff-ness, racy jokes, and eventually on beard and girth, to furnish him with manliness.

With his first conducting position, he naturally used the chance to perform contemporary choral music and to add new arrangements and original pieces of his own. Besides that, he was anxious to perform the older choral works he had been searching out in crumbling editions. These sometimes went back nearly three hundred years, antediluvian in the 1850s when J. S. Bach, who had died a hundred years before, seemed ancient to concertgoers and musicians alike. In his first season in Detmold Brahms performed pieces by Rovetta and Praetorius, plus Handel's perennial *Messiah*.[29] Meanwhile he arranged folk songs for the chorus, without feeling particularly happy with the results: "My stuff is so completely impractical!" he groaned to Joachim.[30]

After a sociable Christmas Day spent with Hofmarschall Meysenbug and family, with lots of presents and games with the children, Brahms headed for Hamburg with relief. En route he stopped over at the Hanover railroad station, where for three hours he and Joachim sat in the restaurant over coffee and the score of the D Minor Piano Concerto. After so many years of private labor the monster was scheduled for its unveiling, by conductor Otten in March, with his newly founded Hamburg Musikverein.[31] Whatever apprehensions assaulted Brahms at the prospect, Joachim reported him to Clara as "in splendid spirits."[32] Weather reports on Brahms's mood had become a regular item of news among his friends: is he stormy or sunny these days?

BRAHMS INTENDED THIS RETURN to Hamburg to be his final homecoming. In April 1858 the family moved to larger quarters at No. 74 Fuhlentwiete and reserved the best room for Johannes, his library and piano, his writing table and bust of Beethoven. For the family this was a relatively elegant place—spacious rooms decorated with ivy, an open fireplace, a view of the park.[33] The road ended in a canal crowded with fishing boats. Elise made everything spotless and kept fresh flowers in the pots. Fritz lived at home but paid rent from his earnings as a piano teacher. Johann Jakob's contrabass was bringing in a good 150 courantmarks a month.[34]

Musicians in town became gradually more cordial. Brahms felt one of the group, as much as he was likely to feel part of any group. Yet in the long run, Hamburg could not hold him. His mother had turned into an ailing old woman continually carping at her husband; it was only a matter of time before Johann Jakob left the house for good. When Brahms's one-time publisher Cranz, owner of the only acceptable piano in town, refused to lend it for the premiere of the piano concerto, Brahms indignantly canceled the concert. "The whole thing is typically Hamburgian," Brahms fumed to Clara. "Cranz will not give me his Erard, but with the utmost amiability offers me all kinds of old tin kettles."[35]

Joachim offered to give a private reading of the concerto with his Hanover court orchestra, as soon as he could find time for it in a rehearsal. All the friends felt beset at the end of that spring—Johannes now tensely awaiting the first run-through of the concerto, Clara suffering an attack of rheumatism, Joachim overworked and ill.[36] Moreover, Clara was becoming increasingly involved with Theodor Kirchner, eventually a good friend and champion of Brahms, in those days enjoying the modest success of his keyboard miniatures—which is approximately where Robert Schumann had been when he married Clara. And like Schumann, Kirchner was a fine but fragile artist, chronically depressed and irresolute. In March, Clara sent him a precious lock of Robert's hair.[37]

On March 28 a telegram from Joachim summoned Johannes to Hanover for the test reading on the thirtieth. Given the myriad imponderables in writing for eighty players, the anxiety crackling around the first hearing of an orchestral work can be brutal for a composer, so much the worse if it is the first experience. It is as if you have singlehandedly built a temple stone by stone, without being entirely sure it will stand up.

That day, as Joachim led the orchestra through the tumultuous introduction, Brahms sat trembling at the piano trying to assess his orchestration while preparing for the silvery chains of thirds that begin the solo part. In the audience, Clara and Julius Grimm listened for the first time to music they had seen for years on paper in tattered drafts. After all the sweat and apprehension, the reading went splendidly. On the podium Joachim handled the accompaniment well, Brahms played the solo part with aplomb, even the orchestra seemed inspired.

As the music spun out, much of the orchestration sounded better than Brahms had allowed himself to hope. If awkward spots remained, nearly everything worked. So at last he knew that he had some conception of how to write for the orchestra—the great thing, the ultimate medium. After the adagio, Brahms played the finale prestissimo out of sheer relief. Walking with him afterward in beautiful, hopeful weather, Clara found Johannes as elated as she had ever seen him.[38] Surely, they thought, the joy of completion and discovery everyone had felt that day presaged victory when the work found its premiere.

DESPITE HIS INDIFFERENCE TO APPLAUSE, Brahms dreamed of a great success with the concerto, and not only for self-important reasons. For him success was not abstract but concrete, played out first in his own mind and judgment, then in the judgment of friends, then in parlors and concert halls in front of people who applauded or did not. Surprising as it may appear for someone as independent as Brahms, he considered the verdict of the middle-class public to be the ultimate arbiter. Certainly he allowed himself to challenge listeners, to stretch their capacities, and he always claimed that he did not like going before the public himself. All the same, if his work did not sooner or later please people in the concert hall and in the parlors of amateur pianists and singers, he believed he was not doing his job.

That is what Brahms implies in a letter to Clara of June 1858. In the first lines he plays his familiar game of reproving someone who loves and supports him, in this case complaining about Clara's very efforts in his behalf: "All I would beg of you is not to allow your own enthusiasm to fire others to a pitch which they will afterwards misunderstand. You expect much too prompt and warm a recognition of any talent which you happen to appreciate." He had come to feel she was pushing too hard about his work. But describing himself airily as a "talent which you happen to appreciate" was too much. For her, Johannes no less than Robert was a holy cause. Clara responded with outrage: "Anybody reading what you have written me about my enthusiasm would think me an extremely hysterical person who worships her friend like a god. . . . Do not try to kill it with your cold philosophizing." In her letters for a long time after, Clara made him suffer for his words—at the same time as she lavishly praised his new work and practiced the piano concerto.

Maybe this time Brahms was not as imperious as he seems in trying to damp down Clara's proselytizing. He says she should not fan the sort of emotional, partisan enthusiasm that has little substance behind it. Any hint of propaganda reminded him unpleasantly of the New Germans. He continued:

> Art is a republic. You should accept this principle much more whole-heartedly than you do. You are much too aristocratic. . . . Do not confer a higher rank upon any artist, and do not expect the minor ones to look up to him as something higher, as consul. His ability will make him a beloved and respected citizen of this republic, but no consul or emperor.[39]

In those few lines we find something as close to an artistic credo as Brahms ever expressed, one characteristically forthright and remarkably mature. Probably it had evolved less through experience in the musical world, of which he still had relatively little, than through years of reading and of dialogues with Joachim. The idea of a republic of art suited Brahms's democratic convictions, his love of the process of music-making from the composing desk through rehearsals and even performing, his respect for the fraternity of musicians (always from his own corner, a little apart), and his essential humility.

Brahms was a traditionalist who worshipped the masters of the past, but he took for granted that he must bring something original to his tradition. He was a craftsman among craftsmen, doing his job as best he could in all humility, though to him the work was not ordinary but something at the highest level of human endeavor. Music was Brahms's religion—but music as a private spiritual and intellectual quest, and a shared undertaking. If he assumed a kind of mantle as a priest of art, he did not extend that priesthood outside the confines of his study and the places where music is played. In other words, Brahms did not envision artists in Wagner's monomaniacal terms as prophets redeeming Germany and through Germany the world, but rather art as a communal undertaking to exalt the individual mind and heart and soul.

Thus his term: *a republic*. If in some degree Brahms preached through his hat in saying there are no consuls in art—he had been a golden child and famous at twenty—he still saw his profession as something musicians share democratically, everyone working for the good of music itself. It was his job to write it and that of players to play it, and the part of the public to decide whom to pay for it. He lived that conviction to the end, even if he was often crotchety about the contributions of his fellow composers to the process.

So for Brahms the final court of any musician was the ears, hearts, and minds of listeners—above all of cultivated Austro/German music lovers, who in the later nineteenth century made up a large and remarkably sophisticated audience. It was a time of unprecedented music-making in Europe, not only in new, grandiose concert halls but in homes and private soirees, all that activity new not so much in kind as in scope. Brahms aimed his music primarily toward the thousands of middle-class amateurs he knew could understand his forms and sometimes his modulations, a good many of whom could sing and play his music as well.

Schumann had called this public philistine because they were unadventurous and worshipped shallow virtuosity. Only occasionally, however, did Brahms wield the epithet *philistine*, and never with the vituperation Schumann did. Brahms accepted the bourgeois public as the ultimate judge, even if their verdict was slow to take shape and manifestly unpredictable. (His experience with the D Minor Piano Concerto would be an unforgettable lesson in how slow and unpredictable.) Eventually he spent a fair amount of his time writing commercial dances and a patriotic extravaganza, and piles of the sorts of vocal duets, quartets, and such that were staples of social music-making, *Hausmusik*, in the nineteenth century. None of this is hackwork, but it was largely written to move off the shelves, and did. When the concertgoing public and critics balked at an ambitious effort toward the end of his life, the Double Concerto, Brahms responded not by denouncing the philistines but by renouncing—fortunately with relapses—his creative life.

Thus, in 1858, Brahms adjured Clara: let my music find its own way with the public, in its own time, and don't try to prod them too sharply. He ended that overbearing letter, "You might answer me more quickly; don't often keep me waiting as long as you did this time." Meanwhile, of course, Clara's proselytizing continued to be one of the main forces helping his music find an audience, and Joachim's another. If Brahms rarely expressed gratitude to either of them, he responded amply in his way— with a string of masterpieces written for, inspired by, sometimes dedicated to Clara and Joachim. He felt those gifts would repay them more than mere words of appreciation, and they did.

THAT SPRING, Johannes and Clara were invited on a vacation to Göttingen by Julius Otto Grimm, Brahms's friend from Düsseldorf who now directed music in that college town. To Clara, Brahms groused about even this friendly invitation, threatening not to go. At the end of her long response angrily repudiating his letter grumbling about her manner of promoting him, Clara said, "I am very much upset by what you write about Göttingen. That you so much dislike the idea of going there is hateful to me. . . . I am waiting for another letter, my Johannes. If only I could find longing as sweet as you do. It only gives me pain and fills my heart with unspeakable woe." She meant longing for him, and he knew it, and she knew he knew it. Johannes hastened to write her a pleasant response, to which she replied with relief. To make her happy, he would go to Göttingen.

Grimm had settled into the stone, brick, and ivy environs of Göttingen as conductor of the ninety-voice Cäcelienverein and associated women's chorus. There he married the enchanting Philippine, called Pine, nicknamed "Pine Gur" after the growled R's of her dialect. Grimm meanwhile had been dubbed "Ise" for "Isegrimm," meaning old bear or grouch.[40] In 1857, they had named their first child Johannes, after Ise's admired friend.[41]

Among their circle in the town was a professor's daughter of twenty-three with a lovely soprano voice named Agathe von Siebold, called

Gathe. Thus the friends Ise, Gur, and Gathe, like some fairy-tale trio. They were young and in the first flush of life and work, and Agathe a catch for the best sort of suitor, and the Cäcelienverein was a steady pleasure for all of them. In inviting Brahms to Göttingen, Grimm wrote, "If it would please you to have a few good voices, lodged in very lovely girls, sing for you, they will take pleasure in being at your disposal. Come quickly!"[42] It appears that Pine Gur and her husband aspired to some matchmaking.

At the end of July 1858, Johannes showed up in Göttingen, grumbling. His reluctance to leave Hamburg shows his concern over work—he had begun a serenade for nine winds—but also his lack of interest in singing girls, lovely or not. When Clara and her five youngest children arrived they settled in with the Grimms, and Johannes roomed nearby. Clara's half-brother Woldemar Bargiel joined the party along with Detmold Konzertmeister Karl Bargheer.

It did not take many days for Johannes to succumb to the charm of the place and of the lovely girls, Agathe in particular. Maybe Ise and Pine Gur should have known better than to try to lead him in any direction, if matchmaking is what they had in mind. Maybe they had failed to absorb that their blond friend was almost constitutionally unable to bear any congenial situation for long before putting his foot in it.

Still, Brahms was in his most charming mood on that vacation, as were they all. Agathe had long dark hair and a lush figure, and she was endowed with a soprano voice whose sound Joachim compared to an Amati violin. Brahms drank in that voice, and Gathe with it. She was talented, intelligent, funny, creative, ready for a game or a practical joke. Though her face was plain, by no means did Agathe's appeal lie purely in talent and intellect. "How delightful," Joachim sighed, "to run your hands through such hair!"[43]

At that time Agathe was studying composition with Grimm, who one day berated her for some careless counterpoint exercises. When she complained to Brahms about it he sat down, chuckling, and wrote out her next assignment himself. The idea was to play a joke on Ise by her submitting an impeccably done exercise. Agathe duly went through the charade of presenting it to her teacher. He looked it over and exploded at the "swinish mess." When Gathe stammered, "But what if Johannes did it?," Grimm only replied heatedly, "So much the worse!" Then they realized the joke had been on both of them.[44] Brahms had not done the proper exercises Agathe thought were intended to fool Grimm, but instead systematically fouled them up. Even if he had fallen for Agathe,

Johannes had no intention of conforming to her girlish expectations, even in fun.

It was one of those luminous, enchanted summers. In the quiet old college town the friends felt merry and hopeful and secure in their talent and their prospects for a pleasant course of life. Drunk with summer and happiness, they played blindman's buff and hide-and-seek and made grown-up music. When the friends headed home in the twilight, Johannes and Agathe would linger behind. Then he might whisper to her that he had better go walk with Clara or she would be jealous.[45] What Clara probably felt was old and sad and unattractive in this laughing youthful company. Even when she joined in the games, her propensity for accidents set her apart. Discovered in an asparagus bed during hide-and-seek, Clara was sprinting for "home" when she sprawled headlong over a tree root, and the fun stopped as everyone gathered to help her.[46]

Grimm wrote Joachim, "Johannes has written glorious songs which Gathe sings to us, and we are all agreed that this is a wonderful time."[47] The new works may have included several of the Opus 14 songs and romances, two of the Opus 20 duets (for Agathe and fellow chorus member Bertha Wagner), and the Opus 19 solos. In the late-summer evenings the friends sat listening to Brahms's sweetheart sing "Ein Sonett" in her Amati voice, while he accompanied her:

> *Oh, if I could only forget her,*
> *her beautiful, loving nature,*
> *her glance, her friendly mouth!*
> *Perhaps I could then grow well! . . .*
> *Much better never to grow well!*

No one could miss the accents Brahms placed on "ihr *schönes, liebes* Wesen"—her *beautiful, loving* nature. In all the songs of Opus 19, romance unfolds in gentle, perennial, idealized images: lovers kiss in spring, they part, they rest beside a brook and dream. In these as in most of his song lyrics, Brahms looked not for the kind of poetic subtlety that inspired Schumann (notably Heine's verses, with his broken idylls and oblique ironies), but rather for verse direct, uncomplicated, ingenuously evocative—poetry close to folk verse which welcomed music and offered no competition to it. (This lay in contrast to the lyrics for Brahms's more ambitious choral works, where the texts are substantial, with a preference for Scripture and for Goethe.)

As in the aphorisms of "Des jungen Kreislers Schatzkästlein," Brahms was also adept at finding song texts to articulate his own feelings. The lyrics of his Göttingen summer suited his purpose, which was to love. If the reality of that summer was more exquisite than the commonplace poems he seized on, it was exactly suited to music. In his songs, those six weeks and Agathe find their first apotheosis.

Still, he worked at a good deal more than love songs on this vacation, much of it things begun earlier in the year. They include a group of folk song arrangements dedicated to Clara's children—the *Deutsche Volks-Kinderlieder*, following up on the *Deutsche Volkslieder* he had just sent Clara for comment.[48] He completed the serenade for a nonet of winds; it had been inspired by the Haydn symphonies, the Mozart divertimenti and cassations and such he had heard and studied at Detmold. Grimm assembled players for a reading of the nonet, which revealed trouble in the scoring. Clara advised Brahms that the music was really an orchestra piece and he agreed, probably with a groan after his struggles with the concerto. He would get to work on it back in Detmold—at first, apparently, in a small-orchestra version.

Besides the songs for Agathe that summer, Brahms drafted a *Brautgesang* (*Bridal Song*), and the beautiful, neo-Renaissance *Ave Maria*, both for women's choir. He regaled the friends' gatherings with his party favors, Hungarian dances of the sort he used to perform with Reményi. It was a forecast of how the rest of the world would receive these exotic melodies when he got around to writing them down. Clara began playing some of the dances in her recitals.

Then in his passion for Agathe, Brahms got careless. One day in the middle of September he stepped behind some bushes to embrace her, and Clara saw.[49] One look was enough: *He left me alone with words of love and devotion, and now he falls for this girl because she has a pretty voice.* That night Clara packed up her family and fled Göttingen.

The friends did not spend much time on regrets. They felt sorry for Clara's distress, but she was always upset about something. Besides, she had hardly fit into the spectacle of romantic youth the old town had been witnessing. None of this is to say that Brahms and Agathe had physically become lovers. She was too respectable for that, at least in the setting of a small town where everybody knew her proper, prominent, Catholic family. The friends all felt happy about how properly and respectably things were going, and how much fun it all was. Surely, they thought, Clara would understand too, once she calmed down.

As for Johannes, for the first time in his life he was part of a sociable group of close friends of both sexes and his own age, and he had found himself a sweetheart. The question was whether he would be able to bear all that Gemütlichkeit.

•   •   •

AT THE END OF SEPTEMBER, Brahms dragged himself from Agathe and back to Detmold for three months of court duties and longing for the pleasures of Göttingen. He sent the new *Brautgesang* to Grimm, who played it over for the two women most connected with its inspiration, Gathe and Gur. Grimm confessed, though, that the piece did not seize him. Brahms conceded that the idea of a bridal song had failed to stimulate his imagination: "Thank you for your criticism. . . . The *Brautlied* is disgracefully ordinary and dull. . . . As it is, a poor composer sits sadly and alone in his room and conjures up thoughts which are none of his business. And a critic sets himself between two beautiful ladies—I don't want to imagine it any further!"[50] All Grimm's letters to Johannes were about "we three"—Ise, Pine Gur, and Gathe. In return, Brahms called them the "beloved clover-leaf," maybe picturing himself someday as the lucky fourth.[51]

Through his days of playing and teaching and composing, and exchanging letters with Agathe, his feelings mounted as the tension of separation grew. He sent her manuscripts of songs he was still writing for her and about her. One of his letters to Julius Grimm shows his style: "Greet Agathe from me. I'm enclosing a few lieder for her, which—one of them—well, and I wanted by it, well—in short, really courteously for me."[52] His own passion almost had to be torn out of him, leaving him choking on his words even as he wrote.

As a counterpart to the sunny *Brautgesang*, which he soon suppressed, Brahms composed the startling, powerful *Begräbnisgesang* (*Funeral Song*), for choir and an ensemble of winds and timpani. Thoughts of the grave inspired him more than thoughts of a bride. The two pieces, which he read over with his Detmold group, foreshadowed his habit of producing pairs of works for the same medium—sometimes contrasting in expression, such as the rollicking Academic Festival Overture and its companion the Tragic. The *Begräbnisgesang* returns to the foreboding Brahmsian minor, the *Dies Irae* tone to which he gravitated as evocation of fatality and death. As in the *Begräbnisgesang*, the Brahmsian minor often appears with relentlessly pounding timpani: *Schicksal! Fate!* That tone recurs from *Ein deutsches Requiem* of the 1860s to *Vier ernste Gesänge* at the end of his life.

This season in Detmold, Brahms played concertos by Mendelssohn, Schumann, and Chopin as well as solo and chamber music. Maybe he found more satisfaction in choral performances, which included his first Bach—the cantatas *Christ lag in Todesbanden*, which perhaps inspired his

Begräbnisgesang, and *Ich hatte viel Bekümmernis*. With his choir he read over Palestrina's High Renaissance *Missa Papae Marcelli*.[53]

In December he wrote Joachim asking for large manuscript sheets: "I need the paper to change my first serenade, now and finally, into a symphony. I can see that it is not right to have it in this mongrel state. I had such a beautiful, big conception of my first symphony, and now!—"[54] One day shortly after, concertmaster Bargheer turned up at Brahms's room in the Stadt Frankfurt to find sheets of manuscript draped everywhere from the piano to the bed, the ink drying. Brahms explained that he was orchestrating the D Major Serenade. A symphony? Bargheer inquired. "Ach," Brahms sighed, "if in these days after Beethoven you presume to write symphonies, they'd better look entirely different!"[55] Finally he shied away, however, from letting this cheerful, Haydn-inspired music stand as his first symphony. The manuscript originally called it "Symphony-Serenade," but he struck off the first term.

Clara wrote Johannes at Detmold. Still bitter over his letter of the past summer chastening her efforts for him, between the lines she also stewed over Agathe: "I am sorry I did not write to you about the Hungarian Dances, for you know how I like to please you. I only refrained because I feared you might say something unkind to me, as you have often done in similar cases."[56] She had been feeling wretched all summer, as she wrote to Joachim: "I am so terribly depressed. . . . I do indeed give concerts, but with what torture of heart. My health is giving way entirely."[57]

Brahms sent Clara a roll of music in December, with the demand "tell me particularly what you do not like, or what strikes you as weak, etc." As he probably had anticipated, she noted the lameness of the *Brautgesang* and the vigor of the *Begräbnisgesang*, saying she would like the latter sung at her own funeral. Most of all she was taken with a first movement for another serenade, this one in A major, eventually five movements for an orchestra without violins. In her comments on the new movement, Clara tried to talk Johannes out of a long pedal point on A before the recapitulation, which undercut the return to the main key of A; he ignored the advice. She concluded her letter with another twist of the knife: "Thank you, dear Johannes, for having sent me these things. Leave me my joy in them and do not spoil it by your customary remarks. . . . I am sorry that you should speak so contemptuously about your concerto. So just lock it up in the cupboard— you cannot take it from me even if you can deny me the pleasure of playing it."[58]

His deploring the concerto was a Brahmsian symptom of anxiety. A commitment for the premiere had finally turned up. After more revisions, Joachim had done another reading for him with his Hanover orchestra, and scheduled it for a court concert on January 22, 1859. A second performance had been arranged at the Leipzig Gewandhaus a few days later.

When he left Detmold for Hanover on January 1, Brahms first stopped off in Göttingen to embrace Agathe after three months of love-making restricted to letters. Innocently and unwisely, Julius Grimm and his wife leaned on Johannes a little: there's talk around town, if you don't do something Agathe could be compromised. Graciously or otherwise, Brahms took the hint. We know nothing about how it played out, but during that visit he proposed and Agathe accepted. Secretly they bought engagement rings and exchanged them. He had a photograph taken in Göttingen, the ring on his finger conspicuously displayed. For all the couple's secrecy, surely the Grimms guessed, and surely word went out that Brahms had found his mate, and the perfect one too.

ON JANUARY 8, Brahms took a tender leave from Agathe and went to Hanover to prepare for the concerto premiere. Everything seemed hanging in a balance, love weighing against his first premiere of a large, ambitious piece. He was still reworking the concerto's "unfortunate first movement, that refuses to be born."[59] His mother wrote from Hanover that his old teacher Marxsen sent best wishes, and she knew things would go well: "you were always so certain of your affairs."[60]

At the premiere on the 22nd the Hanover response appeared polite but puzzled. In the words of one critic, "The work, with all its serious striving, its rejection of triviality, its skilled instrumentation, seemed difficult to understand, even dry, and in parts eminently fatiguing." Brahms may have felt relieved to have gotten off that well. He knew what the public expected from concertos: virtuosic brilliance, dazzling cadenzas, not too many minor keys, not too long, not too tragic. To the degree that those were the rules, the D Minor Concerto violated every one of them. The piece was bound to take time to make its way. After all, for decades even the Beethoven Violin Concerto had been too much for the public, until Joachim forced them to accept it.

The day after the premiere in Hanover, neither success nor disaster, Brahms took the train for Leipzig. Optimistically, he told a reporter that he was thinking of spending the entire winter in the city.

The first omens of what he was in for appeared during rehearsals at the Gewandhaus. The old hall was a long room with a balcony set back, the seats laid out in rows facing the center aisle. As in many older halls, the orchestra sat on a low platform at one end, very close to the audience. The crowd practically breathed down a soloist's neck. Since the time when Mendelssohn occupied the podium and made Leipzig the musical capital of Germany, to have a success at the Gewandhaus was by definition to have arrived.[61]

A number of people showed up for the first rehearsal of the concerto, but there were none of the usual smatterings of applause. For the second rehearsal nobody at all came, and the orchestra remained stone-faced throughout. Conductor Julius Rietz had no liking for the piece, and after the concert said so.

As Brahms arrived for the performance on January 27 he hoped to find Clara there, but she had not come. The concert began and he waited through the opening pieces, anxiously looking for her in the hall. When his turn came he stepped onto the platform to polite applause. The conductor raised his baton; the ominous low D filled the hall. Brahms sat through his orchestral introduction which seemed longer than ever, trying to subdue his nerves. He began the first solo and the chains of thirds fell into place; he was playing well. With his mind on his job, he went through the first movement pleased at how the piece was going from all of them.

In those days audiences customarily applauded between movements, and sometimes called for an immediate encore. After the first movement there was a resounding silence. After the adagio, the same. When the finale had raced to its end and Brahms sat waiting at the piano, from the hall he heard three pairs of hands tentatively brought together, their hollow echo followed by an explosion of hisses. It was then that Brahms realized he had a nightmare fiasco on his hands. Trembling, he rose amid that wave of repudiation, bowed curtly, shook the conductor's hand, and retreated from the stage with what dignity he could muster. The hisses followed him like furies.

Next day he wrote a chipper report about it to Joachim. Was it an attempt at deception, or self-deception? Surely Brahms knew the anguish between the lines would be transparent to a friend and fellow performer.

Although I am still quite dazed by the sublime delights with which my eyes and ears have been assailed for the last few days through the sight and sound of the wise men of our musical town, I will force this hard and pointed steel pen of Sahr's to relate to you how it came about that my Concerto has experienced here a brilliant and decisive—failure.

First of all I must say that it was really done very well; I played far
better than I did at Hanover, and the orchestra was excellent. . . . [He
describes the silence, the hissing.] Not a soul has said a word to me
about the work!—with the exception of [concertmaster] David, who
took a great interest in it, and was very kind. . . .

The failure has made no impression whatever on me. . . . I believe
this is the best thing that could happen to one; it forces one to concentrate one's thoughts and increases one's courage. After all, I'm only
experimenting and feeling my way as yet. But the hissing was too much
of a good thing, wasn't it?[62]

He knew that his concerto was bound to be difficult and unappealing
to mainstream tastes on first hearing, and it still had formal and orches-
trational lapses that made it harder to grasp than it needed to be. He
knew all about that. He also knew that the reception had only partly to
do with this particular piece. Since Schumann's "Neue Bahnen," Leipzig
conservatives had looked on him as a threat to their idol Mendelssohn,
and this concerto—at least the first movement—was as un-Mendelssohn-
ian as possible. Now the conservatives had their revenge. The *Signale*
critic spelled out the party line:

New works do not succeed in Leipzig. Again at the fourteenth
Gewandhaus concert a composition was borne to its grave. This
work . . . cannot give pleasure. Save its serious intention, it has nothing to offer but waste, barren dreariness. . . . For more than three-
quarters of an hour one must endure this rooting and rummaging, this
dragging and drawing, this tearing and patching of phrases and flour-
ishes! Not only must one take in this fermenting mass; one must also
swallow a dessert of the shrillest dissonances and most unpleasant
sounds.[63]

If that were not depressing enough, Brahms discovered that one faction was pleased about the programmatic impact of the opening and in
some degree ready to embrace his concerto—Liszt's circle. The *Neue
Zeitschrift für Music* critic wrote, "Notwithstanding its undeniable want
of outward effect, we regard the poetic contents of the concerto as an unmistakable sign of significant and original creative power; and, in light of
the belittling criticism of a certain portion of the public and press, we
consider it our duty to insist on the admirable sides of the work."[64] It was
the ultimate humiliation: his best review came from the enemy, who
claimed his concerto as a blow for their cause. If soldiers of the New Ger-

man School hoped to recruit Brahms, however, he was not going to sign up. Liszt was in town that week to confer with *Neue Zeitschrift* editor Brendel. Brahms pointedly avoided both of them.

He continued to revise the piece after the first performances. Clara wrote in August 1859, "I like the alterations in the concerto, though on the sudden transition to D major after being in F♯ minor so long, in the third solo, is not quite to my mind; but that is a trifle compared with the wonderful beauty of the whole. [That and the Serenade] have given me hours of such joy as only music can give." She went on to recommend Theodor Kirchner's Preludes to Johannes.[65]

SO AFTER THE DEBACLE Brahms wrote his unruffled letters about it to Joachim and to Clara ("You have probably heard it was a complete frost."[66]). There was another letter in the wake of the disaster, short and apparently flippant too, but terrible in its effect: the one to Agathe von Siebold.

Years later, Brahms spoke about this time to his friend George Henschel. Though he did not name an occasion, he was thinking of a particular face and voice, a particular betrayal:

> At the time I should have liked to marry, my music was either hissed in the concert hall, or at least received with icy coldness. Now for myself, I could bear that quite well, because I knew its worth, and that some day the tables would be turned. And when, after such failures, I entered my lonely room I was not unhappy. On the contrary! But if, in such moments, I had had to meet the anxious, questioning eyes of a wife with the words "another failure"—I could not have borne that! For a woman may love an artist . . . ever so much . . . still she cannot have the perfect certainty of victory which is in his heart. And if she had wanted to comfort me—a wife to pity her husband for his lack of success—ach! I can't stand to think what a hell that would have been.[67]

The fiasco in Leipzig showed Brahms in stark terms where he stood: only a musician, adrift, with talent to spare but no dependable income and few saleable pieces. He saw he was going to be a vagabond still, for who knew how long, living with his parents when he was not on the road. He could not imagine how he could support a family on his earnings without compromises that threatened his work. That he must not allow. And above that dreary ostinato of the quotidian, the siren call of freedom and independence sang in his mind.

After Leipzig, the balance tilted for him. Brahms wrote the letter to Agathe that nearly destroyed her. He may even have considered the way he did it gallant. In fact, it may have been the ugliest gesture of his life. The only echo that survives of it is this:

> I love you! I must see you again! But I cannot wear fetters! Write to me, whether I am to come back, to take you in my arms, to kiss you and tell you that I love you.

That essentially says *I will romance you, sleep with you, but will not marry you.*[68] Agathe was not the kind of woman you said that to. In his letter, if that was all there was to it, she found no trace of explanation, empathy, or regret.

Of course, both of them burned their letters. Near the end of her life Agathe wrote a small, sad, forgiving novel about their relationship, quoting those words to her. In the book, after she receives his letter "the girl fought a hard battle, the hardest of her life. Love would have held him at any price, come what would. Duty and honor counselled renunciation; and duty and honor won."[69] She wrote Johannes breaking it off, returned his ring, never saw him again.

Brahms appeared to skip away from the business unscathed, but he did not. Her letter woke him up to what he had done. He told a friend, "I've played the scoundrel toward Agathe."[70] Julius Grimm and his wife broke off relations, in disgust. None of them were ever quite the same again, quite as innocent. There were no more youthful summers like the one past. The Grimms' first child had been christened Johannes; the first girl would be Agathe. After several empty and aimless years, Agathe von Siebold left Göttingen, to get away from the memories. Ten years after the break with Brahms she found a happy marriage, but her novel shows that the pain endured.

We see Brahms mourning in his songs, as earlier they had voiced his joy. The ones for Agathe were full of love and summer: in Opus 19, "You kiss me as we part, I press you to my breast!" In the next set of lieder, in no. 2 of Opus 32, we hear some of the bleakest pages he ever penned, G. F. Daumer's lyrics set to a sinking, keening, gasping melodic line:

> *I decided not to go to you any more,*
> *and I swore it,*
> *and I go every evening,*
> *because I have lost all my strength and all my steadfastness.*

I would like to stop living,
wish in this moment to expire.

We hear in no. 4 of that set:

Where is the rose my loved one wore on her heart,
and that kiss which intoxicated me, where is it now?

And that man I used to be
for whom I have long since substituted a different self, where is
  he now?

Then, in the next song of Opus 32, we hear Brahms's answer, his cry of freedom and prophecy of triumph in a surging allegro:

Alas, you want to hold me fast again, you impeding fetters?
Up and out into the air!
Let my soul's desiring flow forth in thundering songs, breathing
  ethereal fragrance!

For Agathe, renunciation won the battle; for Brahms, once more, smashing the fetters. Both of them were devastated. From then on, in his lieder Brahms sang more of love lost than won. But only after five years did he write the songs of Opus 32 and there say his true farewell to Agathe—after callous words and sad songs, ravishing music for strings.

CHAPTER NINE

Rebirth

AT THE END OF MARCH 1859, Brahms had two extraordinary concerts at home, the first featuring the D Minor Piano Concerto with the Hamburg Philharmonic, Joachim conducting. In Hamburg only ten years before, Brahms had debuted as a composer with the little "Fantasia on a Favorite Waltz." Now, on his next appearance in town as soloist and composer, he offered his immense and notorious concerto. After the debacle in Leipzig, Brahms was stunned to find some homegrown enthusiasm gathering around him. The concert was a sellout, with hundreds turned away. Directly afterward he wrote Clara that he, Joachim, and Julius Stockhausen (who contributed an aria) had all been encored and the reviews appreciative: "In short, the Leipzig critics have done no harm."[1]

A couple of days later the three friends presented a program including Tartini's virtuosic "Devil's Trill" Sonata from Joachim, Schubert and Schumann lieder from Stockhausen, and the small-orchestra version of the D Major Serenade. Rehearsals and concert in the small hall were again packed, and the audience applauded everything warmly. "You would not have recognized the people of Hamburg," Brahms wrote Clara.[2] Receipts from the concerts turned out inspiring too, and in his euphoria Brahms proposed giving the Serenade a try in Leipzig.[3]

Clara replied from Dresden. She had been brooding about the debacle with the concerto and wrote him: "If I were you I would not move a finger to let Leipzig hear another note from you. The day will come when they will clamor to hear you. Overjoyed as I would be to hear the Serenade I would rather forgo this pleasure than have you produce it before such an unfriendly audience. You must strike Leipzig out of your map—this much pride you must and can have." She reported that out of duty—Wagner had been flattering her lately—she had gone to see *Lohengrin* in Vienna and "could see only too well how such an opera succeeds. . . . The whole thing is full of romanticism and thrilling situations, so much so indeed that even the musician himself at times forgets the horrible music. Nevertheless, on the whole, I like *Lohengrin* better than I do *Tannhaüser,* in which Wagner goes through the whole gamut of abominations."[4]

Brahms, not well acquainted with the operas yet but ready to countenance Wagner up to a point, took care not to interfere with Clara's disgust. However he respected Wagner's craft and imagination, he usually allowed his friends to flay the competition unimpeded. Of course, at that point Brahms was no rival at all to Wagner or to Liszt. His reputation in the greater musical world still went hardly beyond Schumann's "Neue Bahnen." A potential challenger to those revolutionaries he certainly was, and no doubt he planned to become one in fact. As part of that ambition he was working himself up to a fight. This year he wrote Joachim, "My fingers often itch to do battle, to begin to write anti-Liszt."[5]

WITH HIS LARGEST PUBLIC SUCCESS filling his confidence and his pockets—and in Hamburg, of all places—Brahms still had no compelling sense of where to go or what to do, either in his composing or his career as a soloist. The new A Major Serenade in progress pleased him, but he knew it represented no real direction. As he tarried in limbo, once again luck lent him a hand.

Shortly after the Hamburg concerts, at a rehearsal of the women's contingent of his Akademie choir, conductor and Brahms friend Karl Grädener asked the ladies if they would like to perform something by Brahms. To the conductor's surprise the whole alto section jumped to their feet. Some of the choristers had been singing Brahms's folk song arrangements with Friedchen Wagner and her sisters; more had been among the admiring crowds at the recent concerts.

In the middle of May, Grädener pupil Jenny von Ahsen was to be married at St. Michael's, with the Akademie women singing for the ceremony. Brahms offered to play organ for the wedding. That day, as he listened to the women's voices spin through the church, his imagination spun a fantasy of those voices in the *Ave Maria* he had composed at Detmold, and other things he might write for them. Presumably he knew about Grädener's plan to sing something of his, but he preferred to handle it himself, and Grädener approved. Brahms asked Friedchen Wagner to see if any acquaintances in the Akademie and elsewhere might be interested.

On June 6, twenty-eight women turned up for the first rehearsal at Friedchen's house, along with Karl Grädener, Theodor Avé-Lallemant, and other local lights. Brahms was so befuddled at the crowd of eager young women that Grädener had to calm him down before he could start the rehearsal. Finally Brahms led them through his *Ave Maria* and two new neo-Renaissance sacred choruses, *O bone Jesu* and *Adoramus te* (they would appear in Opus 37). Two days later, after another rehearsal, the choir presented the three pieces at a private performance in St. Peter's.[6]

Brahms followed that experiment with a proposal for meetings on Monday mornings, the repertoire to be varied but including his own things. The women agreed immediately. Thus began the Hamburg Frauenchor, the women's chorus that occupied him for much of the next three years.

By the end of that June 1859, Brahms had begun a new set of pieces for the choir with the first two of the eventual six *Marienlieder*, settings of folktales of the Virgin in a style as lilting, sweet, and ingenuously folklike as the verses. Most striking of them, in music and lyrics, is *Marias Kirchgang*:

> *When Mary once to church would go*
> *She fain would cross a deep, wide sea.*
> *And as she reached the waters' flow*
> *A boatman there she chanced to see.*
> *"Oh boatman safely ferry me*
> *What e'er thou ask I'll give to thee."*
> *"I'll bear thee safely over the sea,*
> *If thou wilt come and marry me."*
> *"Before I deign to marry thee,*
> *I'll swim alone across the sea."*
> *Now as she neared the other side,*
> *The church bells rang out far and wide,*
> *Both large and small, with one accord*
> *Proclaimed the Mother of our Lord.*
> *And when the shore they did regain,*
> *The boatman's heart was broke in twain.*

The singers soon grew to about forty, including daughters of Avé-Lallemant and Grädener.[7] Some of them also belonged to a select choir, a dozen or so of Friedchen's friends who met with Brahms in the evening.

A solo quartet of women worked further with him.[8] Naturally he developed crushes on several of these young women, and they of course the same with him. To his sister Elise, Brahms took to calling Laura Garbe, of the quartet, "your future sister-in-law."

Another favorite was little Bertha Porubzsky, visiting from Vienna with an aunt in Hamburg. From a distance, Brahms had observed Bertha's Viennese ebullience, so different from the starched North German women he was used to. Whether as a joke or in earnest, he went literally down on his knees before Frau Grädener to beg for an introduction to this vision. The good lady obliged and, for a while, Brahms got another voice for his choir and another girl to dream about. As much as anything Bertha diverted him with her renditions of Austrian folk songs. He wrote Joachim that after hearing them, "Vienna, which is after all the musician's holy city, has taken on for me a double magic."[9] Bertha's songs would be one of the things that finally drew Brahms to music's city.

He was hardly less fond of the solo quartet—Betty and Marie Völkers, and Marie Reuter along with Laura Garbe. The Frauenchor and its subsidiaries had some of their rehearsals and parties at the house of the Völker sisters, in the country suburb of Hamm. In later life in Vienna, Brahms had with him a photograph of the quartet. Elise, who stayed close to several choristers, kept him posted on them. The time with Brahms marked these women too; of the quartet, only the Völker sisters ever married—Marie, years later.[10] Some of the singers closest to him seemed to share a sense that to have had Brahms, even if only in music and probably unspoken affection, could not be matched by anything less in their lives.

He set up the Frauenchor with a motto—*Fix oder Nix*, "Up to the mark or nothing"—and got to work composing for them. The music came out mostly light, beautiful, pure as a Palestrina motet but with Brahmsian colorations. Here he found the practical experience he needed in writing choral music, and in conducting. Besides his own pieces, which the girls copied into part-books decorated with elaborate drawings, he indulged his passion for older music. In their three years under his direction the women sang music by Bach, Handel, William Byrd, Hans Leo Hassler, Heinrich Isaac, Palestrina, and other Renaissance and Baroque masters.[11] In his own works for the Frauenchor, Brahms donned his Renaissance and *volkstümlich* (national/folkish) masks, as in his organ fugues he had composed wearing his own style of Baroque wig. He possessed the gift of commandeering history without giving up his temperament, his particular musicality. (He has that in common with Stravinsky, equally himself as neoprimitive and neo-classicist.)

With the slight, atavistic period pieces of the later 1850s and early 1860s, Brahms did more than pass the time and sharpen his craft. As with the contrapuntal studies, the Renaissance and Baroque and *volkstümlich* experiments of those years helped free him from the burden of personal reference in his work. In that respect the choir was a signpost pointing toward his mature music.

In his full maturity, Brahms would largely pull back from Schumann-style symbolism. He had discovered that autobiography could only take him so far, to a point of technical or aesthetic uncertainty. Young Kreisler's passion and suffering, and the Schumanns', gave him the first two movements of the D Minor Concerto, three movements of a C♯ minor piano quartet, perhaps the B Major Trio, some lieder and smaller pieces, perhaps the first movement of a symphony in C minor (if he began it then). In turn, that music helped him put his feelings to rest. The trouble was that symbolism and psychodrama could not teach him orchestration, could not give him a finale for a piece when he was unsure how to approach a last movement. Likewise, E. T. A. Hoffmann may have inspired the quartet in C♯ minor, but that was no help when Joachim pointed out, after a couple of readings of the piece, how awkward that key is for strings. In pursuit of the perfection he demanded of his work, Brahms was to conclude that only craftsmanship and patient labor could address problems like those.

So the masks of Renaissance contrapuntist and Baroque Kapellmeister helped deliver him from reliance on autobiography, though the weighty events of his life would always find an echo in his work. In going beyond autobiography, he developed an interior dialectic between a composer born to Romanticism and (another mask) a willful Classicist. Eventually four centuries of Western music, from Palestrina to Schumann and even Wagner, became part of Brahms's persona, the masks overlapping and blending as in a Hoffmann story. What else could he do if, as he confessed to Clara, he had perennial difficulty getting music to flow from his heart?

In his maturity, Brahms had at his command an unprecedented historical eclecticism, to go with the wide-ranging skills he had taught himself. He would carry off that eclecticism so impeccably that it almost—almost—obliterates the question: where do the masks stop, and Brahms begin? As in so many other things, in his extraordinary self-consciousness Brahms might not have posed the question that way, but he was chronically aware of it. Part of his singular solutions to that dilemma began with the Hamburg Frauenchor.

IN AUGUST Brahms wrote Clara, "Tomorrow my girls are rehearsing a psalm [the thirteenth] which I have composed for them. I wrote it in the evening a week ago last Sunday, and it kept me happy until midnight. . . . I feel more and more convinced that you are my friend and the thought fills me with the greatest joy. To think it has become a necessity of my life!"[12] (This was scant affection after what they had been through.) Brahms was unaffectedly dazzled by the feminine companionship and admiration he got from the Frauenchor. If they were enthralled by him, he felt similarly about them. As he explained to Joachim, he was not taking an excursion to the country this summer because "a little singing society (ladies only) detains me. Otherwise, I would have been on the Rhine or in some beautiful forest."[13]

Like any number of choristers, Franziska Meier had a crush on Brahms, and for all the reticence of the time when it came to such things, her girlish passion left traces in her diary. After the March 28 concert in Hamburg, Franziska wrote rapturously, "I spent an almost sleepless night during which I wrote in my diary, made poetry and drew sketches of Joachim and Brahms."[14] He sometimes played piano for the girls and their visitors after the rehearsal. Franziska wrote of one occasion in her diary:

After our poor director had worked so hard to beat these new things into us, he was besieged by Mme. Peterson to play something for us! He has the reputation of being unaccommodating, proud, arrogant, and disagreeable. O, how can one wrong a person like that? He played some [Schumann] Kreisleriana which . . . he had not played for a long time. The poor man—when he made a mistake, he blushed purple, made an angry face, and shook his head. (30-1)

In September, Brahms showed up at Franziska's house to retrieve some music she had taken to copy into her part-book. She swooned.

I could hardly believe my eyes . . . I asked him to come in and speak to my parents but he looked around the corner and said: "I have not a moment's time." He hunted in the dark with me for the music on the piano, and then he hurried quickly away. But the goblets of bliss were

spilled, the fair fruits scattered and night was darkening round about.
(33)

The Frauenchor rehearsed through late summer toward a September 19 performance at St. Peter's, for invited guests, of *Psalm 13* and some of the *Marienlieder*. In one of the last rehearsals the girls offered their conductor an honorarium they had collected. He turned the money down, saying he had enjoyed the work so much that money would only ruin it. In a preconcert rehearsal at the church, there were problems coordinating organ and choir. Franziska watched Brahms turn white as chalk and clench his fist to try and calm himself. (37) They decided to sing from the organ loft, from where the performance came off splendidly for a large audience.

At the end, everyone gathered around Johann Jakob and Christiane Brahms and Elise, who basked in reflected glory as they had been doing for years now. At a repeat performance a week later the girls wore black, they announced, in mourning at losing their conductor to Detmold for the winter. This time the pieces went badly, which did not seem to disturb Brahms at all. Afterward a crowd collected in the loft. When he asked what was going on, he was told that a lady was being shown how to pump the wind chest of the organ. Brahms had a look and the choir heard him exclaim, "Oh God, it's my sister!" (41)

Soon after he reached Detmold, Brahms received a silver inkstand buried in a wreath of flowers and inscribed, "In memory of the summer of '59 from the girls' choir." He responded chivalrously to Friedchen Wagner:

> Esteemed Fräulein . . . I have done so little to deserve it that I would be ashamed if I did not hope to compose a lot more music for you with it; and really more beautiful tones will resound about me when I see on my writing desk this lovely and beautiful gift. / Will you give my heartiest greetings and thanks to all those you are able to reach. / Seldom has a more pleasant joy come to me and, indeed, our gatherings will always be to me one of my favorite recollections. But not, I hope, till later years! (42)

To Clara he wrote more directly, "Oh, my dear girls, where are you now . . . On Monday in the church, what a touching farewell it was! . . . I am becoming something of a cult in Hamburg. But I don't think that can do any harm. In any case I am writing with ever more zest, and there are signs in me which suggest that in time I may produce heavenly things."¹⁵ The women had stirred him, he had fallen for several of them—and as if to illustrate a future psychological theory, he apparently had not seduced any of them. As Freud would have it, Brahms sublimated his libido into music, some of it indeed heavenly.

Certainly it is conceivable that Brahms had an affair with one or more of his Frauenchor singers, but if so, everyone concerned was remarkably discreet about it. In fact one finds no real record of Brahms ever having more than a Platonic connection to any "respectable" woman. An exception may be in March 1858, when Joachim wrote him teasingly from Hanover that a certain Fräulein, "an enthusiastic friend of your artistry, is here and greets you." Brahms replied, for once, like a proper young rascal: "Don't be seduced by the bosom of her dress; she herself hasn't got one."¹⁶ From the perspective of a later time it is hard to imagine that so famous and lusty a man as Brahms was never intimate with anyone but prostitutes, but in later years he said as much. He fell in love with virgins real or imagined, he bedded with whores. If there were exceptions to that, he managed to obliterate them from the record as effectively as his rejected pieces.

During the 1859 season at Detmold, Brahms finished the A Major Serenade, the opening numbers of the Opus 42, Three Songs for Mixed Chorus, and the Opus 31, Three Quartets—the vocal pieces intended for the kind of sociable music-making that the Frauenchor and its smaller units exemplified. Meanwhile, he wrote Bertha Porubzsky charming and affectionate letters: "Shall I send songs? Gay, fresh little songs. I would like to give them directly to you, if you wish." In the same letter he noted, almost in the tone he used with Clara and Joachim, his sorrow at the death of Ludwig Spohr. Now remembered as a minor and pedestrian composer, to Brahms Spohr appeared "probably the last of those who still belonged to an artistic period more satisfying than the one through which we now suffer. . . . At no time has any art been so mistreated as is now our beloved music. Let us hope that somewhere in obscurity something better is emerging, for otherwise our epoch would go down in the annals of art as a manure pit.¹⁷ (The ripest manure, of course, Liszt and his disciples.)

Bertha's Hamburg auntie kept a close eye on these exchanges. To her niece she sternly quoted Goethe's famous lines from "Trost in Thränen," which the previous year Brahms had set so memorably: "One does not crave to own the stars, but loves their glorious light." Soon Bertha Porubzsky returned to Vienna, another singing girl Brahms allowed to escape, stayed loyal to in his fashion, and commemorated in song.

Clara responded with extravagant praise and small caveats to the new choral pieces and the movements of the A Major Serenade. She sat with the adagio of the serenade, playing her favorite moments over and over. Perhaps hours like those alone with Johannes's new works, lavishing her heart and craft on them for her own pleasure, were the most profound experiences Clara had with his music. She felt, on the whole justifiably in those years, that Johannes composed for her first and the rest of the world after. Given the kind of people they were, with their ideals, a physical connection could not have meant more to either of them than that kind of communion.

For his part, Johannes was no less pampered on his third visit to the court of Detmold, but he felt more bored than ever with the stilted atmosphere and dusty finery, the aristocratic aesthetes who were his students, the chorus of Highnesses and Excellencies and their friends who could barely sing the Bach and Handel he gave them. Probably the most enjoyable part of this sojourn was a couple of days that began with a visit from Theodor Avé-Lallemant. As Brahms and Avé returned from a walk in the woods with Bargheer, they found a boisterous Joachim waiting in Johannes's room at Zur Stadt Frankfurt. He was fresh from a tour of England with his new Hungarian Concerto in hand, looking for advice. All that night they happily worked over the piece together.

With his Detmold students Brahms had become curt and snappish, among other faux pas managing to drive away Frau Hofmarschall Meysenbug after a few lessons. Only the genuinely talented Princess Frederike engaged his interest. He pressed the prince to let him conduct the orchestra more, but Leopold resisted in deference to Kapellmeister Kiel, who after some spats over concertos was no admirer of Brahms.

All the same, his creative elation lasted through the Detmold sojourn. Since "Neue Bahnen" he had been awaiting a creative rebirth. In fact it had not quite happened yet, but with the inspiration of various muses— Clara and the singing girls in Hamburg—and his own patient years of waiting and study, he could sense something gathering inside him. After the emotional torments of the last years had sorted out in his creative consciousness, a rebirth would take shape, fueled by the talent that everyone had seen in him from the beginning.

When he received more kind words from Clara about his new pieces he gushed again, "I don't mind saying that I am very much pleased with my things. I really believe, dear Clara, that I am growing . . . how delightful it is to work with buoyancy and strength, and to know that you and others are showing such keen interest. . . . I long for nothing more than to have my things performed."[18]

BRAHMS GOT LEAVE from the Detmold court to play a December concert in Hamburg with Grädener's Akademie. It featured the premieres of the *Begräbnisgesang* and the *Ave Maria* in his orchestral arrangement, and Brahms soloed in the Schumann Piano Concerto. His Frauenchor also sang in the program. This amounted to their public debut and one of their few appearances in mainstream concerts—in those days a rare event for any women's chorus. Most of the Frauenchor performances were in private houses and churches; there was an air of unseemliness about the idea of respectable young women singing on the concert stage.[19]

As a stopover on the return to Detmold, Brahms spent a day in Hanover with Julius Otto Grimm, who was ready now to end their estrangement over Agathe. The reunion had been engineered by Joachim. After all, Brahms agreed with everybody that his treatment of Agathe had been shameful. Grimm was happy to perform the new choral pieces Johannes had brought with him from Hamburg. Relieved to be back in the good graces of this influential conductor, Johannes made haste to supply Grimm with material.

His creative wave continued to rise at Detmold. He produced vocal works including several of the Opus 44 Twelve Songs and Romances for four women's voices—another testament to his solo quartet back home— and some of the choruses of Opus 62. And around then he began the piece that would herald his early maturity in chamber music, the B♭ Major String Sextet.

At the end of 1859, Joachim wrote Clara, more enthusiastically than accurately, "Johannes has sent me the greater part of his Serenade instrumentated; most of it is just as though he had never had anything else to deal with but the orchestra. Well, he was born with it, of course!"[20] (The labors of the past years showed that Brahms was hardly born with an instinct for instrumentation.) In January, back home in Hamburg, he wrote Joachim what he was doing for inspiration: "I let a dozen girls sing old German songs to me. I keep them constantly at it."[21]

For the first time in years he had a little sustained creative momentum going, and after four years of publishing nothing he was ready to issue new work. Clara would be relieved to stop explaining to everyone why Johannes was not producing anything. The following August Prince Leopold's invitation for another season at Detmold would receive a brisk refusal, Brahms citing the pressure of impending publications.[22] He was too busy composing now to take on jobs just for the money. When he needed it, there was always performing.

Not surprisingly, 1860 saw one of his great outpourings of vocal music, much of it written for his circle of women in Hamburg. The music also includes mixed choruses, probably directed to Grimm's choir, among them the two intricately polyphonic motets of Opus 29. Some of this music amounts to Brahmsian *Gebrauchsmusik*, the German term for occasional pieces written for practical purposes, but none of it is tossed off. Only in his teens did Brahms produce true potboilers, and even at that age he would not put his name on them.

Though his heart remained with his choristers, at the beginning of the year the main excitement concerned back-to-back premieres of his two serenades, the D Major and the A Major. Joachim read over the Second Serenade, the A Major, in January and Brahms felt reassured by what he heard. Then on February 10 he had another great day in his hometown, premiering the A Major Serenade with the Philharmonic under his own baton, and as soloist played the Schumann concerto. On the program Joachim contributed the Beethoven Violin Concerto and the Tartini "Devil's Trill." Then on March 3, Joachim took the podium in Hanover to premiere the D Major Serenade.

BRAHMS FELT TOO PLEASED with both serenades to hold them back, but even if his path was still uncertain he knew they were orchestration exercises, *Kapellmeistermusik* of no great consequence nor aspiring to be. He would not give them the exalted name of *symphony*. Yet they endure in the context of Brahms's later and greater music as stretches of fresh air. For modern listeners the serenades are a gemütlich respite from the expressive intensity and formal complexity of so much Brahms. Where else did he find the rustic gaiety that opens the D Major, the charm of the scherzo in the A Major? He never again allowed himself to be quite so unbuttoned in orchestral music; only in the 1880 Academic Festival Overture did he come close. Otherwise the tone in his later orchestral music would be largely sober and monumental, as he believed symphonic music ought to be. In contrast, the serenades resound with the spirit of his youth, the Romantically ancient atmosphere of Detmold and the Teutoburger Wald, and echoes of Haydn and Mozart.

In the D Major, Brahms begins to integrate his studies, reaching toward an unprecedented kind of historical eclecticism. We hear that in the first measures of the First Serenade, the D Major, in the bagpipe drone and pealing hunting-horn tune that starts the first movement. The music is tuneful, Haydnesque in Papa Haydn's folksy vein, as Brahms underscored with the archaic menuettos that make up the fourth movement. At the same time, the effect and style of the music also recall the Baroque suite. The forms are the familiar Classical models of sonata, rondo, scherzo, and the like. One after another for nearly an hour they unfold at a leisurely pastoral pace, without undue surprises. Inside the breezy opening allegro and the closing playful rondo are a pair of scherzos (one subdued, one brash), inside those a long adagio (awkwardly long, transparently recalling Beethoven's *Pastoral* Symphony) and the minuets.

To a later age the D Major speaks differently than when it was first heard, by people who had no experience of Brahms's orchestral music except, if anything, the problematic D Minor Piano Concerto. If it were not for the defining frame of the rest of Brahms's orchestral music the First Serenade would be a period piece—cheerful, inconsequential, and likely forgotten. Through time it has grown and deepened because it is by Brahms; as such, it would inspire later composers, including Dvořák. As a blurry youthful portrait of the artist, studiously ingenuous, self-limited, unassuming, the D Major manages to be enchanting.

Its charm was opaque, however, to some of the first listeners. Soon after the Hanover premiere, Joachim received a letter from a concertgoer: "Brahms's Serenade is a monstrosity, a caricature, a freak, which should never have been published, much less performed *here:* we say here, whilst the piano concerto served up to us last winter still sticks in our throats! It is inexcusable that such filth should have been offered to a public thirsting for good music." Joachim's employers, the king and queen, quite liked the serenade, he reported to Clara, but as for "the public— rather amusing, to use no harsher word."[23] The livid letter-writer heard the Serenade through the distorting prism of the Piano Concerto; despising that, he felt obliged to deplore the other.

The Second Serenade, in A Major, has more expressive and contrapuntal depth, greater concentration and intimacy, a more unfettered treatment of form than the First. (None of which is to say it is more entertaining.) There are five movements this time, a scherzo and menuetto flanking the striking central adagio. The choice of instruments is novel in concept, if not particularly in orchestral sonority: no trumpets and no violins, only pairs of woodwinds and horns, violas, cellos, and basses. Though sometimes the viola part stands in for violins on the melody, the real point is to give the bulk of the melodic material to the winds. If the tone of the music is generally more sober and introspective than the D Major, Brahms compensates with one of his most vivacious scherzos.

In both serenades there are awkward patches in the scoring, but the instrumentation still manages to be effective, sparkling when it needs to be, also noncommittal and anonymous. In his melodies and harmonies and textures and rhythms, Brahms had possessed a singular personality from the time of the piano sonatas in the early 1850s. If by the end of that decade he had brought his orchestration to a point of professional competence, his orchestral voice had yet to find a definable accent. Thus the startling thing about the serenades: while Brahms's first surviving piano music sounds conspicuously Brahmsian, his first purely orchestral works are far less so.

There may lie a prime reason for the fourteen years it took Brahms to issue his next piece for orchestra. With his implacable patience, he waited until he had found a voice with instruments as distinctive as everything else in his work. And as it has been with too few artists, the fates granted him the lavish endowment of time he needed for that to develop. Time always treated Brahms kindly. Even in the happenstance of a month and year for his death, he would be lucky.

THE AGREEABLE EXPERIENCE of delivering the serenades into the world preceded, by a reliable Brahmsian rhythm, a burst of ill humor. This one, however, was not visited privately on friends but was public and historic.

As he had observed to Joachim and probably others, by 1860 Brahms was itching "to write anti-Liszt." Joachim, having made public his break with his old mentor, was ready now to swing a sword alongside Johannes. Together they had been stewing over Liszt's sensationalism, his rambling and histrionic music, the credo of the New German School that music required other arts to buttress it. It was the last-named above all that insulted the friends' faith in "absolute" music, in forms and tonal patterns crafted powerfully enough to stand on their own. To them, the New German agenda was the death of music as they understood it.

Finally, their hatred for the Music of the Future took the form of a manifesto, cooked up during Brahms's stay in Hanover after the Serenade performance. To be published with as many and as imposing signatures as they could round up, the text proposed to refute the New Germans' claims of final victory, and to rouse the opposition. As Joachim wrote to compatriot Robert Franz with an entreaty to sign on: "I, friend Brahms, and several others have lately discussed the evil influence exercised by the 'New Germans' . . . who, in their vanity and arrogance, regard everything great and sacred which the musical talent of our people has created up to now as mere fertilizer for the rank, miserable weeds growing from *Liszt*-like fantasias." While Franz refused to sign, a number of musicians would agree to—but only after a fatal slip.

It has never been clear whether Brahms or Joachim had the larger hand in drafting the manifesto, but it articulated a mutual sentiment: the swindlers are trying to take over the shop, and it is time to expose them.

> The undersigned have long followed with regret the proceedings of a certain party whose organ is Brendel's *Zeitschrift für Musik.* The said *Zeitschrift* unceasingly promulgates the theory that the most prominent striving musicians are in accord with the aims represented in its pages, that they recognize in the compositions of the leaders of the New School works of artistic value, and that the contention for and against the so-called Music of the Future has been finally fought out, especially in North Germany, and decided in its favor. The undersigned regard it as their duty to protest against such a distortion of fact, and declare, at least for their own part, that they do not acknowledge the principles avowed by the *Zeitschrift*, and that they can only lament and condemn the productions of the leaders and pupils of the so-called New German School, which . . . necessitate the constant setting up of new and outlandish theories contrary to the very nature of music.[24]

Though it is not clear in the article—they should have made it clear— their main target was Liszt and the Music of the Future propaganda machine, not Wagner in his capacity as an opera composer. Propaganda was a formidable presence in the age's musical life. Critic Eduard Hanslick wrote in 1862, "Liszt's and Wagner's compositions have the force of military commands. As soon as any work by one of these gentlemen appears, a small literature of explanatory articles, brochures, etc. follows in its footsteps."[25] Much as Brahms and Joachim hated Liszt's music, they hated his influence more—the stream of literature emanating from Weimar that decreed program music and the Wagnerian Total Work of Art to be the only authentic path to the future. For the friends, as for Hanslick, that agenda threatened to turn most music written for the concert hall into formless fantasias. (And in their terms, that is exactly what had happened by the end of the nineteenth century.)

In contrast to the galvanizing elements in most feuds—power and money—this one was largely aesthetic and intellectual, at least on the side of the aggressors. After all, Joachim had found about as much success as is possible for a musician, and Liszt had been one of the people responsible for that. If Brahms did not command the kind of fees Joachim did, he was doing well enough by his own lights. As far as they were concerned, the battle was not for glory or money, but for the soul of music.

Their attack aimed to contain the spread of ideas they believed could taint not only the future but the past. Wagner had declared the work of Bach, Mozart, Haydn, and Beethoven superseded by the new music that, directly or symbolically, incorporated the Word. Wagner wrote: "These tone-mechanical, contrapuntal pieces of art handiwork were altogether incapable of filling a *spiritual need.*" Beethoven, said Wagner, discovered the Word in the choral music of the Ninth, and thereby wrote the last symphony, "the redemption of Music from out of her own peculiar element into the realm of *universal art.* . . . Beyond it no forward step is possible; for upon it the perfect artwork of the future alone can follow, the *universal drama* for which Beethoven has forged for us the key."[26] In other words, the only logical, perfect, indeed ethical future of music was Wagner's own concept of music drama, his *Gesamtkunstwerk*, Total Work of Art—or, in the concert hall, program music in the vein of Berlioz and Liszt. For Wagner, the ultimate meaning and value of Beethoven was that he paved the way for Wagner.

As far as Brahms was concerned most of Wagner's writings, which presaged similar tracts from generations of artists to come, were so much self-serving gobbledygook. Yet neither he nor Joachim was prepared to dismiss Wagner's operas as such, even while they considered his ideas, like Liszt's, lethal to impressionable minds. At that point probably neither of them had heard or studied the operas extensively. Brahms's acquaintance with Wagner's stage works was to be an endeavor of decades, which little by little grew into a strange, extravagant, but resolutely private admiration.

Liszt's writings, in fact mostly ghostwritten by his aristocratic mistress, were less categorical and dismissive of the past than Wagner's, but still he insisted that the future did not lie in "pure" music—what he called "the *posthumous* party"[27]—but in program music and the unity of the arts. Anything other than that was mere formalism, a shallow worship of the past: "The purely musical composer, who only values and emphasizes the formal working-out of his material, does not have the capacity to derive new formulations from it or to breathe new vigor into it. . . . The formalists . . . can do nothing better or more clever than to adopt, propagate, rearrange, and perhaps work over the others' hard-won achievements."[28]

From that one can discern the more pragmatic part of the agenda. In trying to claim the future for themselves and their heirs, Liszt and Wagner also attempted to save the musical present from the encroachments of the past. They understood what the growing worship of history and its formal procedures was leading to in the nineteenth century: concert halls dominated by the music of dead composers and their living epigones. With their music and with a gigantic theoretical and philosophical apparatus, Liszt and Wagner attempted to forestall that process, to keep the living composer in the forefront. The attempt proved a historic failure.

Much of the hatred Brahms and Joachim felt for Lisztean ideas rose from what became of program music when it percolated out among the petit-Liszts of the time—say, Joachim Raff, whose symphony *To My Fatherland* won a prestigious prize from the Vienna Gesellschaft der Musikfreunde in 1863. Raff supplied a brave program for his symphony:

First movement: Allegro. Image of the German Character: ability to soar to great heights; trend toward introspection; mildness and courage as contrasts that touch and interpenetrate in many ways; overwhelming desire to be pensive.
Second movement: Allegro molto vivace. The outdoors: through German forests with horns a-winding; through glades with the sounds of folk music.
Third movement: Larghetto. Return to the domestic hearth, transfigured by the muses and by love.
Fourth movement: Allegro drammatico. Frustrated desire to lay a foundation for unity in the Fatherland.
Fifth movement: Larghetto—allegro trionfale. Plaint, renewed soaring.[29]

In the 1860s, Raff stood among the most famous German symphonists, his work the Music of the Future à la mode. (Actually Brahms, perverse as always, had a certain fondness for Raff's music.) And in the future these ideas did triumph. In literary quality Raff's program may be sillier than the ones for Richard Strauss's later tone poems, but it is not so different in concept. It was that future Brahms and Joachim tried to obstruct with their meager manifesto. In that, they would fail as completely as Liszt and Wagner would in trying to keep living composers in the ascendancy. As Brahms and Joachim hoped, despite the steady presence of progressive composers and program music, in the concert hall the past became established as the unsurpassable foundation of the future.

But their manifesto, however noble in intention, came in too little and too late, and turned into a debacle. How it happened remains obscure. Brahms was distracted in those days by composing, by the Frauenchor, by a big concert at the end of March in which he conducted Grädener's orchestra accompanying Joachim in his newly revised Hungarian Concerto. The two had been careless about sending the manifesto around to prospective supporters—some emphatically rejected it, and one of these was apparently offended enough to sabotage it.

By whomever and for whatever reason, the manifesto was leaked to the Berlin *Echo* and/or the *Neue Zeitschrift für Musik* when it had only four names on it: Brahms, Joachim, Grimm, and their conductor friend Bernhard Scholz. As a result, a parody of the manifesto was published in the *Neue Zeitschrift* on May 4, 1860, actually two days before the leaked original, its pathetic four signatures huddling at the bottom, appeared in the *Echo*.

The *Zeitschrift* parody may have been ham-fisted ("All is *out!*—I learn that a political coup has been carried *out*, the entire future world rooted *out* stump and branch, and Weimar and Leipzig . . . struck *out* of the musical map of the world. . . ."), but it sufficiently called attention to how puny and small-minded the manifesto appeared. Brahms and Joachim had attempted to assault the mighty New German propaganda edifice with a thumb of the nose, and a careless one at that. Even after the manifesto finally collected a number of impressive names—among them Bargiel, Grädener, Theodor Kirchner, Niels Gade, and Clara Schumann—it could be nothing but a futile gesture.

The repercussions did relatively little to harm the careers of Brahms and Joachim, though it made them look plenty ridiculous. It did more damage to music itself. In those years music was more important, more powerful, more visible in the spectrum of Western art and culture than it had ever been before. In such a milieu factions are inevitable, but before the manifesto the parties had overlapped and sometimes cooperated: Liszt had once been a friend of Schumann and remained generous and broad-minded; Raff originally was a Mendelssohn protégé; Schumann had championed Berlioz; and Franz Brendel of the *Neue Zeitschrift* tried to keep channels open among all parties.

All the same, in 1859 Brendel had organized the twenty-fifth anniversary of the journal Robert Schumann had founded, and did not invite Brahms, Joachim, or Clara Schumann to the ceremonies.[30] If there had been skirmishes like that before the manifesto, after it a war raged: the War of the Romantics, one side lined up behind Liszt and Wagner (the unity of the arts, loosening the bonds of abstract form), the other side at length behind Brahms ("absolute music," traditional forms, and especially sonata form). The lines were drawn and defended with power struggles, propaganda, demonstrations, and sabotage. In the later stages of the war, both sides resorted to organizing cadres to disrupt the other side's concerts. Finally by the end of the century, the musical battles were subsumed into larger political tides.

The War of the Romantics was never an equal contest. The conservative faction was more inclined to stay home and study counterpoint than go out and man the barricades. Only in the concert hall did the conservatives win out. Naturally the party of dissent needed a leader and found one—but not Brahms himself, who after his thrashing over the manifesto retired from public musical politicking once and for all. It would be critic Eduard Hanslick, author of *Beauty in Music*, who became the tireless helmsman of the abstractionists.

For himself, in the six years before 1860 Brahms had experienced sufficient calamity and humiliation to sink most people, not to mention artists: the madness and death of Robert Schumann, the break with Clara, the fiasco of the D Minor Piano Concerto in Leipzig, the disaster of Agathe, the years of creative groping, now the embarrassment of the manifesto. After all that, his election as Messiah seemed little more than a hollow joke. He appeared fated to join Schumann's other ordained saviors in obscurity.

Clara chose an especially bad time to rub salt in his wounds. Nothing survives of what she thought of the Agathe business—nor much of what Brahms thought, for that matter. It is entirely possible that the two of them never really discussed it at all. But in February 1860, Clara wrote him, "I was very miserable in Cassel. I could not get poor Agathe, and many other things, out of my head. I kept on seeing the poor lonely girl. . . . Ah, dear Johannes, if only you had not allowed it to go so far!"[31] In April, when Brahms repeated the Piano Concerto in Hamburg, audience response was so rancorous after the first movement that conductor Otten had to talk him out of bolting from the stage.[32] By that point his self-confidence, his self-esteem, his entire career, should have been in ruins.

Of all the things that can be admired about Johannes Brahms, perhaps the most impressive is that he not only survived this string of catastrophes, but found in himself the courage and resources to sail out of them a composer of the highest rank. That year and the next two, among other works he completed the B♭ Major String Sextet, the G Minor and A Major Piano Quartets, and the Handel and four-hand Schumann Variations, and drafted the first movement of the First Symphony. In 1860, at the lowest ebb of his career, his creative rebirth was at hand. Nothing and no one else mattered so much to him as that.

CHAPTER TEN

A Garden Full of Nightingales

EVEN AS HIS MATURE POWERS RIPENED, Brahms fell into a restless and dejected mood in the spring of 1860. Staying with his parents, he said, even at the larger place on Fuhlentwiete, was like living in the kitchen. He wrote Clara in Berlin, imploring her not only to visit him for the summer, but to consider moving to Hamburg.[1] In lieu of that, she made a surprise visit for his twenty-seventh birthday on May 7, and stayed on for a couple of weeks. "I spent the time very pleasantly on the whole. I tried to teach myself to be indifferent to Johannes's fits of ill-humor, and sometimes I succeeded. . . . We had a great deal of music together.[2]

The music-making included the Frauenchor rehearsing the *Marienlieder* and *Volkslieder,* and the Four Songs for Voice, Two Horns, and Harp, Opus 17, the finest of his women's-choir pieces. Of the Harp Songs Clara wrote when he first sent them, in what was for her a remarkable burst of flippancy, "There must have been a very pretty girl in your choir who happened to play the harp and for whom you composed the piece."[3] She had begun to push Johannes toward other women. It was one of the few subjects on which she could be playful with him.

Clara's signature appears on a jocose set of rules Brahms drew up for the Frauenchor that spring. In the grandly copied document he used the Latin- and French-laced macaronic of old learned works like Mattheson's musical treatises. An English equivalent might read:

AVERTIMENTO
Whereas it is absolutely conducive to *Plaisire* that it should be set
about in right orderly fashion, it is hereby declared and made known
to such inquiring minds as may desire to become and to remain mem-

bers of the most profitable and delightful Ladies' Choir, that they must sign *Partoute* the articles and heads of the following document before they can enjoy the above-mentioned title and participate in the musical recreation and diversion . . .

Pro primo be it remarked that the members of the Ladies' Choir must be *there*.

As one should say: They shall *obligiren* regularly to frequent the meetings and practices of the Society.

And if it so be that any one do not duly observe this *Articul* and (which God forbid!) it were to come to pass that someone were to be so lacking in all *Decorum* as to be entirely absent during a whole *Exercitium*:

She shall be punished with a fine of 8 shillings . . .

Pro Secundo it is to be observed that the members of the Ladies' Choir are to be *there*.

As one should say: they shall be there *praecise* at the appointed time. [There follows a fine for lateness.]

1: In consideration of her great merit in connection with the Ladies' Choir, and in consideration of her presumably highly defective and unfortunate constitution, a subscription shall be established for the never-enough-to-be-favored-and-adored *Demoiselle* Laura Garbe, in accordance with which she need not pay the fine every time, in lieu of which a moderate accounting shall be *praesentiret* at the end of the quarter:[4]

Pro tertio: the moneys so collected shall be given to the poor, and it is to be desired that none of them get too much . . .

To whom it may concern: such is our opinion and we await your judicious and much-to-be desired approbation thereof.

In expectation whereof, in deepest devotion and veneration to the Ladies' Choir, their ever-ready scribe and time-beater is always theirs to command.

Johannes Kreisler, Jun.
(alias Brahms)

The Frauenchor had a halcyon spring with their leader. There were excursions and picnics in the country that ended with singing in the moonlight. Brahms, sometimes rowdy by the end of the evening, might climb into a tree to conduct. "The girls are so nice, fresh and enthusiastic, without being soft and sentimental," he wrote Clara. "On the way home . . . we usually have a lot of fine singing and serenading. . . . My girls, for instance, will walk quite calmly into a garden and wake the people up at midnight with their singing."[5] The choir members made up silver badges with the letters H F C for Hamburg Frauenchor circling a B for Brahms.

The season ended in late May, when he went to the Lower Rhine Festival in Düsseldorf and afterward stayed away from Hamburg for the summer. But he brought the ladies' solo quartet with him to the festival, where Clara arranged for them to sing his part-songs in a private recital, Joachim and Stockhausen among the audience. (When one of the quartet took sick before the performance, Clara sang the part herself.[6])

That year the festival featured the Schumann B♭ Major Symphony, and Joachim played his Hungarian Concerto. Though the concerto garnered some hearings and enthusiasm over the next decades, it was too hard, and too unreliable a crowd-pleaser in other hands, for many soloists beyond its composer to take on. In the end it had been Johannes more than anyone else who encouraged Joachim about his compositions—and in the next years that enthusiasm faded. As Clara had left behind her composing and Johannes eventually his solo career, Joachim finally decided to stick largely to playing the violin and conducting.

For two months after the festival, Brahms settled into a Rhine vacation near Bonn with Joachim, Dietrich, and Stockhausen. It began in blossoming spring, with warm nights and the song of nightingales and the Siebenbirge in the distance. Clara wrote him as he got down to work, "men like you are always watching Nature and drinking in her charms. . . . In this way a fine stormy sky can lead to a symphony—who knows what may have happened already!"[7] (This again, by Clara's standards, a knee-slapping letter.) Resisting the temptation of a symphony or any other orchestral work, Brahms instead finished the B♭ Major Sextet.

He was anxious now to get new work in print. That summer he offered a stack of music to his main publisher, Breitkopf & Härtel, including the D Minor Piano Concerto. To his disgust, they only accepted the D Major Serenade. "I'm sorry," he wrote Breitkopf, "that you have so little faith in my concerto. But I would not have thought that the outcome could be so terrible. Of the other pieces I sent, you vouchsafe not a word. I believed I had given you my best and most practical things."[8] The firm of Rieter-Biedermann took the *Ave Maria*, the *Begräbnisgesang*, the Op. 14 Songs and Romances, and, grudgingly, the piano concerto (only the solo part—the full score did not appear for fourteen years). He got modest fees from these sales, but still made most of his income from performing—and did that as little as possible.

Another work Breitkopf rejected, to its everlasting contrition, went to a firm owned by the father of a new Brahms acquaintance from that summer, Fritz Simrock. Fritz was a canny and jovial young Rheinlander, looking to sign up new talent for his family's publishing concern. Brahms took to him right away, and thus the house of N. Simrock got very lucky that year. The publication of the A Major Serenade was the first of a long association between Brahms and Simrock, both Fritz personally and the company he took over from his father around 1870. Before long, Simrock also had in hand the Harp Songs and the B♭ String Sextet.

JULY FOUND BRAHMS in Hamburg again, conducting the Frauenchor again, restless but composing steadily. Joachim and a chamber group premiered the B♭ Sextet in Hanover on October 20, 1860. The date marks the public debut of Brahms as a master of chamber music. The piece endures as one of his most popular and accessible.

For Brahms, string sextet was a characteristic choice of medium in those days, partly because it sidestepped his apprehensions. As he put off composing symphonies because of what he was famously to call "the tramp of giants" behind him, for years in his chamber music he published nothing for the most essential chamber medium, string quartet. In fact he had been writing quartets all along, but did not let one out of the house until some twenty attempts had been consigned to oblivion. He claimed to have papered the walls and ceiling of his room in Hamburg with rejected pieces: "I had only to lie on my back to admire my sonatas and quartets."[9] For years he could not settle on what his approach to the string quartet might be. So in the 1860s Brahms concentrated on fresher, acoustically richer, more nearly orchestral chamber mediums that happened to be less thunderous with the tramp of giants—string sextets, strings with piano, a horn trio.

The B♭ Sextet starts with a warm, floating lyric theme, with the *moll-Dur* (minor-major) coloration of so many melodies to come: a poignant mingling of minor and major, sometimes with short excursions into distant keys. Despite subtle games with the phrasing,[10] the first movement unfolds in "textbook" sonata form, the second theme in the "correct" key of F major. Brahms contrasts the genial spirit of the opening with a startling minor-key slow movement almost in a different style: variations on a bass line and harmonic sequence, clearly related to the slow movement of Beethoven's Seventh Symphony, but with a strange, melodramatic, archaic feel—say, Brahms harking back two centuries in German music to the mode of Heinrich Schütz, the predecessor of Bach, with the cello raking across the strings in the manner of old gamba music. Then the scherzo and rondo finale return to gay and ironic deportment, both of them submitting like the first movement to the expected formal layout of their genre.

In other words, in this work of his early maturity Brahms appropriated traditional models of sonata, variations, scherzo, and rondo more or less at face value, then filled them with his melodic and harmonic personality, his singular expressive world: Romantic emotion bridled by Classical form. In the formal orthodoxy of the B♭ Sextet we see still relatively unsullied the teachings of Eduard Marxsen, and his student who copied down in the "Schatzkästlein":

> Form is the product of thousands of years of the greatest master's efforts and something that each new generation cannot assimilate too quickly. It is but the delusion of misguided originality to seek in one's own limited universe to achieve a perfection that already exists.[11]

Having conformed to that outlook in the B♭ Sextet and made a conspicuous success of it, in his next works Brahms was to move on to a more imaginative dialectic with tradition.

Meanwhile despite Clara's entreaties to wipe Leipzig off his map, in November 1860 Brahms conducted the D Major Serenade at the Gewandhaus. If no fiasco on the order of the piano concerto, it still fell as flat as expected. Clara, who attended, wrote in her journal, "I should have liked to throw myself on Johannes's neck, I was so moved by it, and the coldness with which the audience received it made my heart bleed."[12] (On the same program, Joachim raised a furor with his Hungarian Concerto.) There was at least some compensation next day, when Joachim's group played the B♭ Sextet at the Leipzig Conservatory and students and faculty took to it enthusiastically. Clara insisted on two airings of the A Major Serenade at the Conservatory, she and Johannes playing it four hands at the piano, and with fierce satisfaction she noted some warming of opinion among the faculty.[13]

With new pieces to fan interest, performances accelerated in 1861. Clara came to Hamburg for concerts in January that included the premiere of the Harp Songs with the Hamburg Frauenchor.[14] "They are pearls," Clara wrote in her journal. "How can one help loving such a man!"[15] The last chorus, a setting from the pseudo-bard Ossian, seemed to be the favorite, and for good reason—like the "Edward" Ballade, it unfolds in the Brahmsian bardic tone, the music like the lyric seeming an echo in relentless dactyls of primeval blood-battles:

Weep on the rocks
in the blustering sea-wind,
weep you, O daughter of Inistore! . . .
Your love he has fallen,
now lies overmastered
pale as a ghost
under Cuthulin's sword.

On the program with the Harp Songs, Clara played the Beethoven Op. 47 Sonata with Joachim, soloed in works of her husband and Chopin and Bach, and played Robert's andante and variations with Johannes. In those weeks, as they shared other concerts, Johannes played Schubert hour after hour in the nights as Clara sat listening. Maybe she felt happiest in the times when she was making music with him, and he managing to be a little gracious.

THE CONCERTS AND GOOD FEELINGS of that January 1861 inaugurated one of the most serenely productive periods of Brahms's life. At the same time, something of the old warmth kindled between him and Clara, even as the possibility of actual romance faded. He wrote her at the end of the month: "It was very dreary after you left. . . . I am beginning lots of new lessons. Whenever I go into a strange house and have to meet new people . . . everybody looks like everybody else . . . I sometimes wish to see [you] for the first time again, so that I might be able to fall in love with you all over again. But all the same things are well as they are. Don't you feel the same?" She replied almost in a lover's voice, "I by no means wish you to see me again for the first time in order that you may be able 'to fall in love with me' (if indeed that can ever have happened); rather love me dearly, truly, and for ever and ever—that is the best of all."

On his urging she had gone to Detmold to hear two Mozart piano concertos which, as he hoped, fired her to take up that repertoire. He wrote her, "The fact that the public in general does not understand and appreciate the best things [such as the Mozart concertos] is . . . the reason people like me become famous. If they only knew that from us they get in dribbles what they could otherwise drink to their heart's content!"[16] In those years, Clara began the long project of editing and overseeing the complete edition of her husband's music, with Brahms and Joachim much involved in the process. With so much personal feeling involved among three giant egos, their consultations were bound to come to grief eventually, but at this point there was an easy cooperation. In 1860, for one exchange, Brahms wrote her that, despite doubts from all of them, he and Joachim advised her to go ahead with publishing the *Mass* and the *Requiem*.

With Clara, however, good spirits and halcyon days never lasted long. By summer she had fallen into a brutal depression: "The loneliness is so dreadful that often I can hardly breathe," she wrote a friend. "Dark thoughts crowd upon me, and I think of all the terrible experiences I have known, and live through them once more, and then my longing for Robert becomes so violent that often I hardly know how to control myself. My happiness went with him."[17]

Nor could the harmony between her and Johannes endure. Picking up a theme that was eventually to bring on one of their worst quarrels, he wrote in February, "If only I could hear from you that you had formed a firm resolve to work no more than you are obliged to." This time Clara responded with patient explanations: she needs the money for the children, she feels younger and fresher than she did twenty years before, she is not overdoing it. In fact, she often worked at the edge of physical and emotional collapse.

Her rationalizations, good and bad, were wasted on Brahms. He worried about the effects of touring and performing on her health and on her children, whom she parceled out to family and boarding schools, left in the care of servants, dragged along on concert tours that often took ten months of the year. She saw to the children's education and united the family for summer vacations, but she was rarely home for birthdays, holidays, or even sometimes Christmas. It was not unusual in those days for children to spend periods in the care of other people than their parents, or to be sent off to school, but all Clara's children were deprived of her for long periods. They got sick, got well, and sometimes died without her.[18]

The world saw Clara Schumann as a priestess, something like a saint. If there is such a thing as a secular saint, surely she was one. But saints are not so easy to live with. They tend to inflict on everyone the same kind of unforgiving discipline they do on themselves. Clara's customary admonition to her children amounted to: Be perfect and cause me no trouble or expense, because I am killing myself for you. An 1866 letter to son Felix is characteristic: "Your report makes me very unhappy. What will be the result, if you are not more industrious? . . . I hope that you will take more pains in the future if only for my sake. Think how I exert myself all the winter in order to be able to give you a good education, and

therefore how doubly wrong it is if you distress me by your want of industry and make me anxious about you."[19] The next year, when bright,
imaginative Felix was thirteen, she tried to squelch his creative ambitions: "I would impress upon you that with your name you are justified
in choosing a musical career only if you are a genius. . . . I am equally
sure that your gifts are not such as will carry you to the summits of art."[20]
(To her complaints about the boy Brahms told Clara, "I don't know how
I should contain myself with happiness if I had a son like Felix."[21])

If Clara's seven children suffered for her career, and in some degree
they did, certainly she endured more. Maybe she felt her suffering
paid for her children's. In any case, she was going to perform. "We
would sometimes wonder," Eugenie was to write, "whether our mother
would miss us or music most if one of the two were taken from her, and
we could never decide."

Brahms observed these effects of her career with foreboding. At the
same time, given his blinders with respect to women's ambitions and intellect, he could never quite grasp that Clara was an artist like himself, as
scornful of charity as he was, with ambitions like his own and his kind of
ruthlessness in pursuing them.

In April 1861, Brahms conducted the Hamburg Philharmonic, once
more accompanying Joachim in his Hungarian Concerto; on the program the two also contributed a Beethoven violin sonata. Now Brahms
had determined to show himself as much as possible on the podium, to
enhance his potential as F. W. Grund's successor with the Philharmonic.
At some point the idea of conducting his hometown orchestra had become a ruling ambition.

At the end of the same month in Altona, Brahms and Julius Stockhausen presented three programs (one including the A Major Serenade)
in which they performed three lieder cycles—Beethoven's *An die ferne
Geliebte*, Schubert's *Schöne Müllerin*, and Schumann's *Dichterliebe*. With
Brahms's help, Stockhausen had become a great favorite in Hamburg.
Regular rehearsals with the Frauenchor ended that spring, though the
women continued to meet on their own and appeared in a few performances. Brahms felt too busy with composing, teaching, and performing
to keep working with them. Though his affection remained, maybe he
had tired of the choir, having learned from them what he needed.

With great relief Brahms moved out of the family house in July 1861
and took an apartment in Hamm, a country suburb on the left bank of

the Alster. The house was owned by widow Elisabeth Rösing, aunt to Betty and Marie Völkers of the solo quartet. The Völkers' thatch-roofed house next door had seen a number of Frauenchor gatherings.[22] From Frau Dr. Rösing Brahms had a large sunny studio with tinted glass, once a billiard room, and a balcony looking out to the garden and its old trees full of nightingales.

After years of his family's cramped apartments, mostly in shabby sections of town, he was charmed by the beauty and quiet of Hamm. The A Major Piano Quartet has a dedication to Frau Dr. Rösing, who provided him with such inspiring accommodations. Only at his insistence did she accept any rent at all.[23] The idyll produced an extraordinary outpouring of music during the next two years.

Most days after working hours Brahms showed up cigar in hand for the sociable and musical gatherings of the Rösing and Völkers houses. Laura Garbe and other Frauenchor veterans came to visit the Völkers sisters, and him: houses full of the bright voices and laughter of young women. Brahms accompanied the daughters and their friends in songs, his own and others' music twining in the scented air with the nightingales', and he played late into the night. "It was so wonderful," Marie Völkers wrote, "that I cannot describe it or re-create it in words."[24] Frau Dr. Rösing recalled Brahms in those days:

> Of medium height, and delicately built, with a countenance beneath whose high, fine brow were set flashing blue eyes, with fair hair combed back and falling down behind, and an obstinate lower lip! An unconscious force emanated from him as he stood apart in a gay company, with hands clasped behind his back, greeting those who arrived with a curt nod of his fine head.[25]

He invited friends to visit, and among those who took him up on it were Albert Dietrich, who stayed in Johannes's room in Hamburg and marveled at the esoteric and antiquarian depth of his friend's library, and also at the collection of toy soldiers carefully sorted in boxes in the writing desk. Dietrich spent much time with fragile, toothless Christiane, listening to her chatter on about Johannes, and noted that Johann Jakob was rarely to be seen around the house. He remembered enchanted evenings in Hamm, the quartet of Frauenchor girls singing to them from an arbor in the garden.[26] Another visitor that summer was a young conductor named Hermann Levi, newly Kapellmeister of the German Opera in Rotterdam. Levi had become enthusiastic about Brahms's music and wanted to have a look at its creator.[27] A few years later they would begin a long friendship and collaboration.

Brahms had not anticipated a visit earlier in the summer of 1861. Lischen Giesemann, his friend from the summers at Winsen, announced herself and her new husband at the family house in Fuhlentwiete, but found Brahms away (this just before he moved out to Hamm). Lischen had not seen her old playmate since his teens. Christiane, groaning and cooing, roused herself to show off her son's room, where a freshly copied manuscript of four lieder lay on the music desk. When Lischen took a look at it, indelible moments of her childhood rushed back. Through the crabbed scribble of Brahms's handwriting she made out lyrics of songs from *The Beautiful Magelone*. They came from Tieck's adaptation of the old romance she and Johannes used to read to each other in the fields and woods of Winsen. Brahms had begun a song cycle on this story from his youth and his Romantic wellspring.

The songs of Count Peter of Provence and his ladyloves had stayed with Brahms until the musical friendship with Julius Stockhausen released them. Written for that masterful singer, the cycle absorbed and worried Brahms for some seven years more before he finished it. For Lischen Giesemann in 1861, finding them on his desk was a magical event. She never saw Brahms on that visit, or ever again. Eventually he was to play a part in her daughter's life by financing the girl's musical studies, and in his age he wrote Lischen, "The remembrance of your parents' house is one of the dearest I possess. . . . All the youthful pleasure and happiness I enjoyed there live secure in my heart with the image of your good father and the glad grateful memory of you all."[28]

The first products of his stay in Hamm were the G Minor and A Major Piano Quartets, parts of both sent to Clara for comment in July, and the Handel Variations that bear the date September '61. Clara and Joachim both complained about the somber first movement of the G Minor, its strange concentration on the secondary key of D and its looseness of outline. They were not yet accustomed to the dialectic Johannes had begun with tradition, his ingenious explorations of forms his "Schatzkästlein" called "the product of thousands of years of the greatest masters' efforts."

MUCH OF THE MUSICAL STRIFE of the nineteenth century, the War of the Romantics, would be fought over the issues of traditional versus literary-based formal models, with sonata form as the great sticking point. Brahms was associated with the camp upholding the old patterns, and rightly so. Yet he never used them less than creatively, always adapting them to the nature and expression of the work at hand; and in a few pieces his material drove him to carve unique forms. (Actually it was Wagner who invented the term "absolute music," meaning instrumental music with no explicit connection to a text—and usually using traditional formal models. He invented the idea in order to condemn it.)

The procedures to which nineteenth-century theorists applied the label "sonata form," most often used in the first movements of pieces, were rationalizations of what for Haydn, Mozart, Beethoven, and other Classical-era composers had been almost instinctive reflexes of musical grammar and syntax. A Mozart first movement, for example, unfolds for the listener's ear as logically as a drama or an essay: here is a theme or connected themelets, which we string out like so, and then with this little transition we are carried to another theme, in a new but not too distant key (and if the leading theme is bold to get our attention, the second is apt to be gentler for contrast). Then after the second theme runs its course there is a closing section, maybe touching on a new theme or quasi-theme. Theorists named this whole process the *exposition* of a sonata-form movement, because it presents the principal themes of the discourse.

To drive home the basic ideas and revisit their pleasures, the exposition is repeated. Next we enter a section in which one or both themes, like characters in a drama, are caught up in a restless flux of fragmented themes and shifts of key and texture and rhythm, known as the *development* section. Then, with a transition dramatic or mysterious or playful as desired, we are brought from the instability of the development back to the stability of the *recapitulation*, where we hear the leading theme and the other ideas of the exposition restated with an important difference—everything is now heard in the main key, resolving the harmonic tensions of the exposition and development into stability. The movement usually closes with a section called a *coda*, which anchors us with a strong finish in the main key. Thus the theoretical, textbook norm of sonata form: exposition with two (or more) contrasting themes, repeated; development that amounts to a quasi-improvisation on the themes; recapitulation resolving all the material into the main key; coda to round things off.

As with most statistical norms, few pieces actually conform to that pattern. Yet by the time of Brahms's maturity, generations of musicians and concertgoers had absorbed this organizational framework as if it were an eternal archetype, almost a Platonic form: as Eduard Marxsen taught Brahms, part of the "eternally uncorruptible" in music. During the nineteenth century, like hearing a familiar story fleshed out in new ways, connoisseurs listened for the landmarks in the first movement of a symphony, a sonata, a chamber piece: the first theme, second theme in its new key, closing section, repeat of the exposition, dramatic development, the suspense before the recapitulation, and so on. Likewise, they could identify a scherzo, an A B A slow movement, a set of variations, or a rondo (A B A C A D A, etc.) when they heard them—or when they played and studied the score in piano arrangements, as many amateurs could do in those days. (As soon as he finished an orchestral or chamber piece, Brahms hastened to make an arrangement, usually piano four hands, and those arrangements sold much better than the full score.)

Rather than these timeworn formal landmarks, Liszt and the New Germans handed listeners stories, poetic or philosophical ideas, or vocal music. Their models were first, Beethoven's *Pastoral* Symphony, in whose course we arrive in the country, watch peasants dance, flee a thunderstorm, and so on through a little story. The other model was Berlioz's *Symphonie fantastique*, with its tale of an artist who takes opium in a fit of despair over a lost love, and experiences a series of hallucinations, which are the movements of the symphony; in each movement the beloved is represented by a recurring melodic idée fixe. For both programmatic and absolute music, the new institution of the program note kept listeners squinting into their literature during the performance, to help find their way through increasingly long, mazy works.

Maybe as an inevitable result of theoretical codification, in the nineteenth century traditional forms tended to fossilize into dogma—part of what drove the New Germans to search out alternative shapes in literary and dramatic models. Charles Rosen writes that for the theorists who defined sonata form in the first half of the nineteenth century, "the purpose of the definition was not the understanding of the music of the past but a model for the production of new works. The definition does not work well for the eighteenth century because it was never intended to."[29]

In other words the Classicists Mozart, Haydn, and Beethoven, none of whom knew the term "sonata form," treated its principles far more freely and dynamically than theorists pretended. Many Haydn movements, for example, are more or less monothematic. One of Brahms's advantages over most of his contemporaries was that he understood all that. If he encamped with the traditionalists, he was still too intelligent, canny, and historically aware to fall into the trap so many composers did and theorists encouraged, of treating form mechanically, as a mold to pour notes into.

An entry in Clara's journal from November 1861 shows him pondering these issues: "An interesting conversation with Johannes about form.

How the old masters had the freest form, while modern compositions move within the stiffest and most narrow limits. He himself emulates the older generation and Clementi in particular ranks high in his opinion, on account of his great, free form."[30] Even in the scope of freedom and innovation he allowed himself, Brahms was looking further backward than his contemporaries.

BRAHMS'S DIALECTIC WITH TRADITION takes graphic shape on the manuscript of the G Minor Piano Quartet, from his first summer in Hamm. In the opening movement he wrote down the usual repeat sign at the end of the exposition. Then he scribbled it out and inserted a new section of ten bars, beginning the development without a repeat. These added bars are deliberately misleading—a literal restatement of the first ten bars of the piece, *a false repeat of the exposition*. At the end of those ten measures there is a pause, then the listener finds himself not in the expected place, back at the beginning, but in a new continuation of the material—the development. In turn, this uncertainty over where we are in the form creates a tension that itself becomes part of a dramatic, edgy development section dominated to the point of obsession by a driving sixteenth-note figure. The onset of the recapitulation is similarly blurred, beginning with one of the subsidiary ideas in G major rather than the main theme in G minor. Clara Schumann was the first of many to be uncertain about where the recapitulation actually begins—which she perceived as a miscalculation rather than a willful device.[31]

These kinds of formal adaptations mark Brahms's mature style. In work after work he maintains the expected elements in some degree, but may withhold a clear announcement of them, the kind of help that Mozart usually provides us. Complicating matters more, in Brahms's sonata-form movements the development of ideas tends to spread out of the development section and pervade the whole movement; he wanted that richness of elaboration. A Brahmsian movement is often made of succinct melodic ideas that begin to transform as soon as we hear them, and continue to evolve and recombine throughout, accompanied by the sort of abrupt key changes that used to be confined to the development section. It is this innovative aspect of his style that Arnold Schoenberg admiringly named "developing variation."[32]

Of course, given that there is little new under the sun, and that we can find a cue in the past for nearly everything "new" in Brahms, his games with formal expectations are not unprecedented. Haydn regularly teases listeners with false or withheld recapitulations, in the same playful way

as he might begin a piece with an ending gesture or end with an opening gesture. These are jokes for the connoisseur. Brahms is innovative
more in the extent, seriousness, and subtlety of his formal explorations,
his up-to-date chromatic harmony, his constantly developmental
approach that also tends to blur formal outlines. A primary reason
Brahms was perceived for so long to be a "difficult" composer, despite
the manifest expressiveness of his style, is his complex handling of form,
his obscuring of the boundaries. Critics said: he can't just do something
simple and beautiful and let it be; he's driven to snarl it up with complexities.

Certainly Brahms's experiments with inherited patterns did not begin
all at once with the G Minor Piano Quartet. As early as the A Major Serenade he used a false repeat of the exposition. But in his maturity the
games become more systematic than in his earlier works. At the same
time, in the G Minor Quartet he counterbalances the formal complexities by clarifying other dimensions. The exposition, for example, has an
unusually restricted key outline: a little G minor, then a lot of D major—
which simplifies the key structure while deliberately unbalancing the
overall effect.

Besides, if the formal outline of the G Minor first movement is innovative and sometimes confusing, the ideas are more compact than in
Brahms's earlier large-scale pieces. The austere, measured opening unfolds like a microcosmic demonstration of developing variation: a four-
note motive in even quarter notes, the second measure the same shape
inverted and varied in intervals, the third measure the second transposed,
and the fourth measure the inverted shape transposed again, with the
middle two notes juxtaposed to make a harmony:

The movement grows and intensifies from that opening motive, its
shape turning up again and again in fresh configurations. Finally a new
figure, tense and driving, is superimposed contrapuntally in piano under
the main motive in strings:

The calm opening, then, is like a coiled spring that gradually releases its power (an effect Brahms would make explosive in the F Minor Quintet). Before long the tense subsidiary figure drives into the foreground, to become the main rhythmic and dramatic force in the movement. To keep the thematic evolution in focus, Brahms characteristically makes his music almost unceasingly melodic. In contrast to the stretches of chordal figuration common in Mozart and Beethoven, many Brahms movements can be whistled practically from beginning to end, as if they were a single melodic line. He intended to keep in our ears the essential logic of developing and transforming motives, expressed within a formal framework traditional in concept but often surprising in execution.

After the difficulties he posed in the first movement of the G Minor, Brahms compensates listeners in the rest of the piece. The second movement Allegro he first called "Scherzo" as expected, but at Clara's suggestion struck that off the score and substituted "Intermezzo." He was beginning to move away from the old Beethovenian scherzo toward a new kind of graceful, medium-tempo inner movement of his own invention, for which "Intermezzo" is an apt term. The Intermezzo of the G Minor is liltingly tuneful in its simple, scherzo-like A B A-coda pattern. The formal simplification continues with a yearning, melodious Andante, enlivened with an Animato, A B A again but with elaborate thematic developments that blur the outline.

For the finale, Brahms supplied something he knew would cinch the popularity of the quartet: a breathless, pounding, irresistible movement in gypsy style, *rondo alla Zingarese*, complete with a torrential cadenza for the piano that recalls the wild violin roulades of Hungarian music. One imagines patriotic Joachim, composer of the Hungarian Concerto, smiling when he wrote Johannes: "In the last movement you beat me on my own turf." With this movement Brahms broke once and for all, and with manifest exhilaration, out of his uncertainty about finales. (Once again, he got his cue for this "innovation" from Haydn and Schubert, who seized on the gypsy style.) In pieces of the next years his gypsy voice would continue to develop, even if never presented quite so directly again. The evolution of his *alla Zingarese* style, meanwhile, was part of a broader evolution toward the essential Brahmsian symphonic finale: more moderate in tempo, serious, monumental.

At the same time as his treatment of sonata form became more subtle and adventurous, his approach to theme-and-variations got relatively tighter and more traditional. His earlier sets were close to Schumannesque "fantasy-variations." Then in 1856 he wrote Joachim that he had rethought his approach: "From time to time I reflect on variation form and find that it should be kept stricter, purer. The Ancients were very strict about retaining the bass of the theme, their actual theme." By "Ancients" he mainly meant Bach and the Baroque. The traditional primacy of the bass line—as in Bach's Goldberg Variations—became his model, in theory. In practice, as scholar Elaine Sisman observes, he "sought to reconcile older and newer models in his works"[33]—say, joining the imaginative freedom of Schumann's fantasy-variations with the strictness and "purity" of Bach's.

In 1861 Brahms's conscious turning back to the past, and perhaps unconscious integration of the present, produced perhaps the finest set of piano variations since Beethoven's—the Opus 24 Variations and Fugue on a Theme by G. F. Handel. Besides a masterful unfolding of ideas concluding with an exuberant fugue with a finish designed to bring down the house, the work is quintessentially Brahms in other ways: the filler of traditional forms with fresh energy and imagination; the historical eclectic able to start off with a gallant little tune of Handel's, Baroque ornaments and all, and integrate it seamlessly into his own voice, in a work of massive scope and dazzling variety. The Handel Variations are dedicated to a "beloved friend"—Clara.

Without pausing for breath, in November 1861 Brahms produced a companion piece to the Handel Variations, his second set of Schumann Variations, Opus 23, for piano four hands. Maybe in Brahms's mind this work, with its concluding funeral march, laid to rest the turbulent, improbable, glorious, and wrenching last eight years that saw the end of his youth and his enforced maturity. That autumn, still without a break, he finished the A Major Piano Quartet.[34]

·   ·   ·

AMIDST THIS CASCADE OF WORK, Brahms wrote Clara a remarkably ab-
ject letter, however ironical in tone. She was scheduled to perform in several Hamburg programs starting in mid-November 1861, which would
include the premiere of the G Minor Quartet (that concert also featuring the Frauenchor), the D Minor Piano Concerto with Johannes conducting the Philharmonic, and the premiere of the Handel Variations.[35]
Brahms had written asking her to come to Hamburg in September and
stay for the duration; twice she put him off. Finally in October he wrote
with mock exasperation veiling a real longing:

> Your letter has just reached me and I am certainly not at all satis-
> fied. . . . In all things that concern me you have always treated me, and
> always will, as though I belonged to you, and yet in everything that
> concerns you I am allowed to do nothing. If I had not a farthing I
> should live with you. If I had a house you would certainly live with me.
> But now I have a purse full of superfluous pelf, which I shall scatter
> very shortly out of sheer wrath (the Treasury bonds) simply because it
> is of no earthly use to me as I am not allowed to spend it. . . . I assure
> you that I shall be really furious if you refuse to be my guest here with
> Julie. If you will not do it, I shall throw all my money out the window.[36]

He continues with no less than ten numbered and elaborate reasons,
some serious and some joking, why Clara must come immediately to
Hamburg.

She finally arrived a few weeks before her engagements, on October
21. Why was Brahms so insistent about her coming when he was extraordinarily busy with new work? To a degree it may have been concern
over her persistent gloom. Another part of it, perhaps the major part,
would be hard to believe if not for how it played out, somewhere between
pathos and pathetic, over the next years. The clue lies in the phrase "be
my guest here with Julie." This was Clara's third daughter, by all accounts an ethereal, magical beauty. Brahms had just dedicated the Opus
23 four-hand Schumann Variations to this Schumann daughter.

In fact, he had fallen in love with Julie, who was now sixteen and in full
bloom. Though he was prepared to wait patiently for the right time to
declare it—whatever inconceivable time he imagined that to be—he
wanted to be around her, watch her, admire her from a decent distance.

Clara, sunk in her own concerns and troubles, remained oblivious to Johannes's infatuation with her daughter. During her Hamburg performances in November 1861, she seemed on the verge of nervous collapse. She wrote daughter Marie, "I . . . am often terribly sad although Johannes gives me many hours of glorious pleasure. He does everything he can to please me, but I have had some dark days, when everything has been in deep shadow . . . Johannes has written some wonderfully beautiful things."[37]

Yet another unmentionable matter lay between them, which Brahms might have suspected if he had not been as oblivious to the symptoms as she was in regard to his. Clara was having an affair, or about to enter into one, with composer Theodor Kirchner.[38]

The dates and duration of their intimacy are uncertain, but it had been building for a long time. Probably she lived in terror that Johannes would find out, or her children, or anybody. Thus, perhaps, her depression in 1861. In the end, she and Kirchner managed to keep their relationship extraordinarily discreet. He wanted to marry Clara, but year after year she held back, and finally turned him away. Apparently Brahms never suspected. It would have horrified him to find out: for him Clara existed in some crystalline never-never land. And he and Kirchner were not only colleagues but good friends.

Two decades later, Clara would write in her journal:

> Today I succeeded in making myself read through the old letters from Kirchner. . . . If only I could wipe this old friendship entirely out of my life! for I gave my heart's best to a man whom I hoped it might save. . . . I wished to make one so highly gifted into a worthy man and artist, to ennoble his character which had suffered so much from being spoiled, and through friendship to give him new joy in the happiness of life: in short, I dreamed of an ideal and never thought that I had a fully matured man before me. It was a sad experience. I suffered much, and found comfort only in the thought that I had meant all for the best.[39]

In her early forties, Clara had fallen once more, and for the last time, into an old pattern. She could only cloak her need for love as a duty to inspire another troubled creator to great work, as she had already done with two first-rank artists. It appears that in Clara's mind if Kirchner did not leave behind his melancholy and lack of discipline and under her attentions blossom as a composer, then she had betrayed her husband's memory and her loyalty to Johannes, and given herself to a man for nothing. The trouble was that, though Theodor Kirchner was a superlative pianist and able composer, he was no Schumann and no Brahms. Clara's sufferings for Robert and Johannes had been redeemed by glorious music. This affair was unredeemed; she failed as muse for lack of raw material, and that devastated her.

Since the time of Clara's affair during the 1860s remains unclear, the connection to her frame of mind has to be speculative. But toward the end of 1860 she seemed unusually spirited in her letters to Johannes—say, in this one of October 1860: "You have been tempted to laugh at what I said about the choral motet, have you not? . . . You are a regular good-for-nothing; first one is to say all that one thinks, and then if one does, one gets a rap over the knuckles." Through most of this period she was especially warm to him, without necessarily trying to draw closer to him. In other words, this may have marked the beginning of the affair with Kirchner, during which she wanted to reassure Johannes partly out of anxiety that he might find out. The depression that appeared around the summer of 1861 may mark Clara's disenchantment, her guilt, her mounting fear of discovery. It may also be worth mentioning that her affair followed on the heels of the relationship of Brahms and Agathe von Siebold, which had driven Clara from Göttingen. For all her saintliness, revenge may have played a part in the story too.

Despite the unmentionable, almost unthinkable subtexts that lay between Clara and Johannes, the Hamburg performances of late 1861 thrilled both of them. "The joy of the [Piano Concerto] so overcame me," Clara wrote, "and the fact that he was conducting, that nothing else, not even the stupidity of the audience, could annoy me—the public understood nothing and felt nothing." Four days later, her performance of the Handel Variations was a triumph despite "agonies of nervousness." She rarely felt comfortable playing in Johannes's presence. Afterward, instead of congratulating her he felt obliged to declare his utter indifference to the piece. "I cannot help finding it hard," she wrote in her journal, "when one has devoted all one's powers to a work, and the composer himself has not a kind word for it. . . . Otherwise we had many a happy hour, and Johannes especially delighted me with the A Major Quartet."[40] No wonder she didn't like playing around him.

Clara left Hamburg to perform the Handel Variations with great success in Leipzig. Just after Christmas, Brahms joined her and Joachim in Berlin for New Year's, and growled and snapped for the duration.[41] Maybe tension over the impending vacancy with the Philharmonic was wearing on him. He had conducted both Hamburg orchestras now, besides his solo appearances, and musicians there had a good idea of his skills. (Perhaps that was part of the trouble; Brahms never really became a virtuoso conductor.)

In March, as he worked and worried in Hamburg, Clara made her first visit to Paris. There she rounded up musicians and forced them to listen to Brahms—but in private "séances" as she put it, not in public soirees. For all the efforts of Clara and others, for many years the French did not take to Brahms, and his opinion of the French was no more charitable. Like many Germans, he recalled the atrocities during the Napoleonic invasion; his mother had filled him with those stories in childhood. (Of course, Brahms showed little enthusiasm for any culture at all other than his own.)

Brahms went to Hanover in early January 1861 for a two-month stay with Joachim. They played much together in public and private. While he was there another landmark arrived—a performance of the A Major Serenade in New York, not only the first Brahms orchestral piece heard in the United States but the first outside the orbit of Hamburg, Leipzig, and Hanover. Brahms would make some headway in the United States in the next decades, especially when his German disciples began turning up there. As late as the 1890s, though, Boston critic Philip Hale proposed that the new Symphony Hall should have a door marked "Exit—in case of Brahms."

Early in 1861 Brahms responded to an invitation from Albert Dietrich, by now serving as Court Kapellmeister in Oldenburg. Brahms's letter to Dietrich demonstrates to what extent he expected his friends to make these invitations, and to provide him with useful introductions and generous fees. With a playfulness appropriate to their friendship, Brahms remained magisterially in control of the arrangements:

> I am much drawn to visit you, and to get to know so many whose names I have so often heard mentioned as your friends, otherwise I would say no. So I shall come to you, and shall then stay as long as I can allow myself to be idle.
>
> What shall I play? Beethoven or Mozart?. . . . Advise me!
>
> And for the second part, Schumann, Bach, or might I venture upon some new variations of my own?
>
> Of course you shall conduct my serenade. We have played my quartets a good deal here; I shall bring them with me, and shall be glad if they meet with your approval.
>
> *Apropos!* I suppose I must have fifteen louis d'ors remunerations, but would like it arranged that if I play at Court, that would be paid for extra. Money is very necessary to me, consequently my time is precious, and I am unwilling to allow myself to be tempted to concerts; but if *the one* has to be, the other must follow.[42]

The Oldenburg concert in mid-March—including the D Major Serenade and Beethoven G Major Concerto—found an agreeable reception, likewise an informal performance of the Handel Variations for the orchestra musicians. Brahms had a good visit with Dietrich and his brood: "Like a child with the children," Dietrich wrote. There were sociable evenings with family friends, musical and otherwise. At one party a young lady caught Brahms's eye. After the guests left he rambled to Dietrich: "I should like to marry her; such a girl could also make me happy." Next day, sober again, he came to himself—the girl does not show up again in the chronicle. Brahms went back to Hamm and the nightingales in the trees, and an early-April concert with Stockhausen that saw the premiere of the first *Magelone* song.[43]

THAT SPRING OF 1862 a prophetic series of articles on Brahms appeared in the *Neue Zeitschrift für Musik*. Despite simmering resentment over the Brahms/Joachim manifesto of two years before, editor Franz Brendel stuck by his determination to calm the waters. The five articles in the *Neue Zeitschrift*, analyzing five pieces, fell within a larger series called "Schumanniana" by one Adolf Schubring. Brahms and Schubring had exchanged letters since 1856, but still had not met when the articles appeared. Afterward, not surprisingly, they became friends.

Despite inevitable lapses, Schubring's commentary remains astonishing for its insight, given that Brahms had only published eighteen pieces by then. The series begins by citing Schumann's "Neue Bahnen" and the ensuing factional responses: elation in the Schumann camp, otherwise disapproval to dismay. Schubring notes "the unfortunate fragmentation of musical Germany. Here, Guelphs! Here, Ghibellines! The battle cry is sounding, and the Schumann banner, which stands between the two warring parties, gets dragged into the fray."[44]

In his musical analyses, Schubring identifies thematic logic as the essence of Brahmsian discourse. From a larger perspective, he follows musicological fashion in dividing the work into periods. If that seems nonsensical for a composer not yet thirty, Schubring still astutely examines the development of the music: the early sonatas "Sturm-und-Drang," the B Major Trio transitional, the D Minor Piano Concerto "middle period," and so on. He uncovers the formal uncertainties in the trio and shrewdly implies a more general problem: if in sonata form Brahms likes to develop material from the exposition onward, that tends to compromise the meaning and function of the development section. In varying degrees, that problem bedeviled Brahmsian developments for the rest of his career.[45]

Most strikingly of all, as of 1862, when Brahms had just arrived at his early maturity, Schubring discerned his essential direction:

> Brahms may well have felt that the path he had trodden up to now was a remote dead-end of Romanticism . . . he turned [his work] back to the eternally clear forms . . . of the classics. . . . He understands how to be Classic and Romantic, ideal and real—and after all, I believe he is appointed to blend both these eternal oppositions in art.

Much of the subsequent history of Brahms criticism has built on that insight of 1862—the joining of Classic and Romantic, which Nietszche characterized as the eternal dichotomy of Apollonian and Dionysian spirits: restraint or ecstasy, ideal form or unfettered intuition. That raises the question, To what extent did Brahms himself build on Schubring's insight, in trying to reconcile apparently antithetical spirits? Brahms had an ongoing correspondence with the critic, read the articles, visited him shortly after they appeared. Certainly Brahms had already taken to the path Schubring describes, but criticism of this subtlety could sharpen his focus, confirm his path. Schubring not only may have begun mature Brahms criticism but at a critical point may have helped the composer understand his own maturity. If that is true, Schubring's articles proved nearly as important to Brahms's creative life as Schumann's "Neue Bahnen" had—maybe even a more productive contribution, because more accurate and less intimidating.

In April 1862 Brahms sent the critic a copy of the Handel Variations, saying, "I am fond of it and value it particularly in relation to my other works." (This shortly after Clara's performance, when Brahms told her he could not stand to hear it.) While in this and similar ways he transparently courted Schubring, Brahms generally behaved toward him as he did toward all critics; he stroked them but did not genuflect, kept a certain imperious distance. That is observable in a note Brahms wrote Schubring in 1869. The critic had gotten carried away with thematic derivations in *Ein deutsches Requiem*, and Brahms dispatched a reprimand: "I disagree that in the third movement the themes of the different sections have something in common. . . . If it is nevertheless so . . . I want no praise for it. . . . If I want to retain the same musical idea, then it should be clearly recognized in each transformation, augmentation, inversion. The other way would be a trivial game and always a sign of the most impoverished invention." For pre-Freudian Brahms, an unconscious motivic relationship is a meaningless relationship. He wants credit only for the ones he wilfully crafted.

There is one more thing to note about Adolf Schubring: he was by profession a judge, not a musician. In other words he was another of the cultivated Austro-German amateurs of those days. If professional performers were the cutting edge in spreading Brahms's music, middle-class amateurs were the core of his audience. Thus the conclusion to Schubring's 1862 articles boded very well indeed for Brahms's future:

> The greater public . . . does not yet seem to have any idea what a colossal genius—one completely the equal of Bach, Beethoven, and Schumann—is ripening in the young Hamburg master.

In early June of 1862, Brahms made his usual visit to the Lower Rhine Music Festival, held that year in Cologne. There he met the operatic soprano Luise Dustmann, a great friend of Wagner, and eventually likewise of Brahms. Luise impressed him with her enthusiasm for Vienna and its musical and other pleasures. They began a flirtatious relationship that lasted for years.

After the festival, Brahms stayed for a fortnight with Albert Dietrich in a large house under the Ebernburg, near Clara, who was taking the baths at Münster am Stein. In those weeks Brahms began the E Minor Cello Sonata and an F minor string quintet (with two cellos like Schubert's quintet rather than Mozart's two violas), and apparently drafted a symphonic movement from previous sketches. Dietrich remembered a jolly vacation—he and Johannes both composing in the house, hikes in the countryside, Clara playing in the evenings. The temper of their relations can be found in a Brahms letter to Joachim: "Now I am sitting in a tavern . . . under the Ebernburg. . . . Dietrich is in the next room belaboring his bride. The bride in question being a ballade for choir and orchestra."[46]

Dietrich wrote his regrettably distant wife, "The longer I am with Brahms, the more my affection and esteem for him increase. His nature is equally lovable, cheerful, and deep." He noted that with women Brahms had a habit of straight-faced teasing that was often misinterpreted—especially by Clara, who generally missed the joke and waxed indignant.[47] Thus many scenes of sad-eyed, earnest and hypersensitive Clara bristling at Johannes, who surveyed her tears and reprimands with a mean twinkle in his blue eyes. Joachim had understood from the beginning that Johannes liked to goad people as a way of dominating them. Not even Clara would be spared that. In contrast to Dietrich, she wrote Joachim about that summer: "He made life with him almost unbearable."[48]

At the end of June, Brahms went hiking in the Pfälzer Bergland with Dietrich and Heinrich von Sahr, visited Julius Allgeyer and other friends in Landau and Karlsruhe, and stopped off in the resort of Baden-Baden to see Anton Rubinstein. By mid-August he was back at work in Hamm.

Just after leaving the Ebernburg, Brahms sent a sheaf of manuscript to Clara. In shock, she wrote Joachim on July 1, "Johannes sent me the other day—imagine the surprise!—the first movement of a symphony." For Joachim she jotted down the beginning, which she found "rather strong, but I have soon become used to it. The movement is full of wonderful beauties, and the themes are treated with a mastery which is becoming more and more characteristic of him."[49] It was the first movement of the C Minor Symphony, without the introduction added later. Sketches for it may have gone back to the middle 1850s, the Werther years.

News spread that Brahms had a symphony going, and that year he played over the movement on piano for friends. From London, Joachim wrote Clara, "Perhaps I shall be able to invite you to Hanover for Brahms's symphony at the end of October."[50] Those hopes would not pan out, not by a long shot. He still felt uncertain about how to manage a symphonic finale—apparently another *alla Zingarese* did not appeal to him at that point. And he was moving toward discarding the whole idea of the symphonic scherzo. But if not a scherzo, what? There were to be twelve years, and much water under several bridges, before Brahms's friends heard the First Symphony to the end.

As summer turned into autumn he continued composing at a furious pace, full of juice, the ideas almost tumbling over each other to be heard. If some pieces spent years in gestation, most often Brahms wrote extraordinarily fast, from ideas he had been putting in order in his mind with his remarkable memory for music. Clara received the first three movements of an F minor string quintet in Lucerne and gushed in response: "What an adagio! How rapturously it sings and rings from beginning to end! . . . Yesterday I played it to Kirchner and Stockhausen—they are as delighted with it as I am—and afterwards we drank your health in champagne."[51] But after a reading Joachim declared the string writing ineffectual—maybe in part because of the two cellos—and the piece went back into the oven. It would reemerge twice more before Brahms and Joachim decided it was done.

During all this creative moil and deliberation, the question of Grund's successor at the Hamburg Philharmonic was coming to a head. The aged conductor was finally ready to retire. Having tried to make his availability known to the relevant parties, Brahms decided it might be a good time to let things run their course in Hamburg and to pursue an old fantasy: he would visit Vienna, the holy city of musicians, and with luck return in a few months with the exalted title Music Director of the Hamburg Philharmonic. Flush from performing fees and the sales of new pieces, he could afford a little sightseeing.

As he prepared to leave, someone, perhaps Theodor Avé-Lallemant, made a preliminary inquiry if Brahms wanted the job of assistant conductor of the Hamburg Singakademie; that would give him a leg up for the orchestral position. Certainly that appeared auspicious. Avé, who had much influence in these decisions, wrote an acquaintance, "Brahms . . . thinks of going to Vienna . . . then I shall be quite alone, but thank God I have learned to know the man so well."[52] Brahms felt he could depend on his old friend, who knew him so well, to promote his cause.

Just before he left Brahms wrote Albert Dietrich:

> Dear friend, I am leaving on Monday *for Vienna!* I look forward to it like a child.
>
> Of course I don't know how long I shall stay; we'll leave it open, and I hope we can meet some time during the winter.
>
> The C Minor Symphony is not finished; on the other hand, the string quintet . . . in F minor is [so he thought then]. . . . Enclosed are my Handel Variations; the Marienlieder have not come yet.[53]

In saying good-bye at home, where his mother was recovering from a fall and broken bone, Brahms counseled his father, "Now if things should be going badly with you, music is always the great consolation. Go and study my old score of [Handel's] *Saul.* You'll find great comfort in it." Some time later, when Johann Jakob followed the advice, he discovered that Hannes had filled the leaves with banknotes.

His favorite pupil and Frauenchor founder Friedchen Wagner entreated him not to leave. On his departure Brahms consoled her, in both tangible and symbolic form, with the manuscript of his organ prelude *O Traurigkeit, O Herzeleid* (*O Sorrow, O Grief*). Only after several days of *Herzeleid* herself did Friedchen discover the gift where he had concealed it under the lid of her piano. When Brahms did generous and affectionate things, and he did many, he tended to carry them out in secret and leave the scene. More and more, in person, among his peers, he was prepared to be charming and sociable in good bourgeois fashion, or to be impossible, and not much in between.

BRAHMS TRAVELED TO VIENNA VIA DESSAU, where he visited critic Adolf Schubring, probably to express appreciation for the *Neue Zeitschrift* articles. He arrived in Vienna in the middle of December 1862, planning a short exploratory visit.

After his lifetime of experience with mercantile Hamburg, at last Brahms saw the City of Dreams, where of all places in the West great music was the most famous industry. Dazzled as any musical tourist, he walked through the streets with their endless landmarks. He knew all the places, all the stories. Here behind the Baroque facade of the Lobkowitz Palace Beethoven first conducted the *Eroica* for his aristocratic patrons, and in a small plain room of the Schwarzpanierhaus he died shaking his fist at the sky. Twenty-four years before, in the alcove of another small room, Schubert had muttered, "Here, here is my end," and died at thirty-two, eight months after his first triumph in Vienna. Here was the Esterhazy palace, built by Haydn's employers. On Domgasse, those small stone steps rising from the courtyard echoed to *The Marriage of Figaro* as Mozart composed it; five years later and a minute's walk away, in a chapel attached to the towering Gothic mass of the Stephansdom, Mozart's mourners filed past his coffin before he was buried in a communal grave. Here by the river the first Theater an der Wien produced the triumphant premiere performances of Mozart's *Zauberflöte*, and the new theater that opera helped build on the site saw the disastrous premiere of Beethoven's *Leonora*.

In Vienna, then as now, one could almost see little Mozart bustling through the streets in his dandy's clothes, see the chubby bohemian Schubert with his curly hair and minuscule spectacles, see Beethoven strolling distractedly up broad Kärntnerstrasse, his tall hat crooked back on his head, clutching a roll of music behind his back. In Vienna in 1862 you could speak with old people who said: yes, Mozart, Haydn, Beethoven, Schubert, I saw them, I heard them play, I was there when Beethoven tried to mark time for the premiere of the Ninth Symphony at the Kärntnerthor, and he was so deaf he didn't know it was over, and they turned him around to blink uncomprehending at the roaring ovation. The streets echoed with the memories of giants, and their footsteps, and in the city their music and the applause had never stopped.

Besides touring Vienna, listening to the echoes, Brahms called on leading musicians, who proved curious to meet him. Immediately he made the acquaintance of people destined to be lifelong friends and colleagues. A typical mix of Brahms acquaintances, they included chamber and orchestral violinist Josef Hellmesberger, pianist and professor Julius Epstein, musicologist Gustav Nottebohm. He renewed his acquaintance with conductor Karl Grädener, who had moved to Vienna from Hamburg, paid a call on critic Eduard Hanslick, and had a reunion with his cherished Hamburg chorister Bertha Porubzsky, who was now engaged.

From home Elise wrote: "Mother and I were sad after you left, we were so used to your having coffee with us. . . . You haven't written us anything about the beautiful young Vienna girls." Later Elise reported that some Frauenchor alumni had sung his duets for her and Mother, and his favorite Laura Garbe wanted something to remember him by—a few notes, a lock of hair.[54] Clara Schumann wrote from Düsseldorf that she had bought a little house in the resort of Baden-Baden, and at Winterthur and Bâle, "I was particularly charmed with Kirchner's organ playing."[55] On November 16, Brahms made his Vienna debut, playing the G Minor Piano Quartet with Hellmesberger's group.

A day or two after that came the news of the failure or insult or historic blunder that threw his life into turmoil, years of wandering, and endless bitterness. Theodor Avé-Lallemant wrote apologetically to say that they had offered the podium of the Hamburg Philharmonic to Julius Stockhausen.

Brahms was thunderstruck. Certainly his friend Stockhausen was a superb musician and singer, but he had never held an orchestral position in his life. The members of Brahms's circle were as stunned as he was. Joachim wrote Avé, "The insult to Johannes will not be forgotten in the history of art."[56] Clara, in Hamburg at the time, got the news from Avé himself. They sat talking about it late into the night, Avé offering a number of reasons, perhaps convincing, for the board's decision: there was much to be done in developing the orchestra and that was not Brahms's forte; let Stockhausen build up the group, then Brahms could take it over. Avé probably did not mention the more likely reason, that Julius Stockhausen was internationally famous and unequivocally admired, and Brahms neither.

Brahms could accept no rationalizations. He still longed—or convinced himself he did—to stay in his hometown, to lead a musical life there, to settle down as a proper Kapellmeister. Not least, perhaps, with this position he had dreamed of a kind of redemption for his father and family: to turn Johann Jakob Brahms the *Bierfiedler* and descendant of peasants into the father of the conductor of the Hamburg Philharmonic.

Brahms could not shake the suspicion that his family's place on the social scale had something to do with it. Maybe he was right. He had come from people you saw playing tunes in the street, and for some in Hamburg that was all the Brahmses would ever amount to.[57] It is as if when he heard the news he suddenly saw no redemption for his family's name, and for himself infinite loneliness stretching ahead. He wrote Clara one of the most candid and poignant letters of his life.

I feel I must send you the enclosed letter [from Avé]. It represents a much sadder event for me than you can imagine or perhaps grasp.

As a man I suppose I am a little bit old-fashioned . . . but I am as attached to my native town as I might be to my mother.

Now you must be aware that as early as this autumn the Singakademie were seriously thinking of engaging a second conductor . . . and just before I left Hamburg to come here I was asked privately whether I would be inclined to accept. And now this hostile friend [Avé again] comes and ousts me—forever.

How rare it is for the likes of us to find a permanent niche and how glad I should have been to find mine in my native town. Happy as I am here with so many beautiful things to gladden my heart, I nevertheless feel, and shall always feel, that I am a stranger and can have no peace. . . .

If I could not fasten my hopes on my native town, what claims could I have elsewhere? Where should I care to go even if I had the chance?

Apart from what you experienced with your husband you know that, as a general rule, what our fellow-citizens like best is to get rid of us and allow us to flit about in the wilderness of the world.

And yet what one wants is to be bound, and to acquire everything that makes life worth living. One is naturally frightened by the thought of solitude. An active existence in lively association with others and with plenty of stimulating intercourse, the happiness of a family circle,—who is so little of a human being as not to long for these things?[58]

Brahms never lost that sadness, that rage, that regret, for the rest of his years as an exile in the wilderness of the world. He believed the podium in Hamburg represented his last best chance to be a complete human being. He was mistaken about that, mistaken that he would have enjoyed the job, mistaken about his need for family and home. But that was the way he was made, to yearn for things even as he fled them. He had been handed a destiny, some of it glorious and some of it wretched. Yet if like all men he felt what he had lost and grieved for it, fate once again had dealt him the right card. It took Brahms over a decade to understand it, but when he wrote his anguished letter to Clara from Vienna, he was already in the place he belonged.

CHAPTER ELEVEN

City of Dreams

AFTER THE DRAMA AND TURBULENCE OF THE 1850s, when Brahms bounced from obscure music student to Messiah to frustrated lover to blocked composer and reluctant soloist, the main thing he aspired to in his creative and personal life was this: no more turbulence, no more drama. To that end he was willing to pay the requisite price, which was loneliness. In the decades after he first came to Vienna in 1862, amid the gemütlich cafés and elegant concert halls and a growing crowd of admirers, Brahms carried around with him an unremitting, inescapable solitude. He was a man with many friends and no intimates.

His final conquest of the city took many years and was never unopposed. Still, with him the story would not go as it had with his father's migration to Hamburg, a slow rise to a middling position. The Old World's capital of music welcomed Brahms from the beginning, and the Viennese were prepared to give him applause, favor, and finally love when he had earned them in competition with the local lights—who happened to include Haydn, Mozart, Beethoven, and Schubert. Slowly and warily, he came to love the city in return.

But no more drama. Brahms wanted time and peace for his work and to an extraordinary degree he found them. Time and luck smiled on him as they had not on his predecessors. At twenty-nine, Brahms's age when he came to Vienna, Schubert had two years to live and Mozart six, Beethoven was going deaf, and Wagner had fled Paris after nearly starving. In 1862, Brahms had over three decades of vigorous health and relatively unfettered time ahead of him. In those years he would often be generous with his time and fortune, but only when and where he chose. Mostly he had no employers, answered to no one and submitted to no one (except, sometimes, to Clara Schumann). He never accepted a commission for a piece. The longest position he ever held lasted three years. Every post he occupied he resigned, with nothing in hand to replace them, because the jobs irked him. Though he hardly cared to make a lot of money, eventually he made so much that he simply gave it away by the handful or let it sit in the bank.

Brahms was a faithful minister to his music and eventually Vienna rewarded him for it. Otherwise no drama, no distraction if he could help it. He waged a perennial battle to escape the emotional consequences of life and love, to dominate his life and everyone in it with the same relentlessness that he dominated the fabric of his music. If in the end the world wanted to make a living monument out of him, he found that another useful way of keeping the world at bay. The loneliness he would endure, if never relish.

His life was composing, after that family and friends and study and performing. His music naturally evolved over the years, but more subtly than with other composers of his stature. In nearly four decades after his mid-twenties, there is no journey in the development of Brahms's work nearly as great as the difference between the Beethoven of the First Piano Concerto and of the late string quartets, the Mozart of *Il re pastore* and of *Don Giovanni*. Few composers could have spent twenty years and more on a unified piece, as Brahms did at least three times. It worked because his language and ideas had not changed enough as to make the seams stand out.

Inevitably, now and then, life broke in on his lonely peace and his bachelor routine. Brahms had more unlucky infatuations to get through, but the episodes were unwanted and he escaped them as soon as he could. Night after night he took his bows before audiences, or left a jolly company or the clamor of a bawdy house, and walked home with relief to his narrow bed, to rise next morning before dawn and light a cigar and make strong coffee and contend with the sea of notes again. Always, he slept well.

IN NOVEMBER 1862, Brahms wrote Julius Grimm, "Well, this is it! I have established myself here within ten paces of the Prater [at No. 55 Novaragasse, today Praterstrasse] and can drink my wine where Beethoven drank his." From beginning to end he loved Vienna's Prater, once the hunting preserve of emperors, in the nineteenth century a four-mile-long wooded park dotted with cafés and beer gardens and restaurants. Like every Viennese, Beethoven and Schubert had relaxed there after work and listened to music gay and melancholy from little orchestras. Many of Brahms's works would be laid out in his mind during early-morning walks on the paths of the Prater, turning the luminous input of inspiration into solid notes and forms. Sometimes he spent all day eating and drinking in the park, roaming the woods in his rocking stride, his head thrown back, swinging a hat in his hand.

Brahms was a particular aficionado of the gypsy bands at the café Czarda, where over the years he sat for countless hours steeping himself in that exotic, perfervid music for violins and cimbalom and bass, its rhythms soaring free of the tyranny of musical notation. Otherwise, he could lunch with the babbling hordes in the beer gardens and have his coffee under the trees listening to the Ladies' Orchestra. He picked up the Viennese inflection for its favorite brew: Kaffee. At the cafés there was always good beer and wine, and the Viennese specialties of goulash, beef with vegetable garnish—Tafelspitz—and pork knuckles.

No less did Brahms enjoy the vulgar side of the park, the dusty, crowded Wurstelprater on the western end, its games and rides and food stands and Punch-and-Judy shows (Wurstl is the Viennese name for Punch). There children screamed with delight, lovers walked arm in arm, and Brahms took a turn now and then on the carved horses of a carousel. Eventually, writes biographer Max Kalbeck: "All the restaurant proprietors, stall owners, clowns, carousel operators, acrobats, swing pushers, salami men, bakery ladies, and peddlers knew him."[1] So did the prostitutes, who at dusk, reliable as bats, stalked the Prater in the bright lights of the amusements and the shadows of the woods.

Across Vienna from the Prater, south of the palaces and cathedrals of the Old City and across the River Wien, sits the Karlskirche, most remarkable of the city's Baroque cathedrals. For the last twenty-four years of his life Brahms would look out his front windows across Karlsgasse to its portico and triumphal columns. Between his first arrival in 1862 and his taking an apartment there in 1874, Brahms saw Vienna's last boom and the beginning of its decline toward what Karl Kraus, the fin-de-siècle social critic, called the "Proving-Ground for World Destruction." Yet the place that called itself the City of Dreams never lost its vivacity, its love of life that included love of music and the arts. The splendor of the city lingered on as incomprehensibly as Austria's ancient, incomprehensible empire.

At the time of Brahms's arrival in Vienna the city was approaching its greatest boom. Perhaps no one could have suspected how soon on the heels of that boom the decline would begin. In 1857, the young Hapsburg emperor Franz Josef had decreed that the Renaissance walls of the city, built to hold off the Turks, would be razed and replaced by a broad circling avenue, to be lined with what aspired to be the grandest monuments of art and architecture in the world. So began the Ringstrasse and, in the later 1860s, the period of middle-class boom and speculation called in Austria the Ringstrasse Era—the equivalent of the *Gründerjahre* in Germany, the Victorian period in England, the Second Empire in France, the Gilded Age in the United States.

The first Ringstrasse building finished—before Parliament or Town Hall or the University—was the giant Hofoper, Court Opera, begun in 1861 and opened in 1869. As part of his official duties Franz Josef regularly attended the productions, dozing week after week in the Imperial Box. If the Ringstrasse project originated by royal decree, however, it was carried out by other forces, with their own agenda. Vienna historian Carl E. Schorske calls the Ringstrasse "a visual expression of the values of a social class"[2]—that class being the prosperous bourgeois builders and speculators and art lovers, the *Grossbürgertum*, who shaped modern Vienna in its splendor, its fragility, and its madness. As in Germany, that class was the main audience for classical music.

An essential conviction of the bourgeoisie was that truth in the modern world comes from science and law; only the past contained beauty. So, writes Schorske, "whenever [the *Grossbürgertum*] strove to express its values in architecture, it retreated into history."[3] Translated into architecture, that conviction meant that the structural elements of modern building and technology had to be concealed behind a screen of borrowed tradition.[4] For the Ringstrasse project Franz Josef assembled celebrated architects from around Austria and all over Europe, and formed them into committees to plan a unified development. It amounted to an urban building project unprecedented in history. The committees decreed that each building was to have a style appropriate to its function: the Hofoper in early French Renaissance style, the Town Hall neo-Gothic, the University Italian Renaissance, the Law Courts German Renaissance, the Parliament neo-Hellenistic, the Hoftheater a wedding-cake improvisation on the Baroque, and so on in a ramble through nearly everybody's history except Austria's. The buildings were intended to look like ancient stone, but the look was fake: they were made of poured and molded concrete.[5]

Thus the Historical Style. Its admirers included aspiring young artist Adolf Hitler, who in *Mein Kampf* recalled of his first encounter: "For hours I could stand in front of the Opera, for hours I could gaze at the Parliament; the whole Ring Boulevard seemed to me like an enchantment out of 'The Thousand and One Nights.'" Hitler would plan the

Berlin capital of his thousand-year Reich on the model of the Ringstrasse.

The Hofoper, designed by August Sicard von Sicardsburg and Eduard van der Nüll, can stand for all the Ringstrasse's bold, monumental, ultimately barren plundering of the past. The outside of the Opera is a riot of Renaissance elements, from where one entered a many-arched grand-staircased gloom like a Turkish harem, and finally arrived in an auditorium of similarly eclectic style.[6] In Vienna where everything artistic was a matter of ongoing dispute in every coffeehouse, the Opera's potpourri of historical expropriations was captured in a little rhyme: *Der Sicardsburg und der van der Nüll haben beide keinen Stül*—Sicardburg and van der Nüll have neither any style. In good Viennese style, architect Sicardsburg responded to the slander by killing himself. Vienna had one of the highest suicide rates in Europe, especially among the upper bourgeoisie. In the talented, prosperous, highly musical Wittgenstein family, made famous by philosopher Ludwig, three of the four brothers took their own lives.

So oddly isolated, Brobdingnagian new buildings sprang up around the Ringstrasse, design and symbolism regularly foiling practicality. In the Hoftheater one could hardly hear the actors, in the Hofoper half the boxholders could barely see the stage. The Opera's capricious relation of outside and inside was echoed again and again in the avenue's other buildings, among them the Musikverein, completed in 1869 as home of the Gesellschaft der Musikfreunde (Society of the Friends of Music). The serenely classical exterior of the Musikverein is outshouted by the candy-box extravagance of the "Golden Hall" inside, the audience flanked by rows of gold-plated caryatids. The dominant painter of the era was Hans Makart, brought to Vienna by the emperor in 1869. Makart fashioned a style at once riotously Baroque and turgid, with the same *horror vacui* that characterized the architectural decoration of the day. The Ringstrasse Era is also the Age of Makart.

The period began with supreme extravagance in the 1860s and stumbled in the stock market crash of 1873 and ensuing depression. Those years exactly matched the decline of Austrian power that was to begin with the German victory in the Austro-Prussian War of 1866, which made Austria irrelevant to the further history of German peoples, and the sapping of power after 1867 that came from the Austrian crown's Dual Monarchy with Hungary. Thus the supreme irony of Ringstrasse Vienna: the more impotent the Austrian empire, the more inflated its monuments. Yet as the empire declined the bourgeoisie prospered, immoderately until the crash, more temperately afterward.

So what was Johannes Brahms doing there, this austere North German living in a city halfway across Europe from the homeland he loved, and which considered Vienna second only to Paris in decadence? At least some of the reasons are easily found. Brahms shunned Hamburg after the Philharmonic snubbed him, and by lingering on in Vienna took a path of less resistance. After all, whatever its contradictions the place remained incomparable in the Western world when it came to music. In Brahms's day as in Mozart's, the finest artists gravitated there. One found contacts to be made, powers to court, and both critically and financially the rewards of success were unbeatable. (Now the movers and shakers came more from the *Grossbürgertum* than from the court circles Mozart and Beethoven depended on, though there were still aristocratic patrons.) Brahms was to conquer the powers in Vienna with historic success. After fumbling his campaign to get the job he wanted in Hamburg, he made himself quite a canny careerist, wooing the influential while not appearing to care in the least.

All the same, though his old friends concertized regularly in Vienna, none of them felt obliged to live there. Clara Schumann and Joachim thrived in Berlin, Julius Grimm made do with Göttingen and Münster, Albert Dietrich with Oldenburg. Brahms could have made a living in any number of German cities, even Hamburg. Why Vienna?

Certainly the temper of the place appealed to him as much as its music: the city that loved rib-sticking food and wine made to be drunk in quantity, the atmosphere of romance, the ongoing intellectual and artistic and political debates of the coffeehouses, and in the Vienna Woods the gardens of little *Heuriger* taverns surrounded by vineyards and serving endless mugs of new wine; and everywhere music lilting and bittersweet when it needed to be, incomparably magnificent when it needed to be. The city suited Brahms for those reasons, and deeper ones. More and more as nineteenth-century Romanticism slipped toward decadence and denouement, a melancholy prowled beneath the gay mirage of life and art in the theaters and cafés and streets. The quintessential Viennese playwright Nestroy wrote, "The noblest of all the nations is resignation." The sentiment characterized the place. The gaiety of Vienna was a mask, and Brahms understood masks.

Much of Vienna's tone and humor reflected an empire not exactly conquered but increasingly irrelevant, stewing in its glory. Brahms resonated with that too: a lost past full of glories haunting the present. The past of Viennese music was the audible embodiment of a splendor, the traditions pervading the Baroque churches and palaces, the court and society balls throbbing to the lilt of waltzes, the concert halls worshipful of the past and leery of the present.

The comic-opera court was presided over by the colorless and implacably dutiful Emperor Franz Josef, in his sixty-eight years on the throne one of the longest-reigning monarchs in the history of the world. The empire slowly withered and staggered along with the royal person. The word *helplessness* embodies a good deal of the Viennese tone, and its later history: an ancient empire lurching toward dissolution; a middle class frustrated before a social ceiling that left the top of society frozen and unattainable; eleven constituent peoples and their mélange of languages making up an ethnic bedlam—Slavonic, Hungarian, Bohemian, Italian, Jewish—so ungovernable that the name "Austria" did not even officially exist in the later nineteenth century. The muddle is preserved in the untranslatable polycultural stew of Wienerisch, the city's singular dialect. "Was there perhaps never a rhythmic social whole at all," Carl Schorske wonders, "only an illusion of unified movement resulting from an accidental articulation of fundamentally incohesive, individuated parts?"[7]

Yet again there is the paradox of Vienna, that it remained, and remains, such a particular, singular place. And through all its tumultuous modern history music flowered extraordinarily, in the human and professional tragicomedy of triumphs and disasters and struggles and cabals and boundless ambitions. The city possessed a *Grossbürgertum* eager for art and unprecedentedly educated to it. In Vienna a man like Brahms who felt himself from nowhere, a vagabond belonging to no one, could find a home full of marvelous music and musicians and a strange joie de vivre touched with weariness and despair.

There is still a deeper level of Brahms's connection to Vienna, why he and the city belonged to each other. Born in poverty, he reached adulthood rooted in the rising middle class, the *Grossbürgertum* that built the Ringstrasse and all it symbolized, who were the amateur friends of music who primarily founded and ran and often participated in the orchestra and chorus of the Gesellschaft der Musikfreunde. Politically liberal, capitalistic, constitutional, long the most dynamic force in the city but by the end of the century incapable of hanging on to power, the middle class believed in hard work, in competition, in success, science, rationality, rules, railroad timetables. They honored the arts and culture extravagantly, but they also respected the military and political strong men.[8]

If the arts were near the center of life for the Austro-German *Grossbürgertum*, that class shaped Brahms and his art, and in turn his art confirmed the values of that class. What is his music after all, even before he arrived in Vienna, but another manifestation of the historicism that dominated attitudes and design in his era? Brahms's work, like the Ringstrasse, is an eclectic assemblage encompassing the whole of a tradition. His music arises from the bourgeois art-loving milieu that built the showplaces of the Ringstrasse to glorify itself, and plundered history to do it. And his music was written largely *for* that milieu and its equivalents elsewhere. Brahms imagined his work in the setting of middle-class *Gründerjahre* concert halls. When in his last years he saw his era lurching toward its end and his class withering on the vine, he despaired for his work and for all music.

The differences between Brahms and the Ringstrasse lie in the vital intangibles of unity, integrity, quality. By the mid-nineteenth century, Vienna had for a time lost its way in architecture and painting. That never quite happened in music. Brahms's art is a kind of transcendent historicism in sound, fashioned with immensely more mastery than the committees of artists who planned the Hofoper and Parliament and Burgtheater. If the method is similar, the difference is that between genius and something close to kitsch. If the Opera House has no style, Brahms for all his eclecticism has a style as singular and dynamic as any composer who ever lived—as singular and dynamic as the whole of Vienna itself. Romantic Classicist, Classical Romantic, neo-Baroque and -Renaissance polyphonist, Brahms embodied the self-conscious and contradictory aesthetic that hobbled the Historical Style, but he made that approach breathe and live. If the Ringstrasse only assembled historical themes, Brahms assimilated and masterfully synthesized them. It should not have worked, but he made it work.

Inevitably, seams and contradictions show here and there. The innovations of his technique strain the inherited assumptions of his formal patterns. His self-consciousness shows especially in the genres of which he felt most in awe—string quartet and symphony. He had written Clara early on: Mozart could go into a tavern and compose; I can't. Yet integrity remains the overwhelming impression of Brahms's art. In it nearly the whole of Western classical music sings in a single voice, from the polyphony of Palestrina to the somber spirituality of Schütz, the counterpoint and tonal architecture of Bach, the grandness and formal subtlety of Haydn and Mozart and Beethoven, the gentle lyricism of Schubert.[9] Only Mahler approached Brahms in such resonance with history, and in Mahler the seams, the despair and dissolution, are left to be heard and contemplated.

Brahms's achievement required all the immense talent he was born with, and all the skills he so painstakingly taught himself. The very tension among his sources is part of his style, his triumph: his singular assimilation of Classical logic and form and Renaissance/Baroque polyphony pervaded with a Romantic *moll-Dur* lyricism, his characteristic mingling of bright major and shadowed minor. At the same time, his music stands like the Ringstrasse, but far higher, as a testament and validation of the Austro-German *Grossbürgertum*. Despite his fears, Brahms's music survived the end of his milieu and the golden age of his class because, while it was deeply imbedded in its setting, it also transcended its setting. (Perhaps that is a thumbnail description of the most enduring art.)

Nobody ever shaped a musical career more shrewdly and had more luck in it than Brahms. His historical image seems to be that of a plodder, an artist who made himself great by sheer hard work. In fact he was blindingly gifted, as nearly every musician who heard him understood (he made sure they understood it). Brilliant as he was, Brahms faced dilemmas his predecessors had not, above all the burden of history, and he could not accept the New German answers to them. He faced these dilemmas heroically, head on, and mastered them one by one. That his music has a decisive color is a measure of his achievement. He avoided so many traps, and his music pulled together so many contradictions so beautifully. Loneliness was the price, and he paid the price faithfully if without pleasure. The plight of a homesick North German bourgeois living in and loving Vienna can stand for all his contradictions, and those of his age and adopted city.

WHEN BRAHMS ARRIVED in the city in 1862, two organizations dominated Viennese concert life—the Opera/Philharmonic and the Gesellschaft der Musikfreunde (Society of the Friends of Music). At the end of the decade both were slated to move to new quarters the Ringstrasse development planned for them, the Hofoper and the Musikverein. In 1862 the Opera still mounted its productions at the historic Kärntnerthor Theater, where Beethoven had premiered the Ninth Symphony. The Opera orchestra, conducted by Otto Dessoff, became the Vienna Philharmonic for eight instrumental concerts a year at the Kärntnerthor, the tickets precious and generally reserved for prominent families. The orchestra of the Gesellschaft der Musikfreunde, still mostly amateur in the 1860s, presented its concerts under Johann Herbeck in the Redoutensaal of the Imperial Palace, a room seating six hundred and imperially decked out with long mirrors, Gobelin tapestries, and crystal chandeliers à la Versailles. Everyone was familiar with the proclivities of both groups: the

Philharmonic conservative and largely devoted to the pedestaled dead from Mendelssohn backward, the Gesellschaft more receptive to living composers.

Likewise, among the amateur choral groups in town two dominated, the Singverein associated with the Gesellschaft der Muskfreunde and conducted by Herbeck, and the Singakademie, perennially overshadowed by the Singverein. The Gesellschaft, largely founded and run by amateurs of the *Grossbürgertum* but also with aristocratic members, sponsored a library, a museum, and a Conservatory headed by Philharmonic concertmaster Josef Hellmesberger.

All the same, in the Vienna of Brahms's day the majority of performances were given in smaller chamber and recital halls, and in private soirees in homes and palaces. By 1890, there were around 240 public concerts a year in Vienna in the Bösendorfer, Ehrbar, and Musikverein halls, but only seventeen of them full-scale and professional. If Brahms wanted to hear Beethoven's Ninth in town, he had thirteen opportunities in the thirty-four years he was based in Vienna, and it took around ten years to have a chance to hear all nine Beethoven symphonies played professionally.[10] Many of the amateurs hearing an orchestral program in the later nineteenth century had played or heard the same works in their homes, or had taken the music-appreciation classes that proliferated at the time. Often they came to the concert hall for the full, live experience of music they already knew and loved from piano arrangements. If the public was slow to appreciate living composers, Brahms knew that if he kept supplying them with music for the concert hall and the parlor, both serious and light, they would come around to him. Slowly, they did.

Nineteenth-century Europe created modern musical organizations, modern concert life and concert halls and music education, and the modern sense of a canon of historic masterpieces. As integral accompaniment, that process generated a lively interest in music criticism. Of the critics in Vienna, only one was inescapable in Brahms's years there: Eduard Hanslick, Professor of the History and Aesthetics of Music at the University of Vienna, critic of *Die Presse* from 1855 to 1864 and of the *Neue Freie Presse* until he died in 1904.[11] The latter was one of the leading papers in Europe, and Hanslick one of its leading lights.

Born in Prague in 1825, son of a middle-class philosopher/musician and trained to the law, Hanslick developed a fervor for Schumann's music and writings that tempted him into journalism. He came to Vienna to finish his legal studies and there expected to hear marvelous music night and day. Instead he found, "How trivial was public musical life at the end of the thirties and in the early forties! . . . Cut off from all great intellectual interests, the Vienna public abandoned itself to diversion and entertainment. . . . Musical life was dominated by Italian opera, virtuosity, and the waltz."[12] Ending up a professor and critic, he aspired to raise standards by improving music education, thereby helping to reawaken Vienna to its incomparable past in music. To a considerable degree, he succeeded. And he promoted progressive living composers from Germany—at first including Wagner, or at least *Tannhäuser.*

Hanslick's fame spread beyond Vienna with the 1854 publication of his brochure *On Beauty in Music.* Eventually translated into several languages and running through ten editions in German, it proclaimed a doctrine summarized in its more notorious aphorisms:

> Definite feelings and emotions are unsusceptible of being embodied in music. . . . To the question: What is to be expressed with all this material? The answer will be: Musical ideas. Now, a musical idea reproduced in its entirety is not only an object of intrinsic beauty but also an end in itself, and not a means for representing feelings and thoughts.
>
> The essence of music is sound and motion.

For the nineteenth century those words defined the concept of "absolute music," an instrumental art pure, abstract, objective, beyond words. Among those who kept that faith, Hanslick's pamphlet became sacred text, a small but potent counterblow to the New German/Wagnerians aesthetic edifice. Brahms's first reaction to *On Beauty in Music,* written to Clara Schumann in his Kreisler years, had been: "I found such a number of stupid things in it that I gave it up." In the next decade, when Brahms got to know and need the critic, he sang a contrasting variation.

Like those pronouncements, Hanslick's ideas tended to the grandiose and absolute, even though as a writer his style was finely honed and aimed to a broad audience. Those features suited a time when high art was more broadly popular than it had ever been. Knowledgeable in music history and competent at the keyboard, Hanslick still managed to be oddly and tellingly unmusical. His friend, the surgeon and musical amateur Theodor Billroth, once complained after a session of chamber music, "The schoolmasterly way he performs everything, with his dry tone and without the slightest grasp of the whole, often drives me nearly to distraction."[13] Hanslick could not play legato to save his life, and Brahms's favorite two-against-three rhythms left him floundering at the keys.

Hawk-nosed, bushy-eyebrowed, fiercely vain though essentially good-natured and honest, in lifestyle (like Brahms) a North German bourgeois, Hanslick was one of the last critics to present his judgments as something approaching dogma. The reason so few followed suit was that he so often managed to be imperiously, impeccably, historically wrong. Hanslick swung his sword at the tide of history so uncompromisingly that ever after, in judging new work, music critics have tended to hedge their bets. Since Hanslick, reviewers have looked anxiously to the past and its collections of stupid reviews, whose star attraction is always Hanslick, and reviewers have not wanted to be part of future collections. This is the man who after viewing the premiere of Wagner's *Das Rheingold* at Bayreuth listed a few of its undeniable virtues and then went on for page after page about its "deceit, prevarication, violence and animal sensuality . . . this unctuous pedant [Wotan] revered as the godly ideal of the German people?" His infamous review of another new work concluded, "The violin is no longer played; it is yanked about, it is torn asunder, it is beaten black and blue. . . . We see wild and vulgar faces, we hear curses, we smell bad brandy. . . . Tchaikovsky's Violin Concerto brings to us for the first time the horrid idea that there may be music that stinks in the ear." (Tchaikovsky could recite that review word for word.) Meanwhile, like most Viennese, Hanslick had no great affection for pre-Classical music, confessing that he would burn all of Schütz and a good deal of Bach for a few more works by Brahms and Schumann.[14]

Following a similar road as Schumann's from progressive to counterrevolutionary, Hanslick became a formidable power in keeping Vienna's concert halls conservative citadels. Already in 1858, in his review of *Lohengrin* (a wildly popular work, in fact), Hanslick had begun questioning Wagner's direction. His final metamorphosis from enthusiast to naysayer perhaps came one evening in Vienna, with a typically Wagnerian piece of nastiness. In 1862 the composer invited the critic, among others, to a reading of the new libretto for *Die Meistersinger*. The opera's villain is a blustering pedant the world knows as Beckmesser, but at that time he was pointedly named "Hanslich." As Wagner declaimed the libretto he savored the spectacle of his victim turning various colors and bolting out the door. Wagner professed sincere surprise at the critic's change of heart afterward.[15] In his essay "Jewry in Music," Wagner made Hanslick the archetype of anti-German sentiment in the arts, which he called "music-Jewry." (Hanslick was half-Jewish, though he denied it.)[16]

Through his years of largely futile Wagner-bashing the critic kept up a show of objectivity, insisting that after *Tannhäuser* the work he most admired was none other than *Die Meistersinger*. In his autobiography he came clean: "I know very well that he is the greatest living opera

composer and in a historical sense the only one worth talking about . . .
[but] Wagner's operatic style recognizes only superlatives, and a superlative has no future. . . . he broke a new path, dangerous to life and limb.
This path is for him alone."[17] Privately, Brahms would arrive at an as-
sessment that, while far more generous than Hanslick's, was not so different in drift.

If Hanslick knew all along that it was hopeless to fight Wagner and
Wagnerism, he later, with Brahms egging him on, turned his guns on a
more guileless target, his fellow university lecturer Anton Bruckner.
Timid, nervous, perpetually the Austrian peasant lost in the big city (or
acting the part), the little man stewed miserably in Hanslick's bile. After
the premiere of Bruckner's Eighth Symphony Hanslick wrote: "It is not
out of the question that the future belongs to this muddled hangover
style—which is no reason to regard the future with envy. For the time being, however, one would prefer that symphonic and chamber music remain undefiled by a style only relatively justified as an illustrative device
for certain dramatic situations."[18] Since for years Bruckner had few powerful champions in the city, words like that took great chunks out of him.
"Without Hanslick," he groaned, "all is lost in Vienna. Ever since 1876 I
have been outlawed, because I accepted the position of Instructor at the
University." Once when Franz Josef asked Bruckner what he could do as
a favor, the composer begged the emperor to have a word with Hanslick
about toning down his stuff.

A century later, when the principals and the passions of their causes
have faded into print, these battles seem distant, pointless, laughable. For
those who fought them, they were a matter of something like life and
death—their own fiscal and professional life, and the life and death of an
art in its prime. As music went, as art in Vienna went, so in some degree
went the future of all the arts. And as that future played out in the century before the millennium, Hanslick and Brahms lost the battle. Wagner and the progressives set the course toward Modernism, leaving
Brahms the perpetual outsider.

If a century later the battles are not so important or so central to the
culture, it is because the end of Modernism left music no longer central,
no longer the art to which all others arts aspire. Brahms met people in
Vienna who had known Beethoven and Schubert personally, when those
artists and their predecessors Haydn and Mozart were among the most
exciting things happening in the Western artistic world. You could still
feel that excitement on the streets of Vienna in Brahms's time, and in the
concert halls and schools and cafés and newspaper columns. In some de-

gree the echoes of that excitement still resonate now, at the end of the millennium, nowhere more than in Vienna.

All the same, time exacts its toll and the bravos fade into history and dust gathers on the monuments, and the excitement once palpable in the streets threatens to become a ceremonial relic, a marble cenotaph. That process had begun when Brahms died in Vienna, by then himself almost a monument of the past. It took the city only eleven years to erect its memorial to him. Today his marble double faces the Musikverein, scene of his frustrations and triumphs. He is seated lost in thought, with the Karlskirche at his back, and the Muse lies prostrate at his feet.

CHAPTER TWELVE

Farewell

Soon after Brahms came to Vienna in September 1862, long before he admitted he had settled there, he became a fixture of the musical scene. He presented himself as composer-pianist, and the city often liked his piano playing better than his compositions. For a long time Brahms may have been the only person to call himself simply a composer, but neither to him nor anyone else did it appear possible to get by on writing music. So, away from Hamburg, he resigned himself to what he called an "amphibian" existence, concertizing and teaching for his keep.[1] His sporadic efforts to establish himself as a conductor remained inconclusive. During the 1860s, on a good night, he was still a splendid pianist, his repertoire ranging between Bach and himself but centered on Beethoven, Schubert, and Schumann. If no virtuoso on the level of Clara Schumann or Joachim, he could still put across a piece by sheer insight and musicianship and force of personality.

His first two performances in town came by way of Conservatory professor Julius Epstein, a darling of the town as pianist and teacher. Brahms met him through his one-time Hamburg chorister and devotee Bertha Porubzsky, now Faber. Like so many others, on their first meeting Epstein experienced the Brahms Epiphany: this slight, quiet blond youth who played the piano with such authority, who appeared so certain of himself, who wrote things so manifestly fresh and vital.

Epstein lived in Schulerstrasse, in the building where Mozart had composed *The Marriage of Figaro* in the 1780s; where Joseph Haydn had said to father Leopold, "Before God and as an honest man, your son is the greatest composer I have ever known or heard of"; where Mozart had declared after listening to a teenager named Beethoven play, "Someday the world is going to hear something from that one." Brahms likely knew all that when he showed up at Epstein's for a rehearsal by the Hellmesberger ensemble, bringing with him his G Minor Piano Quartet. If Julius Epstein was a generous and earnest sort, Josef Hellmesberger was a hard-bitten old pro. Son of a famous musical family (his father had taught Joachim), concertmaster of the Philharmonic, leader of the most celebrated string quartet in town, Hellmesberger was a master of the intrigues and political maneuvering that pervaded the musical life of the city.

On this first meeting at Epstein's, things went profitably, almost like Brahms's old days, and the event contributed another piece of history to the *Figarohaus*. Hellmesberger's group read through the G Minor Quartet. After the *rondo alla Zingarese* the violinist leaped up, threw his instrument on the bed, embraced Brahms and theatrically proclaimed, "This is the heir of Beethoven!" A fine start, though hardly representative of how their relations were to play out over the years. Clara Schumann, who performed with Hellmesberger in Vienna, despised the man—to a large degree because he blew hot and cold about Johannes's music and refused to stick his neck out for it, as she did all the time. From this first encounter onward, Hellmesberger and Brahms would be much involved in each other's history, but the violinist watched out very carefully for his own interests and would never be in anyone's pocket. Brahms understood that and behaved accordingly.

So, shortly afterward came Brahms's first performance in Vienna, on November 16, 1862—the G Minor Quartet with members of Hellmesberger's ensemble, the composer at the piano. The old Gesellschaft der Musikfreunde Vereinsaal was crowded with music fanciers wanting a look at Schumann's Messiah. Probably the Brahms friends in town assembled too—Bertha Faber and new husband Arthur, conductor Karl Grädener, soprano Luise Dustmann. Audience response to the quartet was cool until the *alla Zingarese* finale lifted them out of their seats, as it has audiences ever since. After that concert a group of Brahmsians began to form in Vienna.

Two days before, the Gesellschaft orchestra under Herbeck had played the D Major Serenade, not particularly well but to a generally good reception.[2] Critic Eduard Hanslick liked the first minuet best, and for all his abstract ideals could wield a flowery metaphor in a review: "The instrumental coloring and the grace of the melody give [the minuet] the characteristic of night music, and it is full of moonlight and the scent of lilac." The city seemed to be welcoming Brahms entirely pleasantly.

Then came the devastating letter from Avé-Lallemant saying that Julius Stockhausen had been offered the Hamburg Philharmonic. Brahms had to pull himself together for a debut solo concert Epstein had set up for November 29, which fell three days after Stockhausen accepted the offer. His rankling disappointment did not seem to trip Brahms in the least. Assisted by Hellmesberger's group, he played his A Major Piano Quartet, a Bach toccata, Schumann's Op. 17 Fantasia, and his own Handel Variations. The audience was polite at the quartet, enthusiastic at the Variations. Just before his despondent letter to Clara about the Hamburg job, he wrote his parents his own review of the concert. Probably he was bucking up their feelings as well as his own; surely Christiane and Johann Jakob had wanted him on the podium in Hamburg as much as he wanted to be there. His letter shows an uncharacteristic bravado:

> I was very happy yesterday, my concert went quite excellently, much better than I had hoped. After the quartet had been sympathetically received, I had extraordinary success as a player. Every number met with the greatest applause. . . . I played as freely as though I had been sitting at home among friends, and certainly this public is far more stimulating than our own. . . . Tell the contents of this letter to Herr Marxsen.[3]

Hanslick had met Brahms years before at the Lower Rhine Music Festival, but this may have been the critic's first encounter with Brahms playing his own work. Hanslick's review of the recital shows that, like the rest of the world, he had not forgotten Schumann's "Neue Bahnen." Brahms's compositions, wrote Hanslick:

> are hardly to be counted among those immediately enlightening and gripping works which carry the listener along with them in their flight. Their esoteric character, disdainful of popular effect, combined with the great technical difficulties, makes their popularization a much slower process than one had been led to expect from the delightful prophecy Schumann gave his favorite as a parting blessing. . . . Will the natural freshness and youthfulness continue to bloom untroubled in the costly vase that he has now created for them? Will they grow even more beautiful and free? Does that veil of brooding reflection which so frequently clouds his newest works presage a sudden burst of sunlight, or a thicker, less hospitable twilight?[4]

Here Hanslick sounded themes that were to become staples of Brahms criticism, including his own: Brahms the brooding, thick, and esoteric.

The review conceded that this artist "is already a significant personality, possibly the most interesting among our contemporary composers." But Hanslick came down hard on the A Major Quartet: "For one thing, the themes are insignificant . . . dry and prosaic. . . . There is a continual pulling together and taking apart, preparation without objective, promise without fulfillment." He raved only about Brahms's performance of the Schumann Fantasy. No doubt Brahms gritted his teeth over all that, but he was not going to let something like a mere lack of insight stand between him and the most powerful critic in Vienna.

Of the pair of piano quartets from that period, the G Minor has often had an easier time of it with audiences, maybe because the *alla Zingarese* ends the piece so irresistibly. Comparing it with the A Major, its slightly later partner (and both from earlier sketches), shows a characteristic pattern in Brahms's pairs of works for the same medium: the first looser and more extroverted, the second relatively tighter and more subtle. If the appeal of the earlier piano quartet grows with each movement to a peak at the finale, for much of its course the A Major stays engaging and also demanding for the listener. The forms of its movements are comparatively straightforward. The complexity comes in the working-out of the material, some of the earliest examples of mature Brahmsian developing variation.[5] As Hanslick's review shows, the technique is not so easy to take in on first hearing. Often, as in the opening movement of the A Major, a theme is no sooner stated than it begins evolving both melodically and harmonically, often with new keys washing through it.

Whatever the complications, the A Major Quartet's melodic material is winning, the tone largely good-natured. The second movement is one of Brahms's stretches of nocturnal music, the tone sweet verging on sentimental, interrupted with mysterious and vaguely ominous piano swirls (recalling Schubert's eerie lied "Die Stadt"). The A section of the third-movement scherzo is lyrical and light, the trio an exercise in the demonic-canonic, echoing Haydn's famous minuet for string quartet called the "Witch's Round."

Perhaps the most arresting new element in the A Major is its rhythmic explorations. In contrast to the gaunt quarter-note theme that opens the G Minor Quartet, the A Major begins gently, undulating between eighths and triplets, a pattern to recur through the movement, sometimes expressed as two-against-three: in the second theme section from measure 53, for example, the eighths of the melody are based on the eighths of the opening, while the cello counterpoint comes from the

from Frisch, *Developing Variation*

triplets of the opening. Beyond this distinctive use of two-against-three, now Brahms plays remarkable games with meter. The extended and gracious closing theme of the first movement—at the end of the exposition and the most elaborate melody so far—is still written in $\frac{3}{4}$ but as Walter Frisch observes, for three measures the perceived downbeat is shifted to the third beat, followed by three two-beat groupings in a row, before the perceived and written downbeats settle down together.[6] (See above.)

From now on in Brahms's music the apparent, audible metric groupings are apt once in a while to drift around the written measures. He carries that idea further in the driving, vivacious last movement of the A Major. The eruptive beginning defies us to find the barline, then the second phrase almost convinces us the downbeat is in the middle of the first beat. After a series of similar diversions, for several measures (from 47) Brahms superimposes a five-quarter-note pattern over the $\frac{2}{4}$ meter—a wild, almost disorienting effect for its day, mitigated by the larkish tone of the movement.

Where did these metric subtleties come from? For all its unprecedented theoretical and historical investigations, the nineteenth century concerned itself little with rhythm, had few theoretical concepts to apply to it and scarcely even the language to analyze it. In the hundreds of pages of detailed response to Brahms's music from contemporary friends and critics, we rarely find any comment on his rhythmic ideas and no systematic analysis at all. It is as if Brahms were the only musician of his age aware that he was doing remarkable things with rhythm—and since he seldom talked about his own technique, he never brought it up either.

Walter Frisch notes that some of Brahms's ideas developed from his studies of Renaissance and Baroque composers,[7] whose rhythmic patterns can treat the barline more flexibly than later music—before the Classical period, composers did not necessarily think in regular, dance-like measures. Certainly Beethoven's metric games (as in the *Eroica* first movement) contributed to Brahms's love of *hemiola*, which usually means redefining a 3+3 metric division into 2+2+2. The "Hungarian" style in general gave him all sorts of fresh ideas for *ritmico* movements. For Brahms's habit of shifting the perceived downbeat for long stretches, maybe Bach was another model—for example, the B♭ Minor Prelude from *The Well-Tempered Clavier* Book I, where the sense of downbeat drifts to the third beat of the measure, back to the first, to the second, and so on over the course of a languid, beautiful adagio. Schumann's music also provided models of metric freedom. By the finale of Brahms's First Symphony, obscuring the meter for long stretches has become a feature of both local and larger structural organization, and also a highly expressive device: moments of wrenching intensity are created partly by uprooting the pulse.

Besides the bold games with meter, the A Major Quartet's exhilarating last movement evolves a step away from the "gypsy" finale. If the G Minor last movement is a full-scale lusty *alla Zingarese*, the A Major is gypsyish, keeping some of the characteristic rhythmic drive and tonal coloration of the "Hungarian" tone, but more abstracted. The finale of his next chamber piece, the F Minor Piano Quintet, would go a degree further into an abstraction of the Hungarian accent, and a step closer to solving one of the questions that still confronted and maybe baffled Brahms: if this kind of chamber-music finale suited him, what did he want for a symphonic finale? For that, the *alla Zingarese* vein did not feel right to him.

Brahms already had the draft of an opening movement for a C minor symphony awaiting answers to that and at least two other questions, one abstract and one mundane. First: If not a scherzo movement, what instead? Second: How could he earn enough to give him time and peace to write a symphony at all, given that a symphony is the sort of project that can lose one a lot of money? The financial side of creative life was to become even more pressing when Brahms found himself the main support of his family. As it played out, though, the decade following 1862 would provide both the aesthetic and practical questions with agreeable answers.

HISTORY CAN ONLY FOLLOW a little of the process by which he arrived at one approach or another in a piece, because Brahms the avid student of Beethoven's sketchbooks destroyed most of his own sketches. He did not want the world snooping in his workshop any more than in the rest of his life. Maybe too he did not want history to discover how relatively little sketching he did, compared to Beethoven. (Brahms's friend Gustav

Nottebohm made the first important study of the Beethoven sketches, and Brahms eventually owned some originals.)

One of the few surviving sketches concerns fourteen measures for the first movement of the A Major Piano Quartet. The fragment consists of two lines, mostly bare melody on top and bass on the bottom, with figures under the staff indicating the harmony.[8] These measures show how much Brahms composed in terms of a continuous melody unfolding over a strong bass line. In later years, when composers showed him their songs, he was apt to cover up the middle parts with two fingers and critique only the melody and bass.

From the evidence of the few surviving sketches on paper and from observation, it appears that Brahms did not need the painful forging of ideas on paper that became, after Nottebohm's studies were published, part of Beethoven's Romantic mystique. Beethoven's sketches *look* like a heroic struggle with fate and human fallibility. Brahms got his ideas like everyone else, from the unconscious or the angels or the Muse, or whatever one's metaphor for inspiration. Then he put the ideas aside, to let them work in his mind. Given his tenacious memory for music (and for all else good and bad), Brahms did not necessarily have to write things down to work on them, as apparently Beethoven did. Much of his composing was done in his head, pacing around the room or during long walks outside. Brahms sometimes called composing "walking." People who eavesdropped on him at work usually only heard the piano now and then, quietly, a few notes, and otherwise mainly the sound of him pacing and mumbling and humming to himself.[9] (Beethoven at work was famously given to howling, cursing, pounding the piano until the strings broke.)

It appears that for a given piece Brahms would generally jot down a few rough ideas, lay them out in his mind, then do a skeletal continuity sketch like the one that survives for the A Major Quartet: melody and figured bass, to settle the unfolding of ideas and the overall form. When he was satisfied with that he would go on to a rough score of the whole with inner parts added. From that he made his fair copy, with further revisions. Then, sooner or later, the preliminary labor went into the stove.

Brahms's fair copies are not impeccable pieces of calligraphy but rather working documents. He copied in a hurry, without a ruler, the stems canted and the notes made with a quick slash, generally using a quill pen because it was easier on the hand. (In letters he continually complains about having to use a steel pen on the road.) He might make corrections by rubbing out the wet ink with his thumb and writing over the smudge. His copying is always legible, but he did not care how elegant the page looked—neatness was his copyists' business.

The first performances of a piece were usually done from manuscript, both to give him time for revisions and to collect fatter fees before publishers took their cut. As seen in many manuscripts, in the course of trial read-throughs and first performances and consultations with performers, Brahms went over and over his fair copies making revisions, mostly in dynamics and phrasing and the like, but also note and scoring changes. For larger revisions he pasted patches over the manuscript with sealing wax. When he got the copyist's score the refining continued, and likewise with the printer's galleys.

For all his pains in the creative process he still managed to be a sloppy and impatient editor and proofreader, in his editions of other composers' work and in his own. Sometimes he appears to have corrected galley proofs off the top of his head, if the original manuscript was not to hand. A number of his letters ask friends to send him his own pieces, in manuscript or in print, because he did not have any copies. (He apparently never lost a score, surprising since he sent new pieces to friends constantly, by ordinary mail.)[10] Brahms could also be skimpy and arbitrary with dynamic marks, phrasings, and the like; the B♭ Major Sextet, among others, was dispatched to Joachim to put in the bowings, and from there went right to the publisher. Apparently, as far as Brahms was concerned, if the notes and the form were right, the rest of it was icing on the cake and he could afford to be casual about, say, lining up the hairpins for a crescendo. If pressed he might have said: that was good enough for Bach, it's good enough for me.[11]

BRAHMS SPENT CHRISTMAS 1862 alone in Vienna, for the first time in his life neither with family nor with Clara Schumann. Perhaps he spent the holiday contemplating his sins. He seems to have been in one of his fractious phases, and his being alone was not an accident. Clara wrote Joachim in December, "I really could not wish for [Johannes's] presence here at Christmas, because when he was here a year ago, and again in the summer at Kreuznach . . . he made life with him almost unbearable."[12]

On January 6, 1863, he mounted his second solo concert in Vienna, playing the Beethoven *Eroica* Variations, the Bach Chromatic Fantasy and Fugue, and the Schumann F Minor Sonata. For his own offering he accompanied soprano Marie Wilt in songs including "Liebestreu" and played the F Minor Sonata. The audience for this recital included Richard Wagner.

If Liszt had been the advance guard of the New German revolution, Wagner, with his work of the 1840s and '50s—from *Der fliegende*

Holländer to *Tristan und Isolde*—became the most imposing leader of the progressives. His gigantic music dramas and his polemics aesthetic, philosophical, musical, nationalistic, racial, and crackpot, had made him at once the object of quasi-religious adoration and the most reviled composer in history. If the economic nexus of Wagnerism was soon to lie in Munich with the extravagant admiration and financing of King Ludwig of Bavaria, Vienna and the Hofoper were the real home of what Hanslick called the Wagnerian "Dalai Lama cult," until the Master founded his own shrine at Bayreuth.

In 1863 there were surprisingly benign feelings between Brahms and the Wagner camp. After all, Brahms found a good deal to admire in his rival's music: the uniqueness of voice and technique, the theatrical instincts, the ingenuity and sure-handedness with the orchestra, the epic imagination. Brahms did not hate Wagner's music but rather the trappings and hysteria of his cult. Probably he also knew enough about Wagner's boundless ego to hate the extravagance, manipulativeness, pretension, antisemitism—everything for which so many despised Wagner in his own time, and for which history has judged him severely since. Outside the Wagner camp, there is a tone one finds again and again, lying between the words of Brahms and of others who wrote with a certain respect for Wagner. The tone suggests a grudging admiration for the achievement combined with disgust for the man. Wagner was hard to like but impossible to ignore. He made sure of that.

In December 1862 Brahms wrote Joachim from Vienna: "Wagner is here, and I shall probably be considered a Wagnerian largely because of the contradictions to which any intelligent person must be provoked by the irresponsible manner in which musicians here rail against him. I am also particularly in touch with Cornelius and Tausig, who claim not to be, nor ever to have been, followers of Liszt."[13] The two men he mentioned were both part of Wagner's circle, and more Lisztean than they admitted. Both also became close friends of Brahms—because he liked them, maybe also because he found it useful to have connections in the enemy camp.

Brahms originally met the gentle-spirited, chronically impoverished composer Peter Cornelius during the 1853 visit to Liszt at Weimar, and appreciated him immediately. It is a sign of his personal affection that during their short friendship Cornelius was one of the relatively few musicians close to Brahms who had neither influence, skill, nor money to do anything for Brahms. The small, fiery virtuoso Karl Tausig had studied piano with Liszt, and lived in his teacher's house during several half-barbaric child-prodigy years. Once during that time Tausig sold the manuscript of Liszt's *Faust* Symphony to a servant, who disposed of it in a batch of wastepaper. Liszt's response when the manuscript was miraculously recovered: "Kärlchen, you'll either become a great imbecile or a great master."[14] Tausig had grown up the latter, a diamond-brilliant, steel-fingered virtuoso in the Liszt mold, always with a touch of the wild child—something Brahms enjoyed as much as the playing.

In 1863 Brahms wrote the two sets of Paganini Variations for Tausig, an essay in exactly the kind of keyboard pyrotechnics that the rest of his piano music avoids (perhaps the reason Brahms insisted on calling these variations *Studies*). Clara, for whom the Paganini Variations were too Lisztean for comfort but too delicious to resist, always called them *Hexenvariationen*, Witch's Variations. She took them up with the full ferocity of her determination.

Brahms enjoyed visiting Tausig's sumptuous Vienna apartment, where he spent hours playing four hands with his host or lounging on the sofa sipping old cognac and smoking Turkish tobacco, listening to the pianist dispense the latest dirty jokes. It was delightful, being young geniuses together. After some initial interest, Brahms resisted Tausig's attempt to convert him to Schopenhauer, the consecrated philosopher of Wagnerians.[15] Brahms was ready to read anything and to debate ideas all night, but using philosophy to motivate music was not his style. (His "Des jungen Kreislers Schatzkästlein" had been mostly practical advice and idealistic cheerleading.) The tone of relations between Brahms and Tausig can be seen in this 1867 letter from the pianist, after he had premiered the Paganini Variations and moved to Berlin:

> I am very well satisfied to have been the first to introduce the Variations to the public; in the first place, I had the devil of a time with them, and then I am glad that they have caused such a commotion. Everybody considers them unplayable, yet secretly they nibble at them, and are furious that the fruits hang so high. . . . Perhaps we can meet somewhere? Do you still remember the first Pressburg trip, when we three [Cornelius probably the third] got so tremendously drunk? and you insisted on your "Kaffee"?—I do hope we can have such good times together again—life is too sullen.[16]

Likely it was Cornelius and Tausig who enticed Wagner to Brahms's solo recital in January 1863. That Wagner listened to the F Minor Sonata carefully, and maybe had a look at the score, is audible in a few measures of *Die Meistersinger.*[17] And naturally the enticing would have gone in the other direction too. In March, Brahms showed up at a party organized to copy music for some of Wagner's Vienna concerts, and sat quietly to the side writing out instrumental parts for *Die Meistersinger.* Wagner claimed hardly to have noticed him. In later years Brahms spoke of other encounters, said he listened with pleasure to Wagner's endless monologues, heard him tell Cornelius and other disciples, "You must work in another direction than I."[18] Brahms would cite that directive, from the highest authority, to reinforce his own opinion that Wagner was a great genius but a dangerous example.

WHETHER OR NOT there were other meetings between Brahms and Wagner, the historic one came a year after Brahms's concert of January 1863. It took shape rather like a conference of opposing diplomats. Tausig and Cornelius laid the groundwork, and the meeting proper was set up by Wagner's Vienna champion Dr. Joseph Standhartner. Presumably the intention was simply to introduce two important figures of their respective generations and see what happened. As of then Brahms was hardly a serious rival to Wagner, and it appears the older master did not particularly hold the New German manifesto against him—Wagner had understood well enough that it was aimed at Liszt.

The meeting was arranged for a house in Penzing, near the Schonbrünn Palace, where Wagner had settled while he put together some Vienna performances. (These came in the wake of the collapse of the planned *Tristan und Isolde* premiere at the Hofoper in 1862. After seventy-seven rehearsals the opera was declared unperformable.[19]) Wagner had decked out the Penzing place, as was his custom, with a remarkable nonchalance about money. Though quite broke, he kept decorators busy rigging his rooms with silks and satins and wall hangings, until the interior looked like some fantastic seraglio. As negotiations over the meeting with Brahms took shape, Wagner pressed Dr. Standhartner to expedite things.

On February 6, 1864, their encounter turned out a muted and polite affair, with a few observers swiveling their heads back and forth at every exchange. Both principals were small in stature compared to their reputations and the impression of their photos. At thirty, Brahms was still in his beardless blond youth. At fifty, Wagner looked flinty and peculiar, with a face like a hatchet and a penetrating, calculating gaze. For all his physical vigor, his health had always bedeviled him, everything from chronic skin disease to heart trouble.

That day Wagner was in his most charming mode. After some pleasantries he asked the younger man to play piano for him. Brahms obliged with some Bach and then his Handel Variations, as usual sounding his best among musicians who appreciated the subtleties. Wagner, a fine conductor but proverbially wretched pianist, may have felt jealous of the keyboard skills that gave Brahms an advantage in promoting his own work. Only one remark survives from the occasion. When the brilliant fugue had climaxed the variations, the older master pronounced benevolently, "One sees what may still be done in the old forms when someone comes along who knows how to use them."

They were remarkable variations and Wagner recognized that. At the same time, perhaps hidden in his remark was a barb something on this order: *I and my compatriots have revolutionized music, delivered it from the stale abstractions of the past into a world of infinite freedom, and achieved a unity of the arts toward which the entire history of humankind has evolved. Then this boy comes along writing sonatas and variations and fugues like some damned periwigged composer a hundred years ago, and Schumann declares him the Messiah.* In his memoirs, Wagner wrote that he could tell from the Handel Variations that Brahms was "no joker." That is the nicest thing he ever wrote about his rival.

The two men shook hands, parted with flattering words, and never found it necessary to pursue their acquaintance. Brahms maintained a private respect for Wagner that mounted over the years; over and over he declared to friends, "I am the best of Wagnerians." He claimed to have said it to Wagner too. Brahms meant that he saluted the musical achievement and ignored the rant and cant—or rather ignored it with one exception, a long time back: it seems that he had read Wagner's seminal essay "Opera and Drama," probably around the time it came out in 1851, because he copied down a few lines in "Des jungen Kreislers Schatzkästlein":

> The generator of the artwork of the future [Wagner writes] is none other than the artist of the present, who anticipates the life of the future and longs to be contained in it. Whoever cherishes the longing within himself already lives in a better life; but only One can do this: the Artist.[20]

On at least that point of idealism the two men probably agreed. Both looked to art as a prophecy of a better life, and both expected themselves to be contained in that future. It was the nature of their hopes for the future that diverged radically. For Wagner the better life was in the social and political world, a new artistic/political dispensation led by visionaries like himself—above all by himself. Brahms's sense of the better world created by art was personal, private, interior: from the heart and mind of the individual creator to the heart and mind of each listener. As he wrote Clara: *art is a republic.*

Still, whatever his respect for Wagner's achievement, over the years Brahms never tried to dilute the poison in Eduard Hanslick's pen or Clara's hatred for the operas, and never defended Wagner publicly. (Their relations resembled those between Stravinsky and Schoenberg, Picasso and Matisse, always one side more generous than the other.) Few people suspected how rivalrous Brahms actually was. If he generally appeared free of envy it was because, for all the frustrations of his career, few composers have ever had a more enviable one than his, and he knew it.

One has to sniff out Brahms's competitiveness. For one example, he prized many excerpts from Wagner operas, among them the *Ride of the Valkyries* with its exhilarating orchestral fireworks. At the same time he claimed to be often bored with the operas as a whole. Yet in his later years he insisted that it was a mistake to perform parts of them separately: "One can't do a greater disservice to Wagner than by bringing his music into a concert hall. It is created solely for the theatrical stage, and that is where it belongs."[21]

The logical result was to tie up Wagner entirely: the operas don't necessarily work, but neither do the famous excerpts. The game here seems to be that Brahms was willing to respect Wagner's achievement considerably—always with reservations—as long as his rival was shut away in the opera house with his "great moments and very dull quarters of an hour" (as Oscar Wilde put it). In the halls where orchestral and chamber works were heard, Brahms wanted no living competitors. Toward Bruckner, his only challenger as a symphonist, Brahms would prove more deliberately spiteful than toward any other contemporary except Liszt.

Wagner the author of "Jewry in Music" was not the sort to keep his opinions to himself. Everything he did was geared to the public, however arrogant, blundering, self-defeating, and malevolent some of those efforts turned out in practice. His attitude toward Brahms's music was simple contempt, as his wife's diaries display over and over. One day after playing through the Second Symphony Wagner exclaimed to Cosima, "'There is nothing in it, but the public cheers!' . . . [she added:] The symphony . . . we find utterly shocking."[22] After hearing another piece played for them by Anton Rubinstein, Cosima observed for herself and Richard: "To laugh at clumsiness, bombast, and falsity in art is no pleasure. Not a single melody, beginnings of themes from Beethoven and other masters, the composer's realization that it is not his own, hurried resorts to oblique harmonies and contrived curiosities."²³ Once in 1880 when Brahms was advertising in the paper for opera librettos, Wagner unbelievably declared: "I have described my views on composition in the [Bayreuth] *Blätter*, and now he thinks he's got a recipe."²⁴

Beyond sniping in private, when Brahms had become an actual rival Wagner was quite prepared to be malicious in print. In his essay "On Poetry and Composition" of 1879, after Brahms's Hungarian Dances and neo-Handelian *Triumphlied* had become immensely popular, and after the First Symphony had been dubbed "Beethoven's Tenth," Wagner produced his most pungent diatribe. In it he manages to conflate Brahms and his own favorite subject, the Jews: "Compose, compose, even when you have no ideas! . . . I know famous composers whom you can meet at concert masquerades, today in a ballad singer's disguise . . . tomorrow in Handel's Hallelujah wig, another time as a Jewish czardas player, and then again as genuine symphonists decked out as a number ten."²⁵ Wagner was shrewd enough to perceive Brahms's masks and borrowings; he lacked the magnanimity to see the integral style his rival made of them.

Wagner had decreed art the new religion and the artist its high priest, the crown and savior of nations, "demonically suffering, godlike." He insisted on visibility and acceptance not only of his work but of himself and his ideas. To Wagner the public had a duty to follow the artist wherever he led them, whether or not they understood his art or his godlike utterances. Brahms's very determination to disappear behind his music was something else Wagner held against him. Brahms was no less a leader than Wagner, and in his most ambitious and innovative work challenged listeners no less. But Brahms still considered it his duty—as had his heroes in the past—to meet the public partway, to write music ultimately comprehensible to his middle-class audience. Now and then he was even willing to amuse them with light music. All this baffled and outraged Wagner—the humility of Brahms's doctrine of craftsmanship and allegiance to the past and the public, his seeming indifference to politics, his willingness to turn out commercial items.

So in February 1864, early in the struggle, the Brahmsian and Wagnerian camps sat embodied on two sides of a room in Vienna. (Brahms did not have a camp at that point, but it was developing.) Within a decade of that meeting, many had come to believe—correctly, as it played out—that which side won the battle would in some degree determine the future of music.

All that was latent in the Penzing parlor in February 1864. Soon afterward a smaller and more mundane matter divided Brahms and Wagner, as token of the larger rivalry. Knowing Brahms's enthusiasm for historic manuscripts and first editions, Tausig gave him Wagner's hand-written score of the "Venusberg" music, written for the Paris production of *Tannhäuser*, and the manuscript of Wagner's concert ending for the *Tristan* Prelude. Cornelius meanwhile gave Brahms, warmly inscribed, a deluxe printing of the *Tannhäuser* score.[26] From that point if not earlier, Brahms made himself a knowledgeable student of Wagner, and attended the operas regularly. He took his line about being "the best of Wagneri-ans" entirely seriously.

A year after their meeting, Wagner was preparing a production of *Tannhäuser* in Munich and needed the Venusberg music. Furious to learn that Brahms possessed the manuscript, Wagner ordered Peter Cornelius to get it back. Meanwhile, on his own, this Wagner disciple had been bruised once too often by Brahms's rough friendship. Cornelius wrote in his journal in late 1864, "With one person I am now definitely through, and that is Mr. Johannes Brahms. He is a completely selfish and auto-cratic individual. . . . May he walk the path of his glory! I will henceforth neither disturb nor accompany him."[27] Cornelius's letter to Brahms ask-ing him to hand over the *Tannhäuser* manuscript, declaring it had not been Tausig's to give, was distinctly frosty. No doubt Brahms knew why, but it was rarely in him to explain or apologize. He refused to part with the manuscript and Tausig took his side. There the matter lay for some time.[28]

AT THE END OF 1862, Brahms was not thinking of Wagner particularly, but rather practicing for concerts and contending with chronic feelings of aimlessness and homesickness. In December he wrote "An die Heimat," published in the Three Quartets of Opus 64: "Homeland! Homeland! Wondrous-sounding word! How on feathered pinions you draw me back to you." He wrote Joachim, "Everything is perfectly nice here, but I'm still going back to Hamburg."[29] Yet he lingered in Vienna, playing concerts, usually to good if not fevered receptions. A women's choir formed by his pupil Julie von Asten diverted him; for them he com-posed the canonic *Salve Regina*.[30] (Women's choirs often inspired him to sacred canons—suggesting a kind of pious, virginal purity.) By the fol-lowing March he felt good enough about Vienna to write Adolf Schubring, in the careful and positive tone he generally used with this critic:

> The gaiety of the town, the beauty of the surroundings, the sympa-thetic and vivacious public, how stimulating all these are to the artist!

In addition we have in particular the sacred memory of the great musicians whose lives and work are brought to our minds. In the case of Schubert especially one has the impression of his still being alive. Again and again one meets people who talk of him as of a good friend; again and again one comes across new works . . . which are so untouched that one can scrape the very writing-sand off them.[31]

He was not exaggerating. Schubert had composed so much and in 1828 died so young that it took most of the remaining century to track down the manuscripts shoved in cupboards and drawers all over Europe. Robert Schumann had unearthed the C Major Symphony in 1839; only in 1865 was the *Unfinished* discovered and premiered at the Gesellschaft der Musikfreunde, to become the most popular of all Romantic symphonies.

Early in Brahms's Viennese stay, publisher Carl Anton Spina lent him a stack of Schubert manuscripts to look over. Brahms opened some of them to find the ink-blotting sand still stuck to the paper, and realized with a shiver that he might be the first person since Schubert to lay eyes on those pages. The sand itself he reverently preserved in a little box, as a talisman of a personal connection, hand to hand. Among the manuscripts he considered Schubert's Easter cantata *Lazarus* the great discovery. He sent Dietrich some excerpts he had copied out and gushed, "Oh, if I could send you the whole, you would be enchanted with such loveliness!"[32] The impact of *Lazarus* on Brahms would be observable in his cantata *Rinaldo* and in the *Deutsches Requiem*. And from then on, Schubertian lyricism would be a steady presence in Brahms's work—though less in his lieder, for some reason, than in the cantabile moments of his instrumental music.

In the middle of all the performing and the heady excitement of discovery, Brahms lost another bachelor friend to marriage, this one the biggest blow of all: Joachim wrote in February 1863 that he had become engaged to contralto Amalie Schneeweiss, who in her operatic career beginning at age sixteen had gone under the name Weiss. In the letter Joachim sternly reassured Johannes that his bride, despite the temptations of the theater, had remained safely intact: "Do not run away with the usual notions which are unfortunately connected with the life in our operatic circles . . . her mind and her appearance have remained simple and refined."[33] Perhaps to placate her constitutionally jealous husband, Amalie agreed to give up the stage and sing only in the concert hall. Clara wept, for joy perhaps, at the news of the engagement. Johannes wrote the expected manly felicitations, with an accompanying sigh:

You lucky dog! What else can I write but some such exclamation? No-body will feel your happiness as I do, more particularly since your let-ter came upon me when I was in a dark mood. The whole time I have been here I have not stopped wondering whether, since I have to guard against phantoms of another kind [he means loneliness], I had not bet-ter experience and enjoy everything with that one exception, or whether I should . . . go home and let all the rest slide. And then you turn up and boldly pluck the ripest and most beautiful apple in Paradise for yourself. . . . I shall look forward to the time when I can come and see you and, as I have already done at the house of many a faithless friend, bend over a cradle and forget everything in the contemplation of the laughing baby face.[34]

Brahms did bend over the cradles of Josef and Amalie Joachim's chil-dren, and for their first—a boy, naturally christened Johannes—wrote the "Geistliches Wiegenlied" for low voice, viola, and piano. As a token of their friendship he wove his own beautiful lullaby melody around the old Christmas song "Josef, lieber Josef mein," played by the viola. As the marriage was to play out, though, this Josef was no lucky dog or Amalie a lucky *Frau*.

JULIUS STOCKHAUSEN WROTE BRAHMS in April 1863 from Hamburg, "Your little mother is looking more depressed than ever."[35] Christiane Brahms was seventy-four now and drained by age. Elise with her debili-tating headaches, Christiane with her ailments and apathy, weighed on Johann Jakob, but the two women also ganged up on him. Christiane was now demanding that he practice his bass up in the drafty attic. He had been threatening to move out of the house for some dozen years, and was at it again now. Brahms headed for home in May, to make one more at-tempt to patch up his family. With him he brought for his library a col-lection of engravings of Madonnas from Vienna's Belvedere Gallery, and the complete works of Schubert printed to that point, the latter a gift from publisher Spina.

On the way to Hamburg he stopped off in Hanover to hear Amalie Weiss's farewell opera performance, in Gluck's *Orpheus*. Brahms was en-chanted equally by the person of Joachim's fiancée and by her artistry. Amalie had a dark fiery contralto that Max Kalbeck compared to an old Italian viola, a voice uniting masculine power with a womanly soul.[36] As with Julius Stockhausen, Brahms was to write many songs with Amalie's voice resounding in his inner ear, and she was often their first and finest interpreter. During that visit in Hanover, Joachim organized a second reading of Brahms's F Minor String Quintet; once more, the friends did not like the effect. Soon Brahms arranged the music for two pianos, not entirely satisfactory either, and eventually destroyed the string quintet version.

Going on from Hanover to Hamburg, Brahms managed to calm his squabbling parents for the moment. Then, for want of anything better to do, he decided to stay on in town. Even though the apartment on Fuhl-entwiete was roomier than the ones he had grown up in, with a room reserved for him and his library, he had no intention of living with his parents again. Instead he took a place nearby on the Elbe in the suburb of Blankenese, and got to work. The main products of the next three months would be his strange, barely Brahmsian cantata *Rinaldo*, originally intended to be submitted for a composition contest of the Aachen choral society. (He missed the deadline, and wrote a new last chorus only in 1868.)

Brahms was not likely to compose a piece purely inspired by a competition. Most likely he viewed the cantata as an experiment in the direction of an opera. The fantasy of composing opera and confronting Wagner on his own turf was to possess Brahms for years. (In the same spirit, Wagner periodically toyed with the notion of writing symphonies beyond his early one in C Major.)

The Goethe text for *Rinaldo* (after a Tasso tale) concerns the eponymous crusader, enticed from the siege of Jerusalem by an enchantress, lured back to duty and arms by his fellow knights. The parallels of the story with Brahms's life—with Clara and Agathe and all his flights from women to art—are manifest. If *Rinaldo* has virtues enough to make it worth hearing, in the end it is arguably among his least characteristic and least satisfying large works. Since the subject is heroic and the forces are solo tenor and men's chorus with orchestra, one might expect Brahms to use his "bardic" tone. Instead, the feeling of the arias, at least, is often precious, emotionally unengaged, uncomfortably "operatic." The men's choruses come off as lusty and effective, if sometimes less interesting than the instrumental touches that accompany them. The scoring points up that Brahms used his choral works, including the later *Requiem*, to experiment with orchestration while hiding it behind voices. But while he wrote superb music for choir and orchestra, he would never hit on an approach for opera that suited both the requirements of the theater and his personality as a composer. If *Rinaldo* is a clue to what a Brahmsian opera might have been, then his instincts would serve him well in keeping him from the stage.

In some degree relieved to be back in his hometown and working away, Brahms still felt adrift. Joachim's critical response to the *Rinaldo* sketches did not reassure him about how he was spending his time.[37] He did, at least, reconnect with an amiable group of friends. One afternoon some of the old Frauenchor girls, picnicking in Blankenese, noticed their old leader in the distance in a pose they recognized: lumbering along, hands cocked behind his back, thinking. After some hasty discussion the ladies got Brahms's attention by launching into one of his favorite folk songs, and he turned in his tracks with a smile.[38] He began seeing the choristers again, some of whom visited on May 7 for his thirtieth birthday. For them he apparently wrote on the spot one of the canons that would end up in Opus 113, and composed several more of those women's-choir canons that month.

Around then, from her new summer house in Baden-Baden, Clara Schumann wrote him that daughter Julie was just back from Nice where she had suffered from anemia, cough, periodic catatonia, and nervous problems; but the eighteen-year-old was still in cheerful spirits as usual. In the same letter Clara wrote that Theodor Kirchner was expected for a long visit. After he came she wrote, "both Kirchner and I are fascinated by your [A Major] Quartet. I have played it at two parties at my house. . . . I must confess that you were right after all, it is more beautiful than the G Minor, and finer altogether."[39] As Clara saw nothing of Brahms's infatuation with her daughter, so he, despite her perhaps deliberate hints, suspected nothing about the real relations between Clara and Kirchner. Beyond their affair, Brahms's friend and fellow composer continued to struggle to convince Clara to marry him. But for her, in all things, it was first-rate or nothing. If Kirchner had written her better music, Clara might have become his bride.

ONCE AGAIN ENJOYING his circle of female admirers, Brahms toyed with the idea of reviving the Frauenchor. At the same time, it must have felt as if he were back where he started, in Hamburg, having made no progress at all during the last years. He still felt humiliated about losing the Philharmonic. Vienna seemed like a dream, delightful and sympathetic, but not in his blood, not home. What should he do?

His indecision was broken by a summons from Vienna: the conductor of the Singakademie had died and Brahms was offered the position. The main engineer of the offer was a big, bearded, music-loving jurist named Josef Gänsbacher, later to become a fixture in Vienna as voice teacher, cellist, and composer. Part of a small group of Brahms devotees in town,

Gänsbacher had recommended Brahms to the Singakademie directors as the man to bring the group out of its chronic doldrums, always in the shadow of the Gesellschaft-sponsored Singverein. After due hemming and hawing (his instinct was to suspect most suggestions about most things), Brahms agreed to conduct. He wrote the Singakademie board: "The resolve to give away one's freedom for the first time is exceptional; but anything coming from Vienna is doubly pleasant to a musician, and whatever may call him thither is doubly attractive."[40]

If Vienna was drawing him back after all, it could not hurt to pay court to its preeminent critic. In a letter from Hamburg informing Eduard Hanslick that he had accepted the position, Brahms added a flowery tribute to the critic's famous *On Beauty in Music*, the pamphlet about which he had once written Clara: "I found such a number of stupid things on first glancing through it, that I gave it up." Now, on his way to Vienna to conduct concerts, Brahms wrote the man who would be reviewing those concerts,

> I must also send you my most sincere thanks for your book *Beauty in Music*, to which I owe many hours of enjoyment, of clarification, indeed literally of relief. Every page invites one to build further on what has been said, and since in doing so, as you have said, the motives are the main thing, one always owes you double the pleasure. But for the person who understands his art in this manner, there are things to be done everywhere in our art and science, and I will wish we might soon be blessed with such excellent instruction on other subjects.[41]

The letter is a brilliant exercise in Brahmsian irony. On the surface it appears an earnest endorsement, and so Hanslick received it, even quoting it proudly in a memoir. In fact, in his circuitous way Brahms is saying that he considers the critic's book no more than a well-intentioned starting point in thinking about music, and does not see Hanslick as the man to continue those speculations.

As the letter reveals, Brahms and Hanslick in this first year of real acquaintance were already using the familiar *du*. In this case the intimate word denoted not only affection but mutual dependence. Brahms needed Hanslick for obvious reasons, and for all his social ineptitude he remained resourceful in courting useful people when he set his mind to it. By then the critic had probably realized that he needed this composer too. As the Schumanns, Joachim, and any number of others had long since concluded, regardless of how they felt about Johannes personally or how much they liked a given piece, he was the only figure of stature standing against the New Germans and Wagnerism. (After all, that conviction of Joachim's and Robert Schumann's had been a large reason for his premature fame, before he had done much to earn it.) Despite his regard for Wagner, Brahms was ready to become antipope as long as he did not have to fight the battles himself, and could maintain a posture of lofty detachment. He allowed Hanslick to become leader of the Brahmsian camp.

Hanslick's final moment of conversion may have come with an 1863 concert where he heard Wagner conduct excerpts from the *Ring* and *Tristan* in a matinee, then took in Brahms's B♭ Major Sextet that evening. The critic wrote of the sextet: "We believed ourselves suddenly transported into a pure world of beauty, it seemed like a dream; so contrasted was their music, so wholly at variance also was the personal appearance of the two. With rather awkward modesty, Brahms approached the piano. Only reluctantly and timidly did he respond to the stormy call to come forward."[42]

Brahms genuinely liked Hanslick, Hanslick genuinely admired Brahms as composer and man. Genuine and honorable affection notwithstanding, political exigencies tinted both perspectives. Richard Specht notes that the composers really closest to Hanslick's heart were ones like Auber, Rossini, and Johann Strauss—music light, tuneful, unchallenging. Hanslick resisted Brahms's more difficult work, though readers of his columns may not have suspected it. To composer/critic Richard Heuberger Hanslick complained once, "I have just come from [a concert] where Brahms's new quintet was played. I could scarcely bear to stay to the end, so much did his music bore me. . . . Brahms no longer has any ideas and is becoming more and more leathery. After this piece, the Suite by [Ignaz] Brüll that followed was a veritable feast."[43] Next day a befuddled Heuberger read Hanslick's review, with extravagant praise for the Brahms Quintet and a hasty couple of sentences on Brüll.

In 1875, conductor Hermann Levi wrote Brahms: "That notice of Hanslick's of Frau Joachim's concert, where he classes you with Franz and opposes you to Schubert, is worthy of having appeared in a local Munich paper. I hope you have broken off your friendship with him, for anyone capable of writing this sort of thing cannot possibly have an ounce of understanding for you."[44] This was no news to Brahms, but he was too canny to break with the most important critic in Vienna.

To the end composer and critic would walk in step, one of Brahms's few friendships without an interruption somewhere. Each relied on the other as friend, and no less as ally in battle. All the same, the only work Brahms would ever dedicate to Hanslick, in 1865, shows that he knew his man: it was the sixteen light, tunefully Schubertian piano waltzes of Opus 39.

HAVING ACCEPTED THE CONDUCTING POSITION with the Sing-akademie, Brahms wrote urgently to old friend Albert Dietrich for advice on conducting and repertoire: "I am extremely shy of making my first [professional] attempt in this line at Vienna of all places."[45] Dietrich, however, had fallen into a period of mental turmoil and was of little use to anyone for a while. Recently Clara's half brother Woldemar Bargiel had also suffered a breakdown. For Brahms, who had a healthy man's lack of sympathy with illness, one madman in his life had been enough. He had a horror of watching anyone else go the route of Schumann. To Joachim he wrote, "Good lord, the ghastly specter strikes out! First it seized poor Bargiel, and one can't help marveling at his getting free of its embrace, and now it has our poor, dear friend in its grip."[46] (As Bargiel had pulled out of it, so eventually did Dietrich.)

In August, Brahms returned to Vienna to take up the conducting position. The ailing Singakademie had dubbed him, apparently without irony, "der Retter," the Savior. As it had once been with his career as Schumann's Messiah, this tenure as salvationist did not turn out as expected. Though he got off to a shaky start, the Singakademie never doubted their conductor's musicality or energy, though they did wonder about the depth of his commitment.

For his debut concert on November 15, 1863, Brahms conducted the Bach cantata *Ich hatte viel Bekümmernis*, Schumann's *Requiem for Mignon*, Beethoven's *Opferlied*, and three songs by German Renaissance master Heinrich Isaak. The program went agreeably for choir, audience, and critics in unison. For the next concert Brahms had about seven weeks to prepare. By the time he spent Christmas with Bertha Faber and family, he was anxious about the performance on January 6. For that program he had chosen short pieces, mostly old, by Mendelssohn, Johannes Eccard, Giovanni Gabrieli, Giovanni Rovetta, Beethoven, Bach (the motet *Liebster Gott wann werd' ich sterben?* "Dear Lord, when shall I die?"), and Heinrich Schütz's electrifying "Saul, was verfolgst du mich?" ("Saul, why persecutest thou me?"). This time the performance turned out disastrously. The Gabrieli broke down and had to be started over. A critic called the singing "almost without nuance" and described the effect of the Schütz as "an oasis passed by all too quickly in the middle of a hyperaesthetic desert."[47] Only Brahms's arrangement of German folk songs found approval.

The results of the two concerts foreshadowed the rest of Brahms's conducting career. He was an admirable conductor of his own work but otherwise erratic behind the baton. Supremely sensitive and knowledgeable regarding all the music he performed, he tended to be hazy in the mechanics of conducting and offhanded in rehearsal.[48] He occasionally produced an inspired performance, interspersed with scrambling ones. A new age of virtuoso maestros was approaching, heralded by musicians like Hermann Levi and Hans von Bülow. By the end of the century, specialists would supersede composer/performer/conductors like Brahms and Joachim, who conducted on the side and never developed the particular skills the job demanded. (An observer described Joachim's conducting as limited in much the same way as Robert Schumann's—he heard what he saw in the score rather than what was actually being played.[49])

Besides his shaky performance in the second Singakademie concert, in general Brahms gave the Viennese a heavier dose of older and gloomier music than they were used to. Hanslick was typical of local music lovers in having little enthusiasm for music before Haydn. In those days the public generally considered Bach strong medicine—good for you, but hard to get down. A quip by a local wit began circulating: "When Brahms is feeling really frisky, he sings " 'The Grave Is My Joy.' "

After the mostly-Bach third Singakademie concert on March 20, Brahms wrote Clara, "The *Christmas Oratorio* went excellently . . . but a work of Bach has a difficult time with the critics here. Hanslick may have suffered the pains of the damned during the week, for two days afterwards Herbeck's *St. John Passion* was performed." He added, "I have unfortunately to decide at once whether I shall remain at the Akademie next year. If only somebody else could decide for me!"[50] The position was already irritating him, not only the practical responsibilities of arranging for soloists and instrumentalists and the other myriad details of concertgiving, but the very idea of submitting to anyone else's schedule and expectations.

The choir had requested that the season include an extra all-Brahms program. He scheduled it with misgivings. Requested or not, the concert might be seen as self-aggrandizing. He wrote Joachim ironically, "The concert is supposed to bring in money and be put together in two or three weeks. Before I prostitute myself as a mere Kapellmeister and bore the audience with a long row of choruses, I'd rather be patiently tolerated as a composer. Then the people who show up will know what sort of joke they're in for."[51] The choir remained enthusiastic about their maestro and savior, and on April 17, 1864, the Viennese public got a collection of Brahms works mostly new to the city: the premiere of the Opus 29 motet *Es ist das Heil uns kommen her*, two of the Opus 42 songs, two of the Opus 31 solo quartets including the hypnotic, minuettish *Wechsellied zum Tanz*, the *Ave Maria*, and two of the *Marienlieder*. Also in the concert Hellmesberger's group played the B♭ Major String Sextet and Brahms and Tausig the Sonata in F Minor for Two Pianos—his reworking of the discarded F Minor String Quintet (and not its final stop).

After a private Singakademie concert in May, the directors unanimously elected Brahms conductor for three more years. He accepted, but in fact he was chafing at the job and still, in spite of the remarkable progress of his reputation in town, unhappy with Vienna. He wrote Clara a long rumination:

> Life is too gay, and during the short season no person or institution can survive which does not rush to participate in the hurly-burly, instead of doing what they want to do, which is to live quietly and find pleasure and culture in their own pursuits. But everybody wants to live, to dance from one concert to the other, and from one sensation to another. The financial and artistic side of my work is also jeopardized because no really distinguished person with refined artistic feeling is at the head of affairs to help me [here revealing what he thinks of Hanslick's artistic refinement]. . . . My real friends are the old ones. . . . Here I can find nobody to take their place. . . . My Folk Songs arranged for choir have pleased the people here extraordinarily, and Spina very much wants them. But since Rieter rather insists on having them and does not care what he pays, he will get them. I still have the Schubert song. . . . I got it for you from a very pretty girl with whom God knows I might have made a fool of myself if, as luck would have it, someone had not snatched her up at Christmas. My people are all well but my love makes me feel anxious, for my mother is growing old and who knows how soon a heavy blow will fall on me.[52]

The pretty girl in question, Ottilie Hauer, was one of his periodic infatuations, once again a singer. (He knew Clara would not mind his mentioning a woman in his letter. By now she was prodding him to find a wife, preferably rich.) With this singer, though, Brahms came within actual hours of making a fool of himself. Ottilie had been part of the Vienna women's choir with whom he had been working, and sang in the premiere of his *Wechsellied zum Tanz*—a piece quite seductive for him, in fact. The fair Ottilie had been troubling Brahms's quietude for some time until, after who knows what mental thrashings and gnashings, he actually set out on Christmas Day 1863 to ask for her hand. But when he arrived at Ottilie's house he discovered to his great dismay and even greater pleasure that earlier that very day, she had accepted the proposal of a Dr. Edward Ebner.[53] As usual, the friendship persisted and Ottilie's new husband, who had done Brahms a great service in relieving him of an obsession, was received into Brahms's good graces.

ALSO AS USUAL, Brahms got some songs out of the bargain when fate extracted him from Ottilie, to whom he gave an astounding sixteen song manuscripts. One of the lieder she inspired may have been "Von ewiger Liebe" (Of Everlasting Love) from early 1864—one of his most enduring, a particular favorite of his own, and a classic illustration of Brahmsian lieder design. Amplifying the song's connection to Ottilie, Brahms based one of its themes on his rejected *Brautgesang (Bride's Song)*.

Generally he wanted no great subtleties or ambiguities in his lyrics for lieder, but rather a simple situation with direct emotions, succinctly set forth. To a friend he once described his taste in texts as "the best, the most passionate, or those most like folk verses."[54] By "best" he was probably thinking of the ones from classic sources—especially Goethe and the Bible—that he used for his larger choral works, which on the whole are first-rate poetry. The passionate little lyrics of love and loss and the more ingenuous poems in folk style are the sort that tended to end up in his lieder.

Taken from a folk song, the text of "Von ewiger Liebe" begins, "Dark, how dark in forest and field!" A boy meets his sweetheart outside the village, tells her (Brahms may be thinking of Agathe), "If you are suffering disgrace before others on my account, let our love be sundered as quickly as we were formerly united." The girl replies with a burst of passion: "Our love cannot be sundered! . . . Iron and steel can disintegrate; our love must endure eternally!" (That is an avowal Agathe had not made.) The surging, forceful melody in which the girl proclaims her certainty is the one that recalls the *Brautgesang*.

This is the kind of song Schubert might have dashed off on a napkin at dinner, and if the tune went well then fine, and if not there were plenty more where that came from. Even in a little lied, though, Brahms would not allow himself that sort of spontaneity. Nor did he chase after every image in a poem, as Schubert could do so memorably. With this text the older master might have suggested the distant lights in the village, the smoke from the chimneys. Not Brahms. Overt pictorialism and passionate outbursts of emotion were not his style personally, nor his style of expressiveness in music (though there are exceptions to that—in person and on the page).

Brahms's approach to a song text is to wrap it in a form that more subtly evokes the scene and feelings. "Brahms," writes Eric Sams, "inhabits that hinterland of the lied where song borders on absolute music."[55] Characteristically, he sets "Von ewiger Liebe" straightforwardly and without theatrical passion in the vocal line; it is like a folk song where stories of blood and thunder unfold in the placid repetitions of strophic form. Here the dark setting of the poem is not evoked in details of tone-painting but rather in the sound and feel of the opening two strophes—the low, murmuring B minor of the beginning, the dark alto or baritone voice startlingly low. We don't forget the dark dejection that opens this song. The straightforward declamation of the melody is inflected in the piano by drifting chromatic harmonies, but they evolve with a linear logic that veils to the ear how Wagnerianly far-ranging they are.

As customary with Brahms the vocal line follows the poem syllable by syllable, poetic foot by foot, line by line, and in its formal divisions the music strictly reflects the poem's stanzas. In songs, he shapes thematic relationships as carefully as in his instrumental pieces. Here the bass line of the piano introduction prefigures the melody of the voice. (Once again: in Brahms the first considerations are form, melody, and bass, then the rest.)

The opening narrative of the scene between the lovers is set in a calmly striding, shadowed introduction. Then the boy speaks, the accompaniment repeating a figure over and over as his apprehension grows, until the piano part swells into the foreground, expressing at once the musical impetus surging to its logical climax and the boy's breathless anxiety. With a turn to B major the girl responds firmly and confidently, "Our love cannot be sundered!" The rhythm of her reply is a lilting slow $\frac{6}{8}$ that calms the tense $\frac{3}{4}$ that preceded it. For her the piano figure repeats like the boy's and rises to its climax, but in a different tone—her music logically derived from his, but with her own voice and emotions: he ambivalent, she assured. Thus *expressive form*. This lied was to become one of Brahms's abiding hits.

As in "ewiger Liebe," in a Brahms lied we are not likely to find the spontaneity of Schubert or Schumann, or Schubert's conspicuous scene-painting. And it is significant that we tend to think of Brahmsian lyricism more in terms of his instrumental music rather than where we would expect it, in his lieder. It is as if when confronted by a lied text that demanded direct expression of emotion, he pulled back. Brahms was a personality hidden, indirect, oblique. His warmth and longing blossomed more often in the abstract context of instrumental music than in his lieder. There more often we find in the voice part the straightforward syllabic setting and simple rhythms of folk song, the piano accompaniment restrained, often within the capacity of amateurs who performed these songs at home. The characteristic ending is a brusque, efficient cadence. In those respects Brahms was closer to Schubert than to Schumann as a lieder composer.[56] Brahms told his biographer Max Kalbeck that in his youth he set to music all of Heine and Eichendorff and the other complex, emotionally tangled high-Romantic poets Schumann had made his own. Those early songs, stacks of them, went into the stove, and in his maturity Brahms turned to less ambiguous kinds of lyrics.

But if everything in his songs is calculation and craft, often with a nod to practicality and saleability, and if on the whole they have never claimed the audience of Schubert's and Schumann's lieder, in the great ones like "Von ewiger Liebe"—many of them clearly from Brahms's own life and feelings—there is an enfolding warmth and subtlety of expression that places his lieder among the finest of German lyric art, in the line that stretches from Schubert through Schumann to Brahms, and beyond him to Wolf and Mahler. Brahms wrote lieder throughout his life and straight to the end of it, gaining strength as he went, and in them he maintained the same extraordinary consistency as with nearly every other genre he took up.

SOON AFTER RECOVERING from his crush on Ottilie Hauer, Brahms had to contend with another intimidating female—which is to say, one beautiful and talented. Elisabet von Stockhausen was born in 1847, daughter of Freiherr Bodo Albrecht von Stockhausen, Ambassador at the Court of Vienna, the family an old Hessian noble line tracing back some eight hundred years. (They were no relation to Julius Stockhausen.) Elisabet came to Brahms as a sixteen-year-old piano student with creative ambitions. This blond girl was not so much lovely in her features and form as in an inner and outer grace that enchanted everybody who knew her, male and female alike. Her extraordinary talent and intelligence, always gently expressed, seemed only a natural part of her radiance.

Elisabet inflicted on Brahms a kind of trembling awe. Especially just after his recent brush with the altar, he was terrified of touching her, of falling in love with her. With the skewed sexuality the *Animierlokale* of Hamburg had bequeathed him, he could only imagine himself soiling such a creature with his passion. In those days, in that culture, an affair with a respectable woman was a dangerous and rare escapade, while at the same time men were expected to wait years to marry, until they had made their fortune. Janik and Toulmian write, "If a man was to find a sexual outlet . . . he had to turn to prostitutes, for sexual relations with a girl of 'good breeding' were entirely out of the question."[57] With Elisabet the choices were marriage or frustration.

After coaching her on a few pieces including Schumann's *Kreisleriana*, Brahms handed Elisabet back to her former teacher, Julius Epstein, who had declared that it was impossible not to fall in love with her. Eventually, married to composer Heinrich von Herzogenberg, Elisabet would reenter Brahms's life and become a rival of Clara Schumann for his affection.

Yet another Vienna pupil Brahms briefly fell for in that period was Amalie von Bruch-Vehoffer. On her death in 1871 she left him a trunkful of music. Hidden in it he discovered a pile of money with a note saying it was for him. Rather than keeping the cash, Brahms returned it to her widower, saying it had been left in the trunk by mistake.

For a finale at the end of summer 1864, Brahms extracted himself from one more ball and chain when he changed his mind and resigned as director of the Singakademie. His reasons for quitting after one season he never exactly spelled out, but they seem clear enough. The job was a drain on his creative time and energy and its practical responsibilities one more threat to his freedom. (There is no indication it ever occurred to Brahms that conducting the Hamburg Philharmonic would have been worse, and he would have soon quit that position too.) So by preference he was jobless again, even as he observed that his purse of late "has been leading a remarkably limp and inactive existence."

While he was making up his mind to leave the choir, in the middle of June Brahms journeyed wearily from Vienna back to Hamburg to oversee the long-delayed, long-anticipated separation of his parents. As de facto head of the family it was up to him to try and contain the upheaval. He found his father a room in the Grosse Bleiche. Christiane and Elise stayed on for a while at the Fuhlentwiete place, then moved to a small, pleasant apartment on the Lange Reihe, reserving a room on the garden for Johannes. That year Johann Jakob had been accepted into the bass section of the Hamburg Philharmonic, the end of his long ascent from the streets to the higher ranks of Hamburg musical life. Though he was a perfectly adequate player, the job had probably come about after a word from Johannes to his friend Stockhausen. Despite his grief over the shattering of his family, at least it gave Brahms great satisfaction that after so many years of struggle his father had finally, in his late fifties, ascended to a comfortable middle-class life.

His mother and sister, meanwhile, were devastated, ailing, helpless. Grimly Brahms tried to calm his blustering father and two weeping women. Elise, long devoted to her mother and utterly dependent on her, broke completely with her father. Meanwhile Johann Jakob balked at providing any support. Fritz, "the wrong Brahms," by then doing well as a piano teacher, had always promised to take care of their mother if their father left her. In the event Fritz did nothing, and Johannes never really forgave him for it. Now it would be mainly Johannes who kept his mother and sister afloat with regular infusions of cash. Amid the recriminations he declined to take sides, but still his old feeling for his father took precedence. Clara noted, with shock: "I should not be surprised at your standing by your father, but in this case, knowing as I have for years your preference for your mother, it is incredible to me."[58]

When the crisis in his family had settled down enough for him to escape, Brahms made the long journey south to Lichtental, a village next to the Black Forest resort of Baden-Baden, to live for the summer in the Hotel Bären near Clara's house. There began a sociable, brooding, and splendidly productive period.

BADEN-BADEN WAS THEN the most fashionable European watering place, with pleasure palaces and mansions full of royalty and *Gross-bürgertum* making merry, taking the waters at the Kurhaus in hours away from gambling at the casino. It was said in midcentury, "When someone wants to know what is the principal city of Europe, one must answer him: in winter Paris, in summer Baden."[59] Artists found good pickings among the well-to-do French, English, Russian, and German vacationers blanketing the landscape in search of health, or at any rate entertainment. A number of musicians besides Clara had established summer houses around the resort. Concerts at the Kurhaus and in villas, by the local orchestra and prominent soloists, were a regular adornment of town life. That summer Brahms got to know Clara's circle of Baden friends, and despite his own generally spartan style discovered he could find pleasure and profit in frequenting elegant spas.

The cottage Clara Schumann had bought for a retreat in adjoining Lichtental was so small and plain, in comparison to the great houses all over town, that her children, mortified, called it "the kennel." Later they remembered their summers there with their mother as the happiest of their lives. In her memoirs, daughter Eugenie wrote of breakfast in an arbored garden, and watching the king and queen of Prussia, later Kaiser Wilhelm I of Germany and his empress, promenade through town. As her father had done with her, Clara had the children's days laid out like a military schedule: now time for piano practice (the older two girls taught by Clara, the younger ones by the older), now sewing, now exercise, and so on. Eldest daughter Marie ran the household, and in winter toured with Clara as her manager. Because of Marie, Eugenie wrote, their mother "could live entirely for her profession, untroubled by the onerous demands of everyday life." Marie stayed at her post as long as Clara lived, packing the bags for tours, dressing her mother and arranging her hair before concerts, living in Clara's shadow.[60]

Julie remained the darling of the family—blue-eyed and palely beautiful, vivacious, most of the time sick. Her sister Eugenie wrote of "her eyes, blue as the sky, beautifully set in her face . . . her hair, luminous as gold and fine as silk, framed her exquisitely white forehead . . . a face of such unusual charm that no one could look upon it without joy. Yet this would not convey the nobility which those features expressed, their radiance, the sweetness of disposition, the vivacity of her emotions and her mind."[61] Her sisters loved Julie as hopelessly as did Brahms and nearly everyone else.

In the relatively little time she could spend with them—mostly the Baden vacations—Clara was affectionate with the children. Eugenie remembered her mother's shining smile whenever one of them entered the room while she was playing, and how she could read letters and carry on conversations while the music flowed from her fingers.[62] At the same time Clara was stern and inflexible, like her father. The children were never allowed to forget that they owed everything to her performing. Rarely if ever, regardless of what happened to her children and her own suffering and guilt over it, did Clara cancel a concert for their sake or any other reason, unless she was physically unable to play. An 1867 letter from a touring Clara to Eugenie runs:

> Your accounts of your life have interested me very much, and I am glad that you have found several friends. . . . Your mistake in the Adagio from the Sonata Pastorale has made me laugh very much, for—fancy! the same thing happened to me when I was first studying this sonata. . . . I played the last six bars in the major. . . . A thing like that is certainly annoying, as it is due to want of attention, but it should not make one furious. That would be unseemly in any man or woman, but especially in a woman, to whom only gentleness is becoming.

In another letter Clara instructs Eugenie, "When people pay a child compliments on her parents' account . . . a look of pleasure in her face is quite enough; no clever repartees are expected from a young girl." And again, "You say you wish you were dead—do you think so little of your sisters' lot in life? Are they not a prop to me, and the dearest friends of my heart? And are you not as dear to me as they?"[63]

In Baden-Baden Brahms shared the Schumann household daily, at meals and music-making. For the children he was simply a fixture and always had been—part of the family, taken for granted.

His name was widely known, but not his face or his music. In other words, Brahms was not yet a celebrity, was still being discovered by musicians and the public. He made important connections that summer of 1864. Among the luminaries around Clara was Pauline Viardot-Garcia, a friend since their teens. Clara called Pauline the most talented woman she ever knew. A pupil of Liszt and friend of Chopin, gifted as mezzo-soprano soloist, opera singer, pianist, composer, teacher, and painter, Viardot had retired from opera and now taught voice in Baden-Baden. For all his resistance to lady artists and forceful females in general, Brahms was taken by her talent and her flamboyance, maybe even her looks: Viardot had a face heavy-lidded and spanielish; one observer cited her "picturesque weirdness."[64] That she owned the original score of Mozart's *Don Giovanni* endeared her to Brahms even more.

In 1864 Pauline was engaged in building her "Palace of Art" and writing operettas with librettos by her devotee, the Russian novelist Ivan Turgenev. He summered in Baden to be near her.[65] Viardot produced, directed, designed, and performed in her own operettas. Later Brahms directed one of them in a private performance,[66] and she soloed in the premiere of his Alto Rhapsody. By the 1890s she and Clara ended up what Pauline called "the oldest friends in Europe." As two extravagant egos, they naturally had their spats en route. In November 1864, Clara indignantly wrote Johannes, "Madame Viardot consecrated her Palace of Art (as she calls it) the other day, and when she invited high society (the Queen of Prussia etc.) to the first ceremony she naturally did not want me; and afterwards she had a reception for the ordinary folk, for which I was considered good enough."[67]

"Waltz King" Johann Strauss, Jr, also had a grand villa in Baden-Baden. Anton Rubinstein rented another, and was often found dispensing his considerable wealth in the casino. Brahms may have met Strauss that year, among those he got to know and in some degree impressed. On a short earlier visit he had stayed at Rubinstein's villa. (In that period Brahms and Rubinstein formed something of a friendship despite their annoyance with each other's music.)

That summer came a renewed acquaintance with Julius Allgeyer, a friend from Düsseldorf days, then working at his brother's photography atelier in nearby Karlsruhe.[68] By then the dour, slow-speaking Allgeyer had become a protégé of the painter Anselm Feuerbach. Further acquaintances included Princess Anna of Hesse, who was transported that summer by Brahms and Clara's performance of the F Minor Sonata for Two Pianos. As a result he dedicated the piece to the princess, likewise its later incarnation as a piano quintet. That dedication brought an extraordinary response. The princess asked Clara what she could buy for Brahms as a token of gratitude, and as a result he received the crown of his manuscript collection, the original score of Mozart's G Minor Symphony.

In Baden-Baden Brahms and Turgenev amused themselves speculating over their cigars about operas. Eventually the novelist drafted six pages of a libretto, a drama about an inn in the Alps, but the project evaporated.[69] All the same, just as Brahms kept notebooks of quotes, aphorisms, folk sayings, jokes, and poems for prospective lieder, he began keeping another one of ideas for operas.

Yet another connection from this summer turned out for many years the most productive of all for both men. Brilliant, mercurial Hermann Levi had just become court Kapellmeister in Karlsruhe, which involved operatic as well as orchestral conducting. Years before, Levi had introduced himself to Brahms in Hamm; this summer they became intimates. From the beginning Brahms valued Levi's ebullience and wit as much as his skill on the podium. Eugenie Schumann recalled Levi's bleating, infectious laugher and his practical jokes. There was the time Levi hid himself as Brahms walked in to meet him for an appointment: when in some embarrassment Brahms turned to leave, he was startled to hear emerging from a clothes trunk the famous opening of the vocal part to Beethoven's Ninth: "O friends, no more these tones. . . ."[70]

There was a great deal more to Levi than wit and talent. He lived with contradictions as part of his triumph, his peculiar career, in a way finally his undoing. He was a rabbi's son and unconverted—unusual in his time and in his circles, and something none of his friends let him forget. His features were exotic, inescapably Semitic in a society with fine-tuned antennae for that. Even Brahms, who was unusually free of the bigotry of his time and his culture, joined in the supposedly good-natured joking everyone visited on Levi's Jewishness. Levi accepted it with an anxious smile. For all the man's gifts, his ambition and precocious success, his enthusiasms shaded into something obsessive, neurotic, finally self-destructive. He was desperate for heroes, for messiahs. Brahms would be the first, Wagner the last. After a growing professional and personal closeness with Wagner during the 1870s, in 1882 Levi became the anointed conductor for the premiere of *Parsifal*—an opera that was, among its qualities for good and ill, perhaps the highest expression in art of pseudo-spiritualized Germanic antisemitism. A century later, Levi became historian Peter Gay's archetype of the German self-hating Jew.[71]

In 1864 he and Brahms became intimate friends, *Duzenbrüder.* The way it came about shows Brahms's style of affection, and how much he felt for Levi. One night after a visit, when the conductor was hurrying from Baden-Baden for the late train to Karlsruhe, Brahms accompanied him with a mysterious package under his arm. As the train pulled out, Brahms suddenly tossed the package into the compartment and vanished. Levi unwrapped it to find the original manuscripts of the first three piano sonatas, inscribed on the front, "In heartfelt friendship, your Johannes." There for the first time Brahms used the familiar *du.*[72]

Around then Levi wrote Clara Schumann: "This close contact with Johannes has had, I believe, a deep and lasting influence on my whole character. . . . In him I have seen the image of a pure artist and man."[73] Brahms would not have gushed like that, but he was deeply taken. Part of it was that he expected to benefit from the conductor's orchestral expertise, but they had plenty of good times too, which resound in a Brahms letter to Levi that November: "Are you seeing to your health? Drinking good coffee? You and Fräulein Elise amusing yourselves? Got yourself a Frau Kapellmeisterin?"[74]

Their collaboration began immediately. In late July, Clara wrote Brahms that she and Levi had been playing the F Minor Sonata for Two Pianos, and "it is masterly from every point of view, but—it is not a sonata, but a work whose ideas you might—and must—scatter over an entire orchestra. . . . Levi . . . said the same thing, very decidedly, without my having said a word. . . . Please, for this once take my advice and recast it." Brahms probably conceded that this music worked with two pianos hardly better than it had with string quintet (though he published the piano version). He remained loath, however, to risk a purely orchestral work. Instead he got to work recasting the piece as a piano quintet, asking advice from Clara and Levi and Joachim.

FOR SOME REASON that July of 1864, despite the sociable diversions of Baden-Baden, Brahms was overwhelmed with memories of the euphoric, evanescent love he had found in Göttingen six years before. He wrote one of his oblique inquiries to old friend and host Julius Grimm, now working in Münster: "I'd like to know how it is in all the houses where one used to go so happily. Also write me of that house and gate—" He meant Agathe's. Grimm replied without mercy:

> At that house and gate things have sadly changed: the old Professor died three years ago. . . . Since last year Agathe has been a governess in Ireland, she teaches music and German to the two young girls of a rich English family. . . . Finally it got too much for her in Göttingen, she wanted to find a job for herself and get away from the shadowed pages of her life. She wrote me just the other day that . . . she's yearning to come back to Germany—How much she's had to endure—at least she has a strong nature and hasn't lost her sense of humor. . . . But what a gloomy lot is that of a girl alone.[75]

Grimm knew there was no question of Johannes's rescuing Agathe from her lonely wandering. Johannes had made his choice and that was that. With no danger of running into Agathe, Brahms returned to Göttingen and revisited the streets they had walked together. In September, back in Baden-Baden, he composed the devastated and exalted songs of Opus 32, most telling of them "Nicht mehr zu dir zu gehen": "I would like to stop living, to perish instantly, and yet I would like to live for you, with you, and never die."

The same month he composed the first three movements of the G Major String Sextet, completing it the following May. On the face of it this sextet is another magnificent chamber work, more complex, integrated, and mature than its predecessor the B♭ Sextet (and therefore never as popular). To outline it is comparatively simple; the expressive implications are not. First movement warm but with an undercurrent of unrest. Second movement a "scherzo" medium in tempo and in ²₄ rather than the usual ³₄, a Brahmsian intermezzo though not so called (its leading idea comes from a neo-Baroque gavotte of his from the 1850s). For contrast to the gentle elegance of the gavotte theme, a *presto giocoso* middle section in ³₄, entirely scherzolike. Then a set of adagio variations based on a sketch Brahms had sent Clara in 1855; despite a brightly rhythmic fugal variation in the center, the dominant tone of this movement is wandering, empty, tragic. The finale, not the least *alla Zingarese* this time, explodes with something like the racing vivacity of a proper scherzo, immediately contrasted with a warm section of *moll-Dur* melody with the gentle lilt of a dance—say, a last dance, at the end of an affair.

Brahms composed the sextet at the top of his form. Even though it adapts earlier material, it creates its own emotional world; hints of darkness, tragedy, and regret drift through the graceful surface. There is nothing of the monumental quality of his symphonies to come, or the relentless tension of the F Minor Quintet he was reworking at the time, and few hints of the naked anguish found in some of the contemporaneous Opus 32 songs. Rather there is a twilight quality, wistful and high-Brahmsian but still particular to this piece.

The opening movement shows what he had learned by age thirty-one as a shaper of expressive and inventive sonata forms. It begins with a babbling half-step ostinato on G-F♯ by the first viola. With interruptions, this figure persists through much of the first theme group. In that figure lies the main technical gambit of the opening section: what harmonies can be superimposed on a given half-step ostinato? At the beginning Brahms makes a striking tonal shift out of two distant keys that can contain the G-F♯ oscillation, G major and E♭ major (the oscillation gives a major-minor inflection to the latter key). The linked rising fifths of the opening melody, G-D, E♭-B♭, define those two keys, which dominate the opening pages—thus a motive element produces a larger-scale tonal element. The half-step oscillation goes on and on, stopping only to resume, changing to other pitches, ushering in new keys.

To spell out these devices, this depth of craftsmanship, seems terribly dry applied to music this lovely, its gentle wistfulness shot through with quiet obsession. But the technical and expressive are inseparable in this work. The oscillation, for example, is nominally an accompaniment figure, yet it moves continually from foreground to background, functioning like a theme. It is like an obsession—say, with a woman—that moves in and out of consciousness but never really stops. As to the technique: once again, and never more strikingly, Brahms thematicizes accompaniment figures, integrates melody and accompaniment, unifies foreground and background, and the fifths of the opening unify motivic and larger harmonic structure. Meanwhile, for all their simplicity, the half steps of the ostinato never tire the ear because he continually superimposes fresh harmonies around them, finding the right moment to change the pitch and finally to leave the idea.

Maybe the most arresting thing in this movement is the overall thematic process, beginning with the rising fifths of the opening melody. From that point scraps of themes succeed one another, seeming to accumulate rather than just pass by. Step by step, each turn of melody building on the last, we move toward something hinted in a motivic fragment here, a rhythm there. The second theme group arrives with a melody more extended than any so far, and builds yearningly toward a dancing, ecstatic climax that has been gathering since the beginning of the piece. That climax flares in a simple but urgent line with a poignant suspension underneath:

It is the climax of the exposition, a moment of breathtaking beauty and emotional power, more remarkable for the simplicity of means: a line in even quarter notes, as simple and ingenuous as a little waltz. The impact of that climax, its *meaning* for all the abstractness of meaning in music, is created by a marshaling of every musical dimension: a coalescing of thematic elements that seems to produce the melody as inevitably as a flower blooms; the brilliant scoring, the instruments soaring into the high register; the position of the phrase within a subtly original sonata form exposition in which everything points to the end of the second theme group; the rhythmic complexity of the buildup paying off in the lilting simplicity of the climax, which soon falls into metric shifts combined with breathtaking harmonies, rhythm and harmony together almost sexual in the way they mount to a luminous culmination and afterglow.

There is also a secret lying behind that climax, those particular notes: the pitches spell out Agathe's name. They are A-G-A . . . H-E (H being the German name for the note B). The missing letter T is represented by the suspended D that comes in under the melody—so, A-G-A-D-H-E. At the same time the D forms part of another word, made of the second A of the upper melody, the suspended D, and the E of the next melody pitch. The other word is *ADE*, farewell. *Agathe, farewell.*

By this work," Brahms told Joseph Gänsbacher, "I have freed myself of my last love."[76]

In it Brahms freed himself of more than love—if he did that, if it can be done at all. For the listener, the impact of the climax is as "absolutely" musical as anything Eduard Hanslick could have asked for. Knowing the secret (Joachim sometimes referred to Agathe by whistling her theme) adds nothing definable to the effect: the magic works the same if the symbolism is not understood. In contrast to some of the cabala in Brahms's earlier music, the emotional weight of that climax did not strain against the musical dialectic, did not seduce him into neglecting any part of his job as composer.

The meaning of those notes to *him* resounds breathtakingly in the music, but he shaped their effect for the listener by craft, every dimension contributing its part. Melody, harmony, texture, timbre, and form coalesce to make the climax what it is: *those* notes, *those* rhythms, at *that* moment in the form. Musical logic has overtaken personal symbolism. In the end, Agathe's name in the first movement of the G Major Sextet is as good a demonstration as one can find of what *composition* is about, at its most subtle and moving—and abstract.

Which is to say, with the G Major Sextet Brahms freed himself not only from the memory of love and gnawing guilt but from the burden of his life in his art. After this there are few games with pitch-symbols in his music. From now on, in large degree Brahms disappears behind his work as behind a mask. That is not to say that his own experience vanished from his music. Rather, in most of it his experience receded into the background, as private inspiration and impetus. With Brahms as with most creators, art may arise from the artist's life, but that does not make it *about* the artist. To whatever degree possible work should be about every feeling person living in the world. For Brahms as for others, autobiography was part of the inspiration, a tool among other tools, not ultimately the meaning of his art. In his maturity he came implicitly to understand that while the personal may motivate many things in a work, it justifies nothing, excuses nothing.

So in this work in effect Brahms refutes, in sound rather than in prose, the New German doctrine that the music of the future must be derived from literary sources. At the same time, in its inspiration and its hidden message, the piece refutes Hanslick's doctrine of pure abstraction in music. This is a piece inescapably about love and loss—Brahms's particular love and loss, and anyone's. And by that, from at least the point of the G Major Sextet, he stood alone in the aesthetics of his time. No less, in its universality soaring beyond any personal anguish of its creator, this work like all Brahms's mature music refutes the common late twentieth-century doctrine that autobiography is the main point of art. At exactly the moment of deepest subjectivity in his music, Brahms repudiates autobiography as an essence.

In the paradox of his music, his unshakable individuality combined with a determination at once to challenge his audience and to meet it partway, Brahms preserved a pre-Modernist conception of art as a social act, part of the fabric of society rather than opposed to it. He wrote music for the bourgeois audience who supported him and for the musical institutions that class supported—the symphony orchestra, the amateur choir, the chamber ensemble, the private performance at the parlor piano. With his waltzes and Hungarian Dances, he was one of the last first-rate composers to write manifestly light, sociable *Hausmusik*.

If Brahms has always appeared to lie outside the story of late-nineteenth-century aesthetics and of Modernism, it is because his music and its implications, like the man himself, followed no path but his own—yet at the same time a path continuing a social and artistic tradition and fully aware of (even if mostly resisting) the present. Brahms wrote only a few sentences implying a philosophy of art, not much more than "art is a republic," but his music itself builds a persuasive esthetic, in the century when music was king of the arts and much of the dialogue about it carried on in propaganda tracts.

His retreat behind his work, of course, is part of Brahms's biography. From early in life he found his identity in hiding. He read poetry as he played piano in brothels, assumed the masks of Young Kreisler and Werther, used his music to intimate songs and ballads without words, and stories and people he loved. Finally music itself became the veil Brahms drew across his life, even as his life resounded in his music. In that paradox he touched a deep stratum of German Romanticism, its sense of music in the abstract as a manifestation of an unseen world—the inexplicable powers that E. T. A. Hoffmann suggested in his Doppelgängers, his labyrinths of stories within stories, his games of identities, the cryptic sufferings and designs of Kapellmeister Kreisler. In Brahms, the line where autobiography shades into abstraction cannot be drawn. For most of his later and greatest music—including the symphonies and most of the chamber music—he left no hint of unseen implications.

Which, again, is not to say that after the G Major Sextet he drew nothing from life. Every great sorrow, perhaps every great joy, Brahms encountered found its echo in his work. One of the few advantages of being an artist in the first place is that unlike any other profession, your very sorrows and joys are stock in trade, grist for the mill—always the sorrows more than the joys. Brahms made use of his life at the same time as he patiently taught himself the craft to transcend it, to a degree his mentor in subjectivity, Robert Schumann, never entirely achieved.

Agathe, farewell. Brahms asked the G Major Sextet to be his farewell to love and the agitations of the heart. He wanted the story of his life to be finished, leaving only music and uncomplicated Gemütlichkeit with friends, which he pursued avidly but without promises. Much of the time, outside music, he lived like a boxer between rounds.

Yet a desire to escape life and its consequences could not work for one living as gregariously as Brahms did after the day's work was done. His old dream of existing monklike, above the regrets and yearnings of the human comedy, could never be realized. He tried to hide behind sarcasm, peevishness, discipline, jokes, and fame. When one friend fell away he turned without apparent regret to others. But now and again the world and his feelings broke through every barrier he erected against them. He would have another consuming love to trouble and inspire him, in some ways the most lacerating of all, because the most hopeless.

CHAPTER THIRTEEN

They That Mourn

CLARA SCHUMANN came to Hamburg on tour in December 1864 and visited the Brahms family, troubled before, broken now. She reported to Johannes in Vienna:

> My heart was filled with anguish at your mother's to see everybody scattered like that. Oh what misery! Your mother and Elise cried the whole time, and then there was your father who unburdened his heart to me. Each of them in turn said they could answer before God for every word they had uttered. I tell you, it has made me thoroughly ill.[1]

Clara's sympathies lay unequivocally with mother and daughter. With dismay she had discovered that Johannes seemed more concerned for his father. He had sent the women of his family a hundred talers, but that had barely covered their dental bills and rent.[2] Stepping into the crisis, Clara told Johann Jakob that he must contribute more to their upkeep; his son could not be expected to support mother and sister. Johann Jakob told Clara the women could damned well take him to court if they wanted to. Johannes began dispatching cash to Hamburg whenever he had enough, half of it to his father even though Johann Jakob still had his position with the Philharmonic and his freelance work. When his father complained about Clara's meddling, Johannes replied heatedly, "I'm telling you, you don't have to explain one word to Frau Schumann."[3]

Through it all Johannes sustained a fantasy of coaxing his parents back together. In October he wrote his father, "That Mother and Elise have reserved a room for me would please me indeed if I could think that you would occupy it frequently."[4] And in a Christmas letter from Vienna:

"You must receive my greetings for this festival, though we lonely men don't get to see much of it. Didn't you spend even an evening with Mother? Did Fritz do anything to bring you there? I'll sit alone and think lovingly of you!"[5]

Despondent, burdened by her seventy-six years, at the end of January Christiane Brahms spent five days laboring over a letter to her golden boy. She wanted him to understand her life now and her journey there, and the unlikely destiny that engendered him. "I am alone and will try to write you, you can't believe how bad it's gotten for me. The eyes weak, the hand uncertain." An uncertain hand is terror to a seamstress. Father did not come here for Christmas, she wrote, only Fritz. Then Fritz went to a party on New Year's, Elise and I were alone. "There was a concert on the 4th, it was rather full and everything pleased, your Trio and the rest. Both Herren Marxsen, whom I hadn't seen for a long time, were very friendly, and congratulated me saying that I must feel great joy over my children." She rambled on. When I was a child I used to go out all day sewing, then for ten years I was a maid to honest folk, and there was sewing for the company and the Dutch Wares shop with Auntie, and then one day your father, almost a stranger, asked me to marry him. I couldn't believe he was serious, but Uncle said he wasn't joking, take your only chance, "and so I considered it Destiny."

Now Christiane Brahms understood that it had been a profound destiny that joined her with a man young enough to be her son and too handsome for her, and the toilsome and finally unhappy marriage that produced a child as extraordinary as Johannes. "I have written something every day," she wrote toward the end. "It is Thursday evening at nine . . . and since we might not be speaking with each other soon I write you now, so that I may die in peace, that my child should have no misgivings about me. . . . And now I close with the hope that we can look forward to a better year."[6]

Three days after she mailed her letter a telegram from Fritz Brahms arrived at Johannes's door on Singerstrasse: "If you want to see our Mother again come at once." Johannes reached Hamburg on February 4, two days after Christiane Brahms died of a stroke. "God took my mother away as mercifully as possible," he wrote Clara. "She had not changed at all and looked as sweet and kind as when she was alive."[7]

Now most of all he worried about his sister, still suffering chronically with headaches, who had never gotten through a day without her mother's orders, never owned more than her one taler a month allowance. In Clara's letter of consolation she echoed his concern: "Poor Elise! She will be the one to feel the loss most. . . . Could I help you at all by my presence in Hamburg? I would come gladly."[8] There was no question of that. Johannes could find nothing useful to do himself after the funeral, and only stayed in Hamburg a week. His sister became hysterical at any mention of their father; the two would remain estranged. For the moment Johannes arranged for Elise to stay with the Cossels, the family of his first piano teacher (where his old chorister Laura Garbe lived). In the spring Elise took a room with friends of Fritz Brahms.[9] Like Johannes, their brother had long been on his own, earning enough as a piano teacher to support his dandyish lifestyle, but he hardly concerned himself with the family. Now and then Fritz performed his brother's music, once even trying the Handel Variations in public; Clara heard the performance and reported that the piece was quite beyond him. After their mother died the brothers broke almost completely, and so the family lay in ruins.

Johannes told Clara that Theodor Avé-Lallemant had stood "nobly" by his side through the whole misery, and Avé persuaded him to go immediately back to Vienna.[10] After he returned there, singing teacher Josef Gänsbacher visited his apartment at the "Deutsches Haus" and found him playing Bach's Goldberg Variations on piano. As Brahms spoke of his mother's death, tears streamed down his face, but he never stopped playing. "When this sad year is over," he wrote Clara, "I shall begin to miss my dear good mother ever more and more." Beyond that he said little about her, then or afterward.

Accident-prone Clara was then in Cologne for medical reasons, having injured her hand in one of her falls. She was taking the treatment, medieval and unbelievable but approved medical practice, of "animal baths," which meant plunging her hand into the entrails of some freshly killed creature.[11] As soon as her hand improved for whatever reason, she decided to head for London. Her news about going there again, she wrote Brahms, "will not please you," but the money was too good to resist. "You will scold me, won't you, dear Johannes? And yet if you were the father of seven children you would certainly do the same."[12] In fact, Brahms was about to start touring more extensively than he ever had or wanted to, for the money. No England or France for him, though, not now or ever.

It was in this period that he sent Clara new sketches for "a so-called *Deutsches Requiem*." The work was to be a memorial for the dead—not the liturgical, Catholic requiem mass in Latin, but a personal testament in his own language. Brahms gleaned his text from Luther's German Bible and the Apocrypha, shaping it to his own vision. Certainly the death of his mother was a catalyst, but the idea went back some time, maybe as far as the crisis of Robert Schumann. The basis of the second movement, "All flesh is grass," came from the symphony Brahms had sketched—a somber sarabande standing in for a scherzo—just after Schumann jumped into the Rhine. For him the commemoration in the work would always be of both: Christiane Brahms, and his tragic mentor Schumann. Characteristically, Brahms never spoke of the connection with his mother, and growled when anyone asked him about it.

He probably started working on what he finally called *Ein deutsches Requiem* (*A German Requiem*) in Vienna shortly after his mother died. Its biblical atmosphere, and the joy he felt in conceiving the music, shines in a playful letter he wrote Clara from Vienna in March 1865, after she called off a visit to him. He begins with a musical notation for crescendo and diminuendo:

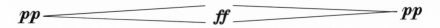

I send a sigh as big as that for starters!

I half expected it, though I have spent all these days cleaning up my room and trying to make everything nice. I had ordered new coffee cups, had the plates cleaned, and bought fireworks! preserves! . . .

I should be sincerely glad to hear that you had simply drawn a thick line through this winter in your book of receipts . . . and that you are thinking of bracing yourself with all sorts of edifying things, such as philosophy. The world is round and it must turn; what God does is well done; consider the lilies, etc.: or better still, don't think at all, for things cannot be altered, and a wise man repents of nothing.[13]

He mailed her a draft for no. 4 of the *Requiem*, "How lovely is thy dwelling-place, O Lord of Hosts," telling her not to show it to Joachim, who was with her in England. "It's probably the least offensive part. . . . But since it may have vanished into thin air before you come to Baden, at least have a look at the beautiful words. . . . I hope to produce a sort of whole out of the thing and trust I shall retain enough courage and zest to carry it through."[14] The letter was prescient—the courage, the zest, and the "sort of whole." *Ein deutsches Requiem* would be his abiding concern through the next year, interwoven with smaller but no less intimately felt projects.

.   .   .

WORKING VACATIONS of four or more months were a reliable feature of his spring and summer now. In May 1865, Brahms returned to Lichtental near Baden-Baden, where he secured from a Widow Becker two quiet and gemütlich rooms on the top floor of a house on a hill. "I came, saw and immediately took the first and best place," he wrote Hermann Levi. There was a small bedroom, and for a study the "Blue Salon," named for its blue-gold wallpaper. From the windows he had a Brahmsian view of fir-decked mountains and the road to Baden.[15] (Today it is Brahmsstrasse.) To his father he reported that the rooms were "unbelievably cheap" and he would stay on until autumn. For several summers over the next years he would return to the house and the Blue Salon. His daily schedule on vacation had become an unvarying routine: rise at dawn and make strong coffee, then take a long walk to mull over the day's work; back to his rooms for four hours or so of composing; lunch with Frau Schumann and family or at an inn in town; four o'clock coffee and talk or walk with the Schumanns, and back to their house for dinner, where his place was always set at Clara's right hand.

During the first two months in Baden he composed the last movement of the G Major String Sextet and the fugal finale to the first solo sonata he would own up to, the E Minor for cello and piano, begun three years before. The main effort was a new piece whose opening theme found him as he sat among the mountain firs near his house—a keening melody, sentimental in almost Schumannesque fashion, for violin, horn, and piano: the Horn Trio, Opus 40.

Not for this music nor any other of his did Brahms want the newly developed chromatic French horns with valves. For the trio Brahms specifically asked for the open, valveless Waldhorn. He had grown up hearing his father play the instrument, and with his father's coaching tried it himself in childhood. At the same time, in practice Brahms knew that open horns were obsolescent. From the beginning, the trio has most often been played on a modern valved French horn.

In his horn writing in the trio—and in all his music—Brahms *felt* the instrument as he did the piano, and perhaps no other until he became wedded to the clarinet near the end of his life.[16] The open horn, meanwhile, had been the one used by the gods, the horn of Haydn and Mozart and Beethoven, noble in sound but limited in available notes. (The virtuosic high horn players for whom Bach wrote had died out by Haydn's time.) In their orchestral music, Classical-era composers often used natural horn for long pedal notes, as tonal anchors. Now and then, as Beethoven did in the scherzo of the *Eroica*, a composer might let the horn loose on its ancestral hunting calls: "Waldhorn" means forest, or hunting, horn.

A valveless horn can largely only produce pitches in its key unless the player creates a kind of artificial pitch by "stopping," which means shoving a hand into the bell to raise the pitch. Besides being the only way of playing notes outside the single, always-major key of the horn, stopping also mutes the instrument's normally bright sound. Brahms wanted both qualities: the particular tone of valveless horn on the open notes of its compass, and the veiled, from-afar quality of stopped notes. Since the requested horn for the trio is in E♭, every movement had to be in that key— the tuneful opening, a scherzo as ebullient and rhythmically fanciful as Brahms's youthful ones, a slow movement in E♭ minor, a finale where the horn finally gets its hunting calls.

The first movement is laid out in an A B A B A pattern, the only opening movement in a major work of his not in sonata form.[17] All the movements count among the more delicious in Brahms's chamber music, but the telling one is the adagio third movement. It is a mournful dirge in $\frac{6}{8}$, in which the minor key and chromatic motives require the horn to use stopped notes much of the time. At the last cadence Brahms deliberately brings the horn to rest not on an open E♭ but on a stopped G♭; he wanted the veiled effect. In the solemn ritual of the music and the faraway stopped tones, this slow movement reveals itself as a gentle memorial for Christiane Brahms, the first of a son's requiems for his mother.[18]

DESPITE THE DEATH of his mother and its reflection in the trio, Brahms was in one of his agreeable phases in summer 1865. He traveled to Basel in June to hear Bach's *St. Matthew Passion* and play his own music in concert, staying with Julius Stockhausen and Theodor Kirchner, the latter now the most effectual Brahms champion in Switzerland. Then Brahms went back to Baden, from where with unwonted gaiety Clara wrote Hermann Levi in July, "We made a delightful excursion to Ebersteinschloss and Gernsbach yesterday, Johannes and Dietrich going with us. We were all in the rosiest mood under a beautiful rosy sky."[19]

Perhaps part of Brahms's mood that summer came from his new closeness to his father. Christiane and Elise Brahms had always handled most of the family letters from Hamburg. After the separation from his wife, however, Johann Jakob began writing regularly to Hannes. It was necessary in any case because Hannes demanded an acknowledgment every time he sent money, which was often. Johannes's letters to his father are earnest and affectionate, studiously without nuance, unlike his correspondence with anyone else. For his father's part, there appeared little for the aging, inarticulate man to report in a letter, though in summer 1865 there was one aside that implied more than it appeared to—he wrote that he had finally found a good place to eat lunch. At the moment Johann Jakob still had his old jobs in the militia band and in the Alster Pavilion, and sawed away at his bass in the Philharmonic ignoring the snickers of the younger musicians around him.

Then, in October 1865, Johann Jakob had news indeed for his son, about the woman who had been serving him lunch at her dining room frequented by musicians. Anxious about his son's reaction, he presented his news carefully:

> Life as I am now living, contains so little that is agreeable, it is so dull and empty, that I have decided to make a change. . . . It is easily understood that I, who for thirty-four years had lived with my family, if not always very happily, must find it hard to accustom myself to the life I have led for the past two years. Therefore, if you think it over, you won't hold it against me if I tell you that I am thinking of marrying again. . . . She is a widow, a homely body, forty-one years of age. . . . I hope . . . my dear Johannes, that we shall see each other soon, and I hope until then that you will think kindly of my intention, even if it surprises you.[20]

The widow's name was Karoline Schnack, and she was eighteen years younger than her fiancé—just as Johann Jakob (fifty-nine now) had been seventeen years younger than his first wife. Abashed and uncertain about his proposing, Johann Jakob had finally approached the handsome widow with this transparent ruse: "You're a sensible woman, Madam Schnack, who may well give an old muddlehead a piece of good advice. I have a mind to get married again. Now tell me to whom." Laughing, Karoline had taken her cue and named herself.[21] Johannes, astonished at the news but never other than indulgent with his father, wrote in reply:

> When I opened your letter and found three handwritten pages, I looked with some trepidation for the news that caused you to write that much. I was indeed greatly surprised. . . . Dearest father, a thousand blessings and the warmest wishes for your well-being accompany you from here. How gladly would I sit at your side, press your hand, and wish you as much happiness as you deserve, which would be more than enough for one earthly lifetime.[22]

Johann Jakob married Karoline Schnack the following March and moved into a comfortable apartment, with space for boarders, in the Valentinskamp business quarter. Once again a room was reserved for Johannes, and his library installed there. It turned out a fortunate union, which is not to say without contention. Despite his new wife's attempts to keep him to a tight budget, Johann Jakob was apt to cruise secondhand shops for bargains, coming home with pounds of honey or a pile of wardrobe hooks and answering his wife's protests, "Well, I couldn't let it stand at that price, Lina!" For all Johannes's consecration of his mother's memory, he formed an affectionate bond with his stepmother. Karoline seems to have been a staunch and straightforward sort, her cooking revered by Brahmses senior and junior. Soon Johannes began calling her "Mother." Karoline's ailing son Fritz, whom Brahms dubbed "the second Fritz," became a special concern and beneficiary of his tireless generosity.

BY THE MIDDLE 1860s Brahms could expect to see everything he produced in print, but he still could not rely on a given publisher to accept a given piece. In early October 1865, Hermann Levi wrote Brahms indignantly that Leipzigers Selmar Bagge and Carl Reinecke, advisors to Breitkopf & Härtel, had quietly sunk the G Major Sextet with that house. They consider the piece, wrote Levi, "vile music, that one should suppress." Clara also boiled about these machinations. In fact, Brahms had first offered the sextet to Simrock, who returned it. After Breitkopf did the same, and backhandedly in the bargain, he never submitted anything to them again. Finally in October 1865 Simrock relented and accepted the sextet along with the E Minor Cello Sonata, and so took a step closer to becoming Brahms's primary publisher.[23] At this point, though, Brahms also maintained a good relationship with the firm of Rieter-Biedermann, and with its eponymous proprietor.

At the end of October, Brahms joined Levi in Karlsruhe for a performance of the D Minor Piano Concerto. The piece was well received there, as it managed more and more to be in that decade. With people on the level of Levi, Clara, Joachim, and Kirchner promoting him, the public was coming around to the more difficult work. Surely over the decades of his playing the D Minor to growing applause, however, Brahms never sat down before an audience to begin it without remembering the hisses that baptized the concerto in Leipzig.

After the performance with Levi he went on to Basel, from where he wrote another champion, Albert Dietrich, "On my big tour I shall see

Zürich, Mannheim, Cologne, and at Christmas or New Year, *you* at Oldenburg. . . . Could we not venture my D Minor Concerto at the orchestral concert? . . . For a quartet evening, I can with good conscience recommend my Horn Trio."[24] This concerned plans for a Brahms Week that Dietrich had arranged in Oldenburg.

Before that pleasant prospect Brahms made the trip he described to Dietrich, his first real grand tour as a pianist. (The one with Reményi in 1853 had been entirely small-time.) Outside his own music, the repertoire would include Beethoven, Schumann, Schubert, and Bach (the latter's Chromatic Fantasy and Fugue was one of his showpieces). The coming months would see one of the periods of touring and living with friends that marked his life until he settled in Vienna. For all its satisfactions, Brahms considered the occupation of traveling virtuoso a vagabond existence, and if he enjoyed it now and then he never really approved of it.

All the same, Brahms could not deny that touring gained him a steady supply of new friends, patrons, and enthusiasts. This time in Zürich, musical amateurs including Theodor Billroth and Otto Wesendonck hired an orchestra and set up a special concert, Kirchner conducting, so they and anyone interested could hear the Piano Concerto and the A Major Serenade again. "They all spoilt me outrageously," Brahms happily wrote Clara.[25] Otto Wesendonck was a wealthy silk merchant, best known in the musical world as the accommodating husband of Mathilde, wretched poet and corporeal inspiration of Wagner's hymn to crazy love, *Tristan und Isolde*. Wagner had since taken up with Cosima von Bülow, née Liszt, wife of conductor and leading Wagnerian Hans von Bülow.

For all Mathilde Wesendonck's persevering if now platonic devotion to Wagner, she had no scruples about showering her (platonic) attention, and her unfortunate poetry, on Brahms. Besides, Wagner had given the Wesendoncks the original manuscript of *Das Rheingold*, which helped entice Brahms to their house. Some time later Mathilde invited him to visit her and sleep in the very garden cottage that had been the scene of the famous dalliance.[26] No doubt that desecration of their sacred bower would have made Wagner apoplectic, and no doubt sleeping in the place would have tickled Brahms enormously, but he never took Mathilde up on the invitation.

Theodor Billroth, some four years older than Brahms, was a surgeon as well as expert musical amateur. Soon he would be called to the University of Vienna, a nexus of modern medicine, where he joined Brahms's inner circle of friends and patrons. Already when they met in 1865, Billroth was becoming one of the most acclaimed surgeons in the world. He was among the first to explore procedures made possible by the discoveries of anesthesia and antisepsis, so that surgeons no longer had to restrain screaming patients during operations, and infection was no longer commonplace. Big, bluff, blond-bearded, loquacious in disposition, and unhappily married, Billroth was driven to get out of the house and indulge his love of music and society as well as medicine, and attended them all with superhuman energy.

Another Zürich encounter of this year, who only later turned up in Brahms's life as friend, was Swiss pastor and writer Josef Viktor Widmann. This winter he saw Brahms for the first time, in a Winterthur concert with Kirchner. Widmann recalled his impression:

> Brahms, then in his thirty-third year, at once impressed me as a strong personality. The short, square figure, the almost sandy-colored hair, the protruding underlip which lent a cynical expression to the beardless and youthful face, was striking and hardly prepossessing; but yet the total impression was one of consummate strength, both physical and moral. The broad chest, the herculean shoulders, the powerful head which he threw back energetically when playing, the fine thoughtful brow shining as with an inward light, and the two Teutonic eyes, with the wonderful fiery glance, softened only by the fair eyelashes—all betrayed an artistic personality replete with the spirit of true genius. In his countenance there lay such a promise of victory, such radiating cheerfulness of a mind revelling in the exercise of its power.[27]

So for all his indifference to performing, Brahms had a dashing platform manner in those days. In fact he was elated at the tour, not to mention considerably enriched by it. He crowed to Clara with uncharacteristic bravado, "I will tell you in detail how successful I have been, as a matter of fact quite beyond expectation in every way. What has pleased me most is that I really have the gifts of a virtuoso." (That conviction would not last.) In reply Clara, as fastidious about finances as everything else, wrote him, "I wish you would give me your money to keep for you! . . . Why do you always carry it about with you?" Since Brahms regarded the handling of money as a bore, her offer was agreeable. He began sending Clara his earnings, which she invested to great effect in stocks and securities. Later, not wanting to trouble her with a growing fortune to which he paid little attention, Brahms would let friend and publisher Fritz Simrock handle his finances. As it turned out,

Simrock the businessman invested them less wisely than Clara the pianist.

As the end of 1865 approached, Brahms traveled to the court of Detmold where he had worked in the decade before, to visit Karl Bargheer and other old friends and concertize for a few days. Not expecting to see him for the holiday, Clara sent a traveling bag for his Christmas present and reported, "Thank heaven we have fairly good news of Julie. She has got over the danger of typhoid, but it will be a long time before she has completely recovered." To surprise them on Christmas Eve, Brahms made the seven-hour journey from Detmold to Düsseldorf, where they were spending the holiday. Before he arrived the family had been too despondent to rouse themselves to light the candles on the tree. Always when Brahms arrived in Clara's house, the energy and spirits soared. In her diary she wrote that she was "very pleased and excited" when Johannes turned up.[28] She might have felt otherwise if she had known that part of his reason for coming was apprehension about Julie. In some vague and confused way, he had come to consider Clara's daughter his own.

In Hanover two days before New Year's, Joachim's wife, Amalie, began a gloomy letter to Clara: "I was particularly sorry that Brahms again failed to come. I am firmly convinced he did not come on my account . . . he thinks he takes Jo away from me, and that I resent it. If Brahms only knew how gladly I give Jo up to his friends. . . . I am so sorry for Jo, buried here in dull Hanover, by the side of an unskillful housewife . . . [who] does not suffice him in other directions, as an artist—still less stimulate and inspire him!" This from one of the most admired concert singers of the age. As Amalie was finishing the letter, Brahms suddenly walked in the door, to both Joachims' delight.

In the coming year, after the birth of their second boy, Amalie would come down with acute rheumatism that left her hobbling painfully on a cane.[29] At the same time she grew stout well beyond the already stout Germanic womanly ideal, and with her chronically weak health she could no longer tour with her impatient Jo. As Amalie's letter to Clara that Christmas shows, her husband was critical of her as both housewife and artist. Less than two years after it began, the Joachims' marriage was in trouble.

Brahms's visit with them in Hanover was preparatory to a tour of Switzerland with Joachim, set for January 1866. Before that came the

Brahms Week in Oldenberg that Albert Dietrich had organized; Brahms manned the keyboard in the D Minor Concerto, Horn Trio, A Major Piano Quartet, and works from his repertoire by Bach, Schubert, and Schumann. Then came the Swiss tour. One got a little crazed in a journey like that, the times onstage a blare of glory, otherwise hours and days of boredom in trains and hotels. During a post-concert banquet in Aarau, Brahms suddenly declared that he and Joachim must "divvy the swag" from their "crimes." As the dinner guests cheered them on, the two began brigand-style to alternate grabbing from a pile of "doubloons" on the table until only one twenty-five-franc piece was left. Over that they fell into a brawl convincing enough that one guest fled the room and returned with change. Brahms and Joachim theatrically fell on the neck of their savior.[30]

After the tour, however, Brahms's zest for performing waned and thoughts of *Ein deutsches Requiem* waxed. He visited Hamburg for three weeks, then headed for a stay with Julius Allgeyer in Karlsruhe to get back to work. This time he would keep at the piece until it was done.

While he was on tour, Clara had written him affectionately, "At last I am once again in my beloved Vienna, but you, dear Johannes, are not here; a thought that makes me sad, for Vienna seems to me almost like your home. Everybody asks me why you don't come."[31] In Vienna as in most places, her concerts had caused a sensation; when Clara did not cause a sensation she might sink into depression. Meanwhile in getting onto a stage she had taken a bad fall and injured her foot.[32]

Vienna hurt Clara in other ways too. She had planned to do Johannes's Horn Trio in a concert with Josef Hellmesberger, but "What a hornet's nest of intrigue and pettiness I fell into!" After some gestures at rehearsing the Trio and the A Major Quartet, Hellmesberger finally refused to perform either one. Furious, but needing the violinist for her concerts, Clara bit her tongue and substituted another piece,[33] but she did not forgive. "One cannot help thoroughly despising a fellow like Hellmesberger," she wrote Johannes, trying to drive a wedge between him and a performer he needed even more than she did. "He plays me the dirtiest tricks and then proceeds to crawl before you."[34] None of that was news to Johannes. "He's always lying," he once said of the violinist, adding with a certain backhanded admiration, "Only when he plays does he stop lying."

BRAHMS FINISHED the second and third movements of the *Requiem* in Karlsruhe and then took with him to Winterthur the growing pile of manuscript—of varying makes and sizes because at that point he could not afford music paper in bulk. This was a working visit with J. M. Rieter-Biedermann, whose firm would publish the piece. Then, continuing his wanderings with the *Requiem* as unifying thread, he settled to work at the beginning of June in a rented house on the slopes of the Züricherberg, where he could look out to an epic panorama of lake, mountains, and the glaciers of the Bernese Oberland. The view from his window may have contributed to the grandiloquent conclusions of the fourth and sixth movements of *Ein deutsches Requiem.*[35] After all, a great deal of his music, in its inspiration and spirit, rose from mountains and forests and open sky.

In Zürich, Brahms once again had the company of Theodor Billroth, the Wesendoncks, and conductor Friedrich Hegar, and on this visit he made the acquaintance of poet Gottfried Keller, who one day would supply him with song lyrics. He found Theodor Kirchner in a dismal frame of mind, and unwittingly wrote Clara about it. With everything else, it must have cost Kirchner agonies to spend so much time with Brahms in the last years, to be intimate with the connection to Clara lying unmentionable between them. Yet Kirchner was too much the admirer to avoid Brahms, who also sought out this friend and champion.

Music was always part of the socializing. One evening during this Zürich stay Billroth invited Brahms to a gathering to include a reading of the G Major String Sextet. An expert amateur pianist, the surgeon had learned violin and viola so he could play more of the chamber repertoire. Before this reading he had dutifully practiced the sextet's second viola part. But on the sweltering summer evening, with the composer listening, Billroth's mettle failed and his fingers turned to rubber. The G Major finally coasted to a halt and to Billroth's mortification another violist present had to take over the part. He never had the nerve to play viola in Brahms's presence again.

It is unlikely Brahms cared about a few missed notes. Their developing friendship was gratifying to both men. Among other things, both were hikers and liked to trade stories of mountain routes. They shared passions and hatreds. Around the time of the sextet reading Billroth wrote a medical and musical friend, "This morning [Brahms] and Kirchner played the *Symphonic Poems* of Liszt on two pianos . . . music of hell, and can't even be called music—toilet paper music! I finally vetoed Liszt on medical grounds and we purged ourselves with Brahms's G Major String Sextet [meaning the piano arrangement]." Billroth was no admirer of Wagner either, but like Brahms and even Hanslick he knew the man could not be dismissed with the high-handed satisfaction with which one damned Liszt. (It is a sign not only of Wagner's genius but of his hold on the age that resisting Wagnerism demanded knowledge and discipline.) Naturally, when the surgeon moved to Vienna he and Hanslick became close.

Billroth's feeling for music, an amalgam of the emotional, practical, poetic, and medical, is shown in a letter of his to Hanslick, attempting to turn around the critic's ambivalence about Brahms's G Major: "This Sextet demands a small hall, even better a moderately large room. It leaves an intense auditory after-image and has only a few places where a physiological emotional effect arises, as for instance the second theme in the first movement [the "Agathe" theme] and the close of the adagio, which resembles the heavens over Rome."[36]

Working away on the Züricherberg, Brahms kept his mind on the *Requiem* as war erupted between Austria and Prussia. The Seven Weeks' War, to settle who was the dominant power in Germanic territories, ended on July 3 with Austria's defeat at the Battle of Königgrätz. With the ensuing Treaty of Vienna, the old balance of power shifted forever in Europe; never again would Austria have any sway over German lands. Here commenced the long unraveling of the Austrian Empire from within and without, hastened by the next year's creation of the Dual Monarchy with one-time subject nation Hungary. Prussia, with Prime Minister Otto von Bismarck as its guiding energy, now annexed Schleswig-Holstein, Hanover, Hesse, Nassau, and Frankfurt. The Hohenzollern crown dissolved the German Confederation and created a new North German one under Prussian dominance. In a half dozen years, by means of pragmatic reforms and relentless militarism, Bismarck's realpolitik would stage-manage the unification of Germany.

In Vienna on July 3, the day of the worst defeat in Austrian history, thousands of partiers jammed the Venetian Summer Festival in the Prater.[37] Through defeat and its aftermath the city kept waltzing and singing and drinking new wine, and the cafés and theaters and concert halls stayed as full as ever while the empire began to evaporate. In 1867, Johann Strauss, Jr., supplied the Viennese with his most celebrated waltz, *The Beautiful Blue Danube*, to help salve the regrets over a lost war. Preoccupied with work in the summer of 1866, Brahms seems to have paid little attention to the conflict, but unification when it came would arouse his dormant German patriotism with a vengeance.

Despite his labors Brahms was not too busy to remember family and friends elsewhere. In August he sent his father and stepmother money to buy furniture.[38] That month he wrote Eduard Hanslick to notify him of another sort of gift:

Just now, writing the title of the four-hand Waltzes, which are to appear shortly, your name occurred to me quite of its own volition. I don't know, I was thinking of Vienna, of the pretty girls with whom you play four-hands, of you yourself, the lover of all that, the good friend and whatnot. In short, I feel the necessity of dedicating it to you. . . . It consists of two volumes of innocent little waltzes in Schubertian form. If you don't want them and would rather see your name on a proper piece with four movements, "your wish is my command."[39]

Hanslick was happy to accept the dedication and did not ask for more than these lovely trifles. He probably hoped for something bigger with his name on it in the future. If so, he never got it.

THAT AUGUST Brahms came once again to his gemütlich rooms in Lichtental next to Baden-Baden, with Clara and family nearby. In the same month he wrote at the end of the *Requiem* score, "Baden-Baden in summer 1866." He had finished it except for the fifth movement, an afterthought following the premiere. On a memorable September afternoon at Clara's he played and sang through the whole piece for guests including Levi and Allgeyer. She noted in her journal, "Johannes has played me some magnificent numbers from a German Requiem, and also a string quartet in C minor. But I am most moved by the Requiem; it is full of thoughts at once tender and bold."[40] (The C Minor String Quartet had been in the works at least since 1865, and it would be years more before Brahms felt ready to let it go.)

Because of work or the weather or his inner barometer, Brahms stayed in good spirits during this Baden summer, distributing presents to Clara's children and amusing them in all sorts of ways—especially Julie. "I often saw his eyes shining when he looked at her," Eugenie remembered. Clara wrote with relief of his mood on that visit, but noted that she did not at all like the beard he had grown that summer: "It quite spoils the refinement of his face."[41] Maybe because of Clara's disapproval, Brahms abandoned this second attempt at whiskers (the first had been when he left Hamburg in 1853), but the aspiration remained. On both sides of the Atlantic men of the later nineteenth century sprouted beards, bespeaking maturity and patriarchal dignity. Most who could manage it raised some sort of shrubbery, from the full flowing style of Stockhausen, Allgeyer, Billroth, and eventually Brahms, to the tighter trim of Joachim and Levi, the under-chin chaff of Wagner, the cloudy sideburns of Julius Epstein, the Van Dykes of Hans von Bülow and Hugo Wolf, the military cut of the young Gustav Mahler. Among Viennese concert crowds, clean-shaven Anton Bruckner stood out like a baby in a sea of bristles.

After the Prussian victory in the war, Joachim had been relieved of his job at the court of Hanover when King George was relieved of his throne by the Prussians. (Being a music lover, the king moved to Vienna.) Brahms was scheduled for more appearances with Joachim in the autumn, but had turned cranky over the idea. "I am not keen on concerts," he growled to Joachim. "It would be too delightful if I could only feel at home in my virtuoso getup. Now you have grown sky-high as a virtuoso, and I have my own notions and don't like strumming in your company, etc. etc."[42] The violinist had heard it all before. Somehow the tour got off the ground anyway, and Brahms astonished Joachim by actually taking an early train to Winterthur to practice. "He makes a new resolution to do it every day," Joachim wrote Clara, skeptically.[43]

An old friendship between Joachim and Hans von Bülow, interrupted when the violinist broke with the Weimar crowd, was renewed during the tour when Bülow turned up in Mühlhausen for one of the concerts. That did not mean the high-Wagnerian conductor was quite ready to defect to the enemy camp, even though he performed Brahms's Horn Trio that year. Bülow wrote composer Joachim Raff just after the Mühlhausen concert, "I respect and admire [Brahms], but—at a distance." Four years later he wrote Raff again, peevishly but with a prophetic ring for the man who was to invent "the three great B's of music": "What do the Br.'s matter to me? Brahms, Brahmüller, Bruch, etc. Don't mention them again! . . . The only one who interests me is Braff!"[44] Joachim surely bent the ear of his new-regained friend about Johannes, but as things turned out it was to be largely an unmusical matter that precipitated Bülow across the divide into the Brahmsians—his hero Wagner was fathering children with Cosima von Bülow.

AT THE END OF NOVEMBER 1866 Brahms gravitated back to Vienna, settling at Postgasse No. 6. Shortly after he arrived a letter came from Clara with more resounding between the lines than he could possibly have realized. Tweaking him, Clara writes that her Oldenburg performance of the A Major Piano Quartet went so well that "If I did not know how much the composer dislikes hearing his works played by anybody else, I should have wanted him to be there."

She goes on to more somber matters. Brahms had reported to her that during his last Winterthur stay Theodor Kirchner had rambled on and on about killing himself. For all their friendship Kirchner could not tell

Brahms the likely reason for his despair: Clara had jilted him. In this letter to Brahms she imperiously dismisses the sufferings of her ex-lover.
Kirchner's "suicidal ideas are not at all dangerous. . . . A man who talks
so much about it is not really serious. But you are right in saying that one
cannot think of him without real sorrow; his is a fine nature ruined by
outward and inward circumstances."[45] Around those lines surges their
carefully kept secret, and her ruthlessness in spurning anything or anybody that failed to meet her standards.

All that, of course, went right by Brahms. Now with what he thought
to be the whole of *Ein deutsches Requiem* finished, he turned his attention
to the practical side of finding a premiere. He made a piano reduction for
the purpose of showing the work around. Clara was the first to see the
arrangement, which he had promised her for a Christmas present. Before
anyone else, she understood the value of the work. "It has given me unspeakable joy," she wrote him.[46] Soon, though, she had pinpointed a nagging problem in the piece—"The only really troublesome thing in it is
the fugue with the pedal note."[47] That fugue at the end of the third
movement was destined nearly to sink the first performance.

The music went the round of friends and performers. Besides soliciting advice, with this process Brahms saw to it that a number of important
people knew he had a big choral piece in hand. Sending the score to
Dietrich in Oldenburg, he dropped a clue: "Write to me seriously what
you think of it. An *offer* from Bremen would indeed be extremely welcome. . . . Reinthaler would have to like the thing particularly, in order
to do something for it." Dietrich took his cue and showed the *Requiem* to
Karl Reinthaler, town music director in Bremen and organist of the
cathedral. Results proved substantial.

Another important premiere had been settled more directly. Despite
Josef Hellmesberger's set-to with Clara over playing Brahms, the violinist was agreeable to premiering the G Major Sextet, which he did with his
group on February 3, 1867. Somehow Vienna took this work of enormous warmth and charm, intimately involved with his feelings about a
lost love, for another of Brahms's passionless exhibitions of intellect. The
reviewer of the *Wiener Zeitung* stormed with Biblical wrath, "We are always seized with a kind of oppression when the new John in the Wilderness, Herr Johannes Brahms, announces himself. This prophet,
proclaimed by Robert Schumann in his darkening hours . . . makes us
quite disconsolate with his impalpable, vertiginous tone-vexations that
have neither body nor soul and can only be products of the most desperate effort."[48]

Just after the sextet premiere Brahms began an Austrian tour with a concert in nearby Graz. Maybe that helped distract him from a development that could not have improved his frame of mind. After less than five years on the podium, Julius Stockhausen resigned as conductor of the Hamburg Philharmonic (though he stayed on for two years more). With a sigh almost audible between the lines, Joachim in London once again wrote to Theodor Avé-Lallemant, prime mover of the orchestra board in Hamburg: "I suppose . . . it's no good hoping that you will rouse yourselves now and offer a fitting appointment to the *greatest musician of our day* (I know what I am talking about), to Johannes Brahms of Hamburg." As Brahms understood, that hope was no good at all, which does not necessarily mean he stopped hoping. Sure enough, for the second time the orchestra committee presented him the back of its hand, to his great disgust and his great good fortune. This time he said little about it. Soon he wrote Clara that he had decided to settle in Vienna, though with his habitual inertia concerning large matters he took a long time to act on it. He had several years of wandering ahead of him.

Joachim returned from London in spring 1867 for a concert in Vienna with Johannes, after which they toured Austria. Then Brahms headed out alone on a Hungarian tour. Much of the considerable proceeds of all this performing flowed to his father and sister in Hamburg. Clara wrote him that month that she had bought a thousand talers' worth of securities in his name and he could pay her back later. She cautioned the fiscally nonchalant Johannes, "You are sure to earn some more in Pest. But don't forget to change your guldens into Prussian money in Vienna, otherwise you'll lose too much on them."[49]

Brahms followed the huge creative outpouring of the *Requiem* with some songs that ended up in Opuses 48, 49, and 58. He had last released instrumental pieces in 1865, and from then until 1873 he completed only vocal music. Meanwhile, that spring an evil humor built up in him.

He visited Baden for a while in the summer, where Clara found him so insufferable that for the first time she disinvited him to meals. There was a break with Hermann Levi too. When the conductor—who had been giving useful advice on the *Requiem* and other pieces—showed Johannes some of his own compositions, the response was sufficiently disdainful to interrupt their friendship for months. Levi wrote Clara: "I am afraid that Brahms, the man as well as the musician, is now at a crossroads. . . . If he should not succeed in snatching his better self from the demon of abruptness, of coldness, and of heartlessness, then he is lost to us and to his music, for only all-engendering love can create works of art."[50]

Likely there were several reasons for Brahms's biliousness this year. Being spurned again by the Hamburg Philharmonic may have accounted for part of it. Besides, after delivering a big project a certain postpartum depression is common with artists. Inevitably, Brahms felt great anxiety about the prospects of *Ein deutsches Requiem*. He knew that its manifest beauties aside, the work was perfectly suited for the dozens of amateur choirs that dotted Europe. He also knew there are no sure things in art.

Beyond all that lay the chronic, unspoken infatuation weighing on him: Julie Schumann, more beautiful year by year and seemingly sicker as well. Clara anguished in her diary in July 1867, "It makes one wretched to see Julie, she looks so miserably ill."[51] She wrote that note in Baden while her daughter was staying in Divonne. When Julie suffered a serious crisis there at the end of the year, Clara was about to begin a tour of Belgium, so in her stead she sent Marie to take care of Julie.[52]

From whatever causes, in summer of 1867 Brahms felt more ill at ease in the world than usual. He sent Clara new songs including "Herbstgefühl" ("Autumn Mood"), written that spring and the bleakest of the bleak songs of Opus 48: "Thus does a cold day, somber as night, send chills through my life. Why should you still tremble at death, my heart, with your eternal beating!" Brahms scholar Ira Braus calls "Herbstgefühl" a "pessimistic, disillusioned grandchild of Schubert's 'Der Lindenbaum.'" Its neighbors in the set are "Trost in Tränen" ("Consolation in Tears") and "Vergangen ist mir Glück und Heil" ("My happiness and joy have fled"). Clara responded that she could not play "Herbstgefühl" without tears. She had no idea what was oppressing him, but she did her best to address it: "I should be pained indeed if I believed that you often felt like that [meaning "Herbstgefühl"]. No, dear Johannes, a man like you with all your gifts and in the prime of life, with his career still before him, ought not to harbor such gloomy thoughts. Make a home for yourself soon, find some well-to-do girl in Vienna . . . and you will become more cheerful." Thus perennially doleful Clara gives advice she would be no likelier to accept than he would. (Her letter continues on a practical note: "Send as much money as you can to the new Government Stocks.")[53]

If Clara's platitudes could not get Brahms out of his funk, something else did—a banner event, a vacation with his father.

AT THE END OF JULY 1867, a young violinist called on Johann Jakob Brahms at Valentinskamp and found him packed and dressed for the trip.

"My Hannes has invited me," the old man announced gravely. "I am to travel with my Hannes."[54] (In Plattdeutsch: *"Min Hannes het mi inladt; ick reis mit min Hannes."*) His son had extended the invitation a few days earlier, writing, "Don't think about it too much, just consider that in your old age the trip will get harder and less enjoyable with every year."

Johann Jakob had hardly been anywhere in his life outside the vicinity of Hamburg and Heide. And he had little idea of the torments his son planned for him. But he studied the railway schedules Hannes forwarded, said his first farewell to Karoline, and set out for Vienna. Just after he arrived, Josef Gänsbacher found the legendary forebear in his son's flat and, on the son's request, sang some Brahms for the occasion. Though Hannes's music like his person was a closed book to him, Johann Jakob expressed something in the area of pleasure. In Vienna, Brahms got visible delight from showing off his father to friends, displaying the old man's country Plattdeutsch and his yarns and his attempts at dignity. Brahms's beaming face seemed to say: *This* is what I came from. One Frau von Bruch was so charmed with Johann Jakob that she traded letters with him for the rest of his life, mailing him reviews of Johannes's music.[55]

During the next days father and son toured the Schönbrünn Palace, catching the splendiferous sight of Emperor Franz Josef holding court with the Pasha of Turkey. Then, in company with Gänsbacher for the first part of the trip, father and son headed for the Styrian Alps. The old man had never seen an actual Alp before and gawked to his son's satisfaction. The Gründlesee Johann Jakob declared "just like the Alster back home in Hamburg." Then he discovered that Hannes actually planned to drag him to the tops of the mountains. His father had to submit to the regime of everyone who traveled with Brahms: he did what he wanted, and you either went along or he was gone, usually after some acid remarks.

Wishing to be a good sport, Johann Jakob found himself riding and hiking through the mountains alongside Hannes day after day, climaxing with an ascent of the 5,850-foot Schafberg. A horse carried Johann Jakob much of the way up, but he had to dismount for the scramble to the summit. There another climber heard their exchange: "Oh, father! Isn't it magnificent here? The air! And the view!" Tentatively the old man agreed and added, "But Hannes, you're not going to do this to me again, are you?" They descended on horseback to an inn where, Johann Jakob noted in his travel diary, they "saw the sunset and full moon, got quite merry on the punch."

They ended with a stopover in Salzburg to have a look at Mozart's birthplace. Then Johannes headed home and gleefully reported on the trip to Joachim: "Through my father's visit and through the little trip we had together, I experienced the greatest happiness I have felt in a long time. Not the least of the happiness was the enjoyment my father derived from everything new that he saw. Until then he had never even seen a mountain, let alone looked down from one. . . . My soul is refreshed like a body after a bath. My good father hasn't the slightest idea how much good he has done me."[56]

In that frame of mind he made another tour with Joachim beginning in Vienna, then off to Budapest and nearby provinces. They found an enormous success, and the friends would play more concerts in Budapest at the end of the year. But Brahms continued to feel Joachim's dissatisfaction with his accompanying, not to mention his own impatience with the touring business.[57] It was clear that Joachim's favorite accompanist was Clara Schumann. After this year the duo would take a long vacation. In 1868, Joachim moved his family to Berlin, where he took over direction of the new music school of the Royal Academy of Arts. Clara would resist his efforts to lure her there as a teacher.

Brahms returned to Vienna with much to occupy him. Before the premiere of the whole *Requiem*, the first three numbers were to be done in Vienna by the forces of the Gesellschaft der Musikfreunde. The December 1, 1867, concert, under Johann Herbeck, was presented in the old Gesellschaft hall. Legend says that the excerpts were hissed at the end. So they were, vigorously, by a few people. But in fact approval overwhelmed the complaints, and in the several minutes it took Brahms to make his way onstage for a bow, the applause stayed strong.[58] The main reason for the ambivalent reception is suggested in Hanslick's review: "While the first two movements of the *Requiem*, in spite of their somber gravity, were received with unanimous applause, the fate of the third movement was very doubtful. . . . During the concluding fugue of the third movement, surging above a pedal-point on D, [one] experienced the sensations of a passenger rattling through a tunnel in an express train."[59]

In other words, this trial run ended with the spot Clara had warned Johannes about, a thirty-six-measure fugue over a sustained D in the bass. It seemed a dubious idea on the face of it, to write an elaborate fugue tied down to a drone, so that harmonically it spins its wheels throughout. But Brahms felt wedded to this effect as an expression of the assurance in the text: "The souls of the righteous are in the hands of God and no torment shall touch them." The already problematic fugue was not helped by conductor Herbeck's underrehearsed performance and a timpanist who felt inspired to play his repeated D as loud as he could. Thus Hanslick's

train-in-a-tunnel effect, and thus the hisses. After long expanses of delicately lyrical, poetic music, the piece seemed to end by clubbing the audience about the head.

After the Vienna airing of the opening movements and its ambiguous
success, Brahms went to work on the score again. He sent it for advice to
his old teacher Eduard Marxsen, saying: "I enclose also something from
my Requiem and *on this I earnestly beg you to write to me*. It looks rather
curious in spots and perhaps . . . you would take some music paper and
put down useful remarks. *I should like that very much*. The eternal 'D' in
No. 3. If I don't use the organ it doesn't sound [well]. . . . There is much
I should like to ask."[60] (After the Bremen premiere Marxsen would advise his still-respectful pupil to add a fifth movement for soprano solo,
and that suggestion Brahms accepted.) It is no surprise that the manuscript shows Brahms making the most extensive revisions in the fugue
with "the eternal D." He tried to head off future timpani disasters by
adding to the part the elaborate expression *piano ma ben marcato*, soft but
well-marked. Originally the whole fugue had been fully scored; now he
returned to the manuscript and struck out wide swaths of instrumental
doublings, trying to provide contrast and climax by holding back a *tutti*
until the end.[61] In that form the world came to know the fugue—improved but still troublesome, arguably the largest miscalculation Brahms
ever let stand in a work of his maturity.

When Dietrich showed Karl Reinthaler the score, the Bremen music
director enthusiastically offered his forces for the full premiere. It was set
for the following year's Good Friday in Bremen Cathedral. Rheinthaler
agreed to conduct most of the rehearsals—some three months' worth—
with his choir, then hand them over to Brahms for the final polish and
performance.

In the middle of January 1868, Brahms went for a stay in Hamburg,
partly to visit family and do some performing, partly to be near Bremen,
where Reinthaler was starting rehearsals for the *Requiem*. While there he
joined with Julius Stockhausen and the Philharmonic in Beethoven's G
Major Concerto and soloed in the Schumann Symphonic Études, plus
conducting some of his own orchestral arrangements of Schubert songs,
with Stockhausen soloing. It was Brahms's first appearance in six years
with the orchestra that had spurned him twice, and his last for a decade
more.

During what turned out to be a remarkable collaboration for the premiere of *Ein deutsches Requiem*, Brahms and Reinthaler had only one
recorded disagreement. Besides being a respected conductor, organist,
and composer, Reinthaler had studied theology. One detail of the *Re-*

quiem rather troubled his religious sensibility: somehow the piece never gets around to mentioning Jesus Christ. Reinthaler wrote Brahms an earnest and carefully reasoned entreaty to address this little oversight.

> Forgive me, but I wondered if it might not be possible to extend the work in some way that would bring it closer to a Good Friday service. . . . In this composition you stand not only on religious but also certainly on Christian ground. The second movement, for example, touches on the prophecy of the Lord's return, and in the penultimate movement the mystery of the resurrection of the dead. . . . But what is lacking, at least for a Christian consciousness, is the pivotal point: the salvation in the death of our Lord. "If Christ is not raised, your faith is vain," said St. Paul in connection with a passage you used. Now it would be easy to find, near "O death, where is thy sting," a suitable place. . . .[62]

He continued, in high theological mode.

Brahms was not about to put up with that sort of thing. He was a humanist and an agnostic, and his requiem was going to express that, Reinthaler or no. *Fix oder nix*, as the old Frauenchor motto ran—up to the mark or nothing. With the title *A German Requiem* he intended to convey that this is not *the* liturgical requiem mass in Latin, nor a German translation of it, but a personal testament, *a* requiem. Brahms avoided dogma in the piece for the same reason. He fashioned an inwardly spiritual work, full of echoes of religious music going back hundreds of years, yet there is no bowing to the altar or smell of incense in it. Even if the words come from the Bible, this was *his* response to death as a secular, skeptical, modern man. Brahms responded to Reinthaler politely but unequivocally:

> As far as the text is concerned, I confess that I would gladly omit even the word *German* and instead use *Human;* also with my best knowledge and will I would dispense with places like John 3:16. On the other hand, I have chosen one thing or another because I am a musician, because I needed it, and because with my venerable authors I can't delete or dispute anything. But I had better stop before I say too much.[63]

He had already said a good deal. The verse he tells Reinthaler he would "dispense with" is none other than "For God so loved the world, that He gave His only begotten Son, that whoever believes in him should not perish, but have everlasting life." Brahms means that he could do without that verse and that dogma, in *Ein deutsches Requiem* and in his life. If he was North German Protestant by tradition and temperament, he was not that in his faith, which like all his convictions Brahms held close to his chest. For himself he would not call Christ a particular son of God. Meanwhile, to Reinthaler he downplays the theology of some verses he does use, saying "I can't delete or dispute anything" from Scripture. With that he obliquely confesses that even the hints of resurrection lingering in his texts are not his own sentiments. At the end of his *Requiem* the dead are not reborn but released: "they rest from their labors." It is that rest from his own lonely labors that Brahms yearned for someday, as his mother rested from her life of poverty and toil.

The central message of *Ein deutsches Requiem* is in its first lines: "Blessed are they that mourn, for they shall be comforted." Brahms wrote his *Requiem* to bless those left living in the world, not the dead. The work aspires to comfort those who mourn. And it has done that through the generations since it was first sung in Bremen.

After their friendly theological debate Brahms and Reinthaler actually came to a compromise. In the performance Amalie Joachim would sing "I know that my Redeemer liveth" from Handel's *Messiah*, to placate the pious. Hearing the effect of that may have helped Brahms conclude that the piece could use a nice solo for a female voice. But when he added that solo after the premiere, it still pointedly made no allusion to the eponymous founder of the Christian religion.[64]

Just before the premiere, Brahms set out from Hamburg with Julius Stockhausen for a tour beginning in Germany and ending in Copenhagen. The Danish part of the tour was cut short by an archetypal demonstration of Brahms's thickheadedness and incapacity to make good on his own insensitivity. The concerts in Copenhagen had been set up by Robert Schumann's old friend, composer Niels Gade. The first ones created a sensation and the city buzzed with admiration for both artists. Then at a Gade party in his honor, full of dignitaries and admiring music lovers, Brahms lavishly extolled Bismarck to the open-mouthed guests and added (playfully, maybe) that it really was a shame the main museum of Thorwaldsen's sculpture was in Denmark rather than in, say, Berlin. Since Denmark had recently lost Schleswig-Holstein to Prussia and the sculptor was a beloved national figure, Brahms had managed with a few offhanded remarks to trample on an extraordinary collection of sensitivities. Stunned, Stockhausen reported to his wife, *"Do you know what Brahms has done in my absence?"* (implying that the singer usually kept track of his partner's tongue).

There was an uproar all over the country, complete with satirical poems and indignant newspaper articles, the remaining concerts were canceled, Brahms took the first boat out of town.[65] His music would not be welcome in Denmark for years afterward. Stopping to visit Klaus Groth in Kiel after the debacle, Brahms gaily called the Ditmarsh poet to the window and slapped his pocket, shouting, "Come out quick, I've made a pile of money!" Brahms related the story to Groth and shrugged it off with, "I've got so much money I won't need any more for a long time, so I couldn't care less."[66]

Besides, by then Brahms may have come to the realization that he had put his foot in it much worse with Clara Schumann.

HE DROPPED THE BOMB in a long letter of February 2, 1868, in which he sounded an old theme. He began by pressing her to come to the premiere of *Ein deutsches Requiem,* which she had told him might be unworkable because she would just be getting back from another English tour. From other matters, with Julie as transition, Brahms modulated into dangerous territory.

> If only you could be a listener on Good Friday [in Bremen] I should be more happy than I can say. It would be as good as half the performance for me. . . . I am resigning myself to the thought that this time, as in Vienna, it will go . . . too fast and too sketchily. But do come!!
>
> I never thought that you had spent your Christmas without Julie. How sad for you that the poor girl (of whom one cannot think without a certain emotion) was so far away and ill into the bargain. For when one sees Julie one thinks of all illness as being far away, although she is so delicate. But I still hope that she will eventually grow out of it. It is true that she is now grown up, but if I were in your place I should still have this comforting hope. Only I can't very well talk to you about it. . . .
>
> I'm now feeling sorely tempted to find an unfurnished apartment for myself in Vienna. . . . How much it would help me to know whether you might be thinking of moving there sooner or later. . . . I should like to implore you to bear in mind that someday your unsettled way of life must come to an end. There is only one thing you have to consider, and it applies . . . to me too, and that is, whether it is necessary for you to earn money this way.[67]

He rambled mildly on. Clara had given him Robert's old Graf piano and it was kept by Frau Rösing in Hamm, but she was moving, so what should he do with it? He had gotten too stout for his fur coat. He railed about his sister Elise's accepting a proposal from a Hamburg watchmaker. About this "unsuitable" marriage Brahms wrote, "Surely it is enough that I should have refrained from putting this sweet draught to my own lips [i.e., getting married] on her account!" One can hardly believe Brahms would pass up marriage in deference to his sister.

No amount of changing the subject would save him now. Surely Brahms did not suspect how hugely his words about Clara's "unsettled way of life" would blow up in his face, or how long she would make him pay for them. Was it a carefully planned campaign of his, or another offhanded remark that hit the wrong note? And what lay behind it?

Given her fury, Clara's response, written from London, was measured:

> You really seem to be living under the illusion that I have enough and am touring for my own entertainment. But surely one would not make all these exertions merely for pleasure! But apart from this, the present moment when my powers and success are at their zenith is hardly the time to retire from public life, as you advise me to do. The whole of the past year I have been received so enthusiastically everywhere, all my concerts have been so packed . . . and with but few exceptions I have played so well, that I can hardly understand why I should stop precisely now. . . . But I will think the matter over, for I cannot weigh it properly until I know what reasons you could have had to say all these things to me, and why you should have done it at a time when they might make such an impression upon me as to paralyze all my powers. . . . It was inconsiderate of you, I shall say no more.[68]

Behind what was to become one of the most painful episodes in their over four decades of relation lay a morass of feelings, prejudices, habits, old frictions, resentments, and guilt. Some of what underlay the quarrel is obvious, some of it perhaps so secret as never to be spoken between them or even admitted to themselves.

Despite his boundless respect for her, Brahms never took Clara's performing career as seriously as she did. She knew that and resented it. Partly it was because he did not take piano-playing seriously for himself, so had trouble conceiving why anyone else would—motivations outside his own were perennially incomprehensible to Brahms. Besides that, his letter resonates with the misogyny that made him suspicious of all women. His letters and conversations were peppered with disdain for female musicians. (Around then he wrote Joachim in planning a tour, "Unless your wife is coming, may we spare ourselves the boredom and vexation of songstresses?")[69]

Moreover, the stain of Hamburg prostitutes continued to taint all his response to women. He feared their sexuality, and like many self-protective, solitary men, feared even more the sexual and emotional power women wielded over him. In his comments about his attraction to women like Elisabet von Stockhausen and Ottilie Hauer, he used terms like "much to fear" and "make a fool of myself"—jokes, but symptomatic ones. The women artists he respected—Clara above all but also Amalie Joachim and any number of others—he treated as exceptions. In his mind, a manifestly superb musician transcended her sex. It was exactly those women he tended to imagine as virginal, untouchable—Clara, Elisabet, the singers he fell for. (Which is not to say that he did not flirt zealously with any number of singers.) If one of the young sirens married somebody else, fine. He at least would not despoil them, or allow them to weaken him. *Degradation in erotic life.* Even Clara could not completely escape the taint of her womanhood, if sexuality came into the picture. If he had discovered Clara's affair with Theodor Kirchner it might have shattered his idolization of her. Near the end of their lives Brahms would say of Madame Schumann, "she is as fresh and virginal as ever."

That is the more obvious import of Brahms's letter to Clara. Still, he had written and probably spoken similarly of her performing over the years, and she had never responded with this outrage. Clara reacted according to her own anxieties, within another wretched period in her life.

Her immediate reaction was to see Johannes's letter as an attack on her playing. In her biography, Nancy Reich writes that for Clara, to love her playing was to love her completely, to reject her playing was not only to reject her but to threaten her sense of meaning, her existence. Besides, she had been angry with Johannes for a long time, even before his foul temper of the previous summer. In September 1868, in the long miserable point and counterpoint that followed his letter of February, Clara wrote him, "The fact that for the last two years—that is to say, long before your letter—I have held aloof was owing to your last visit here. You appeared to be so uncomfortable with us and were so disagreeable . . . day after day . . . and gave so little thought to cheering me or making your visit as a friend at all pleasant, that it really was a more uncomfortable not to say miserable time for all of us."[70] The children felt the same, she informed him grimly. Meanwhile, in another letter (destroyed, but she cites it with appropriate disbelief), he had managed to charge her with "hatred" of him and/or his music. With these kinds of accusations going back and forth, things were spinning out of control.

Given Clara Schumann's determination in her art, it is surprising how attuned to others and concerned about them she was—more so than most artists of her caliber, far more so than Johannes. The solitary labor of becoming and staying a virtuoso always threatens to drag one away from the rest of the world and its struggles. Clara did live in the world and in her family and friends, whatever the pain they caused her. In her endless list of tribulations, the sorrows of the Brahms family counted too, and the same with the Joachims and others close to her. She was entirely genuine in those concerns. But the piano came before all of them. If among the people in her life her children were her greatest concern, the piano still came first. It was true that Clara had to provide for her children, but she also used that as an excuse to justify her own drive to go before the public. As Brahms knew, Clara could have supported her family in other ways closer to home—teaching in a music school, for example. (There is no record that he ever urged her to get married, as she did with him.)

In other words, the vehemence of her response to Johannes's letter has much to do with how depressed and vulnerable Clara felt about her family during those years in particular. Felix was now showing early signs of consumption, Ludwig's mental state was declining, Julie's health lurched from crisis to crisis. While all these sufferings seem to have been congenital and not the least her fault, nursing ailing children also had to take second place to the piano.

Clara's own sufferings mental and physical were so unremitting after her husband's collapse, and her resilience so heroic, that when it came to the misfortunes of others including her children, she tended to address them by grieving and weeping and entreating, but left it at that. Suffering was Clara's normal mode of response, her way of showing concern. Performing was her religion, her only real therapy, and sometimes it was her cross. Besides a steady catalog of cuts, falls, breaks, and sprains, in later years she was afflicted with bouts of what seems to have been tendonitis and bursitis, and often played in wretched pain. If she could move her body and fingers she went onstage, regardless of what it cost her or anyone else. While one can't exactly say that Clara expected the same of others, her own heroism gave her the hardness we find in her response, say, to Kirchner's talk of suicide, and finally to the deaths of three children and two grandchildren, and the madness of a fourth child. Few people could match the tragedies in Clara's life, or the temperamental depression that she survived for over half a century. Part of her hardness was that she knew that.

Clara had not gone to Julie during her ailing daughter's crisis, and spent no more time than before with her other variously ailing children. She had to have felt guilty over that, somewhere inside her perennially melancholy consciousness, somewhere beneath her ingrained self-righteousness. Brahms's letter about her performing struck through Clara's self-righteousness, deep into her guilt. He never quite blamed her children's sufferings on her career, but in the letter of winter 1868 he came as close to that accusation as he ever dared.

So in their exchanges of 1868 there is a buried dialectic—his anxiety for her children, her guilt over them. And as his letter shows, of the seven Schumann children Brahms's thoughts were always most on Julie. He deliberately hinted at his feelings for this daughter: "the poor girl (of whom one cannot think without a certain emotion) . . . only I can't very well talk to you about it." Clara did not take the hint. Which is all to say that his anxiety over Clara's children and the effect of her career on them was not entirely irrational, or misogynistic. Nor was it entirely disinterested. It was permeated by his mounting infatuation for Julie as she reached adulthood. Bluntly: what if somehow Julie died because of Clara's neglect?

Julie was beautiful, lively, intelligent, ethereal, magical. Men are apt to fall in love with women like her. But Brahms's passion was hopeless. Given that he was a kind of surrogate father to Clara's children, his feelings verged on incestuous. His long relationship with Clara made the idea of marrying her daughter nearly unthinkable, an affair more so. Beyond that, this was the daughter of Robert Schumann, his mentor, almost his second father, and Clara had always been to him some inextricable tangle of mother and forbidden lover. Too much was mixed up in Brahms's feelings beyond attraction and admiration. His fantasy of Julie emerged from that psychological morass, stirred further by his reflexive view of feminine sexuality—and his own—as something for the brothel. Julie herself suspected something of it and avoided his glowing eyes when he came to the house. (That may have played a part in his vile spirits of late, when he visited Clara's family in Baden-Baden.) For Brahms, Julie was a fantasy part inevitable, part neurotic. When finally confronted by the reality of her life and feelings, which did not include him at all, he would react to the revelation as if it were a betrayal.

This quarrel would not be resolved easily or soon, nor would Brahms's fantasies about Julie. Meanwhile the Bremen premiere of *Ein deutsches*

Requiem loomed in the spring of 1868, keeping him keyed up. Some two weeks before Good Friday in Bremen came another significant occasion when the F Minor Piano Quintet (reworked from the string quintet and the two-piano sonata) had its world premiere in Paris. At the piano with the Erard group on that occasion was Luise Japha, now Dr. Langhans-Japha, Brahms's friend from his teens and maybe the first lady pianist exempted from his scorn. Luise had found Brahms himself a chore and they had not kept up a friendship, but she had not forgotten his music as she made a distinguished career as a pianist in France. A decade before, Clara had not dared to play his music in public on her first visit to Paris. That country and Brahms still did not suit each other, but this first important French premiere, and a well-received one, at least sustained a presence for his work in a country he never considered visiting.

The F Minor Piano Quintet is often called the crown of his chamber music. Brahms scholar Michael Musgrave calls it Beethovenian in its intensity, Schubertian in its lyrical moments; that combination is the essence of Brahms's full maturity.[71] In expression the quintet ranges from the high-Romantic passion and drama of the first movement, to a lushly lyrical slow movement, to a demonic scherzo and dashing finale. It also carries his familiar techniques to a higher level of thoroughness and mastery. Like the G Minor Piano Quartet, the F Minor begins with a pregnant theme in octaves, of great import to the piece.

But this theme is more varied and songlike than the skeletal opening of the G Minor; despite its quietness it has a coiled-spring intensity that resonates to the end of the piece. The way it will dominate the four movements in all its moods is revealed immediately, when with an explosive gesture like a spring releasing, Brahms transforms the flowing beginning into a passionately surging piano line made by speeding up the opening theme:

The F-G-A♭ of the opening echoes all the way to the main theme of the last movement, which begins with the same notes. The triadic mo-

tives of the opening theme resonate through the piece as well. Yet
Brahms gives priority to the simple half-step outline G-Ab and Db-C (the
latter first heard with an intervening F). That half-step relationship not
only dominates the thematic work throughout the quintet, but has large-
scale implications too. In earlier works Brahms integrated the dimensions of melody and harmony; now he moves another step toward the
future by conflating tiny motivic elements with local harmonic structures
and with large-scale tonal ones: the melodic half steps of his themes extend into a series of key changes moving by half step; the blisteringly intense scherzo is full of melodic semitones including the driving Phrygian
Db-Cs at the end, but also startling harmonic changes based on half-step
part movement. (The Phrygian is the "E-mode," one of the old ecclesi-
astical scales that were common before Western music settled into using
major and minor scales almost exclusively. Phrygian can be thought of as
minor with a poignant lowered second degree: in effect darker than minor, and as such a favored color of Brahms's when he indulged in modal
touches.)

Nearly a century later, Arnold Schoenberg wrote his article "Brahms
the Progressive" partly to claim that the essence of his own twelve-tone
method—that everything in the music, from melody to harmony to the
overall pitch structure derives from a single twelve-note thematic kernel
called a *row*—is the culmination of a progressive development in musical
thought epitomized by Brahms. Mainly Schoenberg was thinking of the
unification of the "horizontal"/melodic with the "vertical"/harmonic,
and the extension of that logic into the larger structure of a piece.
Brahms demonstrated that idea masterfully in works including the F Minor Quintet.

At the same time, in this piece Brahms carries on his metric and formal innovations, displacing the perceived downbeat from the barline for
long stretches, creating a deliberate metric disorientation that adds to the
intensity of the notes. The last movement, with elements of both sonata
and rondo forms, verges on free-form: a slow, ghostly introduction, then
an allegro moderato during which he eventually conflates the functions
of a quasi-development and return of the rondo theme.[72]

Brahms's prime achievement in the piece, though, is more intangible
than a matter of expanding and refining his technique. He had already
created original forms, fashioned intricate thematic work, written plenty
of expressive music. Now from movement to movement there is a unity
of expression that perhaps he had not found before in his chamber
and orchestral music. In the quintet the sweetly nocturnal lyricism of the
second movement seems a retreat from the surging passion and grim

determination of the first; the demonic scherzo drives the intensity of the first movement to a higher level; the finale, after the eerie and desolate introduction, brings everything to a certain emotional equilibrium—though without the expected resolution of minor into "hopeful" major. In the racing rhythms of the finale the coiled-spring intensity of the first movement drives to the last beat, which in its descent from A♭ to G to F seems to answer the question posed by the ascent of those notes at the very beginning of the piece.

The model for that kind of expressive integration is above all Beethoven, who somehow can carry us through four movements of an abstract work like the Fifth Symphony, with its immense variety of character and color and texture, and at the end make us feel we have heard *one story*. Beethoven said his means for helping him achieve that quality in his instrumental music was to imagine a parallel story as he composed the piece. In only one important work, the *Pastoral* Symphony with its program of a visit to the country, did Beethoven spell out his narrative. In other cases he did not provide a story because that was not the point of the music, but rather a private device for achieving dramatic consistency.

Of the subtleties composers aspire to and only occasionally manage to achieve over the course of long pieces, that unity of feeling—within emotional variety—is one of the most elusive. It has little to do with technique as such, or motivic and tonal relationships as such; it cannot be taught, can hardly be analyzed, only felt intuitively by composer and listener alike. For Brahms it began to happen, perhaps, with the F Minor Quintet. Maybe the work reflected his feelings in the middle 1860s, maybe not. In any case, the emotional intensity he achieved in it seems at times anguished, at times (in the scherzo) demonic, at times tragic. Yet the whole quintet remains a unified dramatic plot without becoming monochrome: one story.

In the past that unity-in-variety had eluded Brahms, in one way or another. *Ein deutsches Requiem* is consistent in mood, in fact too consistent, without enough variety of texture and tempo and feeling to create the illusion of a satisfying story unfolding throughout. The *Requiem*, as Brahms predicted as he got to work on it, is only "a sort of a whole" despite melodic interconnections uniting its seven movements (among them the derivation of several themes from the Lutheran chorale "Wer nur den lieben Gott lasst walten"). For all its magnificence and limpid lyricism, sameness of tone is the abiding problem of the *Requiem*. Meanwhile, earlier Brahms masterpieces are satisfying from beginning to end, with plenty of expressive variety, but lack an overall sense of dramatic progression. To name one: each movement of the B♭ Major String Sextet is compelling, but each also stands alone.

Brahms found a sense of *one story* in the F Minor Quintet. It is another quality he needed to have in his grasp before he returned to the sketches toward a symphony that he had carried around with him for so many years. As has been often said about the F Minor, the quintet did not lead to later developments in his chamber music so much as to his mastery of the symphony in its formal, technical, and expressive dimensions. Now the principal remaining hurdle was orchestration, and before long Brahms would address that question with a genre he invented for the purpose—a set of variations for orchestra.

THERE WAS ALSO A PRACTICAL MATTER on which Brahms's ability to write a symphony depended: the public and financial fate of *Ein deutsches Requiem*. It was not that everything hinged on the premiere at Bremen Cathedral. His pieces often insinuated their way slowly into public affection; even the D Minor Piano Concerto managed that to a degree during the 1860s. But a quick success with the *Requiem* would certainly help the cause, and at this stage of his career a disaster in Bremen would have done him a great deal more harm than the one in Leipzig had. Brahms was fearless in doing what he wanted on the page, but at the same time cagey and cautious in managing his career. To write a symphony he required a long stretch of undisturbed time, i.e., money, and needed the kind of reputation that would provide a symphony first-rate early performances and respectful hearings. So as the *Requiem* premiere approached he felt more than usually lacerating apprehensions. The hisses at the Vienna premiere of three movements of the *Requiem* lingered in his ears, blending with memories of the concerto's fate in Leipzig.

On top of it all, Clara his touchstone had said she could not come, and they remained at odds over his letter about her "unsettled way of life." In Oldenburg a week before the premiere, Brahms sighed to Albert Dietrich, "Only Madame Schumann will be wanting now, but I shall sadly miss her presence." Taking the hint, Dietrich contacted a miserably depressed Clara, just back in Baden-Baden from her British tour. Prodded by friends and family, she gave in and agreed to make the trip to Bremen.[73]

The premiere of *Ein deutsches Requiem* in Bremen Cathedral on April 10, 1868, came a month before Brahms's thirty-fifth birthday. That Good Friday was beautiful with its aura of holiness, the overflowing crowd prepared for something extraordinary (and inevitably, some hoping for a fiasco). Clara surprised Brahms at the dress rehearsal the night before.[74] Among the assembled next day, many arriving from a distance, was Johann Jakob Brahms, come to enjoy a little reflected glory from his son. Also in the audience were composer Max Bruch, old friends the Grimms and Dietrichs, and J. M. Rieter-Biedermann, whose firm was to publish the piece.[75]

Spread out before the altar of the cathedral were a chorus of two hundred and a large orchestra. Karl Reinthaler had meticulously prepared his choir during three months of rehearsals. Josef Joachim led the violins and contributed solos during the performance, Amalie Joachim added Handel's "I know that my Redeemer liveth," and the two joined in an aria from Bach's *Saint Matthew Passion*. Julius Stockhausen had come to sing the third-movement solo that Johannes surely composed for the deep bells of his baritone. Among the chorus sat four veterans of the Hamburg Frauenchor, who had come to sing one more new work of their director.

Just before the performance Brahms took Clara's arm at the door of the cathedral and escorted her up the nave. Many of the hundreds watching knew something of what had passed between them. There was almost an air of a marriage ceremony about that moment, their walk down the aisle arm in arm that ended not with ring and vows, but with the consecration of music.

Leaving Clara in her seat, Brahms took the podium. A silence, then he lifted the baton and the quiet pulsing of the basses began, then the gentle lines of cellos and violas rising and falling (he had kept the brightness of violins out of this somber movement). For the first time, listeners heard the simple, unforgettable opening words of the choir, foreshadowing the purpose of the *Requiem* and its progression from darkness to light: *Blessed, blessed are they that mourn, for they shall be comforted. They that sow in tears shall reap in joy.* In the echoing spaces of the cathedral the first movement unfolded, mostly quiet, its immense subtlety wrapped in noble simplicity. The style is at once utterly Brahmsian and in its gentle sweetness unlike anything he wrote before or after. At the same time it is suffused with the history of German religious music, back through Beethoven's *Missa Solemnis* through Mozart and Haydn to Bach and Handel, beyond that a century earlier to the austere gravity of Heinrich Schütz, and back further to the German and Italian polyphonists of the Renaissance.[76] As in Schütz, the music of the *Requiem* seems to rise directly from the German of Luther's Bible: *Selig sind, die da Leid tragen, denn sie sollen getröstet werden.* The music gives voice to the spirit of those words, which return at the end of the first movement distilled to their essence: *getröstet werden,* be comforted.

There would have been a pause in Bremen Cathedral, the audience rustling, turning their texts. They looked to the little figure of Brahms on the podium, giving one of his awkward but forceful upbeats to begin the second movement. Even before the choir enters, this music is unmistakably a funeral sarabande, as it had been when Brahms first sketched it in the days after Robert Schumann leaped into the Rhine.[77] The dark minor of the themes is counterpoised by pealing, Bachlike high chords of strings and winds, and beneath it all the fateful and relentless pounding of drums. In stark octaves the voices enter on a Brahmsian *Dies Irae: Denn alles Fleisch es ist wie Gras und alle Herrlichkeit des Menschen wie des Grases Blumen: For all flesh it is as grass and every splendor of men like the grasses' bloom.* Then the gentle answering phrase, *the grass has withered, and the flowers fallen.* A contrasting moment evokes patience, then the funeral march returns, building to something near despair before the radiant answer: *But the Lord's word endures forever . . . and sorrow and sighing shall flee away.* If the beginning evokes the Gothic severity of Schütz, the end recalls Beethoven's Ode to Joy: *Freude! Freude! Freude! They shall find joy!*

Julius Stockhausen stood to intone the opening of the third movement: *Lord, make me to know my end, and the measure of my days.* Choir and soloist exchange the chastening words of scripture, *Surely every man walks in a vain show . . . he heaps up riches, and knows not who shall gather them.* Yet for Brahms this work ends not in despair but in joy, consolation, quietness—here the pealing fugue over the fixed pedal point of certainty in the bass, *But the souls of the righteous are in the hand of God and no torment shall touch them.*

Then came *How lovely is thy dwelling place, O Lord of Hosts,* as apparently artless as a folk song. Many of the listeners were in tears now. Certainly Clara was. Sitting in the church with thousands at her back, seeing nothing but the musicians and that maddening, beloved genius on the podium, she felt that Johannes was with a magic wand calling masses of instruments and voices together in a great work, and so at last her husband's prophecy in "Neue Bahnen" had been fulfilled. In her depression of that time, for all the tragedies of her family and the troubles between her and Johannes over the years and never more than now, Clara wrote in her journal of that day, "It was such a joy as I have not felt for a long time."[78] They were two much-wounded people for whom music could heal everything, and that lay at the heart of their relationship.

The fifth (later sixth) movement began, with its dark colors and old /new harmonies, on *Now we have here no dwelling place but seek the one to come.* Nearly everyone in Bremen Cathedral was inside the music now, sensing that this work would not let them down but sustain its uncanny aura of grace to the end. This movement, with its simple rhythms and quiet plainspokenness, displays one of the main driving forces of the *Requiem:* harmonies at once archaic and fresh, piercingly expressive with every turn. The movement ends with a grand fugue on Handelian verses and, for the first time, with Handel as its manifest inspiration: *Lord, thou art worthy to receive glory and honor and power.* The fugue reveals the gift Wagner had noted, that Brahms could make tradition his own without negating an inch of it. Yet the *Requiem* is one of the few large choral works of its time not dominated by echoes of Handel.

The music of the finale is full and rich but not showy. It is a finale with the same lyrical sweetness, the same austerity, humility, and limpid ecstasy that the *Requiem* possesses from its opening measures. It ends gently as the work began, without Beethovenian perorations or Handelian kettledrums, but with submission to the inevitable, a peace not of paradise but of deepest rest. *Blessed are they that mourn,* the work begins. It ends, *Blessed are the dead which die in the Lord from henceforth: Yea, said the Spirit, they rest from their labors.* With a radiant gentleness the music dies away on its opening word: *selig,* blessed.

The audience appears to have left Bremen Cathedral that Good Friday in an atmosphere of awe and grace. Perhaps they suspected they had been present at the birth of something that would live long in music and in the heart of humanity. A more direct response came when a visitor, having sat in tears throughout and watched Clara, Joachim, and a good many others weeping, discovered Johann Jakob Brahms taking a pinch of snuff outside. The visitor asked what he had thought of this effort by his son. "It didn't sound bad," the old man said, with a sniff that may have been from the tobacco.

After the performance a large party retired to the Bremen Rathskeller to celebrate. The Joachims and Dietrichs and Stockhausens and Grimms were there, with Max Bruch and Clara Schumann and daughter Marie, the women from the Hamburg Frauenchor, and as many others as could squeeze into the old restaurant. Reinthaler gave the formal speech, including:

What we have heard today is a great and beautiful work, deep and intense in feeling, ideal and lofty in conception. Yes, one may well call it an epoch-making work! . . . It was an anxious, a sad and melancholy time we endured when we laid to rest the last beloved Master [meaning Schumann]; it almost seemed as if the night had come. But today . . . we can predict that the followers of that great master will complete what he began. . . . I know that you all rejoice with me in the fact that we have the author of this splendid work sitting amongst us, and you will willingly drink with me to the health of the composer—*Brahms!*

Everyone responded in his and her style—some applauding, some cheering, Clara sobbing. Brahms rose dutifully but said only,

If I allow myself now to say a couple of words, I must preface them with the remark that I have not the gift of speech at my command. But there are so many in this company to whom I would like to say a word of thanks . . . and especially that applies to my honored friend Reinthaler, who has devoted himself with tireless zeal to the study of my *Requiem*. Therefore I lay my thanks for all at his feet, and call for three cheers for Herr Reinthaler![79]

Afterward he pressed Clara to stay for another day. "I wish I had not given in to him," she wrote in her journal. In the morning they quarreled, she left town in tears. Without even fully understanding the causes, of which Julie was the secret one, they were heading toward a crisis neither of them could foresee. Brahms retired to Hamburg and his father's house for six weeks, there to follow Eduard Marxsen's advice and write a soprano solo to add to the *Requiem* as fifth movement. If the work in his own mind was written in memory of both Robert Schumann and his mother, in this last music for the *Requiem* he evokes unforgettably the memory of Christiane Brahms: *I will comfort you as one whom his mother comforts.*

At its premiere the *Requiem* found success that relatively few works and composers have ever achieved by the beginning of middle age. Carl Dahlhaus calls the *Requiem*, as an individual confession of faith, "one of those works in which the 19th century recognized its own identity."[80] Reinthaler repeated the work in Bremen a few weeks later, and during the next year it was done twenty times across Germany. From there it spread to Russia and England and Paris and to choral groups around the West, in an age when there were able and enthusiastic amateur groups everywhere. (Sending it to publisher Rieter-Biedermann, Brahms stressed, "Above all the work is practical, in that every movement can be done alone.")[81]

Ein deutsches Requiem was the foundation of Brahms's later career, his work, reputation, and fortune. After the *Requiem* he was not unassailable because no artist is (the more famous, the more assailed), but his pedestaled place at the center of the European musical world was assured as long as he could maintain that level of work. And he did maintain it, gloriously. His predecessor Mozart had lived and worked in almost a show-business atmosphere, with hits and misses and flops, without pretensions. Brahms would have liked to work like that, but history would not let him. Nor did he ever compose to order like Bach and Haydn, with the inevitably fickle results. The world depended on Brahms to make masterpieces, and he reliably did. The overall level of the work he published in his lifetime is perhaps higher than that of any other composer. Pieces of the sort Beethoven and Mozart put out as minor but workable, Brahms put in the stove. As far as he could assess what he had written, he wanted to issue nothing but masterpieces.

Yet however predictable Brahms's achievement became in the last three decades of his life, it was never easy, never unearned. He worked from a solid body of technique built on a phenomenal inborn gift, but he followed no formulas and took nothing for granted—least of all his talent. With the courage, relentless discipline, and fierce determination that had brought him to accept the burden of Robert Schumann's prophecy and to fulfill it—as historic genius, if not epochal Savior—after the premiere of *Ein deutsches Requiem* Brahms ascended his lonely pedestal and occupied it to the end of his days.

CHAPTER FOURTEEN

Ruthless Beauty

AFTER THE TRIUMPH of *Ein deutsches Requiem* in Bremen had been repeated in cities across Europe and England, Brahms assumed a com-
manding place among composers of his time, with Wagner his main rival
and that rival on a different stage. Brahms cared little about the rewards
of the position he had earned, the money and glory, so long as he had
them. He took his genius for granted and the recognition of it for
granted. (That is not to say his humility was false. It was not.) More important to his mind, musicians and critics across Europe, in England and
the United States, were taking up his work. Even if few of Vienna's leading performers were wholehearted advocates, Brahms had still woven
himself into the fabric of musical life in the West's capital of music. As it
had been with his illustrious predecessors, the Viennese reserved the
right to scorn him when they felt like it, but as one of their own. For that
reason, his triumphs in the City of Dreams would be the sweetest of all.

In his middle thirties, his burden now was no longer to live up to his
promise but rather to maintain what he had achieved. After 1868 the *Requiem* would be heard around the Western world, and his chamber music and songs were making inroads everywhere. From this point on,
Brahms seems to have felt no necessity to change the craftsmanship he
had learned, but rather sensed that he had reached a level he could refine
but not leap beyond. After the *Requiem* his music would most often be
characterized by a magisterial perfection, with less of the Young Kreisler
left on the surface—no Romantic excesses, fewer surprises, instead great
beauty and resilient architecture. His feelings were still capable of giving
rise to music, but he no longer relied on that inspiration as Young
Kreisler had. Only sometimes now did his life trouble the surface of his

work (certainly one occasion was the Alto Rhapsody). To an increasing degree, in the arrangement of his days Brahms approached his solitary goal: for the story of his music to become the story of his life.

All the same, in ascending to his pedestal Brahms fulfilled Schumann's prophecies only to be confronted by new trials. Looming in his path lay three historic genres he had skirted so far—symphony, string quartet, and opera. The musical world waited to see him wrestle the masters of the past on their own ground, and Wagner on his. No composer had put pen to paper with more expectations hanging over him, and Brahms understood that better than anybody else. During his lifetime the weight of the historical repertoire accumulated steadily, less and less in new works than in the preservation and resurrection of old. Above all, the full magnitude of J. S. Bach's legacy was slowly revealed through the century. By its end, an unprecedented burden of past masterpieces lay on the shoulders of anyone trying to add to them.

It was in the early 1870s, still terrified at the prospect of going up against Beethoven, that Brahms spoke his famous words to conductor Hermann Levi: "I'll never write a symphony! You have no idea how the likes of us feel when we're always hearing a giant like that behind us." The closer he came to string quartet and symphony, both of which he had attempted and so far failed to bring off, the louder the tramp of Beethoven and the other giants resounded in his mind. Yet he still felt driven to take up the challenge of symphony and quartet—was already doing it, in fact, when he vented his fears to Levi.

However cautious he was in practice, Brahms's instincts drove him to master the most exacting trials. In the end, though, after years of toying with the idea of opera, he would hold back from that ordeal: *as soon write an opera as marry*, runs another of his famous lines, ones often repeated. His experiments toward the stage, mainly the cantata *Rinaldo*, had not boded well, nor was he particularly satisfied with most of the lieder he had composed by 1870. After the enormous effort of *Ein deutsches Requiem*, he struggled for years before he hit his stride again with a big piece, and that would be neither symphony nor quartet.

With the *Requiem* Brahms fulfilled Schumann's prophecy—except for assuming the pose of Messiah. Schumann had made that prediction in hopes that Johannes would drive Liszt and his philistine minions from the temple of art, along with their blueprints for redeeming music. But after Brahms's one attempt, with Joachim, to challenge the opposition with the ill-fated manifesto, he left musico/political ambitions to others. The manifesto widened a crack between factions into a gulf, but Brahms was too private a man to lead a faction, the direction of his art too personal, and he felt only disgust for the apocalyptic ambitions of Liszt and Wagner. Brahms was quite prepared to pull strings behind the scenes, but as an artist he modestly aspired to redeem only himself, to exalt only his listeners. If there are prophecies of the coming Modernist revolution in his work, in his own mind any approach to innovation was solitary, and must rise from a foundation in the past.

So while in the flush of success after the *Requiem* premiere Reinthaler declared it "an epoch-making work," for all its popularity it remained a singular gesture, initiating no epoch, not even a new phase in Brahms's style. He was ready to let epochs take care of themselves. As far as he was concerned, they were all headed downhill anyway. Meanwhile, Brahms understood Wagner's achievement to be at once profound and no direct threat to him—unless he did take on an opera—and conversely felt certain that Liszt's music for the concert hall could never challenge his own. (He wrote Karl Reinthaler in December 1871, "We experience Liszt's *Christus* here on the 30th, and the thing appears so incredibly boring, stupid, and absurd that I can't imagine how the necessary swindle will be perpetrated this time.")[1]

For those who could not swallow the New Germans and Wagnerism, Brahms was the available alternative. The Schumanns and Joachim had understood that from the beginning—Johannes the antipope. Now Brahms fully inhabited that role, uneasily, with tacit acquiescence. It would be mainly the upstart symphonist Bruckner who succeeded in getting under his skin. Otherwise Brahms kept his protests private and let others fight the public battles for him. His own energies he husbanded for battle with the lines and spaces of music paper.

Certainly in the three decades of his preeminence Brahms was to influence countless composers, not only with his music but by sitting on committees and placing people he approved of in positions of power. Still, with the exception of his help to Antonin Dvořák— a relatively mature artist when they met in 1875—it is arguable that Brahms's influence on his time was a mixed blessing. When he examined the work of young composers he went at their voice leading and bass lines like the most dogmatic Herr Professor, and usually sent them off to study counterpoint with Nottebohm or some equally exacting pedagogue. Maybe one of Brahms's secrets was that he had the instincts of a pedant and the gifts of a genius, or rather: he had the genius to withstand his own pedantry. Most of his followers did not. Even Dvořak, whose fertility of invention and freshness of voice enchanted Brahms, would be gently entreated to clean up his counterpoint. To the degree that lesser talents than Dvořák took Brahms's advice or followed his example, it may have done them harm. After encountering the dogmatic Brahms, Hugo Wolf sensed the danger and fled to the opposition.

By the end of his life, Brahms's efforts to erect barriers against the future had failed. Modernism overtook him, and Vienna would provide much of the model for the coming revolution, for good and for ill. Brahms would leave no school and mostly minor imitators, though his work enriched composers of the next century as diverse as Sibelius, Elgar, Ives, and Schoenberg. More than any of his contemporaries, Brahms had the kind of technique that can teach something to every composer, of every stripe: what musical logic amounts to.

IN MAY 1868, after the premier of *Ein deutsches Requiem*, Brahms returned to his father's house, to Hamburg's familiar streets and canals, the old gabled houses, and composed the new soprano solo as fifth movement for the piece. With that he gratefully laid the *Requiem* to rest after over ten years of gestation. Then he set off for the Lower Rhine Music Festival, where this year he formed a desultory but persistent friendship with Max Bruch. As with other composer friends, the admiration flowed more strongly toward him than in the other direction; Bruch would often feel the lash of Brahms's sarcasm. All the same, that year Bruch proposed to dedicate his First Symphony to Brahms and the dedicatee accepted with pleasure.

For several weeks after the festival Brahms worked in Bonn. During hours away from his desk he spent much time with Hermann Deiters, philologist and music critic of the *Allgemeine musikalische Zeitung*, a steady champion and in 1880 author of a short Brahms biography, the first of many. That summer Brahms showed Deiters some of a piano quartet in C minor, a reworking of the old C♯ minor quartet from 1855. To introduce to the critic this music from the heart of his Clara-madness, his Werther years, Brahms said to Deiters, "Imagine a man who is just about to shoot himself, and to whom no other course is left." He echoed the sentiment many times in the next years—often to writers, in fact.

By Brahmsian musical/emotional logic, he recalled a period of intense longing for a woman with music that stood for the longing. Picking up the quartet briefly again (it had years to go) he relived the agony of its inspiration. The woman he longed for this time, though, was the daughter of the first one—Julie Schumann, twenty-three now, palely beautiful in her fragile health. Maybe that infatuation drove Brahms to take up the piece again. In any event, he was about to recapitulate an old pattern of his with women, in every way but one: now the woman he had fallen for had not fallen for him.

After a relatively fallow period in the wake of finishing the *Requiem*, he enjoyed a small creative surge during the summer of 1868. In June he visited Albert Dietrich at Oldenburg, and one afternoon went with Dietrich and family to have a look at the naval port of Wilhelmshafen. At the harbor Brahms seemed quiet and brooding. He told Dietrich that early in the morning he had opened a collection of Hölderlin taken from the family bookshelf, and was riveted by the poet's "Hyperions Schicksalslied." After they had toured the harbor for a while, he walked away from his hosts. Dietrich saw him sitting alone on the beach, writing as the waves lapped beneath him.[2]

There began the *Schicksalslied* (*Song of Destiny*), with its uncanny opening framing Hölderlin's evocation of the gods: "You walk up there in the light / Upon soft ground, blessed genii!" After making the sketch Brahms put it aside for three years, to tend to more practical matters. In the choice of the poem itself, though, he had already prophesied an imminent destiny of his own. The text moves from the meditation on divine rapture to a brutal descent: "Suffering humanity falls blindly from one hour to the next, like water hurled from crag to crag."

In the same summer Brahms wrote a new final chorus for his 1863 cantata *Rinaldo* and finished a collection of lieder to be distributed among Opuses 46–9, and maybe Opus 57. Nearly every lyric from that period, mostly by his favored poet G. F. Daumer, seems to echo his undeclared infatuation for Julie Schumann. In those songs a mélange of images of obsession and flight poured out of him:

I gazed into the sweet miraculous glow of the wondrous beauty's eyes, and thereby forfeited the cheerful gleam in my own. . . . I shall plunge your image, obstinate and imperious woman, and those laughing lips full of the sound of lutes, the shadowy shimmer of the hair, and that heaving white breast, and that conquering gaze that darts through me—I shall plunge them into the cup of oblivion. . . . Do not pour down your love-inflaming songs so loud from the blossoming bough of the appletree, O nightingale! . . . Can I conceal the wild flame here, all the pains that torture me, when all the winds round about cry the causes of my sorrow? . . . O lovely visage, you make me yearn for this red, this white, and that is not all I mean; to see, to greet, to touch, to kiss—that is what you make me yearn for, O lovely visage!

In his next lieder collections Brahms mingled these new songs with old ones from the Agathe period—the present fascination with a woman echoing an old, the new songs likewise echoing old ones. His emotional life altogether was becoming a series of fading echoes.

An exception to the passionate tone of most lieder from that summer was the little "Wiegenlied" ("Cradle Song"), from Opus 49, written in honor of Bertha and Artur Faber's second child.

Before long a considerable percentage of humanity was to know the Wiegenlied simply as "Brahms's Lullaby," if they knew its author at all. Out in the world it became part of the human community like so many faux "folk songs," when millions took the melody into their hearts. Its verse (a second was added later) comes from the texts of *Des Knaben Wunderhorn*: "Good evening, good night; with roses bedecked,/with clove pinks adorned,/slip under the blanket./In the morning, God willing,/you will waken again." In fact, the ingenuous little tune unfolds (so much of Brahms in this) as counterpoint to a lilting Viennese Ländler that Frauenchor visitor Bertha Porubzsky used to sing to him in Hamburg, when Bertha was young and he loved her, before he let her slip away. In the same way he had worked the old song "Josef, lieber Josef mein" into the "Geistliches Wiegenlied" for the Joachims' child. The new "Wiegenlied" is entirely symbolic then, as Brahms hinted when he sent the song to Artur Faber in July: "Frau Bertha will realize that I wrote the 'Wiegenlied' for her little one. She will find it quite in order . . . that while she is singing Hans to sleep, a love song is being sung to her."

So Bertha became the first person to sing Brahms's Lullaby. Soon the song spread around the world in all sorts of ramshackle arrangements, which finally caused Brahms to grumble to publisher Simrock: "Why not make a new edition in a minor key for naughty or sick children? That would be still another way to move copies."[3] Brahms didn't mind the money, but he didn't like lesser hands mangling his counterpoint, even in a lullaby.

Presumably Brahms showed Clara Schumann that summer's lieder as a matter of course, but she remained oblivious to their mingling of old lost love and yearning for an impossible new love, in the person of her daughter. Clara was still stewing about Johannes's letter saying she must cut back on performing, with its implication that she should spend more time taking care of her children. Despite their quarrel, correspondence between Brahms and Clara had not slacked particularly, and she was still busily investing his money for him.[4] The tone of the letters remained chilly and tense, with periodic eruptions that not only inflamed the current feud but reopened old wounds.

By then Brahms understood well enough how insensitive he could be. He also knew that he could not explain Julie's part of the reason why he had behaved so offensively for so long in the Schumanns' house. But Clara's onslaught in her letters was relentless. Before long, he began to crack. He would let his offending letter stand for everything that festered between them.

> I cannot get the matter out of my head, dear Clara. I should like to answer your letter, which certainly contained many hard things, without any anger. . . . But I cannot. . . . You refer to my moods in Baden . . . I too had reason to complain that I had not been as successful as usual in trying to win sympathy in your house. . . . But I cannot get my letter out of my mind. I see it as a great wall standing between us. . . . I acknowledge that I may have spoken those words of truth perhaps at the wrong time, and perhaps in the wrong way. . . . But so much of the good friend remains that you can surely forgive him what needs to be forgiven. The crux of the whole matter is his old besetting sin—that he cannot write letters and cannot write diplomatically either.

He hoped this concession, a rare quasi-apology from him, would settle her down. Soon he followed it with a more personal token. On September 12, from the Bernese Alps during another vacation with his father, Brahms sent Clara a gesture of reconciliation more meaningful than she could have understood until years later. On a postcard he offered a few measures of music underlined with a greeting to her, noting, "Thus blew the shepherd's horn today":

Hoch auf-'m Berg, tief im Tal, grüss' ich dich viel tau - send-mal!

His text reads, "High on the mountain, deep in the valley, I greet you a thousandfold."[5] That melody of an alpine shepherd's horn—real or imagined—was to become the horn call soaring over strings, like sun breaking through clouds, that transfigures the introduction of the First Symphony finale. His greeting to Clara was a sign that now Brahms was preparing to pick up the C minor symphony movement he had drafted years before, and go on with it. So a horn call sent as a peace offering, destined to part the clouds of his first symphonic finale, can also stand for a breakthrough of his own—out of his lingering uncertainties in the weights and balances of a symphony.

But Johannes's clarion call did not resolve the issues between him and Clara. She was not ready to forgive him yet. He had to cajole her still more abjectly, and he had to understand something about her and her art. She was not apologizing anymore for her need to play, or claiming the need for money as a reason:

> That letter of yours is not the wall that stands between us. . . . It is not a matter of destroying any wall between us, but only of showing a little more friendliness and a little more control of evil moods. . . . I confess that my children were often angry when they saw how I suffered from your unfriendliness. . . . But I cannot help thinking that your view of my concert tours is an odd one. You regard them merely as a means of making money. I don't! . . . The practice of my art is an important part of my ego, it is the very breath of my nostrils.[6]

Devotion like that Brahms could understand. Maybe now he did respect something about her more than before. Whether he did or not, he was prepared to make a full capitulation. From his point of view it was a straightforward if thorny matter: he loved Clara, he needed her, he could not imagine living without her. And their estrangement kept him from Julie. So he made a careful reply, in the affectionate and forthright terms he used with no one else, but this time with perhaps more secret motivation than usual:

> I wanted a very quiet hour, dearest Clara, in which to put into words my heartfelt thanks for your letter. . . . There is so much that is true in your letter—if not all—and I must confess that with remorse and regret; but with pleasure and satisfaction I realise how kind it is—only an angel like you could have written so kindly. . . . Life is a wild polyphony, but often a good woman like you can bring about some exquisite resolution of its discords.

AT THE END OF OCTOBER 1868 they got together in Oldenburg and re-claimed their old closeness. Clara reported in her journal, "He is as nice to me as he can possibly be."[7] They performed in several concerts in the area, the repertoire including Brahms's four-hand waltzes of Opus 39. At a party they read through some new Hungarian dances that thrilled her. Probably they mulled over this month's surprise: out of the blue Theodor Kirchner—Johannes's old friend and champion, Clara's still-secret ex-lover—had married a singer.[8]

Perhaps Brahms showed Clara other things he was working on, an-other collection of *Hausmusik* designed to sell like the four-hand waltzes. He called this set the *Liebeslieder* (Love Song) Waltzes. They are confec-tionery tunes with a large helping of Viennese *Schlagobers* (whipped cream), for four-hand piano and vocal quartet. Daumer had translated their amorous texts from Slavic dances. The music testifies to Brahms's love of both Strauss and Schubert waltzes, but like most such testaments of his they hardly resemble their inspiration; this is the Viennese waltz à la Brahms.

If he did show the *Liebeslieder* to Clara in Oldenburg, certainly he did not tell her that they were mainly inspired by Julie—written about her or to her, or to his dreams of her. Nor did Clara tell Johannes her news: in Divonne, a nobleman was courting Julie.

Happily unknowing, on into the new year Brahms added one lilting *Liebeslied* to another, and dreamed whatever dreams he allowed himself. The poems he chose for these waltzes suggest some of them:

Tell me, maiden dearest, who has with your glances roused these wild ardors in this cool breast of mine, will you not soften your heart?

When your eyes rest on me so kindly and lovingly, every last trouble that besets me flees. . . . No one will ever love you as truly as I.

Love is a dark pit, an all too dangerous well; woe is me, I fell in, and now can neither hear nor see.

These are typical Brahms song texts—evocative, slight, and by Daumer. There may well have been more Daumer songs composed that summer, on poems whose forthright eroticism would scandalize some of Brahms's friends when he published them as Opus 57, in 1871. If 1868 is

their date, they show the kind of fantasies occupying him near the denouement of an infatuation that seemed to possess him even as he recognized its unreality:

*I dreamt I was dear to you; but I scarcely needed to awaken, for while still
dreaming, I already felt that it was a dream.*

*In the yearnings of my nights, so utterly alone, with a thousand, thousand
tears, I think of you. . . . Ah, the man who has looked upon your face . . . who
has ever lost all his senses for joy upon your bosom.*

*The string on which pearl after pearl is arrayed about your throat—how hap-
pily it rocks to and fro on your beautiful breast! . . . What, then, must we
feel . . . whenever we are permitted to intimately press such a breast!*

*In my mind burning desire swells, but in my veins life is flowing and longs for
life. . . . Come, oh come, so that we can give each other heavenly satisfaction!*[9]

TOWARD THE END of November 1868, Brahms left Clara and Julie and
returned to Vienna for the winter, settling into the hotel Zum Kronprinzen on the Aspernbrücke. There he kept busy with arrangements
for premieres, engraver's proofs and negotiations relating to new publications, and editing Schubert's Impromptus and Ländler for a new
edition.

Besides his daily routine of early rising, strong coffee, walking, working, and loafing, by age thirty-five Brahms had refined the seasonal routine to which he remained faithful. In four months or so of spring and
summer in the country, he drafted most of his music. He returned to Vienna in autumn to polish new pieces, read engraver's proofs, edit other
composers' work for publication (done for the instruction and pleasure
more than money), study old masters' scores and peruse the competition's, and enjoy the company of Theodor Billroth, Ignaz Brüll, Julius
Epstein, the Fabers, and a widening circle of friends from among the eminent artists and *Grossbürgertum* of the city. During the first two or three
months of most years he toured as pianist and conductor, traveling
around Austria, Germany, and as far afield as Holland and Switzerland;
but he never crossed an ocean. Brahms remained deathly afraid of sea-
sickness, or sailing out of sight of land.

From now on, as a pianist, he mainly performed his own music. Practicing bored him to distraction, and as he never tired of saying, concerts

meant little to him anyway. The applause he enjoyed more than he was prepared to admit. While he generally remained competent at plowing through his own music, including the very difficult concertos, his old subtlety of touch at the keyboard gradually deteriorated to what Clara bewailed as "thump, bang, and scrabble."[10] Still, for all that, he toured. By the 1870s he was collecting handsome fees, and his concerts not only provided income but an important means of spreading his work. Even if Brahms was not the ideal performer of his own music, as either pianist or conductor, he came up with marvelous readings sometimes, and in any case audiences showed up in force to have a look at him. So he claimed to hate performing and performed all the time, just as he hated writing letters and wrote them constantly.

He started 1869 with a rush of things to attend to. After years of playing his Hungarian dances for friends, and occasionally giving Clara a manuscript to play from, he had decided to have them published. The pieces had accumulated since the early 50s, played for friends and at parties, rarely written down. Eduard Reményi initiated Brahms into the "Hungarian" style in his teens, and since then he had sought it out wherever he could find it. He could still sit for hours under the trees at the Café Czarda in the Prater, nursing mugs of beer and listening to gypsy bands, who seemed to play with particular fire when the Herr Professor showed up. And Brahms may have browsed published collections of authentic Hungarian folk songs, or what purported to be authentic, looking for tunes.

For Brahms this music had always been a recreation, a way to let go of his usual sobriety and escape into a music perfervid, exotically colored, elastic in rhythm, improvisational in style. Friends remembered his flashing eyes when Brahms played his dances, the rhythm darting and halting, his hands all over the keyboard at once. Part of the reason he resisted writing them down was that he felt unsure how to capture that protean freedom in the cold black-and-white of notation. Meanwhile the style lent a driving rhythm and exotic tone to allegros in his chamber works.

Finally, in hopes of good return, he did write down some dances, setting them for four hands to get the orchestral effect he wanted. In 1867 he offered seven to a publisher in Budapest, who to the man's enduring remorse turned them down. A few years later Brahms sent them to Fritz Simrock, as "perhaps the most practical [pieces] so impractical a man as myself can supply." Simrock understood their practicality to say the least, and in taking them ensured his own and his firm's prosperity for the foreseeable future. (Simrock also published the *Liebeslieder* and the piano Waltzes.)

When the immense appeal of the first four-hand books of Hungarian Dances became manifest, Brahms readily made two-hand versions. Many would eventually be arranged for orchestra too, numbers 1, 3, and 10 by Brahms and more by artists including Dvořák. Joachim supplied violin-piano arrangements. At Brahms's request the dances appeared without opus number. Likewise he wanted his name on the title page under "arranged by." The idea, he wrote Simrock in a torturous metaphor, was that these were "genuine gypsy children, which I did not beget, but merely brought up with bread and milk." In fact, among the twenty-one dances eventually published in four sets (the first two volumes in 1869, the second two in 1880) Brahms slipped in a couple of faux-gypsy children of his own creation. To enhance their appeal, Simrock put out the second batch "as set by" Brahms, who on finding out concluded an irate letter to his publisher with: "yours set beside himself, J. Br."[11]

Brahms received a one-time fee for each edition of the Hungarian Dances and let Simrock get fat on them. As long as he had money for his own generally spartan lifestyle (often spartan in expensive resorts), and plenty to hand out to family and friends (by the later 1870s he did have plenty), Brahms was happy for his publisher to claim most of the manna.[12] At the same time, this kept Simrock extremely grateful, attentive, and generous to his star composer and good friend.

So during the 1860s and '70s, with a fervently proclaimed indifference to money and to commercialism, in composing the *Requiem* for amateur choruses everywhere, and *Hausmusik* including the Waltzes, *Liebeslieder*, Hungarian Dances, and "Cradle Song" for concerts, parlors, nurseries, beer gardens, restaurants, and parks all over the world, plus a steady flow of more serious but still practical vocal duets, quartets, small choruses, and the like, Brahms marshaled his craft to secure himself the wherewithal for an independent creative life few composers have ever enjoyed. For comparison among other Austro-German composers: Bach was employed by courts and churches, who worked him like a slave. Handel was a freelancer who went bankrupt several times before his comfortable old age. Haydn spent most of his career composing for one aristocratic family, with whom he had the status of a servant. Mozart lived independently but had to perform and teach for much of his income. Beethoven received support from the aristocracy and early in his career was a keyboard virtuoso. Schubert mostly lived off friends. For much of his life Wagner existed largely by extracting funds and services from admirers, tradespeople, and King Ludwig of Bavaria, and slipped out of town when creditors caught up with him. Robert Schumann had a small inheritance supplemented by paid positions, journalism, and Clara's performing.

None of those composers earned so extravagantly from publishing their work as Brahms did, and none except Wagner, in his fifties, reached the position Brahms reached in his thirties—composing what he wanted, when he wanted, prospering without ever accepting a commission to write a piece. By Brahms's time, a living like that had been made at least conceivable by the enormous growth of the audience for classical music, and the tens of thousands of pianos in bourgeois parlors, all of them requiring material from light to heavy. At the same time the later nineteenth century saw a proliferation of music schools, which enormously improved the overall level of professionalism and knowledge.

All of that amounted to Brahms's milieu, the setting in which he saw his music. And for his audience the flood of light works he provided for them paved the way for his substantial pieces. Music lovers of every stripe began growing up between Brahms's "Lullaby" and his *Requiem*, from the cradle to the grave.

IN EARLY 1868, amid the labor of negotiating the Hungarian Dances and getting them out, Brahms went before the public steadily. In the space of two weeks at the end of February and beginning of March he participated in seven concerts,[13] which overlapped a series of lieder recitals with Julius Stockhausen in Vienna and Budapest. (Because of this tour Brahms missed the premiere of the complete *Deutsches Requiem*, with the new fifth movement, in Leipzig.)

Among the performances was the premiere of *Rinaldo* in Vienna under his baton. Maybe Brahms had sat on the cantata for so long out of uncertainty whether to air it at all, and the premiere hardly persuaded him. He let his publisher decide whether or not to hold it back: "*Rinaldo* was not as soundly hissed as my *Requiem* was last year," he wrote Simrock, inflating the negative in both cases, "but I don't think I can call it a success. And this time the critical bigwigs listened and really wrote quite a lot. . . . Thus this time everybody expected a crescendo of the *Requiem*, and certainly beautiful exciting voluptuous goings-on *à la* [Wagner's] Venusberg. . . . Therefore I ask you to think matters over more."[14]

Simrock accepted the cantata without question. Even if it might not turn a profit—and probably it did not—he owed the composer any number of favors. One critic who did enjoy *Rinaldo*, at least as a gesture contra Wagner, was surgeon Theodor Billroth. His review of the premiere for the *Allgemeine musikalische Zeitung* concluded, "That which must astonish the modern public in *Rinaldo* is that the hero, far otherwise than in *Tannhäuser, Tristan* . . . etc. is not constantly in an emotional orgasm but really sings melodies of the deepest and truest feeling."[15] Privately, Billroth was unenthusiastic about the piece.

As spring arrived and Brahms geared up for another summer sojourn on his "pretty hill" in Lichtental, once again near Clara and family in Baden-Baden, he made an epochal decision: the city to which he intended to return after this and future vacations would be Vienna. He wrote his father in April not to reserve a room for him in Hamburg anymore. "Apart from you there is no one I want to see. You know well enough how little, in any respect, I get out of the place. . . . I think I shall try to make myself more comfortable in Vienna next autumn."[16] He curtly declined entreaties from family and friends to attend a gala Hamburg performance of *Ein deutsches Requiem*.[17]

Declaring himself rejected by Hamburg—an embellishment, but with reason—Brahms called himself a vagabond for the rest of his life. Much as he loved Vienna, for all the good music and companionship and food and drink he found there, for all the affection the City of Dreams gave him along with the snubs, in his heart it always appeared a place of exile.

BEFORE SETTLING into Lichtental in summer 1869, he stopped off in Karlsruhe, where Hermann Levi was training his choir for a performance of *Ein deutsches Requiem* set for mid-May. A letter from Levi during the rehearsals shows the kind of affection the work already claimed among amateur choristers:

> Yesterday evening after the rehearsal, when most of them had already gone away, I was still sitting lost in my thoughts at the piano, and without any real intention I began to play the first bars of the Requiem. Immediately the girls who were already at the door turned round, their cloaks flew off, they arranged themselves round the piano and began to sing, with beaming faces, until we eventually got stuck in the third movement.[18]

After conducting the Karlsruhe performance Brahms went on to Lichtental and got to work. The first items of business were to finish the *Liebeslieder* and the Romances from L. Tieck's *Magelone*, the cycle of fifteen songs he had been hammering at desultorily since starting it in Hamm in 1861.

The *Magelone* Lieder, Opus 33, stand as his testament, on one hand, to the admired baritone of Julius Stockhausen, on the other to the Winsen idylls of his teens, reading old romances like *The Beautiful Magelone* in the fields and woods with Lieschen Giesemann. Tieck had reworked the story from the version Johannes knew in childhood; in both cases the tale was interspersed with song lyrics, which he set without trying to convey the actual story.

The parallels of the Magelone story to Brahms's own life and loves—to Clara and Agathe especially—are manifest. Young Count Peter of Provence is inspired by a minstrel to go adventuring; in a tournament he wins the love of Magelone, beautiful daughter of the King of Naples; they elope but are parted when Peter is swept out to sea; for two years he lives as a prisoner of the Moors, yearning for his love, but meanwhile captivates the Sultan's daughter Sulima; finally he escapes to be reunited with Magelone, who has faithfully awaited him in a hermit's cabin. Thomas Boyer, examining Brahms's identification with fair-haired Count Peter, notes the dichotomy between lustful Sulima and Magelone, avatar of his matron saint Clara. It mirrors exactly what divided Brahms all his life: the virgin and the whore. Lines from the songs seem to capture his dilemma with women: "How shall I bear/ This joy, this rapture?/ Will my soul not take flight/From the beating of my heart?" And more poignantly, *Nur lieben heisst leben:* Only loving is living.[19] Perhaps the tragedy of his life is that Brahms believed that sentiment but could never bring himself to act on it. Always, he fled the beating of his heart.

Echo of his life, testament to his Romantic *Bildung* and to his admiration for Julius Stockhausen, the *Magelone* Romances are also Brahms's contribution to the German-Romantic tradition of the *Liederkreis*, the song cycle. The genre involves an integrated series of lieder presenting a narrative or other literary unit, epitomized by Schubert's *Die Schöne Müllerin* (The Beautiful Miller's Daughter) and Schumann's *Dichterliebe* (Poet's Love). In fact Stockhausen, often in performances with Brahms, did as much as anyone in the nineteenth century to popularize the Schubert and Schumann cycles.

Naturally, as Brahms carried yellowing sketches for symphonies and string quartets with him all over Austria and Germany, he also wanted to take on the *Liederkreis*. He approached it stealthily, as he did other genres resonant with the tramp of giants. But on the face of it, who more likely to make momentous contributions to the *Liederkreis* repertoire than Brahms the protégé of Schumann, experienced composer and performer of lieder, who during the long period of writing the *Magelone* Romances concentrated largely on vocal music? Yet he hardly seemed to draw on his experience. Their style is notably unlike that of Schubert or Schumann, for that matter unlike most of Brahms's other lieder or vocal music. His songs tend to be laconic, relatively understated, often with a flavor of folk song including a distinct preference for strophic form. The *Magelone* songs are lush, expansive, passionate, mostly through-composed, at times almost operatic.

For all his experience and skill, they are also notably spotty, everything from wonderful to bland. The cycle did not really work as a whole, not in Brahms's mind or for most critics since. Scholar Malcolm MacDonald calls it "a mass of fascinating detail . . . in search of an overall musical rationale."[20] To name one conspicuous problem—in contrast to Schubert's song cycles, the point of the *Magelone* lyrics is unaccountable if the listener does not know the story. Some performances get around that by adding a narrative to connect the songs, but Brahms neither made provision for that nor encouraged it. In fact, his position after surveying what he had wrought was to try to obviate the notion that the songs were a cycle at all. He wrote critic Adolf Schubring: "In the case of the Magelone Romances one does not need many at one go, and should not pay any attention to narrative. . . . It was only a touch of German thoroughness which led me to compose them through to the last number."[21]

His feeling about the results is also shown in this: the *Magelone* Romances are his first and last song cycle. Afterward Brahms returned to his usually laconic miniatures, issued in sets, each opus tending to be loosely related in literary theme (usually love, usually lost) and perhaps in a general musical unfolding. Opus 57, for example, sets a group of passionate love songs by Daumer.[22] Brahms sometimes called his song opuses "bouquets." Still, with the exception of the *Magelone* songs, his lieder opuses are conspicuously *not* cycles in the traditional narrative sense, though the *Four Serious Songs* of Opus 121 approach it.

If the *Magelone* Romances disappoint as a set, they also represent another Brahmsian experiment toward opera that did not quite pay off. Yet he continued to solicit opera librettos from every quarter, and seems to have spent nearly as much time mulling them over as he had in composing the *Magelone* Romances.

BESIDES FINISHING THE *Magelone* songs with perhaps a looming sense of irrelevance and mere diligence, his final work of that summer and fall, torn vehemently from his life, began in a lightning stroke on May 11, 1869. That day Brahms visited Clara in Baden-Baden and she told him she had news that he must be the first to hear: Count Vittorio Radicati de Marmorito had proposed to Julie, and she had accepted. Clara was astonished to see Brahms choke out a response and run from the house.

So that was it. Suddenly everything became clear to her: the reason not only for his flight but for his moods going back years, his rudeness, his awkward kindness toward Julie, her confused withdrawal, his restiveness in the Schumann house. Surely somewhere in his mind he had known that sooner or later, for a reason hopeful or tragic, the moment of losing his fantasy was inevitable. But when it came, the moment was no less terrible for that.

Now he suddenly went limp. "Johannes is quite altered," Clara wrote in her journal; "he seldom comes to the house, and speaks only in monosyllables when he does come. And he treats even Julie the same way, though he always used to be so specially nice to her. Did he really love her? But he has never thought of marrying, and Julie has never had any inclination towards him."[23] Hermann Levi confirmed it to Clara: Brahms had spilled his feelings to Levi and probably to others. Likely there had been late-night sessions with Brahms anguishing, entreating friends to tell him what to do about her, what to do. Rumors that Clara never heard had been going around. That spring in a Hamburg shop, somebody innocently observed to Elise Brahms that a Viennese gentleman with her name was engaged to Clara Schumann's daughter.

Clara had responded to the news of Marmorito's courtship with her usual brooding and anxiety. She would be losing her favorite child, and she was frightened, for good reason, that childbearing might kill the delicate Julie. Clara's customary response to most unexpected or unwelcome things was some mixture of suffering, despair, physical breakdown, outrage, and scolding. And now, after all that had happened between her and Johannes through the years, and just after they had come to a shaky resolution of a long quarrel, one or more of those would be her expected response to the revelation.

Her response was the opposite. The magnificent side of Clara Schumann came forward when Johannes's helpless infatuation revealed itself. If she had no great insight into human nature, Clara seems to have understood the irrational impetus of love and respected it. She had broken with her father for the sake of a passion she regarded as holy, and maybe she saw all love as no less holy, even if hopeless. She could have taken Johannes's love for Julie as a betrayal of herself. Instead, she saw it for the sad spectacle it was, between two people whom she loved. The chances are that she and Johannes never spoke directly about it at all. But for a long time Clara would be very gentle with him.

For his part, Brahms at first treated Julie's engagement as a betrayal of himself, as if despite his unspoken feelings, despite the impossibility of the connection, despite Julie's persistently avoiding him, he somehow owned her. So the news broke over him and he fled to his hill in Lichtental and probably did his crying there, alone. He was quite capable of that; his tears flowed easily. In those tears began one of the most affecting works of his life, the Alto Rhapsody.

To everyone he called it—whether wrathfully, sentimentally, or jokingly—a bridal song. It is an evocation of despair and a prayer for peace, addressed to a God who may not be capable of hearing it. When he sent the Rhapsody to publisher Simrock, Brahms snarled, "Here I've written a bridal song for the Schumann countess—but I wrote it with anger, with wrath! What do you expect!"[24] To Clara, he named it not Julie's bridal song but his own. At other times, with more bitter irony than anyone could have understood, he told friends that the Rhapsody was the epilogue to the *Liebeslieder* Waltzes[25]—maybe also, as he would have been ashamed to confess, epilogue to the amorous dreams of the Opus 57 songs.

In any case, Brahms portrayed the Rhapsody to friends and, perhaps deliberately, to history as the avatar of his struggle with grief and loneliness—victorious like all his struggles, but no less grueling. This wound, though, would be the last one like it, the last note of melodrama in his life. And he came out of the fiasco with joy: still free, and with the Rhapsody to show for it.

By autumn of 1869, as Julie's wedding approached, and as Clara worried, Brahms had turned defiantly cheerful. Besides finding a measure of solace in the Rhapsody, he was flirting in Baden with a young Russian pianist and would-be composer, recalled by Max Kalbeck as Mademoiselle Anne de D. Brahms sent a nocturne of hers to Simrock to consider, submitting a whimsical bill for his own improvements:

Fresh modulation, per key	3 pfennigs.
(i.e., from C to E♭ through F to B♭)	12 pfennigs.
A new bass for the melody	1½ silbergroschen.
Rapturous finish of four measures	5 sgr.
Repairs to a section	2½ sgr.
Whole new middle part	15 sgr.[26]

On September 21, the day before Julie's wedding, there was a gathering at Clara's for the couple and family friends. "We spent a very pleasant evening with the lovers," she told her journal. There was music and laughter, they drank *Ananasbowle*, they cooed over the presents. Brahms's personal gift to Julie was a daguerreotype of her mother. He, Levi, and Allgeyer together gave the couple an embossed brass platter, and had a photo made of themselves contemplating the gift. In the picture the towering Allgeyer indulgently leans over so as not to dwarf Brahms, who seems barely to reach his friend's shoulders. Levi is seated for the same reason, holding the platter on a table. Brahms stands hands on hips, also admiring the objet d'art. He is still clean-shaven but getting round-faced and thick about the waist now, moving toward the stubby figure of his later years. Still, he looks the brash, bright-eyed young man in the company of bearded grown-ups. Not long before this he had been turned away from the Baden casino because he looked underaged.[27]

A week after attending Julie's wedding Brahms turned up at Clara's house and played her the Alto Rhapsody. He did not have to say more than that it was his bridal song. She understood. The children heard the great solemn music coming from the study, and after he left their mother came to them shattered.[28] From that first time Clara loved the piece unreservedly. In her journal she wrote, "It is long since I remember being so moved by a depth of pain in words and music. . . . This piece seems to me neither more nor less than the expression of his own heart's anguish. If only he would for once speak as tenderly!"

THE TEXT OF THE RHAPSODY is a fragment from Goethe's "Harzreise im Winter," chosen with Brahms's reliable gift, going back to "Des jungen Kreislers Schatzkästlein," for finding others' words to speak for him. For all the intimacy of the piece it is no less meticulously crafted, hardly less magisterial and impersonal in tone than Brahms usually was now. His anguish permeates the music all the same. It begins in tremolo strings with an extraordinarily agitated dissonance, the colors dark, the tonality drifting.[29] The chill of winter invades the music, but a chill of spirit more than body. *But who is that standing apart?* the alto intones, like a woman addressing the solitary Brahms. She continues in a mournful recitative:

> *His steps recede into the bushes,*
> *The thickets close*
> *Behind him . . .*
> *The barren waste swallows him up.*

An aria follows the recitative—almost a true operatic aria and maybe the finest Brahms ever wrote. This time, his feelings outweighed his self-consciousness, the words ringing in his heart and on the page:

> *Ah, who can heal the pains*
> *Of one for whom balm has become poison,*
> *And who sucked hatred of mankind*
> *From the abundance of love?*

After the bleakness of those lines, set to music dark and wandering in both tonality and rhythm (much two-against-three, neither settled), there is a pause. Then a prayer breaks out in men's voices, in C major, direct and heartfelt as a hymn, with the alto soaring above:

> *If in your psaltery,*
> *Father of Love, there is a tone*
> *Which his ear can discern,*
> *Refresh his heart!*
> *Open to his clouded gaze*
> *The thousand springs*
> *Alongside him as he thirsts*
> *In the wilderness.*[30]

The words are transparently chosen to capture Brahms's heartbreak and his purpose in this work. The psaltery of the end, the harp of God's succor that Goethe invoked, was for the poet simply a metaphor. For Brahms the composer, the harp stands for the healing power of music, and so stands for the Alto Rhapsody itself. (The accompaniment of the prayer he scored in harplike pizzicatos.)

Brahms's connection to this text, though, goes beyond that. Maybe he knew that for Goethe the journey to the Harz Mountains came at a turning point—away from his youth toward a more mature vision of his life and work.[31] Certainly Brahms knew about the acquaintance of the poet's who had inspired the poem. It was a misanthropic young man who had fallen dangerously under the spell of a story of Goethe's own: Young Werther. There lies the ultimate connection to Brahms, who identified both with Werther and with the solitary misanthrope of the poem.

As prayers go, Brahms's marvelously fashioned one was answered. Even though it is a short piece—thirteen minutes—with it he returned with his soul refreshed not only to the top of his form as a composer, for the first time since the *Requiem*, but to joy in his creativity. He wrote Simrock that the piece was the best thing he'd ever offered.[32] He told Albert Dietrich that he loved it so much that he slept with it (metaphorically) under his pillow.[33] He took it to his bed, in other words, like a bride.

The Rhapsody also represents a turning point in Brahms's life, as "Harzreise im Winter" had represented for Goethe. In Brahms's case it was an acceptance that all he had, now, was his art. In that sense too it is his bridal song, his embrace of a solitary fate. Whatever succor and redemption from despair he might find in life, he would find henceforth in music. Like the G Major Sextet, the Rhapsody is another farewell to love, a darker and more final one. But he did not finish the Rhapsody on Goethe's last word—*Wüste*, desolation, desert—but rather backed up in the poem, to end with the possibility of healing: *Refresh his heart!* set to the familiar IV-I cadence of a hymn's *Amen*.

So the prayer of the Rhapsody was answered as much as prayer can be, on this earth, for a man like Brahms. Which is to say: there would be no more troubles of the heart like those with Clara, with Agathe, with Bertha Faber and Ottilie Hauer and Elisabet Stockhausen, and most painfully with Julie Schumann. There would be other infatuations but *decrescendo*, the larks of an aging bachelor. The gods had inflicted on Brahms a cruel paradox: an ingrained misogyny, an equally ingrained instinct that without a mate his life was a wasteland. Instead of life and love there would be music, but that no final consolation. Conspicuous in Brahms's letters in the next years would be Goethe's word *Wüste*.

Likewise conspicuous in Goethe's poem is the question rendered in English by *if*: "*If* in your psaltery, Father of Love . . ." There is no final response to that *if*, and the last words of the Alto Rhapsody are gentle but still a plea, not an answer: *Refresh his heart!* In a choral work Brahms had sketched by then and returned to later, the *Schicksalslied*, he already implied a message that had begun to take shape as early as the *Requiem*, which would become more and more imperative in the work of the next decades. The message was bleak, but for Brahms inescapable. The man who felt himself born too late, exiled from homeland, torn from love, came to testify in his art that the bonds between God and humanity are broken.

BACK IN VIENNA as a new decade arrived, Brahms fell into one of his depressive phases, feeling wrung out and uncertain of his direction. The debacle over Julie still oppressed him. He still balked before the symphony movement in C minor he had been carrying around for so many years, the string quartet movements he had drafted. The profits from his *Hausmusik* had not begun to pile up yet, so his livelihood still appeared unpredictable. He performed often but with no great enthusiasm. Once again his bourgeois instincts drove him to yearn for a regular and respectable post. All the same, he turned down two music-directorships in 1869, in Cologne and Berlin (the latter came from Joachim, now head of the Royal College of Music).

For the moment Vienna was turning an indifferent if not hostile face to him. In March 1869 Brahms had gotten some manhandling from the Philharmonic when conductor Otto Dessoff programmed the D Major Serenade. During a rehearsal the "Orchestra of Poets" became so offended by the Serenade—for all its gentle atavism—that they mutinied. White with rage, Dessoff closed the score and left the podium without a word, went home, and wrote a letter of resignation. Unnerved by that, the orchestra agreed to play the piece later in the year.

So in December, Brahms conducted the Serenade himself, but was forced practically to beg the Philharmonic to rehearse it properly. "Gentlemen," he declared to them, "you have rejected my work, and I can only say to you, if you want to compare me to Beethoven: such heights will never be reached again. But my work comes from my best artistic conviction. Perhaps you will find that it is not unworthy of your performance."[34] Spitefully, they did their job. Around the same time the first three *Requiem* movements, *Rinaldo*, and the G Major String Sextet had all faltered in some degree in the city.

To friends Brahms said he felt "useless as usual" as 1870 began. He wrote publisher Rieter-Biedermann in Switzerland, "Names like Winterthur and Zürich give me a great longing. It's cheerless to have to loiter around a big city so entirely uselessly." He dreamed of the perfect, irresistible Kapellmeister position or opera libretto falling into his lap. He told Artur Faber he just wanted to go to Budapest and listen to gypsies play.[35]

His bright new rooms in the hotel Zum Goldspinnerin, with a splendid view of the Old City and the new Stadtpark, did not cheer him, nor did the premiere in Vienna of the complete *Liebeslieder* Waltzes in January (Brahms and Clara at the piano, Luise Dustmann heading the vocalists). Clara wrote him in March, a few days after Pauline Viardot premiered the Alto Rhapsody in Jena, "So you have nice rooms, have you? I cannot tell you how glad I am of that . . . your old rooms seemed to me very gloomy. . . . Now you can take to yourself a nice young wife with a little money—and then it will really be homelike."

The suggestion did neither of them any good. Brahms stayed in his funk, Clara was beset by arm and finger troubles and by son Ludwig, who had finally been decreed incurably insane and had to be put away in an institution, where he remained for the rest of his life. "I have not felt pain like this since Robert's tragedy," Clara wrote Johannes about the son whose mental illness could not help but dredge up memories of his father's.[36] It was, Clara told the other children, as if Ludwig had been buried alive.[37] Felix Schumann's consumption worsened steadily. Julie's health hardly improved after her marriage and a quick pregnancy.

To deepen the gloom encircling Brahms and his loved ones, Joachim was threatening to leave his always-ailing Amalie—though they struggled on together, miserably, for ten years more—and Johann Jakob Brahms had been sick the whole winter, to his wife's distress. His hands and feet paining him, he had resigned from the Hamburg Philharmonic in 1869.

To cap it all off, Brahms still bitterly objected to sister Elise's engagement to watchmaker Christian Grund. He was convinced that her debilitating headaches and lack of experience in the world made her incapable of seeing after a sixty-year-old widower and his six children. Despite Clara's pleading for Elise's right to make up her own mind, Brahms pressured his sister to enter a convent in Hamburg, pledging to donate funds for her upkeep.[38] He kept pressing his campaign right up to the marriage, in October 1871, then grudgingly gave the newlyweds a hundred talers as a wedding gift.[39] Before long, however, when he saw the marriage going entirely happily, he relented and bestowed a pension on them. Elise became pregnant, but the child lived only a few days. That sorrow aside, Brahms's melancholy sister had finally found a little luck.

In March, *Die Meistersinger* had its Vienna premiere, and Brahms took it in for the first of many times. Maybe in deference to Clara's Wagner-hatred he wrote her a hedging letter about it:

> I am not enthusiastic either about this work, or about Wagner in general. . . . I confess that it provokes one to discussion. . . . But this I do know, that in everything else I attempt I step on the heels of predecessors who embarrass me. But Wagner would not hinder me at all from proceeding with the greatest pleasure to write an opera. Incidentally, in the order of precedence among my wishes, this opera would come before taking a job as a music director.[40]

In fact Brahms remained, by his interpretation, "the best of Wagnerians," and *Die Meistersinger* became his favorite of the operas. At the same time he longed to challenge Wagner on his own turf. He entreated Julius Allgeyer and Hermann Levi and other knowledgeable friends to scout out librettos for him. That would turn out a frustrating endeavor for all concerned. In spring 1870, Brahms wrote Allgeyer after perusing some opera ideas, "The only thing I can arrive at after much hard thinking is always a 'No.'"[41] For the next fifteen years he kept asking, and after thinking it over kept coming up with the same answer.

Through it all he continued to study the subject of opera and mull it over incessantly, and continued to behave like a Wagnerian. In July, Brahms and Artur Faber joined Joachim in Munich to see the first performances of two operas from *Der Ring des Nibelungen*—*Die Walküre* and *Das Rheingold*, both under the baton of old friend Franz Wüllner. They took in both operas several times. Joachim reported home to Amalie, "*Das Rheingold* did not teach me anything new about Wagner; it's really almost boring with its eternal mystery and elaboration. Even Brahms was forced to agree with me, though he likes to pose as an admirer of Wagner."[42]

If a libretto could not seduce him, in summer of 1870 a chance turned up to secure exactly the kind of post Brahms yearned for, and it happened to be in Vienna: Johann von Herbeck resigned as music director of the Gesellschaft der Musikfreunde concerts in order to take over the Court Opera.

After the Philharmonic and Opera, the Gesellschaft amounted to the second most important podium in town. The Musikverein, new headquarters of the Society of the Friends of Music, opened for business in 1870. The Philharmonic played the first concert in the Great Hall on January 6, and Clara Schumann inaugurated the chamber-music hall with a recital on the 19th. Brahms would know that building intimately; many great and small moments of his career were played out in it.

The classical facade of the Musikverein intimates a Temple of Art, the most placid and elegant exterior on the Ringstrasse. Inside, manic Viennese eclecticism takes over: from the elaborately domed ceiling of the lobby one moves into the Golden Hall, with its rows of glittering caryatids holding up the balcony, gods and goddesses swarming on the ceiling, a blaze of organ pipes towering over the orchestra's low platform.[43] The space is intimate compared to later orchestral halls. It was designed not only to show off music but its patrons, a place to see and be seen. However, all the Age of Makart flamboyance, the rows of golden nudes and teeming bricabrac, help shape one of the warmest, most lucid acoustic spaces in the world. In that hall even the tumult of an ovation is tamed and civilized. The adjoining chamber-music hall has flocks of golden cherubs, whose chubby cuteness exemplifies much of the Viennese spirit in churches and buildings all over the city. Brahms never liked the sound of the small hall—today, ironically, called the Brahmssaal. He preferred the Bösendorfer or Ehrenbar hall for chamber music.

Knowing that he was on the short list of Herbeck's possible successors as music director of the Gesellschaft, Brahms did his ritual writhing over the matter, which included sounding out friends. Clara responded incredulously, "You're thinking of refusing? Surely you have nothing to fear?"[44] Hermann Levi, on the other hand, articulated what must have been Brahms's own qualms: "I saw in Karlsruhe [with the *Requiem*] . . . that you have a gift for conducting such as no other man possesses. Nevertheless, you are not the man to contend successfully with the thousand-and-one petty vexations which are inevitably connected with any official position. I am afraid they would soon get the better of you."[45] Some years before, the board of the Hamburg Philharmonic had likely concluded the same about Brahms—a fine leader on a good day, but impatient with the quotidian duties of a music director. In any case, for the moment the cup passed: the Gesellschaft committee gave a one-year appointment to violinist Josef Hellmesberger pending the choice of a permanent director, and the following year Anton Rubinstein took over on the same terms. Brahms understood that someday the job would be his for the taking. As usual he was happy to put off the decision.

Meanwhile a more dramatic development arose to occupy his attention. As he finished his Wagnerian pilgrimage to Munich in July, the Franco-Prussian War broke out—declared by Napoleon III but engineered by Prussian Prime Minister Bismarck, who provoked war with the French as a means of drawing together the scattered German states under Prussian leadership. During the six months of fighting the ordinary concerns of life went up in smoke. Brahms wrote Clara that he would come to her in Baden, where she could hear the cannons roaring at Strasbourg and lived in terror of Turkish soldiers, rumored to be barbaric, in the French army. Her son Ferdinand eagerly enlisted to fight with the Prussian forces. "I stayed," Clara wrote him, "but in a state of continual nervousness as we have no man to protect us. Your promise to come seemed to me most kind."[46]

Brahms's gallant offer to save Clara and family from the Turks proved impossible to realize; every train in Germany had been commandeered for the military.[47] Suddenly the exploits of the Vaterland infected Brahms with a fever of patriotism that had only been latent before. The Austro-Prussian War of 1866 had not roused him to sign up for the army, but that is what he resolved to do in this war when, briefly, things were going badly for the Prussians. Later, amused at himself, Brahms told George Henschel that in his martial seizure he felt "fully convinced that I should meet my old father [on the battlefield] to fight side by side with me. Thank God it turned out differently!"[48]

Instead, he returned to Vienna and, by way of doing his bit, wrote the opening chorus of the *Triumphlied (Song of Triumph)*. Scored for two four-part choruses and orchestra, it is a neo-Handelian paean for the victory of Prussia, Bismarck, and Kaiser Wilhelm I. Above all, his hallelujahs celebrated the results of the war: at Versailles in January 1871, Wilhelm was proclaimed Kaiser of a united Reich. After centuries of dreams in the face of the apparently impossible, Bismarck had plotted, negotiated, bullied, bamboozled, compromised, and charmed the fragmented mosaic of German states to join under one flag, with Prussia and the Hohenzollerns at the head. As Austria's Holy Roman Empire sank into malaise and irrelevance, the German Empire now ascended to become the dominant power in Europe.

There is no doubting that Brahms's joy at the unification of Germany was authentic. His patriotism was deep-lying, straightforward, conventional. He trusted the Prussians and idolized Bismarck, whose brazen bas-relief, decked with laurel, would someday preside in his living room beneath his bust of Beethoven. Still, for the moment the *Triumphlied* did not get beyond its rapturous first movement, so at the end of 1870 Brahms could not have been cheered to look back on the first year of his musical life in which he finished not one piece (except for 1867, when he was hard at work on the *Requiem*). The best he could say was that he had two promising shorter works in the oven, the patriotic item and the *Schicksalslied*. They are perhaps the most startlingly divergent of Brahms's many contrasting pairs of works: the *Song of Triumph* rattling the sword, the *Song of Destiny* a sublime hymn to despair.

A LANDMARK for Brahms in early 1871 was the first complete Vienna performance of the complete *Ein deutsches Requiem*, which he conducted on March 5 with the forces of the Gesellschaft der Musikfreunde. He must have been waiting to see if people would hiss the end of the third movement again, not to mention snub the whole piece. In fact, it was received calmly and respectfully. With this performance the *Requiem* began to find a place in the hearts of the Viennese.

By then Brahms had secured a premiere for the opening chorus of the *Triumphlied*. He had sent it to his old reliable Karl Reinthaler, co-director of the historic Bremen premiere of the *Requiem*. Once again Reinthaler lived up to his name, which essentially means "good money." They decided to mount the *Requiem* again in the cathedral, this time adding the new patriotic chorus. Needing reinforcements for the proper grandiose effect, Brahms wrote Albert Dietrich that Reinthaler "com-

With his patriarchal beard in a formal pose.
The cravat he is wearing may be one of those Marie Fellinger made for him.

At the piano in Karlsgasse, with the Karlskirche across the street.

Joachim in his middle years.

Brahms playing the G Minor
Rhapsody, painted from memo[ry]
by his artist friend Willy von
Beckerath, who called it "the [one]
at a moment when, completely
oblivious of his surroundings,
absorbed in his art." Reprodu[ctions]
often omit the cigar with droo[ping]
ashes.

Caricature of the time: "Eduard Hanslick Burns
Incense Before the Image of Saint Johannes
Brahms." The adored image carries the
Messiah's palm-leaf, but his pedestal is worn
and shabby.

Brahms walking with his vigorous stout man's stride, by the celebrated Viennese silhouettist Dr. Otto Böhler. The hedgehog informs us that Brahms is headed for his favorite restaurant, the Rote Igel.

...udy on Karlsgasse in Brahms's later years. From left to right: *his portrait of Cherubini with the Muse covered ...s trick rocking chair; the Sistine Madonna; his table with Kaffee machine; the electric light that the Fellingers ...d as a surprise; the bas-relief of Bismarck with laurel wreath; his bust of Beethoven from Hamburg, and under it a Klinger etching; his Streicher piano, next to the window that looked out on the Karlskirche.*

*Brahms in his library—behind him, books from ancient to new and his collection
of original editions and manuscripts.*

Clara Schumann in old age.
The cliché applies: battered but unbowed.

Waltz King Johann Strauss, Jr., in Bad Ischl in 1894.
s was eight years older than Brahms.

The Brahms Monument, which faces the Musikverein in Vienna: nearly the last gasp of the Ringstrasse styl

The House of the Secession in Vienna, decorated for an exhibition honoring
the city's leading composer of the next generation.

plains of the weakness of his choir. Couldn't you find some volunteers at Oldenburg who could sing in the eight-voiced *forte?* It's not difficult, only *forte.*"[49] At Bremen Cathedral on April 7, the first number of the *Triumphlied* raised a furor with two thousand listeners. Said the Bremen *Courier:* "One again recognises the titanic capacity of the composer. The work is a vocal joy-symphony, of imposing power and exalted feeling."[50]

Encouraged by the response, Brahms spent that summer's vacation in Lichtental writing the last two movements of the *Triumphlied.* In final form it found thunderous acclaim not only in Germany but across Europe (except France, naturally), accomplishing as much as the *Requiem*—though less than the small popular pieces—to spread Brahms's fame and fill his coffers. He viewed the *Triumphlied* as his version of a grand festival piece on the order of Handel's *Dettingen Te Deum,* which also commemorates a thrashing of the French.[51] While Brahms decided against the militant initial subtitle, "On the Victory of German Arms," he dedicated it to the Kaiser in flowery language: "Most Illustrious, Most Powerful, Most Gracious Kaiser and Master!" his dedication begins.

The opening chorus's text from Revelation proclaims, "Hallelujah, salvation, and glory, and honor, and power, unto the Lord our God; for true and righteous are His judgments." Brahms omitted the Scripture's indecorous following lines—"For He hath judged the great whore, which did corrupt the earth with her fornication." Privately, though, he copied the beginning of that verse into his own score, under an instrumental phrase that exactly represents it. He took great glee in pointing out the spot to friends.[52]

Certainly Brahms knew you can't go wrong with grandiloquent, *forte* patriotic rhapsodies, especially when combined with the kind of Handelian hallelujahs that struck familiar resonances with concertgoers. Besides the popularity of Handel's oratorios generally and the *Messiah* in particular, in Europe and England that magisterial choral style was coming to be associated with empire-building. To friends Brahms was forthright about the popularistic intentions of the *Triumphlied,* gaily calling it "the imperial *Schnadahüpferl.*"[53] That term is the name of a Swiss yodeling ditty, a harvesters' song. He liked the ironic association (an American equivalent might be "the Kaiser Boogie"). Even that indicated no cynicism on his part; he would later apply the same term to the most solemn of all his works, *Vier ernste Gesänge (Four Serious Songs).*

Whatever the mixture of earnestness and opportunism behind it, Brahms's paean for Prussian militarism rang the public like a gong, retaining its popularity down to the catastrophic apotheosis of that spirit in the First World War. Afterward the *Triumphlied*, an echo of times presumed past, vanished from concert halls, rarely to be heard from again.

Somehow, with his mind full of blood and iron and the whorish French that Baden-Baden summer of 1871, and conversely with evenings spent enjoying Johann Strauss's band in the Kurpark,[54] Brahms also finished the sublime *Schicksalslied* (*Song of Destiny*).

Its orchestral introduction, perhaps the one he sketched on the beach in Wilhelmshafen in 1868, is a singular moment in his music. Ethereal and dreamlike, the timpani softly adding the Brahmsian fate-motif to the texture, the E♭ major introduction forms one of his most yearning, piercing *moll-Dur* stretches. Even the opening major chords sound minor, with their scoring in low, muted strings. Brahms never achieved a more subtle orchestral texture, more expressive in its very sound. The introduction rises to a peak of longing, then sinks for the entrance of the altos declaiming Hölderlin's vision of the unreachable bliss of the gods:

> *You walk up there in the Light*
> *Upon soft ground, blessed Genii!*
> *Gleaming divine breezes*
> *Touch you gently,*
> *As the fingers of the woman musician*
> *Touch sacred strings.*

After the full choir enters, the verses unfold like a hymn. Then, following an echo of the introduction that draws a line under the evocation of the gods, the middle section plummets to earth and human fate:

> *But it is our lot*
> *To find rest nowhere;*
> *Suffering mankind*
> *Wastes away, falls*
> *Blindly from one*
> *Hour to the next,*
> *Like water hurled from crag*
> *To crag,*
> *Down into endless uncertainty.*[55]

The music here is the most violent Brahms was capable of, climaxing on frenzied cries of *Blindly! Endlessly!* He repeats the verse, the second time wrenching the music up from C minor to D minor, rendering the voices more shrill and intense. The end of the section sinks to an exhausted whisper: *Down into endless uncertainty*.

Then comes a gesture recalling one in the Alto Rhapsody. Brahms did not want to end the piece, as Hölderlin's verses conclude, with an unequivocal gesture of uncertainty and despair—not quite. The obvious thing to do (as he had done in the Rhapsody) was to back up, to repeat the opening stanza with the opening music, as if the work turned its gaze once more to the heavens. In fact Brahms sketched that approach, but found it wasn't sitting well, for reasons perhaps musical, perhaps personal. So he visited the man he most trusted for advice at that point, Hermann Levi, and together they went through the piece.

Finally Levi said: leave out the chorus entirely at the end, let the music of the opening have the last word. Brahms did as advised, with gnawing uncertainty. Even after the piece was printed he wrote Reinthaler, "I had already gone as far as writing something for the chorus, but it didn't work out. It may turn out to be a miscarried experiment, but such grafting would only result in nonsense."[56] Besides leaving the chorus tacet for the entire last section, he reorchestrated the haunting first phrases (winds taking the earlier string music) and changed the opening key of E♭ to C major—an uncommon example, for those days, of a piece ending in a key different than its beginning. Brahms conducted the premiere, with Levi's orchestra and choir, in Karlsruhe in October 1871.

There remains the question of what he finally meant by the wordless ending of the *Shicksalslied*, however it took shape. The more apparent answer is the kind of stoic, agnostic reassurance that pervades *Ein deutsches Requiem*. But ending in a new tonality—in the terms of the time, the "wrong" key—is a disconcerting gesture for all the quietness of the end. Donald Francis Tovey wrote of the "ruthless beauty" of the conclusion, with the drums still whispering *fate* as in the "All flesh is grass" movement of the *Requiem*. Fate always an ominous thought for Brahms. "Because this vision rouses our longing," Tovey continues, does not mean "it is an answer to our doubts and fears."[57] With the ending in a new key, Brahms denies us a true resolution, a return home.

If he would not exactly end the *Schicksalslied* on a note of despair, neither could he bring himself to finish it with hope and consolation like the *Requiem* or the Alto Rhapsody. So he finished with music alone, its ruthless beauty the only solace he knew now. In October, acknowledging his fee for the piece from publisher Fritz Simrock, Brahms wrote with *moll-Dur* irony, "Here's the receipt for my heart's blood, also my thanks for the purchase of the poor little piece of soul."[58]

CHAPTER FIFTEEN

Herr Musikdirektor

In 1871, Brahms was thirty-eight and had been famous since he was twenty. During most of his adulthood spent in the public gaze he had outspokenly yearned for a settled life and position, a wife and family and happiness. Meanwhile he fled every opportunity to secure them. The one position for which he ever seriously made a play, the podium of the Hamburg Philharmonic, was the only serious position that ever turned him down. Though like all artists he had a steady familiarity with rejection, he treated the Hamburg rebuff, of a post he would surely have soon given up, as the great tragedy of his life—the blow that prevented him from gaining wife and family and happiness.

As of late 1871 a job had been stalking Brahms for nearly two years while he took evasive maneuvers—Artistic Director of the Gesellschaft der Musikfreunde in Vienna. That autumn he learned that the Gesellschaft board intended to offer him the post again. Once more he commenced his ritual of advancing and retreating. By that point, after all, he had settled into a way of life that allowed him to get his creative work done with remarkable efficiency. When a schedule and lifestyle function that well, one is loath to change them. Adding to his ambivalence was his instinctive resistance to being tied down to anything or anybody.

Still, still, the Gesellschaft position was perfect: a large orchestra and the finest chorus in the city at his disposal, and the promise of a free hand in developing them. As had not been the case with the Singverein, Brahms was being offered a podium with the understanding that he would give the Viennese a stronger dose of Bach and other "difficult" old music than they were accustomed to. At length he concluded, despite himself, that the Gesellschaft was too good to pass up. In December

1871, he wrote Hermann Levi, "I've as good as taken the director position—I don't see any hole to escape through."[1]

Just after Christmas, he did something that implied he might be settling down in life. He took his first apartment in Vienna: two rooms on the fourth floor (called third in Austria) of Karlsgasse No. 4. While that represented a step up from the hotels he had inhabited for years in the city, it hardly seemed a suitable place for someone like himself. It was a plain stone building like any number of others in Vienna, next to the looming Baroque dome of the Karlskirche. The big windows of the living room looked past the cathedral to the plaza and little Resselpark, and the River Wien. Just beyond the river lay the Musikverein, home of the Gesellschaft der Musikfreunde. A short stroll over the Elizabeth Bridge brought him to the horse-drawn streetcars of the Ringstrasse; a ten-minute walk at the brisk Brahms pace took him past the Hofoper to Kärntnerstrasse and then the middle of town, or with a turn east, to the trees and cafés of the Stadtpark. Beyond the plaza of St. Stephen's Cathedral, the woods and amusements of the Prater spread north of the city, below the Danube.

A practical apartment, then, actually in sight of his place of employment, but, when all was said and done, hardly adequate for a famous artist. The painter Hans Makart, whose neo-Rococo kitsch was now the rage of the city, had a house decked out like a Turkish harem, a riot of palms, peacocks, and wall hangings, dripping with objets d'art. That, or as close as means allowed, was the way famous artists and their *nouveaux riches* admirers lived in Vienna (Wagner was a great admirer of Makart and his lifestyle). Brahms's place looked, Max Kalbeck wrote, like the apartment of a student, a minor civil servant, a salesman just starting in trade.[2] One entered the building on Karlsgasse through a plain door from the street, crossed a vestibule past French windows opening to the garden, and ascended winding stone stairs. At apartment No. 8 there was an old-fashioned iron bellpull that jangled loudly in Brahms's living room. Landlady Frau Vogl would open the door on a narrow hall leading past her kitchen, and visitors entered the apartment through Brahms's bedroom.[3]

In 1877 he rented a third attached room, but for the first years he had only the bedroom and living room, both small and plain though sunny, the larger holding his piano and stacks of books and music. (Most of his library stayed in Hamburg until he got the third room.) There was no bath. The furniture, scanty and shabby, was provided by Frau Vogl, and later and somewhat less shabbily by her successor, Frau Truxa. His landladies took care of his mending and housekeeping. Since chairs were in short supply and usually held books or music, there was a perennial problem with places for visitors to sit.⁴

Brahms ate lunch, with friends whenever possible, at one of his habitual restaurants—earlier the Kronprinz, Goldspinnerin, or Zur Schönen Laterne, later Zum roten Igel. At night in the 1870s he generally had a sparse dinner sitting at his little table, often cold meat and a tin of sardines; the latter he carried home in the pocket of his coat and finished by drinking off the oil from the tin, peasant-style.⁵

In short, Karlsgasse No. 4 seemed a stopgap sort of dwelling, a degree better than hotels, but entirely inappropriate to Brahms's station in life. He lived in the place for twenty-four years, and died there.

ONE OF THE FIRST of many prose portraits of Brahms comes from Florence May, a young British pianist. In summer of 1871, when May arrived to study with Clara Schumann in Baden-Baden, she had barely heard of Brahms and had no idea what a rare experience she was in for. He had taught piano a great deal in his twenties, but now neither needed nor wanted pupils. As a favor to Clara, who had to be out of town for much of the summer, Brahms agreed to give Miss May some lessons.

This student's descriptions of Brahms would be echoed by many observers. The short square figure, the long fair hair brushed back, the intense blue eyes under a broad forehead, the outthrust lower lip. Still clean-shaven, clothes plain and neat in those days, notably a short black alpaca coat (soon he would need larger ones). Pince-nez on a cord around his neck (nearsighted as he was, Brahms never wore spectacles for a photograph). His manner usually kind and sociable but always reserved (others found him awkward unto crude). His fervent interest in politics and science; his love of walking; his visible affection for Frau Schumann as he sat beside her every day at table. His dislike of celebrity hounds and autograph seekers, and of the French and English generally (the list of aversions would eventually extend to his fellow Germans). Outdoors he walked vigorously, usually with one hand swinging a soft felt hat, the other cocked behind his back. Most nights in Baden-Baden he went out to hear Johann Strauss's orchestra. Few made note, maybe because it was so common in those days, that he smoked cigars and cigarettes incessantly. There are few candid photos of Brahms without a cigar in his hand. When Florence May lent him a score that summer, it came back smelling lustily of tobacco.

May noticed that even if Brahms sniffed at gratuitous compliments he still responded with a boyish blush of pleasure to any sincere expression of appreciation. He did nothing overt to ingratiate himself with anyone, but she observed that he was tacitly but no less acutely aware of the effect his music or his playing had on people. He seemed to treat servants and tradespeople with more consistent friendliness than he did his friends. One of his landladies in Lichtental told May that Brahms would often show up in the afternoon to help her chop vegetables for dinner. Chambermaids, innkeepers, and Florence May called him kind and cheerful; Clara and Joachim certainly did not.

May found him an ideal piano teacher, even though, "I do not wish to rhapsodize; he would have been the first to object to this." He was calm, patient, and persistent, required daily finger exercises from Clementi's studies, explained everything with absolute clarity. When she did well he tended to respond, "That will make a great effect with Frau Schumann." At the end of lessons he usually played for her, most often Bach. She found his touch exquisite and his Scarlatti breathtaking, but he said his playing was not what it used to be. "You must learn by the faults also," he told her. They had one tiff, when she insisted he play and he didn't feel like it. That day he left in a huff, but showed up for her next lesson as if nothing had happened. Soon afterward he allowed her to charm him into playing for her, and he never refused again.[6] Only later did she discover Brahms's crusty and sardonic side, and she never noted the misogyny.

Florence May's lessons, however, ended precipitously that summer. When Clara Schumann returned, May announced that she wanted to study "the technical" side of music with Clara and "the spiritual" with Brahms. Clara immediately threw her out, and Brahms felt obliged to do the same. There were no hard feelings. May kept in touch with Brahms for the rest of his life and he invariably welcomed her visits. As a performer she became one of his greatest champions in Britain, and in 1905 published the first major Brahms biography in English.

In October 1871, Brahms returned to Vienna, spent two months at Zum Kronprinzen, then made his move to Karlsgasse No. 4. At the beginning of January, Johann Jakob Brahms wrote his son a report on the illness that had been dogging him: "It is nothing more than liver disease, it is not fatal, but still very painful." He added that Fritz Schnack, Karoline's son, was near death from a back injury and Karoline had gone to St. Petersburg to bring him home. "I visited Herr Marxsen, he greets you heartily. He is glad you have taken the position [as Gesellschaft director]. Your loving Father and Mother wish you a joyful and happy new year."

When Fritz Schnack arrived with his mother in Hamburg they called in a doctor to examine him, and while the doctor was there Johann Jakob agreed to a once-over as well. The report was devastating. Two weeks later, Brahms received the news from Karoline: "Unfortunately I have to write you that this time it's very bad. . . . Father can't even stand up. His strength has vanished all at once."[7] Soon Brahms learned the full story, that his father was near death from liver cancer.

Feelings of regret and nostalgia washed over him. "My father is very seriously ill," he wrote Reinthaler just before leaving for Hamburg. "That the two lucky people were not granted a long time together, that after a long laborious life he could not longer enjoy a comfortable old age, how sorrowful that makes me!" Brahms had been more the child of his mother than his father—of Christiane's intelligence, her kindness, even her lapidary skills as a seamstress—but in the end it was Johann Jakob who claimed the larger share of his son's heart. It had been one of Johannes's greatest pleasures to provide his father with the kind of luxuries Johann Jakob had never known, in his long struggle from the streets and dives of Hamburg to the Philharmonic and a measure of respectability. Only the year before, the couple had taken another place on Anscharplatz, a first floor with fewer steps for Johann Jakob to climb. In the last few years he had taken to signing himself Johann instead of Jakob Brahms, in honor of his son.

For the father the talent and success of his boy had seemed a mysterious, inexplicable force. When Johannes was home in Hamburg he was treated with deference, spoken of in hushed tones. Once when family friend Karl Bade came to visit at Anscharplatz, Johann Jakob greeted him solemnly with finger on lips. To Bade's surprised look the old man whispered cryptically, *"He is there,"* silently pushed the visitor into Johannes's room, and closed the door quietly after him. (Brahms, busy packing books to send to Vienna, turned around brandishing an old volume at the befuddled Bade and said, "See here, Kuhnau was a capable musician!")[8]

Johannes arrived in Hamburg on the first day of February 1872 and spent ten days sitting by his father's deathbed. During that time he and Fritz Brahms reconciled as much as was possible for two brothers who, despite their shared musical careers, had never had anything between them. Fritz was still getting along as a piano teacher, no doubt in part because he was the famous man's brother. (To get away from the family, Fritz had recently spent two years in Venezuela.) They would maintain a polite distance. Elise, estranged from her father since he left Christiane, stayed at home with her new husband while her father faded.

On the tenth, Johann Jakob roused himself to say good-bye, then sank into silence and died peacefully the next day. From Hamburg, Brahms wrote Julius Stockhausen that his father's death marked "an epoch in my lonely life. . . . You know my weakness for the homeland and you can imagine with what special feelings I went through the streets this time— which I certainly won't see again for a long time."⁹ In 1874 he would compose three songs on Klaus Groth's lyrics, all called "Heimweh" ("Homesickness"). It was after Johann Jakob's death that the last word in the text of the Alto Rhapsody—*Wüste*—began haunting Brahms's letters.

After the funeral he gathered mementos—Johann Jakob's old Certificate of Apprenticeship, the fanciful Brahms family coat of arms, the certificate of Hamburg citizenship. He gave Karoline a small oil portrait of Johann Jakob as a young man, asking her to leave it to him when she died. In the end, Karoline outlived her stepson, who was some six years younger. If the deepest part of his connection to his hometown was severed now, Brahms never slacked in his attention to his stepmother, stepbrother, and sister. As he had from the beginning of his career, he continued to dispatch a large percentage of his earnings to his family. All of them would receive steady appeals to ask for more when they needed it, and they rarely asked for anything when he did not give more than asked. Karoline returned to her old trade of taking in boarders. The unlucky Fritz Schnack, with his back injury from which it took years to make an incomplete recovery, was the particular beneficiary of Brahms's generosity and concern. Brahms hired medical care for his stepbrother, "the second Fritz," and finally set him up in a watchmaking shop in Pinneberg near Hamburg, where Karoline joined him.

After settling his father's affairs Brahms returned to Karlsgasse for the spring, then in May to Lichtental. There he perhaps worked on string quartets or songs, perhaps tinkered with the symphony long in progress, but finished nothing. At the same time he prepared for his duties as Gesellschaft artistic director, set to begin in September.

Most of all, echoing a pattern from the fallow years of the 1850s, he studied counterpoint while lamenting his aimlessness. "What for?" he wrote Clara. "The better to run down my beautiful things?—I did not need counterpoint for that. To become a Professor at the Academy?—no, not that either. To be able to write . . . music better?—I don't even aspire to that! But there is certainly something tragic about becoming in the end too clever for one's needs." He and Clara were exchanging kindnesses in this period, which had lasted since the debacle with Julie. Brahms wrote her in the same letter, "What a joy it is to me then to remember how big with love is a certain human breast. . . . You see everything so warmly, with such beautiful serenity, just like a reflection of yourself."[10]

If his creative juices were running low that summer, there was no lack of excitement. He played the Schumann Concerto and conducted the A Major Serenade in Baden-Baden in August, for which he was paid a thousand francs. Hermann Levi had scheduled the premiere of the complete *Triumphlied* for June 5, his farewell performance as *Hofkapellmeister* in Karlsruhe. Levi was about to take over the Court Theater in Munich, where through the next years he would be mesmerized by Wagner, the artist who dominated King Ludwig's capital. Levi the rabbi's son had already written Brahms in defense of Wagner's antisemitic screed "Jewry in Music": "I've never been able to join in with the general howling about Wagner's foolishness and questionable character; you will remember that I myself defended the Jewish brochure insofar as I believe it to come from serious artistic conviction."[11] As of summer 1872, though, Wagner's spell had not threatened the highly productive collaboration of Levi and Brahms, nor the affection between them.

Inviting friend Theodor Billroth to the *Triumphlied* premiere, Brahms wrote, "It is said that my song is very merry." Indeed, the crowd found its patriotic raptures merry on June 5, at the Karlsruhe Hoftheater; it garnered stupendous acclaim. Clara and Joachim came for the concert. She had written in her journal, "Johannes's *Triumphlied* is certainly the deepest and grandest piece of church music since Bach."[12] (That may have been the deepest and grandest misjudgment of Clara's experience with Brahms's music. Like him, she was carried away by patriotism.) Billroth could not attend but in his stead sent a beaker engraved "Master of German Music. Johannes Brahms, in remembrance of the fifth of June, 1872." Moved, Johannes wrote Billroth after the concert:

> I cannot in any way write and really thank you as I feel. It would have to be a description of my feelings as I held your letter in my hand or as Clara Schumann's noble face beamed as we sat together with Levi and talked about men of your sort with awe and love. It is so natural for you to do the extraordinary that you can't imagine how it impresses. The beaker was filled on that evening and afterwards, how many times! . . . I will never again hear my song, which after all was calculated for the great masses, with more joy. The artists really performed, as did our soldiers in France.[13]

In the same month, Brahms wrote in quite another mood to Reinthaler: "How often I have upbraided myself that I haven't written you—but it is a desolate life [*wüstes Leben*] and so many letters must be written." That summer Julie Schumann, having borne two children to Count Marmorito and carrying a third, had come to Baden-Baden to say farewell. Clara's worst fears had been confirmed; childbearing had proven too much for Julie. "We saw her growing worse and worse day by day," Clara wrote, "and could do nothing. No doctor could help her; she had worn out her delicate frame with all the cares of household and children. . . . I knew indeed that this loss must come, but I little guessed how soon the blow was to fall."[14] Julie died on November 10, the day of Brahms's first concert with the Gesellschaft der Musikfreunde.

BEFORE BRAHMS LEFT LICHTENTAL to take up his duties as artistic director, he made another historic connection. That summer he and pianist/conductor Hans von Bülow, having spent years avoiding each other, formed a friendship based at first on a mutual affection for Johann Strauss's waltzes.[15] Conductor and composer took to spending evenings together sitting over beer in the summer air, plunged in the lilting stream of Strauss's melodies, watching their driving force swaying around his fiddle in front of the band. "African and hot-blooded, crazy with life," a rather shocked German observer said of Strauss, "he exorcises the wicked devils from our bodies and he does it with waltzes, which are the modern exorcism."[16] Brahms and Bülow may have enjoyed more temperately than that, but they basked in the heat and felt maybe a little exorcised.

Bülow had once studied piano with Liszt, then as conductor had been among the best of Wagnerians until Wagner stole his wife. High-strung and obsessive at the best of times, Bülow had nearly been destroyed by the experience. After the divorce with Cosima was settled in 1870 he was still depressed, but available for a new hero. (His replacement as favored conductor in the Wagnerian ranks would be Hermann Levi, though Bülow continued to perform Wagner.) While Bülow had long resisted Brahms's music, as pianist he had occasionally played it. Now, as sign of their new friendship, Bülow played the E♭ Minor Scherzo, the Ballades, and the Handel Variations in Vienna, in November 1872.

Some observers, including Clara Schumann, called Bülow's sinewy and analytical performances overintellectual, but Brahms appreciated them. (Another of Bülow's teachers had been Clara's father, Friedrich Wieck.) His orchestral conducting showed the same refined, meticulous, but still intense style. During the 1870s he joined Clara and Joachim as a leading Brahms champion. All that was necessary was to provide him with more orchestral music to champion, and Brahms was about to see to that.

In September Brahms returned to Karlsgasse No. 4, trying to subdue his ambivalence as he geared up for the Gesellschaft season. Each year as artistic director he earned 3000 florins for presenting four regular subscription concerts and two special, nonsubscription ones. The Gesellschaft board had agreed with his requirement of full control over programs, hiring, and all artistic decisions. Brahms immediately replaced nearly three dozen of the weaker amateur players in the orchestra with professionals from the Philharmonic/Opera orchestra, making up an ensemble of a hundred. Josef Hellmesberger, still the town's leading concertmaster, headed the violins. The Gesellschaft choir numbered three hundred; Brahms for the first time required of them a second weekly rehearsal. Immediately the level of performance in Gesellschaft concerts shot up.

His own level went up and down, from shaky to inspired, as his performing generally tended to. As with his piano playing, Brahms could be nervous on the podium, especially when presenting new work of his own. Still, as artistic director he made an impact not only on the Gesellschaft der Musikfreunde but on the musical life of Vienna—and from there, to a definable degree, on the musical world.

Brahms was determined to extend the concert repertoire backward to the Baroque and beyond. His programs featured more Bach than perhaps any previous group in history; during his tenure he mounted several cantatas and the complete *St. Matthew Passion*. After the performance of the cantata *Christ lag in Todesbanden*, Theodor Billroth probably voiced the feelings of many Viennese when in a letter he called it "damned dry music, though here and there lofty in effect." He added that the audience took it well, out of respect for the conductor.[17] Critic Eduard Hanslick, who gave still less of a damn for Bach, usually managed to be civil toward the old master in his reviews. But when Brahms put together on one program a Cherubini Requiem and Bach's cantata *Liebster Gott, wann werd' ich sterben?* (*Dear Lord, When Shall I Die?*), Hanslick could not resist grumbling in the *Neue Freie Presse*, "It is not the custom here . . . to go to concerts for the sole purpose of being successively buried according to Protestant and Catholic rites."[18]

It was that sort of attitude Brahms had in mind when writing a sardonic pseudo-Biblical note to Amalie Joachim, by way of inviting her to solo in Handel's *Saul:* "Therefore David inquired of the Lord, saying, 'Shall I go forth and smite the Philistines?' . . . And the Lord answered unto him and said, 'Arise . . . for I have delivered them into thine hand.' . . . But as you know, David always plundered mightily from the

Philistines. . . . As a Music Director puts it: What kind of money are you getting?"[19]

Brahms never relented in his own smiting of Philistines, especially the Viennese variety, and did much to establish the monumental works of Bach in the repertoire (Joachim was doing the same for Bach's solo violin music). If Brahms's performances of Handel, including the oratorios *Saul* and *Solomon*, perhaps went down easier with the Viennese, he also gave them therapeutic doses of Renaissance composers Palestrina, Isaac, Gallus, and Lassus.[20]

As Virginia Hancock has detailed, Brahms's way of performing older music in general and Bach and Handel in particular represents a middle ground between the "modernized" Baroque of his time and the "historically informed" approach of the next century. When Felix Mendelssohn made his epochal revival of Bach's *St. Matthew Passion* in 1829, he decked out the music with the full Romantic forces of giant orchestra and chorus, and the contemporary expressive palette of sighing swells, sweeping crescendos, varied articulations, and arching legatos. Brahms had the time's love of huge choruses doing Bach and Handel (Bach himself premiered the *St. Matthew* with less than fifty), and did not use harpsichord and other "obsolete" instruments. Still, he was more discreet than most conductors of the day in adding dynamic effects and such to the music (though he added some). He also avoided reworking the instrumentation to the degree Mendelssohn and others had.

Of mainstream composers Brahms naturally concentrated on Haydn, Mozart, Beethoven, Gluck, Mendelssohn, Schubert, and Schumann. The surprising thing, for that age and for a composer, is how little contemporary music he played, and how few premieres. Most of the living composers he presented were friends of his, the pieces including a violin concerto by Albert Dietrich, Joachim's Hungarian Concerto, and works by Goldmark, Hiller, Rheinberger, and Rubinstein. Brahms's farewell Gesellschaft concert was entirely taken up by Max Bruch's *Odysseus*. (There is a legend that after Bruch first plowed through the long oratorio for him at the piano, Brahms's sole comment was: "Say, where do you get your music paper? First rate!"[21]) If Brahms felt dubious about Berlioz, most admiring his pastoral oratorio *L'enfance du Christ*, he still programmed the hyperbolic Frenchman's *Harold in Italy*. Of his own music, over three years Brahms played the *Schicksalslied*, the Alto Rhapsody, and the *Triumphlied*, and in 1875 conducted a performance of *Ein deutsches Requiem* that turned out to be one of the great triumphs of his life.

On the podium Brahms was graceless but decisive, the baton sweeping vigorously around the stubby figure, the pince-nez on its cord flying in loud passages. In adagios he might conduct dreamily, left hand shoved in his pocket. He always memorized the scores. Sometimes he allowed his troops to get careless. In his third concert the harpist brought Schumann's *Sängers Fluch* to a halt by turning over two pages at once, and on the same program an early entry by a timpanist led to a breakdown as Ferdinand Hiller conducted his Concert Overture. That night only Mendelssohn's *Walpurgisnacht* had an uninterrupted journey. These do seem to have been the last sweat-drenched episodes of the kind in Brahms's tenure, but there were a number of conspicuously subpar performances, including *Harold in Italy*.

Brahms managed rehearsals with incomparable musicianship and ready wit. He knew how to be self-deprecating, as when he echoed the town's (and probably his own) favorite joke about himself: "I'm in a really good mood today, so let's do *Dear Lord, When Shall I Die?*" Behind the scenes, managing the thousand details that Levi had warned him about— programs, budgets, scheduling, hiring soloists, and on and on—Brahms did his job scrupulously and with only a hint of impatience. Even though he insisted on keeping his summers sacrosanct as prerequisite for taking the job, as time went by he was composing less and knew it.

In history the overwhelming stature of Brahms the composer has tended to obscure his significance as a performer, whether presenting Schubert and Schumann lieder with Stockhausen, or conducting orchestras and choruses. When Brahms was born, Beethoven and Schubert had been dead less than ten years and Schumann and Chopin were in their prime, Bach was still a novelty and earlier composers hardly known, and most of the music heard on concerts was new or less than a half century old. By the time Brahms died, the repertoire was made up largely of the great dead from the Baroque to the mid-nineteenth century.

Brahms's tenure as Artistic Director of the Gesellschaft der Musikfreunde represents a landmark in that process of tilting the repertoire away from the present in favor of the past. It was exactly this state of affairs that Liszt and Wagner and the New Germans had attempted to forestall, by keeping the living, revolutionary composer in the forefront of the art. But in the end Brahms had more clout than Liszt, he wrote more successful orchestral music, and his aesthetic prevailed in the middle-class temples called concert halls. Eventually, when the conservative/revolutionary, Brahms/New German factions faded and the world had embraced both sides, and the leading figures were all dead, a curious echo of the factions lingered. Among artists the Wagnerian model of the artist as high priest and redeemer persisted as an article of faith for Modernist artists: the creator as revolutionary leader. In the concert hall, Brahms-style conservatism endured, preserving much of the same canon he favored in his tenure at the Gesellschaft. The few living composers he performed in those years—friends who wrote music he approved of— would mostly vanish from the scene.

As the bitter factionalism of the nineteenth century subsided, the split between artist and public steadily widened. Less and less new work was allowed into the standard repertoire, and Vienna became one of the most reactionary musical centers of all. If in the end the factional feuds of the nineteenth century did not hobble the course of music, the split between composers and the middle-class audience, a development to which Brahms contributed, would be a defining, initially freeing, ultimately debilitating, condition of Modernism.

BRAHMS'S FIRST CONCERT with the Gesellschaft went off on November 10, 1872, the program Handel's *Dettingen Te Deum*, Joachim's orchestration of the Schubert Grand Duo, a Mozart concert aria, and *a cappella* choruses by Renaissance masters Eccard and Isaac. His tenure began as it would proceed: as composer and conductor, Brahms remained aware of his audience and ultimately considerate of them, and at the same time challenged them to go beyond their experience.

Creatively, at the end of 1872 he seemed to have recovered from the aimlessness and depression of the last couple of years, but he still had no particular plans. He wrote Hermann Levi that he had been much occupied with story possibilities for an opera, notably Calderón's *The Open Secret* and two fantastic plays of Carlo Gozzi, *King Stag* and *The Love of Three Oranges* (the same story Prokofiev later used).[22] Levi had been scheming for some time now to tempt Brahms with one libretto or another; a couple of years before it had been *Sulamith*, based on the Song of Songs.

As Brahms meticulously considered and regretfully rejected one idea after another, he developed various rules of thumb about opera. Among other notions, he did not want continuous music but rather numbers linked with spoken dialogue, like Mozart's Singspiel *The Magic Flute*. As did Wagner, Brahms rejected realistic drama in favor of myth and legend; but the magical tales of the Italian Gozzi, in their puckish unreality, are as far as one can get from Teutonic epics, and so would keep Brahms at a useful remove from Wagner. Brahms also clearly preferred texts that did not demand realistic emotions from him. It is boggling to contemplate that for a while he seriously considered a story about gold prospecting in California. For Brahms that would also have been a foray into the fantastic.

In short, he knew what kind of librettos he wanted and the form he wanted them in, ones that would demarcate his own territory as distinct from his rival's; and he had several experienced friends plying him with librettos. What he could never settle on was a musical style for opera that suited the medium and suited him. *Rinaldo* and the *Magelone* lieder had been experiments in that direction, and they had not satisfied him. Yet year after year he kept mulling over ideas for the stage, and probably made musical sketches for some of the librettos.

As of 1872, if opera was preoccupying Brahms and nothing else particularly demanded to be done, at least he and Clara were maintaining a general cease-fire. At Christmas 1872 he wrote her affectionate greetings:

> May many New Years go by without robbing you of so many precious things as the last one [meaning the deaths of Julie and of Clara's mother]. . . . Often, by way of making a miserable joke, I have said you look upon me as the police look upon one who has undergone three jail terms. I can only hope that this unfavorable opinion of me has frequently proved unjustified, just as I fear your more favorable opinions of my artistic work have been. . . . But neither of them need rob you of the feeling and belief that no one can be more attached and devoted to you than I am.[23]

Among his inner circle the next wrangle was with Joachim, and it was largely Brahms's fault, or rather the product of his habitual obliqueness. It took shape in a contrapuntal series of misunderstandings. Bonn had planned a Schumann Festival in August 1873, to help build a fund for a memorial at Schumann's grave. Joachim was named director of the festival. As plans developed, the Committee asked Brahms to compose a new work for the occasion. He declined. Instead, Joachim made plans to do the obvious thing— mount *Ein deutsches Requiem*, and do it on the opening day of the festival.

In responding to that proposition, Brahms seemed oddly ambivalent: "As to your wanting to put on my Requiem—yet—I can indeed not tell you my reasons against it—so further. . . ."[24] He thereby attempted, he thought, to be properly restrained and modest about the honor of having his work performed, especially since some of the Committee were resisting the *Requiem* idea and Joachim was having to fight for it.[25] If the *Requiem* were going to be done, meanwhile, Brahms preferred to conduct it himself, but he didn't make that clear either. He simply assumed that Joachim could read his mind.

Instead, Joachim felt he had been battling for the piece and Johannes had let him down in the letter, so he allowed things to fall into a muddle. The result was that in June, staying in Tutzing, Brahms learned from a newspaper article that the *Requiem* was not going to be done at the festival at all. The confusion was complete and everybody angry at everybody else. Despite his disgust at the outcome, Brahms appears to have understood that some of it was his own doing. That shows in the tortuous letter he wrote Joachim:

> I see from the newspapers that my Requiem is not going to be performed at Bonn, and what annoyed me still more, I heard that you justified your action on the grounds of a letter from me.
>
> I am supposed to have written diplomatically and not to have made it clear whether the performance would please me or not.
>
> If my letter really made this impression, I should, naturally, have preferred that you write and tell me so, or ask me a second question. . . . It is easy to attribute all sorts of motives to a man who is not keen on answering and explaining. . . . I certainly said *nothing* on a good many subjects which I had very much at heart—and on the matter as a whole. But that was not diplomacy, merely my dislike of letter-writing. . . .
>
> If, in this case, you had considered the matter quite *simply* you would have known how completely and inevitably such a work as the Requiem belonged to Schumann, so much so that, in my heart of hearts, it seemed to me a matter of course that it should be sung for him.[26]

Brahms required his friend, in other words, to understand that even an apparent withdrawal might express a fervent desire. As he wrote to Clara in later years, "I always write only half-sentences, and the reader himself must supply the other half."[27]

From that point ill will shuttled back and forth among a collection of highly prickly personalities. Clara had been put out over some recent words of Johannes as well, and showed them indignantly to Hermann Levi, who in turn wrote in an effort to placate Joachim, "I could not help giving Frau Schumann a lecture or two on her behavior towards Brahms. . . . She showed me a letter from [him] which I was expected to consider inconsiderate, cold, and unkind, which . . . I was not able to do. . . . He is just himself. . . . Will you not write to him now in a friendly, pleasant way, and just explain why you are not singing the Requiem?"[28]

Meanwhile, Clara wrote similarly to Joachim, trying to calm him down about Johannes's letter: "I do not think the letter to you is so very bad, merely cold. I fancy he would really have liked to conduct, and was perhaps offended because he was not definitely invited to do so *by the Committee,* and I think he is justified in this."[29]

Joachim would have none of these attempts to calm the waters. Now that his blood was up he dispatched a blast to Johannes that looks like one he had been saving up for a long time:

> Let us be quite frank. For the last few years, whenever we have met, I have always felt that your manner towards me was not what it used to be. . . . No doubt I have disappointed many of the hopes you set on my development, and have been more indolent that you liked in many respects. . . . What more natural than for me to imagine that you regarded our old intimacy . . . as something embarrassing rather than desirable. . . . You wanted a reassuring answer. I wonder if this is one?[30]

It was of course not at all reassuring, but Brahms made no counterattack. (The "disappointed hopes" probably refers to Johannes's old ambitions for Joachim as a composer.)

In the middle of all this bile and trouble, Clara discovered something that made her really apoplectic. She had been accepting a stipend from the Schumann Committee, but learned that some of it came from concerts other people had been advertising and presenting for her benefit. Nothing could have outraged Clara more than the idea of lesser musicians performing on her behalf. In an ecstasy of rage she spluttered to Johannes:

> I am now to allow other artists to give concerts for me, and to this end to suffer the publication of such mendacious advertisements for the collection of more money! It is an indignity. I am so thoroughly infuriated, I do not know what to do. . . . I must be vindicated. The fact must be stated in the leading Vienna newspapers that the whole thing is a lie and that I knew nothing about the concerts. . . . Then steps must be taken to prevent so much as a farthing of the receipts from coming to me.[31]

After the tempests had run their course the main repercussions fell on relations between Joachim and Brahms. Their friendship had been deteriorating for years, and after the misunderstandings over the *Requiem* the decline only accelerated.

Everyone expected Brahms to boycott the Schumann Festival because of the imbroglio, but that August he turned up in Bonn. If studiously glum, he refrained from making a scene. Finally he was cheered by Clara's performance of the Schumann Piano Concerto and its reception. There was an extraordinary demonstration as Clara appeared onstage, with trumpet fanfares from the orchestra, thousands of the audience standing and shouting and waving handkerchiefs. Eugenie Schumann described it to a friend:

> At last Mama was allowed to seat herself at the piano. She looked so beautiful—like a young girl, a bride, a child. Her dress was lovely, and the effect was heightened by a rose in her hair. . . . Brahms himself said that he had never heard the concerto so well played. When it was over a tremendous storm of applause broke out again, there was a flourish of trumpets, and Mama was overwhelmed with flowers.[32]

After the excitement of the festival, the friends returned to their cares and their sour grapes. Though Joachim had a wife and children, he was destined to remain a lonely and even tragic figure. When he and Johannes first met, they had been precocious geniuses on the threshold of glittering careers, at the same time clumsy and immature in their dealings with people. With the incomparable success that had attended their lives since then, many of those years in close friendship and collaboration, their emotional and social selves had hardly matured. Joachim's need for love had always been insatiable. Among his other suspicions and jealousies, he had begun to imagine that his wife was unfaithful to him. Over that a disaster was in the making, one that took excruciatingly long to run its course, and which nearly consumed one of the most remarkable collaborations in the history of music.

IN THE SPRING OF 1873, Clara took a flat in Berlin and eventually sold her house in Baden-Baden, making the move partly to provide a better home for her consumptive son Felix.[33] She spent the summer in the resort that year, but Brahms sought another vacation spot for himself. In April he took rooms at Gratwein, in Styria, only to come under siege by some "aesthetic ladies." After suffering through two days of that he packed his bags and fled to the village of Tutzing on the Starnberger See, taking lodging at an inn called the Seerose (Water Lily). (Levi and Julius Allgeyer had recommended the town to him.[34]) Immediately he received an invitation from a group of young artists to join their meetings at the inn. Next morning the maid found the invitation ripped to shreds on the floor.

Still, Brahms rented the inn's broken-down piano and settled in for the summer, with visits to Levi in Munich for purposes sociable and practical. Keeping him company in town were soprano Luise Dustmann from Vienna, quite married but still flirtatious in her relations with "Hansi," and a young musician from the Dutch East Indies named Lucie Coster, who was more or less willing to put up with the relentless teasing to which Brahms subjected the women who appealed to him.

Brahms seemed to be rekindled by that landscape in the Bavarian foothills of the Alps. The weather in Tutzing was glorious, he wrote Levi, and the view "more beautiful the other day than we could imagine . . . the lake was almost black, splendidly green on the shore, but usually the lake is blue, a more beautiful, deeper blue than the sky. And besides there was the chain of snowcapped mountains—you never get tired of looking at it."

With the inspiration of lake and mountains and feminine company, Brahms had a more productive summer than any in years. There were many new songs this summer and the next, and he was ready to finish a couple of string quartets long in the works. He made the acquaintance of the singers Heinrich and Therese Vogl, Wagner's anointed Tristan and Isolde, who were enthusiastic to try out his new lieder.

The first item on his agenda, though, was another piece planned for some time. After a hiatus of ten years, Brahms returned to the genre of theme-and-variations. His theme would be a jaunty little tune attributed to Haydn, called "Chorale St. Antoni" on an old manuscript. Scored for pairs of oboes and horns, three bassoons, and the archaic serpent horn, it had been discovered by Gesellschaft librarian, Haydn biographer, and Brahms friend C. F. Pohl. In 1870, Pohl had showed the chorale to Brahms, who copied it down as something that might turn up ideas.

Later scholarly heads have decided that the attribution to Haydn was probably spurious.[35] (In Haydn's time there was something of a cottage industry devoted to faking his music.) The attribution probably would not have concerned Brahms. The tune, attractive and sinewy if slight, suited his purposes. Besides, a slight theme is not necessarily a liability in this genre; variations can progressively add color to the relatively blank slate of the theme. As Brahms would have noted right away, the chorale has a simple and sturdy harmonic structure, a gently swinging rhythm, and phrases with a nice touch of irregularity, respectively 5 5 4 4 4 4 3 measures. In variations you can do things with features like those—a sturdy structure here, a slight irregularity there. A piece based on Haydn would also allow Brahms to touch another of his talismans, as he already had Beethoven, Bach, Schubert, and so many others. So began the Variations on a Theme by Joseph Haydn, in its two renderings.

Brahms first drafted the Haydn Variations (theme, eight variations, and finale) for two pianos, during June and July of 1873. As it turns out, what appear to be most of his sketches and drafts for the piece survive—the only substantial set of sketches he ever allowed, deliberately or not, to escape destruction.[36]

In his study of this material, Donald M. McCorkle notes three levels of work: shorthand rough drafts (often two-line continuity sketches), detailed sketches of tricky places, and finally relatively full drafts for two pianos, from which Brahms made his fair copy. The material tells an interesting story, both in what it contains and what it does not. As in the other surviving scraps of Brahms's sketches, one does not find the slow, painful development of ideas, often beginning in the commonplace and ending in the sublime, that Brahms's friend Nottebohm detailed in the Beethoven sketchbooks. Instead, Karl Geiringer notes, "In the first sketch all the characteristics of the complete work are already evident."[37] One sees further evidence of Brahms composing fast and efficiently, then solving the remaining problems during read-throughs and early performances, and in the copying and engraving process. (Any number of pieces he quietly smothered in the cradle, before or after private readings.)

In other words the compositional process revealed in the Haydn Variations sketches duplicates what is implied in the surviving sketch of the A Major Piano Quartet: by the time Brahms started putting notes on paper he had already worked out in his mind much of the continuity and general drift of a piece. That is what his early-morning walks (or, in Tutzing, swims) were devoted to. His main tool in this method was his superb memory—the kind of memory Mozart possessed. Like Mozart, though, in the complex contrapuntal passages with which the Variations are studded, Brahms needed to work out things on paper, including the skittering Variation V and the intricate presto of Variation VIII. (There may, of course, be lost sketches.)

By the time the Variations were finished for two pianos Brahms had apparently decided to make an orchestral version of the piece, if that was not the idea from the beginning. In both versions the music represents a watershed for him, marking his return to instrumental composition after seven years of concentrating on vocal, and to major piano works after ten years (not counting the two-piano version of the F Minor Quintet). As it turns out, the Haydn Variations in the piano version is the last large keyboard work of his life. In grander garb, meanwhile, it is his first purely orchestral work since the early serenades of 1858–9.

In the spectrum of Brahms's compositional output the Haydn Variations amount to a tour de force. As McCorkle puts it:

> the most distilled essence . . . of the compositional craft and musical aesthetics of Brahms, as well as a phenomenal artistic amalgam of Baroque, Classical, and Romantic formal and stylistic components. . . . [A] synthesis of the Romanticist's miniature character piece and Beethoven's type of character variations climaxes in a Bachian passacaglia, the first time a basso-ostinato construction was used to conclude a set of character variations.

At the same time the instrumentated version constitutes an entirely new genre—the first freestanding orchestral variations in history.

Pervading all this we see Brahms's singular melding of historicism and originality: a piece in concept like none ever written for orchestra, that begins with Haydn, in its course touches on Beethoven and the expressive high noon of Romanticism, and ends by evoking Bach. In all those respects, it nonetheless epitomizes Brahms. Yet it also represents a turning point for him. McCorkle calls it "a transition point in Brahms's development from impressionable young Romantic to maturity as a classicist Romanticist. It was, moreover, the culmination of his efforts as a composer of independent variations and large-scale piano works."[38]

If such heavy historical and personal baggage seems a lot to lay at the feet of a relatively short—about twenty minutes—and apparently unpretentious piece, that is an illustration of the issues with which Brahms grapples, sometimes, even in his more straightforward works. And he addresses these formidable aesthetic and stylistic matters with as little apparent effort as he negotiates invertible triple counterpoint in the lyrical Variation IV.

There is still another matter that surely absorbed Brahms as much as any, as he composed the Variations: they are his final orchestral study before taking up the C minor symphony sketches again. That summer of 1873 he made several visits to conductor Hermann Levi in Munich, where the two presumably sat working through the scoring. Certainly by then Brahms was far more experienced with the orchestra than he had been in the 1850s, when he dived into the D Minor Piano Concerto and found himself over his head. But he still depended on Levi's expertise for ideas and corrections, as he had once relied on Joachim and other friends.

After writing the Piano Concerto he had come to terms with orchestral technique in the two Serenades and in the accompaniments to his choral music—most strikingly the *Schicksalslied*, his breakthrough as an instrumental colorist. With the Haydn Variations, Brahms reached his full bloom as an orchestrator: very late for someone of his stature, never as concerned with sheer color as Wagner and Berlioz nor as thoroughly at home with the orchestra, nor as consistently imaginative as those two; but still with a personal voice that ideally projects his musical intentions.

It is characteristic of his autodidactic approach that Brahms could hardly have designed for himself a more practical scoring exercise than a set of variations, in which each number has to be characterized not only in texture and figuration but in color. From theme to finale, the scoring demands, and nicely achieves, ten distinct environments. Which is to say, it requires an orchestral virtuosity that Brahms did not possess in the previous decade, and might not have achieved at all without Hermann Levi to advise him.

Among other things the orchestral Haydn Variations clarify his debt to the past in the instrumental dimension. Brahms begins by evoking the sound of Haydn and the eighteenth century; he scored the theme largely for winds, close to the original chorale. (During rehearsals for the premiere he corrected a blunder—strings had doubled the winds in the beginning, making a bland scoring instead of the neo-Haydn effect we know today.) The sound of the beginning evokes quite specifically the *early* Classical period. Brahms probably knew how the wind section had developed in the history of the Classical orchestra: pairs of oboes and horns and bassoons added to the string section, with trumpets and drums for festive effects; then in Haydn's day flutes were added, followed by clarinets; and Beethoven first introduced trombones to symphonic music in the Fifth Symphony. Brahms begins the Haydn Variations with the woody sound of winds dominated by oboes and bassoons, without flutes, and he left trombones out of the piece entirely.[39] That sound, with its characteristic Classical-era doublings, was to turn up often in his later orchestral music.

In the first variation, its sweeping lyrical lines in vinelike intertwining, appears fully emerged the mature Brahms string sound: octave doublings making a weightiness (perhaps gleaned from studies in Wagner) that suits his compositional personality better than the lighter, paler orchestral voice of the Serenades. And he regularly uses arpeggio figures of pianistic cast. Now as an orchestral colorist no less than in his notes and forms, Brahms unites Classical and Romantic in a singular voice. In many ways his mature orchestra is the Classical one expanded in range and made thicker and darker. In the Haydn Variations that process takes place before our ears, in the change from Haydnesque theme to Romantic first variation.

If the rhythmically driving second variation recalls the sonic world of Brahms's serenades (but with more octave doublings in the winds than before), another of his thumbprints turns up in the wistful and flowing third variation, in which he moves from rich, full scoring to (at letter B) delicate effects of instruments used soloistically. There we hear an early example of his way of integrating full-orchestra and chamber textures, alternating the monumental with the intimate. At letter C in the same variation we find Brahms's new mastery of characteristically Viennese *durchbrochene Arbeit* ("broken work"). As Karl Geiringer defines that technique, "The motives and themes rove continually from one instrument to another; long-drawn-out melodies are divided among the various instruments, so that the lead is permanently changing from one section of the orchestra to another."[40]

The liquid lines of variation IV make up a contrapuntal tour de force that at the same time is the most poignantly expressive moment of the piece. Its mood is contrasted immediately by the darting, *vivace* chromaticism of variation V, that recalls the exhilarating scherzos of Brahms's younger days (now with a steady exploration of polyrhythm, playing 3+3 against 2+2+2 in the $\frac{6}{8}$ meter). After the next variation's robust pealing of hunting horns, variation VII presents another contrapuntal extravaganza in the form of a lilting *siciliano*.

That sighs away into the finale, at once the most original and most backward-looking of the movements. Having taken bits and pieces of the theme and its harmonies for his material throughout, Brahms fashions elements of the theme's harmony and melody into a five-bar bass pattern repeated over and over, underlying a gradually unfolding contrapuntal development above. It makes for the first set of variations ever to be concluded with a "ground bass" movement, a genre whose most famous exponent is Bach (especially the Chaconne for solo violin, a specialty of Joachim and a favorite of Brahms).

As much as anything else in this work one remembers its sound—massive here, delicate there. Only perhaps in the *Schicksalslied* does Brahms's sheer orchestral voice say so much. As one of the more subtle examples of originality: who would expect him to deal so lovingly with so un-Brahmsian an instrument as the piccolo? The Variations has one of the most elaborate piccolo parts written to that time. Besides making use of its usual function of adding a top to the orchestra, in the eighth variation

Brahms became one of the first to explore the fragile lyricism of the instrument's middle register. Most memorably, in the finale the piping voice of the piccolo seems to pull the other instruments up an octave, to create a glittering reminiscence of the "Haydn" theme. There, in a prophetic suggestion of what the avant-garde of a hundred years later would call "tone-color composition," the silvery tones of the triangle blend with the piccolo and high winds to produce a music-box effect of magical charm, which casts its nostalgic glow backward over the whole piece. With that gesture Brahms capped one of his most delightful, most popular, and most far-reaching works.

THEN, immediately after the scintillating Variations he completed, at age forty, two of his most severe, introspective, and ultimately least popular works—the String Quartets in C Minor and A Minor, Opus 51.[41] Both had been going for some time, with provisional versions read over by Joachim and his group (he formed his renowned quartet in 1869).

Brahms claimed that Opus 51 had been preceded by twenty discarded quartets. The quartet genre/medium was a territory Haydn had laid out in its developed form, Mozart carried forward, and Beethoven in his sixteen quartets explored to a breadth and depth that for composers raised the question of whether he had left anything for anyone else to say. Since Beethoven, only Schubert and in some degree Schumann and Mendelssohn had shown that the quartet could still produce fresh ideas—but as of the 1870s the Schumann and Mendelssohn quartets had not taken hold, which means that none since the 1820s had entered the repertoire.[42]

So by mid-century the string quartet like the symphony appeared a moribund genre despite the dozens of composers writing them. The intimacy and concentration of the quartet seemed contrary to the spirit of Romanticism, which loved the extravagant and monumental. Wagner, Liszt, Chopin, Berlioz—none of them wrote string quartets. Carl Dahlhaus observes, "It had become virtually impossible to strike the precarious and mutually conditioned balance between subjectivity of expression—as in late Beethoven—and rigorous objectivity of form; composers saw almost no escape from the trap of succumbing either to musical academicism or to programmatic confessions.... After Beethoven, string quartets resembled fossil specimens of an extinct genre."[43]

With a tenacity that he showed in no other genre, not even the symphony, Brahms kept writing quartet after quartet and throwing them away. He insisted on picking up the legacy of Beethoven and carrying it further, but as always he insisted on doing it his own way, which included finding something fresh in the old genre. When he finally issued his pair of quartets in C and A minor, his personal solution to the problem turned out to be what biographer Malcolm MacDonald calls a "remorseless logic" of thematic construction,[44] and a harmonic complexity that Arnold Schoenberg (in "Brahms the Progressive") admiringly compared to the hyperchromaticism of Wagner's *Tristan und Isolde*.[45]

The C Minor String Quartet begins with a rushing theme that casts its urgent tone and its motivic echoes over the whole piece:

Ivor Keys comments that the theme "constantly summons a storm, as it were, to drown any incipient songs."[46] The melodic material of the first movement and much of the rest is fragmentary bits of themes, largely in a dark minor, with none of Brahms's lyrical transports. The instrumental writing is scrupulously without brilliance. Walter Frisch summarizes the approach of the C Minor:

> Harmonies, especially in the first and last movements, churn continuously, carrying aloft very small thematic or motivic fragments. . . . The rising stepwise third that opens the first movement reappears . . . to shape the main theme of the [second-movement] Romanze. Both the main theme and countersubject of the [third-movement] Allegretto also clearly derive from the basic motive. And the finale bursts in with a theme that directly recalls the main idea of the first movement. . . . It is the first work in which Brahms shows a concern for such higher-level thematic processes, rather than mere thematic recall or transformation.[47]

Thus Brahms's manifestly self-conscious solution to the dilemma of following Beethoven and Schubert as a writer of string quartets: not lyricism or subjectivity but objective craft, a heightened attention to structure and motivic development across the movements, a relentless determination to make every note significant to the whole. The expressive intensity of the C Minor is created in large part by the intellectual intensity of that labor—for composer and listener alike. (This "total thematic" approach to composition, and the heated effect of the result, were to be founding elements of Schoenberg's style.) The middle movements of the C Minor, the romanze and the allegretto—both moderate in tempo, neither remotely like a scherzo—relent a little, before the brusque and explosive last movement.

The A Minor Quartet is a degree more outgoing, less intense, less self-conscious, more relaxed in logic than the C Minor. Michael Musgrave observes, "It is the lyrical and improvisatory quality which now claims his attention, and both the main themes of the first movement and that of the second demonstrate his growing interest in the generation of flexible and evolving themes."[48] The first movement is in unusually orthodox sonata form, followed by a traditional unto archaic layout of movements: a slow and songful one, a "quasi *minuetto*," and for finale a lusty fast movement full of rhythmic quirks, integrating a scherzo-like feel with a touch of Brahms's "Hungarian" mode.

The sustained, wistful lyric melody that begins the A Minor has as its most conspicuous motivic element Joachim's old motto F-A-E, *frei aber einsam* (free but lonely). That and the Hungarian echoes in the finale are clues that Brahms had originally intended to dedicate the A Minor to Joachim, until the ruckus over the *Requiem* came between them. Instead,

Brahms dedicated both Opus 51 quartets to Theodor Billroth, and made him a present of the manuscripts. The letter announcing the dedication was the first in which Brahms used the familiar *du* with his medical friend.

If the Haydn Variations and two quartets were not achievement enough for the summer months of 1873, Brahms also wrote or completed the Eight Songs of Opus 59. Their subjects are a mixture of love found and lost, the most famous of them settings of two Klaus Groth lyrics: "Regenlied" with its imitations of raindrops ("Pour down, rain; reawaken in me the dreams I dreamed in childhood") and the anguished "Mein wundes Herz" ("My Wounded Heart").

Before going back to Vienna in mid-September, Brahms ended the summer with a private reading of the two quartets and the two-piano Haydn Variations at Hermann Levi's in Munich. There, with Levi looking over his shoulder, he finished orchestrating the Variations. He had much to look forward to and much to worry about. All three works were slated to be heard before the end of the year, two of them in Vienna, and Vienna itself was in chaos.

At their premieres the string quartets would be received respectfully if without great enthusiasm, which on the whole is how they have been received by audiences ever since.[49] Still, they entered the repertoire, they helped revitalize the medium, they helped inspire quartets from Schoenberg and Bartók and many of the next century's composers. In other words, Brahms had revivified a great but moribund tradition. Having done that with the string quartet, he was finally ready to do the same with the symphony.

CHAPTER SIXTEEN

The Tramp of Giants

IN SEPTEMBER 1873, after his grudging visit to the Schumann Festival in Bonn, Brahms returned home to a capital staggering through one of the turning points in its history—this and most turns to come, for the worse. Vienna had mounted a great International Exhibition to show off the achievements of the *Gründerzeit*, the years of boom and bourgeois prosperity, the time of spreading railroads and grand concert halls and the epic kitsch of the Ringstrasse. Brahms had his stepmother ship Robert Schumann's old Graf piano, which Clara had given him years before, to be shown at the Exhibition. Among other sights drawing crowds to the fairgrounds was Hans Makart's colossal, swarming canvas *Venice Pays Homage to Caterina Cornaro.*[1] Then, a week after the Exhibition opened, the reckless speculation that had fueled an illusory prosperity came to its crisis. The stock market crashed and the country plummeted into depression.

The crash affected every class and institution, the box offices of concert halls as much as anything. Even when the depression eased, the long-term result was a serious deterioration in workers' lives, a chronic housing shortage, and an assault on the parliamentary liberalism that had dominated Austria for years. Meanwhile the Austrian empire continued its inexorable decline, irrelevant to Europe and weakened at its foundations by the Dual Monarchy with Hungary. Yet the government continued to erect colossal structures around the Ringstrasse, their fake-historic grandeur touting a prosperity and an imperial stability that no longer existed.

Now antidemocratic and antisemitic forces that had simmered under the surface of Austrian culture found fertile soil. Jews would be blamed for the crash, and eventually for every ill of an increasingly precarious society. In 1879 the aristocratic Georg von Schönerer, pan-German and prototype of the Nazi, would make suppression of "the Semitic rule of money" and of the free press major planks of his election platform. (The *Neue Freie Presse*, after all, was the leading liberal paper.) These ideas inflamed Vienna's university students, of the sort who had once cheered their parents' liberalism.[2] Vienna historian Carl E. Schorske writes:

> Beginning with the economic crash of 1873, challenges to the liberal hegemony grew ever more powerful. At the same time, within liberal society itself cries for reform mingled with groans of despair or disgust at the impotence of liberal Austria. A widespread, collective oedipal revolt began in the seventies to spread through the Austrian middle class.[3]

The liberal bourgeoisie had not ultimately lost its money or its lifestyle or its love of music, but rather was losing, bit by bit, its power and direction. Among them, writes Schorske, "a sense of superiority and a sense of impotence became oddly commingled."[4] As symptom of that impotence, now began the epidemic of suicide among the *Grossbürgertum* in Vienna. And all over Austria, wracked by the conflicting claims of contentious groups, the wave of reaction rose. Schorske notes that in their politics the liberals had "succeeded in releasing the political energies of the masses, but against themselves rather than against their ancient foes [the aristocrats]." In the 1870s, Vienna entered a twilight that over the next decades would deepen into darkness.

AFTER THE CRASH there were dark forebodings in Brahms's circle over what was gathering, but he had premieres to worry about—the A Minor String Quartet in Berlin by the Joachim Quartet in October, the Haydn Variations by the Vienna Philharmonic in November, the C Minor String Quartet by Hellmesberger's group in December.[5] Brahms was most fearful about the orchestral premiere, in which he would conduct the Philharmonic. His previous experience with them had been memorably unpleasant—when in 1869 they refused to play the scheduled D Major Serenade, relenting only when Dessoff threatened to resign.

For the last rehearsal of the Variations with the Philharmonic, Brahms gathered friends around him, as buttresses. To Theodor Billroth he wrote, "It would be extremely pleasant for me to have you there as an audience, and have a word with you."[6] Klaus Groth, who also appeared as moral support, found Brahms pacing back and forth backstage as the orchestra rehearsed a Beethoven symphony. "I know that piece well enough," Brahms said to Groth. As he stepped on the podium to begin, the orchestra gave him a reasonably friendly greeting, he thanked them in his high gruff voice, and got efficiently to work. Afterward, when Groth reported that he and Billroth had enjoyed it, Brahms had unwound enough to respond with trademark irony: "Ah, so you are also unmusical!"[7]

On November 2 the premiere of the Variations on a Theme by Haydn made a sensation with the Viennese. It would repeat that success across Europe and the world. Brahms could relax a little; he had returned as an orchestral composer. The bad news was that he could not avoid the stack of symphony sketches much longer. Now he had the experience and the skill and the conceptions he needed to get on with them; but he managed to hold the symphony at bay for another year.

At the beginning of 1874 he received the first of a long row of honors: the Order of Maximilian for Science and Art. In other words, he had been knighted and could call himself (though he would not) *Johannes Ritter von Brahms*. The medal came from none other than King Ludwig of Bavaria, patron and fanatical devotee of Richard Wagner. Shortly afterward, Wagner received the Order as well. Livid when he discovered that his knighthood had been sullied by the presence of his rival, Wagner threatened to refuse the honor—but of course did not.

Clara wrote congratulations. She was living in Berlin now, woeful as usual. "There is nothing to hear except Joachim's quartet!!!" she wrote him. "The theater is only so-so, the Singakademie is conventional, the symphony concerts are incredibly dull."[8] Her son Felix was slowly dying, an arm was tormenting her, and her hearing had been acting up—the first symptoms of a growing deafness that would worsen over the years. To her astonishment, Clara had recently received a large inheritance from her late father, Friedrich Wieck, who once had all but disowned her for marrying Robert Schumann.

The previous autumn she had sent Johannes some of Felix's poems with the observation, "Tell me frankly what you think of them—do not imagine that, like a weak mother, I fancy him a genius, on the contrary I am so afraid of overpraising the talent of [Robert's] children that I daresay I often demand too much of them."[9] In December, as his Christmas present for Clara, Brahms made a robust, passionate setting of one of Felix's delicate, slight lyrics, "Meine Liebe ist grün." Clara was hard on her children, but also capable of grandly affectionate gestures. She didn't tell Felix about Brahms's setting of the song but instead made it a surprise.

One night he came in to find his mother and Joachim playing over a lied. As Clara reported in her journal, "Felix came over and asked what the words were, and when he saw that they were his own he turned quite pale. How beautiful the song is."[10] The next summer Brahms sent them his setting of Felix's "Wenn um den Holunder."

If he had finally charmed the Philharmonic with the Haydn Variations, there remained one venue where Brahms had been often and painfully unwelcome—the Gewandhaus in Leipzig, where the orchestra regarded playing any living composer as an act of condescension. Through the efforts of a band of partisans, Brahms's name had been acquiring some luster in the city. At the end of January 1874 he went to Leipzig for a week of his music, in which he would participate as pianist and conductor.

This time Leipzig began to warm a little to him, the Gewandhaus echoing to polite applause all week. Concertgoers heard Brahms playing in the Horn Trio, the Handel Variations, the old piano Ballades, the new *Liebeslieder* Waltzes. The big concert by the Gewandhaus Orchestra included the Haydn Variations and his new orchestral arrangement of three Hungarian Dances. Amalie Joachim sang the Alto Rhapsody, a work she had made her own. Clara came for the concerts, staying in the hotel and breakfasting every morning with Brahms, the Simrocks, and Amalie. In her report to Hermann Levi, Clara described the audience as calm but receptive, the orchestra spirited. For herself, music had once again raised her above the miseries of her life:

> The variations are too wonderful! . . . That is the Beethoven spirit from beginning to end. And then the rhapsody, that marvelous piece, which I've never heard like that. Such pain, such despair, lies in the introduction, and what heavenly joy at the end! Then came the Liebeslieder and the three Hungarians for orchestra, how well done under his direction! . . . My heart rejoiced through the whole evening.[11]

Besides the satisfying memory of applause in a hall that had once resounded with hisses for the D Minor Piano Concerto, Brahms took home with him a new friendship. He had gotten to know Heinrich and Elisabet von Herzogenberg in Bonn, at the Schumann Festival the previous August, and this Brahms Week had largely been their doing. Elisabet was a renewed acquaintance—the former Elisabet von Stockhausen, the brilliant teenage piano student from his first year in Vienna, whom he had handed back to Julius Epstein in fear of falling in love with her.

Now she was safely married and exquisite as ever, thus an ideal object for Brahmsian yearning. He could not realize yet how important her judgment would be to him in the next years, this nominal housewife and helpmate to her composer husband, who could play orchestral scores at sight at the piano and memorize them overnight. Her husband Heinrich was already devoted to Brahms's music and to spreading the gospel in Leipzig.

Elisabet assessed her old admirer and appreciated what she saw. "He was not like the same person," she wrote their mutual friend Bertha Faber in Vienna. "So many people suffer shipwreck on that dangerous shoal called Fame; but we all felt that it had mellowed him, and made him kinder and more tolerant."[12] In future years she had reason to revise that estimate, as she pressed her husband's music on their resistant hero.

BRAHMS WAS BACK rehearsing the Gesellschaft der Musikfreunde in February 1874. On the day he performed Schubert's Mass in B♭ and the Schumann *Manfred* music, Clara wrote him in the afterglow of Leipzig, "How eagerly I drank in your wonderful creations, like the most exquisite nectar of flowers, and how they revived me at a time when I was more depressed than you can imagine. . . . I feel more desolate that I ever have before in my life." She was, as it turned out, in the beginning of an eighteen-month siege when arm troubles—probably tendonitis or bursitis—prevented her from performing. For Clara, being denied the stage was an agony worse than physical pain.

In a following letter from Clara came a bit of gossip: Julius Stockhausen had been appointed head of the Stern Gesangverein in Berlin and, Clara wrote, "Joachim has been imprudent enough . . . to forbid his wife to sing at Stockhausen's next concert. . . . At a large party . . . Frau Joachim exhibited such passion . . . that I was quite angry. Meanwhile, of course, the so-called 'good friends' of whom Simrock was one, egged her on. . . . Just imagine how Joachim's enemies . . . rejoiced that she could make Joachim look such a fool."[13] Clara did not suspect what lay behind all this: Joachim's festering jealousy of the men around Amalie, and of Fritz Simrock—Johannes's friend and publisher—in particular.

Besides the regular Gesellschaft concerts in Vienna, Brahms undertook a good deal of performing elsewhere during the winter. In mid-February he headed for Munich to play the D Minor Piano Concerto under Levi, reporting it to Clara as well received. Around that time his letter of consolation to her about the declining Felix, to whom he was very attached, showed a surge of warmth and affection—of a kind, in fact, that Clara may never have written to him: "I feel your pain and anxiety all much too deeply," he wrote, "to be able to express it to you in words. For I am so thoroughly accustomed to endure even my own suffering in secret and without making a sign. . . . Let this deep love of mine be a comfort to you; for I love you more than myself, and more than anybody or anything on earth."

That July, Clara informed him that he had been elected an honorary member of the Prussian Academy of Arts and Sciences in Berlin. Brahms got the news in his summer quarters at Rüschlikon on Lake Zürich. As usual he was making himself unavailable to Gesellschaft queries, to the annoyance of the Committee, who needed decisions from him. The gemütlich setting of Rüschlikon was epitomized in a letter from friend C. F. Pohl, stuck in the Gesellschaft library in sweltering Vienna. Pohl imagined Brahms sitting "far away beside Lake Zürich, admiring the view at Nydelbad; he drives to Küssnacht, eats freshwater fish and cray-fish in the 'Sun,' drinks the excellent red wine at Erlenbach, or even bet-ter lakeside wine at Mariahalden . . . and saunters along to Horgen, which is one fragrant rose garden in June."[14]

In Rüschlikon, Brahms completed the waltzes he called *Neue Liebes-lieder*, written to capitalize on the tremendous popularity of the first set, and perhaps some of the Opus 61 and 63 lieder and Opus 64 vocal quar-tets. Then he picked up the symphony whose first movement, possibly begun in the mid-1850s, he had showed to Clara and Joachim and other friends in 1862, when they expected to hear the premiere at the end of that year. By that summer in Rüschlikon the alpenhorn theme Brahms had sent Clara on a postcard in 1868 may have found its place in a sketch of the finale, which had always been the sticking point of the symphony. Brahms attacked the piece obliquely, however, picking it up and putting it down over the next two years.

As always he looked for distraction in afternoons and evenings away from his desk. On July 11, at dinner in the house of composer Hermann Götz after a Zürich festival performance of the *Triumphlied*, Brahms made the acquaintance of the Swiss pastor, writer, playwright, and trans-lator Josef Viktor Widmann. Among his other interests the polymathic Widmann produced opera librettos, including one for Götz's new, much-celebrated, eventually forgotten *Taming of the Shrew*. Brahms felt kindly toward the chronically ill Götz, but once on a visit greeted the sight of the younger man's chamber scores with a curt, "Ah, do you also some-times amuse yourself with such things?" Götz spoke bitterly of that mo-ment for the rest of his short life.[15]

Josef Widmann came from a family of fervent musical amateurs. His mother had improvised for Beethoven, his father had sung for Schubert, and among other treasures they owned the Graf piano that had belonged to Beethoven when he died. The night of the dinner at Götz's, Widmann managed to enchant Brahms by the surprising method of getting into a red-faced argument with him. Widmann was expressing his support of the Theological Reform movement in Switzerland when to his astonishment he found Brahms not only cognizant of the issue but with forceful and contrary opinions about it—he declared it a half-measure that would satisfy neither the pious nor the freethinkers. During the next few days of the music festival Widmann found Brahms seeking out his company.

With his writer's eye, Widmann surveyed his famous new friend, whom years before he had observed from a distance on the concert stage. He immediately noted Brahms's delight in children. At restaurants Brahms would fill his pockets with sweets to hand out to urchins on the street. Widmann appreciated the wit, often at the expense of innocent admirers: say, the small-town musician who claimed to know everything Brahms had written, whereupon Brahms convinced the man that an inane tune played by a nearby band was his. Widmann observed that Brahms did not like having his nearsightedness noticed so walked the streets without his pince-nez, claiming the ladies looked prettier that way. When somebody pressed Brahms about needing glasses when he conducted, the reply was that he used them only during Schumann's *Faust*, when the score directs "here women pass by."[16] Brahms and Widmann fell into a long-lasting friendship fueled by an ongoing dialogue on art, literature, politics, and philosophy.

Besides the *Neue Liebeslieder,* Brahms had apparently worked at something else that summer on Lake Zürich. Soon after leaving Switzerland for Vienna and taking up his third season with the Gesellschaft—he had scheduled himself to play the Beethoven *Emperor* Concerto in the first concert—Brahms surprised Theodor Billroth with the manuscript score of a piano quartet in C minor. In the accompanying note he cautioned disingenuously, "The quartet is only a matter of curiosity! Perhaps it can be considered an illustration to the last chapter of the man in the blue coat and yellow vest"[17] (Young Werther).

Perhaps in person Brahms explained to Billroth the cryptic reference to Goethe, which he was repeating to any number of friends: this was none other than the piece begun in 1853 as a quartet in Kapellmeister Kreisler's key of C♯ minor. He had returned to the quartet a couple of times since his own Werther period, and finally finished it. The first, dark murmurings of the strings outline (transposed) Robert Schumann's Clara theme of C-B-A-G♯-A, of which Brahms had also made use several times in his twenties. So now he completed his collection of three piano quartets with the C Minor, its material spanning, with few discernible seams, over twenty years.[18] (If Clara recognized herself in the first theme, she still never much cared for the opening movement.)

So Brahms wrote variants of the Werther story to friends, among them Simrock: "You can put on the title page a picture, namely that of a man with a pistol to his head. Now you can get an idea of the music. For the purpose I will send you my photograph. You can also use a blue coat, yellow trousers, and boots with it." To critic Hermann Deiters: "Now think of a man who is going to commit suicide and for whom nothing else is left."[19]

Why did he explain the piece so much? It was not the only time Brahms hinted to friends about a personal resonance, but this was the most elaborate of his explanations—and more or less the last (and for a piece going back a long time). After the G Major Sextet he had largely moved away from that kind of personal symbolism. He did not want his art inspired by powerful personal experiences, because he did not want the experiences—he hoped to close that kind of unpleasant inspiration with the Alto Rhapsody. So why did he keep hinting about the story behind the C Minor Quartet? Certainly the piece had passionate associations, but there is no discernible indication that they were troubling him at that point—say, no infatuation to dredge up old memories (unless the recent reacquaintance with Elisabet von Herzogenberg had roused a new sense of loss).

One surmise for Brahms's insisting on the Werther connection is that he wanted history to note it. The charge of manipulating the record is one he would never have confessed to—he professed indifference to such matters. Yet history was always on his mind. The first time he heard of someone buying a letter of his for the autograph, he vowed from then on to suppress intimate details in his correspondence. As he observed to friend George Henschel, "A person has to be careful about writing letters. One fine day they get printed!"[20] He took to signing letters "J. Br." to foil autograph collectors.

During the years of his fame Brahms parceled out his life to future generations in all sorts of ways, sometimes by withholding information, sometimes by priming potential biographers with a few discreet facts and caveats. At times, knowing it would be noised around, he went out of his way to provide a personal anecdote about a piece to several people, most notably the story about the C Minor Piano Quartet. Likely the references were authentic, but he may have made a point of them with the public and history in mind. After all, in his covert and desultory way Brahms had always promoted himself shrewdly, finding champions in the highest ranks of musicians and critics. Now to some ambiguous but detectable degree he had begun to do the same with his own history. He was trying to manipulate the future as he manipulated the notes on the page. That the C Minor would come to be called the Werther Quartet was his own, perhaps deliberate, doing.

THIS PERIOD began the heart of the relationship between Brahms and surgeon Theodor Billroth. After one of his crowded days, his grueling rounds at the hospital often followed by a play or a concert and late-night dinner with friends, the insomniac surgeon would sit at his desk and pen long ruminative letters to people like Brahms, Hanslick, and his medical compatriots.[21]

In October 1874, responding to the *Neue Liebeslieder*, he issued the kind of thoughtful response that Brahms treasured, even if at the same time he tended to receive it with a certain patronizing impatience. This surgeon was another exemplar of the ideal amateur for whom Brahms mainly composed, Billroth's responses a model of how Brahms expected to be perceived. In other words, this letter, one of many like it, may stand for the terms—intuitive and analytical, poetic and technical—in which the age and the Austro-German *Grossbürgertum* thought about music.

> The day's work and sorrow is past, and midnight is approaching. I wish that you were here and that we could chat with each other or be silent, just as we pleased. But since you can't be here, you will have to put up with an answer to your good notes in one of my almost unreadable letters. I am very proud that you have sent me your Neue Liebeslieder and that I have seen them *avant la lettre*. You have given me innermost joyous hours. . . . One can say of a beautiful poem really nothing better than, "How beautifully poetic." But when you say about a composition, "How beautifully musical," that means much more. This is really music from the heart. It should only be sung and played together in late hours by good friends. You know, I suppose, that an impresario from Leipzig is traveling about with a quartette of a black and a brown piano player and a white fiddle player, playing your Liebeslieder. . . . I love the romantic, idealistic magic which is spread over all your songs. . . . I can, with you, feel Daumer's verses very deeply. They are like the poetry of Goethe as an old man, more beautiful musically than

beautiful in the way the words express the context. I have the feeling
that here the outermost boundary in the expression of words is occasionally reached, and sometimes exceeded. . . . Wagner's poetry is not
so far removed from this boundary, but moves only toward the edges
of this domain when music accompanies it. You lead poetry out of the
hyper-romantic into the area of the most beautiful and clear musical
feeling.

To all that—there was much more—Brahms made one of his laconic,
grateful, hedging, perceptibly impatient replies:

> Even a long letter from you does not read so badly, but that in this
> case it was not only the length that impressed me, I do not have to tell
> you. It is too bad that I have such a talent for finding good texts—the
> best, the most passionate, or those most like folk verses; but we will
> have to have a word with each other about Daumer. In that matter I am
> somewhat ticklish, in spite of the fact that I know myself a layman in
> the art of verse. I will bring a few poems with me next time so that you
> can see what I find beautiful. But what you have to criticize in Daumer,
> I really would like to hear more clearly!
>
> The praise of me I will stick in my pocket. I can honestly and seri-
> ously say to that—it's too bad about me![22]

So artist and public fortified one another, when music was in its glory.

In fact, having set to music so many of G. F. Daumer's love lyrics,
Brahms had decided a few years before to pay a visit to the aging versi-
fier, as an act of homage. Perhaps he imagined a touching moment, a
heartfelt exchange between colleagues, a new insight into the poems,
maybe the beginning of the sort of easy friendship he had found with another elder poet, Klaus Groth. So Brahms made his pilgrimage to
Würzburg and there, he related to Klaus Groth, "in a quiet room I met
my poet. Ah, he was a little dried-up old man! . . . I soon perceived that
he knew nothing either of me or my compositions, or anything at all of
music. And when I pointed to his ardent, passionate verses, he gestured,
with a tender wave of the hand, to a little old mother almost more withered than himself, saying, 'Ah, I have only loved the one, my wife!'"[23]

The Gesellschaft der Musikfreunde continued to occupy most of
Brahms's time in Vienna. Shortly after his December performance of the
Beethoven *Missa Solemnis* came a letter from Hermann Levi that hardly
suggests the looming breach in their friendship—or maybe marks an attempt to forestall it. Responding to Brahms's duet "Wenn zu der Regen-

wand" Levi gushes, "If only I could tell you how this song has seized and moved me! I wish you were lying in my bed again, and I could sit beside you and stroke your brow—I have a terrible yearning to see you again."[24] Levi was getting carried away in those days, but the main thing carrying him away was Brahms's rival. Shortly afterward came a letter from Levi rhapsodizing over *Götterdämmerung*. Brahms was willing to be generous toward Wagner up to a point, but Levi was passing that point. All that was lacking between them now was a match to light the fuse.

In February 1875, Brahms found enormous, city-wide acclaim with his Gesellschaft performance of *Ein deutsches Requiem*. Next month he mounted the complete Bach *St. Matthew Passion*, a monumental work still rarely heard in those days. Shortly after the Bach performance, he gave notice that he was resigning the Gesellschaft directorship effective at the end of the season.

For an immediate reason he blamed his predecessor, who wanted the job back. Brahms wrote Levi, "It is certainly said in a word: Herbeck! I will neither wrangle with him nor wait until he eases me out." Johann von Herbeck had left the Gesellschaft directorship for the Hofoper and Philharmonic, but in four years there had become disgusted with the intrigues and politics involved in the position. So he was determined to reclaim the Gesellschaft.

Brahms had the power to put up a fight, but he lacked the will. Why should he use his time and energy to resist Herbeck, who was a master intriguer and politician himself? Instead, Brahms took the excuse to bow out. (Herbeck regained the directorship only to die two years later.) Brahms had plenty of unspoken reasons for quitting: the unfinished symphony, his almost embarrassing performance of the *Emperor* that revealed how much his playing had deteriorated (from now on he rarely attempted any concertos but his own), friction with the board over his spending summers incommunicado, a feeling that in his three years and eighteen concerts with the Gesellschaft he had sufficiently made his mark on the city. Meanwhile his experience on the podium had solidified his own understanding of the orchestra and his confidence in composing for it. Mainly, though, he quit because he wanted his freedom back.

His last concert as director of the Gesellschaft der Musikfreunde came on April 18, 1875, with a matinee performance of Max Bruch's *Odysseus*. History would hardly embrace Bruch's oratorio, but it went over handsomely in the Musikverein. After the concert, baritone George Henschel, who soloed in the performance, observed Brahms's boredom and irritation during a farewell ceremony that included a long poetic eulogy. Brahms responded to it all with a gruff "Thank you very much," picked up his grandly inscribed certificate, and headed for the door. A celebratory dinner that night was more his style. Still, he parted on good terms, remaining an honorary member of the Gesellschaft committee, a position that gave him great weight in local musical affairs. Thereafter, whenever Brahms attended concerts at the Musikverein, he sat in the director's box. His tenure with the Gesellschaft der Musikfreunde marked the high point of its history as a performing organization.

On his way to summer quarters, Brahms stopped off in Munich for a baneful rendezvous with Hermann Levi. At one point during the visit Levi was making a comparison between the operas of Wagner and his predecessor Gluck, to the advantage of Wagner, when Brahms interrupted: "One doesn't pronounce those two names like that, one after the other!"[25] After perhaps adding some more personal and insulting things Brahms stalked out of the house, and next day left town without saying good-bye. Levi wrote a dignified letter about it, reminding Brahms that he had always deplored Liszt and his crowd: "The fact that I shun even the most distant intercourse with the Futurists' band, and that I am thoroughly hated by them, ought to make you consider whether I really deserve your truly harsh words."[26] Brahms did not reply.

They made a few gestures at restoring the friendship, and visited later that summer, but each man knew a boundary had been passed. For Brahms, acceptance of Wagner was one thing for a friend of his; Hans von Bülow, Franz Wüllner, and Joachim all conducted Wagner, and singers George Henschel and Luise Dustmann were famed for Wagnerian performances. But Levi's intoxication was another matter. Besides, neither man needed the other as much as before, and probably both of them knew it. Now Brahms had Bülow on his side, and the brilliant and self-destructive Levi was turning into the figure Peter Gay calls "Richard Wagner's favorite conductor and Jewish whipping-boy."[27]

BRAHMS SETTLED for the summer of 1875 at Ziegelhausen near Heidelberg, in the house of painter Anton Hanno. The usual train of visitors showed up, as he reported to Karl Reinthaler: "Levi and Dessoff were here today, tonight Frank [a Viennese conductor] is coming, tomorrow some charming lady singers from Mannheim—in short, life is only too gay."[28] When old friend Franz Wüllner invited him to a performance of *Ein deutsches Requiem* in Munich, Brahms gently declined: "Your letter was a great temptation to leave my pretty house . . . but all the same I stay sitting here, and from time to time write highly useless pieces in order not to have to look into the stern face of a symphony."[29]

The "useless" efforts included final polish on the C Minor Piano Quartet and the Five Duets of Opus 66. And he composed the String Quartet in B♭ Major—his most buoyant, with its dancing rhythms and droll themes. Joachim read it over in June with his group and professed great pleasure. Clara wrote Brahms that the end, into which he interweaves the jaunty opening theme of the quartet, "is too fascinating for words with its delightful, mocking conclusion."[30] For Brahms and for his friends, the B♭ was like a shout of liberation after the austerities of the earlier two quartets. Years later he admitted to Joachim that it was his favorite of the lot. Hanslick preferred it too, as "more cheerful, clearer, more human."[31] Brahms chose as favorite, in other words, the quartet in which he escaped his anxiety before the medium and managed to have fun with it. And with that, he quit while he was ahead—there were no more string quartets.

Another visitor in Ziegelhausen that summer was Anselm Feuerbach, who was vacationing nearby. Brahms had met the artist in 1867 in Baden. A nephew of philosopher Ludwig Feuerbach, he had studied in Antwerp and Paris and in his maturity arrived at a somber neoclassic style, his subjects usually taken from Greek mythology or Italian literature.[32] Brahms came to admire Feuerbach more than any other painter alive, seeing him as embodying virtues Brahms also aspired to: clarity, restraint, subtle lyricism, respect for tradition, an aesthetic that exalted form over color. Eventually it would be Brahms who encouraged Julius Allgeyer to write his biography of Feuerbach, published in 1894.

The two artists had a long association and were nominally friends, even if never entirely comfortable with each other. Brahms not only admired Feuerbach's work but also his person, his classically beautiful features and ringing voice.[33] Yet for all his admiration, Brahms could never break through the painter's personality. Vain, defensive, a womanizer, nearly as dandyish as Wagner, Feuerbach proclaimed himself a genius and demanded the world acknowledge it.[34] Though he had a circle of acolytes, the larger public failed to take its cue.

Against Brahms's advice, Feuerbach came to Vienna in 1873 to take a position as Instructor of Historical Painting at the Imperial Academy of Plastic Arts. What happened to him during his three years in the city was exactly what Brahms predicted: the public diverted by the bright, cherub-ridden trivialities of Hans Makart had little patience for Feuerbach's muted mythology, and that public could be brutal. Writes biographer Richard Specht: "The Viennese Feuerbach baiting takes its place worthily beside similar diversions . . . : the Bruckner baiting, the Hugo Wolf baiting, the Klimt baiting, the Mahler baiting."[35] Having some experience with public scorn but far more resistance, Brahms watched Vienna ruin his friend's career and health and could do nothing about it.

At length Feuerbach in his rage and frustration would turn on Brahms. The moment came during work on a portrait to which Brahms, who resisted such things, had agreed out of respect for the painter. As he dutifully showed up again and again at Feuerbach's studio for sittings, he became alarmed over an epic painting called *The Battle of the Amazons*, with which the painter proposed to conquer the city and expose the vulgarities of his rival Makart. Uncertain of the validity of his own response, Brahms brought in Klaus Groth to have a look at the giant canvas. Groth confirmed it: in his opinion this was a misconceived picture, in any case dangerous to put before the Viennese. When Brahms gently pressed Feuerbach to hold it back, the painter treated that expression of concern as a betrayal. "Another evening spoiled by Brahms," he wrote in his journal. He turned the unfinished portrait to the wall and never took it up again.

When he finally exhibited *The Battle of the Amazons* it gained Feuerbach nothing but humiliation. "A storm broke over my head," he wrote, "by which I could at least reassure myself as to the importance of my pictures. I could not sit down to table without finding jests, raillery, caricature . . . beside my plate. . . . I was told that everyone, from the professor to the porter's boy, was laughing at my bad picture." Relations between him and Brahms reeled but did not quite break. When Feuerbach made a visit to Rome in winter 1875, he noted gratefully that Brahms showed up to lend him a fur coat for the trip. After suffering a nervous breakdown, the painter left Vienna in 1876. He died broken in Nürnburg, four years later. That Brahms never lost his admiration and affection would be demonstrated by his response to Feuerbach's death—*Nänie*, a somberly beautiful setting of Schiller verses with their unforgettable opening line: *Even the beautiful must die!*

THE MELANCHOLY STORY of Feuerbach's final collapse lay in the future in summer 1875, when the two visited and Brahms kept himself busy and cheerful in Ziegelhausen—free of the Gesellschaft, still putting off the symphony. He came back to Vienna in mid-September with good spirits persisting, and in November manned the piano with Hellmesberger's group for the premiere of the C Minor Piano Quartet. Among the audience at the Musikverein sat Richard and Cosima Wagner.

They had come as a symbolic and conciliatory gesture. That year had seen a skirmish between the two men, settled peaceably through

Brahms's magnanimity. It had to do with the manuscript of the "Venus-berg" music from *Tannhäuser,* which pianist Karl Tausig had presented to Brahms over a decade before. Naturally the score became a valued item in Brahms's manuscript collection. An early attempt by Wagner to re-claim it had been blocked by Tausig, but the virtuoso had died (at thirty) in 1871, and Wagner had not forgotten the matter. Brahms's possession of the score seemed a standing outrage.

In June 1875, Brahms received a peremptory demand from Wagner to give him the manuscript ("it can only be of value to you as a curiosity"). Brahms made a studiously chilly reply ("I do not collect 'curiosities'") agreeing to hand it over, but not without compensation: "If you are go-ing to rob my manuscript collection of such a treasure, it would please me very much if you would enrich my library with something else of yours, such as the *Meistersinger.*"

At first Wagner was livid, exclaiming to Levi, "If a lawyer wrote to me like that—so what? But an artist!" Finally though, Wagner responded with a slightly warmer note and sent a deluxe printed copy of *Das Rheingold,* disingenuously inscribed "To Herr Johannes Brahms, a well-conditioned substitute for a sloppy manuscript." Probably Wagner was befuddled by Brahms's response, which was entirely sincere: "Your en-closure has given me such extraordinary pleasure that I can hardly man-age with these few words to express to you my heartfelt thanks for the splendid gift that I owe to your generosity."[36]

Thus with a show of generosity Wagner and Cosima dutifully turned up at the premiere of Brahms's quartet. Maybe Brahms felt some of the bad feelings that he and Joachim had sparked with their manifesto of 1860 had been resolved by his good behavior. That he made himself minutely acquainted with the *Rheingold* score is shown in corrections he entered in the trombone parts.[37]

Brahms's behavior may have created something of a truce, but if so it lasted only until satirist Daniel Spitzer published in the *Neue Freie Presse* some astounding letters of Wagner's to his one-time Viennese milliner Bertha Goldwag. In them Wagner lovingly details his requirements for deep carpets, embroidered cushions, plush chairs and poufs, satin breeches with matching fur-lined jackets and Oriental slippers, reams of silk and velvet wall hangings, and silk dressing gowns by the dozen.[38] (At the time he ordered these luxuries he was completely broke.) In the cafés of Vienna the publication of the letters elicited the amusement Spitzer had hoped for. It was as if Wagner had satirized himself better than any-one else could. Since Spitzer was one of Brahms's circle, Wagner was convinced that Brahms had put the satirist up to publishing the letters.

Well, Wagner may have been right—though that sort of trick was more Wagner's style than Brahms's. In any case, it put relations between the two men back on their normally bad terms.

Through an admirer Brahms later came into possession of the letters to the milliner and liked to give dramatic readings of them, with great gusto, to his friends. Wagner was never likely to become reconciled to Brahms anyway; contempt for rivals was axiomatic with him. Not long before, his young disciple Friedrich Nietzsche had undergone a spasm of Brahms-fervor, mainly over the *Triumphlied*. When the philosopher went so far as to press the piece on his mentor, a tragicomic scene ensued. As Wagner mockingly recalled it:

> When I entered his room at the hotel I saw a suspicious-looking little red book, some songlet of triumph or of destiny by Brahms, with which [Nietzsche] made ready to attack me. But I was not going to have any of it. Towards evening the Professor came to Wahnfried [Wagner's palace at Bayreuth] and behold, he had the accursed red book under his arm. He now had a mind to put it on the piano desk and play it to me. . . . At last I became violent. . . . I was rude and—heaven knows how—Nietzsche was thrown out.

It is said that on this occasion the philosopher crowed to Wagner, "Look, that is absolute music, yes, *absolute music!*" (Nietzsche owned a well-thumbed copy of Hanslick's *On Beauty in Music*, which Wagner had denounced as written "in the interest of music-Jewry.") Nietzsche's short-lived passion for Brahms and his futile attempt to bring the two composers into détente did perhaps mark a stage of the disciple's apostasy, as Wagner obviously suspected. But the course of this odd triangle would continue to run unpredictably in the next years.

Now THAT HE WAS NO LONGER tied to the Gesellschaft, Brahms's winter performing schedule actually accelerated. January 1876 saw a tour of Holland that enhanced his already considerable prestige there. At the end of a deliriously applauded program in Utrecht featuring his performance of the D Minor Concerto, there was a ceremony emblematic of the time: two beautiful girls marched to the platform carrying cushions bearing wreaths, one decked with ribbons in Austria's black and gold, the other with Dutch red, white, and blue. With embarrassment and pleasure Brahms brandished the wreaths to the cheering throngs.

In Utrecht he stayed with the family of Professor Wilhelm Engelmann—like Billroth a music-loving physician—and his pianist wife Emma. To Engelmann went the dedication of the B♭ Major String Quartet. Fellow quartet dedicatee Billroth revealed much of his feeling for art when he wrote Engelmann: "I am afraid these dedications will keep our names in memory longer than the best work we have done; for us not very complimentary, but beautiful for humanity, which, with the correct instinct, considers art more immortal than science."[39]

After Holland, Brahms toured in Germany, enjoying the usual interludes of sociable dining and drinking. From an evening in Koblenz at the house of Geheimrath Wegeler came a famous anecdote when the host presented the company a prized bottle with the conceit, "What Brahms is among composers, so is this Rauenthaler among wines!" Instantly Brahms's voice was heard: "Ah, well let's have a bottle of *Bach*, then." After a matinee in which he performed with some Frankfurt musicians, the Princess of Hesse-Barchfeld presented Brahms with a silver laurel wreath, each leaf engraved with the title of one of his works. He was tickled to find the name of the minuscule "Wiegenlied" (Lullaby) engraved alongside the monumental *Triumphlied.*[40]

Awards of all sorts turned up steadily now. That April, Joachim wrote that England's Royal Academy was offering an honorary Doctor of Music. Brahms was agreeable to the idea until he learned that he must receive the degree in person. Suspicious of the British as of most other foreigners, still childishly fearful at the prospect of the Channel crossing, Brahms let the idea slide. (Joachim conducted the First Symphony from manuscript at Cambridge the next year.)

After a frenetic winter of performing, in June 1876 Brahms sought out his seasonal idyll, this time choosing Sassnitz on the Isle of Rügen. He found a wild, heroic landscape with chalk cliffs plunging to a crashing sea—just the thing to inspire a symphony. To Clara and family he wrote:

> Rügen is really very, very beautiful, apart from the dear old Low German, in which I am at last able to indulge again. There is the most beautiful forest coming right down to the sea. . . . My room is beautifully situated, my window looks out on to the sea, the village straggles up the hill to my left, and cornfields in front of me for the present stand in for the murmuring roll of the waves.[41]

To baritone and song composer George Henschel, who of late had become a good friend, Brahms dispatched an invitation: "I should find it charming if you could soon decide on coming. We shall not disturb each other in the least. For you the place swarms with ladies. In *your* free hours you can *com*pose songs for them, the badness of which I in turn will *ex*pose in *my* free hours! It is quite beautiful here and the bathing enchanting."

Around then Brahms received, simultaneously from Elisabet and from Heinrich von Herzogenberg, each unaware of the other's efforts, copies of Heinrich's new Variations on a Theme of Johannes Brahms. With that began a relationship beautiful and excruciating. For the first of many occasions in regard to Heinrich's compositions, Brahms squirmed out of forced compliments in his reply. Instead, he turned to a sighing evocation of Elisabet: "Forgive me if my thanks begin, and my critical remarks end, sooner than you would like. How can I be disinterested, when, as I open the duet and play it in imagination, I have a distinct vision of a slender, golden-haired figure in blue velvet seated on my right? If I say any more I shall offend one or the other of you." There followed a brief disquisition on variation form ("Beethoven treats it with extraordinary severity") intended as a lesson to Heinrich.[42]

Soon George Henschel was in Sassnitz happily diving for pebbles in the surf with his host. Despite the high spirits, the task Brahms had set himself in those cheery surroundings was as terrifying as he ever faced. With the heroic landscape of Rügen as provocation, he was determined to finish the C Minor Symphony at last. The question of how to handle the finale had been the lingering dilemma, but now he knew what he wanted to do with it. He completed the symphony that August, while staying near Clara in Lichtental.

WHEN AFTER ITS PREMIERE Hans von Bülow, with his gift for historic quips, dubbed Brahms's First Symphony "The Tenth," he encapsulated what was on everyone's mind. Brahms's relation to Beethoven had long been manifest to the public (his debt to Schubertian lyricism less so). That spirit shone unmistakably in the First Symphony, from the monumental sound of the orchestra to the chorale theme of the last movement—the latter so inescapably reminiscent of the Ninth Symphony finale that Brahms could only snap in response: "Any jackass can see that!" Many saw too that this was the first truly historic symphony since Beethoven's Ninth, which is to say that with it Brahms restored to full viability a genre that Wagner, among others, had pronounced dead.[43]

Yet with all that looming history as a given, the C Minor is one of the most innovative symphonies that the later nineteenth century produced.

Once more, and never more powerfully, Brahms achieved a paradoxical resolution of conservative and progressive elements, and did it with a magisterial finality that no symphonist of stature would ever match again.

The piece begins with a searing, anguished adagio, with relentless pounding timpani. That extended introduction, going through several stages, poses the essential "plot" of the First Symphony: call it *fate*.[44] Brahms added this defining introduction some time after he first showed the movement to Clara Schumann in 1862, when he had a better conception of the overall expressive shape. Besides posing the great question that sparks the dramatic unfolding of the symphony, the introduction lays out much of its thematic material—notably a "fan" of chromatic lines, striving upward in cellos and violins, sinking downward in winds and violas, all pervaded by the ominous pulse of the drum:

It is one of the most spine-tingling beginnings of any symphony, plunging us into a world dark, questioning, shifting, striving toward some indefinable goal. The intensity of its question is carried into the body of the movement, a surging allegro in $\frac{6}{8}$, scherzo-like in tempo and rhythmic momentum but tumultuous in expression. This is music first sketched in the early 1860s or before; in feel it is the Brahms of the Werther years, the opening of the D Minor Concerto, the passion and frustration of Young Kreisler. *Fate! Fate!*

In the first movement we hear the fully developed Brahmsian orchestral sound. There are clear connections to the Classical past, especially in the scoring of the winds, but made monumental in sound partly by octave doublings and the steady thickening of bassoons. (As Beethoven did in the Fifth Symphony, Brahms saves the trombones for a memorable entry in the last movement.) Yet for all the richness of sound there is a general clarity of texture that projects a continually contrapuntal conception.

That conception is critical in the beginning of the allegro, in which Brahms departs from the tradition, in a sonata-form exposition, of exposing the principal theme and then a contrasting one. Instead, from the outset there is a *double theme*, a contrapuntal joining of two ideas from the introduction[45]: a restlessly surging line in thirds and sixths (*b*), and under it the rising chromatic "fate" theme of the opening measures (*a*):

These ideas, plus a rushing figure (*c*), dominate the movement, in continually new juxtapositions and inversions, here tender, there searing. From these, other ideas grow: racing triplets outline a minor third that dominates the end of the exposition (under them is an inversion of the (*b*) theme); then those triplets are boiled down to lurching minor thirds. In the storms of the development the racing triplets become imperious repeated notes—the fate-motive of the timpani at the beginning, echo of the four-note fate-motive of Beethoven's Fifth. At the end of the movement—another innovation—the tempo slows to a pensive coda that looks back to the introduction and the fateful drumbeats. There Brahms in effect reopens the dramatic question of the introduction, and leaves it hanging in the last chords.

The *Andante sostenuto* provides lyrical contrast to the stormy first movement, as in Beethoven's Fifth. The essential plot is woven into its main theme with reminiscence of the introduction's chromatic fan. (This reference—in measures 5 through 8—was added after the first performances, when Brahms also simplified the form of the movement from rondo to A B A.[46]) This slow movement ends with an exquisitely longing melody in high solo violin, anticipating the intimate, chamber-like scoring that in the later symphonies relieves the monumentality of the full-orchestra writing.

The key of the slow movement is E major, a major third up from the previous C minor/major. The next movement, continuing the pattern of third-relations, is in A♭ major. Marked *Un poco Allegretto e grazioso* (A little fast and gracefully), short and tripartite, it forms another contrast to the monumental first and last movements. It is one of the intermezzos with which Brahms replaced the scherzo in many later works. (Here the first movement is closest to a symphonic scherzo in rhythm and tempo.) A blithe clarinet tune begins the movement, the effect reminiscent of the serenades of Brahms's Detmold years; the theme is stated and then, in the consequent phrase, turned exactly upside down. The middle section, dominated by grand flowing woodwind and brass lines, has a touch of fatalism in its insistent repeated notes.

So in layout (if less in material) the symphony's movements recall Beethoven: serious opening movement in moderate-to-fast tempo, contrasting lyrical slow movement, relatively light third (though not the usual minuet or scherzo), then a "heroic" allegro finale. In the 1860s, Brahms had first solved his uncertainties about last movements with the "Hungarian" style wedded to rondo form. That approach did not suit him for a symphony finale, though it did for concertos. For a symphonic last movement he wanted something more serious. After years of mulling it over he finally conceived an approach for the C Minor, but one that placed an enormous burden on his imagination.

The symphonies of Haydn and his time were "top-heavy"—the first movement the weightiest, then lighter middle movements, then the finale usually a "last dance" in tone: a light, spirited movement usually in rondo form (A B A C A, etc.). Mozart in his last three symphonies began to build up the intensity of the finale, but (except perhaps in the *Jupiter*) the first movement remained the most substantial. From the *Eroica* onward, Beethoven added weight and intensity to the finale, in the process quickening the rhythm of the third movement with the creation of the scherzo, until his middle movements hung suspended between the pillars of the first movement and finale. Following Mozart's cue, Beethoven thus changed the "last dance" idea of the symphonic finale into an *apotheosis*. The end result of that process was the epic choral finale of the Ninth Symphony.

Picking up mainly from the Ninth, in the C Minor Symphony Brahms continued in a logical but supremely difficult direction. He inverted the top-heavy symphony of Haydn's day, making the finale the weightiest movement, a culmination of the motivic and dramatic unfolding—the "characters" and "plot"—of the entire symphony. To that end he made the middle movements less intense, the third lightest of all. Following the daunting assignment he had given himself, to intensify between first movement and last, Brahms was now obliged to write a finale of extraordinary impact.

He begins the finale with an unprecedented gesture: an extended slow introduction, calling to mind the introduction of the first movement. That is its function, to return to the dark intensity with which the symphony began, the fatalistic question it poses and leaves unanswered. In the finale, though, the terms of the introduction are new: the timpani rumbling rather than pounding, the main theme a keening minor one that is about to undergo a remarkable transformation into major:

So the plot of the symphony, posed in the searing introduction that begins it, reaches its denouement in the finale. As Reinhold Brinkmann puts it: "Brahms [takes up] that 'plot archetype' of nineteenth-century music which might be paraphrased as the resolution of a conflict of ideas through an inner formal process aimed toward a liberating ending—in a nutshell, the 'positive' overcoming of a 'negative' principle."[47] As in Beethoven's Third, Fifth, and Ninth Symphonies, Brahms's First is a symbolic journey from darkness to light, from fatalistic uncertainty to apotheosis, from tragedy to joyous liberation.

Yet in taking up that archetype Brahms finds fresh ways to realize it. With the F Minor Piano Quintet he had mastered the Beethovenian sense of dramatic plot in his own terms, and carried that personal interpretation into the First Symphony. The final liberation of Beethoven's Fifth, for example, begins with the outbreak of the finale—resolving C minor to C major—and ends in the coda with the falling fate-motive of the famous opening transformed into a triumphant rising figure.

Brahms's transformation in the First occurs instead in the introduction of the finale, when after stormy minor-key rustlings a horn emerges in a soaring C major, like sun breaking through clouds.

It is the alpenhorn theme Brahms had sent to Clara on a postcard in 1868, as a gesture of reconciliation in a stormy time between them. Here it is the great resolution of the symphony, presented as a transformation from minor to major—an old trick done a million times, but here as fresh and moving as if Brahms invented it. More than that, to accompany the horn he added an extraordinary shimmering tremolo in muted strings, creating an atmosphere Debussy would have been proud to own (and probably, in Brahms's case as in Debussy's, owing much to Wagner).

If the keynotes of the First Symphony's plot are *intensification* and *joy overcoming darkness and fatality*, Brahms demands of himself continually fresh, striking ideas in the finale. And with a marvelously sure hand and strength of inspiration, he found them. After the first horn call is echoed by a soaring flute, Brahms brings in trombones for the first time, joining bassoons in a quiet, archaic, chorale-like moment like a benediction that floats effortlessly from D minor to B♭ to F to C:

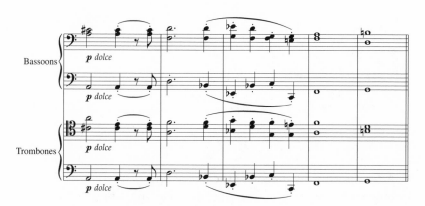

In this symphony, as in most of his music now, Brahms no longer overtly draws on his own life and sufferings, but there is still a personal resonance in those two gestures. Surely the alpenhorn call suggested to his mind *Clara;* and in the trombone chorale the upper notes A E F re-call F-A-E, *frei aber einsam,* and Joachim. Such Young Kreisler note-cabala, however, if intended at all, no longer determines the music or its meaning, either for us or for Brahms. His terms now are the terms of music in its dynamic, self-creating form.

After the trombone chorale the alpenhorn theme returns, horns calling to each other as if in an Alpine valley, within the shimmering sunlight of strings. The music reaches a pause like a held breath. Then comes a chorale theme in strings (above), its melody transformed from the dark minor of the introduction, unforgettable from the first time one hears it. It has a noble simplicity that like its model in Beethoven's Ninth was written to intimate the highest qualities in life—and written to conquer the world.[48] The turn from darkness has already been made, with the emergence of the alpenhorn. The chorale theme then is like a revelation on top of an epiphany, a melody of extraordinary folklike directness that bears a mysterious power. (Still, its sighing accompaniment at *x* is a transformation of the fateful chromatic lines of the first movement.)

For all this melody's echoes of Beethoven's Ninth Symphony theme, however—its position in the finale, its hymnlike quality, its scoring—the chorale is still unique. Beethoven's theme is joyous and finally heroic. Brahms's theme is gentle and noble, its second half touched by his *moll-Dur* yearning, the whole more lyrically sustained than Beethoven's. Once again we find in Brahms's music something manifestly inspired by the past that he carries to an utterly individual place.

What follows the finale's chorale theme is one of Brahms's most extraordinary personal adaptations of traditional form. The music unfolds as a combination of rondo and sonata: the return of the C major chorale theme after letter H seems to be a repeat of the exposition but isn't—more like a return of a rondo theme, quickly modulating to the distant key of E♭ before dissolving into what turns out to be more or less the development.[49] The development features a thematic dialectic in which the chorale melody is systematically transformed into the alpenhorn theme:

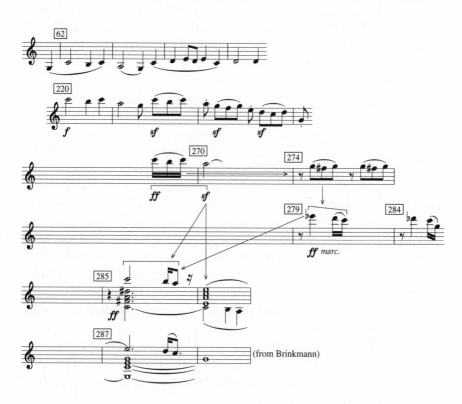

(from Brinkmann)

The end of that process of transformation is the recapitulation after letter N, which therefore presents the alpenhorn rather than the expected chorale theme. (The second theme recapitulates normally, even in the "right" key of C, at measure 302.)[50]

The finale has moments of conflict, with Brahms more ingenious than ever in dislocating the meter to intensify climaxes—either displacing the downbeat or leaving even the pulse uncertain for long stretches. At the high point of the pealing, ecstatic coda, what Brahms turns to as his final apotheosis is not the string chorale or the alpenhorn theme, but rather a full-orchestra proclamation of the introduction's trombone chorale. It is like an eruption of holy joy, capping both the symphony's progress from darkness to light and Brahms's personal triumph.[51]

The year he completed the First Symphony is the same year Wagner brought the titanic *Der Ring des Nibelungen* to the stage, in his own theater at Bayreuth. Brahms's achievement was no less stunning in his terms: to compose at the top of his skill and imagination despite the tramp of giants thundering around him, to epitomize his singular integration of Classical formalism and Romantic expression, to integrate Western musical technique stretching from Palestrina through Bach to Haydn and Mozart, and symphonic form from Haydn through Beethoven to Schubert, Mendelssohn, and Schumann. In sheer ambition, tenacity of purpose, and power of expression, what Brahms achieved in the forty-four minutes of the C Minor Symphony rivals Wagner's achievement in the twelve hours of the *Ring*.

IN AUGUST 1876, as Brahms was finishing the symphony, Eduard Hanslick journeyed to Bayreuth to review the first performance of the *Ring*. He conceded it to be "a remarkable development in cultural history," admired bits and pieces of the music and Wagner's "astonishing mastery of his orchestral technique." But in the end Hanslick deplored the drama and the "repugnant and absurd" device of the magic potion; he declared Siegfried "not a hero but a puppet," called the pattern of leitmotivs "of meagre melodic and rhythmic substance," complained of the "indigestible German . . . offered as poetry," and on and on.[52] While sharing some of Hanslick's sentiments about the *Ring*, Brahms stayed apart from the fray, but meanwhile found himself increasingly fascinated with Wagner and what he had wrought.

Also as Brahms was completing the C Minor, he received an offer of the position of music director in Düsseldorf—Robert Schumann's old post. After months of mulling it over and exchanging flocks of letters with most of his friends and with town authorities, he said no. The best explanation he could offer was in a letter to Billroth:

> My chief objections to accepting are also of a childish nature. I must remain silent regarding some. Perhaps they include the good restaurants and winehouses in Vienna and the, to me, disagreeable and rough tone in general in Düsseldorf. In Vienna one can be a bachelor without any more discussion. In a little city, an old bachelor is a caricature. I do not plan to marry, and have some grounds left to be a little frightened by the fair sex.[53]

At this point Brahms was actually still considering the Düsseldorf offer, and told Billroth he was planning a second symphony as a farewell to Vienna. As it turned out, he did not need the farewell but wrote the symphony anyway, and wrote it to suit the Viennese.

Naturally Brahms took the First Symphony to Clara as parts of it were done. At the end of September, in Baden-Baden, he played her the outer movements on piano. She expressed tentative approval in her journal: "These two . . . are grand, full of life and of thought from end to end; only certain of the melodies seem to me rather thin." On a drive one afternoon he provoked her ire by defending Wagner. (The previous year Clara had seen *Tristan und Isolde* and declared it "the most repulsive thing I ever saw or heard in my life."[54]) During this visit she also observed, "I have often been amazed . . . that he can so delight in the old masters before Bach . . . for with the exception of certain isolated passages they are not interesting, musically. But always I love to watch Johannes when he is losing himself in a work of that sort, there is something touching about him."[55]

Finally on October 10 Brahms played her the complete symphony. For herself after that first exposure she said, "I cannot deny that I was grieved and depressed, for it does not seem to me to compare with other works of his. . . . I miss the sweeping melodies."[56] Clara tempered her response to Brahms in person, but her lack of enthusiasm could not have escaped him. He decided to offer the premiere to Otto Dessoff, now conducting the ducal orchestra in Karlsruhe where Levi had once presided. Brahms knew the conductor from his years with the Vienna Hofoper and Philharmonic, and had no great admiration for his abilities. But his intention was to have the C Minor heard at first in a relatively small town with a relatively good orchestra. If the results turned out embarrassing, the repercussions would be more containable in Karlsruhe.

Brahms meanwhile played cat-and-mouse with publisher Simrock, who failed to take the hint when Brahms wrote him of a lovely symphony left hanging in the trees and cliffs of Rügen. Receiving no response, Brahms wrote Simrock in disgust either real or mock,

> Too bad that you are not a music director. Otherwise you could have a symphony. It will be performed on the 4th [of November] at Karlsruhe. I expect from you and other friendly publishers a nice present in recognition of my not bothering them with such things.[57]

At that point Simrock got the message and hastened to snap up the work. From the mid-1870s on, the publisher was to claim nearly all Brahms's new pieces (*Nänie* the main exception), and eventually bought from Breitkopf & Härtel the early works in their catalog.[58]

Given the complexity of the music, the Karlsruhe premiere of the C Minor Symphony on November 4 was surprisingly well received. Already a number of other cities were eager to hear it. First came Mannheim, then Munich and Levi's orchestra, Brahms conducting both performances. The Mannheimers were polite, but Munich not the least receptive to this symphony nor to Brahms generally. This was Wagner's town. Levi had serious reservations of his own, writing Clara, "The last movement is probably the greatest thing he has yet created in the instrumental field; the first movement comes next. But about the two middle movements I have certain doubts. . . . They seem to belong in a serenade or a suite rather than in such a spacious symphony." To the conductor's complaints about the middle, Brahms replied laconically, "the finale must be considered." Levi missed, or had no sympathy for, the realignment Brahms had wrought on symphonic form. Their visit during the Munich rehearsals was the last time they set eyes on each other.

Finally came the first Vienna hearing, Brahms conducting the Philharmonic. Billroth returned the score of the symphony with words encouraging and astute, though he went beyond his mandate in advising Brahms how to rehearse his own piece:

> The last movement I have conquered fully. It seems to me one of the greatest and most glorious of your endings. . . . That the whole symphony has a somewhat similar emotional groundwork as Beethoven's Ninth occurred to me in my study of it. And yet . . . your own artistic individuality stands out clearly. . . . I would lay the greatest weight in the rehearsals on the introduction of the first and the last movements . . . they are the most difficult of all the parts of your work to grasp. . . . I repeat my invitation of Thursday evening to eat oysters with you and Hanslick after the concert.

There were more raves from Billroth after the first rehearsal. Brahms, probably in an ecstasy of nervous anxiety, seized on the kind words like a drowning man and wrote Billroth a poignant letter:

> I wish there were two words . . . to tell you very distinctly how thankful I am to you. . . . I would not like to say that a little composing is vain labor and trouble and only a continual nuisance and outrage, that nothing better will come of it. You may scarcely believe how wonderful it is and how it warms my heart to find the understanding and sympathy which you feel. In that moment, one does believe that's the best thing about composing and all . . . connected with it.[59]

On December 17, 1876, Vienna received the symphony respectfully if a little coolly. Brahms knew that this reception—similar to that in Karlsruhe, Mannheim, and eventually Leipzig[60]—was the best he could hope for and better than he could have expected, with a work as hard to swallow as this. (It would have depressed him at that point to know that during his lifetime Vienna never really warmed to the C Minor.) Hanslick's review of the Vienna performance, written after his postconcert oyster dinner with Billroth and the composer, probably spoke for many in the city:

> Seldom, if ever, has the entire musical world awaited a composer's first symphony with such tense anticipation. . . . But the greater the public expectation and the more importunate the demand for a new symphony, the more deliberate and scrupulous was Brahms. . . . The new symphony is so earnest and complex, so utterly unconcerned with common effects, that it hardly lends itself to quick understanding. . . . Even the layman will immediately recognize it as one of the most distinctive and magnificent works of the symphonic literature. . . . Brahms recalls Beethoven's symphonic style not only in his individually spiritual and suprasensual expression, the beautiful breadth of his melodies . . . but also—and above all—in the manly and noble seriousness of the whole. Brahms seems to favor too one-sidedly the great and the serious, the difficult and the complex, at the expense of sensuous beauty. . . . Having relieved myself of these minor reservations, I can continue in the jubilant manner in which I began. The new symphony of Brahms is a possession of which the nation may be proud, an inexhaustible fountain of sincere pleasure and fruitful study.[61]

In other words, as Brahms of course realized, Hanslick was making something of a disingenuous case for a work he did not particularly like. Seven years later, reviewing the Third Symphony, Hanslick called the First "almost pathological . . . the expression of a suffering, abnormally agitated individual."[62] Brahms understood that like most Viennese, Hanslick preferred pleasant, pretty stuff. On his next symphonic outing he would provide them something closer to that.

If things were nonetheless going better than he had allowed himself to hope, his foreboding about every new performance is shown in a note of warning to his hosts Heinrich and Elisabet von Herzogenberg, as he prepared to leave Vienna for the Leipzig premiere: "Three days before the concert I begin to sweat and drink camomile tea; after the fiasco (at the Gewandhaus) attempts at suicide, and so on. You shall behold the lengths to which an exasperated composer will go!"[63]

Yet amazingly enough, Leipzig was generally receptive to the symphony on January 14, 1877. Clara, who heard it live for the first time there, called the effect

> grand, overwhelming; the last movement, with its inspired introduction, made an extraordinary impression on me . . . then it gradually brightens in the most marvellous manner until it breaks into the sunny *motif* of the last movement, which makes one's heart expand like a breath of spring air after the long, dreary days of winter. . . . The Leipzig audience behaved as it always does—respectfully; enthusiasm was shown only by a few.[64]

Brahms was content with respect; he could wait for the piece to settle in. And certainly it did, at least outside Vienna. The C Minor Symphony may in some ways be less seamless and sophisticated than Brahms's later orchestral works, but it became his most popular and one of the most beloved of all symphonies—mainly due to the beauty of its themes, the lyrical charm of the inner movements, and the electric emotionalism of the outer ones. Meanwhile, the piece in one blow (Bruckner being still largely offstage) resurrected the genre of the symphony from years of failure, made it once again the king of musical forms, and so in some degree made possible the achievements of Dvořák, Mahler, Elgar, Sibelius, Nielsen, Ives, and generations of symphonists to come. Carl Dahlhaus wrote that with Brahms's First begins "the second age of the symphony."

For himself, Brahms knew what he had accomplished: he had wrestled with the giants. If he had not beaten them at their game and could never beat them, he had at least respectably held his own and added to music something genuinely new and manifestly powerful. In a sense, after that he had nothing left to prove, either to the public or to himself, unless he proposed to test his mettle on an opera. That the rest of his career was hardly an anticlimax is a sign of his continuing tenacity of purpose. But if Brahms had surpassed himself with the First Symphony, he had done it for the last time.

CHAPTER SEVENTEEN

———

Late Idyll

IT WAS IN THE MIDDLE 1870S that Brahms befriended baritone George Henschel, as he would do with several promising young musicians over the next decades. While he never accepted formal composition students and disdained disciples, Brahms enjoyed having a circle of men around him and liked to encourage talent. Few of his protégés had a career to compare with Henschel's. A superb concert baritone, Henschel had been engaged by Brahms to sing in Gesellschaft der Musikfreunde performances. Also a composer and conductor, he would eventually be called to Boston as the new Symphony's first music director. Henschel published a diary of his encounters with Brahms that provides a striking sketch of the composer in his prime—still beardless, but in the long high tide of his art that began with the First Symphony.[1]

Brahms was getting stout then, in his forties, the long blond hair turning sandy. While the truculent underlip was soon to disappear under foliage, the forget-me-not twinkle of his eyes—kindly or roguish in a good hour, steely in a bad—lasted to the end. Henschel seemed usually to find Brahms in jolly moods. One of their first encounters came when the two were soloing with the orchestra in Koblenz in 1876. At the public dress rehearsal Henschel was pained to hear the famous man losing notes by the handful in the Schumann Piano Concerto. Next day he found Brahms alone in the concert hall, red-faced with frustration as he belabored the piano. "Really, this is too bad," Brahms groaned.

> Those people tonight expect to hear something really good and here I'm likely to treat them to a swinish mess. I assure you, today I could play . . . far more difficult stuff, with wider stretches for the fingers—

my own concerto for example—but those simple diatonic runs are ex-
asperating. I keep saying to myself: *"Now Johannes, pull yourself together—do play decently"*—but it's no use. It's really horrible.

As it turned out, Brahms's years of dodging practice did not embarrass
him too much that night, so at the postconcert dinner the eyes were
twinkling, and he even made a small speech.

With young composers Brahms liked to try a bit of mentoring. What
little he said about his craft comes down from those neophytes who
joined him for the lively suppers, who tried to keep up on his walks, who
sat trembling as he went through their music page by (usually defective)
page. On the train to Wiesbaden after their days in Koblenz, Brahms was
relaxed and willing to talk shop with so avid a listener as Henschel.

There is no real *creating* without hard work. What you can call invention, which is to say a thought, an idea, is simply an inspiration from
above for which I am not responsible. . . . It is a present, a gift, which I
even ought to despise until I've made it my own by dint of hard work.
And there doesn't have to be any hurry about that . . . it germinates unconsciously and in spite of ourselves. For instance when I've found the
first phrase of a song, say,

I might shut the book there and then, go for a walk, do some other
work, and maybe not think about it again for months. Nothing, however, is lost. If afterward I approach the subject again, it is sure to have
taken shape; now I can begin to really work at it. But there are composers who sit at the piano with a poem before them, putting music to
it from A to Z until it's done. They write themselves into a state of enthusiasm that makes them see something finished, something important in every bar.

With that Henschel heard the most extended statement Brahms may
ever have made about his method—which says something about the results too. Brahms knew that the galvanizing ideas come on their own, in
their own time, to whomever the Muse favors. Yet he distrusted the irra-
tionality of inspiration at the same time as he relied on it. Even in com-

posing the kind of lieder that Schubert and Schumann famously could
dash off in a sitting, Brahms shunned spontaneity. (Ironically, it was
Schumann who with his prophecies had choked off Young Kreisler's
spontaneity.) At the same time, Brahms had a distinctly modern feeling
for the workings of what Freud would name the unconscious: ideas can
grow in the back rooms of our minds whether or not we know we are
working on them. Brahms would wait for an idea to ripen in his unconscious; when it was ready, it would announce itself.

If not spontaneity, what? Craftsmanly perfection, or the closest possible approach to it. On the isle of Rügen in the summer of 1876, as
Brahms labored on the First Symphony, he told Henschel after looking
over some of the younger man's songs:

> In some . . . you seem to me too easily satisfied. One should never for-
> get that by actually perfecting *one* piece one gains and learns more than
> by starting or half-finishing a dozen. Let it rest, let it rest, and keep go-
> ing back to it and working it over and over again, until . . . there is not
> a note too many or too little, not a bar you could improve on. Whether
> it's *beautiful* too, is an entirely different matter, but perfect it *must*
> be. . . . I never cool down over a work, once begun, until it's perfected,
> unassailable.

There lies important and dangerous advice for Brahms's heirs in the
art. *Perfection before beauty*, he said—*perfection* meaning unassailable in
logic and craft, *beautiful* implying expressive. In preaching that ideal to a
protégé Brahms exaggerated for effect; he knew nothing is perfect. But
for good and ill his words echoed through the next generations of composers, some of whom did exalt thematic logic and harmonic logic over
expressiveness. (Schoenberg and his pupils Berg and Webern were accused of that, usually wrongly. It could be argued that in lesser hands
Schoenberg's twelve-tone method, which owed much to Brahms in logic
and in spirit, did prove amenable to a pedantic elevation of logic over expressiveness.)

For himself, on the face of it, Brahms did elevate craft above expression. Years before, in the counterpoint exchange with Joachim, the violinist berated him for letting the logic of the lines create ugly harmonies
or textures. That objection became an occasional but persistent refrain
from Clara, Elisabet von Herzogenberg, and any number of critics. His
music proves, though, that in his secret heart Brahms cared more about
beauty than he admitted, just as he turned away to hide his tears when a
little folk song setting of his moved him. With the North German bour-

geois craftsman censoring his tongue, Brahms never spoke of the yearning, lyrical Young Kreisler voice that flowers so often in his work.

Yet that yearning voice has been a prime source of his popularity all along. The lyricism and emotion draw listeners into his music before they come to grips with the complexities—the sheer difficulty of absorbing his constant protean variation, his tonal deflections, his experiments with conventional forms. The middle-class audience loved the beauty and warmth of his music, not the logic. Surely Brahms understood that. Even if he made considerable demands on his listeners, even if he never coddled them in his big pieces, he still never forgot their feelings or his own. He made sure the warmth stayed in his work. But he would never admit it.

The results show the value of his method. Few major works of his caught on unequivocally right away; most of them, like his reputation as a whole, had a slow steady ascent to a summit of acclaim from which they never fell. (Some, notably the Violin Concerto, had not reached that summit when he died.) If Brahms's advice to composers was pedantic, he had the genius and the passionate secret life, and the unsearchable favor of the Muse, to transcend an aesthetic that placed craft over beauty. Most of his protégés did not have those advantages. History has largely forgotten the names of the ones who took his advice.

In a letter Brahms had jokingly invited George Henschel out to Sassnitz for the company of the ladies, so that the young man in his spare time could "*com*pose songs for them, the badness of which I in turn will *ex*pose in *my* free hours." When Henschel turned up on the island Brahms kept his promise, pounding away at the exigencies of craft as he understood them, in words he would repeat with any number of composers.

> In writing songs you must endeavor to invent, simultaneously with the melody, a healthy, powerful bass.... Then, my dear friend, let me counsel you: no heavy dissonances on the unaccented parts of the bar, please ... I'm very fond of dissonances, you'll agree, but on the heavy, accented parts of the bar, then let them be resolved easily and gently.

Here he spells out the composing technique that his few surviving sketches imply: he worked out the continuity of a piece largely in terms of unbroken melody and bass line (with an almost obsessive preference for the two in contrary motion), then added the inner voices, textures, and instrumental colors. No doubt in practice the process was rougher, less linear than this tidy model; but Brahms's lifelong efficiency as a composer shows his methods to be direct and habitual.

In the celebrated man Henschel discovered the humility too, the unaffected awe before the giants. Brahms's modesty became more pronounced as he grew older, and sensed that his work had reached a plateau he was not likely to rise above.

I . . . confess that it gives me the keenest pleasure if a song, an adagio, or anything of mine has turned out particularly well. How must those gods, Bach, Mozart, Beethoven, have felt, whose daily bread it was to write things like the *St. Matthew Passion, Don Giovanni, Fidelio*, the Ninth Symphony! What I can't understand is how people like myself can be vain. As much as we men . . . are above the creeping things of this earth, so these gods are above us.

Most of the time, after the morning's struggle with the page, Brahms wanted to talk anything but shop. That summer the two men took to the ocean regularly, Brahms teaching Henschel how to swim underwater with eyes open so they could amuse themselves diving for coins and colored pebbles. At table Henschel noticed that Brahms's conversation stuck to trivialities of weather or excursions, while with friends it was books, plays, ideas, politics, and gossip of the artistic world. (Brahms kept a notebook of the latest jokes and sometimes got caught repeating one to the person who told it to him.[2])

At Sassnitz one afternoon, Brahms took Henschel on a long walk across the moors to listen to what he called *his* bullfrog pond. "Can you imagine," he said of the echoing amphibian chorus, "anything more sad and melancholy than this music . . . ? Here we can understand the origin of fairy tales about enchanted princes and princesses. . . . Listen! There he is again, the poor King's son with his yearning, mournful C♭!"

Henschel saw plenty of Brahms's teasing side, now brash and provoking, now wounding. On one tour they shared a hotel room and Henschel had to flee in the middle of the night from his mentor's symphonic snoring. Next morning Brahms found the fugitive and intoned with mock apprehension, "When I awoke and found your bed empty I said to myself, *'There, he's gone and hanged himself!'* But really, why didn't you throw a boot at me?" Another evening they visited the house of a composer of popular but thin music who habitually worked all day long. When their host left the room his wife told Brahms that she had finally prevailed on her husband to walk with their daughter, to give himself at least two hours a day away from composing. "Oh that's good, that's *very* good!" Brahms broke in earnestly, while Henschel tried to squelch his giggles.

As they walked home that night the younger man waxed sarcastic about a music-loving aristocrat who had published some pretentious attempts of his own. Brahms broke in, "My dear Henschel, let me warn you to be more circumspect when speaking of a nobleman's compositions—because you can never tell who wrote 'em!"

Henschel may have been surprised to find Wagner a recurring theme between them. Brahms knew that Henschel had established his fame partly by singing Hans Sachs in *Meistersinger*; but that was not the reason the subject came up. Brahms seemed constantly to be turning over the matter of Wagner in his mind, sometimes critically, sometimes respectfully, sometimes in puzzlement, but never questioning the significance of his rival. As they walked home one afternoon after sharing a couple of hours of *dolce far niente* in a hammock (Brahms was amused by the problem of how both of them could climb in it at once), Henschel rhapsodized about sections of the *Ring*. Brahms replied mildly:

> Certainly these are fine things, but I can't help it, somehow or other they don't interest me . . . when Siegmund in *Die Walküre* pulls the sword out of the tree, that's fine, too; but it would . . . be *really* powerful and carry one away, if it all concerned—let's say young Bonaparte, or some other hero who stands nearer to our feelings, has a closer claim to our affection. And then that stilted, bombastic language. . . . What really happens with the ring, anyway? Do *you* know?

Brahms the contrarian usually responded like that when he heard enthusiasm about the operas. He had an old habit of taking the opposite of whatever happened to be the going opinion: the eternal devil's advocate. When he brought up the subject of Wagner himself, or when he heard criticism of his rival and suspected it was done to curry favor, Brahms was apt to put on his mask as best of Wagnerians. "I repeatedly heard *Rheingold* and *Walküre* at Munich," he told Henschel, "and admit it would greatly interest me [to go to the full *Ring* premiere at Bayreuth], but—well, we'll think about it." He had an abiding distaste only for *Tristan und Isolde*, probably its harmonic vagaries that herald what a later age would name atonality. Brahms said he usually studied Wagner with enthusiasm, but "with the *Tristan* score it is different. If I look at that in the morning, I'm cross for the rest of the day." (All the same, he fleetingly alludes to the opening of *Tristan* in the second of the Opus 117 intermezzos, and in the song "Mein wundes Herz."[3])

With Henschel Brahms was voluble about his own life, in the forthright but still circumscribed way he spoke with friends. "I sometimes regret that I didn't get married. I ought to have a boy of ten now; that *would* be nice. But when I was at the right age to marry I didn't have the position to do it, and now it's too late." He supported his sister Elise, he told Henschel, but had little in common with her, and hardly any connection with brother Fritz except to send him money now and then, on request. (He had his publisher Simrock forward new piano pieces to his brother.) He relished stories about his father, "a dear old man, very simple-minded," the tales an excuse to indulge in some Low German dialect. There was the time Johann Jakob scolded a beggar who had walked into the house: "Why, you could've easily stolen my overcoat that's hanging in the hall! Get out o' here and don't you come back!" Naturally, Brahms added, when it came time for his father to go out, the overcoat was missing.

"Brahms is looking splendid," Henschel reported to his diary from their summer in Sassnitz. He was the sort with whom you use the word *splendid:* handsome and ruddy of face, rambunctious when you caught him on the right day, a lusty eater who attacked his plate with manifest pleasure and likewise the accompanying mugs of beer and Kaffee afterward. Even to those who didn't recognize the famous figure, Brahms stood out in a crowd, walking with his vigorous rocking gait, soft hat in hand, waistcoat unbuttoned, the wool-flannel *Jäger* shirt collarless whenever possible: the archetypal tie-hater. Likely Henschel was not the only person who thought "his whole appearance vividly recalls some of the portraits of Beethoven." Brahms might not have taken amiss that comparison, but he did not cultivate it: for one thing, Beethoven never grew a beard and Brahms was working up to one.

DURING THE WINTERS in Vienna he had a circle of friends on whom he relied for society. (He followed some of them, or vice versa, to summer vacation spots.) Most of the friends naturally were musicians, but there were also writers, physicians, businessmen, and other professionals from the upper *Grossbürgertum*. The group included pianist Julius Epstein, cellist Josef Gänsbacher, composer/pianist Ignaz Brüll (Brahms's preferred partner for trying out new pieces four hands), and Conservatory professor Anton Door. C. F. Pohl, the Haydn biographer and Gesellschaft librarian, lunched with Brahms regularly in Zum roten Igel, his preferred restaurant of the 1880s. Eventually Karl Goldmark, composer of the exotic and in those days famous opera *The Queen of Sheba*, joined the circle of regulars.

Satirist Daniel Spitzer of the *Neue Freie Presse* (who published Wagner's letters to the milliner) and his fellow journalists made Brahms an honorary member of their "Board of Scoffers" that met at Gause's Pilsner Beer Hall. One of the group's trademark ditties satirizing the members ran this way, to the tune of an old bawdy song:

> *At Gause's sang Johannes Brahms,*
> *And whatever good he found he brought*
> *Into the realm of airy spirits;*
> *but since there already existed a Master,*
> *He became Assistant Master.*

Everybody knew *The Master* referred to Richard Wagner.[4]

Further regulars of the Brahms circle included the crabbed, thick-bearded scholar and composer Gustav Nottebohm, student of Beethoven sketchbooks, to whom Brahms dispatched novices to be drilled in counterpoint. (Nottebohm had been a pupil of Mendelssohn and Schumann.) At postconcert dinners Billroth often joined the table, and also Hanslick— a cozy cohabitation between a composer and the critic who was often slated to review him next day.

Brahms appreciated the knowledge and skill and brains that had made these men eminent in their fields. He also required companions who, like him, could light up a cigar and down a few glasses and make a back room ring with gossip and good talk and manly laughter. Given the constitution of artists and the art-loving public in Vienna, many friends had a Jewish background—Epstein, Brüll, Goldmark, Spitzer, Henschel, Hanslick, and more in later years as the circle evolved. Toward the end of his life, responding to the antisemitism that had become endemic in Austrian politics, Brahms was heard to growl, "Next week I'm going to have myself circumcised!"[5] It was a statement not only of principle but of solidarity with an important faction of his audience—the educated, assimilated Jews who formed the leading cadre of the liberal Austrian *Grossbürgertum*. With the weakness of his class for strong men and the military, Brahms may have idolized Bismarck and the authoritarian Prussians, but he remained a liberal and a democrat at heart.

His friends enjoyed Brahms's teasing and practical jokes, at least when they were not his targets. One of his more ingenious pranks was visited on Gustav Nottebohm. On a piece of old manuscript paper Brahms expertly faked what looked like a sketch by Beethoven, but in fact was a current popular tune. He bribed a strolling food-seller in the Prater to give it to Nottebohm, wrapped around a hunk of cheese. Came the delicious moment when Brahms saw the old pedant step beneath a streetlight, put on his spectacles and peruse the paper with eyes popping, then slip it in his pocket with a sly air and begin munching his greasy cheese bare-handed.[6] Brahms dined out on that story for some time.

Besides his Beethoven studies and composing, Nottebohm did important work with the Schubert complete edition and with composers of the pre-Bach era who were still new territory in musicology. If Brahms admired Nottebohm's contrapuntal authority and scholarly meticulousness, though, he did not appreciate the inflexibility that went with it. This friend was the sort who tried to get mailmen and waiters fired for minute infractions real or imagined. Sometimes Brahms trailed after Nottebohm patching things up.[7]

Several composer friends may have had distinguished reputations, but not as distinguished as Brahms's, and he was apt to let them hear about it. Ignaz Brüll was admired for his light touch as both composer and pianist, and Brahms admitted that he wished he had a comparable fertility of melodic invention. But Brüll had not subjected himself to the sort of contrapuntal discipline Brahms had, and Brahms was unforgiving of shortcomings in technique. Besides, Brüll was surrounded by his adoring mother and sisters and wife, and to Brahms that household of women seemed a dismal setting for an artist. One of his wounding sarcasms ran, "One day 'Nazy really intended to write a modulation from F major to B♭ minor, but the whole family objected so he gave it up."

He subjected gentle Karl Goldmark, then Vienna's second most celebrated composer, to relentless teasing, like a teenager whose notion of affection merges into cruelty. "Goldmark is such a terrific guy, both as a man and as a musician," Brahms said by way of excuse. "The only trouble is that he's so sensitive that I can't go without teasing him. I'm often sorry afterwards; still, he . . . ought to know how to take a joke." The prodding came to a head in the eighties when Brahms was awarded a high state prize, the Order of Leopold. Goldmark received the same award later on, but not before Brahms had spent years declaring himself the "superior" and watching his victim squirm. Biographer Richard Specht, who witnessed some of this, observed that in Brahms's company Goldmark tended to be visibly on edge.

One evening when Brahms was in an evil humor he went beyond teasing. At a dinner at Brüll's house the guests were complimenting Goldmark's setting of a psalm in Luther's translation, when Brahms broke in angrily, "Don't you think it's extraordinary that a Jew should set Martin Luther's words!" Goldmark went pale and probably the rest of the company with him. Brahms would not let it go, pontificating on and on about the impropriety of setting things outside one's own faith and experience, until the dinner came to an abrupt end. It was the only time on record that Brahms sounded an antisemitic note. If he had explained himself, he might have said that it was intended as a statement about authenticity. That was not how the company took it. Certainly he could see that, and certainly the implication did not reflect his real sentiments. As usual Brahms never apologized. The two men avoided each other for a long time after.[8] Eventually, maybe to clear a little room for himself, Goldmark moved out of Vienna for the lakes and mountains of Gmunden, near Bad Ischl.

BRAHMS REMAINED A LONE WOLF in the midst of friends and fame, as happy alone in his Karlsgasse rooms as out in company. In Vienna he did little fresh composing; instead he polished work done in the summer, saw pieces through the publishing process, attended to his correspondence. And he did regular editorial work. In the 1860s it was collections of pieces by Bach's sons, Schumann, Schubert, and Handel; in the 1870s he worked on more Schubert, Couperin, Schumann's *Études Symphoniques*, Mozart's Requiem, and a good deal of Chopin; in the 80s and 90s Handel, the Schubert symphonies for the complete edition, and much Schumann—the latter supplementing Clara's edition of her husband's work (Brahms advised her in that as well). He kept up a friendship and correspondence with the leading musicologists of the time—not only with Nottebohm the Beethoven scholar and Pohl the Haydn, but with Karl Franz Friedrich Chrysander whose Handel edition Brahms worked on, Philipp Spitta the biographer of Bach and editor of Schütz, and Otto Jahn the biographer of Mozart.

For company at home he had his reading and his little projects, including the notebook habit going back to "Des jungen Kreislers Schatzkästlein." Besides collections of song lyrics, opera ideas, and so on, they included a collection of parallel octaves and fifths—a cardinal sin in counterpoint—that he had gleaned from the works of the masters. Each infraction he copied down with an annotation as to whether he deemed it forgivable.

Sometimes Brahms accepted the usual pay for his editorial work, sometimes not. He no longer particularly needed anybody's money. By the 1870s he was living mostly on performing fees and interest, the accounts managed by friends. For a while Clara made investments for him; later the banking brothers of both Hermann Levi and Felix Mendelssohn saw to some of it; finally he put everything into the hands of publisher Fritz Simrock. Brahms usually asked Simrock to deposit fees for his works into the bank in Berlin, no questions asked. Once when Levi pressed him to look for investments with higher interest, Brahms replied testily, "I earn what I need. I don't want to pursue any kind of business with what's sitting there; I may never need it for myself but rather can bequeath it to my family. I understand absolutely nothing about money matters and they don't interest me in the least."9 At home he stuffed bundles of uncounted bills in his closet and rarely had any idea how much he had in his bank account.10 All the same, he commanded top fees for his conducting and playing. With Simrock and concert producers he named his prices and they were not skimpy, and he got what he asked for.

Except perhaps for a few people writing opera, Brahms was the first composer in history to prosper like that from creativity and personal appearances. He did not accumulate an enormous fortune as fortunes go, but by his forties he was exceedingly comfortably set up, and that with minimal attention to his finances. When in the 1890s Simrock lost 20,000 marks of his most famous client's money in some disastrous speculation, Brahms simply wrote back, "I haven't given it a moment's thought," and that was that.

Likely Brahms could have paid for Wagner's notorious wardrobe and furnishings with his spare cash. His own lifestyle was famously frugal and unadorned. Any luxury in his accommodations he was apt to describe as "Wagnerian." Even if he summered in fashionable resorts, he ferreted out bargain rentals and cheap cellars to dine in. On the train he traveled second class, the comfortable but simple middle of three ticket classes in those days. (Third class had wooden seats. Some trains had a fourth class like a cattle car, with no seats at all.) Instead of using his money for his own comfort and glory, he showered it on family, on friends in need, on promising young musicians. "Why don't people come to me?" he complained in later years. "I've got plenty!"11 Eventually he would accomplish the rare feat of finagling Clara Schumann into accepting cash.

Which is all to say: the operative concept in Brahms's financial philosophy was "plenty"—less for himself than for friends and family, and for what he perceived to be investments in the future of music. In an age when many artists spent their last years in garret or gutter, and the body of Johann Strauss, Senior was famously found naked on a bare bed in an empty apartment, Brahms never lacked for plenty.

·   ·   ·

IN FEBRUARY 1873, Heinrich von Herzogenberg wrote Brahms from Leipzig, "My little wife plays [the First Symphony] accurately now, and is not a little proud of her feat in reading the score. But how shall I express our great admiration for the composer, and our thanks?"[12] It is not clear whether in her teens Elisabet von Herzogenberg learned from Brahms to play orchestral scores at the piano, during the short time she studied with him. She was safely married now to Heinrich, diligent composer and Herr Musikprofessor. For Brahms to reestablish relations with a married woman for whom he had once fallen, and befriend the husband too, was a pattern of his going back to Bertha and Artur Faber.

Elisabet von Herzogenberg, amateur musician of genius and an artist in living and friendship, reentered Brahms's life at exactly the time he needed her. In some ways, for some years, she came to occupy the place in his affections and his creative life that Clara Schumann had once held.

Another admirer of Elisabet was British composer Ethel Smyth, who during her studies in Leipzig lived with the Herzogenbergs for most of the 1870s. Smyth first heard of Elisabet, then around thirty, as a legendary figure, "said to be the most gifted musician and fascinating being ever met or heard of"[13] and a close friend of Brahms. Smyth wrote of her as "not really beautiful but better than beautiful, at once dazzling and bewitching; the fairest of skins, fine-spun, wavy golden hair, curious arresting greenish-brown eyes. . . . With her sunshine came in at the door."[14] Her circle called Elisabet Lisl. To Brahms, in deference to Heinz, she was Frau Lisl. The Herzogenberg marriage Smyth reported as "notoriously happy," but it had its afflictions. Lisl was unable to bear children and never stopped mourning it. She struggled with chronic asthma and a weak heart. Smyth remembered her idol painfully ascending stairs with her trademark stoop (that was somehow lovable too), stopping every fourth step to catch her breath.

In the next decades Ethel Smyth became a prominent composer and suffragist in England, and a marvelous memoirist. (Her connection to Lisl had an element of frustrated passion, since the Englishwoman was a noted "Sapphist." Eventually—and fatally for the friendship—Smyth's only male lover of record was Lisl's still-married brother-in-law.) During her student years, Smyth was an incisive observer of the musical life she found in Germany. George Henschel first mentioned her to Brahms, sending an introduction for this "jolly and amusing" young Englishwoman who "wrote some quite charming little songs, even before she had any lessons. . . . Besides all this she can jump over chairs, back and all, she rides, hunts, fishes, swims etc."[15]

When he first met Smyth Brahms greeted her: "So this is the young lady who writes sonatas and doesn't know counterpoint!" Her initial challenge with the famous man was to convince him she had actually composed the songs—Brahms half-seriously accused Henschel of writing them. Given his experience with Clara, the concept of female composers was not new to Brahms or necessarily anathema, but there remained his abiding skepticism of female artists and of thinking women in general. (To Henschel, Brahms claimed he could always detect a female pianist at a distance, even a "masculine" one.)

As Smyth understood, the habit of relegating most women to "Kinder, Kirche, Küche" was the culture's problem. But Brahms possessed a virulent case of it. Smyth saw his misogyny in high relief and was not inclined to make excuses, as Lisl von Herzogenberg did. After all, Lisl was one of the great exceptions. With her and Clara and the favored few "his attitude was perfect . . . reverential, admiring and affectionate, without a tinge of amorousness." As to the rest, "if they did not appeal to him he was incredibly awkward and ungracious; if they were pretty he had an unpleasant way of leaning back in his chair, pouting out his lips, stroking his moustache, and staring at them as a greedy boy stares at jam tartlets."[16]

Like most who knew Brahms, Ethel Smyth never let conflicting feelings about him cloud her admiration of the music, or of the humility that balanced the arrogance and callousness: "He knew his own worth—what great creator does not?—but in his heart he was one of the most profoundly modest men I ever met."[17] Besides, in the Herzogenberg household he could be a charmer and a pushover. Smyth had indelible memories of Lisl emerging flushed from the kitchen where she was cooking one of his favorite dishes at the stove, and declaring with mock imperiousness, "Begin that movement again; that much you owe me!" At such moments Brahms rolled over like a puppy.

Obviously the Herzogenbergs were something like ideal friends for him, their circle a welcoming setting. He was their shining hero, his friendship their great prize, Lisl one of his most admired heroines. He appreciated the couple's talent, the pleasures of their company, and Lisl's skills in the kitchen. That Heinz led a Bach chorus endeared him to Brahms too. (In every performance of the Bachverein Lisl led the soprano section.)

In 1877, Brahms began sending Elisabet von Herzogenberg new work for criticism—nominally to Heinz as well, but really to her. And for over a decade Brahms kept a photo of this blond, velvet-clad muse on his writing desk in Vienna.

In those years, Elisabet returned to him minute critiques and a great deal of praise, becoming one of the friends he relied on for both caveats and approval. Once again, Brahms the misogynist allowed a woman to remake him. Among his circle Lisl filled an important niche. At one end were Clara and Joachim, both virtuosos at the top of the profession who had once composed extensively. At the other end was the amateur Billroth, who could read an orchestral score at the piano and had tried his hand at composing. (He exterminated the results, observing that "it was beastly stuff and stank dreadfully while burning."[18]) Billroth remained a surgeon by trade, though; he had not studied music like a professional and his scientific side tended to take him into musical speculations of no interest to Brahms. As an amateur with professional training, Elisabet's background lay between those extremes. Though Brahms may not have known about it during her lifetime, she composed too—including some songs published under Heinz's name.

Meanwhile, in the later 1870s relations among Brahms and Clara Schumann and Joachim had become strained, for reasons sometimes tangible and sometimes not. To a degree it was simply because they were three formidable people, and after twenty-five years of intensive personal and professional association they were bound to get on one another's nerves. With Elisabet Brahms now had another trusted advisor to fill in for them.

If he rarely followed anyone's advice to the letter, his friends still had a steady influence on his work—if not in the details of a given piece, in his larger direction. It is notable that he never included a full-time composer as one of his closest circle of advisors. (Timid Heinz was not as critical as his wife, though she voiced his concerns for him.) It is still more notable that at no time on record did Clara, Lisl, Joachim, or Billroth encourage Brahms to be more innovative, or ever comment on his novelties in rhythm and meter. More likely, with their complaints at his boldest touches, they helped restrain him from adventuring too far. The main constraint, of course, was his own backward-looking consciousness.

Still, there are no unclouded relationships, and nothing near that was possible with Brahms. There was the matter of social graces, his lack of them. The Herzogenbergs had formed a circle of Brahms admirers in Leipzig, and when he was in town they gave many parties with the great lion as centerpiece. Ethel Smyth remembered the occasions as unpredictable. To begin with, Brahms often felt obliged to harangue the Leipzigers about how much he loathed their city, would never so much as set foot in the place if not for the Herzogenbergs. Compliments were another problem. While he might receive a sincere compliment from a friend with blushing pleasure, enthusiasm from a stranger, especially a female one, say at a party, was apt to draw the full blast of his scorn. Some were lucky, like the lady who asked him, "How do you write such divine adagios?" and he replied, amusingly enough, "Well, you know my publisher orders them that way."

When he was not feeling generous, things got ugly. If expected to play the lion, he could also snarl and bite. Smyth saw him humiliate a timorous fan during a party, crooning with a cruel smile, "And did the gracious lady have all those beautiful feelings thanks to my poor quartet? . . . and where did they lodge? Beneath the little blue shawl? Or perhaps under the . . . bird on her hat?" He dominated the occasions, getting through them downing ham rolls and one mug of beer after another, taking on anybody intrepid enough to approach him. But at the end of the evening Smyth sometimes found "a sort of 'after the battle' atmosphere. . . . Some of the injured had been removed in stretchers; others were licking their wounds, brooding over a sortie that had gone awry."[19]

For Brahms, the chief trouble with the Herzogenbergs was Heinrich's music. The man was hugely prolific and had extraordinary technique that allowed him to dash off complex canons and fugues in a sitting; his daily schedule of composing reeled off like clockwork.[20] The results, however, did not tend to be inspired. Heinrich had two distinct styles in his work, one manifestly Brahmsian, the other relatively more original.[21] Brahms found both wearying. Unfortunately, Heinz also had a chronic and forlorn craving for approval from his hero. Early in their friendship he wrote Brahms:

> You know how much a word or two of recognition from you, however relative, means to me, even a well-intentioned refusal or condemnation I can . . . appreciate as a kindness. . . . If you realized how I turn over in my mind any casual remark of yours, you would understand why I am always coming to you in spite of your anything but encouraging attitude.[22]

Such pathos from a friend would be nerve-wracking to anyone, to Brahms with his brutal honesty all the more so. Besides, while he liked Heinz well enough, there was probably a nagging itch of jealousy that this second-rater had managed to claim such a prize for a wife. To make it worse, the usually modest and self-effacing Lisl fought for her husband's work like a tigress, and never let up about it. The most painful moments in their long correspondence consist of Brahms trying to squirm off the hook when she had sent him another frustrating opus of her husband's. "Best thanks for your package," he noted circumspectly of one new submission from Heinz, "which takes me back for the moment, with an ominous sigh, to certain tricks of my own in the old days."²³ Translation: He's imitating me, and not even my best.

At times Brahms's disdain for Heinz's work spilled out in person, and then Lisl let him have it. After an incident in 1878 she wrote,

> You were so sweet and good at Schillerstrasse, and I can't tell you how much I enjoyed hearing you talk in the window-seat (after spilling all that liqueur). . . . Then the name of that work—cropped up, and, sure enough, you treated us to the old story of [my brother] praising Heinrich's quartet and . . . contemptuously dismissing yours (the B♭)—all this with a certain complacent irony, as if to say: Of course the man made a fool of himself once and for all. Now it was not a disinterested third person to whom you were speaking, but exactly the man whom you know to be the first to laugh at such an ignoramus . . . one who does not think himself worthy to unlace your boots, a seeker, a humble learner, who is a thousand times more upset by such over-rating than by the most withering criticism. . . . I cannot understand how you . . . could twice be guilty of such ungenerosity. . . . But let me tell you straight out that it was neither kind nor just in you, and therefore so unlike you that I can only hope it was a drop of alien blood.²⁴

The little story that put Heinrich in his place had been, of course, quite like Brahms. Ethel Smyth heard of one bathetic scene in the house when Lisl tearfully chewed him out about Heinrich, and Brahms, near tears himself, could do nothing but kiss her hand. Lisl did not get over those episodes for a long time. A couple of them led to silences in the friendship.

All the same, there is nothing surprising about the persistence of the relations of Brahms and the Herzogenbergs. Whatever the frictions and disappointments among them, it was nothing on the order of what he was used to in dealing with Clara, Joachim, and any number of friends, not to mention his enemies. For over a decade, at least, the admiration outweighed the resentment. Heinrich after all had a distinguished career as composer and educator; only with Brahms was he the humble searcher. Each of them, even the earnest and hapless Heinz, received great gifts from the others, and each of them understood their value.

WHATEVER WAS ON BRAHMS'S MIND in the spring of 1877, something prodded him to compose a stack of lieder in April and May—the nine folk lyrics of Opus 69 (he subtitled them "Girls' Songs," then changed his mind), two for Opus 70, the five of Opus 71, two for Opus 72. At the end of April he mailed a batch to Clara, Lisl, and Billroth. In the accompanying note to Clara he observed, only half jokingly, "If possible write me a short comment on each. You need only give the opus or the number; for instance, Op. X, 5, bad; 6, outrageous; 7, ridiculous, and so on."[25] He warned her that the racy import of "Mädchenfluch" ("Girl's Curse") in Opus 69 would "horrify" her: "May God in the bright heavens grant that he should hang himself on a fatal tree—on my white neck!/May God in the bright heavens grant that he should be imprisoned deep in a dungeon—on my white breast!" (Was he thinking of Lisl's white neck, which Ethel Smyth declared her chief beauty?)

"What a wonderful surprise!" Clara replied. "And how glorious the songs are!" She added a few qualms, with a suggestion "to publish the best of them in two books, and omit the few unimportant ones altogether." (He published them all.) "Mädchenfluch," she wrote, "is one of my favorites, the music is so full of swing and interesting from beginning to end, which makes me forget the ugliness of the words."[26]

Once again the ongoing tragedies among Clara's children were tormenting her. During his service with the Prussian army Ferdinand had come down with rheumatism and from the treatment acquired an addiction to morphine. At the same time Felix had upset Clara by proposing to publish his poems, which she feared might prove unworthy of the Schumann name. In despair, she turned to Brahms, who had already set two of Felix's verses: "I wrote to him . . . that he must write under a pseudonym at first, in order to spare us any unpleasantness in case his attempts should prove unsuccessful. . . . This seems to have upset him very much. . . . Couldn't you try to influence him a little regarding his aims in life . . . and try to revive his sense of duty toward his family?"[27] Felix was then suffering from advanced tuberculosis. At least daughters Marie and Eugenie had never troubled Clara; both were unmarried and lived at home. Marie, who looked uncannily like her father, continued to run the house and serve as Clara's manager and dresser.

Billroth responded to Brahms's new songs with appropriate lustiness, writing Hanslick that "Salome" from Opus 69 should be sung by "a rather original sixteen-year-old, black-eyed little girl, full of fun, full of spirits. . . . When after that song that girl meets her John, she embraces him as if to crack his ribs!"[28] Lisl, from Berlin, where she and Heinz were visiting Clara, responded, "How your ears should burn when we drink your health [on your birthday]! Let me tell you it is a red-letter day for us, the day when you graciously condescended to visit this planet." She added a brief list of songs she liked and didn't, but had to break off and fetch Joachim for an evening of music-making.²⁹

If writing the mostly spirited lieder of spring 1877 and receiving mostly delighted responses from his friends cheered Brahms, it did not show in the cheerless congratulations he sent the Joachims upon the birth of another son, which happened to be on Brahms's own forty-fourth birthday. He wrote: "One can hardly in the event wish for him the best of all wishes, not to be born at all." Then he came to himself and appended ceremonial good wishes: "May the new world citizen never think such a thing, but for long years take joy in May 7 and in his life." Soon afterward Brahms headed for Lake Worth, where he composed two works in which those felicitous and despairing spirits mingle.

BRAHMS WOULD SUMMER for three years at the village of Pörtschach on Lake Worth, near Bertha and Arthur Faber's summer place. The first season he stayed in two plain rooms of the housekeeper's quarters at Castle Leonstain, with its cool, linden-shaded courtyard. He shipped his piano from Vienna only to discover that it wouldn't fit up the stairs, so he exchanged it for a local doctor's smaller one. In the next two summers the numbers of visiting friends would send him to a more spacious place on the lake. Drawings of Pörtschach in those days show a gaslit path leading down to the water, where Brahms took his daily swim at dawn. As usual he had vistas of snowy mountains and water and good eating for inspiration—he reported to Billroth that there were "crabs to be enjoyed in quantity."

The summer before, after over fifteen years of uncertain and interrupted labor, he had completed the First Symphony. This summer, like a sigh of relief and pleasure after clearing that hurdle, he turned out the Second Symphony in four months. During those same months came the anguished motet *Warum ist das Licht gegeben den Mühseligen?*—Wherefore is the light given to them that toil?

As he wrapped up that remarkable summer's production in the autumn, he teased friends with reports of the new symphony. To Lisl von Herzogenberg: "I shall not need to play it to you beforehand. You have only to sit down to the piano, put your small feet on the two pedals in turn, and strike the chord of F minor several times in succession, first in the treble, then in the bass . . . and you will gradually gain a vivid impression of my 'latest.'"³⁰ Though the harmony he cites is oddly wrong (perhaps it was that way in the drafts), he seems to be talking about the

end of the first movement's development, the raw outbursts in thirds
dominated by trombones. At the same time he wrote Simrock, "The new
symphony is so melancholy that you can't stand it. I have never written
anything so sad, so minorish: the score must appear with a black border."[31]

The joke is that on the surface, the D Major Symphony is the most
buoyant orchestral work Brahms ever wrote, immediately identified by
everyone as a pastoral outing in the spirit of Beethoven's Sixth, if more
monumental in tone. So came another association of the sort Brahms
hated: as Hans von Bülow had dubbed the First Symphony "the Tenth,"
others would declare the Second "Brahms's *Pastoral*," and eventually the
Third "Brahms's *Eroica*." The composer himself suggested only that the
charms of Pörtschach inspired the Second Symphony and the other
warm, lyrical masterpieces of the next two years. He wrote Hanslick,
"The melodies fly so thick here that you have to be careful not to step on
one."

For many listeners from then to now, the D Major has seemed a backward-looking, idyllic affair, with all four movements in major keys. The
first is in three-quarter time like a waltz, beginning with lilting themes
that Johann Strauss might have claimed. In a symphonic context, the
symphony's opening seems light, gemütlich, radically retrogressive.
With it Brahms evokes, in his lush, mature orchestral voice, both Haydn
and his own tranquil days in Detmold, and the D Major Serenade. In
other words, he returns in maturity to the tone of his youth to take it in
new directions, technically and expressively.

In fact, anyone trying to waltz to this music will fall on his face. That
this is no longer the world of the Serenades but the fully mature Brahms
is shown right away, the opening bass line answered by motives in the
winds whose phrase begins a bar later than the basses', so a whisper of

uncertainty intrudes already into the gemütlich tone. The apparent lilting simplicity of the beginning will not last either, but fall into the kind of rhythmic and metric explorations Brahms had come to insist on: for the thirty-eight measures between letters E and F in the exposition, the stresses constantly shift within the bar line, never finding the written downbeat. In movements like this, an unequivocal downbeat is a structure-defining event, to be parceled out carefully. As Brahms may withhold harmonic resolution for long periods, now he does the same with meter.

A few figures unify the melodic unfolding of all four movements, mainly the three-note motive that begins the symphony. The little rocking figure recurs right-side-up and upside-down, in constantly evolving guises:

As its rhythmic ambiguities suggest, the cheery pastoral surface of the Second Symphony, the source of its instant and abiding popularity, masks a darker undercurrent. The "black border" Brahms wrote about was only partly a joke. Musicologist Reinhold Brinkmann called his study of the D Major Symphony *Late Idyll*. He means it is an idyll longed for when the idyllic is no longer possible. As a few people realized from the beginning, deep shadows cross the sunny face of the D Major Symphony. If it evokes Haydn, it conjures a world and a time that Brahms understood to be past. The symphony is secretly inflected by the question posed in its complement, the motet of summer 1877: "Wherefore is the light given?" As he did in his Kreisler years, but now more subtly and more thoroughly within the boundaries of an "abstract" musical discourse, Brahms adumbrates in tones his life and his fatalistic sense of life.

The symbolic bearers of that "Why?" in the Second Symphony are the trombones and tuba. Brahms never relished the brass section and the new possibilities of valved instruments nearly to the degree that Wagner and Bruckner did. If he accepted grudgingly that valveless brass instruments were obsolete by the 1870s, his French horns are still largely those of Beethoven, and his trumpet writing barely enough to keep the players awake. (Slide-equipped trombones, of course, had always been able to play all chromatic notes.)

Previously, in the First Symphony Brahms had held back the trombones until the finale, then introduced them with a chorale, the sacred tone traditional to those instruments. Solemn harmonies in trombones had long been associated with sacred music. (That is why the instruments served Mozart to evoke the sacred in *The Magic Flute*, and the perversion of the sacred in *Don Giovanni*.) In the Second Symphony Brahms characteristically wielded his trombones sparingly, but for that reason they are more telling from their first entrance just after the halcyon beginning. Here there is no sacred tone at all. Their quiet, ambiguous dissonance (a diminished seventh chord) appears like a chilly shadow falling across a summer meadow. The intensity near the end of the development, almost shocking in context, has much to do with the braying of trombones and tuba in their low registers. *Wherefore is the light given?* This symphony, as Brahms described it to Clara, for once without irony, is not sunny or light but "elegiac in character." The arrival of the coda in the first movement, the yearning twilight wistfulness of that moment as if looking back on something forever lost, defines what he meant by "elegiac."

After the introduction and the first ambiguous whispers in the trombones, the breeziest of lines breaks out, the first theme proper of the sonata form:

At C comes the second theme, a gracious and ingenuous tune in parallel thirds:

Yet that gentle theme is also touched by the shadow. The normal key of a second theme in a D major movement is A, and the sweet parallel thirds of Brahms's melody imply that key—but the bass harmonizes it in F♯ minor. Throughout the symphony, these four major-key movements are treated to some of the most subtle and pervasive *moll-Dur* inflections in Brahms's long history of mixing the brightness of major keys with poignant tints of minor. At times he went beyond that into modal suggestions, especially the ominous suggestion of Phrygian mode, with its poignant lowered second degree—as in the strings at (C) in the generally untroubled third movement.

The adagio is the longest slow movement in all his symphonies and maybe the most beautiful. It opens with one of his sighing cello themes, this one vaguely disquieting in its ambiguity, at first revealing neither the meter nor the B major tonality. From this beginning Brahms keeps the metric and tonal sense off balance for most of the movement:

This opening is a prime example of what Carl Dahlhaus calls Brahms's "centripetal" tonality, which is to say: how he manages the stresses, tensions, and resolutions within the tradition of the major-minor tonal system. To be technical for a moment: at the beginning of the slow movement the pedal tone is F♯, the dominant of the actual B major, but the cello line begins by descending to a B♯. When the bass falls to B at measure 3 it still sounds ambiguous; only in measure 4 do we more or less understand B as the actual key. Yet Brahms withholds a root-position tonic chord for most of the movement; the first one does not come until the downbeat at C—and that is B minor.

In other words, in contrast to Wagner's frequent "centrifugal" tonal meandering, often seeming to go from anyplace to noplace in particular, Brahms's technique (more formalistic, as one would expect from him) is to hide tonal references within the ambiguity, so the revealing of the actual key is a matter of closing in on an implicit presence. Thus, "centripetal." Another example is the opening of the D Minor Concerto, in which he actually manages to make a pedal point on D unstable. In Brahms's maturity his handling of rhythm and meter can be thought of as centripetal in the same sense: the written meter can be obscured for long periods, with the eventual coming together of written and perceived meter forming a kind of rhythmic "full cadence." (One can't avoid finding in all this a reflection in his art of Brahms's elusive and oblique personality. He was as expert at hiding key and meter as at hiding himself.)

As third movement of the Second Symphony we find another of the charming intermezzos with which Brahms replaced the symphonic scherzo, its leading theme like one of the Viennese proto-waltz pieces called ländler. It is built on an inversion of the three-note motive that began the symphony:

As Max Kalbeck notes, much of the game in this movement is rhythmical, with exhilarating jumps of meter and tempo, the opening melody and its ländler rhythm transformed into a two-beat "Galop," then "a pungent quick-waltz."[32] The touch of shadow in this movement comes in the lapping Phrygian-tinted string lines at letter C, swept away by mocking phrases in $\frac{3}{8}$.

Brahms did not begin the Second Symphony with a gentle idyll simply in order to negate or destroy it, say, as Carl Nielsen tears apart the Brahmsian idylls of his Sixth Symphony with flatulence and madness. In the Modernist century, idylls would tend to be compromised, destroyed, mourned: Mahler in *Das Lied von der Erde*. Brahms had not fallen that far, at least not by 1877, and not in splendid Pörtschach. The idyll is real, but so is the inescapable shadow. His finale is a Haydnesque "last dance" turned up several notches in breathlessness, furiously gay in its dashing and swirling figures that start with these bars:

The symphony ends with a spine-tingling D major chord in high trombones. With that Brahms once again completes a transformation that heralds tone-color composers of a century later: timbre as the bearer of structure and meaning. The trombones, harbingers of darkness in the first movement, are redeemed in the last, proclaiming the triumph of joy—or at least of Pörtschach's sunshine and water and seafood in quantity.

The trouble is, the finale for all its pleasures and ingenuities doesn't really redeem what it proposes to. As Brinkmann expresses it, "the gaiety becomes almost violently brilliant and seems stage-managed." After all, the halcyon past of delirious love and uncomplicated composing is gone indeed—from this composer's life, and from music. The finale is like Brahms on a Prater merry-go-round, or laughing and drinking with friends in a café. He threw himself into the gaiety, but in the end it was mostly show.

That Brahms understood the symphony's ambiguities, and how they echoed his own malaise, is hinted in a remarkable response he wrote in 1879 to an admirer named Vincenz Lachner. In a thoughtful letter about the Second Symphony this older musician took Brahms to task for the "rumbling kettledrum, the gloomy lugubrious tones of the trombones" that sully the first movement, and for darkening that D major expanse with the suggestion of G minor in the last measures.[33]

Brahms's reply to these protests begins, "My letter will hardly tell you what great, sincere pleasure your letters are giving me . . . it is so good to know that what one has created with love and hard work is also being studied lovingly and carefully by another person." For the trombones he has this, for him, astoundingly self-revealing defense:

> I very much wanted to manage in that first movement without us-
> ing trombones, and tried to. . . . But their first entrance, that's mine,
> and I can't get along without it, and thus the trombones.
>
> I would have to confess that I am . . . a severely melancholic person,
> that black wings are constantly flapping above us, and that in my out-
> put—perhaps not entirely by chance—that symphony is followed by a
> little essay about the great "Why." If you don't know this [motet] I will
> send it to you. It casts the necessary shadow on the serene symphony
> and perhaps accounts for those timpani and trombones.

He leaves between the lines that neither in the motet's final dying cries of *Warum?*/Why?, nor in his heart, did he find any answer to the question of *Wherefore is the light given to them that toil?* Thus his birthday greeting to Joachim's child: the best is not to be born at all. The black flapping wings will abide—and certainly they were hovering over Austria and Germany as Brahms wrote the Second Symphony. He would evoke the unanswerable "Why?" in two more magnificent and despairing works of the next decade: overtly in *Gesang der Parzen* (*Song of the Fates*), covertly in the Fourth Symphony.

The darker, more *mollig* import of the D Major Symphony, the "necessary shadow," would have been perceptible even if Brahms had not written his letter to Lachner (maybe doing that with an eye to history and biography). Lachner felt the shadow, though he could not understand it. In the first movement Brahms provides another covert clue. In the music he alludes to a lied he had written that spring, and in his working copy of the score he jotted a few words from it under those measures.[34] The song is Heinrich Heine's "Es liebt sich so lieblich im Lenze," one of the relatively few settings of Robert Schumann's favored poet that Brahms produced in his maturity. Heine's way of secreting lacerating ironies within charming little verses, Brahmsian as that might be in spirit, did not tend to sit well with Brahms's folk-song-inspired lieder—he wanted straightforward texts that cried out for musical setting.

This poem of Heine's amounts to a bittersweet evocation of pastoral poetry, the title a repeated refrain with lilting, ironic dactyls: "O love is so lovely in springtime!" A shepherdess sits on the riverbank weaving "the daintiest wreaths," and as she sighs "To whom may I give my wreaths?" a plumed horseman suddenly appears like a vision of knighthood and romance, and greets her impetuously. Then he rides on out of sight. As the tearful shepherdess hurls her wreaths into the river comes the final refrain, "O love is so lovely in springtime!" The poem inspired not only a song from Brahms but maybe also his late idyll into the form of a symphony, the same sorrowful undertones shadowing both pastorales.

On leaving Pörtschach in September 1877, Brahms visited Hans von Bülow in Baden-Baden and for the conductor played over the First Symphony on piano. Here may have come the moment of transformation like Saul's, when Bülow turned away once and for all from Wagner the betrayer and threw his allegiance to Brahms. It was around then that Bülow dubbed Brahms's C Minor "The Tenth." In a letter about it to a friend, he added his other soon-famous formulation: "I believe it is not without the intelligence of chance that Bach, Beethoven and Brahms are in alliteration."[35] The conceit soon reached the public's attention, and never left it. Brahms would be branded in history, to his infinite dismay (and probably covert pleasure) as one of "the three great B's of music."

Leaving Baden-Baden, Brahms joined Josef Viktor Widmann in Mannheim to take in the premiere of the late Hermann Götz's unfinished opera *Francesca da Rimini*. Brahms could not summon much enthusiasm for this work of a highly popular composer whom he had liked personally but never treated with much respect. Brahms and Widmann stayed in a hotel together and passed the time turning over the idea of an operatic collaboration.[36]

With Widmann and others the correspondence about opera would straggle on through the next decade, but already in the 1870s Brahms had observed to an acquaintance about the idea, "Beside Wagner it is impossible."[37] Of course, he had said the same about Beethoven and symphonies—and so opera continued its feverish round in his mind. Recently he had discovered *Carmen*, going to see it twenty times in 1876 alone. Brahms loved Georges Bizet's vibrant and exotic style; beyond that, it perhaps offered him clues toward a means of escaping Wagner. (Nietzsche was also ravished by *Carmen*, for more or less the same reasons.)

It would all come to nothing. Opera was a great genre and Brahms had taken on the great genres one after another—sonata, theme-and-variations, song cycle (*Magelone*), symphony, string quartet, cantata (*Rinaldo*), oratorio (of a sort, with *Ein deutsches Requiem*), and finally symphony. It had been genres close to opera, song cycle and cantata, that had turned out the most disappointing in his hands. Besides, opera is not ordinarily the medium for a composer who frets over every note, or for one who shies away from the direct expression of emotion in his work. Even the years of labor on the *Requiem* and First Symphony might have paled before what an opera would have cost Brahms. All the signs, in other words, implied that opera did not come naturally to him. And Brahms could augur the signs as well as anyone else.

All that, and then when it was finished he would have to go up against the Wagnerian juggernaut. No, no. Brahms had tremendous courage, but he was also a sane and a practical man. Thus the meaning of his famous formula: as likely to write an opera as to marry. He was talking about resisting the two greatest temptations of his life, and being a little frustrated and more than a little pleased at having escaped them both.

AT THE END OF OCTOBER, Brahms was back in Vienna, gearing up for the premiere of the Second Symphony. In usual form he dropped hints to friends about it, whipping up anticipation. Shortly after his return he summoned a group of interested parties including conductor Hans Richter, Billroth, and Hanslick, to Ehrbar's piano salon to listen to the new piece on piano four hands, Brahms and Ignaz Brüll at the keyboard. The listeners were enchanted. After the reading Billroth wrote Brahms, "That symphony is like blue heavens, the murmur of springs, sunshine, and cool green shadows! It must be beautiful on Lake Worth."[38] Hanslick's review of the premiere by Richter and the Vienna Philharmonic on December 30, 1877, declared it an "unqualified success . . . with nothing of the contemporary tendency to emphasize novelty. . . . This time Brahms has managed to suppress his imposing, but dangerous, art of hiding his ideas in a polyphonic web or exposing them to contrapuntal frustration."[39] The Second was perhaps more to the tastes of the Viennese and their favorite critic than any other symphony of Brahms: gay and lilting and brilliant, if you don't listen too hard.

Around that time Hanslick wrote an encouraging note to an impoverished and obscure Bohemian composer, notifying him that for the third year in a row the Austrian Commission for the Conferring of Artists' Scholarships had awarded him a prize of 600 florins. This time, Hanslick advises, the younger man should do more than express thanks to the committee.

> Johannes Brahms, who together with me has proposed this grant, takes a great interest in your fine talent, and likes especially your Czech vocal duets. . . . The sympathy of an artist as important and famous as Brahms should not only be pleasant but also useful to you, and I think

you should write to him . . . and perhaps send him some of your music. . . . After all, it would be advantageous for your things to become known beyond your narrow Czech fatherland, which in any case does not do much for you.[40]

The letter was addressed to Herr Anton Dvořák, composer, Prague.

Brahms had been on the three-member Austrian Commission since 1875. At that point Karl Goldmark and Hanslick were the other members, but Goldmark was largely living in Gmunden, so the other two did most of the selecting. Hanslick would screen the pile of scores and forward the ones he considered respectable to Brahms, who always returned them fully studied, with marginal comments from enthusiastic to acid.[41]

Dvořák had been at it for a long time, with only middling and local success. The freshness and fertility of his gift amazed Brahms. At the same time, the Czech coloration of his style Brahms perhaps saw as a welcome touch of the exotic, like gypsy music. And as with "Hungarian" music in general, there is no indication Brahms took the ardent nationalistic sentiments behind Dvořák's work particularly seriously. (For another example, as a patriotic gesture Dvořák pointedly avoided using German in company, even though he could speak the language perfectly well.[42]) Like most liberals Brahms tended to look at the nationalism of Austria's subject peoples with suspicion, as a threat to the stability and prosperity of the empire.

None of that came between Brahms and Dvořák, because still for Brahms, music that he admired excused everything. The two men met in December 1877, and visited periodically from then on. For years Brahms's letters to his publisher Simrock regularly drummed for Dvořák. It was one of a number of times Brahms generously promoted a younger artist—but the only time the world would much remember it. Other composers about whom he was nearly as enthusiastic included the names Knorr, Röntgen, Fuchs, and Novak,[43] all men Brahms hoped would lead music into the future. The list did not include Anton Bruckner, Hugo Wolf, or Gustav Mahler, whom history has called after Brahms the three greatest Viennese composers of the late nineteenth century. For none of their work did he have the respect he did for that of Fuchs, Röntgen, et al.

So at the end of 1877 Brahms began to pull strings, writing Simrock that Dvořák's Moravian Duets were "suitable and practical for publication," and the composer should be paid well: "There is no doubt that he is very talented. And then he is also poor. I beg you to think the matter over." (In fact the duets turned out a huge hit.) In gratitude for the help, Dvořák dedicated his D Minor Quartet to Brahms, who wrote a cautionary acceptance:

> You write somewhat hurriedly. When you're filling in the numerous missing sharps, flats, and naturals, it would also be good to look a little more closely at the notes themselves and at the voice leading, etc.
>
> Forgive me, but it is very desirable to point out such things to a man like you. I also accept the works just as they are very gratefully and consider myself honored by the dedication of the quartet.[44]

In the spring of 1878, Dvořák wrote Brahms saying that Simrock, clearly with Brahms's biggest sellers in mind, had commissioned him to write some Slavonic dances. "As I did not know how to set about these, I have tried to obtain your famous Hungarian Dances, and I shall take the liberty of using these as my model."[45] Brahms responded encouragingly.

The Slavonic Dances would do for Dvořák's fortune and fame what the Hungarian Dances had done for Brahms's. Like Brahms, this composer would capitalize on that success with a string of superlative works from the popular to the symphonic. Unlike Brahms, he produced operas as well. In 1879, Brahms and Hanslick arranged a meeting between Dvořák and the head of the Hofoper, which some years later led to a production of *The Cunning Peasant*. But anti-Czech sentiment was raging in the city and that situation turned the production into a fiasco. Due in large part to Brahms's encouragement and steady promotion, however, by then Dvořák could afford a fiasco: he had become a musical citizen of the world.

AFTER THE VIENNA PREMIERE of the Second Symphony, Brahms took it on the road as part of his regular winter concertizing. Mostly the symphony repeated the success it had found in Vienna; only Leipzig was notably chilly. Ethel Smyth observed the occasion. Brahms, she wrote, "had the knack of rubbing orchestras up the wrong way. . . . Moreover . . . the Gewandhaus musicians were inclined to be antagonistic to his music, and indeed considered the performance of any new work whatsoever an act of condescension."[46] After much bitter experience there Brahms was probably more brusque and nervous on the Gewandhaus podium than on any other. One reviewer's opinion amounted to a dig at both the composer and his city for countenancing such frivolous stuff as the Second: "The Viennese are much more easily satisfied than we are. We make quite different demands on Brahms, and require from him music which is something more than 'pretty' and 'very pretty' when he comes before us as a symphonist."47

When he had finished the season's touring in Holland, Brahms realized an old fantasy. After diligent study of travel guides and attempts to learn some Italian, he headed out on a vacation to Italy in April 1878, Billroth and Goldmark in tow. For four weeks they dashed through cities including Florence, Naples, and Rome (without Goldmark after Naples, where Brahms had a sad visit with the critically ill Felix Schumann). During the trip he wrote Clara, "How often do I not think of you, and wish that your eyes and heart might know the delight which the eye and heart experiences here! If you stood for only one hour in front of the facade of the Cathedral of Siena, you would be overjoyed." He meant she would be given solace in the face of her family's tragedies, of which Felix was now the chief. Brahms reported to Simrock that he found church music in Italy "atrocious . . . unbelievably brassy and crude,"48 but that only gave him more time to enjoy the scenery and art and architecture.49 Somewhere in this vacation Brahms made sketches for a piano concerto, but he would not take them up again for several years. For all his delight in Italy, this first excursion was mainly a prelude to later trips—nine in all, Italy the only country outside Germanic ones in which Brahms ever traveled for pleasure.

By the second week of May 1878 he was back at work in Pörtschach, as usual keeping his cards close until he had something to show. For all the pleasures of the town, his temper there could be as variable as everywhere else. Russian composer Iwan Knorr learned that one night when Brahms was invited to the house of a music patroness who he knew was friendly with Cosima Wagner. And whenever Cosima turned up, this lady was careful to hide her copies of Brahms's music. Brahms arrived at her house with Knorr and violinist Richard Barth, to find his works and his picture grandly displayed on the piano. Nudging Knorr, he said loudly, "See here, Brahms everywhere you look! But you mustn't for an instant suppose that this is always the case! Here one modulates into various keys. Well, Frau X, how about singing a bit of Peter Cornelius?"

Earnestly the hostess swore she had no such Wagnerian trash in the house. At which point Brahms began to rummage through her cupboards, the lady becoming more and more distraught, until with a cry of triumph he produced a copy of Cornelius's songs. Sitting down to the piano, he began to play and sing them in his raucous voice, with commentary—"Quite different from that Brahms guy, eh?"—until his victim collapsed in tears. Eventually he ceased the torture and agreed to play a sonata with Barth. "We really wanted to play Mozart," he told his whimpering hostess, "but as you're not worthy of it, we shall, for your punishment, play Brahms's A Major." Recalling the experience, Knorr said, "I have seldom lived through a more painful evening."[50]

THE MAIN PRODUCTION from the summer of 1878 turned up toward the end of August, when in a note Brahms alerted Joachim that "a few violin passages" would be forthcoming. They turned out to be a gigantic first movement's worth of solo part. With thrills of anticipation and anxiety, Joachim saw that Brahms had taken on a violin concerto and was talking about four movements like a symphony, rather than the usual three for a concerto. After their decades of friendship and collaboration, Brahms would write it for Joachim and expected his collaboration—in theory, if not always in practice.

The violinist, whose own Hungarian Concerto still made up a major item of his repertoire, was concerned from the beginning to make sure Johannes's solo part was more playable and idiomatic than his old friend was likely to manage on his own. Joachim knew better than anyone that Brahms had always been impatient over string bowings and fingerings and other matters of the kitchen. In music of the nineteenth century and after, various notational conventions give string players instructions on how to wield the bow and where to change from an upbow to down, all of it having intimately to do with the musical effect. Players regularly tinker with the given bowings and some notations were (and remain) ambiguous, but still it is valuable to have them on the page as a foundation, especially in something as important as a concerto.

Brahms generally ignored the whole question of using slurs to indicate string bowing. Most of the slurs marked in his published scores show phrases rather than bowings, or else the bowings have been put in by a string player, who was usually Joachim. Joachim understood that the single instrument with which Johannes was entirely at home was his own. As Brahms exclaimed years later, working on the Double Concerto: "Oh, how much more agreeable and sensible it is to write for an instrument one knows thoroughly—as I presume to know the piano."

Soon the two fell into steady correspondence over the gestating concerto, Brahms writing out swatches of solo part and dispatching them in the mail. A certain amount of the work they did in visits, Joachim with violin in hand to try out ideas on the spot. Joachim not only made suggestions for the solo part but rewrote passages, mainly ones involving the arcana of virtuoso figuration—complex figures that take ingenious and ear-dazzling advantage of the possibilities of strings and bow. These suggestions Brahms sometimes adopted, sometimes ignored, sometimes used as the basis of a third version. At the same time he beleaguered Joachim for more suggestions, half-seriously threatening to take the piece to a "stricter" violinist. Then often as not he cavalierly rejected the advice offered.[51]

Exasperated by these bait-and-switch games, Joachim kept at Johannes with dogged patience. He was determined that the concerto would be a showpiece for both of them. Near the end of the process Brahms gave his collaborator free rein to compose the single cadenza, in the first movement, the one usually played ever since. (Joachim's cadenza for Beethoven's Violin Concerto is also the standard.) Even the final manuscript of Brahms's concerto is dotted with revisions in the solo part, some in Joachim's hand, some of those ignored in the published version.

Meanwhile separately and together they wrestled with the inevitable affliction of composing concertos in general, which is heightened by the fact that a violin cannot make as much noise as a piano: how can you have every note of the fragile solo part be heard over an orchestra of eighty or more people? That Brahms intended this to be a massive, full-throated piece compounded the usual problems of balance.

If all that were not enough to contend with, Joachim pressured Johannes to have the piece ready for a New Year's Day 1879 concert in Leipzig. Just as the anointed soloist made his push for a quick premiere, Brahms wrote that he had gotten himself in trouble with the four-movement idea: "The middle movements are bust—naturally they were the best ones! I'm writing a wretched adagio instead."[52] (Of the two discarded movements, one would do service in the Second Piano Concerto.)

Through all these frustrations one notes that while Brahms was plainly concerned about the solo part, he was not particularly intimidated by the idea of writing a concerto. Essentially he had two daunting models to live up to in the nineteenth century—Beethoven's sublime one, and Mendelssohn's elegant and melodious one. With one previous concerto and two symphonies under his belt now, Brahms was not as overawed by those giants as he would have been before producing his first symphony and string quartet. Besides, he had always liked some of the minor composers of virtuoso concertos such as Paganini and Viotti, neither of them any threat to him.

Despite the mounting pressures and the sheer labor of writing a concerto substantial even in three movements, that summer of 1878 Brahms wrote several lieder for Opus 85 and Opus 86, and also composed and pulled together his first collection of solo piano pieces since the little Waltzes of 1865—the Four Capriccios and four Intermezzos of Opus 76. The Romantically passionate No. 1 of the new piano set had been written in 1871, the others perhaps later. Given his stated ease in composing for his own instrument, Brahms's relationship to the piano seems almost perverse. At the beginning of his career he wrote three immature but still extraordinary piano sonatas, then some masterful sets of variations and wildly profitable light works; then he largely gave up doing anything like any of them. Only toward the end of his life would he produce piano music again in quantity—and it would again be small, distilled character pieces with vague designations such as capriccio, intermezzo, and rhapsody.

Michael Musgrave writes that Opus 76 stands "stylistically, as chronologically, between the character pieces of Brahms's youth and the rich flowering of the later period."[53] As usual the pieces are distinctively Brahms and at the same time have clear ties to the past, mainly the character pieces of Schumann and Mendelssohn. One is also reminded, for once, that Brahms knew and admired Chopin's music and, during this period, was editing volumes for the Chopin Complete Edition. In Opus 76 Brahms spins out little pieces like Chopin's that move from Romantic fervor to drawing-room grace: two of the set are marked *agitato*, three *grazioso*.

What with the rush of composing and the ongoing bother over the Violin Concerto—he and Joachim kept revising it into the following summer—Brahms seems to have been in a bilious mood toward the end of 1878. He snapped at Simrock, who had been pressing him:

> Done! What is done? The violin concerto! No. You or I! No. . . . One knows nothing definite; even the most credulous doesn't. . . . And I am credulous. Indeed, I believe in immortality—; I believe that when an immortal dies, people will keep on for 50,000 years and more, talking idiotically and badly about him—*thus* I believe in immortality, without which beautiful and agreeable attribute I have the honor to be— Your J. Br.[54]

Eduard Hanslick got another eyeful of ink when he responded to an urgent request from Hamburg authorities to be a go-between. Brahms had been invited to the fiftieth anniversary celebration of the Hamburg Philharmonic and had not responded. To Hanslick's plea to attend he growled:

You have preached the doctrine of deportment to me in public once before; I do not wish that it should happen again . . . and therefore I am telling you that it is the fault of the Hamburgers if I do not appear at their festival. I have no occasion to display good breeding and gratitude; on the contrary, a certain amount of incivility would be appropriate, if I had the time and inclination to ruin my mood with it.[55]

Having delivered himself of that eruption, the product of his undying outrage at being snubbed by the Philharmonic, Brahms decided after all to attend the festival and enjoyed it considerably.

Clara Schumann was there to play a Mozart concerto, and among the guests and visitors were others from Brahms's past and present: Theodor Kirchner, Ferdinand Hiller, Niels Gade, Karl Reinthaler, Klaus Groth, Hermann Grädener, Eduard Hanslick. Brahms was sitting beside Groth at the opening banquet where a flowery speaker cited the proverb of "a prophet without honor in his own country" as fortunately not applying to Brahms. The honored prophet leaned over to Groth and hissed, "Twice they filled the vacant position of director of the Philharmonic Society with a stranger, and passed me over. If I had been elected at the right time I might still have become a proper citizen. I could have gotten married and lived like other men. Now I'm a vagabond!"[56] Years later Brahms told Max Kalbeck that there had been a girl at that banquet in Hamburg to whom he almost turned and proposed on the spot, but once more he resisted the urge.[57]

On the final evening he conducted the Second Symphony with the Philharmonic, Joachim sitting at the head of the violins. Naturally sister Elise, brother Fritz, stepmother Karoline, and stepbrother Fritz Schnack were proudly in attendance, and his teacher Eduard Marxsen and a number of women from the Frauenchor. His first teacher, Otto Cossel, had died thirteen years before, but his wife and daughter—Brahms's goddaughter—had come.[58] As Brahms stepped up to the podium to stormy applause, he was presented with a laurel wreath and the brass broke out in a flourish. At the end of the symphony the audience showered him with flowers. Hanslick remembered him then as "with roses bedecked," like the baby in his Lullaby.

At the end of the trip there was a squabble when Elise wanted to claim the flowers. "So you want to boast with them?" Johannes snapped. Instead he dragged her with him to place them on their father's grave.[59]

The New Year's Day 1879 premiere of the Violin Concerto in Leipzig turned out a scrambling affair, with Joachim unnerved by all the last-minute revisions and Brahms even more tense on the podium than usual at premieres. The response from public and critics was no worse than cool, but it was enough to make Brahms hand over the baton for the Vienna premiere to Josef Hellmesberger, which in turn upset Joachim.[60] Somehow at the Musikverein two weeks later—with Brahms and Joachim furiously revising solo and accompaniment in the interim—the work found a delirious response. Brahms reported it to Julius Stockhausen as "a success as good as I've ever experienced. *Publikus* would not cease its noise."[61] He was even pleased that the crowd had applauded Joachim's first-movement cadenza right into the coda.[62]

The always unpredictable Viennese had fallen under its spell. The first movement, though it recalls the pastoral D major three-beat of the Second Symphony and pretty Pörtschach, still makes us wait a long time for the lyrical flowering. When that breaks out with a ravishing melody at the end of the exposition, it is one of the most memorable of those moments where Brahms the mature craftsman and the poetic Kreisler sing together. That tender lyricism permeates the second movement. For a finale, with Joachim and his Hungarian Concerto in mind, Brahms produced another gypsy-tinted outing, not exactly a rondo but something like it, with dashing rhythms and delirious trills in the winds.

To a later age the work would seem almost irresistible, manifestly joining Beethoven's and Mendelssohn's as the third towering violin concerto of the nineteenth century. Yet most of the world outside Vienna resisted it for a long time. When Joachim took the concerto to Berlin and played it with his Hochschule orchestra, the papers demanded to know why students were required to participate in such "trash."[63] Some of the problem musicians and public had with the piece is suggested in two quotes from violinists. In Vienna, cynical old Josef Hellmesberger famously declared it "a concerto not for, but against the violin." Pablo Sarasate spoke for many virtuosos: "I don't deny that it's fairly good music, but does anyone imagine . . . that I'm going to stand on the rostrum, violin in hand, and listen to the oboe playing the only tune in the adagio?" Once again Brahms had committed the cardinal sin of writing a symphonic concerto in which orchestra and soloist carry on the musical dialogue as equals.

Having mostly put off ambitious orchestral works until his forties, Brahms had now made up spectacularly for lost time, producing two symphonies and a concerto in three successive years, all of them historic masterpieces. From now on his orchestral excursions would appear regularly at two-year intervals, the periods between given largely to chamber and vocal music. Meanwhile, though Brahms perhaps never produced a more warmly melodious orchestral work than the Violin Concerto, he would still have to trust in posthumous acclaim for it. Certainly he had the philosophical patience for that—but not necessarily, anymore, quite the old courage of his convictions. Brahms had drafted a Second Violin Concerto, but after the reception of the first one held the second back. Finally he consigned it to flames.

There was another creative endeavor, of a sort, at the end of 1878: for the third and definitive time, Brahms grew a beard. To queries about why, his favored explanation ran, "With a shaved chin, people take you for either an actor or a priest." To his satisfaction he discovered that whiskers made him almost unrecognizable. For as long as the joke lasted he enjoyed introducing himself solemnly as "Kapellmeister Müller from Braunschweig," and seeing how long it took people to figure it out. Gustav Nottebohm spent an entire evening in polite conversation with "Kapellmeister Müller."[64]

With the flowing blond beard between him and the world, the face of Johannes the Fair, the defiant underlip, the eternally boyish features of Young Kreisler sank once and for all behind the patriarchal mask. Brahms's face became as magisterial and enigmatic as the outer face of his music.

The disguise was complete at last.

CHAPTER EIGHTEEN

Song of the Fates

THE DAY AFTER the first Vienna performance of Brahms's Violin Concerto in January 1879, Felix Schumann died of tuberculosis in Frankfurt, at age twenty-four. Clara had moved there from Berlin the year before, to take the leading piano teacher's position at the Hoch Conservatory. Felix was the last of her children, born when his father was in the asylum, everyone's favorite of the boys as Julie had once been of the girls. He died in the arms of his sister Marie; she had not waked Clara when the crisis came because it would have upset their mother too much.[1] Clara told her diary, "One grows old only to bury one's children."[2]

Brahms rushed to Clara's side to help her through the latest tragedy, but she was suffering from more than her children's sorrows. The previous October she had celebrated her fiftieth anniversary as a performer in her native Leipzig, and played Robert's concerto in the Gewandhaus, once more amid flowers and fanfares and delirious applause.[3] But her arms were aching miserably and her hearing was deteriorating. During the coming year she would try to relearn Johannes's D Minor Concerto, but for the moment its thundering chords defeated her: "I had to give it up, and once more lay it aside with tears. I love the concerto so passionately, that I feel . . . as if it had grown out of my heart."[4] It must have been a sad meeting that February, Brahms still in his robust prime, their fourteen-year difference in age weighing on both of them. For distraction they worked on her edition of Robert's music.

In March Brahms received word of another honor, one he particularly relished: an honorary doctorate from the University of Breslau. Now to go with the distinguished career and distinguished beard, there would be the title Herr Doktor Brahms. Whereupon Richard Wagner, *Ritter* but not *Doktor* while his rival sported both titles, appeared once again lathered with righteous rage in print. These were the lines in his paper the *Bayreuth Blätter* about an unnamed composer who masquerades as a "cabaret singer," poses in his "hallelujah periwig of Handel," dresses as "a Jewish czardas fiddler," and then appears as respectable symphonist and "Number Ten." Wagner of course knew Brahms was not the least Jewish; that was thrown in for effect. Wagner's Jewish disciple Hermann Levi, meanwhile, was now inhabiting the inner circle and following the Master in calling his former hero and *Duzenbrüder* Brahms an "epigone"—a second-rate imitator of his betters. This year the Bayreuth paper also belabored Robert Schumann in a series of articles, surely in part another strike at Brahms.[5]

One more honor of that period came when Brahms was offered the position of cantor at St. Thomas's Cathedral in Leipzig, which would have made him a successor in the post of J. S. Bach. Some in the city resisted the appointment on musical grounds, while others took to mudslinging and accused Brahms of a "dissolute life." It is not clear whether that resulted from word of his taste for whorehouses getting around, or simply that being a bachelor of forty-six put him under suspicion in a proper German-bourgeois town. Clara and the Herzogenbergs united against the idea of his going to St. Thomas. With relief Brahms sent a quick refusal. By the end of May 1879 he was again on Lake Worth at Pörtschach.

The main creative effort of that summer, another characteristic product of the landscape where he said melodies flew thick, was the First Violin Sonata in G Major, Opus 78. It begins with Brahms at his most sweetly, piercingly wistful, and stays on that expressive tack for much of its course:

Brahms had, in typical fashion, written and suppressed at least three previous violin sonatas before the First. The initial thing his friends noticed about this one was that in both melody and accompaniment the third-movement rondo is based on his related settings of two Klaus Groth rain poems, "Regenlied" and "Nachklang," of Opus 59. In sending the piece to Theodor Billroth, Brahms slyly hinted at the connection: "It's not worth playing through more than once, and you would have to have a nice, soft, rainy evening to give the proper mood." Billroth figured it out quickly enough and wrote back, "You rascal! . . . To me the whole sonata is like an echo of the song."[6] Clara responded: "How deeply excited I am over your sonata . . . you can imagine my rapture when in the third [movement] I once more found my passionately loved melody. . . . I say 'my,' because I do not believe that anyone feels the rapture and sadness of it as I do. . . . My pen is poor, but my heart beats warmly and gratefully, and in spirit I press your hand."[7] She always called it the "Regenlied Sonata."

The dotted figure from the Groth songs is part of the dialogue throughout, making a rhythmic motto across the movements. That shows Brahms concerned, as usual, not only with writing something charming and gently lyrical (though it is enormously so) but also with further integrating thematic material throughout the movements. Most noticeably, the main theme of the middle movement and its key of E♭ are taken up and carried to apotheosis in the finale. In its first appearance that slow-movement theme, in its somber beauty, shows another dimension of Brahms's harmonic originality: the harmonies are conventional and unambiguous, but the rhythmic freedom is remarkable, with nearly every structural bass note kept off the strong beats. The music wanders in a rhythmic fog:

In the first movement Brahms plays elaborate games with phrasing, switching the stresses of the $\frac{6}{4}$ meter back and forth between 3+3 and 2+2+2, or superimposing both in violin and piano. (That dichotomy, as we expect from Brahms, is inherent in the principal theme itself.) These ideas gather at the climax at measure 235, with its layering of phrases making an effect that perhaps during the nineteenth century only Brahms could have conceived:

The First Violin Sonata is usually thought of as harking back to the earlier product of Pörtschach, the lyrical Violin Concerto. So it does; at the same time, in its rhythmic sophistication and its integration of thematic and tonal elements across the movements, the sonata looks forward as well to the Third Symphony.

On a copy of the sonata's slow movement that he sent to Clara, Brahms told her that he composed it to "tell you, perhaps more clearly than I otherwise could myself, how sincerely I think of you and Felix."[8] (The thought did not persuade Clara to like the adagio; she preferred the outer movements.[9]) When Brahms sent the piece to Simrock, he asked his publisher to slip the thousand-taler fee anonymously into an account that Clara drew from. She apparently did not detect the gift, or she would have returned it indignantly. For a more tangible memorial to Clara's son, Brahms set a third lyric of Felix's, "Es brausen der Liebe Wogen."

Another product of summer 1879 was the song "Feldeinsamkeit" ("Solitude in an Open Field"), one of his most beautiful and eventually most famous, with its extraordinary second stanza depicting the thoughts of a dreamer lying in the grass:

> *The beautiful white clouds pass above*
> *Through the deep blue, like beautiful silent dreams;*
> *I feel as if I were long dead*
> *And moving peacefully with them through eternal space.*

Also that summer he wrote the two intense, passionate piano Rhapsodies of Opus 79, dedicated to Elisabet von Herzogenberg. If the pieces rise from his feeling about Lisl, they were rhapsodic indeed. For this period of his life, when most of his music had become magisterial and impersonal, the Rhapsodies turned out startlingly turbulent in their harmonic and rhythmic language, and in their emotions.

In the course of this sojourn in Pörtschach Brahms enjoyed his accustomed string of visitors, and made a new acquaintance of considerable enchantment for him. It began with a rehearsal of young women musicians that he attended. Brahms sat nearsightedly watching as a miserable pianist played, followed by a superb violinist, after which apparently the pianist returned to play a second piece, much better. When he commented on the improvement to a neighbor, he was informed that actually the second piano piece had been played by a different girl who was also the violinist, both of them fifteen-year-old Marie Soldat. Brahms sought her out afterward and quipped, "Now that you've played violin and piano so beautifully, why don't you sing for us too?" In August he accompanied Marie during a Pörtschach recital, then he sent her off to study with Joachim.[10] She would later repay Brahms's favors with interest. He gave her the sort of nicknames he bestowed on people he liked: she was "Mietzchen," or "die kleine Soldat," the little soldier.

That September Joachim joined Brahms for a concert tour of Hungary and Transylvania. Despite regular cheers for the First Violin Sonata, Joachim once more had to put up with his accompanist's grumbling and resistance to practicing. As Brahms wrote Clara:

> There has to be a concert every day, and all one can do is to arrive an hour before the concert and be off again an hour after it. I can think of nothing more detestable or more contemptible than this kind of occupation. And yet people like us are so well treated. We are received by the mayor and the Directors at the station, introduced immediately into the best circles, and they all vie with each other in being as kind and as friendly to us as possible.[11]

In fact it would be a long time before Brahms's winter performing schedule slackened; early the next year he and Joachim toured in Poland. If Brahms claimed to hate performing and did not particularly need the (very good) money, he continued to need the exposure. Anyone proposing to perform with him, however, had to be prepared to follow their accompanist's vagaries. Brahms still tended to play chamber music as if he were the only one present. Besides, he had acquired the habit of groaning and growling along as he played. The effect was alarming, if you were close enough to hear it.

Just before his summer's working sojourn of 1880, Brahms traveled to Bonn for the unveiling of the monument at Robert Schumann's grave.

The ceremonies included several concerts. Among the old Schumann circle attending—including Dietrich, Hiller, Grimm, Bargiel, and Stockhausen—was Joachim, who contributed an especially memorable performance of Brahms's Violin Concerto with the composer on the podium. Brahms also conducted Schumann's *Rhenish* Symphony and *Requiem for Mignon*.

The performers did not include Clara, whose arm troubles were not allowing her to play long pieces. Her misery at that was compounded by having to listen to Johannes grope and growl his way through Robert's E♭ Major Piano Quartet with Joachim's group. "I felt as if I were sitting on thorns," she told her journal, "and so did Joachim, who kept casting despairing glances at me."¹² Hermann Levi, once intimate with all of them, neither attended the festivities nor sent greetings. At a party following the ceremonies Clara and Johannes played the second and final set of his Hungarian Dances, which would be published that year. Like the previous set they would be issued first for piano four hands, then in all sorts of profitable arrangements; Dvořák orchestrated nos. 17–21, and Joachim supplied a violin-piano version as he had for the first set.

In Bonn, Clara invited young Max Kalbeck, who had come on Brahms's recommendation to consult with her about editing Robert's letters, to return to Frankfurt with them and stay over to celebrate Johannes's forty-seventh birthday. At home on May 7 she played the new Opus 79 Rhapsodies for the assembled guests. Brahms had been in a foul mood throughout the visit, and Clara asked Kalbeck if he knew why. The young man had no idea. Suddenly Clara's eyes filled with tears. "Would you believe," she said to Brahms's future biographer, "that in spite of our long and intimate friendship Johannes has never told me anything about what excites or upsets him? He is just as much of a riddle, I could almost say as much of a stranger, as he was to me twenty-five years ago."¹³

LOOKING FOR NEW SCENERY and new ideas in the summer of 1880, Brahms chose Bad Ischl, a resort east of Salzburg called "the Baden-Baden of Austria." The place was famed for being the summer home of Emperor Franz Josef and much of fashionable Vienna. To the Herzogenbergs Brahms wrote, "If half of Berlin or Leipzig were here, I'd probably run away, but half of Vienna is very pretty and very easy to look at."¹⁴ (He appears weary of his fellow Germans.) Around his forty-seventh birthday he reported to Billroth, "I live most comfortably in Salzburger Street 51. Some of my rivals are here, meanwhile, in the persons of [Eugen] Franck and Brüll. But now we only rival each other in

seeing how long we can walk and gad around; there I outdo all my colleagues."[15]

Ischl turned out to be wretchedly cold and rainy that year, and from
the weather Brahms developed an ear infection. Given that he was unfamiliar with the whole idea of illness, the onslaught brought on fantasies
about losing his hearing like Beethoven. He rushed in panic back to Vienna and appeared unannounced as Billroth's family were having lunch.
The surgeon calmed him down and led him to an ear specialist, who
found nothing to be concerned about. "My ear decided to catch a cold,"
Brahms reported to the Herzogenbergs.[16] It passed and he went back to
Ischl, but while he sketched several things that summer, only a couple,
and relatively small ones at that, got finished.

Adding to the distractions of the weather and his health was the final
collapse of Joachim's marriage to Amalie. Brahms wrote the violinist in
July, "It has made me very sad and is constantly in my thoughts. You had
so much in common, which gave promise of a long and happy life together. And now!—I find it hard to believe there is any really serious
cause for it."[17] That implies he may not have known yet the reason
Joachim was repudiating his wife: his conviction that Amalie was having
a liaison with Fritz Simrock. Though others joined in Joachim's suspicions, Brahms felt sure the idea was the product of his friend's chronic
brooding and jealousy. From the beginning, Joachim had resented his
wife's performing career; even though Amalie gave up the operatic stage
for him, she still concertized. Meanwhile, he was often away on tour and
Amalie had suffered long periods of illness.

In that lacerating moment Joachim fell back on his old friend for support and sympathy. But he found none—instead, the worst break of their
historic collaboration and their long love/hate relations. For once, it
would not be Brahms's callousness and self-protectiveness that forced the
break, but rather his decency and honesty. He made a special trip to
Joachim's summer place in Salzburg, and there amid the usual playing
tried to talk sense to his friend. Joachim listened, appreciated the concern, but could not be shaken out of his chimeras. He wrote Johannes in
December with a weary, clinging self-pity:

> You know, dear friend, what great weight I attach to your judgment in
> matters of common humanity, that I reckon you as shrewd and upright,
> but in my experiences with the Simrock person I can go only on what
> I have found myself to be true. . . . He has acted toward me like the
> most crafty scoundrel; through him, my life is night. I must learn to

bear my fate like a man; but the poor, poor children!—that grieves me unutterably.[18]

Indeed, Brahms was too shrewd and upright to share his friend's delusions. He knew all about Joachim's suspiciousness and his relentless demands for affection, all exacerbated by years of unrelenting work. (Even Clara found Joachim's schedule appalling; day after day in their English tours he had dashed nonstop from concerts to rehearsals and back.) Brahms admired Amalie, her person as well as her voice, too much not to accept her protests of innocence. At the end of the year he sent her a long reassurance, which said in part:

> Let me say first and foremost: with no word, with no thought have I ever acknowledged that your husband might be in the right. . . . Despite a thirty-year friendship, despite all my love and admiration for Joachim, despite all our artistic interests . . . I am very careful in my association with him . . . and would never think of wishing to live in the same city joined with him in collaborative endeavors. At this point I perhaps hardly need to say that, even earlier than you did, I became aware of the unfortunate character-trait with which Joachim so inexcusably tortures himself and others. . . . The simplest matter is so exaggerated, so complicated, that one scarcely knows where to begin with it and how to bring it to an end. . . . His passionate imagination is playing a sinful and inexcusable game with the best and most holy thing fate has granted him.[19]

After dispatching the letter to Amalie, Brahms wrote Simrock, "I am freed from a burden, that I could finally say to her a small part of what I'd like to."[20] When Amalie asked him if she could use his letter as a character reference if she needed it, Brahms assented. He could hardly imagine what use she would make of it, four years after.

Despite all this uproar, Brahms did not end 1880 without something to show; he began piano trios in C major and E♭ major. Clara preferred the latter when Brahms played them for her, but he destroyed it.[21] He also began a masterpiece that may have had a dual inspiration. His painter friend Anselm Feuerbach had died in January. In June Theodor Billroth asked Brahms to arrange something of his own, perhaps from the *Requiem*, for male chorus and brass, intended someday for the surgeon's funeral. Billroth reminded Johannes that he was not religious, so nothing too pious, please.[22] Johannes replied that he would keep it in mind. That summer, for those and maybe other reasons, he began *Nänie*.

He may also have worked on the Second Piano Concerto and a string quintet in F major. But the only completed works of the year, which he showed to Joachim and other friends in the fall, were a pair of overtures. The Academic Festival Overture amounts to Brahms's thanks to Breslau University for the honorary doctorate; he would premiere it there in January 1881. Long-time friend Bernhard Scholz in Breslau had prompted him that the school expected something in return for the honor: "Compose a fine symphony for us! But well orchestrated, old boy, not too uniformly thick!"[23] In lieu of that Brahms produced the lightly scored and lighthearted overture that he described to Max Kalbeck as "a very jolly potpourri of student songs à la Suppé." The composer he cited was the à la mode Franz von Suppé, master of what a later time would call light classics, among them the *Poet and Peasant* and *Light Cavalry* overtures.

The most thoroughly unbuttoned of Brahms's works, the Academic Festival concerns itself with the life of students rather than the dignity of the institution. Probably Brahms based it on memories of staying with Joachim at the University of Göttingen in 1853—the closest he ever came to student life in the streets and taverns. The overture ranges from bassoons comically puffing the freshman ditty "Was kommt dort in der Höh" to its closing, near-Wagnerian brassy blaze of "Gaudeamus igitur." For all the droll tone and episodic form, Brahms gave it his usual treatment, drafting three versions and holding back the weaker two.[24] At least one of those he kept for over a decade, just in case. As companion piece, with his inclination to pairs of works, he produced the somber Tragic Overture. That freestanding movement developed from sketches ten years old, going back to the period of the Alto Rhapsody.[25] It also recalls Brahms's "bardic" tone going further backward to the Harp Songs, and forward toward *Gesang der Parzen*. Soon after the overtures were finished, Joachim did trial readings with his student orchestra.

After the winter in Vienna, from where he wrote Clara "my music, particularly the chamber music, is having a terrific vogue," and after tours of Holland and Hungary, Brahms took his second Italian vacation. This time he took with him Nottebohm, Billroth, and Viennese friend Dr. Adolf Exner; their main stops were Venice, Florence, Pisa, Siena, and Orvieto. Brahms had gone so far as to hire a language tutor before the trip. It did no good, the words wouldn't come; he would stand stammering before a tradesman until Billroth stepped in with his fluent Italian.

The tone of the trip can be discerned in the surgeon's report to Hanslick, from Taormina: "Five hundred feet above the murmuring sea! A full moon! The intoxicating fragrance of orange blossom! The red-flowered cactus on picturesque, colossal boulders! . . . Add to this the wide, long, snow-covered slopes of Etna, and her pillar of fire! Add to this a wine called 'Monte Venere'! And to crown it all, Johannes in ecstasy! I, in drunken impudence, improvising fantasias to him on his quartets!"[26] Billroth had to go home early, however, and Brahms lost Nottebohm when he refused to depart Venice for Rome. The old pedant had found a Cyprian wine he loved like a woman and could not tear himself away from it. Thus rose another rhyme the Board of Scoffers sang at Gause's beerhall in Vienna:

> *At Gause's too drank Nottebohm,*
> *Who started out to go to Rome*
> *But got to Venice merely,*
> *Old wine of Cyprus made the man*
> *Scorn wandering sincerely.*

This may have been the Venetian occasion when an acquaintance of Brahms spotted her composer sailing along in exalted spirits, perhaps from Cyprian wine, and grabbed him as he was strolling into a canal.[27] Brahms not only loved Italy, he loved to travel it with a few men whose mode of joie de vivre counterpointed his own.

MAY 1881 found Brahms in Pressbaum, an hour from Vienna on the Linz rail line. To Billroth he said he chose the place "desiring to avoid a bad summer in Ischl, which I would not like to expose myself to again." His visitors included Henschel, Widmann, Simrock, and Joachim, the last still pressing Johannes to second his accusations against Amalie and Simrock.

That summer Brahms completed *Nänie* for chorus and orchestra, his commemoration of the death of Anselm Feuerbach. He sent it to Billroth with the reminder that he had not forgotten the "garden"—i.e., funeral—music for which the surgeon had asked him (which he never got around to). Brahms noted in the letter, "Incidentally, if the piece does not please you, reflect upon the fact that hexameter makes a rhythm which is quite difficult for a musician."

The hexameters in *Nänie* are Schiller's, a re-creation of the ancient Roman funeral dirge called *noenia* sung by parents on the death of a child.

In keeping with that Brahms dedicated it to the painter's stepmother, who indeed embraced it as her funeral song. In search of a text that would suit the neoclassicist Feuerbach, Brahms had happened on the verses after begging Lisl von Herzogenberg, "Won't you try to find me some words? . . . The ones in the Bible are not heathen enough for me. I've bought the Koran but can't find anything there either."[28] The text he finally found is an evocation of the pagan and Classical world, a dirge at once tragic and serene:

> *Even the beautiful must die! That which conquers men and gods*
> *Does not touch the brazen heart of Stygian Zeus . . .*
> *See! Then the gods weep, all the goddesses weep*
> *Because the beautiful perishes, because perfection dies.*[29]

Though like most of his texts it spoke deeply to his life, Brahms's setting of it is far from the resignation of *Ein deutsches Requiem*, the anguish of the Alto Rhapsody, the threatening despair of the *Schicksalslied*. He set Schiller's verses to exquisite melodies in richly weaving counterpoint: a ceremonial dance before the grave, a tonal analogy to the quiet gravity of Feuerbach's art, and one of the highest examples of what has been called Brahms's "sublime style." Perhaps no one but Brahms, with his constitutional reserve masking a feeling soul, could have set "Even the beautiful must die!" to a gently lilting, D major soprano melody that captures the sorrow of death and transcends it in the singing. The beginning already embodies the closing words: "Even to be a song of lament on loved ones' lips is glorious."[30] Brahms would conduct the premiere in Zürich in December 1881.

Immediately, mundane matters intruded upon that sublime canvas. Even though Brahms had now been happily with Fritz Simrock's publishing house for years, he gave *Nänie* to Dr. Max Abraham at Peters, to fulfill an old promise of a work. He was thinking of doing the same with the next piece. That news brought an alarmed Simrock flying to Pressbaum in person, with the result that Brahms wrote Dr. Abraham with mock gravity, "Herr Simrock . . . is a much too easygoing and well-disposed colleague of yours. He will take the heavy cross from you and carry it for you!"[31] The "heavy cross" he hints about, a.k.a. "the long terror," turned up in equally ironic form in a letter of July 1881 to Elisabet von Herzogenberg: "I don't mind telling you that I have written a tiny, tiny piano concerto with a tiny, tiny wisp of a scherzo."[32] All the teasing was for the monumental four-movement Second Piano Concerto in B♭

Major, with its giant scherzo (probably the one he had deleted from the Violin Concerto).

As soon as he heard about it, Hans von Bülow offered Brahms a trial reading of the new work with his Meiningen Hofkapelle Orchestra. Bülow had just taken over the court orchestra and was in the process of building it into one of the most finely honed ensembles in Europe. Brahms made some polite demurrals to the offer but allowed himself to be persuaded. He turned up in Meiningen in October 1881 and occupied the piano at the reading as Bülow proudly showed off his men. There began an extraordinary collaboration between Brahms and Bülow, and also the long and surprising relationship of Brahms with the music-loving court of Georg II.

From that point, for as long as Bülow headed the Meiningen Orchestra he placed it at Brahms's disposal as a laboratory for new pieces, and at the same time made the group—despite its having only forty-eight players—the prime model of Brahms performance. In that Bülow outshone the Vienna Philharmonic under the brilliant but mercurial Hans Richter. Like Bülow, the current Philharmonic conductor had been a protégé of Wagner; unlike Bülow he had remained one—Richter conducted the first performance of the complete *Ring of the Nibelungs* at Bayreuth in 1876. Eventually he would champion Anton Bruckner as well. Brahms and Richter were by no means inimical to each other, but understandably wary. Richter was noted for skimpy rehearsing that he made up for, sometimes, by inspired performances. His philosophy was to give "the orchestra of poets" room to poeticize. It worked beautifully sometimes, but such an approach was not Brahms's style in the least. When the Philharmonic gave a characteristically underprepared repeat performance of the First Symphony in 1878, Brahms told friend Richard Heuberger, "Finally I didn't say anything else, but only laughed when things got really sloppy. If you don't want to study it, you should leave it alone."[33] He wrote Clara at the same time about the Philharmonic, "They mean well, but when something has once failed, they don't rehearse it."[34]

In contrast, Bülow was both celebrated and in some circles deplored for his fanatically meticulous performances. As Hanslick put it, he played the Meiningen Orchestra "like a little bell in his hand."[35] Bülow handled not only concerts but rehearsals without a score, which amazed Brahms as much as anyone.[36] The conductor also lectured and sometimes harangued audiences; at one concert, when he felt the appreciation for Beethoven's Ninth had been insufficient, he played the enormous symphony all over again.[37] "He baptizes the infidels," Hanslick wrote, "with a firehose." As sign of their commitment and concentration, Bülow made his musicians memorize the music and play standing; some ridiculed them as the "strolling orchestra." And he took them on extensive railway tours, one of the first conductors to do that.

Both Clara Schumann and, for a while, Elisabet von Herzogenberg considered Bülow's conducting and piano playing cold and intellectual. After hearing the Meiningen Orchestra Lisl sent Brahms a report reflecting what many of the day thought of Bülow's hard-edged style.

> Everybody lay prostrate before this anointed one, who bore himself like a priest elevating the Host in the glittering monstrance for the first time. At times he seemed to be giving a repulsive anatomy lecture. It was as if he were making the experiment of stripping an antique statue of its lovely flesh, and forcing one to worship the workings of bone and muscle. . . . Bülow's affected little pauses before every new phrase, every notable change in harmony, are quite unpardonable.

Quirks aside, Bülow's philosophy of precision and fidelity to the score was prophetic, heralding a new age of conducting virtuosos. Clearly that approach suited Brahms. At the same time some of this friend's affectations, mainly the habit of marking phrases with pauses and generally letting tempos wander, did not please the composer any more than they did Elisabet. In theory, Brahms rejected all such tricks: "I've completely forbidden that in my symphonies; if I had wanted it, I would've written it down."[38] Of course, he had to admit that sometimes he did the same thing himself. Listeners recalled the excitement Brahms generated on the podium at the beginning of the First Symphony finale by accelerating the pizzicatos more than the score calls for. Elisabet discovered with relief that once Bülow knew a piece better his vagaries of tempo and such tended to recede, and the virtues of his lapidary approach shone forth.

In his personality the conductor was famously pinched and prickly, lean and hungry, at times downright weird. (In his later years, for example, he once descended from the podium during a concert and tried to force Gustav Mahler, who was sitting in front, to take the baton and conduct.) Bülow called himself "the little leopard," his plump hero Brahms "the great lion." The lion admired his leopard not without qualification, but immensely all the same. And so the favored conductors of Brahms and the New Germans, once respectively Levi and Bülow, had switched places.

Now his three B's were Bülow's gods. In 1881 he wrote his new wife: "You know what I think of Brahms: after Bach and Beethoven the greatest, the most sublime of all composers. After your love, I hold his friendship as the most important thing in my life. It represents an epoch in my life, a moral conquest. . . . Ah, his Adagios! Religion!" Another side of his devotion he expressed one day to Max Kalbeck, in a sudden paroxysm as they walked together: "I have him to thank for being restored to sanity . . . in fact, for still being alive! Three quarters of my existence has been squandered on my former father-in-law [Liszt], the old mountebank, and his tribe, but the remainder belongs to the true saints of art, and above all to him! to him!! to him!!!"[39] With that he gestured wildly toward Brahms, strolling ahead of them.

After Bülow and Brahms played the Second Piano Concerto in Meiningen at the end of November 1881, the duke awarded its composer the Commander's Cross of the Order of the House of Meiningen. Brahms the son of the Hamburg docks would become something on the order of friends with Herzog Georg II and Freifrau Helene von Heldburg, of the little Meiningen court where the arts loomed large. To add to Brahms's pleasure in Meiningen, Princess Marie had studied piano with Kirchner and Bülow and played his music prettily. If his tastes remained unpretentious, democratic, and tieless, Brahms did not appear to mind staying in the castle, donning his good coat with his medals, and dining from golden plates with footmen at his elbow.[40] Unlike Mozart and Beethoven, Brahms had the luxury of not particularly needing anything from the aristocracy, so he could enjoy what they offered him without ulterior motives. The following year's *Gesang der Parzen* would be dedicated to Georg II.

In February 1882, Bülow gave a historic all-Brahms piano recital in Vienna that included what may have been the formal premiere of the F♯ Minor Sonata, Opus 2, plus the old Opus 10 Ballades and new Opus 79 Rhapsodies, and the Handel Variations. After the last, the cheering went on so long that finally Bülow shouted jokingly, "If you don't stop applauding I'm going to play the final fugue again!" Liszt came to the recital and complimented Brahms for that music and in a note afterward, mildly, for the Second Piano Concerto: "Frankly speaking, at the first reading this work seemed to me a little gray in tone; I have, however, gradually come to understand it. It possesses the pregnant character of a distinguished work of art, in which thought and feeling move in noble harmony."[41] Liszt was not so magnanimous, though, as to break his record of never playing Brahms in public.

The honor of premiering the Second Concerto went to the Budapest Philharmonic on November 9, 1881, with Alexander Erkel on the podium and Brahms at the piano. Bülow was soon playing both concertos as conductor and pianist, sometimes conducting from the keyboard. Florence May saw performances in Berlin that season by the Meiningen Orchestra, in one of which Bülow soloed in the D Minor with Brahms conducting, then vice versa for the B♭ Major. (They repeated the stunt in other cities, sometimes switching places.) May was struck by how much Brahms's playing had deteriorated in the ten years since she had studied with him. Nevertheless, in some fashion or other, and with expert faking, he got his hands around the virtuoso demands of his concertos.

The D Minor Concerto had been emblematic of a young composer finding his way; the Second Concerto is Brahms at his most masterful. If the experience of love and yearning and tragedy nearly overwhelmed the First, the Second turns a lofty, magisterial face to the world. If the Violin Concerto was too symphonic for many soloists to stomach, the B♭ is more so, both in its structure and in the four-movement plan. As with the First Concerto, the treatment of the piano itself approaches orchestral in its sheer mass of sound. (In later years Brahms preferred the modern, thicker tone of instruments like the Viennese Bösendorfer, the Bechstein of Berlin, the American Steinway.[42])

In their material his two mature concertos are more conservative than his symphonies—the B♭ has one of the few real scherzos of his mature orchestral works, and in both of them one finds less rhythmic quirkiness than in the symphonies and chamber music. In the orchestra the principal theme of the B♭ Concerto and its derivatives are largely made of quarter notes in four-square rhythms, while the piano adds resplendent figuration. (If Liszt was in some degree right about the grayness of tone, surely rhythm has much to do with it.) The D minor scherzo of the second movement is marked *Allegro appassionato*. If it does not possess the fantasy of his youthful scherzos, it does have a massive, at times demonic intensity, inflected by subtleties of form and rhythm that only the mature master could manage. Asked about the startling change in tone from first movement to scherzo, Brahms was apt to explain—tongue in cheek, surely—that the first movement was so "harmless" that the piece needed the passionate contrast of the scherzo.[43]

The first two movements omit his sweetly lyrical side, but he lays that on thick in the slow movement, starting with one of his extended, yearning cello melodies. That gives way to the playful two-beat rondo of the finale. Michael Musgrave questions whether this light, "last-dance" conclusion, spacious though it is, succeeds in balancing the textural and emotional weight of the earlier movements, especially the scherzo.[44] Donald Francis Tovey, happier with the effect, metaphorizes the finale:

"We have done our work—let the children play in the world which our work has made safer and happier for them."[45] In any case, with the Second Concerto Brahms commemorated the still living but now neglected Hamburg master who had made his own childhood happier, writing on the score: "Dedicated to his dear friend and teacher Eduard Marxsen."

During the concert season of 1881–2, Brahms took the new concerto around Germany, Switzerland, and Holland, plus the two overtures, the second set of Hungarian Dances, and *Nänie* along with other items old and new. Whether played by Bülow and Meiningen or by local orchestras, the concerto was welcomed rapturously nearly everywhere—though tepidly in Leipzig. Clara wrote in her journal: "Brahms is celebrating such triumphs everywhere as seldom fall to the lot of a composer."[46] She did not begrudge him his success after her husband's lifetime of comparative neglect. Clara considered Johannes hers nearly as much as Robert, and her labors critical for both of them, and so she took a proprietary interest in Johannes's music. She also knew that whatever his triumphs on the world's stage, in many ways he lived a sad life and always would.

BACK IN VIENNA IN MARCH 1882, just before trying Bad Ischl again for the summer, Brahms pulled together the lieder of Opuses 84–6. He sent Elisabet von Herzogenberg a revision for "Therese" from Opus 86, making a more elaborate melody for the beginning of a song she had already seen, and he asked what she thought. "I should feel quite sad if you insisted on it," Lisl replied. "I do beg that you won't meddle with the dear little song any more, but rest satisfied with the simpler version."[47] He did as told. In April he took up and revised the old "Wiegenlied" ("Cradle Song") he had written for alto and viola on the birth of the Joachims' first child, quoting "Josef, lieber Josef mein." He hoped it might help resolve the estrangement of two beloved friends and musicians. Of course it did not. As "Geistliches Wiegenlied" it would join "Gestillte Sehnsucht" to make the lovely Opus 91 for contralto, viola, and piano. For a long time, the alto voice in Brahms's imagination had been Amalie, just as violin and viola were always Joachim.

From Ischl that summer Brahms responded to an invitation of Bülow's, confessing he was tempted to accompany his friend to the premiere of Wagner's *Parsifal* in July: "The fact that I can't come to a decision about Bayreuth probably means that I am unable to produce that 'yes.' I need hardly say that I go in dread of the Wagnerians, who would spoil my pleasure in the best of Wagners. . . . I may take advantage of my beard, which still allows me to trot about so nice and anonymously."[48] It is charming if he really imagined he could sneak into Bayreuth undetected behind his beard, like a spy in disguise.

Shortly after that, Wagner issued a barely coherent harangue in the *Bayreuth Blätter*, perhaps partly by way of revenge on Bülow for his defection from the fold: "But as the Gospel has faded since the cross of the Redeemer has been hawked like merchandise on every street corner, so has the genius of German music grown silent ever since it has been hauled around the world-mart by the métier, and pseudo-professional gutter-witlessness celebrated its progress." He snarled that the success Bülow had found recently with Brahms's symphonies only proved that public taste had become so debased that maybe now Brahms's eventual ten symphonies would survive compared to two by Beethoven. After perusing those thoughts, Brahms wrote Bülow again, turning down the invitation to Bayreuth with his sarcasm running strong: "What a pity, for I was planning nothing for the entire month apart from a pilgrimage to the Prophet who has divined my future in so friendly a way."[49]

A letter of that summer to Simrock, asking the publisher when he was going to Bayreuth, shows that Brahms had heard of the kind of abuse Hermann Levi was getting in the Wagner circle: not only were many of Wagner's disciples, and Cosima, disgusted with the Master's choice of a Jew for a conductor, but the Master himself could not stop taunting his disciple with antisemitic gibes. Brahms wrote Simrock, "The official scribes treat [Levi] with suspicion and praise the assistant Kapellmeister!" Like many in the cult Levi was in a kind of sinister rapture now, making excuses for Wagner to his rabbi father. And to Joachim, to whom he wrote: "I bless the day on which my eyes were opened. . . . But one cannot argue about Wagner any more than one can about religion. . . . I should be glad if you also were granted such a—change one day. (I said 'granted' deliberately, because it comes quite of itself, and you need only to keep quiet and not to fight against it.)"[50]

Yet out of respect for his bygone friendship Levi had still programmed the first two Brahms symphonies in Munich. In part because the conductor did not entirely like either piece, in part because Munich was Wagner's town, both symphonies were a fiasco. A group of citizens informed Levi that in the future he must announce the entire season's schedule ahead of time, and if Brahms were on it they would cancel their subscriptions. Even with the best of intentions, Levi could hardly fight that kind of resistance and keep his job. Whether it secretly pleased him is another question.

Without the distraction of going to Bayreuth, in 1882 Brahms had a remarkable summer in Bad Ischl. He finished the F Major String Quintet, the C Major Piano Trio, and *Gesang der Parzen*—the quintet Brahms at nearly his most ebullient (perhaps enhanced by the daily companionship of Ignaz Brüll and his tuneful music), the trio a mingling of light and dark, and the *Parzen* the most desolate work of his life.

AS IN THE 1860s Brahms, enjoying his liberation from the onus of genres the past had perfected, wrote two string sextets with great freedom and success, so in his maturity he produced two string quintets undaunted by Mozart's great ones. The viola added to the usual quartet of strings allowed him to indulge in some of the textural richness and warmth that had marked the sextets.

The F Major Quintet opens without preliminaries on a gemütlich, almost Schubertian theme, lushly harmonized:

From that uncomplicated (perhaps a touch self-satisfied) beginning, the Quintet goes on to be quirky in all sorts of ways, including being cast in three movements rather than the usual four. The second theme of the opening movement, traditionally in C if you start in F, instead goes up a third to A major; in the recapitulation it comes in down a third, to D major. That heralds a number of other "mediant" key relationships in the piece, an echo of the same in Schubert's C Major Quintet. Among other formal singularities, the development begins in busily contrapuntal fashion, but after a false recapitulation in the middle spends its second half in an extended retransition to the real recap.

The middle movement turns out to be based on two of Brahms's little neo-Baroque piano dances from three decades back. The slow part, which returns three times in varied forms something like a rondo theme, comes from his old A Major Sarabande, now put into C♯ minor. Here the *moll-Dur* quality of the original is made even more poignant.

That theme is marked by penetrating harmonic vagaries, mostly turning around the "Neapolitan" harmonic inflection (a D major chord in C♯ minor). Between those slow, introspective sections Brahms scissors in two fast, dancing interludes derived from his old A Major Gavotte. The effect, in the middle of this three-movement piece, is to put a slow movement together with a scherzo in a kind of collage. At the end comes a veiled, cryptic series of harmonies that cadence not on C♯ minor but rather A major—another rare example of Brahms finishing a movement in a different key than he started it. (And the ending makes a mediant relationship with both the beginning of the movement and with what follows: C♯, A, F.)

For a finale he picks up the cue of his First Cello Sonata—and of Beethoven's third *Rasoumovsky* Quartet—to create a racing, high-spirited sonata form treated fugally throughout. The virtuosity of its counterpoint seems part of the joke. It keeps climaxing with one or another form of a manically polyphonic, absurd little phrase, its leading tune doubled by barking low cello and squeaking high violin:

For some reason this F Major Quintet would turn out to be one of the least popular of Brahms's chamber pieces, at the same time one of his own favorites. He told Simrock, "You have never before had such a beautiful work from me"; to Clara he named it "one of my finest works."[51]

Brahms had a surprising pattern in his favorites. Of the three string quartets he most liked the Bb Major, which stands out from its siblings in its light, almost satirical tone. When in 1880 Eduard Hanslick expressed delight in the tuneful and mocking little song "Vergebliches Ständchen" ("Futile Serenade"), Brahms responded surely with irony, if not forced praise: "I am in an extremely good humor as a result of the good-humored correspondence! . . . And this time you have hit my bullseye! For this one song I would give up all the others. . . . But from you the confirmation is of immensely serious value to me! I have known for a long time that your excellent sniffer doesn't miss any really excellent morsel (this is more annoying when we are eating oysters)."[52] One recalls Brahms's glowing cheeks and flashing eyes when he played his Hungarian Dances.

What it adds up to is that he seemed most to enjoy the pieces of his that came to him most easily and posed neither daunting technical nor emotional demands. In that he was a bit like Hanslick, after all: he liked to relax and listen to something tuneful and delightful, including his own stuff. It does not follow, though, that he would have placed the lighter pieces above his symphonies and choral works, only that like many artists he could not forget or entirely forgive what the hard ones took out of him. (When Jean Cocteau's disaster-haunted production of *La Belle et la Bête* finally ended and Cocteau viewed the uncannily beautiful result, he remarked, "It looks to me like nothing but pain.") At least the public agreed with Brahms about the song: among his lieder, "Vergebliches Ständchen" is one of the enduring hits.

The C Major Piano Trio is his first in the medium since the youthful B Major of 1854, and so a good indication of the distance he had traveled, what had changed and what stayed the same. Young Kreisler had begun the earlier trio with a sweetly lyrical cello tune, and the Herr Doktor still was not above producing gestures like that. The C Major Trio, however, does not particularly try to seduce us at the outset; it starts with a stately unison, a kind of blank slate. It goes on to be an expressive but organic and straightforward first movement, with tense moments here and there. Then comes a remarkable slow movement. By then, Brahms had written a number of driving "gypsy" allegros; now he writes variations on a slow tune of Hungarian flavor. Its hollow, keening tone and its "Scotch snap" rhythm can be heard in some of Bartók's slow movements, which are more authentically Hungarian but hardly more soulful than this:

After a skittering, succinct scherzo, Brahms begins the finale with a flowing tune in Lydian mode on C, with its characteristic raised fourth degree:

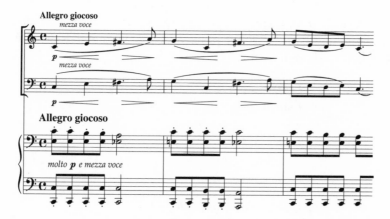

When he flirts with these scales outside the usual major and minor keys (often Phrygian, with its second degree lowered from minor), Brahms does not usually jump whole cloth into modality but rather suggests the coloration of a mode before resolving everything into major or minor. (Here, for example, there is nothing particularly Lydian about the harmony.) In its overall shape the finale is laid out in sonata form, but for most of its course it has the lighthearted, dancing feel of the traditional rondo finale. About a quarter of it is taken up by a coda of ambiguous expressive import: though it winds up with the joviality of the movement proper, it is dominated by a shimmering arpeggio figure that strangely recalls, in both texture and harmony (F♯ diminished seventh) Schubert's unsettling late lied "Die Stadt." In that song the narrator is rowed by a mysterious figure who suggests Charon, across a cold bay to an obscure city, where on the shore he finds the place where he lost his beloved. (Earlier there seems to be an allusion to "Die Stadt" in the A Major Piano Quartet.)

From those moments when a chilly wind seems to blow through the generally affable atmosphere of the trio finale, it is not so far to the world of *Gesang der Parzen* (*Song of the Fates*), for orchestra and six-part chorus, its text from Goethe's *Iphigenia*.

The thought of fate had always been an ominous one in Brahms's work, shadowing the opening of the C Minor Symphony and the *Schicksalslied*. Meanwhile there had grown in his music and in his mind the bleak conviction that humanity in some way has been divorced from God. *Ein deutsches Requiem* ends with the word *selig*, blessed. The Alto Rhapsody portrays a misanthropic separation from the world, but ends with a sublime prayer. The middle of the *Schicksalslied* (*Song of Destiny*) expresses the rift with the gods in an anguished voice, but the work ends in wordless peace. In *Nänie* the gods weep for the death of beauty. Now in *Gesang der Parzen* there is no prayer, no answer, no resolution, neither in its searching harmonies nor in its verses. Now the gods are distant, silent, and foreboding.

> *Let the race of man*
> *Fear the gods!*
> *They hold the power*
> *In eternal hands*
> *And they use it*
> *As they please.*
>
> *Let that man fear them doubly*
> *Whom once they exalted! . . .*
>
> *The rulers turn away*
> *Their blessing-granting eyes*
> *From entire generations,*
> *And refuse to recognize in the grandson*
> *His ancestor's*
> *Quietly speaking features,*
> *Which they once loved.*
>
> *Thus sang the Fates;*
> *In caverns of night*
> *The exile, an old man,*

Listens to their songs,
Remembers his children and grandchildren
And shakes his head.

And so sang Johannes, a man once exalted by fate, named almost a god, now nearing fifty calling himself an exile, and watching his culture fall to pieces. When he said to George Henschel, "As much as we men . . . are above the creeping things of the earth, so these gods are above us!" the gods he spoke of were his personal ones, his real religion: Bach, Mozart, Beethoven, Schubert, and the others. Now he approached his age with the gods of the earth vanished, and the ones in the heavens silent and unapproachable.

The searing introduction that begins *Gesang der Parzen* might be called a distorted echo of the joyful, elevated, Handelian tone of the *Triumphlied*. Perhaps here Brahms takes back the *Triumphlied*'s forthright exaltation of victory and empire: the patriotic work is in D major, the *Parzen* in D minor. Brahms generally called it *Parzenlied* for short—the Song of Triumph found its negation in the Song of Fate.

The opening harmonies are among the most unsettled Brahms ever wrote, not revealing the central tonality of D until the third measure; there is scarcely a solid harmonic resolution in the piece. The beautiful but sorrowful conclusion, its harmonies drifting free of any definable tonality (an evocation of mankind with no foundation left), became a favorite passage of Webern and Schoenberg. (There is a general difference in Brahms's and Wagner's means of obscuring tonality: at least from *Tristan* on, Wagner tends to do it with more dissonant harmonies—mainly ninth chords, diminished and half-diminished sevenths—Brahms with triads changing in unconventional ways. Sometimes his metric instability also works to unsettle the tonal sense.)

Billroth complained about the dissonance and ambiguity of the beginning: "Hanslick . . . will probably get a shock in the first few bars. . . . You will, of course, have your conscious and unconscious grounds . . . to emphasize these abnormal hardnesses of the *Parzen*, but our modern ears are sometimes pained by it." To that Brahms offered another of his few glimpses into the workshop: "Think back for a moment to the minor chord [in the third bar]. Think of how the modulation from then on would be without any effect, and also quite restless, as if one were searching for something, unless one had heard this progression before and very much emphasized!"[53]

He means that the dissonant and unsettled are keys to this work, and that to begin with stability would have created the wrong impression.

Clara, orthodox as she tended to be about such matters, knew exactly what he was getting at: "Words fail me to tell you the joy I have had from the piece—the gloomy beauty of its harmonies. The progression in the second bar, of which Billroth speaks . . . is precisely what stirs me most."[54] For the "gloomy beauty" she is probably thinking also of the chorus part, especially the first entrance on "Let the race of man fear the gods!," another of Brahms's dactylic bardic chants.

To Brahms the musical evocation of *fate* required minor keys, simple inexorable rhythms, and the kind of pounding kettledrums that here accompany the entrance of the choir. That evocation rings throughout *Gesang der Parzen*. Even within the usually abstract and Olympian voice of the mature Brahms, and despite the quiet resignation of the ending, the work is an evocation of universal despair—and Brahms's despair, who had no other children than music: the old man listens to the songs of the fates and remembers his children and grandchildren, and shakes his head in the caverns of night.

In the Alto Rhapsody, *die Wüste* was the wasteland of a solitary and exile. Now Brahms had come to see exile in *die Wüste* as the fate of his culture: *The rulers turn away their blessing-granting eyes from entire generations.*

AT THE SAME TIME, to a degree, from its composer's standpoint *Gesang der Parzen* is a work of what a later age would call "midlife crisis": I'm getting old, music is going to the dogs, I have no children, nobody will remember me when I'm gone. If it had only been his personal anguish that the piece reflected, however, Brahms might not have allowed such self-indulgence. The breakup of the Joachims had shaken him. Surely he was thinking of Clara too: aging, much in pain, a son and daughter dead in ten years, another son mad and another broken by drugs. Beyond these concerns he thought about the state of music, with a few streaks of hope like Antonin Dvořák, but no one in sight who seemed to him to possess the kind of mastery and depth he did, poor as those were in relation to the gods. And he looked with a shudder at the state of his homeland and his adopted country.

The year after he finished *Gesang der Parzen*, 1883, Brahms wrote Simrock, "In a city and a land where everything not rolls, but tumbles downhill, you can't expect music to fare better. Really it's a pity and a crying shame, not only for music but for the whole beautiful land and the beautiful, marvelous people. I still think catastrophe is coming."[55] Later that year anti-Brahmsians in Vienna spread a rumor that he no longer believed a German could live in Austria.[56]

Now Austria's long slide, not only of empire but of spirit, was accelerating toward the era expressed in the term *fin de siècle*. Brahms understood with agonizing clarity that the *siècle* about to end in social and artistic revolution was *his* age, the age in which his music had flowered and found its public: the long, relatively placid interregnum after the Napoleonic Wars, the era that saw the triumph of the rationalistic, liberal Austro-German bourgeoisie that also happened, more than any other class in history, to appreciate music.

The political part of Austria's decline was relatively easy to understand, impossible to resolve. The polyglot Austrian empire was unraveling at its eternally weak seams. The Dual Monarchy with Hungary continued to sap the Crown, and the Hungarians exploited their new power relentlessly for their own purposes. The other ethnic groups, especially the Czechs, followed the Hungarian example with increasing vehemence, all the subject peoples exploiting the turmoil of a government that socialist Viktor Adler famously declared "a system of despotism tempered by *Schlamperei.*" The word mingles inefficiency, sloppiness, and incompetence.

If Emperor Franz Josef grew into an astute politician, he did not become enough of one to find a way out of the maze. His court had become an operetta fantasy world useless if not dangerous to the country. Most of the real power was wielded behind closed doors of palaces and ministries, in secret actions of nameless bureaucrats answerable only to the Emperor. Parliament approached paralysis, leaving the liberals, long the most dynamic and effective part of the leadership, nearly impotent. There was no possibility of nationalistic sentiment uniting the country, because, as Franz Josef well knew, there was no such thing as an Austrian nationality, only a patchwork that had lasted hundreds of years for no particular reason. The name "Austria" did not even officially exist anymore. In other words, Austria ruled its empire by a kind of epic fakery: empire as theater, with nothing behind the stage set. (The Ringstrasse the biggest stage set of all.) Yet this peculiar congeries had long been one of the greatest powers on the continent, and even in its decline wielded a formidable military machine. And as of 1881 Vienna had a population of one million, making it the fifth-largest city in the world.

From 1879 the government had been led by the witty and cunning Count Taaffe. He proclaimed a "no-party" government, with a policy he actually articulated as *fortwürstln*, which means "muddle along," with overtones of bumbling and clownishness. Wurstl being the Austrian version of Punch, the prime minister seemed to place his government on the footing of a violent and insane puppet show. While keeping the liberals at bay, Taaffe set out to placate the Slavs and Czechs and other ethnic groups by letting them use their language in official capacities.[57] German-speaking Austrians on the spectrum from left to right responded with outrage, which in turn helped to breed violently reactionary organizations—particularly the aristocratic, pan-Germanic, antisemitic movement of Georg von Schönerer that so inspired Hitler. It was Schönerer above all who changed Austrian politics from shouting in Parliament to fighting in the streets. When it came to a favored composer, the hero of the reactionaries was inevitably Wagner—social prophet of murky but suitable cast, German patriot, author of the antisemitic classic "Jewry in Music." When Wagner's disciple Bruckner emerged from obscurity, he became another tool the right wing used to belabor Brahms.

To Brahms as to most liberals, Taafe's playing to the Hungarians and other minorities was anti-German and a road to revolution. On the other hand, the liberals were hardly united and had few ideas of their own about the direction of the country—mainly upholding capitalism and Parliament. (Unlike most liberals, Brahms had no objection to Czech-language schools.) The German-speaking right turned toward authoritarianism and demagoguery. The liberal *Grossbürgertum* collected their profits, wrung their hands, and retreated to the world of art and music as if to drink. Thus, to name one example from the later *fin de siècle*, Hugo von Hoffmannsthal's and Richard Strauss's *Der Rosenkavalier*, which hangs suspended like a marvelous unreal bubble in the imagination: Viennese operetta made sublime.

Just as the City of Dreams had kept drinking new wine and waltzing to Johann Strauss after the devastating loss to Prussia at Königgrätz, the spirits of the city continued to sing and dance through the onslaught of social and political chaos. "The situation," runs an old Viennese joke, "is desperate but not serious." Edward Crankshaw writes, "On the surface this beautiful city had never seemed more vital than when it was dying. It drew vitality from its past, which lived in the streets, and also from its incomparable setting between tall hills, with beeches, pines and gemlike meadows, and the great arterial river curving out across the plain to Hungary."[58] At the same time as the muddle of competing ethnic groups spread chaos in the city, so did the singular cultural goulasch of Slav, Magyar, Italian, Jew, and German create the singular vitality of modern Vienna.

Brahms witnessed the city singing through the dying of its empire and its soul, what Karl Kraus called the "Proving-Ground for World Destruction" that in the next century would be realized in Sarajevo and the Third Reich. Brahms feared for music and humanity alike. As he sang in *Gesang der Parzen*, neither for himself nor for humanity could he see any deus ex machina human or divine to step in, no salvation or consolation. That work of 1882 may be the first herald in music of the coming era, in which everything Brahms most feared came to pass except one: his music sang undiminished through the century of death.

CHAPTER NINETEEN

Valedictions

BRAHMS WROTE THEODOR BILLROTH in spring 1883: "Hanslick and I, on Monday evening, want to have a little small sad festival together. Only you, Faber, and we two." The sad festival was his fiftieth birthday, on May seventh. In approaching it he would have remembered that Beethoven died in his sixth decade, Bach had completed most of his greatest work by then, Mozart and Schubert and Mendelssohn were long dead by his age, and he had outlived Robert Schumann. Clara Schumann's infirmity and the deaths of her children weighed on him. The previous autumn he had sat by the bed of his old friend Gustav Nottebohm, to see him out of the world.

Richard Wagner died in February 1883. Hans von Bülow responded to the news of his hero and betrayer's death by falling to the floor in a fit, clawing and chewing the carpet.[1] Given word during a rehearsal of *Gesang der Parzen* in Meiningen, Brahms solemnly laid down his baton and announced, "Today we sing no more. A master has died." He sent a laurel wreath and card to Bayreuth. Clara wrote condolences to the distraught Hermann Levi: "Though we may be unfortunate enough to disagree about Wagner, yet I know what he meant to you, and I feel for you warmly in the sorrow that has come upon you."[2]

Brahms did not know some of the other landmarks of that year, heralding ages passing and beginning: Anton Webern, Edgard Varèse, and Franz Kafka born; Karl Marx dead, John Maynard Keynes born; Nietzsche's *Also sprach Zarathustra* written; the first skyscraper built in Chicago and the Brooklyn Bridge opened in New York; Paul Cézanne's *Rocky Landscape* painted in the prophetic vein of his maturity; Anton Bruckner's Seventh Symphony completed.

Probably Brahms was convivial enough on his fiftieth birthday, dining and drinking with favorite companions. There is a drawing of Brahms and Billroth and Hanslick from this decade: three fat old men in evening dress, holding cigars and raising their glasses, glowing with champagne and self-satisfaction. In 1883, beyond the advance of time and the eternal demands of work, on the face of it Brahms had little to worry about and much to please him. However portly he had gotten from years of enthusiastic eating and imbibing, he remained in strapping good health. He had just produced another springtime flowering of choruses, vocal quartets, and lieder (for Opuses 92–5) and had a symphony growing in his mind. Meanwhile, yet again, he was in thrall to a singer.

He met her in Krefeld, where he had gone in January for a performance of the Second Piano Concerto and *Gesang der Parzen*. The German town had developed a Brahms cult centered around friends there including Rudolf von der Leyen, a music-loving businessman like many of Brahms's circle. In the Krefeld concert the choir and orchestra did the *Parzen* so beautifully that the composer wept on the podium. The audience demanded an encore of the piece, which the performers did even more beautifully. Brahms was heard to cry out "Ah!" at the blazing entrance of the winds in the beginning. Afterward, in gratitude, he sent the manuscript of the piece to the Krefelder Konzertgesellschaft.

Among the performers that day was contralto Hermine Spies, who had studied with Brahms's longtime colleague Julius Stockhausen. At a party after the concert she sang him "Vergebliches Ständchen" ("Futile Serenade"). The heady effects of the performance and the postconcert celebrations, and a slender and lively young woman singing him his sauciest song, acted predictably on Brahms. When she had finished the lied (the maiden leaves her suitor out in the cold with "Go home to bed!") Brahms exclaimed, "I'm sure she'll let him in!"

The flirtation would go on for years, with many songs for alto as symptoms. He called Spies "my songstress," "the Rhine-maiden," "Herma," and "Herminche," and with Shakespeare's queen in mind: "Hermione-ohne-O" (Hermione without the O). Now he had another dark female voice to hear in his imagination, to compete with Agathe's from years ago and with Amalie Joachim's—though no one would replace Amalie, the finer and more enduring musician.

In the first glow of connection with Hermine Spies, that spring Brahms produced his surge of vocal music. Still, the texts he chose speak more of frustration and encroaching age than of new infatuation. Ruckert's "Mit vierzig Jahren" ("At Forty") from Opus 94 begins, "The mountain has been climbed; we stand still and look back." (The first time

Stockhausen tried it over with Brahms, the singer broke down in tears.[3])
"Stieg auf, Geliebter Schatten" is a plea: "Arise before me, beloved ghost,
in the dead of night, and refresh me in my deathly weariness . . . and
make me young again." And ominously, "Das Mädchen" ("The Girl"):
"If I were to know, thou white face of mine, that someday an old man will
kiss you . . . I would pick all the wormwood in the mountains, I would
squeeze bitter juice from the wormwood, and I would wash you, my face,
with the juice, so you become bitter when the old man kisses you." He
would end Opus 94 with a bleak setting of bleak words: "No house, no
homeland, no wife and no child; thus I am whirled like a straw in storm
and wind!"

Infatuation or no, then, most of the lyrics of 1883–4 reflect Brahms's
perennial theme of love lost rather than found. Vigorous as he was, age
weighed on him. The viola song "Gestillte Sehnsucht" (Satisfied Longing), which he added to "Geistliches Wiegenlied" to make up Opus 91
for Amalie Joachim, voices his feelings more than Amalie's: "You desires
of mine, always stirring in my breast. . . . Thou longing of mine that
makes my breast heave, when will *you* rest, when will *you* slumber?"

If those lyrics speak his thoughts, Brahms at fifty felt more torn by life,
more frightened by love than ever. Yet the summer of 1883 he went to
Wiesbaden to work, because Hermione-ohne-O was there.

THERE IS LITTLE RECORD of what went on between the two that sum-
mer in Wiesbaden, but the time looms large in his work. Brahms told
Billroth that his country house with a high airy studio, in sight of the
Rhine, was as luxurious "as if I were trying to imitate Wagner."[4] Back in
Bad Ischl, when it got around that he was not returning there for vacation, he received a mock-tragic letter from the proprietress of the Café
Walter: "In the name of the heartbroken Esplanade . . . I take the liberty
of asking you whether you are not going to honor us with your visit
again. . . . Although your faithful companion [Brüll] has entered into
wedlock, I will do my best to give you good coffee and plenty of newspapers."[5] By then Brahms was ensconced in the vicinity of Hermine and
working on the Third Symphony in F Major.

His First Symphony he had managed, with unrelenting and in some
degree audible effort, to hold together despite the enormous period of
gestation from Young Kreisler to mature master. The Second had been a
sigh of pleasure and relief, completed perhaps a touch too fast and too
easily. Apparently also done in a summer, the Third shows Brahms at the
height of his mastery, confidence, and concentration.

If with the First he had already produced one of the most hair-raising beginnings of any symphony, he nearly matched it with the Third: two pealing wind chords move from stable F major to a rivetingly ambiguous diminished chord, followed by a towering string theme undergirded by a bass line that leaps from a major chord to an ear-churning minor:

Brahms had long favored such *moll-Dur* moments, mingling minor and major, but usually to poignant and yearning effect. The opening of the F Major Symphony is heroic, *moll-Dur* with a vengeance. At the same time it begins with another of his double themes, the violin line on top the less featured, if in the end more significant. The figure that will actually dominate all four movements is the bass line, F-A♭-F: a third up and a leap to the octave, a signature motive of Brahms's that goes back at least to the D Major Ballade of Opus 10.

Yet while that simple three-note bass line (first outlined in the opening wind chords) is the leading motive in a symphony of extraordinary thematic integration, the violins' opening melody is the main bearer of meaning—and this theme comes from Robert Schumann. Specifically, in a symphony composed on the bank of the Rhine, it is taken from the first movement of Schumann's *Rhenish* Symphony. Brahms's version of it has the swinging "hemiola" rhythm of Schumann's opening (in which two measures of three-beat are broadened out into 2+2+2), but it also begins with the exact intervals of a variant Schumann presents during the recapitulation.

from Musgrave, Music of Brahms

What did this theme signify to Brahms? Is it another cabalistic reference like the "Clara theme" that he took from Schumann, or like the songs without words in his early music, or like the portrait of himself as Werther in the C Minor Piano Trio?

In fact he left no clues in this music, never hinted anything to friends about it. If the Third Symphony's monumental opening theme has a personal import, it remains hidden. Maybe he was evoking Schumann's evocation of the Rhine for its own sake. Certainly it is a superb theme, its rhythmic profile hovering (like that of the G Major Violin Sonata) between a 3+3 and 2+2+2 articulation of the $^6_4$ meter. Most likely, if Brahms is getting at any "meaning" here, it is abstract. Rather than digging for personal intimations, one can call the Third a case study of how "meaning" can be suggested in tones—hardly the first such case in Brahms, but one of his most far-reaching.

So he begins with the bold stride from F major to ambiguity in the winds, then presents a heroic double theme moving from F major to a suddenly shadowed, almost brutally proclaimed F minor—all that in the opening four measures, which set up essential motives, gestures, and tonalities for the entire symphony. The motive of the bass, F-A♭-F, will recur in myriad avatars; the turning point between F major and minor, the notes A♮ and A♭, resonate throughout (including in the progression of keys). Yet Schumann's theme is the real bearer of meaning: at the beginning of the symphony Brahms moves it from major to minor; at the close it will return, unforgettably.

There is still another element to that theme, and to this work in which so many ideas and memories and stylistic elements come together. Wagner had died shortly before the work began[6]—Brahms's rival, his respected enemy, his shadow. Several things in the Third hint at connections to Wagner, among them the atmospheric string textures of the end. The opening Schumann melody itself suggests some of Wagner's grand triadic leitmotivs and themes: say, the Rhine motive:

Wagner, Rhine-motive in "Siegfried's Rhine Journey"

Or this theme from "Siegfried's Death"[7] (here transposed to F):

Despite these echoes of Schumann and perhaps Wagner (plus the "cyclic" integration of thematic and tonal elements through the movements, a technique associated with Liszt[8]), Hans Richter dubbed the Third Symphony "Brahms's *Eroica*," after Beethoven's Third. Brahms never escaped that comparison, however little his Third resembles Beethoven's in sound and material.

Yet again: the point is how a self-contained work of absolute music, Brahms's Third Symphony in itself, for all the references to Schumann and Wagner and Beethoven outside itself (there are always such references in Brahms), can create its own meaning in tones—something in the direction of what Hanslick was getting at in *On Beauty in Music*. Carl Dahlhaus has pointed out the most intriguing secret of the opening Schumann theme, which is an abstract one: in its descent toward a ca-

dence it sounds not like an opening, but like a concluding theme.[9] In
other words, the Third's opening, the heroic form of the theme, is not its
ideal form and cannot bring the theme to fulfillment in its essential nature. Beyond that, as a theme that starts in major but is wrenched into
minor—A♮ canceled by A♭—it awaits another kind of fulfillment and resolution.

After the searing opening, much of the first movement is gentle and
beautiful, with flowing melodies and much intimate, chamber-like scoring. The second theme of the exposition is presented by clarinet, in A
major, almost a micro-lesson in Brahmsian "developing variation"—each
ensuing bar is a progressive variation of the first:

In this symphony the clarinet takes a leading soloistic voice; it is the
principal "character" in the wind section. In his handling of the orchestra Brahms may never have equaled the subtle colorings of this symphony, much of it refined during the early performances. (The
manuscript is full of revisions, the first Simrock edition riddled with mistakes—Brahms remained an inexplicably careless proofreader.)

The first movement's themes are flowing and lyrical much of the time;
the dynamic and tension-building element is rhythm. In the G Major Violin Sonata Brahms played elaborate games with phrasings. In the opening movement of the Third Symphony he carries those ideas further,
sustaining the ambiguity of 3+3 versus 2+2+2 for long stretches, and for
further stretches (for example, measures 50–77) displacing the downbeat
or letting the stresses float free of the bar line. Another kind of metric
tension is found in the clarinet's second theme, noted above: clear in
meter, but in the wrong meter, $\frac{9}{4}$ instead of the prevailing $\frac{6}{4}$. The kind
of prolonged harmonic tension Brahms perhaps learned from Robert
Schumann is now fully joined by a technique of prolonged metric displacement, which resolves at a rhythmic "cadence" when written and
perceived meter finally fall together. As in the Second Symphony but
more pervasively, these strong downbeats form the structural articulations.

The gentle opening of the second movement andante—in C major
with clarinet again the leading voice—has one phrasing marked for the
melody and another for the accompaniment.[10]

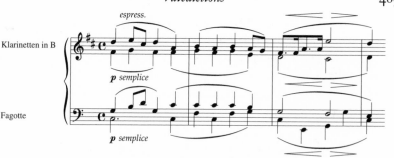

As in the slow movement of the Second Symphony, that metric freedom will dominate much of this sonata-form andante. Its second theme is this keening melody in clarinet and bassoon, the harmonic effect verging on polytonal—the melody in A minor and the accompaniment suggesting G minor:

Brahms withholds that second theme from the andante's recapitulation. Instead, it will reappear, in different garb, in the last movement: here, as he had done in the G Major Violin Sonata, he integrates the material of slow movement and finale.

The C minor third movement, marked *Poco Allegretto*, was the immediate hit of the symphony, regularly encored in concerts during that era when audiences applauded every movement and conductors and composers were happy to repeat one. It features a sighing melody with a lacerating sense of yearning—another of Brahms's intermezzos, another cello tune, but with a fresh and indelible expressive atmosphere. The movement strikes a tone and a voice familiar now but extraordinary to his time: this backward-looking contrapuntalist who can conjure a tonal world like nothing heard before, this conservative allegedly indifferent to orchestral color who can shape a string accompaniment with a magical wavelike shimmer.

Reinhold Brinkmann calls the finale of the Third a "valediction," in comparison to the Second Symphony's "last dance" and the "apotheosis" of the First.[11] Metrically it is the most regular and predictable movement of the symphony, but still ambiguous harmonically. The whispering, flowing opening sounds like C Phrygian, giving little hint of the underlying F minor tonality.

The finale closes in on F minor, as if the opening gesture of the symphony from major to minor finally came to rest on the darker mode. The A♮ that defines the major key seems eclipsed by the A♭ of the minor. In the exposition the "missing" theme from the second movement is taken up again, now in A♭ major—see the facing page.

The finale's surging, lyrical second subject in C major provides some lightness, but it also has a breathless and unsettled quality. Joachim told Brahms that for him it conjured up the image of Leander swimming desperately toward Hero: "I cannot help imagining the bold, brave swimmer, his breast borne up by the waves and by the mighty passion before

his eyes, heartily, heroically swimming on, to the end, to the end, in spite of the elements which storm around him!"[12] Brahms received the idea silently, but he did not try to deny the image: the struggle above the abyss.

The "missing" second-movement theme returns in the towering, trombone-haunted climax of the last movement's development, which leads almost undetectably into the recapitulation. Then, after strains anguished and heroic, Brahms produces the most unforgettable of his codas.

Just before the expected loud and lively wrap-up of a movement or a piece, Brahms often injects a meditative moment, or (as happens in the F Major Quintet) a moment of troubling ambiguity that darkens the customary high spirits of the coda. At the close of the Third Symphony he appears to do something like that again: starting seven measures after letter N, muted violas begin a whispering variation of the movement's

opening theme in the distant key of B minor. So it starts like another of
Brahms's penultimate interludes that will surely be swept away for the
kind of ending—gay or heroic or monumental—that a symphony is supposed to have. But the interlude persists, gentle themes dissolving into a
fluttering atmosphere of strings that reminds us that Brahms had studied
Wagner's "Forest Murmurs." Suddenly we realize we are in the coda and
the symphony is winding to a quiet close.

The very idea of ending a heroic, monumental work like this might
have seemed unthinkable if Brahms had not done it here, with incomparable grace. Fragments of melody from the whole symphony seem to
gather until they return us to where we began: with the opening melody
of the work, Schumann's theme. Now, though, it is resolved into its true
nature as a conclusion, in a gentle F major that flutters downward to its
resolution, and slips into silence. The winds that began the symphony by
stepping away from stability into uncertainty now end the piece in a pure,
long-sustained F major chord. It is the transformation of Schumann's
theme from searching and heroic, major wrenched to minor, to the
peaceful valediction that is the abstract but no less moving "meaning" of
this symphony.

Carrying Eduard Hanslick's half-formed conception of music further,
American philosopher Suzanne Langer said that music works like a symbol, but an "unconsummated" one: it strikes our consciousness full of
symbolic import but does not represent anything specific in the way language does. "Music is 'significant form,'" Langer writes, "and its significance is that of a symbol, a highly articulated sensuous object, which . . .
can express the forms of vital experience which language is peculiarly un-
fit to convey. Feeling, life, motion and emotion constitute its import."[13]
In this sense, music echoes primordial dynamic shapes of emotion, sensation, movement, and experience. In the nineteenth century, this was
what Walter Pater was thinking of when he wrote that in its elusiveness,
its virtual meaningfulness without words or stories or images, "Music is
the art to which all other arts aspire."

Brahms's Third Symphony can stand as a demonstration of these conceptions, how music can "mean" in the abstract. For Brahms the man it
may also stand for his withdrawal behind the mask of music. Whatever
Schumann's theme meant to him, if anything in particular, he no longer
felt obliged to share it. What inspired his work was his business here, not
ours.

The Third reveals something else as well. A paradox of Brahms is that
he functioned within the contexts of musical genres and of concert life as
they existed in his time, yet composed as he lived, a loner in company.

"Brahms's symphonies," Dahlhaus writes, are "directed not at the bourgeois public as a whole but primarily at the individual listener, at the 'subject' immersed in his feelings and thoughts, and are thus perceived . . . as though they were chamber music. . . . A Brahms symphony is virtually a musical attestation of the fact that each member of a crowd . . . is nevertheless entirely on his own."[14] As Langer implies, the music speaks to each listener in that private self, her yearnings, his aloneness—each person's meanings.

FOR BRAHMS AS A COMPOSER, the trouble with the Third Symphony was that from its premiere by Hans Richter and the Vienna Philharmonic on December 2, 1883, and in subsequent performances all over Europe, it received full-throated acclaim. (At the Vienna premiere there had been the usual demonstration by the Wagner Club, but it was shouted down.) Critic after critic declared this symphony the best thing he had ever done.[15] Despite the relief and pleasure at that, for one still at work it is a discomfiting situation. After thirty years of unrelenting labor and profound achievement Brahms suddenly found that the unthinkable had happened: for the first time since the *Requiem* he had conquered audiences and critics immediately with a major work, and therefore the stakes had risen.

That realization likely came over him slowly. As was his habit, in the wake of finishing a big project Brahms relaxed, worried, visited friends, promoted the new piece, arranged performances. By now many orchestras vied for his presence and for every new work. In September he visited Clara in Lichtental for her sixty-fourth birthday. He was in good spirits, she reported, but a little casual about the event: "He said he meant to have brought me a bouquet, but the shop lay out of his way, and then he meant to have given me some photographs of the Germania memorial, but he was too lazy!! . . . the fact that he has written a third symphony only slipped out in the course of conversation."[16]

Brahms surely enjoyed the earnest warmth of Clara's response when he had finally sent it to her—even if she is shockingly, almost Lisztianly, tone-poetic in her imagery:

> I have spent such happy hours with your wonderful creation. (I have played it over several times with Elise). . . . What a work! What a poem! . . . From start to finish one is wrapped about with the mysterious charm of the woods and forests. . . . The second is a pure idyll; I can see the worshippers kneeling about the little forest shrine, I hear

the babbling brook and the buzz of the insects. . . . [In the finale] one's beating heart is soon calmed down again for the final transfiguration which begins with such beauty in the development motif that words fail me![17]

In fact, since Brahms regularly sent Clara critiques from Billroth and Elisabet von Herzogenberg, she had become anxious about her place in his life and music. Now others often saw new pieces before Clara did, and their eloquence in responding to them made her halting phrases seem inadequate. Some of her letters of this period apologize for that: "How wonderfully Billroth understands what to say to you. . . . His comments always make me feel ashamed—not because I think he feels or understands your things better than I do, but because his way of expressing himself makes mine appear so amateurish."[18] Maybe that is why she became more flowery in her prose, trying to match the literary responses of the other two. (Clara had always felt embarrassed about her education outside music.) Eventually, inevitably, that insecurity turned to anger. She suspected that Johannes might value Lisl's opinion more than hers. In this period, he probably did.

For quite different reasons Joachim felt deserted by his friend, who had never sympathized with his accusations against Amalie. Joachim had finally sued for divorce on the grounds of adultery. Amalie challenged the suit, and in court produced in her defense Brahms's 1880 letter: "with no word, with no thought have I ever acknowledged that your husband might be in the right." Largely because of the letter, Amalie was vindicated and won the case. Joachim knew that Johannes had never intended the letter to be made public, but he considered it all the same an unforgivable betrayal. His friends would get many earfuls of his tirades against Johannes's disloyalty. Then, probably many times, Joachim would pick up his violin and go out to give a magnificent performance of Brahms.

Toward the end of 1883 Brahms wrote forthrightly to Joachim: "In the sad affair of your wife I could never be on your side; I always had to deplore most profoundly the way you proceeded in this matter. . . . I can never regret having written that letter. For me, it was a good deed, a release, to be able to say to your troubled wife the same thing that I had often enough said to you. . . . But what a mess was brought out at the trial!"[19] Surely he was thinking back to his old experiences with the violinist's jealousy and insecurity, to the way Joachim used to sit on Johannes's bed and plead endlessly for assurances of devotion.

Yet in this same letter Brahms held out his hand, asking Joachim if he wanted to give in Berlin the second performance of the Third Symphony. In reply Joachim brushed away everything but that gesture: "When I play your Concerto tonight I shall be taking your 'proffered hand,' and . . . I shall regard it as a great privilege if I can give the Symphony." It would be years before their hands touched again in person, and the profound friendship that had lasted them through three decades of triumph and squabbling was gone for good. However, their collaboration endured through it all. Joachim said in 1885, when their near-total estrangement remained in force, "Artist and man are two different things. . . .I can do no other than feel this music with my whole being . . . it works on me like a force of nature."[20]

AMID THE SEASON'S PERFORMING in Germany and Holland, naturally featuring the new symphony, Brahms turned down a second offer from Cologne to succeed Ferdinand Hiller as music director. He wrote his old friend Hiller:

How I used formerly to long for such employment, which is not only desirable and even essential for the creative artist, but is necessary to enable him to lead a decent and fitting existence. I am thinking now of Hamburg, my native city, where, since the time when I consider I began to count for something, my name has repeatedly been—absolutely ignored.[21]

So Brahms remained unencumbered by a decent and fitting job, in his terms still a vagabond, when he took his fourth Italian trip in spring 1884, this time accompanied by his Krefeld friend Rudolf von der Leyen. It ended with a stay at the Villa Carlotta, the Duke of Meiningen's summer house on Lake Como.

Just before he left for Italy, Brahms had written to Hanslick responding to two newly discovered cantatas the critic had sent him: "Even if there were no name on the title, one could guess no other author—it is all Beethoven through and through! There is the beautiful and noble pathos, the grandeur of the feelings and fantasy, the power, yes even violence of expression." In one of these early works Brahms found a presentiment of the glorious end of *Fidelio:* "How deeply Beethoven must have felt the melody in the cantata . . . as deeply and beautifully as he did later when he sang the love of a woman—and of liberation—to its end."

In that letter we find one of the few times on record that Brahms let himself go about music, speaking of his hero Beethoven's work in terms more impassioned than he ever used in speaking of his own. Yet despite his enthusiasm Brahms was opposed to having the cantatas published. He said they should be left in a few copies in libraries, for the use of scholars. He repudiated, in fact, the whole idea of complete editions, which had been a major endeavor of nineteenth-century scholarship. "I cannot find it right and proper for amateurs and young artists to be seduced into filling their rooms and their brains with all the 'complete works' and thus confusing their judgment."[22]

FOR THAT YEAR'S SUMMER working sojourn he tried out a new vacation spot that he hoped might be conducive to a new large work. This was the Austrian mountain village of Mürzzuschlag, some two hours by train from Vienna at the southern end of the Semmering Pass. Brahms's Viennese friends the Fellingers had summer lodgings there. When word got around where he was headed, once again a voice from Bad Ischl complained of his infidelity, this time Ignaz Brüll: "Well, what a fellow he is! He means to take rooms in Ischl for the summer, and then one morning he wakes up in Mürzzuschlag! I had been looking forward to our walks, . . . to our pleasant coffee parties, and much besides—and most of all to playing new duets—and now all my hopes are turned to water (hence all this rain!)."[23]

When he arrived in Mürzzuschlag, Brahms registered with local police as "itinerant musician." He took rooms in a big house with a courtyard on the town's main street, the window in the square bay of his workroom facing not toward the surrounding hills but down Wienstrasse toward the Rathaus (City Hall). There was an expansive adjoining room with rococo plaster ceiling, supplied with a borrowed piano, handy for private performances. The wood-paneled rooms and stained glass of his favored restaurant Zur Post lay just down the street; as company at meals Brahms made friends with several local men, from a baron to a train engineer.[24] For his daily hikes he had the relatively low ring of hills that surround the town—suitable for ascending at, say, the walking tempo of the opening of the Fourth Symphony.

Since he lived in the middle of town he went about his work as quietly as possible. Even his landlady's curious ears usually only detected him pacing around the room and humming to himself. One day a Viennese pianist named Fritzi Braun, also staying in the house, ran into Brahms on the street and he inquired, "So how's it going?" Very well, she replied politely, and how is it with you? "Me?" said Brahms mysteriously. "These days it can only go for me as it does with you, in fact only *exactly* as it does with you." After watching her gape at that, he revealed the meaning of his riddle. The day before he had come upon two women standing in front of the house listening to Frau Fritzi's excellent piano playing, and he heard one whisper excitedly to the other, "Do you hear? Brahms is playing." From then on Brahms called Fritzi his *"Doppelgängerin,"* his lady double.[25] He probably had in mind a comic mirror of Schubert's "Der Doppelgänger," in which the poet sees his double anguishing before an old lover's house. For himself, Brahms was not going to be caught entertaining passersby.

At Mürzzuschlag that summer he completed the first two movements of the Fourth Symphony. This would be no single season's job, like the last two symphonies. He was excruciatingly aware that the new one would be compared to the Third and its instant popularity. Surely it occurred to him that it had been a long time since he had suffered a fiasco, and maybe he was overdue.

Much of his socializing in Mürzzuschlag was with the Fellingers, husband Richard another prosperous, music-loving industrialist, wife Maria a painter, sculptor, and photographer—and to Brahms's equal pleasure, a Hausfrau who cooked a marvelous *Metzelsuppe* (a Swabian peasant dish) and knitted him the kind of socks his mother used to. Frau Maria made many of the pile of silk neckties that now reside in a glass case in the Mürzzuschlag Brahms Museum. He had met the Fellingers shortly after they came to Vienna in 1881. Maria's mother had been admired—by Mendelssohn among others—for singing her own songs to her own accompaniment, and her father was a professor at Tübingen who wrote poetry as "Christian Reinhold." Brahms set several Reinholds to music.

As much as the Fellingers senior, Brahms enjoyed their two girls and boy. He was happy to get down on the floor and play with all his friends' children, basking in their cries of "Onkel Bahms!" In Mürzzuschlag as in Vienna and other towns where he stayed, every street urchin knew him, the short fat man who always had candy and little toys for them in the pockets of his shabby black waistcoat. He would hold up treats and let them jump for them, or shove into their mouths what looked like a river pebble and beam at their delight when they discovered it was sugar candy.

Sunday dinner with the Fellingers became one of his most reliable rituals. To Maria we owe paintings and busts of Brahms, and many candid photos from the last decade of his life. Brahms and the Fellingers would have one of the most untroubled of his friendships—and as with Widmann and most of the other relatively untroubled ones, Brahms and the Fellingers never used the familiar *du*. Usually his *Duzenbrüder* were the ones he bruised most.

Brahms took the train back over the Semmering Pass to Vienna in mid-October and prepared for his winter tours. That autumn he collected funds from friends to give Theodor Kirchner, who was declining in fortune and spirits. Kirchner had always been depressive, but now his health was broken and the vogue for his little keyboard pieces long past. Maybe he spent his dotage brooding about Clara, their long-ago affair. It was that year when Clara, contemplating his decline, wrote the veiled, melancholy reminiscence in her journal: "I wished to make one so highly gifted into a worthy man and artist. . . . It was a sad experience. I suffered much."[26]

During the 1884–5 concert season, Brahms appeared several times with Hans von Bülow and the Meiningen Court Orchestra. In December he went to Oldenburg to stay with Albert Dietrich, who had arranged another of his gala all-Brahms events. The honoree showed up in Oldenburg with seven people in tow including Hermine Spies, who added four of his songs to the concert. (It otherwise included the Tragic Overture, the Second Piano Concerto, the Third Symphony, and the *Liebeslieder*). In a letter afterward to Dietrich's daughter, Hermine raved, "What I value most particularly is to have now enjoyed Brahms *as a man*. How charming he was with us when we were making and guessing riddles. What delightful hours we spent! . . . Of course now I only play Brahms the livelong day."[27]

She had met him more than a year before and spent much of the previous summer at Wiesbaden in his company. If Brahms had undertaken to court Hermine, and in his fashion he probably had, his approach was remarkably oblique. There is every reason to assume, anyway, as with other "respectable" women, that he flirted full-tilt and kept his hands to himself.

AFTER THE OLDENBURG CONCERT, Brahms surprised the Herzogenbergs in Leipzig with a visit for Christmas 1884.[28] Shortly after he left, Lisl wrote him of "the Bruckner excitement here, and how we rebelled against having him thrust upon us—like compulsory vaccination. . . . We are not to consider artistic results everything, but to admire the hidden driving-power, whether it succeeds in expressing itself satisfactorily or not. . . . One can only hold aloof, and resign oneself to be abused by the philistines."[29] She and Heinz were anti-Wagnerian as a matter of course, but like most of their persuasion including Hanslick, they acknowledged Wagner's brilliance and felt a certain resignation about his triumph. (Clara never gave up hope, however. After attending *Das Rheingold* she fumed, "How posterity will marvel at an aberration like this spreading all over the world!"[30])

Anton Bruckner was another matter; Brahms and nearly every Brahmsian despised his ecstatic, brassy, sprawling symphonies. Moreover Bruckner was vulnerable, could conceivably be suppressed. Brahms replied to Lisl's letter with the kind of choler he usually reserved for Liszt's music:

> I understand! You have sat through the roaring of Bruckner's symphony once, and now, when people talk about it, you are afraid to trust the recollection of your own senses.
>
> Well, you may safely do that. Your delightful letter expresses most lucidly all that can be said. . . . He is a poor crazy person whom the priests of St. Florian have on their consciences. . . . You will not mind when I tell you that Hanslick shares your opinion, and read your letter with pious joy!
>
> With supreme ill-humor, deepest respect, and kindest regards, yours,
>
> J. Br.[31]

Bruckner had been brought from the Austrian provinces to Vienna in 1868, to become court organist and professor at the Conservatory of the Gesellschaft der Musikfreunde. In 1875, to Hanslick's disgust, he began lecturing in music theory at Vienna University. Many of his students, among them Gustav Mahler, became fond of the old peasant, not only his music but the piety and ingenuousness (real or apparent) that merged into something more absurd and unbalanced. There were his homely bald head and blinking innocent eyes, the stocky figure and short legs encased in flapping provincial trousers.[32] If the Angelus rang in the middle of a lecture, Bruckner would fall to his knees on the podium and pray, crossing himself, then return to his fugues and canons at the blackboard. While Brahms made a sport of alternately coddling and insulting his admirers, Bruckner was capable of addressing a letter to a patron, "Most Honored, Most Kind and Geniuslike Protector!"[33] Second only to the Dear God and His Son, Bruckner adored Wagner, at whose feet he once fell crying, "Master, I worship you!" At concerts in the Musikverein Brahms sat in the Gesellschaft director's box while Bruckner could only afford standing room in the back, with his students. When the two passed in the halls of the Musikverein, Bruckner bowed and scraped as Doktor Brahms swept past with a curt nod.

Outlandish stories about Bruckner went the rounds in Vienna, many of them true. Part of what Brahms and others could never quite get over was that Bruckner the composer of epic symphonies behaved, much of the time, like a nincompoop. There were, for instance, the incidents regarding the Beethoven and Schubert remains. Both composers were exhumed in 1888 for reburial in "Graves of Honor" in Vienna's Central Cemetery. Before reburial the coffins were opened for the inspection of doctors and scientists. Bruckner, then sixty-four, showed up uninvited on both occasions. When he saw Beethoven's open casket, he shoved past the horrified doctors and seized the skull in both his hands, staring into the empty sockets as if he were trying to divine the sublime riddle of genius, and declaimed in his Upper Austrian drawl, "Now ain't it true, dear Beethoven, that if you were alive today you'd allow me to touch you? And now them strange gentlemen here want to forbid me that!" He had to be forcibly removed. Beethoven's bones may be decorated to this day by a lens from Bruckner's spectacles, which fell out during the ruckus.[34] He pulled the same stunt at Schubert's exhumation, refusing to release the skull until they allowed him to place it in the coffin himself.[35]

As always, Brahms could have forgiven a rival all that (he forgave Wagner much more) if he had been able to find any admiration for the music. He owned and studied some of Bruckner's scores, but they only confirmed his enmity. To Brahms, Hanslick, and most of their circle the scope and ambition of those symphonies were unwarranted, the occasional worthwhile ideas lost in a meandering maze. Carl Dahlhaus writes of "the supreme nonchalance with which Bruckner presupposed symphonic monumentality while casually abandoning everything which the classical-romantic tradition, as represented by Brahms, understood to be musical logic."[36]

At one point Brahms expressed his objections in these terms: "Everything is affectation with him, nothing natural. As to his piety—that's his business, it's nothing to me. But this thrashing around is disgusting to me, completely repugnant. He has no conception of a musical logic, no idea of an orderly musical structure."[37] If Wagner strung his operas together in loose quasi-symphonic form, that approach at least was relegated to the dramatic stage and its traditions. Bruckner appeared to bring the same cavalier approach to the genre of the symphony, intoxicating the public with brassy perorations and soaring themes without making any demands on their intelligence, their understanding of formal conventions. In other words, to Brahms and his followers Bruckner pandered to a public in some degree corrupted by Wagner, who wanted only to plunge into a voluptuous bath of sound and emotion.[38]

While Brahms sniped at Bruckner behind the scenes, Hanslick kept up a relentless attack in print. It was in 1892 that the critic's review greeted the premiere of Bruckner's Eighth Symphony as "interesting in detail but strange as a whole and even repugnant. . . . [it features] the immediate juxtaposition of dry schoolroom counterpoint with unbounded exaltation. . . . Everything flows, without clarity and without order, willy-nilly into dismal long-windedness. . . . It is not out of the question that the future belongs to this muddled hangover style—which is no reason to regard the future with envy."[39] These diatribes, certainly incited, perhaps in some degree even worded by Brahms, caused Bruckner endless agonies and materially impeded the progress of his career. Carl Dahlhaus wrote, "The anti-Bruckner polemics indulged in by the Brahms party in the 1880s form one of the sorriest chapters in the history of music criticism, mainly because they struck a man who, unlike Wagner, was largely unable to defend himself."[40]

Even with Bruckner in his grave, Brahms's outrage still ran strong. Maybe his most sustained volley came in the last year of his life, a testament he vented to Richard Specht that says much about his relations not only to Bruckner but to Wagner, the Wagnerians, and the Brahmsians. As Specht recalled it, Brahms erupted:

> Bruckner? That's a swindle that will be forgotten a year or two after my death. Take it as you will, Bruckner owes his fame entirely to me, and but for me nobody would have cared a brass farthing for him. Of course I had nothing to do with it; in fact it happened very much against my will. Nietzsche once declared that I had become famous through mere chance, because the anti-Wagner party required me as anti-pope. That's nonsense, because I'm not the man to be placed at the head of any party whatsoever. I must go my way alone and in peace. . . .
>
> After Wagner's death his party naturally had need of another pope, and they managed to find no better one than Bruckner. Do you really think that anyone in that childish crowd has the least notion what those symphonic boa-constrictors are all about? And don't you think that I am the musician who knows and understands Wagner's works best today, certainly better than any of his so-called followers, who would like nothing better than to poison me?
>
> I once told Wagner himself that I was the best Wagnerian of our time. Do you take me to be too dull to have been as enchanted as anyone by the joyousness and sublimity of the *Meistersinger*? Or dishonest enough to conceal my view that I consider a few bars of this work as of

more value than all the operas that have been written since? I an anti-pope? It's too absurd! And Bruckner's works immortal and "symphonies"? It's preposterous!⁴¹

In that mélange of spleen, dubious assertion, and good sense, Brahms's admiration of Wagner rings true. He repeated the line many times for many years: "I am the best of Wagnerians." If that seems impossible, there is no doubt that he believed it. Nor was he exaggerating the Wagnerians' need for a new pope. When the first one died, Bruckner was the available candidate.

Brahms did not mention another and more malevolent dimension to the exalting of Bruckner, which he certainly understood as well. Students like Mahler and musicians like Hans Richter took up Bruckner's cause because they heard something in the music. (Mahler later deplored it, but he would do the same with Brahms after early enthusiasm.) As the 1880s progressed, however, music in Austria was caught up in the burgeoning struggle between the ascending right wing and the waning left.

A peculiarity noted at the time was that in their musical tastes liberals were largely conservative (i.e., Brahmsian), while the reactionaries took up Wagner's revolutionary social and German-nationalistic agenda along with his revolutionary music. For the right wing, the exigencies of *form* proclaimed by the old liberals were to be swept away by a music of passion and blood-instinct. Against the tight, intellectualized chamber music of Brahms were placed Bruckner's *fortissimo* rhapsodies: let his pealing trumpets and horns blow away the effete rationalism and elitist aestheticism of the past!

The pan-Germans, the aristocrats, the conservative Catholics and Christian Socialists, took up Bruckner in the same spirit as they had Wagner, as a holy cause. The struggle to gain a hearing for Bruckner was declared identical with the struggle to form a new society purged of the Jew-ridden liberals. There rose the cult of emotion, antirationalism, and German blood that would find its denouement with the Nazis, who exalted Bruckner alongside Wagner. In 1889 the antisemitic organ *Deutsches Volksblatt* proclaimed, "To invent melodies requires only strong feeling and that involuntary, unerring creative instinct which must be inborn.—Both reside unweakened even today in the raw core of the *Volk.*" (Brahms preached distrust of instinct, his opponents that instinct is unerring.) That year the same critic inveighed against Brahms's Third in these terms: "What wretched barrenness of ideas reigns in this . . . movement, which does not even disdain Jewish-temple triplets simply to appear properly 'understandable.'" Soon after, following Wagner's lead, another critic simply transformed Brahms into a Jew, alongside his friends and sympathetic critics:

> We are very curious about the Philharmonic repertoire, which will be assembled, as ever, from some frequently heard symphonies of Beethoven, Schubert, and Schumann, along with the most recent works by Jews. . . . What a pleasing spectacle awaits us when Hanslick, Hirschfeld, Königstein, and Kalbeck again offer the palm to their great fellow-clansmen Goldmark, Goldschmidt, Brahms etc. and lead them into the temple of immortality. Long live the music-loving and music-making Jewry![42]

Bruckner himself, though conservative and Catholic, disavowed antisemitism, or at least kept his prejudices out of sight (the young Gustav Mahler was not his only disciple of Jewish background). If many of Bruckner's supporters were antisemites—that was their affair; he needed all the friends he could get. For Brahms and his circle it amounted to an unholy alliance of a music and a political agenda both of which they abhorred. In 1891, Brahms's friends Theodor Billroth and Viktor von Miller zu Aichholz (neither of them Jewish) helped found the "Party of Resistance to Antisemitism." It was around this time that Brahms groaned to Richard Heuberger, "I can scarcely speak of it, it seems so despicable to me. If the endless [immigration] of Galician Jews to Vienna were hindered, I'd favor it; but the rest is vileness!"[43]

These political ramifications and resonances inflected Brahms's campaign against Bruckner, the only case where he patently did harm to an artist weaker than himself. Yet despite Brahms's power in musical Vienna—and by then there was no one more powerful—he could not stop the slow rise of Bruckner, who in his retirement lived at the Belvedere Palace, supported by the emperor, and, despite the incessant bombardment of Hanslick's heaviest guns, saw the triumph in Vienna of his Brobdingnagian Eighth Symphony.

Perhaps part of Brahms's unwontedly bitter resistance came from something else too. Wagner was not only manifestly a more important composer than Bruckner, he also worked in a medium that essentially resided outside the concert hall. Bruckner was the only serious living competitor Brahms had as a symphonist, at least in Germanic countries. Brahms was unused to competitors on his turf, and he did not appreciate them. Maybe now and then his usually unbroken sleep was troubled by the nightmare that someday, somebody would propose a fourth "Great B" to add to Hans von Bülow's three.

THERE WAS A MEMORABLE MATINEE in Vienna on March 8, 1885. Violinist and Brahms discovery Marie Soldat, now twenty and fresh from her studies with Joachim, gave a dazzling performance of the Violin Concerto at the Musikverein. Brahms was beside himself with delight at this fresh-faced young woman playing his concerto so beautifully. Above the torrential applause afterward, Brahms's broken tenor could be heard shouting from the balcony: "Isn't the little soldier a hell of a fellow? Couldn't she hold her own with ten men? Who could do it better?"[44] After the concert he squired Marie to the Prater's merry-go-rounds and *Wurstl* puppet show, and in the evening took her to see *Macbeth* at the Burgtheater.

That month saw a historic meeting of the newly founded Wiener Tonkünstlerverein, a musicians' club of which Brahms became honorary president the next year. On this evening he had a pleasant chat with visiting guests Liszt and Rubinstein. The only sour note came when a lady insisted on snipping locks of hair from each of the famous men. In the process she stuck Brahms's finger with scissors, at which he exploded in rage.[45]

Every distinguished musician visiting the city was invited to the Monday meetings and dinners of the club, held in the Mozart Room of the Musikverein. The meetings often included a short concert. Members had indelible memories of Brahms at the piano in those congenial surroundings, accompanying the best singers in town in his newest lieder. He also served on committees that determined programs and handed out prizes and commissions to composers. Though the club was an all-male outfit, they gave composition awards to several women. A certain amount of the prize money flowed anonymously from Brahms's pocket.[46]

Monday evenings at the Tonkünstlerverein became a staple of his life in Vienna, along with his regular meals with friends, Sunday dinner with the Fellingers, day-long Sunday walks all over the forests and vineyards of the Vienna Woods. Every weekend those friends proposing to keep up with the brisk Brahms pace would meet at the Café Bauer, opposite the Opera, and take the tram with him out to the suburbs. For walks in the woods he sported one of his few examples of sartorial pride, a dashing green hunting jacket which he topped with a feathered cap. The day generally ended in a favorite *Heuriger*, one of the village inns where new wine flows and little bands dispense bittersweet Viennese tunes.

In and out of the Tonkünstlerverein, Brahms took any number of young composers under his wing to some degree or other, with great concern and generosity, if not necessarily gently or to great effect. He was often able to establish his favorites as teachers and administrators in schools, where they tended to champion his music and his aesthetics. He was not, however, able to make any of his protégés into a first-rate composer. This may not have been news to him. "What I do envy," he once wrote Elisabet von Herzogenberg about Heinrich, "is his power of teaching."

As they had been with George Henschel, Brahms's dealings with aspiring composers were straightforward, brutally frank, and dogmatic on matters of craft. Still, he perhaps felt guilty enough to soften his approach after a tragedy of 1880: Hans Rott, a school friend of Mahler's, asked Brahms for a critique of his Symphony in E, and received such a rebuff that it may have precipitated a breakdown. The next month Rott lost his senses during a trip, raving, "Brahms has filled the train with dynamite!" He ended up in an asylum and died at twenty-six. As far as we know, Brahms never expressed regret. Over a century later, the premiere of Rott's symphony revealed a remarkable if immature talent that manifestly influenced Mahler in his formative years.[47]

In 1879, the composer Hugo Wolf brought Brahms some of his songs. Two years before that he had been thrown out of the Conservatory for general intransigence, climaxed by a (perhaps) joking threat, in a signed letter, to assassinate Director Josef Hellmesberger.[48] One of the most brilliant of the young men who came to Brahms for advice over the years, Wolf was then scraping by on a few students and food mailed from his parents. The diminutive composer looked the classic bohemian: lean and shabby, with burning eyes and endless cigarettes and little beard scraggly from his constant nervous tugging.[49]

From Brahms Wolf got the usual treatment: he took things too lightly, he must study counterpoint with Nottebohm. Wolf returned from the interview spitting with rage to a friend who had been waiting at the Café Imperial. He reported that Brahms had told him, "First you must learn something, then we'll see if you have talent."[50] To his father Wolf wrote, "It's only Brahms's North German pedantry that makes him thrust Nottebohm on me." In any case, he could not afford the lessons.

On the other hand, there seems little doubt that Hugo Wolf had instinctively fled a genuine threat to his creative temperament. From that point he moved decisively from an admirer of Brahms to the opposite camp, and in that camp he found his voice. He was destined, during a short career that ended with insanity, to join the line of great German lieder composers that began with Schubert and ran through Schumann and Brahms to Wolf and Mahler.

However, Wolf came to public attention in Vienna during the mid-1880s not as composer but as music critic of the *Wiener Salonblatt*, a society paper whose columns he graced with fanatical defenses of Wagner and Bruckner and vitriol toward Brahms. Among Wolf's more notorious blasts:

> Through this composition [the D Minor Concerto] blows an air so icy, so dank and misty, that one's heart freezes. . . . Unhealthy stuff!

> Whoever can swallow this pianoforte concerto [the B♭] with relish may look forward with equanimity to a famine.

> He has, to be sure, never been able to raise himself above the level of mediocrity, but such nullity, emptiness and hypocrisy as prevail in the E Minor Symphony have come to light in no other of his works. The art of composing without ideas has decidedly found its most worthy representative in Brahms.[51]

The most famous and outlandish of Wolf's *bons mots* summed up Brahms this way: "A single cymbal-stroke of a work by Liszt expressed more intellect and emotion than all three symphonies of Brahms and his serenades taken together."[52]

Brahms would read Wolf's columns to friends for laughs. All the same, he remained extraordinarily forgiving when it came to musical judgments. When Wolf's songs began appearing in print and causing a stir, Brahms looked them over as a matter of course, observing mildly to Richard Heuberger, "Ja, if you're not concerned about the music, the declamation of a poem is pretty easy. Otherwise one can see that he's a clever, cultured, intelligent man."[53] After enduring years of vicious critical battering himself, Wolf finally found some favor in 1894 with his orchestral works *Feuerreiter* and *Elfenlied*. Then even Hanslick called him "a man of spirit and talent." Among those seen applauding the Vienna premiere of Wolf's pieces was Brahms, who knew very well what his enthusiasm could do for the career of a hungry composer.[54]

One aspirant who stuck it out with Brahms, and took the counterpoint lessons while maintaining something of his own counsel, was Alexander von Zemlinsky. He would turn out to be the only Brahms disciple to be played and spoken of to any extent outside Vienna a century later—

though that in part because of a protégé of Zemlinsky's named Arnold Schoenberg.

Young Zemlinsky sent Brahms a sonata for violin and piano and was summoned for the verdict. He arrived at Karlsgasse to find the master seated ominously before his open sonata score, with an open score of Bach to the left and Beethoven to the right. Brahms proceeded to tear the sonata to pieces bar by bar, with unpleasant comparisons to the flanking masters. This went on relentlessly until the victim jumped up and cried: "Well, under these circumstances, one should really quit composing!" Brahms stuck his face in Zemlinsky's and roared, *"Indeed, one should!"*[55]

With that little episode out of the way, they became friends. Brahms's point had been clear enough: if you want help from me you'd better have guts, because if you don't have them you're going nowhere in any case. Moreover, never expect any compliments (in practice, they bubbled out when Brahms saw something he liked). Brahms gave Zemlinsky a monthly stipend to allow him time to compose, and got Simrock to publish his music. In turn, the youth fell into the master's orbit. "Among my colleagues," he recalled, "it was considered particularly praiseworthy to compose in as 'Brahmsian' a manner as possible. . . . Then came a reaction, of course. With the struggle to find oneself, there was also an emphatic repudiation of Brahms." Still later, as a mature artist, Zemlinsky could afford to love the music again.[56]

Others perhaps never managed the rebellion they needed, to give themselves room to find their voices. For several years during the 1880s Richard Heuberger received informal lessons. He and Brahms remained friends as Heuberger established his career as a critic and composer—best known, though, for operettas rather than his symphonic and chamber music.

Much of what Heuberger wrote in his remarkable diary of their encounters echoes what Brahms told Henschel and other neophytes. When the young man excused something in a song of his with "It just occurred to me that way," Brahms exploded: *"Such things should not occur to you!* . . . Do you think that any of my few decent lieder came to me complete and finished? I took a good deal of trouble with them! . . . You know, one ought to be able—I don't mean this literally—to whistle a song . . . then it's good!"[57]

Gustav Jenner, another protégé whom Brahms devastated and then encouraged, had the temerity to bring the master a scherzo in which "I had attempted to be 'original'. . . . Its originality was slowly but surely transformed into pure nonsense. We came to the end of this movement remarkably quickly, and Brahms said well-meaningly, 'Of course, you *will* promise me not to write anything like this again.'"[58]

Jenner wrote, "When he discussed a song . . . the first thing to be examined was whether the musical form fully corresponded to the text." Whenever possible one should use strophic form—setting each verse of the poem to the same melody, like a folk song. "At those points where language inserts punctuation, the musical phrase has cadences." And he should model his instrumental works on the old masters: said Brahms, "If Beethoven goes from C major to E major, you do the same; that's how I used to do it myself." He repeated to Jenner what he had told Henschel: "'When ideas come to you, go for a walk; then you'll discover that the thing you thought was a complete idea was actually only the beginning of one.' Again and again he would impress upon me that I should mistrust my own ideas."[59] In other words, mistrust raw inspiration. All the same, as he once reminded Jenner, "Have I ever offered you my compositions as a model?"

Probably most bewildering to his protégés was to discover the depth of Brahms's obsession with Wagner. Once when Richard Heuberger declared Wagner responsible for sowing confusion in young minds—something Brahms had said often enough himself—the rebuttal came quick: "Nonsense, the misunderstood Wagner has done that to them; the ones who are misled by him understand nothing of the real Wagner. Wagner is one of the clearest heads that ever lived in this world!"[60] (Surely he exaggerated for effect.) As to Hanslick's eternal naysaying, Brahms observed that the critic had "absolutely no ear, absolutely no understanding for Wagner's work. Hanslick is old and this whole artistic approach is a foreign language to him."[61] When Hanslick made one of his occasional mild objections in print to a Brahms work, Brahms joked to Heuberger that the critic's misunderstanding "puts me in the very good company of Richard Wagner."[62] He even expressed pleasant memories of Wagner's endless monologues at parties, and as for the infamous personality: "Wagner's thick-headed conflict-seeking character was necessary to create such a work as *Die Meistersinger.*"[63]

It appears, implausible as it sounds, that Brahms deliberately pushed his young admirers toward his late adversary, to get from that source what they could. In the long view he perceived Wagner as upholding the same essential principles as his own. To Heuberger, however, he added this caveat: he had personally heard Wagner tell some of his disciples, "You must work in another direction than me."[64]

Through it all, Heuberger did not fail to notice that Brahms never expressed enthusiasm for Wagner in public, never tried to mitigate

Hanslick's fury. Nor, even if he occasionally tweaked Heinrich von Herzogenberg or Robert Fuchs for being too Brahmsian, did he ever insist on his disciples working in a significantly different direction than his own. In fact, the force of his personality tended to fix young composers in the orbit of his music and his principles. Brahms considered those creative and technical principles not his own at all. They were the eternal, sacred road of the gods: melody and harmony reined by immutable laws of counterpoint and form.

As Brahms kept faith with those unchanging laws, the world changed around him, and science contributed to that change. Among the epochal studies of the time, which had an abiding influence on music, was the work of Heinrich von Helmholtz that established the modern science of acoustics. In his 1862 book *On the Sensations of Tone, As a Physiological Basis for the Theory of Music,* Helmholtz attacked the dogmas of Western musical theory:

> At every step we encounter historical and national difference of taste. . . . What degree of roughness a hearer is inclined to endure as a means of musical expression depends on taste and habit. . . . Similarly Scales, Modes, and their Modulations have undergone multifarious alterations . . . hence it follows . . . *that the system of Scales, Modes, and Harmonic Tissues does not rest solely upon inalterable natural laws, but is at least partly also the result of esthetical principles, which have already changed, and will still further change, with the progressive development of humanity.*[65]

Helmholtz's discoveries and their extensions influenced everything from the design of pianos to the international standardization of musical pitch.[66] For composers of coming generations, by challenging the myth of "eternal laws" in music, he not only provided a scientist's sanction to embrace music of the distant past and of other cultures, but also to explore new territories of harmony and tonality and timbre. The message was unmistakable: if science says that many things are a matter of taste and culture, and taste and culture inevitably evolve, then unheard-of things are possible.

Eager to sound out the views of creative artists, Helmholtz managed to get an interview with Brahms. Their meeting turned out badly. The scientist talked of sine waves and spectra, the composer of counterpoint and form. Helmholtz complained that Brahms and Joachim "always give me artistic musical answers to my questions regarding scientific acoustical problems!" Brahms responded: "In musical things, he is an enormous dilettante."[67] Billroth's passion for Helmholtz Brahms wrote off as more dilettantism.

The Scales, Modes, and Harmonic Tissues the scientist and the physician saw as conditional, time-bound cultural constructs, Brahms saw simply as what music was *about*. To his mind, the dissolution of the assumptions and procedures of Bach, Mozart, and Beethoven was not a matter of the "progressive development" of art and humanity, but rather a sign of the decline of art and humanity. In the profoundest sense, Brahms and Helmholtz spoke different languages: one a language of the past, the other of a future that stretched all the way to the advent of electronic music nearly a century later.

BACK IN MÜRZZUSCHLAG in summer 1885, Brahms completed the six lieder of Opus 97 (two of them on lyrics by Maria Fellinger's father), and the last two movements of the Fourth Symphony. Soon after he arrived in town there was a rush of inspiration when, for a fifty-second birthday present, Klaus Groth sent him the poem "Komm bald" (Come Soon), noting that he had also sent a copy to Hermine Spies. Brahms and the aged Groth had been keeping up a nominally joking competition between them for the delightful Hermine's affections. In one sitting Brahms put the little lyric to music: "Why should we wait from day to day? In the garden everything that feels like blossoming is doing it. . . . I wish you were here!" If the text is flirtatious and frivolous, he made of it a warm and tender love song to send Hermine. He told Max Kalbeck, "I've never done anything so fast, so *a tempo*."[68]

His new scores figured in a more dramatic event of his two summers in Mürzzuschlag. One day a carpenter's shop in his house erupted in flames. Brahms ran from his workroom in shirtsleeves to join the bucket brigade to fight the fire, shouting at well-dressed passersby to lend a hand. In the confusion someone pulled him aside and told him his papers were threatened by the blaze. Brahms thought it over for a second, then returned to the buckets. Richard Fellinger finally extracted from him the key to his room and ran to save the score of the Fourth Symphony. When the fire was out—his rooms were not touched—Brahms shrugged off the threat to his manuscript with "Oh, the poor people needed help more than I did." He followed that up by slipping the carpenter money for rebuilding.[69] (He could, after all, have rewritten the symphony from memory.)

In May, Brahms had dispatched the new songs for Opus 96 to the Herzogenbergs for comment. Lisl replied with one of her characteristically long, detailed letters, writing out small passages for approval or complaint, exulting and cautioning and dissenting:

["Wir wandelten"] must be one of the most glorious songs in the world. It is so ideal for the voice, so vigorous in conception, and so happy in the lines of its melody which flatter both singer and listener. . . . Next in order comes "Meerfahrt" [Heine], with those strangely affecting horn-blasts, the F♯ over the A minor harmony, the C♯ over the E minor further on, and last of all the B♮. They come with startling freshness, and must be classed among the wonders which, to the end of time, will be evoked in response to any great force demanding expression, exhausted as the available store of musical material often seems, and actually is, to the non-elect. Tell me, don't you have a special weakness for "Meerfahrt" yourself? . . .

[After approving of others,] I cannot reconcile myself to one song, and that is the "Mond, der sich leuchtend drängel." Either I am quite irresponsible and capricious in my tastes, or it really is not on the same musical plane with the other. To put it brutally, I feel as if it had only the contours of a Brahms piece—what is called mannerism as distinct from style. . . . How can we *Brahmsianer* sanction a melody like this, with its intricacies and its restless harmonies, after all the treasures of inspiration showered on us![70]

It did not escape Lisl that with his atmospheric, ominous setting of "Meerfahrt" Brahms had, for once, seized the Heine effect: an idyllic scene of two lovers rocking in a boat at night, that ends with a chill— "There the music sounded more and more lovely . . . but we floated past, desolate on the wide sea." At the same time, Brahms accepted Lisl's judgment that he had failed with another of the Heine settings. He suppressed the "Mond" and another song she objected to, recast a third based on her complaint, and followed her advice to extend the ending of "Entführung" (Opus 97). This may represent the one time in his maturity that he took someone's advice almost point by point. And it went beyond the notes. He had been thinking of composing a number of Heine settings, returning to a poet of enormous subtlety and ambiguity whom he had loved and set (in discarded songs) in his youth, and who had been a favorite of Robert Schumann. After thinking over Lisl's response, Brahms let go of his plans for the Heine series.

That he may now have trusted and relied on Elisabet von Herzogenberg more than any other friend only made his anxiety more perturbing when, in August, he sent her the first movement of the Fourth Symphony with these words: "Would you have time to look at it, and tell me what you think of it? The trouble is that, on the whole, my pieces are nicer than myself, and need less setting to rights! But cherries never get ripe for eating in these parts, so don't be afraid to say if you don't like the taste. I am not at all eager to write a bad No. 4."[71]

The next two months turned into an agony, though he bore it with his usual stoicism. Nothing said by his friends would give him any real reassurance about this symphony. What happens to all artists sooner or later, most of them periodically, some of them relentlessly, had happened to Brahms for the first time since his twenties: the terror that he was dried up, that in chilly autumnal winds the cherries would never ripen again.

CHAPTER TWENTY

The Taking Back

RETURNING TO VIENNA at the end of September 1885, Brahms steeled himself for a premiere that boded as ill as any since the First Piano Concerto. Responding to the opening movement of the Fourth Symphony, Elisabet von Herzogenberg wrote:

> I can now trace the hills and valleys so clearly that I have lost the impression of its being a complicated movement. . . . At worst it seems to me as if a great master had made an almost extravagant display of his skill! . . . Your piece affects me curiously; the more penetration I bring to bear on it, the more impenetrable it becomes. . . . One never wearies of straining eyes and ears to grasp all the clever turns, all the strange illuminating effects of rhythm, harmony and color. . . . Indeed, the possibilities are so inexhaustible that one experiences the joys of a discoverer or a naturalist at every new evidence of your creative ingenuity.[1]

Lisl's husband Heinrich had not written him, but her response included his. Brahms could not miss that when her attempts to put a good face on it were discounted, these comments amounted to a prophecy of doom. The new symphony threatened to be too cerebral even for the Herzogenbergs. The critics who accused him of placing intellect above feeling were going to have a field day.

As usual Brahms kept his feelings close—in fact, became cagier than usual. At a café early that October Max Kalbeck inquired after the summer's work. A new string quartet, perhaps?

"God forbid, nothing so grand as that!" Brahms exclaimed. "Once again I've just thrown together a bunch of polkas and waltzes. If you really want, I'll play it over for you." Kalbeck jumped up to open the piano. "No, wait," Brahms continued. "The matter isn't so easy. 'Nazy has to help." Then Kalbeck understood: if Brahms needed Ignaz Brüll's two hands to help play it, this must be something big, a symphony.

So Kalbeck found himself, as on earlier occasions, in the Ehrbar piano salon with Brahms and Brüll at the piano, other invited listeners including Hanslick, Billroth, and conductor Hans Richter. Two years before, when nearly the same friends had heard the Third Symphony played in the same place, there had been bravos and Richter had made a toast: "Long live Maestro Brahms's *Eroica!*" This time, after composer and assistant had plowed through the first movement of the Fourth, the response, except for Richter muttering into his beard and Brüll nervously clearing his throat, was a resounding silence.

"Well, let's go on," Brahms growled. Hanslick gave a deep sigh and said, "I feel like I've just been beaten up by two terribly intelligent people." That brought a laugh, at least. The four hands continued. After the andante Kalbeck expressed, as he recalled it, "some resounding banality which probably had a still more disagreeable effect than the uneasy silence that preceded it." There followed the pounding two-beat scherzo and the somber chaconne of the finale. More silence. The friends scattered from the reading in a dismal mood.

Kalbeck spent a troubled night, finally deciding to confront the bear in his den next day. "So fire away!" said Brahms when Kalbeck appeared. "Of course I noticed that you didn't like the symphony yesterday, and honestly, that hurt. If my music doesn't please people like Billroth, Hanslick, or you, then who is it supposed to please?"

Heart pounding, Kalbeck spoke his piece. You must hold the symphony back, he said. Throw away the scherzo with its "abrupt principal and trite subsidiary themes." Make the finale a freestanding work, then compose two new movements. Brahms heard Kalbeck out and responded gravely. He would not try to defend the third movement because you can't argue about the value of melodies; anyway it was conceived for orchestra and so made little effect on piano. The last movement, its thirty variations above a bass line, he justified with reference to a similar structure in Beethoven's *Eroica*. After some two hours of debate back and forth, Brahms announced he would not hold back the symphony. "I don't give a damn about the shouters in the pit—and the rest of the public, between you and me, ditto. You may be right. But first we have to hear how it works with orchestra."[2] He dispatched Kalbeck with thanks.

The symphony seemed to be taking every possible ounce of flesh out of him. A few days later his fears were clanging as he wrote Elisabet von Herzogenberg, "It's very doubtful whether I shall inflict the piece on anybody else [after the premiere in Meiningen]."[3] Later, with a surge of hope, he sent Lisl the two-piano reduction of the whole piece, saying, "You will also have a chance of modifying your criticism very considerably!" There followed a long silence from the Herzogenbergs. Finally Brahms wrote Heinz with wrathful sarcasm: "Many thanks for your kind [nonexistent] letter. My letter-writing pen cannot contain itself for joy at the beautiful example set by your wife. It dances across the sheet just any way." He demanded the scores back. Only then did Lisl respond, quoting sections from memory with hedging praise and stern criticism:

> All that beauty, all that rich tenderness [in the scherzo], and then the . . . almost brutally rapid return to C major! Believe me, it is as if you had played us some glorious thing on the piano, and then, to ward off all emotion and show your natural coarseness, snort into your beard: "All rot, all rot, you know!" . . . It's no modulation, but an operation.[4]

To publisher Fritz Simrock Brahms wrote: "Taking it all in all I haven't the ghost of an idea whether I'll let the thing be printed. . . . You'd be insane to invest a groschen in it!"[5] In mid-October, holding down his dread, he took the train for Meiningen and Hans von Bülow's Hofkapelle Orchestra. His plan was to see the piece through the premiere, then decide whether he and Bülow would take it on tour as planned.

As always with Duke Georg, he was treated royally in the Meiningen castle. "I came here a few days ago and am rehearsing the new symphony," Brahms wrote Clara Schumann. "I have worked long and hard at it, thinking of you all the time, and wondering whether it might prove a very doubtful pleasure to you. The fact is I'm living in the lap of luxury here." By then, having heard the effect of the symphony with full orchestra, he felt a little optimistic: "As the piece pleases musicians (and does not entirely displease me) I can't exactly refuse to let Bülow travel around a bit with it."[6]

The premiere on October 25, 1885, was almost an anticlimax. The Meiningen audience unreservedly applauded every movement and there was a delirious ovation at the end. A great weight must have fallen from Brahms's shoulders, but an unfamiliar apprehension remained. Somehow the triumph at the premiere and in city after city afterward was ambiguous, if there is such a thing as ambiguous triumph. At its first performance Brahms was fifty-two, still vigorous but aging visibly, and had been famous for a very long time. Perhaps he could not shake the suspicion that the applause the symphony found across Europe was not so much for the piece as for him and his achievement. Could these be valedictory ovations? To have the courage to start the next big work, he needed to be reassured not about a body of work already on the books, but about *this piece*, which is to say: reassured that he could still do it.

When they heard the effect with orchestra, expressions of relief and pleasure came from the people he most cared about. Lisl von Herzogenberg called Joachim's performance in Berlin *"overpowering*, beyond all we had imagined."[7] (The Herzogenbergs had moved to Berlin, where Heinrich was teaching at Joachim's Hochschule für Musik.) Clara wrote, "My heart is full to overflowing about your symphony. It has given me some wonderful moments and its beauty and richness of color have held me spellbound."[8] Her response was based on the piano arrangement. By then Clara's hearing had gotten so bad that she could not listen to orchestral music without maddening distortions of pitch. In early 1886 she spent a month in bed with rheumatism.[9] Joachim and Brahms were still not speaking to each other except in letters, but the violinist seized on the forbidding, cloudy Fourth as his favorite of the symphonies. When he wrote a letter expressing his enthusiasm, Brahms responded a little stiffly, "Praise and sympathy such as yours are not only highly gratifying, but necessary. It is as though one had to wait for them for permission to enjoy one's own work!"[10]

After Bülow conducted the Fourth at a repeat concert in Meiningen, he and the orchestra set off with it on a railroad tour of fourteen cities in Germany and Holland. Just at the end of the tour, Brahms managed to derail what should have been a jubilant experience for himself and Bülow, who was now his most eloquent champion.

It was another episode of his bearish insensitivity. Brahms had already directed the new symphony in Frankfurt, where Bülow was due to play it with the Hofkapelle Orchestra in mid-November. After watching Brahms conduct the Fourth, no doubt Bülow intended to show the Frankfurt audience that he could handle the symphony better than its composer could. Maybe Brahms suspected that, and that was part of the reason he allowed himself to be persuaded by an anti-Bülow faction to repeat the Fourth with the Frankfurt orchestra, just before the Meiningen arrived in town. When Bülow learned of it, enraged and humiliated at what appeared to be a calculated insult, he substituted Beethoven's Seventh for Brahms's symphony in his program. At the same time he sent a telegram to Meiningen resigning his post immediately.

The resignation was expressed in such violent terms that the duke felt obliged to accept it.

There lay an unbelievable situation for two men who had worked together so long and so profitably. In his five years in Meiningen, Bülow had made the Hofkapelle Orchestra perhaps the finest ensemble in Europe, and the incomparable model for Brahms performance. Yet from old habit Brahms shrugged off the Frankfurt affair, treating the results of his tactlessness as if he could not care less. No one could know Hans von Bülow without understanding his hair-trigger sensibilities, his fierce pride of place. Yet after the insult of his performance Brahms actually compounded it by writing the conductor, "Once and for all, concerts and all that belongs to them do not count seriously with me, and I find it hard to think of last winter's concerts as anything but a diversion." With those words he waved away Bülow's achievement with the orchestra, his championing of the Fourth and many other works, the meaning of his life. The conductor responded with admirable restraint, his teeth almost grinding on the page: "If *tant bien que mal* I make propaganda to convince people of the glory of your music, it is not done, Heaven knows, with the irreverent object of offering you a diversion. . . . However, each one as he pleases."[11]

By that he meant their relations were at an end. In fact, remarkably enough, the friendship and collaboration would be resurrected—but not in Meiningen, because Bülow had left the orchestra for good. Brahms for his part would continue to enjoy the hospitality of the duke's court, where for a short time the Meiningen orchestra was led by a young composer/conductor and Bülow protégé named Richard Strauss.

The Vienna premiere of the Fourth Symphony came in January 1886. As usual, Billroth geared up for the event by planning a postconcert celebration, this time at Sacher's celebrated restaurant. He wrote Brahms that he would invite friends including Hanslick, Brüll, Richter, Faber, Goldmark, Door, Epstein, Kalbeck, Fuchs, and Ehrbar, all *senza* spouses. "I am in favor of anyone you wish to invite," Brahms rumbled in reply, perhaps thinking of Bülow, "and no one is important to me!" But then he added to the list a few others, including his young friend Eusebius Mandyczewski, soon to take over from the dying C. F. Pohl as librarian of the Gesellschaft der Musikfreunde and regular Brahms companion.[12]

As usual, Richter's skimpy rehearsals with the Philharmonic made Brahms nervous; he observed in comparison, "Bülow has simply miraculous rehearsals." Still, he declared himself pleased with the performance on January 17, 1886. Audience response was respectful but muted: no demonstrations from the Wagner Club, no ringing cheers. The dinner of

Brahms's circle at Sacher's afterward proved a tense occasion.[13] In the next day's review, Hanslick was hesitant and tight-lipped about "the composer's severest test," his "dark well."[14] Privately, Billroth told a friend that this time Brahms had not surpassed himself. When the surgeon wrote the composer, though, he put the best face on it: "One slowly learns to feel, when working at it, that it develops consistently, uncovering riches constantly and becoming more and more magnificent." Brahms replied uneasily, "I gather from your letter that you are now on a better footing with the E Minor Symphony, and that gives me great joy. Hanslick I have read superficially because he writes about affairs that don't happen to interest me."

Privately too, Billroth declared his scientific opinion that no artist could surpass himself after his fiftieth year.[15] Maybe he told that to Brahms, because Brahms suspected the same.

WITH THE FOURTH SYMPHONY Brahms did present a "dark well" to his public, just as Hanslick said. The E Minor has the most concentrated expression of his symphonies, lies the furthest from the effusive Romanticism of his youth. At the same time, with its complexity of design and expression and intent, its pervasive skepticism and foreboding expressed in the rhythms of dance, it represents so many returns for him. It is the beginning of a process of coming full circle in his life and art. Little of that could be perceived by the listeners who first heard the symphony in 1886, but those who knew his work sensed a web of issues musical and personal surging beneath its incomparably crafted surface.

Brahms tried out Joachim's suggestion for a brief chordal introduction and then struck it out of the draft.[16] Instead he began right on the main theme, a lilting minor-key melody of ambiguous expressive import. Its building block is thirds descending and then ascending, a chain of thirds being a Brahms thumbprint going back at least to the "Abend dämmert" movement of the Opus 5 Piano Sonata. They also recall the endless games with thirds in Beethoven's *Hammerklavier*, the model for the opening of Brahms's Opus 1 Sonata. (By the time of the Fourth Symphony, Brahms owned Beethoven's original sketches for the *Hammerklavier*.[17])

The opening theme and its intervals presage a work of extraordinary thematic integration, of a kind Brahms had done before but here perhaps more pervasively than ever. The thematic process begins with the first notes and continues to the end of the symphony. Besides the ever-present melodic thirds, much of that integration will turn on the relations of E and C, the tones respectively of the opening key and the first leap in the melody:

The first movement stays close to a particular tone, call it somber nobility. It is significant as much for what it does not do as for what it does: little of Brahms's games with rhythm and meter, most of the time with a straightforward, dancelike two-beat that develops a sweeping momentum. Nor is there any Kreisleresque lyricism; where that is most expected, in the second theme (at letter C), there comes a melody strained and searching for all its expansiveness, darkly scored in cellos and horns. The curt, stuttering accompaniment to that theme forms another of the work's chains of thirds, and its juxtapostion of thirds with a stepwise line (reaching A♯-B in the fifth measure) presages the thematic culmination of the finale.

In *Sonata Forms*, Charles Rosen writes, "The glory of Brahms's academicism is his almost complete transformation of his models."[18] That was a lifelong process, now reaching its furthest extension. All the movements of the Fourth adapt historical forms and genres and historical resonances to fit this specific frame. In the sonata-form first movement, after stating his opening theme Brahms takes the unusual step (at letter A) of immediately presenting a contrapuntal variation of it—notifying us that the idea of variation is going to figure importantly.[19] For the first time in one of his symphonic opening movements there is no repeat of the exposition; instead, the development begins with another of his false repeats, an idea going back to the Second Serenade and the G Minor Piano Quartet. While the usual transition to the recapitulation in an opening movement

is a moment of drama or anticipation, here the tone is hesitant and mysterious, slipping into a quiet return of the main theme not at its beginning but in the middle, after an extended stretching out (augmentation) of the notes of the first phrase—in other words, the transition to the recap and the recap itself overlap. The movement ends with slashing minor chords and pounding timpani, a fateful close that from long experience listeners expected to be resolved into major-key "optimism" or "triumph" in the finale. One way or another Brahms had done that himself, in three previous symphonies and in most of his chamber music.

For second movement comes a brooding intermezzo, as singular in tone and expressive import as its parallel in the Third Symphony. It begins (see previous page) with a solemn, declamatory theme of wide-ranging tonal import, hovering between Phrygian E and major C. Then, picking up the implications of C and E at the beginning of the symphony, the theme suddenly falls into E major, or rather a mélange of shadowed *moll* and bright *Dur.*

From the tints of Phrygian, darkest of the modes, and the archaic incantation of the leading theme, we are returned to the world of Brahms's bardic voice that stretches back to the "Edward" piano ballade and the Opus 17 Harp Songs. Now that voice is joined with some of his most artful instrumentation, none more telling than from bar 9, where every timbral element is fresh and expressive: theme in the veiled timbre of the clarinet's middle register, middle voices in whispering low clarinet and bassoons, and pizzicato strings doubling the winds, giving the feel of a solemn processional as if for a fallen hero—a Wagnerian scene, but painted as if from afar, and in Brahmsian colors.

The formal outline of this second movement is sonata-like, with a brief development (from measure 74) and a gently lyrical second theme for contrast at letter C. Again the idea of variation pervades the movement, with the main theme undergoing a series of transformations in mode, texture, and tone—among them the twining, beautiful E major variation at letter B. The movement ends in almost pure E Phrygian, only with a raised third on the tonic chord for a touch of E major. The scoring there—horns and bassoons and complex string doublings and accompaniments—has a lush coloration reminiscent of Wagner, prophetic of Mahler if not of Ravel.

The third movement's *Allegro giocoso* is not quite a scherzo in form or meter (two-beat rather than the usual three, again sonata-like), but it functions as the scherzo. Clearly Brahms wanted to move back toward the traditional fast movement, rather than issuing another of his inter-

mezzos. Some have called its pounding, brusque main theme "baccha-
nalian"; Tovey admires its "tiger-like energy."[20]

The movement's second theme, the one Max Kalbeck found "trite,"
seems indeed coy, balletic, almost Tchaikovskian. That reinforces the expressive point of the third movement, which is to contrast the somber
cloudiness of the rest of the symphony with an expanse of major-key an-
imation, lightness, and unbuttoned joyfulness that courses down to the
climactic piccolo and flashing triangle. (The main theme has, of course,
a heavy-footed Teutonic joyfulness.) The symphony's governing chain-
of-thirds motive is preserved in the outline of the opening theme, whose
skeleton is thirds descending from C to D. The larger tonal implications
of third-relations are echoed, meanwhile, in details like the opening
theme's nimble leaping from C major to E♭ major.

The finale stands as Brahms's most remarkable symphonic move-ment—most profound in craftsmanship, most wide-ranging in historical resonances, and most troubling. Likely the conception of this movement was the beginning of the work, which is to say that the finale not only completes the Fourth Symphony in its thematic and expressive design, but may have been its reason for being in the first place. In tracing that reason as far as we can discern it, the dimensions of craft and personal im-petus are indistinguishable. The finale of the Fourth Symphony is a tech-nical tour de force in an archaic genre, expressed in terms of a personal and cultural tragedy.

It appears that the immediate inspiration for the finale came out dur-ing a conversation among Brahms, Bülow, and conductor Siegfried Ochs in 1880. The subject of Bach cantatas came up and Brahms predictably knew that repertoire better than his friends. He went to the piano and played for them the climactic chaconne of the then-unpublished Cantata 150, *Nach Dir, Herr, verlanget mich*. Singling out the repeated bass line on which the movement was erected, he speculated, "What would you think of a sym-phonic movement written on this theme someday? But it's too clunky, too straightforward. It would have to be chromatically altered somehow."[21]

So began the process of thought toward the Fourth Symphony. As he had suggested, for his purposes in the finale Brahms altered Bach's bass line by adding a chromatic A♯ to fill out eight measures of $\frac{3}{4}$.

Bach (transposed)

Brahms

Inevitably, other associations accumulated around the idea of basing a symphonic finale on an archaic procedure—more or less the Baroque idea of the chaconne, a slow, solemn dance built on a "ground bass." This means that as the basis of the finale Brahms repeated the Bach-derived theme over and over as an ostinato, the theme sometimes drifting from the bass into the upper parts, and wove the rest of the music around it. The chaconne Brahms had particularly in mind was another of Bach's, which Joachim had made famous—the epic one from the D Minor Sonata for solo violin. In 1877, Brahms made an arrangement of that work for piano left hand, dedicated to Clara, and wrote her about it:

For me the Chaconne is one of the most incredible pieces of music. . . .
For a little instrument, the man writes a whole world of the deepest
and most powerful expression. When I ask myself if I had written this
piece—been able to conceive it—I know for certain the emotions excited would have driven me mad.[22]

Michael Musgrave notes that as Brahms worked out his ideas for the
finale, other influences and associations collected, among them a favorite
organ passacaglia (a similar genre to chaconne) by Georg Muffat,
Couperin's passacaglias that Brahms edited for Chrysander's edition,[23]
and perhaps the E Minor *Ciacona* of the pre-Bach German master Dietrich Buxtehude.[24] So if the presiding spirit of Brahms's chaconne finale is
Bach and the voice his own, his inspiration characteristically stretches
back through Bach to the early Baroque and perhaps further, to Palestrina and the Renaissance polyphonists. Meanwhile, in the symphonic
literature the clearest predecessors of his finale are that of Beethoven's
Eroica, also a series of variations on a bass line, and the variations on the
"Ode to Joy" theme in the Ninth Symphony finale.

Moreover, if the chain-of-thirds opening of the Fourth Symphony
represents Brahms's return to the *Hammerklavier* inspiration of his early
keyboard music, the finale echoes his own first maturity as an orchestral
composer with the Haydn Variations. The latter, however, was a series of
contrasting character variations by way of an orchestral study—cumulative in effect, highly episodic in practice. Having invented one unique
form in the Haydn Variations, in the finale of the Fourth Brahms wanted
a new and far more rigorous procedure: he unified the thirty variations
on his eight-bar chaconne theme by binding them up in a continuously
unfolding form, an arching A B A-coda design.[25]

To shape a long movement from a short repeating ostinato, thereby
forbidding changes of key (though he moves from E minor to major), and
yet make the music accumulate, expand, turn up contrasts, and finally climax, requires something like the incomparable mastery that Bach wielded
in his solo-violin chaconne. The cumulative effect of Bach's work is so intense, like a spring wound tighter and tighter, that even Brahms said it
would drive him mad to attempt it. Maybe no other composer could equal
that feat, and certainly no one has with a single instrument. Brahms, near
the end of his career and in the full flood of his mastery, accomplished
something like it in the finale of the Fourth—though he needed the full
resources of the orchestra to do it.

Beginning the movement with a series of trombone-dominated wind
chords that present the chaconne theme in the upper voice, he then out-

lines the theme in curt string pizzicatos, around which wisps of melody accumulate. In its A B A-coda design, the finale functions something like a sonata form, the impassioned melody over the chaconne bass at measure 23 (variation 4) serving as quasi-second theme (it ends with another chain of thirds).

The variations succeed one another, the chaconne theme sometimes absorbed into the middle of the texture, the sections at once expressively contrasting but also unified in their steady progress—that perhaps the greatest technical feat of the movement, echoing Bach's. From letter D, variations 10 and 11 serve as a sort of transition to the B section/quasi-development, which begins with a flute solo of unforgettable tragic beauty, exquisitely poised between *moll* and *Dur*, and in the silken lower register. From there, finally, E major emerges like a breath of hope, leading to a solemn, halting trombone and bassoon chorale that recalls the sublime male choruses of Mozart's *Magic Flute*.

The trombone chorale sinks to a meditative pause, then variation 16 erupts fiercely in the winds as a quasi-recapitulation, leading to an expanse of towering and anguished music and a shouting climax. From there flow shimmering strings and gentler, more lyrical variations that complete and unify the melodic unfolding of the whole work. Now the thirds that began the symphony are joined to the scalewise theme of the last movement, finally coming to a moment of profound compositional alchemy: a chain-of-thirds canon at one beat's distance whose downbeats magically form the chaconne theme:

The music builds to the pealing and declamatory coda, the place where in the First and Third Symphonies a transformation of tone took shape. In the First it was a transformation from "fatalism" to "exaltation," in the Third a turn to a quiet, valedictory peace. In the coda of the Fourth Symphony there is no transformation but rather a sustained tragic intensity that reels to the final E minor chords. For the only time in his symphonies, for one of the few times in his work or in any large work before him, Brahms does not turn to major at the end of a minor-key piece. He allows the darkness to stand, gives tragedy the last word.[26]

The significance of that ending was not lost on his era, when listeners and critics had gotten to know the Fourth. After Brahms died, conductor Felix Weingartner wrote of the finale: "I cannot get away from the impression of an inexorable fate implacably driving some great creation, whether it be an individual or a whole race, toward its downfall. . . . This movement is seared by shattering tragedy, the close being a veritable orgy of destruction, a terrible counterpart to the paroxysm of joy at the end of Beethoven's last symphony."[27]

Thus Reinhold Brinkmann, recalling the words of Thomas Mann's haunted, Schoenberg-like composer Adrian Leverkühn in *Doktor Faustus*, speaks of Brahms's Fourth as the "taking back"—taking back the "Ode to Joy" that Beethoven proclaimed in the finale of the Ninth, and so creating an anti-archetype that would go on to speak in Mahler's more tormented and grotesque symphonies, and from there through the shattering course of Viennese and German musical Expressionism. "The chorales in the First and Third Symphonies," writes Brinkmann, "resound with 'hope,' directly and positively. . . . With its negative ending, the Fourth Symphony denies this hope; it is the composed revocation of it." And with this symphony Brahms sealed his "skeptical, broken mastery."[28]

If most of the minor-key symphonies ever written, among them Beethoven's Fifth and Brahms's First, enact a drama from darkness to light, fatality to triumph, minor to major, Brahms's Fourth narrates a progression from a troubling twilight to a dark night: fin de siècle. When he finished it he was fifty-three years old.

With this work, Brahms at the onset of old age shaped his apprehensions and prophecies into a vessel of consummate craft, his dark answer and counterpart to Beethoven's joy. He saw himself as the meager but last-ditch embodiment of the great Germanic tradition, the line of Schütz and Bach through Haydn, Mozart, Beethoven, Schubert, and Schumann. He believed that when he died, that lineage would die. The E Minor Symphony "means" many things, but surely part of it is this: his funeral song for his heritage, for a world at peace, for an Austro-German middle class that honored and understood music like no other culture, for the sweet Vienna he knew, for his own lost loves. In one of the last pieces he wrote, in 1896, Brahms would set the E Minor Symphony's first four notes, B G E C, to the words "O death, O death!"

WITH BRAHMS STILL ESTRANGED from Joachim and Bülow, in spring 1886 there was an interruption of his correspondence with Elisabet von Herzogenberg. This dissonance resulted from some malicious rumors about Brahms that Lisl had gotten wind of. She was even more shocked when Brahms appeared completely to ignore the unexplained interruption in her letters. At the end of the year, when she learned that the rumors had been false, she wrote him about the Second Cello Sonata he had sent her, with hardly a mention of the break, and they simply picked up where they left off.[29] From long experience Lisl knew there was little point in belaboring Brahms for his obliviousness.

Soon after that he made a circuitous gesture of reconciliation to Hans von Bülow. He stopped by the conductor's Vienna hotel and left a message, unsigned, consisting of a few notes from Mozart's *Magic Flute*. Brahms knew the conductor would realize who left the note and remember the text for that line of music: "Dear one, shall I see thee no more?" In his fashion it was a touching, even sentimental gesture. Bülow hastened to Brahms's house to make peace. They were a team again.

Then Clara unleashed a blast. It had much to do with her fears that she had been ejected from the inner circle of those whose opinions Brahms most valued. Her physical woes and hearing loss had made it harder for her to play through his work, and slower to respond to it. Some of his Viennese friends seem to have been hostile to her, and if so that would not have escaped her: she would be brooding on the laughter at her expense during meals in the back room of the Igel. Depression over her ills and jealousy of Elisabet von Herzogenberg's hold on him contributed to Clara's mood as well.

In the middle of all that Brahms wrote her the incredible accusation that she considered his sending her music a "nuisance." His letters from the period have not survived, but they are reflected in hers: First, "Why are you sending me nothing more? Do you want to leave your old friend quite out in the cold?" Then, "Your last letter but one wounded me so deeply that all I could do was to send you a card telling you what was absolutely necessary."[30] Before long the two patched up these disharmonies, but as so many times before the scars lingered.

Clara was feeling eclipsed in other ways too. Franz Liszt had died in July 1886, during a visit to Bayreuth. He and Joachim had made peace by then, but her enmity was unshaken. In her journal Clara commemorated his passing this way:

He was a great piano virtuoso, but a dangerous model for the young to imitate. Almost all the rising pianists imitated him, but they lacked his mind, his genius, his delicacy of touch, so that now we have nothing but great masters of technique and a number of caricatures. . . . [His pieces] are trivial, wearisome, and they will soon disappear now that he has gone. . . . As a young man he was most fascinating but later he let so much coquetry blend with his really intellectual and charming disposition that I often found it disagreeable.[31]

When Clara edited her husband's C Major Fantasy for the complete edition, she deleted from the title page Robert's dedication to Liszt.[32] She had said of her rival, "He has the decline of piano playing on his conscience." But Liszt's bravura style of pianism had triumphed, leaving Clara a relic of the past. Someone who saw one of her late performances of Robert's concerto remembered only:

a dumpy old lady in a cap. She was greeted with long-continued applause. She seated herself at the piano, and after half a dozen elusive settlings of herself and shaking out of her gown, just as the conductor was about to begin, she popped up and went among the instrumentalists, in order to give a special direction to the first oboe. . . . She then came back to the piano and again went through the settling process . . . at last she was ready.[33]

IN MAY 1886, after celebrating another birthday in Vienna, Brahms headed for a new vacation spot, outside Austria. He may have considered himself something of a refugee from Count Taaffe's generally anti-liberal regime.[34] Brahms's new resort was at Hofstetten, just outside the city of Thun in Switzerland's Bernese Oberland. He rented the sunny second floor, with a big porch, of a place owned by a merchant named Spring. The stately house sat at the foot of a hill stretching down to the glass-green water of the Aare River, near where it flows into Lake Thun. The landlord kept a haberdashery shop on the ground floor and maintained a handsome garden. Next door lay the Hotel Bellevue, which would hold many Brahms visitors during his three summers in the house. On the heights above the city loomed a Romantic sight, the twelfth-century Castle of Thun.

Brahms wrote his publisher Fritz Simrock, "The mountain is right in front of my window as if it was deliberately placed there. Then follow to the left the Stockhorn, the Niesen, the Blümlisalp, and a few steps from the house you can also see the Jungfrau and the Mönch."[35] To Max Kalbeck: "It is simply glorious here. I only say quite in passing that there are crowds of beer-gardens—actual beer-gardens—the English [tourists] are not at home in them!" He settled into the habit of whiling away the afternoons with beer and cigar in a nearby casino, where he tapped his foot to the house orchestra and slipped the musicians cash for card games.[36]

As it usually happened, Brahms had chosen his vacation spot not only for the beauty but for the company. This time he mainly counted on Josef Viktor Widmann, who lived to the north in Bern. Soon after he arrived at Thun in 1886 Brahms wrote Widmann, "I have induced the 'songstress' (Fräulein Spies, Hermione-ohne-O) to break in on you a week hence . . . and with my help to torture you with songs." Taking his cue, Widmann invited a good deal of musical Bern to attend. They heard an unforgettable evening of Brahms songs from Hermine and the composer, with interludes of Bach from the keyboard.[37] Brahms became a regular weekend guest at Widmann's, talking for hours, critiquing his friend's newspaper pieces, playing with the children and the dog, and putting away formidable slices of Frau Widmann's plum cake.

In his memoirs Widmann recalled his friend in late middle age. Even when Brahms stayed up past the midnight chimes, he still rose at dawn for a walk and then work, his breakfast still a Havana cigar and strong coffee. His morning brew he made from a Viennese brass coffeepot with a little spigot, on a porcelain stand. An admirer in Marseilles kept him supplied with fine *Mokka* in quantity. Widmann recalled Brahms walking through Thun with the inevitable crowd of children around him, vying noisily for treats.

For weekends in Bern he usually turned up at Widmann's in a striped flannel shirt without tie or collar. He would wear over his shoulder a shabby leather satchel, which he filled with books from Widmann's library that he usually returned read the next week. His clothes still tended to black, the long topcoat graying with age. When it got cold Brahms would throw a brownish-gray shawl over his shoulders and secure it with a huge pin; the effect was grandmotherly enough to set the Swiss staring. He wanted his trousers short, out of the way of his walking boots, and if a pair was too long he was known to chop them off with scissors. Despite his age and girth Brahms continued to take on ambitious mountain treks, though in those days he complained all the way up. Usually on reaching the summit he turned cheerful, and he went downhill like a cannonball.[38]

In his literary tastes he remained old-fashioned, on the whole preferring to reread favorites from his youth like Jean Paul rather than new productions. Yet Brahms was *au courant* in his way, entranced like most of his class by Edison's electric light and phonograph and the other fruits of modern science and invention. On the other hand, he detested the new bicycle craze, mainly because cyclists interrupted his thoughts as they whizzed past. Besides the course of politics both German (always hopeful to Brahms as long as Bismarck was in charge) and Austrian (with mounting alarm), he kept up attentively with the rest of the world.[39] In 1876, Brahms had raised a glass to celebrate the deaths of General Custer and his troops at Little Big Horn, telling George Henschel, "You wouldn't believe the joy that gives me! Of course I know it won't help the poor fellows; but at least it was granted them to take one good bath in the blood of their persecutors!"[40]

In conversation Brahms was ready to debate everything from politics to literature to philosophy. For a while he put off reading Nietzsche's *Beyond Good and Evil*, which Widmann had reviewed enthusiastically in his paper before he lent it to Brahms. "I have placed an Italian novel on top of the Nietzsche," he wrote Widmann, "while I think twice whether I'll walk under a blue or a gray sky!"[41]

It was in 1888, after Nietzsche heard that Brahms had read and enjoyed the book, that the philosopher tried out his musical pretensions on the famous man, forwarding Brahms his own *Hymn to Life*. Brahms found Nietzsche's hymn "much the same as any young student's effort," but out of respect he thought it over before making an uncharacteristically diplomatic response. Finally he announced to Max Kalbeck, "I've done it! I've extricated myself beautifully from this Nietzsche business. I simply sent him my visiting card and thanked him politely for the stimulus he had given me. The amusing thing is that I quietly avoided mentioning the music at all!"

Brahms had written: "He regards it as a signal honor, and he is grateful for the considerable stimulus he has derived from it." Nietzsche chose to regard those words as a seal of approval on his achievement as a composer; he told a friend that his hymn had received signs of "piety and deep recognition from a number of artists, among them Dr. Brahms." That did not impede Nietzsche's disillusionment with the artist whom he had once attempted to make into a new hero. In "The Case of Wagner," written in 1888, Nietzsche issued his famous dismissal:

> What does Johannes Brahms matter now?—His good fortune was a German misunderstanding: he was taken for Wagner's antagonist—an antagonist was *needed.*—That does not make for *necessary* music. . . . I discovered almost by accident, that he affects a certain type of man. His is the melancholy of impotence: he does *not* create out of abundance, he *languishes* for abundance. If we discount what he imitates, what he borrows from great old or exotic-modern styles . . . what remains as specifically his is *yearning.*—This is felt by all who are full of yearning and dissatisfaction of any kind.

Naturally "the melancholy of impotence" became a rallying cry for anti-Brahmsians in perpetuity. Nietzsche's attack probably upset Widmann more than it did its target; nothing like that surprised Brahms anymore. But though the critic took some potshots at Nietzsche afterward—including his play named *Beyond Good and Evil*—Widmann never escaped a certain fascination with the philosopher. Meanwhile Nietzsche, shortly after condemning Bismarck, the Kaiser, and all antisemites to the same perdition, collapsed into syphilitic paralysis in January 1889.[42] The final irony was that as music for his funeral in 1900, his sister chose Brahms's "Wenn ein müder Leib begraben": "When a weary body is entombed."[43]

AMONG FRIENDS, Brahms in his fifties was jolly and joking as always, if still capable of galling insults inadvertent and otherwise. Strangers and hangers-on he held at bay, skillfully keeping the trials of fame from becoming a nuisance. Widmann noted the cunning with which he prevented lady pianists from gaining the bench to play for him. He was equally adept at evading autograph hounds, including the ones who asked him to sign for phony packages.[44]

To a degree few artists have achieved, nothing from the outside world interfered with his work, when he was ready to do it. The remarkable musical products of his 1886 summer in Thun were the Second Cello Sonata, the Second and Third Violin Sonatas (the Third not quite finished until 1888), the Third Piano Trio, and several songs for Opuses 104 and 105, including "Wie Melodien zieht es mir." The latter is one of his most ingratiating lieder, a portrait of the effervescent Hermine for whom he wrote it and who made it her own. By then she was giving acclaimed performances of the Alto Rhapsody. All the same, Brahms had begun to beware of his current favorite songstress: "I'm now getting to the years," he wrote Kalbeck that summer, "where a man easily does something stupid, so I have to doubly watch myself."[45] Before long Hermine would provide him with an excuse to pull back.

If he was warning himself about her, his yearning for Hermine is still written in more music from that summer, especially the Second Violin Sonata in A Major. He composed it as he waited for a visit from her; his means of symbolizing that agreeable longing took the familiar form of a song without words. The song is his own: the second theme of the sonata's opening movement has, in the piano, a quotation of "Wie Melodien zieht es mir," transformed from the original two-beat into a dancing three. But the feeling still echoes the opening words of Klaus Groth's verse: "I feel as if melodies were moving through my mind;/they seem to blossom like spring flowers and waft away like fragrance." (Some writers suspect echoes of two more Hermine-inspired songs in the Sonata, "Komm bald" and "Immer leiser wird mein Schlummer.")

This Violin Sonata, like the First, is largely lyrical and songlike, the mood suggested in its tempo indications: *Allegro amabile, Andante tranquillo* (with three interpolated *Vivaces*), and the warm conclusion, *Allegretto grazioso* (*quasi Andante*). The Third Violin Sonata in D Minor, also sketched but not finished that summer, stands in contrast as the most passionate and dark-toned of the three—and maybe for that reason it is dedicated to passionate, dark-toned Hans von Bülow (the last work Brahms dedicated to anyone).

While the Second Violin Sonata paints a picture of Brahms at his desk yearning for Hermine, the rest of that summer's work in chamber music and song seems to reflect, more starkly than usual, his feelings of age and loss. The Opus 105 lieder begin with "Wie Melodien," but continue with "Immer leiser wird mein Schlummer" and its portrait of a dying girl wishing her lover to "komm' bald"—"come soon, O come soon!" (a grim riposte to the flirtatious "Komm bald" earlier written to Hermine). The folk song text for the next lied, "Klage," is set in a winter landscape: "Sweet girl, don't trust him so he won't break your heart!" Then comes "Auf dem Kirchhofe," a scene in a graveyard, with the "Gewesen"—"departed"—written on the graves transformed into an ambiguous "Genesen"—"healed." Are the dead healed because granted eternal life, or healed *from* life? The final song of the set, "Verrat" ("Betrayal"), is a melodramatic ballad in which a lover murders his rival on a barren heath.

Elisabet von Herzogenberg found the text vulgar and shocking, but Theodor Billroth commended the song as "a treasure for all bassos."[46]

None of these lieder suggests the musician's truce with death, however provisional and secular it is, that Brahms had achieved a couple of years before in his setting of Heine's "Der Tod, das ist die kühle Nacht":

> *Death is the cool night,*
> *Life is the sultry day.*
> *It is already growing dark; I am sleepy;*
> *The day has wearied me.*

> *Over my bed rises a tree;*
> *In it the young nightingale is singing;*
> *It sings of nothing but love;*
> *I hear it even in my dreams.*

Two other products of the Thun summer 1886 also show contrasting trains of thought, musically and expressively. The Second Cello Sonata in F Major is a testament to the rich tone and musical fantasy of his friend Robert Hausmann, of the Joachim String Quartet—the cello that Brahms seemed to carry in his mind in the last decade of his life, as he carried Joachim's violin and the voices of Amalie Joachim and Hermine Spies. The sonata begins recalling the Third Symphony, with a metrically wandering and wildly disjunct theme in a mixture of F major and minor. Arnold Schoenberg would recall how "indigestible" this beginning appeared to the Viennese, himself included, in his youth.[47] Theodor Billroth expressed some of that feeling in his response: "I confess the first movement was somewhat dubious to me. . . . But you always know the right way to the purely musical." With his accustomed lustiness (Billroth seems to have believed the musical instinct to overlap the sexual) he added, "The [Second] Violin Sonata is of unending grace, charm, and lovely feeling—a darling child, so sweet and dear, just to be kissed all over!"[48]

Hausmann's influence on the Second Cello Sonata may be seen in its feeling for the cello *as* cello, a creative involvement with timbre and technique only now and then to be found in Brahms's writing for instruments other than the piano, and which looks forward to his obsession with the clarinet in his last years. The sonata begins memorably with sweeping piano tremolos; in the course of the movement they are transformed into cello tremolos across the strings. The change of the idea of tremolo from one instrumental medium to another is itself a "theme," a coloristic/

structural kind of thinking one hardly expects from Brahms the conservative. And there are novel experiments with pizzicato effects including, at the end, the proto-Bartókian idea of changing pitches on a single pluck of the string.

If the Second Cello Sonata ends with a certain emotional equilibrium, that feeling is counterpoised by the Third Piano Trio in C Minor, which from the first measures contains some of the most Romantically expressive unto anguished music of Brahms's maturity—that contrasted with a flowing, hymnlike, utterly beautiful second theme. Much of the piece exhibits the compactness of form and gesture that marked Brahms's late music. Every idea is stated succinctly, each part of the formal model not only treated with his usual freedom, but making its point with dispatch—such as the tiny two-beat quasi-scherzo of the second movement, in straightforward A B A form.

The Third Trio also carries his metrical explorations in a prophetic new direction. The first movement begins with general metric stability, but for long sections (most of the development, the first part of the recap) there is little sense of meter and sometimes little of the beat. Part of the second-movement scherzo's function is to establish an interlude of stable two-beat. The third movement presents an extraordinary metric experiment in the form of constantly changing time signatures, at first an alternation of one bar of $\frac{3}{4}$ with two of $\frac{2}{4}$, making a seven-beat phrase.[49] Later in the movement he varies that idea, including a section combining one bar of $\frac{9}{8}$ with one of $\frac{6}{8}$, to make a five-beat pattern. (In 1888 Brahms composed the unsettling vocal quartet "Nächtens" entirely in $\frac{5}{4}$. By that point in Brahms's work the twenty-five years to Stravinsky's *Sacre du printemps* seem less of a leap.) The trio's scherzo-like last movement begins on an upbeat that sounds equally like a downbeat, and sustains that kind of ambiguity for much of its course—a quite intense course, though this time there is a concluding turn to C major.

Elisabet von Herzogenberg hastened to declare this work and its optimistic outcome a more satisfactory image of the composer than the Fourth Symphony. The whole Third Piano Trio, she wrote, is "better than any photograph, for it shows your *real* self."[50] That was wishful thinking about Brahms, in 1886.

BRAHMS MUST HAVE GONE BACK to Vienna in October 1886 feeling satisfied over that summer's crop, one of the most prolific of his life, and one of the last richly productive ones. Certainly he had warm feelings about the social part of the vacation. He wrote Widmann: "When I think back on wonderful Thun—the memory of you is the dearest, most valuable, and the most warming." Yet then and later he used the formal *Sie* with Widmann rather than the intimate *du*.

At the beginning of November, Fritz Brahms died, still a bachelor, in Hamburg. Though they had remained contentedly apart throughout their lives, bachelor Fritz left his brother an inheritance of 10,000 marks in his will, the result of a prosperous career as piano teacher and probably, in some degree, professional "wrong Brahms." Apparently Fritz had no one else to leave his money to. Johannes first gave it to Simrock for safekeeping, then to his stepmother Karoline and her invalid son, "the second Fritz." If the death of his brother gave Brahms any particular pause, it did not show. His main concern that month was to act as impresario for the Vienna debut of Hermine Spies.

Preparatory to her recital came a big dinner at Billroth's house for Hermine and guests chosen by Brahms with an eye to people his protégé needed to impress—Hanslick naturally the first. Kalbeck recalled the dinner as a "high feast of life . . . the maestro was in youthful merry mood [and] did everything that one could ask of him. . . . The composer and the singer sat together like a happy couple, opposite the jovial master of the house. Hermine Spies did not pretend for a moment that she did not adore her neighbor at the table, and he also showed, in a way not to be denied, his great interest in her."[51] One would like details of what Kalbeck meant by that, with Brahms falling under the influences of wine, good food, and a pretty singer by his side.

Brahms accompanied Hermine's recital on the twenty-fourth. Afterward, once again, he began the process of extracting himself from the high feast of life. Hermine herself supplied the motivation for his escape, as Lisl von Herzogenberg suggests in a letter to Brahms that November: "How did Spies sing in Vienna? I can't help feeling strongly that she is not developing at all. When I think of Frau Joachim and the way her voice grew steadily fuller, it seems to me that concert work and tearing about is . . . making this one more casual. She sings so many things as if she were reading at first sight, and I do wish someone like you would warn her . . . for she gets terribly spoilt, and understands no hints."[52]

Lisl may have been covertly jealous of Hermine's place in Brahms's affections, but she also knew what she was talking about. In fact, Brahms had already warned "his" singer, obliquely, in a letter of November 4: "I actually dreamed that I heard you skip a half bar's rest, and sing a quarter note instead of an eighth." Hermine understood the hint: "It is very sweet of you only to dream that I am unmusical. I have not only dreamt it, but have known it for ages."[53] This did not mark an end to their relations, or their flirtations, not quite; but the crest had passed. From that point another inspiring musician Brahms had contemplated marrying could be added to the register of ones he let get away.

January 1887 began with a second performance of the Fourth Symphony by the Vienna Philharmonic. Richard Heuberger reported to his diary that it found "zero" success with the public.[54] Maybe by then a Viennese wit had applied a text to the opening melody: *Es fiel . . . ihm wie- . . . dermal . . . nichts ein*—once more he had no ideas. Brahms did not lose any sleep over it. At least elsewhere the piece had found enthusiasm, more than he had expected. That month he attended to his chores of spreading around the fruits of his labor. He wrote Fritz Simrock to send Theodor Kirchner 2000 marks as payment for three Schumann manuscripts Kirchner had given him, 1000 marks to his sister Elise as one of his regular support payments, 2000 to stepbrother Fritz Schnack, "and finally 1000 marks to this poor sinner."[55]

Brahms's relations with Simrock remained close, harmonious, and ironic. For years the publisher had raked in unheard-of profits from a serious still-breathing composer, while that composer paid remarkably little attention to the whole business, only asking to have financial affairs kept off his mind and a favor done here and there. On the whole, Brahms's letters to Simrock are a blend of the expected practical matters dealing with copying and engraving, and his ever-inventive wit when it came to matters of money. His usual game on those occasions was to portray Simrock as tightfisted shyster and himself as humble supplicant. In 1882 he submitted pieces with this note:

> Tell me if this rubbish is worth 1000 thalers apiece to you. Trio, quintet, *Parzenlied*. Speak right out! I shall certainly not complain that you have taken unfair advantage of my temporarily destitute condition. Actually you could have the whole bag of tricks for 1000 marks if you sent it right away. I don't know what I shall have to live on in another week, to say nothing of rent and tailor. . . . In short, mull this over finely. I'm a man you can bargain with.

When Simrock tried, unsuccessfully of course, to buy *Ein deutsches Requiem* from Rieter-Biedermann, Brahms teased: "How were the stairs in Leipzig? Swathed in soft carpets? Fitted with comfortable banisters?" When he asked for money another time:

> The so-often-praised goodness and charity of your Well-bornship give me the courage to approach with a great petition. My situation is

terrible, a horrifying future stares me in the face; the abyss appears yawning before me, I fall therein—unless your saving hand draws me back. With the last one-mark note I must now proceed at once to the Igel restaurant—but with what feelings shall I eat, and indeed drink![56]

Late in their long professional and personal relationship, Fritz Simrock became one of the last people Brahms honored with the intimate *du*.

At the end of May 1887, as Brahms prepared to leave on another Italian trip, he dined with Heuberger at the Café Czardas in the Prater. The day found him crowing with high spirits: "I tell you, the food is decent, goulash delightful, ham salad wonderful, good beer, good wine and a splendid Gypsy band!" Next day he headed for Innsbrück and thence to Italy with Fritz Simrock—and, in an experiment that did not turn out happily, Theodor Kirchner. As Brahms wrote Hans von Bülow, "Simrock's happy thought of giving Kirchner a glimpse of the promised land delighted me, but now I feel it's at least twenty years too late. At least, I suspect he only feels really at home when he sits down to dinner or supper, and can chat about the Gewandhaus and other splendors." His and Clara's old friend was sixty-four now, teaching at the Dresden Conservatory, settled in his gloom.[57] In 1890, Kirchner retired to Hamburg to live out his last years.

WITH HIS UNVARYING SCHEDULE, Brahms returned from Italy and headed directly for his chosen summer retreat, once again Hofstetten near Thun, convenient to Josef Widmann. As he set to work on new pieces he began a new campaign with Clara: he demanded that she return his letters to her, and he would give back hers. The idea was to read them once more for old times' sake, then destroy them while they had the chance. He was especially anxious because he did not have children to look after his legacy, to protect his privacy in history. "It is much more important that my letters should be sent back than that yours should," he wrote Clara. "You can always have the latter, as can also your children. . . . But in case of my death, my letters have no one to go back to. That is why I most earnestly beg you to return them to me, and if I say send them quickly, please don't think it's because I'm in a hurry to send them to the bookbinders!"[58]

Clara agreed, then balked. When he sent some of her old letters she was both moved and horrified to read them: "I found them . . . one wail of sorrow," she wrote in her journal, "and though this was justified by my

hard fate, yet I should be sorry to think they would ever be made public."
She begged him to let her save some of his. Gently, he refused.[59]

Rarely is Brahms on record as being any more free with his writing.
Once when musicologist La Mara asked to include something of his in a
published collection of musicians' letters, he replied to her, "I never write
otherwise than reluctantly, hurriedly, and carelessly, but I am ashamed
when an example like yours comes to my attention . . . no one can do me
less of a favor than to print letters of mine. . . . It pleases me to save a letter from Beethoven as a memento; but I can only be horrified when I
imagine all the things such a letter may be taken to mean and explain!"
He felt similarly about minor works and manuscripts: leave them in libraries for scholars, don't let them fall into the wrong hands (biographers, by definition, being the wrong hands).[60] Still, in his response to
the musicologist all that was preparatory to making an exception for one
letter that he did allow her to print. If he specifically chose to let something out, then fine. More than a particular piece of his private life, it was
the reins over his private life that he never wanted to give over to historians.

As Clara grappled with the letters and memories, her son Ferdinand
had sunk so far into morphine addiction that she had to take over support of his children, and at the same time her daughter Elise's four-year-
old died. One of Julie's children had died as well—her favorite. Still,
while all that was going on Clara became ecstatic over the new C Minor
Trio: "No previous work of Johannes has so completely carried me
away. . . . How happy I was this evening—happier than I had been for a
long time."[61] Taking a break from his labors in June, Brahms attended
the Cologne Music Festival, then visited Clara in Frankfurt. She wrote,
"Sorrowful feelings, as always, when he leaves."[62]

The Cologne Festival was a function of the New German–dominated
Allgemeiner Deutscher Musikverein. Brahms played in a performance of
the C Minor Trio, premiered earlier in Vienna. His old friend Franz
Wüllner was directing the festival, and with Liszt and Wagner both dead
Brahms was ready for a gesture of reconciliation toward the opposition.
He even endured a performance of Liszt's *Legend of Saint Elisabeth*. At the
end he reported to Clara: "Everything went off in the happiest and most
delightful fashion. Wüllner did his work excellently. . . . The company
about me, both young men and girls, were fair to look upon and jolly, and
finally at Rüdesheim we sampled as much of the best wine as we possibly
could."[63]

After returning to Thun he also returned to his campaign about the
letters. "I become abundantly convinced that it would be a crying shame
to destroy them," Clara pleaded, to which he replied mildly,

We are behaving in a remarkable manner about our letters! I have always secretly meditated an exchange but did not dare to utter the word. I then sent your letters, but didn't have the courage to look into them and read them beforehand, because I took it for granted that if I did I would not be able to send them away. But you are a regular fraud. You start the whole ball rolling, send nothing, and go on reading.

Shortly afterward he gave her the rest of her letters to him, and with a flood of tears she handed over his.[64] In reality, Clara appears to have lied about how much she destroyed. She kept back many copies, or perhaps originals. And after Brahms had torn up many of his own letters and consigned them to the nearest river, he also preserved some, perhaps planning to burn more eventually, never quite getting around to it.

In the above letter he also reported to Clara his main project for summer 1887:

As to myself, I can tell you something funny, for I have had the amusing idea of writing a concerto for violin and cello. If it is at all successful it might give us some fun. You can well imagine the sort of pranks one can play in such a case. . . . I ought to have handed on the idea to someone who knows the violin better than I do. (Joachim has unfortunately given up composing.) It is a very different matter writing for instruments whose nature and sound one only has a chance acquaintance with . . . from writing for an instrument that one knows as thoroughly as I know the piano. For in the latter case I know exactly what I write and why I write it as I do. But we'll wait and see.[65]

There is great uneasiness in those flippant words. Brahms generally waxed coy about new works, the more ambitious the piece the more coy, but he did not ordinarily use words like "fun" and "pranks." And it is astounding to find him, at that age and experience and position, still insecure about solo writing. The problem was that this time Joachim would not be on hand to help him. Beyond that, if his anxieties about the Fourth Symphony had been calmed by its reception, his larger fears about his dwindling creative juices had not subsided.

The immediate impetus for writing a double concerto for violin, cello, and orchestra is clear enough: a gesture toward Joachim, from whom he was still estranged. At the same time, it would provide another showpiece for Robert Hausmann, for whom Brahms had written the Second Cello Sonata. In September, after a meeting and rehearsal in Baden-Baden among Clara, Brahms, Joachim, and Hausmann, she told her journal:

"This concerto is a work of reconciliation—Joachim and Brahms have spoken to each other again for the first time in years." The piece was premiered in Cologne in October 1887, Brahms on the podium and Joachim and Hausmann soloing. Brahms told an acquaintance, "Now I know what it is that's been missing in my life for the past few years. . . . It was the sound of Joachim's violin."[66]

But few of Brahms's friends particularly liked the Double Concerto, even after they heard the full effect with orchestra. Joachim was dubious; Clara wrote in her journal: "I do not believe the concerto has any future . . . nowhere has it the warmth and freshness which are so often to be found in his works."[67] Billroth wrote Hanslick that he found it "tedious and wearisome, a really senile production. If the *Zigeunerlieder* [*Gypsy Songs*, a high-spirited product of the previous summer] had not been composed later, one might almost believe it was all up with our Johannes."[68] Billroth may have been reading some of his own infirmity into the Double Concerto. That summer he had been struck by an attack of pneumonia from which he never really recovered. The indefatigable prodigy of surgery was finally feeling his age.

Certainly Billroth did not use such harsh words about the Double Concerto with its creator. But Brahms knew how to interpret what his friends said, and did not say. The trouble was that his own fears about his and his work's viability ran in the same direction. Few if any knew it at the time, but Brahms had drafted a second double concerto, just as he previously had another violin concerto. After gauging the equivocal private and public response to the concertos he did release, he smothered both sequels.

And through it all illness and death gathered around him. His musicologist friend C. F. Pohl had died in the spring, his old teacher Eduard Marxsen at the end of 1887. Besides Billroth's ailments, Heinrich von Herzogenberg had fallen into a wretched siege of rheumatism and mysterious complications that were to cripple him for years, that in turn a burden to Lisl's always-precarious health. (For the next decade Heinrich's place at the Berlin Hochschule would be filled by Clara's brother Woldemar Bargiel, whom Brahms respected more as a composer than he did Heinrich.[69])

Brahms, Joachim, and Hausmann played the Double Concerto together several times in the 1887–8 concert season, and if the performances did not find the usual tumultuous ovations they still brought Brahms and Joachim in some degree back together—if not on the old intimate footing, at least in regular if wary collaboration. The Double Concerto has some of the expected nods to his friend. While Joachim's motto F-A-E is not highlighted as such, those pitches in some arrangement or outline turn up often, notably in the rondo theme of the last movement. The second theme of the opening movement suggests Viotti's Concerto No. 22, a favorite of both Brahms and Joachim going back to their early years together. The "Hungarian" character of the finale is another testimonial.

Eventually, Joachim came around to admiring the piece. It did not hurt that Brahms gave him the manuscript with the inscription: "To him for whom it was written." The public, for its part, would never embrace the Double Concerto during Brahms's lifetime, and since then the requirement for two first-rate soloists has been a steady impediment. The music, consistently beautiful and of course masterful, is hardly the "senile production" Billroth called it. But maybe this time there are signs of Brahms slipping from his extraordinary standard. A decade before, in the successive years 1876 to 1878, he had produced the first two symphonies and the Violin Concerto, then a major orchestral work every second year, each of them an unquestioned masterpiece.

Among those historic orchestral works the Double Concerto seems the most backward-looking, the most Romantic, from the melodramatic unison proclamation of its opening to passages of Schubertian sweetness. Its predecessors probably include Beethoven's Triple Concerto, Mozart's Sinfonia Concertante, and the Bach Concerto for Two Violins.[70] As usual, Brahms absorbed his influences and produced something in his own voice, in fact a unique genre as a solo concerto for violin and cello. Certainly the piece has great tonal and rhythmic fluidity and striking harmonic effects. Yet it is hard to place expressively, neither particularly tragic nor particularly gay, its monumental opening arguably rhetorical and unearned. It has few memorable melodic transports of the kind in which Brahms had always been lavish; perhaps there are too many passages of the soloists rippling through the harmony bar after bar in unvarying figuration.

If Billroth was wrong to call the concerto senile, maybe it is a little weary, or geared mainly to honor two friends and reconcile with one—a holiday before Brahms turned to the more intimidating proposition of a fifth symphony. As Beethoven harked back to the Baroque *concerto grosso* in his Triple Concerto, Brahms in this concerto harkened a half-century back. In that context it is startling to realize that the year of the Double Concerto, 1887, was the year Vincent Van Gogh painted *Moulin de la Galette* and Marc Chagall and Marcel Duchamp were born. The next year Paul Cézanne painted *L'estaque* and James Ensor the proto-surrealistic *Entry of Christ into Brussels*.

In other words, a zeitgeist was taking shape in which the magisterial, backward-looking beauties of the Double Concerto seemed to have no place. Surely Brahms felt it; for all his studied posture of indifference to everybody and everything, he had extremely sensitive antennae for the public, for culture and its moods. He published a revised version of the concerto in 1889, but that did nothing for its popularity or its relevance to the present or the future.

The more relevant developments of 1889 are that Gustav Mahler completed his First Symphony and Brahms's young acquaintance Richard Strauss electrified the world with his tone poem *Don Juan*, the first of his excursions into the minute depiction of stories, in musical style hyperchromatically post-Wagnerian. The year after that Van Gogh died unknown, but at the beginning of a decade whose spirit transformed his once-aberrant paintings into masterpieces. The next year, 1891, Gaugin headed for Tahiti and his greatest work. Likely Brahms knew little of those landmarks, though he certainly kept up, growling, with Strauss's manifestations.

It was in 1887, the year of the Double Concerto, that young French composer Claude Debussy introduced himself to Brahms. Seven years later, the exotic perfumes of his *L'après-midi d'un faune* would open a fantastical tonal world, one in which Brahms's world seems never to have existed. In 1887, Arnold Schoenberg had entered his teens in Vienna and was dreaming of composing. In the United States that year, Charles Ives's father was tinkering with quarter-tone instruments and teaching his son to sing in one key while he accompanied in another. Even if no one could know the import of all that, there was still an encroaching sense of something new and unsettling approaching, in art as in society.

If one arguable metaphor (among others) for Brahms's Fourth Symphony is an act of mourning for Austro-German music, the Double Concerto can be called an aftershock, a memorial service after the funeral. Maybe for the first time in his music, in the Double Concerto one can hear a dissonance between Brahms's art and the spirit of his age.

CHAPTER TWENTY-ONE

Laurels

THOUGH HE DID NOT SPEAK OF IT YET, by 1887 Brahms had begun to feel like an elder composer with the world passing him by. His main professed worry of that year, however, had to do with his lodgings in Vienna. Frau Vogel, from whom he had long been subletting, had died and Brahms was left suddenly helpless.[1] Most of his furniture belonged to the Vogels so he was going to lose it, and he might have to give up the apartment entirely. The prospect of changing his accommodations was an alarming thought for an old bachelor. The situation presaged a period of loose ends for him.

In one of several worried letters to Maria Fellinger in Vienna during the summer of 1887, Brahms called the apartment "my chief topic." When word got around about Frau Vogel's death, a row of ladies—"From the far corners of Europe!" Brahms complained—offered their services as his housekeeper, but he dithered and balked at the idea of having some strange new woman in his rooms. Finally Brahms told Maria that he would keep the place, borrow furniture from friends, and let the aged lady called the *Hausmeisterin*, who dusted the stairs and such, take care of his cleaning.

Maria Fellinger would have none of that. The care of the great man was a serious affair, not to be left to chance. She scraped together some temporary furnishings and prodded Brahms to find a real housekeeper. One day after he returned to Vienna she showed up at his rooms to lift the sofa cushions and reveal triumphantly the dust the *Hausmeisterin* had left under them. Giving in to Maria's prophecies of squalor overtaking him, Brahms let in the door someone she sent over, a stout, no-nonsense journalist's widow named Celestine Truxa. She inspected the empty rooms, brusquely made an offer, and left with his assurance that he would think it over. At home a week later her aged aunt, who lived with Frau Truxa and her two boys, ran in to say that a strange man was measuring the furniture in the living room. The intruder turned out to be Brahms, brandishing a tape measure. To the bewildered Frau Truxa he exclaimed, "The things will go in!"

So Celestine Truxa was installed in Frau Vogel's old apartment with her aunt and sons. From then on she would make a study of Brahms's daily routines and rituals. If he did not consider his housekeeper a friend or confidante, he still appreciated her and delighted in her children, as sign of which he usually spent Christmas Eve with the Truxa family.[2] The holidays made pleasant memories for all concerned, except perhaps the one when Brahms decided to tease the Truxa boys. He solemnly announced to them that the Christ Child had come down with the flu and would not be bringing presents this year. The boys fell to howling and his attempts to ply them with candy got nowhere. Frantic, he ran to their mother and pleaded, "Look here, Frau Truxa, now I don't know what to do! Can't you calm them down? Tell them the Christ Child has gotten well!" As with most situations, she soon brought this one under control.[3]

For the most part Frau Truxa had an easy enough job, since her employer was intensely private and generally fastidious. She learned to clean without moving anything; Brahms even noticed when she turned his spectacles around. His communication of that like everything else, however, was peculiarly circuitous. One had to learn his little games. If he needed a glove or a sock mended he would leave it draped over an open drawer until Frau Truxa got the message, then express surprise and delight to find it repaired. If his boots needed polish he would set them a shade further from the wall. He needed to maintain the fiction of asking nothing, of being no trouble even as he relied on everyone for favors. Once he sulked mysteriously for days before Truxa, after a minute inspection of his rooms, discovered that a maid had inadvertently closed the lid of his wicker wastebasket. He wanted it open, beckoning, at all times: after the piano, the wastebasket was his most important piece of furniture.[4]

During one period a lady downstairs took to playing his music on her piano, to impress her famous neighbor. If that was not bad enough, her playing was appalling. Driven to distraction, Brahms spoke to the lady with his usual degree of tact, which was none. His diplomacy can be judged from the fact that after they spoke the lady hired a conservatory student to come into her apartment and play for hours on end, as loud as possible. Now really traumatized, Brahms took his anguish to Frau

Truxa. After thinking over various plans of attack, his housekeeper decided to extol to the lady downstairs the wonders of the zither, which Frau Truxa played herself. She even offered to give the woman free lessons and persuaded her (this was not a remarkably bright sort of neighbor) that the thing to do was fire the conservatory student and devote her time to that admirable and pleasantly quiet instrument, the zither.[5] Peace returned to the house.

Maria Fellinger's photographs of Karlsgasse No. 4 in later years show Frau Truxa's furniture, mostly simple chairs and tables. Brahms particularly prized her unstable rocking chair. He generally directed visiting ladies, especially pretty ones, to have a seat in it. They would lean back to find their legs thrown in the air and skirts flying, or lean forward and be deposited on their knees, as he watched with blue eyes sparkling. A firescreen served him as a place to hide from guests, whom he would startle with a burst of fiendish laughter.[6]

George Henschel remembered Brahms's rooms as sunny and smelling of coffee.[7] He kept the lid of his Streicher piano closed and draped to mute his playing, and used the top to display a changing collection of medals, awards, and keepsakes. The artworks on the wall were his own, a pantheon of household gods: a great white bust of Beethoven over the piano (he had owned it since Hamburg), Bach's portrait over the narrow bed, Raphael's *Sistine Madonna* over the leather couch, near it a portrait of the neglected composer Luigi Cherubini, with whom Brahms identified as a once-famous craftsman whom the world was determined to forget. In the picture Cherubini was being blessed by the Muse of Lyric Poetry. Brahms found the lady ridiculous, so he cut out a piece of cardboard to cover her up. Eventually there was a bronze bas-relief of Bismarck under the bust of Beethoven, with a laurel wreath circling it.

In the library one wall held his books, original editions, treasured manuscripts from Beethoven and Schubert to Wagner. The shelves looked casually arranged, but he knew every item's place and on his vacations could order things sent him citing their precise location. Facing the bookshelves was a standing desk where he worked in winter, and the room held his trunk, kept packed for a quick getaway. Surprisingly, he was willing to lend out books and even manuscripts, and once while he was away he invited Richard Fellinger to go in and borrow anything he wanted.

Rarely did Brahms eat at home anymore, but now had lunch and dinner mostly at Zum roten Igel, whose name means the Red Hedgehog, in the Wildpretmarkt. He came to call the place his "prickly pet," and himself another: once he invited Frau Brüll to join "the two pricklies." For his money the Igel had the best cheap food in Vienna, and he prided him-self on eating better for less than his companions. When Brahms came alone to the Igel he sat in the lavishly appointed main room, but behind a curtain, or in good weather out in the garden. With friends he retired to the dark rear *Stube* with its barrel ceiling, and a table that could seat six or so. If he preferred those plain accommodations beside working people, the management still reserved a barrel of first-rate Hungarian Tokay for him, and there is no record that he objected. As a meeting place of the Brahms circle, the back room became an unofficial artistic center where Vienna's musical affairs were pondered over and settled.

After his lunch of goulash or roast beef or pork with a glass or two of beer or a *Viertel*—quarter liter—of wine, Brahms might walk to the Café Heinrichshof across from the Opera, to have his *Mokka* and read the newspapers on sticks, then snooze for a while as tourists gawked at the famous beard in the window, motionless as a statue.[8] On sunny summer days he frequented the outdoor casino under towering trees in the Stadt-park. After evenings out he might stop by the Igel late for one more *Mokka*, which never seemed to trouble his sleep.

FOR INTIMATE FEMALE COMPANIONSHIP Brahms still relied on broth-els. His acquaintances, the male ones at least, knew about his regular vis-its to the places. The record of these escapades stops at the door of the establishments; one did not speak in public of such things, and in those days madames had more class than to write memoirs of their famous cus-tomers. For variety there was the occasional compliant serving girl. The names of Brahms's favorites appear jotted here and there on his manu-scripts.[9] Probably friends accompanied him to the whorehouses; it was what bachelors and some married men did in Vienna as in many cities. Some Viennese men acquired a lower-class "sweet girl" as mistress, but that was not Brahms's style. Since his childhood in the dives, sexuality had been for him a matter of secret transactions with the demimonde—efficient, predictable, and without obligations except for the fee.

With his hired companions Brahms seems to have been a thoughtful customer, with the same democratic consideration for working people that he showed to other professions. Once he recommended a prostitute to an acquaintance; when the man followed the suggestion he found that she could not praise the kindness of the Herr Doktor enough. He treated her like a daughter, she said. Streetwalkers affectionately called to him on the street and sought him out when they were short of cash; generally he reached cheerfully into his pocket. One evening when Brahms was out with Frau Brüll a passing streetwalker hailed him. He flushed bright red and muttered sheepishly to his companion: "I want you to know that I have never made a married woman or a Fräulein unhappy."[10]

It was in this decade that Brahms got drunk at a party and branded all women with a word so shocking that it broke up the occasion and nobody would repeat it. Walking it off in the Prater with singer Max Friedländer, Brahms poured over that friend his scorching recollection of the "singing girls" of the Hamburg *Animierlokale*. It was as if he were living it over again. "And you," he snarled to Friedländer in a frightening burst of fury, "you who have been reared in cotton wool; you who have been protected from everything coarse—you tell me I should have the same respect, the same exalted homage for women that you have! You expect that of a man cursed with a childhood like mine!" In that period he wrote another acquaintance, "People always call me rough and tactless. Where should I have learned tact? In my youth in order not to starve I was forced to play in saloons frequented by sailors, and indeed one learns nothing good there."[12] As far as history knows he told the truth to Frau Brüll: he kept his hands off respectable women, and he took pride in that.

The sights and smells and rough laughter of the places on the Hamburg docks never left him, nor the thumping of feet on creaking boards in time to the tunes he had played there night after night. Once late on a cold winter night in Vienna, critic Max Graf, during his student days, was dining with companions in a cheap café when a group of elegant party-goers swept in on a gust of snow and sat down to have a beer. Graf noticed Brahms in the middle of the group. Directly the door flew open again and a well-known streetwalker and two gigolos straggled in, all of them drunk. In short order the lady was shouting for the "Professor" to give them some music, they wanted to dance. She seemed to know the Professor a bit. Brahms got up, went over to the dirty, out-of-tune piano at the wall, and began playing old-fashioned waltzes and quadrilles, one after the other. The trio of rough visitors had an hour of dancing before Brahms rose, paid the bill, and left with his group. Next day, queried by a friend about the scene, Brahms explained mildly, "When I was a boy in Hamburg I used to play in just such a place the whole night. I played dance music for drunken sailors and their girls. . . . The pieces I played were those I used to play every night in Hamburg."[13]

If Brahms habitually flirted with "respectable" ladies, he could not abide any female taking the initiative or showing signs of courting him for his fame. One woman recalled a day when she was fifteen and strolling on the Ringstrasse, and saw Brahms looking over some concert posters near the Opera. "I sidled up and gazed adoringly at him. With his great deep blue eyes, he returned my glance most expressively. We walked along like this, keeping parallel, until we came to where the Goethe monument now stands. Here . . . I blurted out: 'Good day, Herr Doktor!' That broke the spell. He gave out two queer, gruff, staccato sounds, more like the yap of an outraged dog than anything else, and turned abruptly away."[14]

In 1888, Hermine Spies met Brahms at the train in Basel and was shocked by how gray he had become, seemingly all of a sudden. He would not have missed that she was so upset by his appearance that at first she could barely speak. Then she saw his "beautiful blue young-man's eyes and the fresh, dear features," and her gaze softened again.[15] Once his line about marriage had been that he was too poor, a vagabond. Now it was becoming that he was too old. "I could *not* marry now," he exploded to a company one night, in another of his sudden furies. "I could not help despising a girl for taking me for a husband. Surely you are not going to persuade me that anybody could fall in love with me, as I am now? . . . What else could attract them? My money? My art?" He concluded with grim satisfaction, "to be accepted out of admiration . . . I should *have* to despise her."[16] Behind all that he may have had a once-handsome man's horror of losing his looks, the instant attraction women used to have for him.

If he could be brutally curt to friends and strangers alike, Brahms still blushed and wept easily. At Brüll's house Richard Specht saw the tears start from his eyes as he looked over his own arrangement of the folk song "The Fair Jewess." He turned away in embarrassment, growling into his beard, "Why must this thing always get to me so?"[17]

In his fashion, Brahms remained modest and generous and often self-deprecating, but he did not escape the effects of fame. In his age he could not abide being contradicted, took it for granted that he was the center of every company. He maintained his chosen masks: the Master to be approached at peril, the *eminence grise*, the gruff hard-drinking bourgeois preferring the company of men or in mixed company telling naughty stories to the ladies. He played the old scamp, the old rogue, flirting with every pretty face and everyone's daughter. But he looked and did not touch beyond a playful squeeze, laughed and held forth and gave lavish gifts but in the end gave nothing of himself beyond his art. Ruthlessly, he had sunk the fair features and moonstruck soul of Young Kreisler under the patriarchal beard and forbidding bark of Herr Doktor Brahms.

.   .   .

DURING APRIL OF 1888, the month before an Italian trip with Josef Viktor Widmann, Brahms wrote Clara Schumann about a new treasure in his collection, the original version of Robert's D Minor Symphony. The piece had been composed in 1841 and revised in 1851, to adapt it to the deficiencies of Schumann's orchestra in Düsseldorf. After studying the original scoring in the manuscript, Brahms concluded that the later version, the one always performed, amounted to a makeshift, turgid compared to the lighter touch of the original. He wrote Clara, "Everyone who sees [the original] agrees with me that the score has not gained by being remodelled; it has certainly lost in charm, ease, and clarity." Distracted by grandchildren and miserable with rheumatism and neuritis, Clara replied nebulously, thereby setting up the worst fight of their old age. Brahms reported at the end of the same letter, "At Billroth's we had a very pleasant evening with the *Zigeunerlieder* for quartet with piano, sung by myself. They are kind of Hungarian love songs, and beautifully sung as they were and in such jolly company, you would have found listening to them a delight."[18] Billroth had an expansive home in Vienna, laid out for entertaining. The surgeon slept in a narrow bed in a plain room; the lavishly decorated music room was the centerpiece of his house.

In the same month Brahms wrote anxiously to Fritz Simrock, who was about to buy his early piano sonatas and other music from Breitkopf & Härtel. Brahms felt ambivalent about these works being in the public eye at all, and certain they would not earn back the prices Härtel demanded for them. Oblivious to the kind of profits his publisher was piling up from his music, and speaking out of an abiding fear that his work was doomed to obscurity, Brahms wrote:

> You expect me to congratulate you? . . . I can't help your overestimating me immensely . . . but I think it exceedingly unwise of you to buy Härtel's things at goodness knows what high prices, music that cost them approximately a hundred Louis d'or, and which in the near future won't be worth powder and shot. . . . I suggest or propose truly and seriously that henceforth I receive no honorarium, but that you place a certain sum to my credit, which I can claim in case of need, but which is simply canceled by my death. . . . I can live very well without receiving any further fees. And live well I will, so far as a man of my stamp, which is very different from Wagner's, cares to. . . . Well if I must send them, here are my congratulations, but I wash my hands with carbolic and so forth![19]

One would like to know Simrock's response to these proposals—measured? sly? ironic?—but Brahms destroyed his publisher's letters. Simrock would continue to pay for new pieces. In fact, there were not many to come.

After three weeks basking in Italian towns and countryside with Widmann, Brahms arrived at his house in Thun at the end of May. The work of this third summer in Switzerland was more scattered than that of the last two: the setting of Max Kalbeck's "Letztes Glück" ("Last Happiness") and the remaining *a capella* choral settings of Opus 104, some of the Opus 106 and 107 solo songs, vocal quartets for Opus 112. Otherwise, he finished the Third Violin Sonata, arranged the quartet *Zigeunerlieder* for solo voice and piano, and began the choral *Fest und Gedenksprüche* that would prove quite serviceable the following year.

In the June 1888 there was another memorable soiree at Widmann's with Hermine Spies and Brahms. He may have been distancing himself from his songstress, but their relations remained cordial and he wrote that summer's lieder with her in mind. As with most of his friends Brahms was fond of the whole Widmann family, especially daughter Johanna, whom he playfully referred to as his main temptation to wedlock: for example, "Have I never told you of my good resolutions, father of my Johanna? Among these, to try neither an opera again nor marriage. Otherwise I think I should immediately undertake two (that is, operas), "King Stag" and "The Open Secret."[20] The joke about his bride, increasingly tattered, was one he had been indulging in since his flirtation with Laura Garbe in Hamburg.

The affection between Brahms and Widmann can also be read in an 1887 letter of thanks from Brahms in his pseudo-biblical mode: "And they brought unto them meat from his table. But unto B.[rahms] was given five times as much as unto the others. And they drank and were drunken with him. Thus it has been and will be in the palace of Joseph; wherefore the heart of B. rejoiceth."[21] At the end of that season the Widmanns had been saddened by losing their Scotch terrier during a trip to the glacier at Grindelwald, many kilometers from Bern. Brahms grieved with the family: "You'll never see the dear little fellow again!" He was visiting them one morning when a scratch was heard at the door and they opened it to find weary Argos wagging his tail; he had made an astounding journey back home from the mountains. From Vienna Brahms wrote Widmann that autumn, "How is Argos? Would he take it as a tender greeting from me, if you were to give him a nice piece of meat instead of dog biscuit?"[22]

For all the affection between them, that summer of 1888 Widmann's republican and anti-German inclinations clashed with Brahms's patriotism enough to threaten the friendship. It was the "Three-Kaiser Year" in Germany, with the death of Wilhelm I and his son Friedrich III and the ascent to the throne of the rash, vain, militant Wilhelm II. Widmann wrote an article condemning a speech by the Kaiser, and Brahms blew up over it. After some further squabbles over monarchism versus republicanism, with Brahms the liberal democrat perversely defending the Prussian throne, each man retired to his corner. Before long both were trying to smooth the waters, Brahms doing it in his roundabout fashion. He wrote Widmann, leaving the bitterness between the lines,

> Thus all that comes from Germany is severely criticized, though the Germans themselves lead the way. It is the same in politics as in art. If the Bayreuth Theater stood in France, it would not require anything so great as the works of Wagner to make you and Wendt and all the world go on a pilgrimage there, and rouse your enthusiasm for something so ideally conceived and executed as those music-dramas.[23]

The coming years would see a great deal of tension between Switzerland and Wilhelm II's Germany. In their future relations Brahms and Widmann carefully skirted the subject.

IN THE SAME PERIOD as the quarrel with Widmann, Brahms also distanced himself from the ailing Theodor Billroth. It pained him to see the erosion of his friend's once overflowing vitality. Besides, in his decline the surgeon did not go quietly toward the night but angrily, without the least willingness to cut back his exhausting schedule. "I am at the height of my good fortune!" he wrote in this period, "And afraid of the gods!"[24] From his summer house in St. Gilgen, Billroth sent Brahms a note in summer 1888: "I have not heard from you for quite a time, and just a few days ago . . . got your address through Fellinger." They had once been nearly daily companions; now Billroth did not even know where Brahms was staying. Brahms replied with a stiff attempt at warmth: "Your letter has given me enormous pleasure. I have long wished for it and wanted to ask for it. You are so superior to me in goodness, writing, and in all possible things. What you can manage to accomplish!"[25]

There was more than fear of illness behind Brahms's holding back; other matters had drawn them apart. Billroth could be as blunt and roughshod as any of the other extravagant egotists he called friends. He had received with great happiness the dedication of Brahms's Two String Quartets, Opus 51, and naturally was thrilled when the composer presented him with the manuscripts. One day Brahms was visiting the surgeon and noticed a picture of himself framed on the wall, with a clip of his signature and dedication mounted under it. Suddenly he realized that Billroth had cut them out of a quartet manuscript. As a collector of manuscripts himself and preoccupied with their value, Brahms was horrified. He flew to friend Eusebius Mandyczewski, sputtering with rage, "Can you imagine? Billroth has cut up my quartets! Just think! He who should have known that I love him so well I would gladly have made him a new copy of the whole quartet if he wanted! And now he goes and chops a piece out of it!"[26]

Yet another matter rankled between them. Brahms had always proclaimed himself forgiving toward his parents for sending him to work in dives, chalking it up to ignorance on their part and toughening experience on his. To Billroth the scientist, what Johann Jakob had done was an unforgivable abuse of a child, and he saw the results woven all through Johannes's relations with men and women. Billroth never spoke of that to Brahms directly, but he did to others. At one point Hanslick told Brahms about some beautiful letters their friend had written him about the music, in his midnight ruminations. Brahms asked to see some of them, so the critic gathered up three or four rambling Billroth letters and sent them over—forgetting that they also contained an expression of contempt for Brahms's "neglected upbringing."

Though in his cups Brahms had said the same thing himself, he was terribly hurt by that insult to his family from one of his closest friends. As usual, he refused to acknowledge his feelings. He wrote Hanslick, "You need not worry yourself in the slightest. I barely read the letter . . . and only shook my head quietly. I shouldn't mention anything to him about it. . . . I am long since calm and take it as a matter of course."[27] Always he played Brahms the indifferent. At the same time his silence only made his pulling away from Billroth more painful and inexplicable for the ailing man. As with Joachim and others, reconciliation would come eventually, but it would be slow and incomplete.

THAT AUTUMN, Brahms sent Clara the completed Third Violin Sonata. She was suffering from neuralgia and could not touch the piano, so daughter Elise and a violinist played it through for her. Despite her hearing that distorted everything, Clara responded to the piece with youthful warmth: "I marvelled at the way everything is interwoven, like fragrant tendrils of the vine," she wrote him. "I loved very much indeed . . . the third movement, which is like a beautiful girl sweetly frolicking with her lover—then suddenly in the middle of it all, a flash of deep passion, only to make way for sweet dalliance once more."[28]

These are shockingly amorous words from Clara Schumann, especially in her fretful and unhappy age. They sound in fact like an old woman's fond memories rather than a scene imagined. Later, Brahms responded in kind to another letters of hers: "It's really too lovely and delightful to think of my D Minor Sonata flowing gently and dreamily beneath your fingers. As a matter of fact I laid it on my desk and in my thoughts wandered gently with you through the maze of organ-points, with you still beside me, and I know no greater pleasure than this, to sit at your side, or, as now, to walk beside you."[29] Here for once may be a clue, if no definitive one, to what relations Clara and Johannes had had thirty-five years before. Maybe after all there had been some sweet dalliance. We will never know.

More to the point, Brahms spent half the summer of 1888 at the difficult task of forcing 15,000 marks on Clara. He knew that taking over Ferdinand's children stretched her resources at the same time that her health put her performing in abeyance, maybe for good. Ferociously independent as always, even if she had been bedridden much of the time, Clara put him off. Finally he simply sent the money and she convinced herself that she had to keep it, but only as a favor to him: "What ought I to do? Ought I to sent it back to so old a friend? I could not do that. I had to keep it and thank him for it; there was nothing else to do."[30]

In those days the Herzogenbergs were staying in Nice, both of them better after a miserable siege of bad health. "Before, I could not carry a pound's weight without gasping," Lisl wrote Brahms in September. Now, with a little strength back, she returned to detailed critiques of his work. About one of his new songs she observed sarcastically, "Why don't you indulge in a hideous harmony like this one at the end more often, so that our ears might grow accustomed to it!" That letter was largely made up of detailed complaints about most of the songs he had sent her, though she loved the *Zigeunerlieder*. After a following letter, in which she expressed jubilation over the Third Violin Sonata, Brahms responded warily, "If maybe you made the last letter too sugary from sheer kindness, send the pepperbox after it."[31] If history says anything, he was shaken by Lisl's criticism of the songs. He published them, but from that point composed no more lieder until the last year of his life, and those would hardly be songs of love.

With relations in flux between Brahms and Billroth, the Herzogenbergs, Joachim, and Widmann—and another wrangle with Clara gathering steam—he felt drawn more toward friends with whom he remained
on uncomplicated good terms. Those included the Fellingers and especially the bright, domestic, always-helpful Maria. In September 1888,
Brahms notified Maria that he was on his way back to Vienna and would
dearly enjoy a bowl of her Metzelsuppe on his first Sunday visit.[32]

THAT WINTER he busied himself with helping to arrange a celebration of
Joachim's fiftieth anniversary as a performer, contributing a hundred
gulden for a bust to be placed in the Berlin Hochschule that Joachim
headed.[33] Clara had just celebrated her Diamond Jubilee as a performer.
Though she would manage occasional appearances in the next years, at
this point she could only play a few minutes at a time.

If his creativity appeared on the downhill, outwardly Brahms was in
good spirits that winter, still the jokester and prankster as Richard
Heuberger details. After a meeting of the Tonkünstlerverein they were
talking about a well-known lady pianist and composer: "I praise Jaell!"
Brahms said, grinning. "She's an intelligent, gifted person and can write
things herself that are just as bad as Liszt's." He told a story of a woman
who had recently come asking him to suggest something of his to sing.
Straight-faced, Brahms advised her to try some of his posthumous lieder.

"And which?" she inquired politely.

"Just ask Kalbeck, he knows everything." So she did ask Kalbeck, who
dissolved in laughter. When she returned irate to Brahms, he replied
with a certain kindness, "Ja, dear lady, don't ask me about such things. I'll
usually just make some kind of joke—and if a good one doesn't occur to
me, then a bad one."[34]

The Vienna premiere of the Double Concerto in December, Joachim
and Hausmann soloing, was cheered enthusiastically.[35] For Brahms the
gloomy conviction may have deepened that audiences were applauding
him rather than the music. Critic Hans Gal describes the actual feeling
about the piece as "indifferent" among friends, public, and performers.[36]
Recognizing the ambivalence behind the applause, Brahms was visibly
depressed over its reception, no longer as sure as he had been in earlier
times that the public would come around—and no longer as sure of himself.

In his review Eduard Hanslick noted the ovation, but as for his opinion: "I am unable to place the Double Concerto among the first rank of
Brahms's creations." If in the Violin Concerto, "the solo violin is not ac-

corded the sovereign place it deserves, this criticism applies all the more pointedly to the Double Concerto. . . . We feel that it is characterized by a lack of freshness and originality of feeling, of melodic and rhythmic magic."[37] By then both piano concertos had caught on, but critics and public still resisted the beauties of the Violin and Double Concertos. That situation would not change through the 1890s.

All the same, Brahms saw to practical matters, making sure the *Zigeunerlieder* were out before Christmas so Hanslick could praise them and boost holiday sales. The critic duly noted in the *Neue Freie Presse:* "His songs make excellent Christmas presents." Brahms dined with the Hanslick family on Christmas Eve. Next day, after lighting the tree in his library with Frau Truxa's family, he lunched with friends at the Igel, napped at the Café Heinrichshof, then oversaw Frau Truxa packing his things for a visit to the duke's castle at Meiningen, where he was scheduled to celebrate the New Year and conduct the Double and D Minor Concertos.[38] The latter would feature his new favorite pianist, Eugène d'Albert, who had done the most to secure the popularity of the Second Concerto.

After Hans von Bülow resigned from the Meiningen Hofkapelle Orchestra it had been briefly conducted by his young assistant Richard Strauss. Now Fritz Steinbach had taken it over, and this conductor was happy to lend the podium to Brahms. From the duke's castle he wrote Clara, "Oh, how I wish you could have spent the last few days here with us! You would have loved it. At the concert d'Albert played my D Minor and Joachim and Hausmann my Double Concerto. Both went excellently. Yesterday at a rehearsal Joachim played Beethoven's Concerto and mine quite magnificently. . . . In short it was a mixed but sumptuous menu." From Meiningen he stopped by Frankfurt to visit Clara and play in a performance of the Third Violin Sonata. She wrote in her journal, "I once more thanked heaven for sending so strong and healthy a genius into the world in the midst of the Wagner mania, one who counteracts it for the moment and who must soon conquer it entirely."[39]

There were any number of manias about in those days. At the end of that month the Austrian emperor's heir Prince Rudolf, another frustrated liberal, who had despaired of ever gaining the throne and effecting anything, shot his teenaged mistress and himself in his bedroom in the royal hunting lodge at Mayerling. The Crown attempted to call it a stroke and secretly buried the mistress in an unmarked grave, but everyone suspected the truth. In the wake of the royal suicide confusion rattled all over Austria. Anton Bruckner demanded to be driven out to Mayerling to peer at it from the outside, then returned to the city and fell into one of his odd manias, standing outside in the cold and counting the hundreds of windows in the Imperial Palace over and over again.

Like most liberals, Brahms saw the tragedy as yet another sign of despair and dissolution. In that atmosphere the Wagner- and Bruckner-loving reactionaries thrived by preying on the fears of aristocrats and working people alike, blaming the Jews for Austria's ills. Brahms, his monarchical and democratic instincts clashing, wrote Simrock, "The saying that 'everything has happened before' has been dashed to pieces. It is new how emperors and kings kill themselves. They explode, they drown [Bavaria's King Ludwig, Wagner's patron, had plunged into a lake], they kill themselves. And now, in addition to all this, our Imperial tragedy." He asked Simrock for uncensored newspaper reports from Berlin.[40]

Whatever the ominous symptoms of Crown and empire, musical life played on unimpeded. In February, Brahms accompanied Joachim in three concerts that added up to a triumph, the programs featuring the Third Violin Sonata and Joachim's arrangement of the Hungarian Dances. Then the two went to Berlin for the Hochschule celebrations of Joachim's fiftieth anniversary, which Brahms had helped plan and finance. Among the orchestral performances there, Brahms conducted the D Minor Concerto with Hans von Bülow at the piano. Brahms's collaboration with Joachim was the first major undertaking the two had tried in person since their reconciliation, and both had felt apprehensive about it. Brahms reported to Clara that his old companion "was more affable and friendly than usual and . . . we had a very pleasant time together."

From Berlin, Brahms went to Hamburg to visit sister Elise, now widowed but in relatively good spirits, and his stepmother and brother.[41] All were prospering from his generosity. In April he stayed at Duke Georg's "Villa Carlotta" on Lake Como. Billroth was traveling in Italy that summer, this time without his friend. Brahms wrote the surgeon in Palermo, "I never see the beautiful sickle moon without thinking of you."[42] Even as quarrels periodically darkened his relations with Billroth and Clara and Joachim and others, still Brahms's dealings with friends and family alike were taking on a valedictory cast.

BRAHMS WROTE JOSEF VIKTOR WIDMANN at the end of April 1889, "It's a bit of a minor chord that I'm sending you."[43] He had decided to try Bad Ischl once more for his vacation, forsaking Thun after three years there. Widmann knew that their political differences had something to do with it, but received the news as diplomatically as he could. Besides, a new promenade had been laid out along the Aare just beneath Brahms's windows in the Hofstetten house, and Brahms did not want to become an attraction for strolling tourists.

During his two earlier summers in Bad Ischl, Brahms had never quite settled into the emperor's, and fashionable Austria's, favorite resort, despite the presence of friends there including Ignaz Brüll and Johann Strauss, Billroth in nearby St. Gilgen, and Vienna friends Viktor von Miller zu Aichholz and his wife Olga, who kept a grand villa in nearby Gmunden (where Karl Goldmark also lived). This time Ischl, on the River Traun, its air brisk from mountains and lakes, suited Brahms despite the unpredictable weather and hoards of tourists. At least most of the faces in town were Viennese. He would vacation in the resort for the rest of his life.

He composed relatively little new that summer, mainly the Three Motets, Opus 110. He wrote Clara about another project, "With what childish amusement I while away the beautiful summer days you will never guess. I have rewritten my B Major [Piano] Trio. . . . It will not be so wild as it was before—but whether it will be better—? If Joachim and Hausmann happened to be knocking around Baden we might try it sometime."[44] They made sure they were knocking around. Brahms had reworked the piece because Simrock had bought the rights and planned a new edition. He hoped to redo the F Minor Piano Sonata too, but never got around to it.[45]

In his revision of the B Major Trio Brahms preserved most of the charm while tightening the structure. Once again, the seams hardly showed when he returned to an early work. Perhaps no composer in history would have still been close enough to his youth, and to the style of his youth, to tear apart and recompose a piece as he did the B Major—though he left intact long stretches of the outer movements and most of the scherzo. His friends generally resisted the new version, preferring the youthful fervor of the original. Lisl scolded him, "you have no right to impress your masterly touch on this lovable, if sometimes vague, product of your youth." For his part, Brahms felt at first optimistic about the new version, informing Simrock that it would be "shorter, hopefully better, and in any case more expensive."[46] In the end, though, he never summoned any great conviction that he had improved it: "I must categorically state that the old one is bad," he wrote Simrock, "but I do not maintain that the new one is good."[47] For better or worse, the early version fell into neglect.

If he was doing little new work, there were plenty of agreeable distractions that summer. Visitors to Viktor Miller's villa in Gmunden included Brahms and most of his closest Vienna friends—Goldmark, Dvořák, Brüll, Heuberger, Epstein, Gänsbacher, Door, Hanslick, and Mandyczewski. Only the ailing Billroth did not turn up. Brahms also became a regular feature of the lavish parties Johann Strauss produced at his Biedermeier-style villa in Ischl. Strauss was happy to accept the friendship of the distinguished symphonist. Brahms got to know a young pianist named Ilona Eibenschütz, a pupil of Clara's. If Ilona was more of a passing fantasy than Hermine Spies had been, the talented and beautiful teenager still may have helped inspire his late piano music.[48] That winter Ilona played his Handel Variations in Vienna.

As Brahms liked to put it: life was only too gay. Now he let himself be diverted by the gaiety. All the same, in whatever society he still did quite as he pleased. If he went regularly to Strauss's parties, he might spend the evening insulting the guests. Strauss's fashionable friends had to wonder why the famous man was invited and why he showed up, if he found the company so offensive. At Viktor Miller's in Gmunden that summer Joachim played through a Bach solo sonata, then had hardly begun Brahms's G Major when its composer crashed his fists on the keys and leaped up to declare that with Bach in his ears, his own stuff was too banal to endure.[49]

Even his modesty had become a burden to his friends. Still, his affection and admiration endured along with the impossible moments. If Brahms tortured the abjectly deferential Miller now and then, he enjoyed the businessman and his hospitality. If Johann Strauss wondered why Brahms came to his parties only to belabor the guests, there were still moments like the one when his daughter Alice asked Brahms to sign her autograph-fan and he responded gallantly, writing down the beginning of her father's *Blue Danube* Waltz with the note: "Unfortunately not by yours truly, Johannes Brahms!"[50]

ANOTHER DISTRACTION, the most welcome, arrived in May: Brahms had been given his hometown's highest honor, the Freedom of Hamburg. He was greatly touched. The Freedom not only represented the highest accolade his native city could bestow on him, it was also a rare one—only twelve people had ever received the Freedom, the last two being Bismarck and Prussian general Helmut von Moltke.[51] The idea of giving it to Brahms had been promoted by new Hamburg resident Hans von Bülow, with the cooperation of Bürgermeister Carl Petersen.

In the first flush of excitement Brahms drafted a telegram to Mayor Petersen: "Gratefully honor your news, as the most beautiful honor and greatest joy that mankind can bestow on me." Brahms often sent follow-up letters to people, sometimes on the same day, correcting a hasty first thought. This time, dismayed at having expressed his feelings so nakedly, he sent a quick correction by post to the Bürgermeister:

> I feel with my whole heart the need to add a few words to my hasty, short telegram. . . . As the artist is rejoiced by such a distinguished token of recognition, so also is the man by the glorious feeling of knowing himself so highly esteemed and loved in his native city. . . . The precious gift of my citizen's letter . . . becomes more precious and clear to me as I place it by the side of my father's citizenship document. . . . My father was, indeed, my first thought in connection with the pleasant event, and one wish only remains, that he were here to rejoice with me."[52]

There is no record that Brahms had dwelled on his father's memory since Johann Jakob died in 1872. Now with this accolade, the son's first thought was of his father—and apparently none for his mother. For Johannes son of Johann, the Freedom of Hamburg not only elevated him and his labors, it also redeemed Johann Jakob Brahms the peasant and buffoon, and his long struggle that had borne such unexpected fruit. At last the name of Brahms, plain as the broom plant it came from, had found glory on native soil. It was a profound moment in Johannes's life, maybe the highest of all the tributes among his long row of them. Yet he was still embarrassed at himself when he wrote Hanslick that summer,

> My Honorary Citizen adventure was too lovely and agreeable. . . . However, I am alarmed to see my telegram to the mayor in print! It sounds altogether idiotic, 'the greatest beauty, which can come from human beings'—as if apart from that I had been thinking of eternal salvation! But our dear Lord did not occur to me at all in that connection, I was only thinking in passing about the so-called gods and the fact that when a pretty melody occurs to me it is far preferable in my mind than an Order of Leopold, and if they should grant me a successful symphony, it is dearer to me than all honorary citizenships.[53]

The Order of Leopold he mentions was another decoration he acquired in the same summer. This award, one of Austria's highest, had been Hanslick's doing. Grimly, Brahms set to the drudgery of answering a mountain of congratulatory letters and telegrams. More were required when he was named an honorary member of the Beethovenhaus Society in Bonn and a foreign member of the Académie Française. In his letter to the Académie he tried to resurrect his childhood French, but finally gave up and thanked them in German. The accumulation of ribbons and medals on Brahms's coat at formal occasions was becoming formidable. It was in connection with the Leopold Order that he told Richard Specht, "I don't care a rap for decorations, but *have* them I will."[54]

As he tried to get back to work in July, Brahms wrote Clara, "The Herzogenbergs were here for a day. . . . One's pleasure in the man himself is considerably reduced if not entirely obliterated by the composer. I would like to get the better of the latter some time if I could only get him alone, but his wife is always there and one really doesn't know what to talk about."[55] Quite a callous letter, given that the couple he was dismissing, both of them miserably ill, had honored and served him as much as anyone alive. Certainly Brahms was generally unhappy with Heinz's music, and never papered over his opinions despite the couple's insatiable craving for approval. Out of Heinz's voluminous production Brahms had complimented little but a few string trios and quartets, the latter dedicated to him.[56]

The saddest fact is that probably the Herzogenbergs' physical infirmities were what most alienated Brahms in those days—Lisl sapped by asthma and heart disease, Heinz mobile but still racked by rheumatism. Clara, who had met them in Italy, described Heinz to Brahms as "a broken man."[57] As Brahms was increasingly intolerant of friction or contradiction from anyone, he also could hardly bear to be around sick people, as so many of his aging friends were. He had recently written Clara, "Since his illness the sight of Billroth disturbs me, upon my soul I don't like the look of him, and when he makes an effort to appear bright and in good spirits it makes one's heart sink!"[58] Somehow, with the exception of Clara, he instinctively felt the sick to be a distraction, a bother, a threat to his own robust health.

It may have been that period when Elisabet von Herzogenberg's photograph, the golden-haired muse that had presided over his writing desk for many years, suddenly disappeared from view. Brahms gruffly gave Frau Truxa the frame Lisl's picture had resided in.[59]

In Hamburg that September, as a gesture of thanks for the Freedom, Brahms premiered with the Cäcilienverein the three *a capella* choruses he called *Fest- und Gedenksprüche* (Festal and Commemorative Mottoes), as part of the festivities at a Trade and Industry Exhibition. With their biblical texts on civic virtues and aloof, elevated style, these double-choir pieces seemed the ideal occasional piece, and they were dedicated to Bürgermeister Petersen. Actually, Brahms had largely completed them before the honor was announced. His performance with the Cäcilien-verein, as it turned out, was his last appearance on a concert platform in Hamburg.[60]

For all their grandeur, recalling the antiphonal choruses of the late-Renaissance Venetian master Giovanni Gabrieli and his German pupil Schütz, Brahms did not value the *Gedenksprüche* as much as the equally atavistic motets of summer 1889.[61] He took a sneaking pride, though, in his juggling of the biblical text in one of the new choruses. In his setting he makes a sentence from St. Luke, "When a strong man armed keeps his palace, his goods are in peace," evoke the German nation under the firm hand of Prussia and the Kaiser. Meanwhile he knew perfectly well that in the Bible the "strong man" of those verses is actually Satan. This chi-canery he described playfully in a letter to Josef Widmann as "theologi-cal, even jesuitical subtlety."[62]

A s a g e s t u r e o f r e c o n c i l i a t i o n with Widmann after their political quarrels, Brahms invited his republican friend to join him on a visit to Baden-Baden and Clara in September. There he stayed at his old favorite hotel, Zum Bären, but when he discovered that three favorite pine trees near the Bear had been cut down, he informed them he would never come back. Though the two friends skirted politics now and Widmann had given up trying to tempt Brahms to write an opera, they still had long talks about all sorts of things.

For example, there was a conversation that drifted to the subject of bi-ography. In his youth, immersed in Robert Schumann's library, Brahms had written Clara: "What would become of all historical research and biographies if undertaken with an eye to the susceptibilities of the sub-ject? The sort of biography which you might write about our Robert would certainly make very beautiful reading, but would it as certainly have any value for history?"[63]

He had meant, in 1856, that he asked biography to be fearless and honest. In 1889, in his fame and encroaching old age, he told Widmann: "The chief consideration, in the selection of material for a biography of an artist or author, should be whether the facts in question were of a na-ture to make the artist, whom we love and honor in his art, also win our esteem as a man." Brahms observed that after the recent publication of some new Beethoven letters, "our mental image of Beethoven has been disfigured by features so unwelcome that it would have been preferable to have been kept in ignorance of them."[64] When on that trip Widmann met Clara Schumann for the first time—he was enchanted by the youthful smile breaking out on her aged, careworn face—Brahms added, "When you have written something, ask yourself whether such a woman as Frau Schumann could read it with pleasure. If you doubt that, then cross out what you have written."[65]

Eventually it occurred to Widmann that these remarks were not as offhanded as they appeared. Brahms was grooming a biographer, instructing him to defer to the feelings and reputation of his subject, leave the great man on his pedestal. The truth can disfigure a hero. In that spirit Brahms reminisced to Widmann about his life, revealing this and withholding that. To the same end, it was in the next years that he burned most of his papers and sketches and the pieces he had decided to keep back. He would do his best, in other words, to shape his own history, to deny biographers material or motivation for the kind of biography he valued in his youth. Widmann would produce only a thin book of memoirs about Brahms, but in it he followed the counsel his subject had given him. Like most memoirists and biographers after him, Widmann painted a bourgeois hero and kept the shadows out of the picture, just as his hero had advised.

As he returned to Vienna in 1889, Brahms could not have been happy about the last two summers' work. For the first time in his maturity he had not kept to his pattern of a major orchestral piece every other year. What made it more worrisome was that he had toyed with ideas for one or two symphonies, and they had failed to take flight. One of them had been far enough along to play through on the piano for Billroth, but he held it back.

If new pieces would not come, he was not going to occupy his time with performing. After some twenty-five years of exhaustive touring during the winter concert season—and more or less the same amount of time avoiding practicing—Brahms cut back considerably on appearances. Now he would concentrate mainly on presenting new works.

So with little proofreading and less performing than usual to occupy him in the winter of 1889–90, Brahms at fifty-six must have been at a loss as to what to do with himself. Maybe boredom was part of the reason he agreed to a surprising engagement. He had returned to daily dining at his "prickly pet," Zum roten Igel. One afternoon in October, Brahms kept an appointment there for lunch with Anton Bruckner. Though the two composers had lived in the same city and passed each other in the halls of the Musikverein for years, this was their first (and last) formal meeting.

Both turned up with entourage. Everybody crowded around a table, waiting for one of the famous men to say something on this momentous occasion when Brahms had finally deigned to acknowledge Bruckner's existence. There was a long, excruciating silence. Finally Brahms picked up a menu and declared, for history: "Oh, dumplings with smoked meat! That's my favorite!" Immediately Bruckner's peasant voice chimed in, "I say, Doktor Brahms, dumplings and smoked meat! That's where we two agree!" A few seconds of bemused silence ensued, then much relieved laughter.[66]

The occasion was declared a success, though it hardly reconciled the camps. Still, maybe that moment of small agreement and laughter did mitigate some of Brahms's venom toward his rival. Maybe that was what Bruckner and his friends had had in mind. In any case, in 1890 Bruckner was finally made an honorary member of the Gesellschaft der Musikfreunde without overt fuss from Brahms in the director's box, or from Hanslick.[67] The year after that, Emperor Franz Josef installed Bruckner in the Belvedere Palace.

Being the kind of personage he had become, Brahms had to cope with people who wanted to juxtapose him with other personages, as in a sculpture gallery. Sometimes he submitted to it. He shared a table with another nominal rival at the beginning of 1888, while he visited Leipzig to conduct the Double Concerto and play the C Minor Trio. Invited to dinner at the house of Gewandhaus concertmaster Adolph Brodsky, Brahms joined guests Edvard Grieg and Peter Tchaikovsky. Brahms had met the affable Norwegian before and they had always had cordial relations. On this first acquaintance Tchaikovsky and Brahms dutifully attended each other's rehearsals, but neither could stand the other's music and took no trouble to hide it. To Tchaikovsky the German master's work was pretentious and derivative; to Brahms the Russian's was shallow and self-indulgent.

At Brodsky's dinner Frau Grieg was seated as a buffer between them, but she soon leaped up saying, "I can't sit between these two any more, it makes me so nervous!" Slipping around the table to take her place, Edvard Grieg declared, "I have the nerve!" Tchaikovsky wrote a report home: "I have been much with Brahms yesterday and today. . . . We are ill at ease together because we do not really like each other, but he takes pains to be pleasant with me."[68] One gets the feeling that while Brahms was passionately competitive with Bruckner, he did not take the Russian seriously enough to conceive a rivalry. In a diary entry, Tchaikovsky called Brahms "that scoundrel . . . this self-inflated mediocrity."[69]

Besides his involvement in the musical scene, there were novelties and amusements to keep Brahms occupied, if composing and performing did not. A few years before, the Herzogenbergs had introduced him to Thomas Edison's phonograph, and now the Fellingers had a machine at their house. "I have had the opportunity of hearing it often and quite pleasantly," Brahms wrote Clara. "You must have read about this new miracle. . . . It's like being in fairyland again." That December he met an American named Theo Wangemann at the Fellingers. Edison had dispatched this associate to record famous Europeans on his cylinder machine. Naturally Wangemann asked Brahms to contribute.

Brahms returned to the Fellingers' a few days later to try out this Yankee marvel. At first he sat paralyzed by nerves when confronted by the apparatus, then suddenly he went to the piano and, as Wangemann scrambled to get the machine going, played off a section of the First Hungarian Dance and a Strauss polka. The recording survives in mangled condition, revealing a rhythmically free, bass-heavy kind of playing. As intriguing is the voice at the beginning of the recording, so garbled that no one can tell who is speaking or quite what is said. At least one haunting possibility is a mixture of German and English from the high tenor of Brahms himself, shouting at the future: "Grüsse an Herrn Doktor Edison! I am Doktor Brahms . . . Johannes Brahms!"[70]

It was at a party in those years that he heard a young American woman playing a ragtime tune on a banjo. To a friend Brahms recalled the evening wistfully, humming a few bars of what may have been "Hello, Ma Baby." He was fascinated by the effect of the instrument, and by the dancing syncopations of this new American style. Instinctively he saw its rhythm as a fresh resource, as gypsy music had been for his generation. But now he was too old to do anything about it.

His main loyalty remained, of course, to popular music close to home. He reveled in his friendship with the Waltz King, writing Simrock in December 1889: "The evenings with Strauss! And his wife! and the champagne! and the waltzes! and the . . ."[71] Near the end of the year he had an audience with Emperor Franz Josef, to thank him formally for the Order of Leopold. Frau Truxa made a great fuss of dressing her employer for the occasion, using all her powers to persuade him to wear white gloves. No report came from the meeting. The emperor tended to sleepwalk through such occasions, and his musical tastes ran to Strauss and Suppé.

Thus the record of Brahms's life as the new decade approached—laurels, scattered events without focus, without the excitement and anxiety of big premieres in autumn and winter: the life of a famous composer as opposed to the life of composing. Otherwise, everything ran on schedule. He spent Christmas Eve of 1889 lighting the tree and exchanging presents with Frau Truxa's family. Then the next day's holiday dinner with the Fellingers, where as always Frau Maria charmed and cajoled him into accepting gifts.[72]

In January 1890, Brahms skipped the ceremonies Hamburg put on for Hans von Bülow's sixtieth birthday, but to mark the occasion he sent his old compatriot a rare gift—the manuscript of the Third Symphony. Bülow had been given 10,000 marks to dispose of as he wished; Brahms persuaded him to send it to Friedrich Chrysander for his Handel Edition. That month Joachim was in Vienna for concerts with his Quartet, and during a dinner served up an order to Johannes: "What shall we have next? A quintet! We have one, a very fine one; let's have another."

Brahms took his seventh Italian trip in April, this time with Widmann. Then he headed for Bad Ischl and wrote a quintet to Joachim's order, commencing with a spacious cello theme that may have been intended for a symphony that had not taken wing.

The more telling new work of that summer is an unforgettable little piece for women's voices, which Brahms added to ones he had written earlier to make up the Thirteen Canons of Opus 113. As theme for the new canon he quoted a melody of Schubert's—the weird singsong of the last lied in *Die Winterreise* (*Winter's Journey*). In it the narrator, wandering in the wilderness of the world, stands in a frigid waste as sole audience for the keening melody of an organ-grinder who in some way is Death. Schubert's song is one of the most haunting moments in music, shaped by his own impending doom. Brahms, weaving that melody into a dense canonic fabric, somehow heightens the eeriness of the original. He made Schubert's theme into a soft, twining wail of lamentation on a text of Rückert:

> *Changeless is love's sorrow,*
> *a song of monotonous tone,*
> *and yet always*
> *wherever I hear it*
> *I quietly hum along.*

When he reached Vienna that October, Brahms wrote Fritz Simrock, "I tossed a great deal of ripped-up manuscript paper in the Traun upon leaving Ischl." As "The Organ-Grinder" had been one of Schubert's last songs, Brahms when he committed those sheets to the river had decided that the gay new quintet and the deathly canon would be his own swan songs. At fifty-seven, worn by the years of discipline and struggle, fearful that he was drying up, feeling increasingly irrelevant and inimical to the spirit of the age, he had vowed to rest on his laurels and quit the game.

CHAPTER TWENTY-TWO

Secrets and Foreboding

DURING THE SUMMER OF 1890, Theodor Billroth visited Bad Ischl and found Brahms plunged in the thick volumes of Sybel's *Foundation of the German Empire* and disavowing "the idea that he is composing or ever will compose anything." That summer Brahms said to friend Eusebius Mandyczewski in the tones of a retiring bureaucrat: "I've been torment-ing myself for a long time with all kinds of things, a symphony, chamber music and other stuff, and nothing will come of it. Above all I was always used to everything being clear to me. It seems to me that it's not going the way it used to. I'm just not going to do any more. My whole life I've been a hard worker; now for once I'm going to be good and lazy!"[1] In fact, following Joachim's suggestion, Brahms was working on the G Ma-jor String Quintet, and his vow to quit would hardly last out the year. But for the moment he was ready to let the lighthearted and laconic quintet stand as his farewell.

In November the Rosé String Quartet, with added violist, began re-hearsing the new piece. This was a young ensemble founded by the then twenty-seven-year-old Arnold Rosé, who had already served as concert-master of the Bayreuth Festival Orchestra and had led the Vienna Phil-harmonic violins since age eighteen. A decade later the Rosé Quartet was to become an historic champion of Arnold Schoenberg. At their first re-hearsal with Brahms in Vienna, they had a frustrating time of it. Max Kalbeck speculates that the initial theme of the G Major Quintet was originally meant for a symphony—a brash, craggy cello melody under pealing chords in upper strings. As soon as he saw the beginning, Joachim told Johannes that it would take "three cellists in one" to make the line heard above the *forte* accompaniment.[2] Joachim was right as usual, Brahms as usual open to all suggestions and resistant to most. After the rehearsals with the Rosé, after various makeshifts with the opening, after further warnings from Joachim and from Elisabet von Herzogenberg ("the cello . . . must scrape mercilessly to be heard," she complained[3]) and experiments on the manuscript, Brahms let the beginning stand and bequeathed aggravation to cellists in perpetuity.

He simply didn't want to give up the effect he had in mind, and was ready to let musicians thrash out for themselves how to achieve it. When they do succeed, the opening is breathtaking, an explosion of youthful summery spirits whose energy surges through the concise but kaleidoscopic opening movement. When he first heard the beginning, Max

Kalbeck exclaimed, "Brahms in the Prater!" Brahms replied, "You've got it!," and added with a roguish grin, "And all the pretty girls there, eh?"[4]

Moments of *dolce* wistfulness wash through the opening movement as well. That mood changes to gypsy-toned melancholy in the short and quiet second movement in D minor, with its soaring roulades from the viola. (The soulful, dark-voiced viola is surely the most Brahmsian of stringed instruments.) The G minor third movement is closer to waltz than scherzo, marked with the double diminutive *Un poco Allegretto*—a little slightly fast. Its poignant, hesitant main theme is contrasted with a flowing G major middle section. After these two plaintive minor-key movements (Elisabet's favorites), Brahms finishes with one of his zestiest gypsy movements: *Vivace ma non troppo presto*.

Thus he proposed to quit. Maybe that is why Billroth, knowing it, wrote him a beautiful twilight letter after hearing the first rehearsal:

> As I think back over the hours of my life, the richness of which few mortals can have had, you always and still stand in the first place. I have lived with you a great part of our being, and you with me. The experiences which bind us together are a bit like those that tie together the brothers of a good family. . . . Today I heard enthusiastic shouts, "The most beautiful music he has ever composed!" . . . I have often reflected on the subject of what happiness is for humanity. Well, today in listening to your music, that was happiness.[5]

At the end of a career or a life, there could be no sweeter words from an admired friend. Brahms replied to Billroth with a restraint he knew would be understood: "My nature has not changed. Such words in such cases are not only pleasant for me, they are necessary—for I do not say such things to myself. They reverberate in me gently and are damped down delicately."[6] The premiere of the G Major String Quintet in Vienna on November 11, 1890, was a sensation.

THE EXPERIENCE OF COMPOSING the G Major, however, and the acclaim for his gay and poignant farewell to music, led to an ironic puncturing of that drama and poignancy. Brahms told a friend,

> Recently I started various things, symphonies and so on, but nothing would come out right. Then I thought: I'm really too old, and resolved energetically to write no more. I considered that all my life I had been sufficiently industrious and had achieved enough; here I had before me

a carefree old age and could enjoy it in peace. And that made me so happy, so contented, so delighted—that all at once the writing began to go.[7]

If ideas wanted to come he would not submit to a mere vow. But the reawakening of creativity owed at least as much to a couple of new acquaintances as to the pleasant experience of the quintet. One of the inspirations, naturally, was a singer.

That autumn, Brahms raved to Richard Heuberger about mezzo-soprano Alice Barbi: "From somebody like Barbi we can all learn! Above all the Italian lady sings supremely steadily, with a solid pulse, and . . . projects the structure of every piece she sings. Really, we all just fool around at the piano! . . . Most Germans make music in a dressing gown! We know all these tunes so thoroughly, we know the bass, the chords, and then we just doze off on them. From Barbi you can learn a lot, a lot!"[8]

By that point Brahms was, so to speak, on the rebound from Hermine Spies, who had never reached maturity as a musician. Hermine-ohne-O was a delightful presence on a concert stage; Alice Barbi was the same, and a superb artist as well. (She had begun as a near-prodigy violinist.) For Brahms to say that Barbi projected the *structure* is to say that she sang songs the way he liked: a total musical and expressive shape, not a chasing after every scrap of tune and image. Amorous ideas, for Brahms. That the mezzo was a sparkling, black-eyed, dark-haired beauty didn't hurt. The first time he heard her sing one of his own he exclaimed, "Today I've heard my songs for the first time!" Barbi had specialized in Schubert and Schumann in her recitals. Now she added Brahms. Those who heard her sing "Wie bist du, meine Königin" or "Vergebliches Ständchen" were not likely to forget it.[9]

Brahms began to squire Barbi around Vienna. Critic Max Graf remembered seeing them together under the trees in a Prater café. A *Schrammelquartett* was playing the new American hit "Ta-ra-ra-boom-de-ay!" It was the fashion for listeners to wait for the buildup on "Ta-ra-ra . . ." and thump the tables with beer glass or walking stick on the *boom*. Graf watched Brahms lean over on every refrain, beaming with beer and high spirits, and whack his umbrella on the table like a boy while Barbi watched adoringly.[10]

Brahms confessed to Ignaz Brüll that after middle age, Barbi was the only woman he ever really wanted to marry. Brüll suspected that he had actually proposed, but she turned him down over the matter of children: she wanted them, he did not.[11] In 1890, Barbi was twenty-eight, Brahms fifty-seven.

Whom Brahms was squiring around town, marrying or not marrying, was by then a subject of general discussion in Vienna's cafés, restaurants, and concert halls. Some of this was normal gossip-mongering (Brahms loved gossip too), some of it the more serious question, What will this encounter do for or against the master's work, and for or against X, Y, or Z's career? Brahms had risen to a position of fame and influence that tended to invest everything he did, everything he said, everyone he smiled or failed to smile on, with a promise of the Historic.

That is why in mid-December 1890, young Gustav Mahler was electrified when someone passed him a note on the podium of the Royal Hungarian Opera House, just after he had conducted the overture of Mozart's *Don Giovanni*. The note read, "Brahms is in the house!" It had been a dicey thing. Two friends from the Academy of Music in Budapest had invited him to the performance, but he snapped, "I wouldn't dream of it. No one can do *Don Giovanni* right for me. I enjoy it much better from the score. . . . We'd be better off going to the beerhall." However, the professors managed to snooker the famous guest. They led him toward the beerhall past the Royal Opera and mused: Say, since it's so early and the beer won't be ready yet, why don't we just go in and catch the opera for a half hour?

Assured that there was a couch at the rear of the box, Brahms agreed to nap while they listened. Just after the overture, the professors heard a queer snort. Then Brahms was beside them, leaning over the railing with eyes blazing: "Quite excellent, tremendous—he's a devil of a fellow!" At intermission he went backstage to embrace the wiry, nervous figure of Mahler, and they spent hours talking after the performance.[12] No particularly close friendship was born at that point. They were too far apart in age and in taste for that: Brahms the past, Mahler the future. Still, they made a connection of distant but mutual respect.

Brahms would pull strings for Mahler after that, and he had a lot of strings to pull. His word in the right places helped bring the brilliant young conductor first to the Hamburg Opera and then, in 1897, to the podium of the Vienna Hofoper.[13] Naturally in the intervening years Brahms followed the development of the young devil as a composer too, with interest if not exactly enthusiasm.

Mahler was appropriately grateful for it all and, in those years, despite his Wagnerian and Brucknerian sympathies, he admired Brahms's music. At the same time he blamed Brahms in part for being condemned to "my whole cursed operatic career"—in 1881, Brahms had been part of a conservative panel of judges (the others were Goldmark, Richter, and Hanslick) that declined to award Mahler the Beethoven Prize for *Das klagende Lied.* Mahler believed that rejection had made a composer's career impossible for him.[14] Still, for several years the younger artist would make an annual pilgrimage to Bad Ischl from his summer composing quarters at Steinbach, to visit Brahms.

Christmas 1890 Brahms celebrated in Vienna. He wrote Clara, who was distraught at the prospect of physical debilities ending her performing, "Here next door in my library there also stands a beautiful large tree which will remain concealed until this evening from [Frau Truxa's] two darling boys. . . . Frl. Barbi has told everybody here that you made her very happy through your kindness and friendliness."[15] After lighting the tree with the Truxa family, he had his usual Christmas Day dinner with the Fellingers.

Just after the holiday, Brahms came down with flu, which was going around the city. Two years before he had been struck mildly by the same illness, but was so unaccustomed to being sick that he hardly knew what to make of it. It was no different this time. Recently Max Kalbeck had showed up at Zum roten Igel still recovering from flu and Brahms observed with mock disdain, "Naturally, you have to go along with every fashionable foolishness." Shortly afterward, Kalbeck came to Brahms's apartment and found him in the library stripped to the waist, leaning over the washstand and pouring a jug of water over his head. With face flushed and beard dripping, Brahms groaned to Kalbeck in an odd efflorescence of Hamburg dialect: "I feel kind a' out of it. I'm so frightful hot!" He seemed to have no idea what a fever was. To Kalbeck's demand that he summon a doctor or at least go to bed, Brahms insisted that for a cure he would go over to the Igel and dose himself with Pilsner beer and roast beef. When Kalbeck, improvising, raised the specter of Mozart's death as possibly a result of flu, Brahms saw reason in the light of historic precedent. He assured Kalbeck he would be good, "as a favor to you."[16] Then, for one of the few times in his life, he may actually have taken to his bed.

IN JANUARY 1891, Brahms sent Clara the new G Major String Quintet with a warning: "I have always told you that the first [F Major] Quintet is a really beautiful piece—for heaven's sake don't expect anything better or even equal to it!"[17] In early March she ended an enthusiastic letter, "Finally the conclusion, which is just the sort of magnificent confusion that one hears in a dream after a Zigeuner evening in Pest. . . . Poor Frau Herzogenberg is not at all well. She has been in bed now for over six weeks."[18]

That month Brahms went to Meiningen for a weeklong arts festival that included a performance before the playwright of Joseph Widmann's tragedy *Önone*. Brahms was met at the train by a *Hofmarschall* and driven to the castle in the ducal carriage with full equipage. During the visit the court orchestra under Fritz Steinbach played the Fourth Symphony, which moved him so much that he asked them to do it again. At meals, Widmann enjoyed the uncommon sight of Brahms in full evening dress with all his decorations seated at the duke's opulent table, obviously having a grand time. Before going to Meiningen Brahms had told a friend that Widmann "had better watch out for bad jokes." Sure enough, he made a daily ritual of taking Widmann's pulse in the morning to see "whether the thick, sluggish blood of the republican had not yet changed into the thin, swift current that flows through the veins of the courtier."[19] He thereby turned into a joke their recent, bitter argument over the Prussian throne, with Brahms for all his republican instincts defending the Kaiser.

Most important, in that visit to Meiningen Brahms was stunned by performances of the Weber Clarinet Concerto and Mozart Clarinet Quintet by the orchestra's principal clarinetist, Richard Mühlfeld. This musician had come to Meiningen in 1873 as a violinist, and then in three years taught himself clarinet well enough to take over the principal position. He also served as the orchestra's assistant conductor. In the next decade he became principal clarinet with the Bayreuth Festival orchestra, but despite his fame stayed on in Meiningen for the rest of a long career.

Brahms befriended Mühlfeld and sat listening to him play for hour after hour. Maybe for the first time in his life he felt something more than pleasure in a fine musician. Now he experienced an epiphany of an instrument in itself. With the clarinet it was the superimposed layers of its three octaves: the rich reediness of the low register, then the gentle paleness of the "throat" tones; above that the velvety center of the instrument, in Mühlfeld's hands and breath capable of endless nuances of color and volume; and finally the high register, flutelike when soft, swelling to a piercing angry cry.

Here was a musician who could make his instrument sing like a violist or a mezzo-soprano, and so Brahms recognized another incarnation of the kind of dark, soulful voice that had always seduced him. Thus his nicknames for Richard Mühlfeld: "Fräulein Klarinette," "my dear nightingale," "my Primadonna," even sometimes, "Fräulein von Mühlfeld."[20] All Brahms's life, as he had painstakingly mastered the orchestra and chamber media, the influence of his training and of his North

German temperament had pulled him back from the sensuality of mere instrumental sound. In his maturity, even as he shaped beautifully fresh orchestral effects he could never quite concede the possibility that color might exist on the level of counterpoint and harmony and form. And even as he wrote many hours of music for Joachim's violin, whose sound rang in his inner ear, he still felt inadequate in his understanding of any instrument beyond the piano. Other than perhaps in his study of Wagner's scores, he had never systematically tried to overcome that limitation.

Now in his imagination Brahms embraced Fräulein Klarinette like a woman, and as with so many Fräuleins before, this celibate passion inspired him. The fruits of his Ischl summer of 1891 were first the Clarinet Trio in A Minor and then what he called "a far greater folly," the Quintet in B Minor for Clarinet and Strings.

Brahms was fond of the four-movement Trio, which especially in the first movement has some of the subtle novelties in form that characterize his late music—Michael Musgrave calls it "a broad A B with a retransition to the tonic rather than development."[21] For the public ear the Clarinet Trio has always seemed an austere affair, its expressiveness more ambiguous than the Quintet's warm wash of emotion. Malcolm MacDonald notes of the Trio that "in some stretches the work resembles a cello sonata with clarinet obbligato."[22] Which is to say, in the piece Brahms's fondness for Hausmann's cello competes with his newfound love of Mühlfeld's clarinet.

In the Quintet nothing competes with the glory of the instrument. Its beginning is a gentle, dying-away roulade that raises a veil of autumnal melancholy over the whole piece: the evanescent sweet-sadness of autumn, beautiful in its dying. This gentle opening is strikingly different from those of Brahms's recent chamber music—the pounding Romantic melodrama that starts the C Minor Trio, the somber tone of the Third Violin Sonata, the pealing gaiety of the G Major Quintet. Now wistful sweetness pervades the atmosphere. The first movement unfolds with dreamy melismas in clarinet and strings, everything on the edge of sentimentality but late-Brahmsian conciseness keeping the sentiment from being dwelled on.

The music so clearly looks back on lost love with a distillation of Brahmsian yearning, what MacDonald calls "every super-refined shade of silver-grey regret."[23] Yet it is also a song to new love. It is Fräulein Klarinette herself that seems to create the sweetness, and the staccato contrasts. The sighing quality of the music is made from nuances unique to the clarinet. When a flurry of notes sweeps from low to high, it sweeps through the colors of the instrument from the lush low tones to the delicate high ones. The urgent moments are the urgency of the high register when it is loud and piercing. The vertiginous gypsy melismas of the second movement arise from another mood of the instrument, and likewise, the third movement's combination of a flowing *andantino* and a rhythmical *presto* with sharp-tongued staccatos. The finale's variations are portraits of the clarinet in its nuances of timbre, articulation, and dynamics, ending on a dying series of chords, piercingly lonely.

As late as the Double Concerto, after writing hundreds of pages of string music, Brahms had still complained: "It is a very different matter writing for instruments whose nature and sound one only has a chance acquaintance with . . . from writing for an instrument that one knows as thoroughly as I know the piano." Perhaps we can call these late clarinet works his reconciliation with instrumental color and technique, a dimension of music in which he had floundered while composing the First Piano Concerto and in some degree resisted ever since, even as his orchestral skill and imagination mounted. Perhaps the clarinet pieces are the only true love songs to an instrument Brahms ever wrote.

In the quintet even more than in other works, Brahms also demonstrates as well as any composer that some of the greatest art exists near the edge between sentiment and sentimentality, but has a fine sense of where that edge lies, and how to stay on the right side of it.

As HE WORKED on the clarinet pieces in Ischl in the summer of 1891, once more in his rented rooms on Salzburgerstrasse, Clara wrote him a new report on Elisabet von Herzogenberg, sad in what it reveals of both their friend's health and Clara's jealousy: "Frau Herzogenberg is much better. . . . Her doctor, who is here now, declared that she was so bad for a while that she was at death's door. I am not sure that the unbridled ambition of this good lady does not do her a lot of harm by keeping her in a constant state of agitation."[24] Clara Schumann impugning a woman's ambition! Brahms made an abysmally dispassionate reply, saying he was glad to hear Lisl was better but:

> I had no news of them, even indirectly for a long time, and I am growing accustomed to not hearing from them. Yes, ambition! It looks as though the same things were happening with them as has already happened with X—. In both cases intercourse with them has become impossible owing to their otherwise quite amiable wives. . . . One finds it impossible to discuss an artist's work with him, and perhaps to criticize

it, if his wife is listening, not to mention arguing with me. Alone with the men, I could come to some conclusion, and then how happy I should be to enjoy the company of the ladies afterward!

In her last letter Clara had described herself as "continually racked with pain now in one place and now in another." For the moment she could not walk. Still, in his reply Brahms invited her to come to the premiere of the new clarinet pieces in Berlin: "To listen to the clarinet player would mark a red-letter day in your life. . . . You would revel, and I hope that my music would not interfere with your pleasure!"[25] There was no chance she could come.

At the beginning of October, Brahms was back in Vienna with the prospect of something he had never expected to experience again—two autumn premieres. He had a letter from Clara saying she wanted to publish her old Mozart concerto cadenzas, but had forgotten that he had actually composed parts of them. What should she do? "Let the cadenzas go out into the world in your own name," he replied. "Even the smallest of J. B.s [on some of them] would only look strange. . . . Besides, if you did that I ought by rights to put under my best melodies 'Really by Clara Schumann,' for with only myself to inspire me nothing profound or beautiful can possibly occur to me! I owe you more melodies than all the passages and so forth you could possibly take from me."[26]

They had loved each other nearly forty years, and spent the same years periodically torturing each other. Brahms had known other muses than her, and now was happy to find a new one in a contraption of ebony and reed. But that letter was the most touching testament he ever gave Clara Schumann. And there is no doubt that he meant what he said. Besides, of late Brahms had been increasingly mindful of her, mostly on his best behavior.

Her response to his testament was pleased but distant. Clara was seventy-two, suffering and distracted and depressed, no longer able to perform in public and so denied the main thing that had kept her alive and alert. (When she was able, she still played for students and friends.) Her deteriorating hearing threatened even her ability to enjoy music. After years of ghastly decline from morphine addiction her last son, Ferdinand, had died in June. At the same time the failure of her favorite student, Leonard Borwick, to make a splash in Vienna, despite Brahms's string-pulling, had brought her near a nervous collapse. In the wake of that she and Johannes fell into a furious argument during a visit. Then in October 1891, for a completely unexpected reason, he got a fusillade of her wrath in his face.

Several times Brahms had written Clara of his preference for the first version of Robert's D Minor Symphony, the manuscript of which he owned. He felt the revised version, the one then in print, had reflected mainly the weakness of Robert's Düsseldorf orchestra. Clara had never really responded to Johannes's queries. Not wanting to bother her again, he went ahead and did what he thought best in the Schumann Edition, on which they had long worked together. (It was issued between 1887 and 1893.) He arranged for old friend Franz Wüllner to edit the D Minor Symphony for Breitkopf & Härtel, in an edition with the original and revised versions on facing pages.[27] When Clara learned from the newspapers that it was coming out, she was beside herself with fury that she had not been consulted.

Her first letter to Brahms about it does not survive, but his response implies that he did not yet understand how serious a breach threatened. "I hope your annoyance is only connected with the business side of the matter," he wrote. It certainly was not the business, she shot back, but maybe it was Wüllner's fault. "I alone am responsible for the publication of the symphony," he responded with a sigh. "All this may sound too arrogant to you, as in your letter you seem to regard W. and myself not as two upright men and musicians, who are in your opinion perhaps misguided, though in their own opinions they are carrying out a sacred and holy task . . . but as in every respect the opposite." He ended, "For an honorable man your letter of today is too hard and forbids my saying more."[28] It sounds like things Clara was accustomed to say to him. They forcibly calmed the waters for the holidays, but Clara's outrage over the symphony publication would flare up again and again during the next year. In a series of skirmishes through those months the two of them fought bitterly and hard like two old lovers, remembering old wounds as they inflicted new ones.

ON NOVEMBER 21, 1891, Brahms arrived in Meiningen to rehearse the Clarinet Trio and Quintet, the first with Richard Mühlfeld and cellist Robert Hausmann joining him, the second with the Joachim Quartet plus clarinet. They gave a private performance of the pieces for Duke Georg, then got ready for the public premiere in Berlin. Before that, Brahms spent a few days in Hamburg visiting stepmother Karoline, stepbrother Fritz Schnack, and his seriously ailing sister Elise. In Berlin on December 1 the reception of the clarinet pieces was tremendous, certainly more because of the Quintet than the Trio. From the beginning the quintet was understood to be a masterpiece written from the heart and addressed to the heart.

Then he returned to Vienna and sank back into his life there, the round of concerts, plays, politics, meals, and gossip. On January 5 the Clarinet Quintet, played by the Rosé, had what Richard Heuberger declared an "unparalleled success" in the city, the cheers roaring on endlessly. With Heuberger, Brahms scoffed at the news that Bruckner was getting an honorary doctorate from the University of Vienna, which sullied his own cherished title of Herr Doktor: "If somebody overrates somebody as an artist, that's his business. But that a totally uncultured man is made a doctor, that's really pretty hard. . . . I was the guinea pig for music doctorates, and now it's gotten so common!"[29]

The turn of 1892 brought many beginnings and endings for Brahms and his world. That year Bruckner finished his gargantuan Eighth Symphony and Tchaikovsky *The Nutcracker.* To the north the Dane Carl Nielsen produced his First Symphony, carrying on Brahms's legacy, and Jan Sibelius joined that legacy to Finnish accent and mythology with *Kullervo* and *En Saga.* In France, Maurice Maeterlinck wrote the precious, short-lived drama *Pelléas et Mélisande*, which Debussy would spend the rest of the decade making into an ageless opera. Monet began his Rouen Cathedral series, Toulouse-Lautrec painted *The Moulin Rouge.* Across the waters, Alfred Lord Tennyson and Walt Whitman died.

On January 2, Brahms received a telegram that Elisabet von Herzogenberg had passed away in San Remo, of her old heart condition. Many people grieved, in and out of her circle. In Florence the sculptor Hildebrand created a monument to her in Renaissance style, with Elisabet as St. Cecilia seated at the organ. Brahms wrote Heinrich:

> It is vain to attempt any expression of the feelings that absorb me so completely. And you will be sitting alone in your dumb misery, speechless yourself and not desiring speech from others. . . . You know how unutterably I myself suffer by the loss of your beloved wife, and can gauge accordingly my emotions in thinking of you, who were associated with her by the closest possible ties. . . . It would do me so much good just to sit beside you quietly, press your hand, and share your thoughts of the dear marvellous woman.[30]

Brahms was being kindly there and also, between the lines, coldly honest: the only thing Heinrich really meant to him was the connection with the dear marvelous woman. From that point Heinrich, devastated by her death, went into virtual seclusion for years, composing works in his wife's memory. He also published eight piano pieces Elisabet had written, part of a lost body of work from one of the most extraordinary musical figures of her time. Now there would be relatively few letters between Brahms and Heinrich von Herzogenberg. Brahms was no more inclined to smile on Heinrich's work now than he had ever been; he preferred to avoid the subject entirely.

Mühlfeld and the Joachim Quartet performed both clarinet pieces again in Vienna the same January. After one of the concerts they and friends retired to the Igel for a noisy evening, Brahms and Joachim joking the night away. Maybe it was a release for Brahms after the wrenching, if long anticipated, death of Elisabet. At the dinner he passed up sitting beside two attractive and attentive women to sit between the clarinetists who had played his pieces in Vienna that month, Mühlfeld and F. Steiner, making sure they got the best cuts of meat and keeping their glasses full.[31] During dinner he mentioned to Richard Heuberger that he had a second Academic Festival Overture at home, waiting for the right moment.[32] (The moment never came.)

That winter the Fellingers surprised and did not entirely please Brahms by having electric lights installed in his apartment.[33] Maria's photographs show a kind of track light in his living room, a shaded bulb that could travel from the piano to the table beside it that held his coffeemaker. There was a similar setup in the library. On February 20 Frau Maria spread before Brahms a feast of brain consommé, lobster salad, beef filet garnished with vegetables (Viennese *Tafelspitz*), ham cooked in Madeira, hazel grouse, ice cream, pastries, champagne, and coffee.[34] In May he celebrated his fifty-ninth birthday as had become his habit, with an asparagus dinner among friends in Vienna. Clara, who had been forced by worsening health to resign her place at the Frankfurt Conservatory, wrote him a painful birthday note: "I am not allowed to write much, but I feel I must send you my warmest greetings for your birthday with my own hand. . . . May you enjoy good health and once more this year be able to give further glorious gifts to mankind. Oh, how hard it is for me—I could not get to know anything because everything I hear sounds all wrong."[35]

Then Brahms headed back to Salzburgerstrasse in Bad Ischl, indeed with plans for new pieces. There would be no more talk of quitting, but also no more large projects, no more glorious gifts to mankind. Now, he told Clara, he was composing for himself alone.

·   ·   ·

THE YELLOW HOUSE with white trim owned by Frau Grüber, whose second floor he had rented on all his visits to Ischl, lay on a slope above the River Traun. From his windows and porch Brahms had an expansive view of the river and of the surrounding mountains that beckoned him for morning walks and weekend excursions. From there it was a short stroll to the Esplanade along the river, the middle of the "Kaiser Village," and the Café Walter, his favored spot for coffee and chats with Ignaz Brüll and the others who gathered around him.

In the basement of the Hotel Kaiserin Elisabet on the Esplanade he had long ago found a frugal restaurant to his taste. The place became another center for his circle to joke and tope and gossip. The proprietor reserved for them a choice spot under the window, dubbed "the patriarch's table." After lunch they would retire to the Walter to have a *"Schwarzer,"* read the papers under the trees, and watch the elegant tourists stroll by, many of them acquaintances. Since he did not like to wear his pince-nez in public, now and then Brahms nearsightedly hailed a stranger, who would be thrilled by how friendly the eminent man seemed to be toward everybody.

It was in the Kaiserin Elisabet that theater critic Julius Bauer uttered a famous *bon mot* after listening to Brahms's habitual gossip and putdowns. You, Herr Doktor, said Bauer, are "the greatest *Schimpfoniker* in the world." The pun unites *Symphoniker* (composer of symphonies) with the verb *schimpfen*, which is to insult, abuse, revile, affront, use bad language, or scold. Brahms roared with laughter at the line.[36]

In 1892 he was working on little piano pieces that would become the Seven Fantasias of Opus 116 and Three Intermezzos of Opus 117. In connection with them, it may have been that summer when his future biographer Max Kalbeck experienced a peculiar vision. He was visiting Ischl and went walking on a warm early July morning. Emerging from the woods and rushing toward him he saw what he took to be a peasant, or maybe the owner of the property, coming to shoo him away. Then Kalbeck realized it was Brahms, with hat in one hand and his coat in the other dragging on the ground, running through the dewy meadow as if a demon were after him. Wild-eyed, weeping and gasping and sweating, Brahms brushed past Kalbeck and disappeared in the distance, apparently without seeing his friend at all.

Another day Kalbeck came to visit Salzburgerstrasse and noticed the door to the music room open. From inside came pealing piano music, stopping and starting, passages repeated over and over with tiny changes. Kalbeck realized that Brahms was composing or revising a piece. But as the music changed and grew under the composer's hands, there rose an accompaniment of "the strangest growling, whining, and moaning, which at the height of the musical climax changed into a loud howl." Unlikely as it seemed, Kalbeck decided that Brahms must have gotten himself a dog. Hearing the scrape of a piano stool, he went in to find Brahms alone in the room, his face red and beard glistening with tears. Embarrassed, Brahms wiped his face with the back of his hand and slowly returned to his usual joking self."[37]

There may have been more to those episodes than the artistic ecstasies Kalbeck assumed. After all, Brahms usually worked in houses with others in earshot, and no one else reported scenes like those. In Mürzzuschlag his eavesdropping landlady had heard mostly pacing and humming and silence. This summer in Ischl, rather than the lash of the muse, Brahms's wailing may have come from all the illness and death weighing on him. Some of it may have gotten into the music as well—such as the three Intermezzos for Piano that he called "cradle-songs of my sorrows."

Elise Brahms had died in June. Brahms wrote Clara that his sister "lay desperately ill the whole winter. . . . We who were watching could not help wishing for the end long ago."[38] He was more shaken by this death than by that of his brother Fritz; so was Clara, who had long ago befriended Johannes's sickly, simple sister. For all the years since he left Hamburg, Brahms had depended on Elise for news and gossip of home, of Laura Garbe and Friedchen Wagner and the other girls of his Frauenchor who were now becoming old women. Through the years Elise had faithfully attended performances of his music in Hamburg, and sat listening in tearful wonder. Her late and happy marriage to watchmaker Grund had cheered Brahms. All her life Elise had most loved her mother, flowers, a tidy house, friends, and her brother. She had stayed faithful to them all.

Johannes supported Elise for decades and wrote faithfully as well, the many letters of small news that were returned to him after she was gone. He had written her last from Ischl, the day after she died: "I'd like so much to visit you again and am always thinking how to manage the rather long trip."[39] When he got his letters back he pored over them, amazed at how many there were. Then he destroyed them, but he could never quite bring himself to burn hers.

By 1883 he had already liquidated the trunkfuls of youthful songs, sonatas, trios, and quartets that had been stored in Hamburg. Now in a note to cousin Christian Detmering, who had notified him of Elise's death, Brahms asked for all the letters, books, and pictures in the house.

He also mentioned an inscribed silver inkstand, the one the Hamburg Frauenchor had given him in 1859. At the same time he told Christian that he did not have room for the oil paintings of his father and mother. His stepmother kept the one of Johann Jakob in Pinneberg, where she lived with her son Fritz. The painting of his mother—could they find someplace to put it? (The picture was lost. He did have in the house some pieces of his mother's fine embroidery, which he showed off to visitors.) In autumn 1893, Christian Detmering, the last of Brahms's immediate family, died in the great Hamburg cholera epidemic.

At the same time as Brahms shared his news good and bad with Clara, her rage over his publishing Robert's symphony continued to boil (those letters have not survived). If Brahms's style of torturing loved ones was hit-and-run, Clara's was a slow, relentless assault that wore you down. On her seventy-third birthday in September 1892, Brahms wrote her a sad greeting: "Please allow a poor pariah to tell you today that he always thinks of you with the same respect, and out of the fullness of his heart wishes you, whom he holds dearer than anything on earth, all that is good, desirable, and beautiful. Alas, to you more than to any other I am a pariah; this has, for a long time, been my painful conviction, but I never expected it to be so harshly expressed." Then, unbelievably, he went on to dig up a chimerical wrong that he had obviously brooded on for years:

> You know very well that I can't accept the ostensible cause, the printing of the symphony, as the real cause. Years ago I had a profound feeling that this was so, though I said nothing about it, at the time when the Schumann piano pieces, which I was the first to publish, were not included in the Complete Edition. All I could think of on both occasions was that you did not like to see my name associated with them. With the best will in the world I can neither discover nor acknowledge any other reason.
>
> In my dealings with my friends I am aware of only one fault—my lack of tact. For years now you have been kind enough to treat this leniently. If only you could have done so for a few years more!
>
> After forty years of faithful service (or whatever you wish to call my relationship to you) it is very hard to be merely "another unhappy experience." But after all this can be borne. I am accustomed to loneliness and will need to be with the prospect of this great void before me. But let me repeat to you today that you and your husband constitute the most beautiful experience of my life, and represent all that is richest and most noble in it.[40]

Now it was Clara's turn to be dumbfounded. It really had been the symphony matter that enraged her—that, and bad health and depression amplifying her old self-righteousness. In any case, she was not yet prepared to forgive him. For that Johannes would have to grovel properly. She replied:

> You reproach me with having shown you too little consideration in connection with the Schumann Edition. But I cannot for the life of me remember why the pieces did not appear. . . . If, however, I offended you, you should have told me at once quite openly and not have given free rein to the base suspicion that I did not like to see your name connected with Robert's. Such a thought could only have occurred to you in an evil hour. . . . If your suspicion were well founded, surely I could not be reckoned among the more pleasant recollections of your life? . . . [41]
>
> But enough of this! Nothing makes me more miserable than these disputes and explanations. Am I not the most peaceable person on earth? So, my dear Johannes, let us strike a more friendly note, for which your beautiful piano pieces, about which Ilona [Eibenschütz] has just written me, afford the best opportunity if you will only take it. Greeting you with the same old affection, I am, Your Clara.

He took the opportunity offered and groveled, if a little disingenuously:

> From the bottom of my heart I thank you for your kind and comforting reply to my letter. The subject of our altercation, which seems to have upset you so much, I do not even remember, but I infinitely regret not having kept sharper guard over my tongue. With regard to the Schumann Edition I cannot remember whether it was you or I who wrote ambiguously.[42]

Finally the year-long battle, which had threatened to destroy four decades of love, friendship, collaboration, and service, trickled out. There would be no more battles. As Johannes had written: Why fight in the little time left them? They quickly straightened out the business over the Schumann pieces he had edited; the pieces would come out in a supplementary volume, with other opus-posthumous works that Brahms selected, including the variations Schumann had written on the spirits' theme just before his leap into the Rhine. He approved when Clara burned some works of Robert's that they considered unworthy. She was thrilled with his new piano pieces. Their relations went on.

Just before Christmas 1892 Brahms wrote her again about Robert's variations as he worked on them for the supplementary edition. In the letter he used terms perhaps more flowery than he had ever used about music. He knew they were pleasant images Clara would like, but they spoke from his heart too:

> The Variations are remarkable and irresistibly charming. The other day . . . I again sat down at my piano and without any particular object in mind played them over to myself quite naturally and with profound emotion. I felt as though I were walking on a beautiful soft spring morning, in a grove of alders, birches and lovely flowers, with a babbling brook at my feet. One never gets tired of the mild still air, the delicate azure, the tender greens; there is nothing to remind one of the hurly-burly, and one feels no wish for darkling woods, for rugged rocks and waterfalls amid all this beautiful monotony.[43]

So much for Brahms the great abstractionist.

Clara told her journal about eleven new piano pieces he had sent her, "full of poetry, passion, sentiment, emotion, and with the most wonderful effects of tone. . . . In these pieces I at last feel musical life stir again in my soul. . . . How they make one forget much of the suffering he has caused one." At the end of the year she recorded, "I had a dear letter from Brahms . . . it arrived on Christmas Eve, a thing that has not happened for years."[44]

As the latest confrontation with Clara subsided, there remained Brahms's rankling and unspoken resentment of Billroth for cutting up his manuscript, for speaking badly of Johann Jakob, for being sick. The year before, the surgeon had been so weak that he could not climb the stairs to Brahms's apartment.[45] When that October there were festivities marking his fiftieth semester at Vienna University, Billroth wrote Brahms, "The excess of honor and love at my jubilee, was, I admit, wonderful, but it was at the same time a sort of funeral service. I prepared my body with digitalis and other poisons so that I could join in the festivities looking like a well man."[46] Now this old admirer could not find any enthusiasm for Johannes's new piano miniatures. Billroth wrote his daughter, "I like this type of thing the least except for the Rhapsody in G minor. . . . Brahms should stick with the great style."[47] Brahms in turn would have sensed the lack of enthusiasm, even if his friend tried to gloss it over.

It came to a head in November, when Brahms played out one of the calculated scenes he was given to now and then. Billroth had invited him to play some of the piano miniatures in his music room, for a gathering of friends. For himself the surgeon wanted to give the pieces another chance. Maybe suspecting what was going on, Brahms sulked and growled in his beard from the beginning of the party. When asked to play the new pieces he balked at going to the piano at all, then sat down and played something else. When asked if that was Bach he sneered, as if he knew Billroth's appraisal of his new pieces: "Whether Bach or Massenet or me, what difference does it make?" He struck off a few fragments of the new work and then rose imperiously from the piano.

It was a dismal evening and of course Brahms never apologized. Billroth, aged and suffering, was very much hurt, and confirmed in his conviction that such conduct reflected a poor upbringing: "It doesn't make any difference to him," Billroth wrote his daughter, "whether serious men are present who are very much devoted to him or whether he has a crowd of rascals as an audience. . . . In any case this evening has deprived me of any desire to undertake anything similar with Brahms again. He really makes it very difficult for one to keep on loving him."[48] Their friendship would stumble on, mostly in brief notes, but after years of hearing his songs and chamber works regularly in Billroth's beautiful music room amid delightful gatherings, Brahms never set foot in his friend's house again.

In January 1893 he went to Meiningen to play in the Clarinet Trio and Second Cello Sonata. Though he was no longer touring as he used to, he spent the month making rounds of friends. After Meiningen he made a reconciliatory visit with Clara in Frankfurt, then went to Hamburg to see old friends including Friedchen Sauerman née Wagner, and finally in Berlin visited Woldemar Bargiel, Heinrich von Herzogenberg, Marie Soldat, and his godson Johannes Joachim, who was sitting for his doctoral examinations. Shortly after he arrived back in Vienna, he learned that on the day after her thirty-sixth birthday Hermine Spies had died in Wiesbaden, where the year before she had married a lawyer. He grieved, but now Alice Barbi was his songstress.

The musical world, meanwhile, was aware of an approaching landmark: Brahms's sixtieth birthday. He was unaffectedly pleased when, on Viktor Miller's initiative, the Gesellschaft der Musikfreunde struck a gold medal of him. Otherwise, his response to the approach of his birthday, and to the flood of deaths around him, was to bolt the scene. In the middle of April, with Josef Widmann and Zürich friends Friedrich Hegar and Robert Freund in tow, Brahms headed for familiar foreign ports. The world could send him birthday congratulations in Italy, if the world could find him.

The friends ate and drank and sightsaw their way through Genoa and Pisa and Rome and Naples, made a side trip to Sorrento, took a ship from Naples to Palermo, and so on for weeks, with sojourns in Brahms's beloved Taormina. "Fortunately my sixty years come very little into my reckoning," he reported to Clara, "but I was always bad at arithmetic. On our travels I was certainly the most vigorous and had the most staying power. I was always last to bed and first to rise, though my three traveling companions are much younger men."[49] The trip had been a pleasure much of the way, even if at the outset Brahms had managed to lose all his cash. "I cheerfully concluded that it was merely a sacrifice to the gods, and hoped that it might suffice them. But as luck would have it, they demanded more."

With the last he was referring to an incident on the boat from Messina to Naples, when a crane knocked Widmann into the hold. The fall might have killed him if his foot had not caught in an iron ring—but the ring broke his foot. So Brahms spent his sixtieth birthday at the bedside of his crippled friend. Shaken by the painful scene when a doctor set the break, Brahms joked through clenched teeth, "I'm your man if it comes to cutting! I was always Billroth's assistant in such things." As he sat with Widmann he read over the telegrams of birthday congratulations. After seeing Widmann and Hegar onto the train to Bern, he boarded his own train for Vienna. He had seen his beloved Italy for the last time.

On May 13 came the ceremony of presenting the Gesellschaft's gold medal. Designed with a profile of Brahms by Anton Scharff, it was struck in gold for the honoree and dozens more were minted in silver and bronze. At the ceremony Brahms was almost too overcome to speak, but finally he choked out, "I feel myself more shamed than pleased by this great honor. Thirty years ago I would have found the joy and responsibility to make myself worthy of such a distinction. But now it's too late."[50]

IN BAD ISCHL in summer 1893 he got back to his piano miniatures, sending them to Clara as they were finished. Among them was the extraordinary B Minor Intermezzo, in which falling chains of thirds form almost Debussyan ninth and eleventh chords, and create a sighing, dreamlike atmosphere.

Brahms wrote Clara.

I should very much like to know how you get on with it. It teems with
discords. These may be all right and quite explicable, but you may not
perhaps like them. . . . It is exceptionally melancholy. . . . Every bar
and every note must be played as if *ritardando* were indicated, and one
wished to draw the melancholy out of each one of them, and voluptuous joy and comfort out of the discords. My God, how will this description whet your appetite?

Her response surprised him: "You must have known how enthusiastic I should be when you were copying out that bittersweet piece which,
for all its discords, is so wonderful. No, one actually revels in the
discords, and, when playing them, wonders how the composer ever
brought them to birth. Thank you for this new, magnificent gift!" Later
she called the B Minor a "gray pearl." He responded with relief and a
touch of irony: "I must write a line at once to tell you how glad I am that
my little piece has pleased you. I really had not expected that it would,
and now shall be able to enjoy it in peace and calm at my piano as if I
had a license to do so from the chief of police. . . . Most affectionately
yours, Joh."[51]

With these miniatures he returned to the genre of Romantic character piece for keyboard—the kind of music played in nineteenth-century
parlors all over the world. In his own career, he had followed his early piano sonatas and variations with character pieces. The new ones went under the relatively arbitrary names of ballade, capriccio, intermezzo,
rhapsody (he revised the designations of several before publication).
They lie in the tradition of miniatures by Schumann and Chopin, two
masters Brahms knew as both performer and editor.

The inspiration for this flood of pieces in Opuses 116–19 of
1892–3—twenty in all, probably with others that were destroyed, some
of them probably composed earlier—we can trace to matters both personal and "purely" musical. The beauty of playing and person of young

Ilona Eibenschütz likely had something to do with them. (Ilona premiered Opuses 118 and 119 in London in 1894, and in her later years recorded a number of the pieces.) It was the gently beautiful, lilting intermezzos of Opus 117 that Brahms declared "three cradle-songs of my sorrows." Maybe all the pieces with their delicate lyricism are love songs to lost women in Brahms's life, to Ilona and Clara and Agathe and Hermine and Alice, to Elisabet for whom he wrote the rhapsodies of Opus 79, and to all the others known and unknown to history. And no less he may have composed the pieces to try and keep Clara Schumann going in body and soul. Since she could only play a few minutes at a time now, and because she loved these miniatures so deeply, maybe they did keep her alive.

Musically, they were an expressive outlet in a time when Brahms did not feel up to larger projects—and he probably suspected that he never would feel up to them. (At one point he proposed to Fritz Simrock that he might whip several of the piano pieces into an orchestral suite, but nothing came of it.) The main significance of the late piano works, however, is this: they are a summation of what Brahms had learned, almost scientific studies of compositional craft and of piano writing, disguised as pretty little salon pieces.

Expressively they are varied, but the majority slow and gentle. There is a preference for A B A forms. His rhythmic subtleties, his love of two against three and related effects, pervade the pieces. The complexity is in the depth of construction, the thematic relations, the novelties of harmony and modulation. The B Minor Intermezzo, whose dissonance Clara loved, is an essay not only in complex harmonies but in tonal implications, *moll-Dur* carried to a new level: in the first section the right hand implies B minor, the left D major, and the establishment of each key (the A♮-A♯ dichotomy that defines each) is left exquisitely ambiguous until the sweet D major of the middle section.

As shown in his letter to Clara, Brahms was afraid he had gone too far with the dissonances in this piece. In fact, he had not gone as far as Wagner's *Tristan und Isolde*, or Liszt's atonal late piano works. (Debussy had already written piano pieces in which tonality is systematically blurred.) Which is to say: in its harmonies the B Minor Intermezzo may not have gone as far into the future of music as others had, but it represents the furthest Brahms was willing to go.[52]

Yet these late pieces helped inspire the next generation. There is a direct line from Brahms's late piano works to the revolutionary piano miniatures of Schoenberg, twenty years later. Which is to say: Brahms's techniques transcended his own language, his own aesthetics, his own era.

All that can be demonstrated as well as anywhere in the A Major Intermezzo of Opus 118. On the surface it is a wistfully lyrical piece, technically easy, eminently suitable for young women to play in the parlor. Brahms begins it, tellingly, with an upbeat on the tonic (the main chord) and a downbeat on an unstable chord:

The important thematic material in the upper voice is a four-bar theme whose significance is both motivic and rhythmic, and whose most important element is the motive C♯-B-D:

He follows the presentation of that theme with three subtle variations on it, each having the same metric inflection: three *one* two, three *one* two, three-one-two-three *one* two. . . . (At the same time the downbeat, the *one*, is usually compromised by an unstable harmony even as it is perceived as a downbeat.) The next few measures pick up and simplify that metric motif with a new idea.

The melodic motive of measure 17 was anticipated in the bass in measures 11–12; thus the motivic development is not just played out in the top voice but saturates the texture, even when there is no overt counterpoint. In the process, melody creates harmony. After a rising chromatic sequence based on the initial melodic motive of the piece, the music settles down to a sighing section from measure 30, which is another variant of the three *one* two rhythmic pattern. (It features a three-note descending motive that has been growing in the piece since the middle voice in the first two beats, in the bass line in measures 5–6, etc.)

The most striking thing about the moment from measure 30, though, is the sighing, yearning harmonic inflection. There we see some of what excited Schoenberg and his heirs: that harmonic inflection is created by the bass line, which turns out to be the opening melodic motive of the piece, the figure C♯-B-D, repeated over and over; then that *Dur* figure become the *moll* C♮-B-D.

At the final cadence before the B section, the piece's opening theme is buried in the middle voices. The new section, beginning at measure 49, is based on a descending figure apparently new, but derived from the subsidiary descending motive, now extended (but with the original C♯-B-D part of the line too):

At the same time, what appears there to be a countermelody in the left hand is actually a near-canon with the top line—then it departs for another reference to the C♯-A leap of the opening theme.

It was this kind of musical alchemy, this extraordinary depth of construction, these three-dimensional relationships in musical time and space, that helped inspire Arnold Schoenberg's invention of twelve-tone composition: one or two ideas saturate the texture and constantly change and grow in developing variation; a leading melody is submerged into bass and middle voices; melody and counterpoint create harmony. Even though Brahms willfully planted his feet in the musical language of his world, his class, his century, in this kind of craftsmanship at once traditional and innovative we find the genius Schoenberg named "Brahms the Progressive."[53]

. . .

DURING 1893 Brahms felt plagued by Billroth, who was working on a projected book called *Who Is Musical?*. For all his respect for the surgeon's knowledge and judgment in the art, Brahms felt his friend to be out of his depth in theorizing about musicality. Still, he answered Billroth's questions as patiently as he could, ignoring a basic divide between them: Billroth considered the sense of beauty inborn and unexplainable, Brahms considered it a matter of knowledge and craft. For his friend Brahms analyzed Goethe's famous poem "Über allen Gipfeln ist ruh" in both musical and philosophical terms. It is the only evidence that survives on paper of the kind of debates the two men held regularly in person. As Billroth summarized Brahms's analysis:

> The beauty and grandeur of the entire picture, from the heavens to the tops of the trees and downward to silence in the life of nature, and the reference to sleep and death of humanity; humanity is a part of nature, thus taking into itself all of nature. . . . One could not alter one word of it without destroying the poem; the shortness and simplicity of the whole, a beautiful adagio in the form of a song. For a similar analysis, Brahms explained some Sarabandes from the French suites of Bach; the configuration of the whole, the rising of the melody, the question and the answer, cadences in different periods. . . . In contradiction to these, he showed me empty, ugly, unskillful melodies, bad-sounding or empty bass parts. It all confirmed the opinion that I had . . . it is a matter of individual feeling . . . beauty can only be understood by the person born with a specific feeling for that particular art.

To that Brahms replied: "'Feeling is everything!' That's fine for an examination on religion for a young Fräulein! But we have to have more concern than for the moment; Goethe preaches this so impressively with words and deeds appertaining to art." By that he means that every moment in a work must also be understood in the context of the whole. He was even more exasperated by the naïveté of Billroth's theories, such as that cultures only arrive at major keys in the higher stages of development. Sighing, Brahms sent over some folk songs intended to demonstrate the uselessness of such notions. Billroth persevered, but he knew he was not thinking all that clearly. He wrote Brahms in December 1893, "I have such dreadful pains in my left leg that I can scarcely move around. The pain was so violent at night that I took a good deal of morphine, and because of that I'm hardly in a frame of mind to distinguish major and minor."[54]

That December Alice Barbi, still Brahms's favorite singer but now about to marry an Italian aristocrat and retire from performing, presented her farewell concert in Vienna. There was a gasp from the audience when, instead of the advertised accompanist, Brahms lumbered onstage and sat down at the piano. They performed four of his songs, including "Der Tod, das ist die Kühle Nacht."

If that final cadence of a personal and artistic collaboration was a bittersweet pleasure for Brahms, a new collaboration of a sort appeared in January 1894, when he received a series of forty-one engravings, etchings, and lithographs called *Brahms Fantasy*, by the Leipzig artist Max Klinger. Years before, Klinger had dedicated his series *Amor and Psyche* to Brahms. This new *Fantasy* was all interpretations, in the artist's most visionary mode, of the impact Brahms had upon him.

Brahms had known Klinger's work since the 1870s, when Fritz Simrock commissioned the artist to engrave covers for pieces including the *Schicksalslied*. For some time Brahms had been dubious about the eccentric, haunted style of the pictures, and about the whole idea of illustration. He wrote Simrock in 1885, "That would be fine, if I wrote things with titles like Kreisleriana, Humoreske, Phantasiestücke, Noveletten, Karneval! I doubt, though, that a simple title of Sonata can suggest anything in particular to him."[55] But as he pored over Klinger's work Brahms fell into its aura, and so a new figure joined Anselm Feuerbach in his private pantheon of visual artists.

In much of his work this artist grounded himself in the same Classical imagery as Feuerbach, but he took that influence in more idiosyncratic directions. Brahms understood that Klinger, with his strangely gesticulating figures and roiling seas and pianists surrounded by spirits, was not trying to do a pictorial "interpretation" of particular pieces (a familiar game with Wagner-inspired artists in those days), but rather to create a visual analogy to music itself: a compelling design of symbols that elude explanation. Brahms wrote Clara about the *Fantasy*, "They are not really illustrations in the ordinary sense, but magnificent and wonderful fantasias inspired by my [vocal] texts."[56] And he wrote Widmann, "They are perfectly fascinating, and seem to be intended to make one forget all the miserable things of the world, and to lift one into higher spheres. The more one studies them with the eye the more the mind seems to discern their inner meaning."[57] Brahms never spelled out what Klinger's inner meanings said to him, any more than he would have done so in relation to his own work. But for all their oddities these pictures rang old Romantic, Hoffmannesque, Kreisleresque chords in Brahms: music as an echo of another, greater, more magical world.

So we do not know what went through his mind as he studied the most dazzling of the *Fantasies*, called *Akkorde* (*Chords*), in which a pianist plays pealing harmonies beside a stormy seascape that tosses a ship; beyond that lie cloud-swirled mountains with strange temples, and beneath the pianist sea sprites reach toward a wildly carved harp, perhaps that of the *Schicksalslied*. In the picture scholar Leon Botstein sees "dimensions of communication," the pianist an immediate reality whose playing evokes vistas of imagination that spread through the picture, "a narrative within the imaginary world" of nature, spirits, muses, myths.[58] What appealed to Brahms's imagination in Klinger's pictures was their intangibility, their paradox of unfathomable mysteries lucidly delineated: a narrative of unbounded imagination.

He wrote Klinger with perhaps deliberate ambiguity, "I often envy you with your pencil for being able to be so precise; I am often glad that I do not need to be."[59] A pencil can be precise about the intangible, but he preferred to withdraw even further than that, into the endlessly suggestive enigmas of tones. But Brahms also told the artist, "Seeing them it is as if the music resounded further into eternity, and everything that I might have wished to say was said, more clearly than music can, and still so filled with secrets and foreboding."[60]

It is startling to find Brahms declaring that a visual artist can deepen the mystery of his own art, its secrets and foreboding, and in that way somehow complete the music. With that suggestion Brahms touched on New German themes, and he was even more forthright when he wrote Klinger, "all art is the same and speaks the same language."[61] With Liszt and Wagner gone, he was prepared to accept a kind of unity of the arts, if not a *Gemsantkunstwerk*. At least that seems to be what he saw in Klinger—drawing that approached the mystery of music.

Klinger had an indelible memory of standing in the living room at Karlsgasse as Brahms opened the *Fantasy* on top of the piano and turned through them slowly, studying each page with manifest delight, reveling in this echo of his work. Maybe there Brahms was paid for his labor in the coin he valued most: artistry answered by artistry.

There was another artist whom Brahms took up in those years, more conservative in style than Klinger and in fact a considerable influence on Feuerbach. This was Arnold Böcklin, whose personal and intensely evocative reflections of Classical imagery can be seen in his most famous painting, *The Isle of the Dead*: a boat with sails furled drifts toward an island of towering rocks and gigantic cedars looming over a mysterious Classical temple. Brahms visited Böcklin's studio in 1885 and saw the painting *Centaur at the Village Blacksmith*, and the two men got along well. The painter had notions about evocation in pictures that Brahms probably found sympathetic: an image should "touch the eye," he said, "without having to explain or describe the effect with words," to create a "felt impression" beyond the explicit, like music.[62]

In other words, Klinger and Böcklin, late enthusiasms for Brahms who rarely took up living artists, rang his yearning for the inexpressible. At the same time, like Feuerbach, they shaped elements of tradition—images from history and mythology—into a personal expression: not really neoclassical but something more integral, original, and ultimately Romantic: secrets and foreboding.[63] At the same time, in taking up Klinger, Brahms unknowingly made a connection to the future, to Modernism, by way of Klinger the proto-surrealist, creator of the Beethoven sculpture that someday would form the centerpiece of an exhibition of the Vienna Secession, and inspire a fantastical work from Klinger's friend Gustav Klimt.

In 1894, Brahms read Julius Allgeyer's biography of Anselm Feuerbach, which he had encouraged Allgeyer to write. Around the same time he bought collections of Böcklin prints and received from Max Klinger a special printing of the *Brahms Fantasy* on Japanese paper. Since Brahms was barely performing that winter and maybe not composing either, he had leisure to immerse himself in these new pleasures. He wrote Widmann, "These three fill house and heart, and really one cannot call those times evil, which produce such a trio. . . . I realize how luxuriously we live, and how superficially we calculate."[64] (On other days, he was entirely prepared to call his times evil.)

The connection of Brahms and Klinger is most compelling in relation to Brahms the atavist, who kept up with everything that was happening but preferred rereading Hoffmann and Jean Paul and Goethe to steeping himself in modern artists. Yet Klinger seized him. His efforts to get Clara Schumann, Joachim, and Hanslick excited about that artist failed—he was looking further ahead than they were. Still, Klinger is no full-fledged Modernist, and it is hard to imagine that Brahms could have countenanced the kind of painting Van Gogh, Cézanne, Monet, and any number of others were doing in the 1880s and 90s—or the kind of music Debussy was writing. Richard Strauss's tone poems, the *ne plus ultra* of the avant-garde in the 1890s, repulsed him.

Klinger is more a transitional figure between Romanticism and Modernism, influenced by the French Symbolists, foreshadowing Surrealism and other creative exploitations of the Freudian unconscious. At the same time, Klinger was grounded in Romanticism, with a pre-Freudian sense of the mysterious and unreachable. In embracing Klinger, Brahms once more revealed, as he had in his own B Minor Intermezzo, how far he was willing to advance into the future.

IT WAS A BAD FEBRUARY for Brahms in 1894, worse for his friends. Theodor Billroth died in Vienna that month, and six days later Hans von Bülow died in Cairo, where he had gone in hopes of a cure for racking illnesses. Brahms's last note to Billroth had been an answer to some of the surgeon's queries about folk music, to which Brahms wearily replied, "I most certainly know that where the rhythmic and melodic movement of the songs has for me more and more interest, your interest would be totally absent." The letter upset the surgeon in his last days, and his wife never forgave Brahms for it. That guilt hung over him after his friend died, and maybe was the reason he avoided the huge procession that accompanied the casket to the Grave of Honor in the Central Cemetery— the kind of burial Vienna liked to give its great men.

As he walked to the graveyard through back streets with Max Kalbeck, Brahms reminisced about the nearly thirty years of friendship since he and Billroth met in Zürich in 1865. "Billroth was attracted to my music at a time when most people didn't want to hear any of it; this friendship has been a gift of fortune, and his warm enthusiasm has become a necessity to me." After the funeral he wrote Clara, "The grief over Billroth's death is extraordinarily widespread, but you cannot possibly have any idea how unique is the manifestation of sympathy in all circles here. His death had been long expected and for his sake was to be desired." And to Widmann: "I wish you could witness, as I do, what it means to be loved in Vienna. . . . Others don't wear their hearts so openly; they don't show their love as warmly as they do here, and I mean the best of them— I mean the real people, the ones who occupy the cheapest seats in the theater."[65]

The second death, Bülow, left Brahms so shaken that he could not bring himself to write a note to the widow in Hamburg. He asked Bürgermeister Petersen's daughter to buy a wreath for the funeral, and gave money in the conductor's memory to two institutions for musicians. When Fritz Simrock made those anonymous gifts public, Brahms was furious: "Now I look like any vulgar benefactor!"[66] In April, J. A. Spitta, the pioneering Bach biographer whom Brahms had known and corresponded with for years, died in Berlin just as Brahms sent him some folk song settings to look over.[67] Brahms began to repeat his aphorism: "Life robs one of more than death."

In the middle of that wave of loss washing over him, the most brutal of ironies arrived in the mail. The Hamburg Philharmonic, which had twice passed him over and, to his mind, condemned him to the life of a vagabond and exile, now offered him the post of music director. Of course he could not accept it. He might have said a great deal to the gentlemen of the Hamburg Philharmonic. Or maybe in his succinct reply he did say it all:

> There are not many things that I have desired so long and so ardently at the time—that is at the right time. Many years had to pass before I could reconcile myself to the thought of being forced to tread other paths. Had things gone according to my wish, I might today be celebrating my jubilee with you, while you would be, as you are today, looking for a capable younger man. May you find him soon, and may he work in your interest with the same good will, the same modest degree of ability, and the same wholehearted zeal, as would have done yours very sincerely,
>
> J. Brahms[68]

In March there emerged from his living room in Vienna one of his springtime projects: *49 Deutsche Volkslieder*, in seven volumes, with his own loving and subtle piano accompaniments. They are a testimonial to his lifelong inspiration from these nominal products of the German *Volk*. He had never accepted that many of them were ersatz folk music. Their authenticity meant much to him; the connection to the spirit of the German people—or illusion of connection—was another aspect of his sense of the past. He had a great deal of his own work, both vocal and instrumental, to show for his love of folk music. This late collection returns, as Malcolm MacDonald writes, to "a world of gallant knights, deserted maidens, enchanted fiddlers, repentant nuns, lovers both sad and happy, and Death the Reaper—an idealized medieval world, fit for the dreams of Young Kreisler."[69]

The folk songs, in other words, were a return to the Romantic inspiration of his teens, and so another cadence in his life. Deliberately, he ended the collection with "Verstohlen geht der Mond auf," which had been the unspoken text of the slow movement of his Piano Sonata Opus 1. From Ischl that summer he wrote Clara: "I am expecting the proofs of the forty-nine (!) songs. It is probably the first time that I have looked forward with so much pleasure to a set of proofs and to the publication of one of my works."[70] And later that summer:

> Has it ever occurred to you that the last of the songs comes in my Opus 1, and did anything strike you in this connection? It really ought to mean something. It ought to represent the snake which bites its own tail, that is to say, to express symbolically that the tale is told, the circle closed. But I know what good resolutions are, and I only think of them and don't say them aloud to myself. . . . At sixty it is probably high time to stop, but again without any particular reason!![71]

Whether there was a reason or not, he had a few pieces left in him. In the same vein, in Ischl Brahms responded to a friend who attempted to commiserate over the difficulties he had experienced in his career:

> My God, what do you want? I've gotten far enough! People respect me, my friends and enemies both. If people don't also love me—they respect me, and that's the main thing. I don't ask for more. I know very well what position I will occupy someday in the history of music: the position that Cherubini occupied then and now, that is also my lot, my *Schicksal.*[72]

That summer he sent Clara two photos of himself, one fated to be famous: Brahms standing alongside Johann Strauss, Jr., on the porch of the Waltz King's villa in Ischl. Strauss looks dashing, dark-haired, slim, and youthful next to the aged, portly, grizzled figure of Brahms. Strauss was older by eight years. Pictures of both men were already appearing on postcards.

That summer Brahms wrote the two clarinet sonatas, his last testament to Fräulein Klarinette and as beautiful as anything he ever wrote. One never forgets the first time one hears the opening of the Second Sonata, a flowing melody in his warmest and most nostalgic mood. An American tunesmith of the next century remembered that movement when he set a lyric that begins, "Try to remember that time in September, when life was green, and oh, so mellow."

HIS LIFE IN 1894 had been agreeably scattered and patchy, a time of big Brahms concerts and festivals all over the map. In November, Brahms visited Clara and her family, which now included teenaged grandson Ferdinand. Joachim also came to Frankfurt then, to play the Violin Concerto

in an all-Brahms program. Ferdinand was fascinated by this first encounter with his grandmother's celebrated friend, shorter and plumper
than he looked in pictures, the mustache gray on one side and fiery red
on the other.[73]

He still had some of the boyish fervor. "It was astonishing," Eugenie
Schumann recalled, "how full of life the house seemed as soon as Brahms
set foot in it." It was as if he had been saving up talk for Clara. News and
ideas and jokes and stories poured out of him: an operation Billroth had
described to him, Dvořák's new pieces, plays he had seen, Widmann's
books.[74] Joachim could sleep like a rock on tour, Brahms reminisced, but
he was a wretched card player. There was a proposal for a monument
to Hans von Bülow in Hamburg, but Brahms was against it and refused
to contribute: a performer, who leaves nothing behind, is not entitled to
a monument.[75] Brahms would make the same point in objecting to a
Bülow memorial in Vienna: "There's not even a monument to Wagner
yet!"

If he had a performance to give he would put off getting ready, sitting
talking with Clara and family and their guests until Marie Schumann
prompted, "Herr Brahms, you really must practise now or you won't play
properly at the concert." He would rise obediently and trudge into the
next room, stick a cigar between his teeth, and play pealing arpeggios
from one end of the keyboard to the other. "Interesting as this playing
was," Eugenie recalled, "there was always something of a fight or ani-
mosity about it. I do not believe that Brahms looked upon the piano as a
dear, trusted friend, as my mother did, but considered it a necessary evil."
Often in the morning Eugenie came into the dining room to find Brahms
sitting amid clouds of tobacco smoke, and her mother with glowing eyes
and a beautiful smile. After so many years and so much pain between
them, Clara still looked young when Brahms was around.

There were the shadowed moments too, the explosions from some
deep wellspring of sorrow and loneliness. One day he burst out in inexplicable fury to the family who were his dearest friends: "I have no
friends! If anybody tells you he is my friend, don't believe him!" Everyone was speechless. Finally Eugenie said, "But, Herr Brahms, friends are
the best gift in this world. Why should you resent them?" He looked at
her with wide haunted eyes and said nothing.[76]

During the November 1894 visit Ferdinand watched one of the marvelous hours, Brahms playing over a new clarinet sonata with Mühlfeld.
Clara sat beside Johannes, turning the pages. After each movement they
waited for her expressions of pleasure, then Brahms would politely ask,
"Shall we go on?" and she would nod with a smile. That night at the end

of the all-Brahms orchestral concert there was, recalled Ferdinand, a "hurricane of applause, thunderous bravos and cheers. The orchestra played a fanfare."

The year 1895 added to the list of all-Brahms celebrations. After one in Leipzig in January, which included the clarinet sonatas played by Mühlfeld and both piano concertos by Eugen d'Albert, Brahms wrote Clara that it was "really one of the most pleasant concert adventures that I have ever had." This was in the new Gewandhaus, not the one in which the D Minor Piano Concerto had found the worst fiasco of his life. Surely now the noisy success of the D Minor Concerto anywhere in that town was especially gratifying to him. He had always resented Leipzig, and on the whole the city and its musicians had responded in kind. This time the critic of the *Signale*, the very same who in 1859 had declared the D Minor premiered "to the grave," felt obliged to report "what can only be described as extravagant homage" from the Leipzigers.

In February Brahms was back with Clara in Frankfurt for more concerts, this time in ill humor. Clara could not stand his piano playing in the clarinet sonatas, and as the applause at the end of the concert pealed on and on, he made a scene in the curtain call: when as an attempt at homage the first violinist refused to take a bow with him he physically ejected another player out the stage door ahead of him. The audience laughed, but the performers were outraged at Brahms, and he with them.[77] Everybody swore never to play together again.

The next month he led the Gesellschaft der Musikfreunde Conservatory Orchestra in the Academic Festival Overture, part of a concert to mark the twenty-fifth anniversary of the Musikverein. As he conducted the piece in the Golden Hall, Max Kalbeck saw him over and over press his left hand to his breast, meaning: From the heart, from the heart![78] It was the last time he conducted in Vienna.

On his birthday in May, Brahms, Heuberger, and other friends from the Tonkünstlerverein took in a famous gypsy band at the Prater. Brahms greeted the men like colleagues and praised them extravagantly; clearly the band recognized him, and gave him a verse of "Hoch soll er leben!"— "Long may he live!" After dinner the friends indulged in the amusements of the Wurstlprater, ending around midnight with the big slide and the haunted house. On the way home Brahms outdistanced his companions and drew Heuberger with him, to rave about a new collection of Bismarck's speeches he was reading: "And most of it is impromptu . . . an improvisation. A colossal spirit! And eighty years old!" Wilhelm II had fired the Iron Chancellor in 1890, but neither Brahms's loyalty to the

Prussian throne nor his admiration for Bismarck had flagged. He would pore over the speeches for the rest of his life.

His days now seemed to be a cheerful skipping from celebration to acclamation, but through it all he carried abiding apprehensions. The day before he left for Ischl in midmonth there was a somber gathering of the Brahms circle at Zum roten Igel. The Christian Socialists under Karl Lueger had just won the election, ending the long liberal rule once and for all. Lueger had been elected vice-mayor of Vienna as the summit of a brilliant political career that mixed populism, socialism, and pandering to the antisemitic instincts of both the working class and the German-speaking Catholics and aristocrats. With Lueger's victory, successful politics in Austria became antisemitic by definition, from then until Hitler.

In fact, Emperor Franz Josef would refuse to allow Lueger to take office as mayor until he had been elected five times. But that night of May 1895 in the Igel, when Lueger had become vice-mayor and sooner or later was inevitably going to ascend to power, Brahms barked across the table to his friends: "Didn't I tell you years ago that it was going to happen? You laughed at me then and everybody else did too. Now it's here, and with it the priests' economic system. If there was an 'Anticlerical Party'—that would make sense! But antisemitism is madness!"[79]

CHAPTER TWENTY-THREE

Who Shall Bring Him to That Place?

IF BRAHMS COMPOSED ANYTHING in Bad Ischl in the summer of 1895, he did not talk about it. He may have been working on a series of organ preludes, but that year would be the first since 1872 that he released nothing. The recent deaths of friends weighed on him, along with the labors and wounds of a long life in the public gaze. One day as he and Heuberger dined, Brahms was reminiscing about his father's second marriage when suddenly he clutched his fist to his heart and groaned, "Apart from Frau Schumann I'm not attached to anybody with my whole soul! And truly that is terrible and one should neither think such a thing nor say it. Is that not a lonely life! Yet we can't believe in immortality on the other side. The only true immortality lies in one's children."

Calming, he spoke of the Schumanns: "It's the most beautiful memory of my life, to have been close to these two beautiful people, to have known them so well. And today Frau Schumann is as fresh, as virginal as ever." He spoke of Jean Paul's novels: "Enchanting ideas, splendid anecdotes, endless wisdom about life!" Young people today don't know them well enough.[1] At home he still kept the notebook from his teenage years, "Des jungen Kreislers Schatzkästlein," filled with quotes copied from Jean Paul and his other Romantic icons.

In September he went up to Viktor Miller's villa in Gmunden to celebrate Eduard Hanslick's seventieth birthday. It was a moving occasion for the circle who gathered there. Brahms and Hanslick had been *Duzenbrüder* for over thirty years, during which they had sustained an unprecedented partnership for an artist and a critic. During that time, Hanslick had taken it upon himself to lead the Brahmsians, to uphold the antipope to Wagner even as his pope steadfastly refused to take the throne. Together they had resisted Bruckner, but Hanslick had stood alone against Wagner while Brahms stood apart.

One of the most famous musical caricatures of the nineteenth century shows Hanslick as an acolyte swinging a censer before Brahms, who is installed on a pedestal and decked out as Pope. In the picture Brahms looks impassively into the distance, raising one hand in benediction, the other hand holding the Messiah's palm branch. His pedestal is worn and chipped. Year after year the critic and acolyte had pulled his punches and bit his tongue when he did not like his hero's music. For his part, Brahms had let the critic fight battles for his benefit, and bit his tongue so as not to speak too plainly that he believed Hanslick could not understand his music. For three decades they had sustained that peculiar partnership, and for each other a genuine affection.

Brahms was mostly on good behavior at the dinner. Conservatory Professor Anton Door gave a long meandering speech full of superlatives. When he declared that Hanslick's knowledge stretched from Brahms backward to Bach, Brahms was heard to mutter into his beard, "You must mean Offenbach."[2] In his toast to Hanslick, Brahms said some things he had planned (he had written them to Clara a couple of weeks before), his words surely addressed both to those present and to history. For history above all, he wanted to commend his friend and their friendship, and at the same time to distance himself from his best champion. In a choked voice Brahms made his toast:

> We men very rarely have occasion to say tender sorts of things to each other, and the occasion must be unusual for that to happen. But today's celebration is such an occasion. I can say that in my rather long life I have rarely known anyone so consistently faithful, honest, clever, and good as our beloved Hanslick. We all know that he has his weaknesses. His great weakness is the one sitting next to him [Hanslick's considerably younger wife]. But apart from such defects he is quite a man, a splendid fellow, and despite our pronounced tendencies to take different paths—so little do many things interest him that please me, and vice versa—I can only say that I have scarcely known a more discerning and upright man. . . .

At that point tears overcame him and he could only get out, "Well, here's to long life!" Blubbering, the two fat old men awkwardly hugged. Somebody began to play the little Waltzes Opus 39, the only thing Brahms had ever dedicated to the critic. At the end there was another embrace and Hanslick rasped, "God be with you, you old beast!"[3]

From Ischl, Brahms went to Meiningen for a grand festival of the "Three B's," then to Clara in Frankfurt for a quick visit, only a day. He was in splendid form, smoking and storytelling and opinionating for hours. Meiningen had been very fine, he said, with some wonderful renditions of his songs. He no longer composed for the public, only for himself. After all, the clarinet music notwithstanding, you can only create until your fiftieth year, then the ideas begin to run out. In the evening there were many songs and much laughter.

Next morning Eugenie heard the sound of the piano from the music room. It was Bach, followed by two pieces from Brahms's Opus 118, music he had written to sustain Clara, and which she loved. When the music stopped Eugenie went into the room and found her mother at her writing table, her cheeks flushed and eyes shining, and Brahms sitting opposite her with tears in his eyes. Gently he said to Eugenie, "Your mother has been playing most beautifully for me."

After a moment he asked Eugenie to get a particular volume of Beethoven Sonatas from the shelf. In it he pointed out a place where Clara had long ago corrected a mistake that had appeared in every edition. "No other musician has an ear like that," he said.

It came time to say good-bye, his train was due. They embraced and kissed, as always. Brahms had dispatched young Ferdinand to get him some of his favorite Caporal tobacco and packs of cigarette paper. When her grandson arrived with the goods and Brahms was stuffing them in his bag, Clara asked Johannes what he was going to do with all that tobacco.

"Smuggle it through, Clara!" he said laughing, and set off for the train. They never saw each other again.[4]

IN OCTOBER, Brahms went to Zürich to conduct the *Triumphlied* for the inauguration of the new Tonhalle. Looking up at the paintings on the ceiling, he saw portraits of Beethoven, Bach, Mozart, and himself. On December 1 there was a performance of the First Symphony by Hans Richter and the Philharmonic. Suspecting what was going to happen— the piece had never gone over well in Vienna—Brahms went for a walk during the concert. Heuberger reported that it had been "bad, without understanding, and unpoetically played." Brahms replied bitterly, "Well, if my symphony were really such insipid stuff, so gray and mezzoforte as Richter performed it for people today, then the people who speak of the 'brooding, melancholy Brahms' would be right."[5]

A couple of weeks later there was a dinner in Zum roten Igel with Mandyczewski and Antonín Dvořák, who regaled them with stories from the two years he had just spent in America. (The following February, Richter's Vienna premiere of Dvořák's *New World Symphony* would make a sensation.) While Dvořák was away, Brahms had edited his music for Simrock. Here and there he discreetly cleaned up his careless Czech friend's counterpoint.

Another holiday, lighting the tree on Christmas Eve with Frau Truxa and the boys, next day dinner at the Fellingers. And then it was 1896. That year Alban Berg was eleven, Anton Webern thirteen, Igor Stravinsky fourteen, Béla Bartók fifteen, Charles Ives twenty-two, Claude Debussy thirty-four, and Gustav Mahler thirty-six. Brahms was sixty-three, Joseph Joachim sixty-five, Karl Goldmark sixty-six, Theodor Kirchner seventy-three, and Giuseppe Verdi eighty-three. That year Richard Strauss wrote *Also sprach Zarathustra*, Mahler his Third Symphony, and Puccini *La Bohème*. And Arnold Schoenberg, at age twenty-two, composed his D Major String Quartet.

On a visit, Alexander von Zemlinsky showed Brahms the Schoenberg quartet. (Zemlinsky had become something like the mentor for Schoenberg that Brahms had been for Zemlinsky.) The old man was intrigued with the music and asked about this new name. Zemlinsky said that for years this promising composer had been doing workaday musical copying and arranging to get by. Immediately Brahms offered to supply him with a stipend to study at the Conservatory. When Zemlinsky went to Schoenberg with the offer, the young man proudly turned it down.[6]

Schoenberg must have seen the old-fashioned figure of Brahms in the streets and concert halls of Vienna, but there is no record that he ever shook Brahms's hand. In his creative maturity, just a decade and a half from then, Schoenberg would challenge much of what Brahms believed to be eternal in music: tonality, lyric melody, an abiding loyalty to the bourgeois audience. All of it changed under the assaults of Schoenberg, his pupils Webern and Berg, his followers, his time. Yet Schoenberg the revolutionary would declare himself a traditionalist, and count himself among the most devoted students of Brahms in his time, the first to declare Brahms deeply relevant to the twentieth century and thus to Modernism. If Brahms accurately prophesied the ruin of his ideals, he could not have prophesied that his own innovations would help shape the revolution.

In the middle of January 1896, Brahms conducted the two piano concertos with Eugen d'Albert and the Berlin Philharmonic—another milestone, his last appearance anywhere as a conductor. At a dinner hosted by Joachim the violinist was trying to propose a toast, "To the greatest composer . . ." when Brahms jumped up and shouted, "Quite right, here's to Mozart's health!" and went around clinking everyone's glass.[7]

In that trip to Berlin, Brahms also visited a new friend, the eminent historical painter Adolph von Menzel. Brahms had met him in Berlin, at the premiere of the clarinet pieces. In 1854, Menzel had sketched the young Joachim playing a recital with Clara Schumann. In 1891 he sketched Mühlfeld in the premiere of the Clarinet Trio and Quintet, making him look a sort of Greek demigod, and sent the drawing to Brahms with a note: "We often think of you here, and . . . we confess our suspicions that on a certain night the Muse itself appeared in person (disguised in the evening dress of the Meiningen Court) for the purpose of executing a certain woodwind part. On this page I tried to capture the sublime vision." Both Menzel and Brahms sported the high Prussian order "Pour le Mérite." Brahms was charmed not only by the art but the artist, scampish and indefatigable in his late seventies, who could keep up with anyone at eating and drinking and banter. Menzel's nephew wrote Brahms after a visit in 1892, "We have never yet had such fine and enjoyable carousals as those of the December days when you were with us."[8] Menzel may have represented the joie de vivre Brahms aspired to in his next decade, if in fact he aspired to live that long.

FRIEND MARIE RÜCKERT SAID that in these years Brahms looked like a lion from the front, from the rear—in his characteristic walking pose of arms cocked behind his back—like a loafing literary man. In Vienna he appeared antiquated, a figure from the past: his black clothes, hefty frame (it was something of a strain for him now to reach past his belly to the keys), bowler hat, and pince-nez stood out from the more fashionable, trimmer clothes and figures of his younger friends.

Among those friends was newspaper critic Max Kalbeck, who had been part of the circle for years. Surely Brahms, who had set a couple of Kalbeck's early poems, viewed this young journalist as a candidate for a biographer. So it turned out: the four dense, rambling volumes Kalbeck produced in the first decades of the next century would be the perennial source of information on the composer. As he had with Widmann, Brahms may have groomed Kalbeck for the job. At the same time, Kalbeck made an ideal contribution to the Brahms entourage—witty, articulate, dashingly handsome, selflessly devoted. Richard Specht wrote that Max was "ready to go with [Brahms] through thick and thin, to love what he loved . . . , to hate what he hated, and to follow him and his work unconditionally."[9]

Brahms treated this devotee with a mingling of kindness, concern, and backhanded contempt. Specht was present for a dinner at Ignaz Brüll's when Kalbeck was rhapsodizing on Cherubini as an opera composer, at the expense of Wagner. He become so caught up in his eloquence that he did not notice Brahms's color rising, until suddenly the master smashed his fist on the table and shouted, "For God's sake, Kalbeck, don't talk about things you can't understand!" Kalbeck went pale and left without a word. A few days later Specht ran into him on the street. "What do you think of what I have to put up with?" Kalbeck said. "This is my reward for years of work and faithful friendship and active devotion! But this time I didn't pocket the revered master's insults: I wrote him a long letter and told him exactly what I think of him." Specht was naturally curious to know Brahms's reaction. Kalbeck smiled sadly. "Oh, well, I never mailed him the letter."[10]

They all knew that Brahms admired Cherubini as well as Wagner. The explosion at Kalbeck had simply been his contrariness, his obliviousness, his compulsion to put an acolyte in his place. Forty years before it had been Joachim who wrote, "Brahms is egoism incarnate. He knows the weaknesses of the people around him, and he makes use of them, and then does not hesitate to show . . . that he is crowing over them."[11] In old age, Brahms was unchanged. Usually he was forgiven for the same reasons Joachim forgave him: his essential honesty and decency, his genius.

With friends Brahms pored over his life and career, his upbringing and education, his fears for the future. In February 1896, as he and Richard Heuberger waited for the train back to town after a walk in the Vienna Woods, Brahms rambled on. He spoke of Haydn, who after a lifetime of indefatigable production wrote the expansive oratorios *The Creation* and *The Seasons* at the age Brahms was now:

> *That* was a man indeed! How miserable we are in comparison to something like that! And if you ask the reason why everything is going to the devil today . . . it's due to those who won't learn anything. If there's somebody with a little talent here and there, he certainly won't learn anything. Even the better ones are like that. Neither Schumann nor Wagner nor I learned anything right. Talent was the decisive thing. Schumann went one way, Wagner the other, I the third way. Yet none of us learned what was right. None had correct schooling.—Ja, *afterwards* we learned.[12]

By "school," scholar Imogen Fellinger speculates, Brahms apparently meant "standing in a continuity of tradition," and also a mastery of musical technique, above all the rules and regulations and lapidary skills of counterpoint. Brahms envied Mendelssohn's training; having the best teacher in town brought to the house every day to drill the boy in counterpoint and form from the examples of Bach and Mozart, the teenager writing fugues and quartets and symphonies that his parents hired the finest musicians to play. *That* was learning, that was a school! "What indescribable efforts it has cost me to recover this lost ground," Brahms said to Heuberger.[13] "Look at France, were a *school* exists to this day. . . . Cherubini was the great master from whom everything had proceeded, beside him the excellent Halévy, then Auber, who also mastered his craft to a remarkable degree." Maybe Heuberger did not know what Brahms omitted: that he saw himself as another Cherubini, his work doomed to be obliterated by the decline of schooling, of art itself.

The train approached. "Really, I don't know where music is coming from," Brahms concluded painfully to his young friend. "It seems to me it will completely stop!" On the way home, relenting a little, he praised the fugues of Julius Röntgen. And of course there was Dvořák, "a spontaneous talent, who knows from inside himself what's right. That belongs on its own page!"[14]

That March, Clara wrote in her journal, "My evenings are terrible. I am always so exhausted that I can hardly hold up my head, and the pain and sickness are dreadful. . . . Poor Marie tends me morning and evening, and weeps with me when I am miserable." On the twenty-sixth she had a slight stroke.[15]

In the same month, Brahms, Dvořák, Röntgen, and others of the circle sat in the director's box of the Musikverein for a Grieg concert. (Backstage when Heuberger told the Norwegian that Brahms admired his piano-playing, Grieg sighed, "Oh, that's just one of his stupid jokes."[16]) During Dvořák's visit Brahms tried to persuade him to move to Vienna and teach at the Conservatory, to be a buttress against the encroaching decline: "Look here, Dvořák, you have a lot of children, and I have practically no one dependent on me. If you need anything, my fortune is at your disposal." Though he was deeply touched by the offer, Dvořák could not bring himself to leave his beloved Bohemia for Germanic territories.

As the two of them talked, Brahms rambled on about his agnosticism, his growing interest in Schopenhauer the philosopher of pessimism (Wagner's favorite). On the way back to his hotel with violinist Josef Suk, Dvořák was thoughtful and silent. Suddenly he exclaimed with real anguish, "Such a man, such a fine soul—and he believes in nothing! He believes in nothing!"[17]

．　　．　　．

WHEN BRAHMS HEARD from Marie Schumann of Clara's stroke he wrote, "What a fright your mother has given us. I must ask you, if you think the worst is to be expected, to be so good as to let me know, so that I may come while those dear eyes are still open; for when they close so much will end for me!"[18]

The prospect long dreaded was at hand. Clara the indestructible was sinking. A few days after her stroke Brahms heard from his old friend Julius Grimm that his wife, "Pine Gur," of the days in Göttingen with Agathe von Siebold, had died. Brahms wrote a short, concise note to Grimm. He was getting very experienced with letters of consolation.

Yet at his sixty-third birthday celebration in the garden salon of Zum Hirschen he was jolly and tipsy among friends from the Tonkünstlerverein. Brahms said he enjoyed the "pathos-free, gay tone" of the occasion, and after the usual ironic encomiums and toasts he made a wry little speech himself, in honor of the Verein board and "the beautiful pianists who have played and *not* played, the singers who sang and the young composers who have brought their first works to performance" in the year's concerts.[19] In later life everyone there treasured the memory of that evening, because there were no more like it.

He received a muddled birthday greeting from bedridden Clara: "Heartiest good wishes from your affectionate and devoted Clara Schumann. I cannot very well do anything more yet, but or soon Your—."[20]

In the middle of May, Brahms made his seasonal pilgrimage to Bad Ischl. When he arrived at the Attnang junction at lunchtime, the chef of the train station emerged to say, "Herr Doktor, we have reserved the Salzburger Nockerlin for you!" Brahms was befuddled but pleased. Heuberger had arranged by letter the treat of a favorite dish, roast pork with plenty of fat, and dumplings.[21]

Brahms arrived in Ischl carrying the manuscript of four lieder he had drafted in the first week of May, just after the news of Clara's stroke. He called them *Vier ernste Gesänge* (*Four Serious Songs*), for low voice and piano. The texts are scriptural meditations on death, but still he called them *serious*, not *sacred*. To friends, with his usual irony, he dubbed them his "godless *Schnadahüpferln*," meaning pagan harvest revels, yodeling ditties. In public he always denied that he had written them about Clara, and he dedicated them to artist Max Klinger, who had lost his father.

But in reality they are about Clara, who was the main thing on Brahms's mind in those weeks. Later he admitted it privately when he played through the songs with Heuberger in Ischl: "They have to do with [Frau] Schumann. I didn't exactly compose them on the occasion of her death, but the whole time I've been thinking about death, on which I have very, very often had opportunity to reflect! I wrote the lieder in May. I wanted to give myself something for my birthday! Don't tell anybody . . . that I wrote the songs on the occasion of her death. I also don't like to hear that I wrote the Requiem for my mother!"[22]

With the *Vier ernste Gesänge* Brahms once more found words from Luther's translation of Scripture to speak for him, this time out of the secret recesses of his heart. In public, shrouding his feelings was second nature to him. Rarely did any tragedy or terror stop the flow of his garrulousness, the lusty appetite for food and drink and laughs, the evenings in the brothels. The real feelings he saved for his music, and usually there he sank them deep. But not this time, even though he would still wrap his grief in the highest perfection his craft was capable of.

For the purpose he once more invented a new kind of piece, but an invention erected firmly on his and his culture's past. Malcolm MacDonald says that the *Vier ernste Gesänge* "extend the Lied tradition to accommodate the searching ethical idealism previously explored in his sacred choral works, particularly the *Requiem* and the motets."[23] The whole course of Brahms's life and art resound in these four somber and deceptively straightforward death chants.

The first one returns to the bardic Brahmsian minor, his *Dies Irae* that in the *Requiem* set "For all flesh, it is as grass." Here in quiet phrases is another stark and relentless funeral dirge like those from his youth. In a larger sense it may be said to stand for *the past:*

> *For it goes with man as with the beast;*
> *as that dies, so dies he also;*
> *and they have all the same breath;*
> *and man has nothing more than the beast;*
> *for all is vanity.*

Then, allegro in a swirling of dust, death overtakes mankind and there is no reassurance:

> *All are taken to the same place;*
> *it is all made of dust*
> *and goes back to dust.*

Who knows if the spirit of man ascends upward,
and that of the beast descends into the earth?

Brahms had said to Richard Heuberger that the only real immortality is in one's children. His works were his children, and he despaired for them. Yet his work had been all he truly possessed.

Therefore I saw, that there is nothing better,
than that man should be happy in his work;
for that is his lot.

For who shall bring him to that place
where he may see what shall come after him?

Call the second song *the present*. What Brahms saw in the present, for himself, for Vienna, for humanity, was terrifying. Austria was succumbing to a ferocious mythology of blood and authoritarianism under the cloak of populism, all of it fed by an evil wellspring of hatred. *Antisemitism is madness!* Brahms had cried. From all the madness, he could not know when or how, rivers of blood would flow. For all its gentleness, his second Serious Song is suffused with that prophecy, and with compassion for the victims to come.

I turned and looked on all who suffer oppression under the sun:
and behold, there were tears from those
who suffered oppression, and had no savior;
and those who oppressed them were so mighty,
that they could find no savior.

Then I praised the dead . . .
more than the living,
who still have life.

Years before, when Amalie and Joseph Joachim had a son, Brahms had written them before he could stop his pen: "One can hardly in the event wish for him the best of all wishes, not to be born at all."

And he who has never been . . .

(There is a terrifying silence, then a single low tone in the bass:)

is better off than both,
and is not conscious of the evil
that happens under the sun.

The third song is in a stark E minor, the key and the very pitches of
the chain of thirds that begin the Fourth Symphony. Technically the music is a distillation of minute thematic relationships in three dimensions:
melody becoming counterpoint and harmony and form, and so erasing
the divisions between them.

Call this song *the future:* what happens to all, what is about to happen
to Clara Schumann to end her years of suffering.

> *O Death,*
> *O Death how bitter art thou*
> *when on thee thinks the man*
> *who has good days and wherewithal,*
> *and lives without sorrow . . .*

Into the accompaniment comes the pattern C-B-A-G♯-A, Robert
Schumann's Clara theme, the musical cabala that Brahms had inherited
and used in the days when he loved Clara as a young man loves. At the
same time the descending thirds of the beginning are turned upward to
rising sixths in a hopeful E major. With Clara's name in the accompaniment, these words:

> *O Death, how well you comfort the needy one*
> *who is feeble and old,*
> *and mired in trouble,*
> *and has nothing better to hope, or to expect!*
> *O Death, how well you comfort!*

In the last song we find Brahms's final word—if not quite that in tones,
his final message to the world and to himself. We have heard songs of
past, present, and future. He concludes as one speaking to all time a consolation to the bereaved—as in the *Requiem,* without illusions of eternal
life. Antonin Dvořák said Brahms believed in nothing. Speaking in a later
and more skeptical age, conductor Wilhelm Furtwängler said Brahms
proclaimed "that there can be no development without man, beyond
man. As a result he became the arch-enemy of all illusions."[24] In Dvořák's
terms, the terms of religion as he knew it, Brahms did not believe. But
what Brahms expressed in this last song, setting Paul's words from the
Gospels, was nonetheless a credo for himself and as best as he knew, for
humanity, without illusions. For himself, however, it was a despairing
testament.

It begins in E♭ major with almost an ardent sweep, a little rhetorical like the gallant love songs in *Magelone*. But gradually that theme, and that sense of love, fall into tenderness and meditation: Youth becomes age, *eros* melts into *agape*.

> *Though I speak with the tongues of men and of angels,*
> *and have not love,*
> *so I would be like sounding brass,*
> *or a tinkling cymbal.*

(Brahms says in that: *without love, music is empty*.)

> *And though I could prophesy*
> *and understand all mysteries and all knowledge,*
> *and have all faith,*
> *even if I could move mountains,*
> *and have not love,*
> *so I am nothing . . .*

> *We see now through a mirror in a dark word;*
> *but then: face to face.*
> *Now know I in part;*
> *but then shall I know, as I am known.*

> *For now, though, remain faith, hope, love, these three;*
> *but love is the greatest of them.*

With those words, set to a gently lilting three-beat, Brahms took his leave of music.

For himself it was a far more tragic leave-taking. Clara was dying: Clara whom he would not marry but could never let go. He had clutched his heart and cried out to Richard Heuberger: "Apart from Frau Schumann I'm not attached to anybody with my whole soul! And truly that is terrible and one should neither think such a thing nor say it! Is that not a lonely life! Yet we can't believe in immortality."

For Brahms, love had the face of Clara Schumann, his strange and eternal bride, his art and his life. When she died, love would die for him, and for him then music would be no more than sounding brass and tinkling cymbal. And so he would be nothing.

·   ·   ·

THE TELEGRAM came to Vienna on May 20, 1896, from Marie Schumann: "Our mother fell gently asleep today." Clara had lingered since suffering a devastating second stroke on the night of the sixteenth. Earlier that afternoon, the last music she had heard was Robert's, played by his grandson Ferdinand. Her last intelligible words, spoken to her daughter: "Poor Marie, you two must go to a beautiful place this summer."[25]

The telegram set in motion a series of horrifying mistakes. Brahms's housekeeper Frau Truxa, not realizing what the telegram contained, forwarded it to Ischl by mail. When he received it two days later, Brahms had only an hour to get on the train for Frankfurt, where he assumed the funeral service would be held. Exhausted, he decided to nap on the train and asked the conductor to wake him at Attnang, where he had to catch his connection. The conductor forgot and Brahms woke up to find himself speeding in the wrong direction. He was forced to wait all night in the Linz station for the next train. Finally after a full day's travel he got to Frankfurt, only to find that the funeral was in Bonn, where Clara would be buried beside Robert. After a nightmare journey of over forty hours he arrived nearly prostrate in Bonn the next day. They had delayed the funeral, waiting for him, but when he arrived the procession to the grave was underway.[26]

Instead of joining the procession, Brahms stumbled behind some funeral wreaths, fell on the neck of his friend Rudolf von der Leyen, and sobbed.[27] Finally he recovered enough to throw three handfuls of earth into Clara's grave, next to her husband's where Brahms had also thrown his handfuls, under the Schumann monument he had helped consecrate.

Afterward he visited von der Leyen and other friends for nearly a week, joining in an ongoing musical memorial for Clara. He said to Alwin von Beckerath, "Now I have nobody left to lose."[28] For a collection of friends, he played and sang though the *Vier ernste Gesänge* with tears streaming down his face. He could never bring himself to hear them sung in public.

Brahms returned to Ischl apparently in fair spirits and good appetite, but friends became concerned over his appearance. He looked ill, his skin yellowish. But he got down to work again, now at some chorale preludes for organ that he perhaps never intended to publish. Concerned about Marie and Eugenie Schumann, who had never married and lived with their mother until the end, he wrote Marie Fellinger, "Neither young nor healthy, the poor maidens sit alone in that big house."[29] In July he sent Marie the *Vier ernste Gesänge*, saying,

These songs really concern you very closely. I wrote them in the first week of May. Some such words as these have long been in my mind, and I did not think that worse news about your mother was to be expected—but deep in the heart of man something often whispers and stirs, quite unconsciously perhaps, which in time may ring out in the form of poetry or music. You will not be able to play the songs yet, because the words would affect you too much, but I beg you to regard them and to lay them aside merely as a death offering to the memory of your dear mother.[30]

It may have been that July when Gustav Mahler, recently through Brahms's influence appointed to the Vienna Hofoper, made a visit to Ischl that lives in legend—because of a quip, but one that said much about the divide between Brahms's generation and the next. As they walked along the River Traun, Brahms was singing his familiar refrain: music was going to the devil, after he was dead it would be finished once and for all. Suddenly Mahler took Brahms's arm and gestured excitedly toward the river, exclaiming, "Look, Doktor, just look!"

"What is it?" Brahms said, taking the bait.

"Don't you see?" said Mahler. "There goes the last wave!"

Maybe that got a cheerless chuckle from Brahms. He said only, "That's all very fine, but maybe what matters is whether the wave goes into the sea or into a swamp."[31] By then, with his usual meticulous care he had studied the score of Mahler's Second Symphony. That work, with its glowing instrumentation and grandiose Brahmsian close, perhaps intrigued him at the same time as it made him shudder. Yet the second movement, the scherzo with its juxtaposition of the ecstatic and grotesque, Brahms declared a work of genius—a term he did not use lightly. But he also said, "I used to think Richard Strauss was the Chief of the Insurrectionists, but now I see it's Mahler."

As Mahler left from that last visit to Ischl, he glanced through the window to have one more look at Brahms. He saw the old man wearily taking a sausage and a slice of bread from the stove for his lunch. It all comes to this, Mahler thought.[32]

Brahms's other break from Ischl that summer was a quick trip to Vienna in July, for the silver anniversary of Maria and Richard Fellinger. There are photographs of Brahms in the Fellingers' garden during the party. He looks just detectably shrunken and strained. The exhaustion he had felt at Clara's funeral lingered through the summer. One hot day he walked eight miles from Ischl to Steg, further than he had intended, then turned around and walked back most of the way. That night he felt so sick he thought he was going to die; he passed out again and again.

Still, he seemed stunned in July when Richard Heuberger confronted him, saying his eyes and skin looked yellowish and he must see a doctor. Brahms had rarely visited a doctor in his life, though he had submitted to a dentist to have his upper teeth pulled and a plate made. He put up a brief resistance, then held his head in his hands and said to Heuberger, "I'm no hypochondriac. . . . Nobody has told me that I seem to be altered. I thank you from my heart. You know I don't like to have anything to do with doctors, but if it's something serious, it ought to be looked at. But it's annoying . . . the few years one has left to live . . . and to go to the doctor!"

Three weeks later, at the end of July, Brahms called on Dr. Hertzka in Ischl. He received a diagnosis of jaundice and an order to take a cure in Karlsbad. The doctor also placed him on a strict diet.

"But no goulash?" Brahms asked anxiously.

"Absolutely not!"

"Really?" Brahms groaned, but added slyly, "Then I'm going to tell people I didn't see you till tomorrow, and eat goulash at the Eibenschützes' today—after all, it was cooked especially for me."[33]

Protesting, he made his reservation in Karlsbad. With his healthy man's habit of seeing illness as a sort of moral failure, Brahms dubbed his condition "my petit-bourgeois jaundice." Visiting Viktor Miller's villa just before he saw the doctor, Brahms seemed in high spirits: in a photo he stands between two laughing attractive women, Viktor's wife Olga and their daughter, brandishing his cigar and looking roguish.

He stopped off in Vienna, then headed for Karlsbad in early September. The petit-bourgeois jaundice had gotten worse. He arrived in Karlsbad feeling poorly on September 3, then seemed to respond to the cure and the scene. Soon he was working at the organ chorale preludes and writing letters to friends in his vacation mode. To Hanslick: "I am grateful to my jaundice for having at last brought me to famous Karlsbad. I was at once greeted by glorious weather. . . . What is more, I have an absolutely charming lodging."[34] To Widmann: "My indisposition need not make you in the least uneasy: it is quite a commonplace jaundice, which unfortunately has the idiosyncrasy of not wanting to go away. But it has no further significance, as affirmed by the doctors. . . . Besides, I have not had pain or suchlike for a single day—nor even lost my appetite for a single meal."[35]

In Vienna that autumn Richard Heuberger ran into Dr. Schrötter, a specialist who had earlier examined Brahms. The doctor kept shaking his head saying, "Poor fellow! Poor fellow!" When Heuberger said that Brahms was in Karlsbad taking a cure, the doctor could only respond, "For Brahms's illness there is no Karlsbad! It doesn't make any difference where he spends his money!"[36]

At the resort Brahms consulted a Dr. Grünberger. The physician asked to examine him a second time, privately hoping it was not as bad as it looked. The second examination confirmed his worst fears. On September 3, 1896, the doctor noted in his book: "Hr. Johannes Brahms— Wien. hep. hyp. m." It stands for *hepatitis hypertrophia maligna*, cancer of the liver. The same had killed Johann Jakob Brahms.[37] The doctor did not reveal the diagnosis to his patient, who had expressly requested, Widmann reports, "on no account to tell him anything unpleasant."[38]

At the same time it is clear that soon enough Brahms came to understand that he was under a death sentence. There were many evidences of it, but the most poignant were his neo-Baroque choral preludes for organ, eventually eleven, part of a larger planned set that he never finished composing. Most of the old chorales on which he based the pieces concern death, and two are based on "O Welt, ich muss dich lassen": "O world, I must leave thee." The preludes would be found in his apartment after he died.

He returned to Vienna at the beginning of October, trying to convince himself he was on the mend. He told everyone he could not be getting thinner because his clothes fit just the same. In fact, his housekeeper Frau Truxa had quietly been taking them up, in hopes he would not notice how much weight he was losing. Most of the time, he felt miserable.

On October 11, Anton Bruckner died. Wearily, Brahms descended the stairs to attend the funeral next door at the Karlskirche. He arrived to be told he was late and the church full. An attendant offered to let him in, but Brahms shook his head and turned away, muttering, it is said, "Never mind. Soon my coffin."

His condition went up and down, inevitably more down than up. On some occasions he was his old joking self in company, at other times subdued, drifting, visibly in pain though he rarely admitted it. He continued through the autumn to try to put the best face on his condition. At a dinner in October he reported to Heuberger that he felt better, was eating and drinking fine, and the doctor had permitted him half a bottle of champagne at night to help him sleep. "I'm fit as a fiddle . . . if I'm a little yellow, it's all the same to me!" he proclaimed, and struck the table hard enough to make the plates rattle. When Anton Sistermans premiered the *Vier ernste Gesänge* in Vienna in November, however, Brahms stayed away.

Then he began joking about losing weight, saying he had exchanged his rounded Romanesque physique for a pointed Gothic arch. In fact he looked wretched: gaunt, eyes yellow, skin yellow going to brown and papery. Eventually his complexion became almost ivy-green. He told Kalbeck that at home he kept the piano closed most of the time, never played or listened to music anymore, just sat and read through Bach scores. He needed company more than ever. He dined out steadily with friends old and new—the Fellingers, Fabers, Millers, Kalbecks, Heubergers, a number of others, all of them leading figures in the business and artistic *Grossbürgertum* of Vienna. He continued to attend concerts, trying to convince himself and everybody else that everything was as always. But now he sometimes fell asleep at table or in the theater box.

Brahms's incapacity to face his dying straight on was more than being unused to illness. Dying was the first thing in his adult life he had not been able to figure out, to conquer by force of will, or to flee. At least one day during those months he was practical enough to spend several hours with the Fellingers discussing a new will to replace one he had written at Ischl in 1891, in the form of a letter to Fritz Simrock. Since then his sister and his cousin Christian Detmering had died, so he needed to make changes in the disposition of his estate.

Fellinger drafted a new will with all his requirements. Brahms needed only to copy it out, date it, and sign. Instead, heading out for a dinner when Fellinger arrived with the draft, Brahms stuck it in a drawer and never got around to signing it. The result would be eighteen years of litigation over his estate, with distant relatives as far away as Chicago making claims on it.[39] He always said he was no good with finances; here was the proof. Eventually most of the money—some 50,000 crowns—was parceled out to those relatives, not to his stepbrother Fritz Schnack as Brahms had intended. His scores, historic manuscripts, library, and what papers were left went mostly to the Gesellschaft der Musikfreunde, as he had wished. Eventually the papers included many letters he had asked to be destroyed or returned to the senders.

He knew he was dying and he didn't want to know. Everyone played along with the game. Yet it was unmistakable that something had gone out of him. Though much of the shoptalk and gossip and conviviality was the same, he had gone limp, inside and out. As symptom he became kindlier, at one point exclaiming in wonder at himself, "I've even given up being rude to people!"[40] Several times he went to visit Theodor Billroth's widow and children in St. Gilgen. Once, when he was very sick, he sat Billroth's grandchildren on his knees and stared moist-eyed into their faces for a long time. They looked much like their grandfather.[41]

By the end of the year his condition had become impossible to ignore. As he sat down to dinner at his friend Hugo Conrat's at the beginning of December, he groaned to the hostess, "If you knew how wretched I feel!" During that dinner he warmed up and joked a little. A week later he told Heuberger that he could no longer enjoy life, though he still ate and slept well. They talked about Richard Strauss's new tone poem *Also sprach Zarathustra*, which purports to express in music the eponymous work by Nietzsche. Liszt and his followers had done poetry, novels, patriotic programs with the orchestra; now Strauss proposed to express philosophy. "Have you seen the end?" Brahms said, "B♭ major and C major together! I wouldn't have anything against it, if something would happen in both keys that in itself was really compelling and inescapable. But like *that?*"

He spent Christmas Eve with the Fellingers, then invited himself to meals there on the next three days. At the last one he made a toast: "To our meeting in the New Year," he began, then gestured downward: "But I shall soon be there."[42]

On January 2, 1897, Joachim's group had a tremendous success in Vienna with the G Major Quintet. Only occasionally in his last years had the two men been able to bear seeing each other, but the violinist had never slackened in championing the music. Brahms listened to the quintet from the artist's room, declaring that he would not take a bow. But the applause went on so long that he was obliged to come out on the platform. The audience gasped at the sight of his brownish-green complexion, stringy hair, shrunken frame and bony hands, and they redoubled their cheers.

On February 12 he was in good spirits with Heuberger, talking shop. In lesser religious pieces, he said, Christ was a tenor, whereas in the greatest ones—mainly the Bach Passions—Christ was a bass, a *man*. Brahms admitted to Heuberger that he was getting weaker, but observed resignedly, "Food and drink are still good and so long as *that's* good, I'll eat and drink away! When I see that no longer works, then I'll go to the Rudolfinerhaus [the hospital Billroth founded]."[43]

Death advanced on him, slowly here, quickly there, agonizingly, gently, matter-of-factly. A stroke on February 18 temporarily paralyzed the left side of his face. His appetite finally declined and that shook him, though doctors permitted unlimited wine, and morphine when there was pain. He took out his old notebook "Des jungen Kreislers Schatz-kästlein" and in a trembling hand wrote down a few more pieces of wisdom. From Bismarck: "After nine o'clock it's all over, says the actor." From Luther: "As the musicians, when you ask them, won't sing, but when you don't ask them, then they can't quit." And the last, from

Solomon: "But no man knows either the love or the hate that he has before him."[44]

He spent much of the days now looking out his windows at the portico and minarets and dome of the Karlskirche. And he sat before the parlor stove reading through old letters and musical manuscripts he had held back, burning them one after another. "It's so sad," was all he said when friends found him surrounded by papers, before a stove full of ashes.[45]

INEVITABLY CAME the last time he heard his music in public, the matinee of the Vienna Philharmonic on March 7. Hans Richter had, for a change, carefully rehearsed the Fourth Symphony, so that the orchestra would play at their magnificent best. Gesellschaft der Musikfreunde conductor Richard von Perger accompanied Brahms to the Musikverein. As they turned up the stairs Perger went on ahead. Brahms called up peevishly in his cracked tenor, "Don't just skip up ahead of me like that, youngster!" He faltered, "Ja, ja, I'm done for. . . ." But when Perger offered to give a hand Brahms snapped, "Don't talk nonsense! I'm not an old lady!"[46] He struggled up the stairs to the director's box.

And the Golden Hall rocked with cheers after every movement of the symphony. Surely in Brahms's mind there was a sense of a coda, a great cadence in that half hour of his most despairing work. It had come to this, these minor chords. If at moments Brahms still hoped for long life, he knew that it was past dark and the comedy nearly done. It had come to this, so he wept.

At the end of the symphony the ovation roared on and on, hats and handkerchiefs waving all over the hall, men of the Philharmonic on their feet bellowing and waving along with the crowd. Brahms stood weeping quietly in the torrent of love the Viennese were giving him, his wasted hands clutching the balustrade. Finally, with a nod of his head he stepped back, and the Golden Hall saw him no more.[47]

A WEEK after hearing the Fourth Symphony in the Musikverein Brahms did rouse himself to go out for one more performance. In company with Hanslick he slipped into the premiere of his friend Johann Strauss's operetta *Göttin der Vernunft* at the Theater an der Wien. But after the first act he asked for a cab home. A week later he was brought to a rehearsal near his apartment at the house of his friend Karl Wittgenstein, father of the future philosopher. There Marie Soldat and her Women's String Quartet, with Richard Mühlfeld as guest, were preparing the Clarinet Quintet. Complaining that he had heard his own piece quite enough, Brahms asked them to play instead Weber's Quintet in B♭. After an embarrassed moment, the group did as asked. The Wittgenstein music room was full of guests, who stole shuddering glances at the sepulchral figure. When the piece was finished Max Kalbeck escorted Brahms home.

On March 24, Brahms wrote Joachim in England, "I'm going downhill; every word spoken or written is a strain."[48] Next day he dragged himself out to have lunch at the Millers', with Mandyczewski and Richard Mühlfeld. At the end he did not want to leave, sighing, "Oh, let me stay a bit, it's so beautiful here!" Next day, feeling deathly weak, he took to his bed under the picture of Bach, writing a note to stepmother Karoline: "Dear Mother, For the sake of variety I've lain down for awhile, so can't write easily. But don't be afraid: nothing has changed, and all I need is patience as usual. From the heart, your Johs." It is the only time on record since childhood that Brahms was bedridden. Next day he wrote a final note, to Ignaz Brüll saying he would not be able to make a dinner invitation set for the following day.

He would not leave the house again alive. In the last days Frau Truxa saw to him faithfully, friends and doctors slipped in and out, Antonin Dvořák among the visitors. On the piano rack lay a large volume of the monumental Bach Gesellschaft Edition, completed the previous year. The book was opened to a motet, the margins of the music covered with Brahms's notations. Watching over the piano were the bust of Beethoven and the bronze relief of Bismarck.

Now Brahms was a shrunken face on the bed, his breathing labored, the famous beard flowing over the white nightshirt and covers that Frau Truxa kept fresh. At times he became delirious and had to be restrained. Near the end of March there was an episode of bloody diarrhea. A doctor told him it was a necessary climax to his jaundice, after which he would recover. Brahms accepted the lie.

His humor did not desert him. Frau Truxa would help him up and across the room to the washstand; he called it "washing with police escort." Once when she came in to bathe him he snapped, "You want to give me my last bath? I'm not a baby!" She said she was just trying to save him the trouble. Relenting, he whispered, "You're a sensible woman. One can negotiate with you."

That was hours before he died. He had gotten a morphine injection from his doctor's son. In the early morning of April 3 Artur Faber came by and gave him a glass of Rhine wine for his thirst. Brahms took the glass in both hands and sipped slowly. With a sigh he said, "Oh, that tasted fine. You're a kind man," and sank back down.

Just before nine A.M., Frau Truxa came in and when she looked at him could not stifle a sob. Brahms struggled to sit up and say something to her, but the words would not come out. Great tears rolled down his face and he fell back on the pillow. Then, with no struggle, he stopped breathing.[49]

VIENNA LOVES A GREAT FUNERAL and every Viennese aspires to one. The city had donated a Grave of Honor for Brahms in the Central Cemetery, and the Gesellschaft der Musikfreunde supplied funds for the ceremonies. Friends and admirers arrived from all over Austria and Germany. George Henschel came to Brahms's apartment in the afternoon of April 3, to find the rooms already overflowing with a display of funeral pomp ironic for an agnostic who had lived plainly: silver crosses on black velvet, a huge brass candelabrum with candles blazing, flowers piled higher than the coffin. The Gesellschaft der Musikfreunde handled the arrangements. Engraved invitations went out for the funeral on April 6. That morning, thousands gathered in the streets, crowding Karlsgasse in front of the house and lining the miles-long route of the procession. A stream of friends and deputations went up and down the stairs with wreaths and flowers and palm branches.

Finally the coffin appeared at the doorway and the thousands removed their hats. The coffin was draped with two huge wreaths, one from Hamburg, the other from the civil administration of Vienna. (Flags flew at half-mast that day in the harbor of Hamburg.) The procession set off past the Karlskirche, led by a standard-bearer in old Spanish costume on a black charger; the funeral car was followed by six more riders carrying lighted tapers on poles and a second mounted standard-bearer. Then came six funeral cars heaped with flowers, laurels, palms, and ribbons. The sun broke out on what looked to Henschel like a gigantic moving garden.[50] There followed officials, friends, honored guests including directors of the Gesellschaft der Musikfreunde, professors of the Conservatory, musical ensembles including Marie Soldat's Women's Quartet and the Männergesangverein, and deputations from the Hamburg Senate, the Berlin Philharmonic and Hochschule für Musik, the Amsterdam Musikgesellschaft, the Budapest Konservatory, the Leipzig Gewandhaus, and many other organizations. Herzog Georg II of Meiningen and his wife Freifrau von Heldburg had sent a colossal wreath that moved slowly along the procession. Marchers included many names from Brahms's past: Marie Schumann, George Henschel, Frau Johann Strauss, Arthur Fellinger, Karl and Luis Wittgenstein, Josef Hellmesberger, Max Kalbeck, Viktor von Miller zu Aichholz, Artur Faber, Heinrich von Herzogenberg, Antonin Dvořák, Fritz Simrock, Anton Door, Richard Epstein, Eusebius Mandyczewski, Richard Heuberger.

The procession crossed the River Wien to the Musikverein, its entrances and pillars draped in black. There the Singverein that Brahms had once conducted sang his Opus 93 "Farewell," accompanied by choruses of birds from the Resselpark across the way. The procession continued on past the great bulk of the Hofoper and thousands of onlookers, to a service at the Protestant church on Dorotheërgasse, the throngs listening to the ringing incantation of the minister: "A High Priest in the shrine of true Beauty has entered the Holy of Holies of glory, a mighty Sovereign in the kingdom of tones has laid his scepter aside, a soul full of wondrous melodies has breathed his last sigh, and a noble man has ended his earthly pilgrimage!" Then official Vienna joined as the procession continued to the Grave of Honor in Central Cemetery—a herd of robed magistrates and chancellors and dukes and *Landmarschalls*, and Dr. Karl Lueger, who was finally about to take his seat as Bürgermeister of the city.

The procession reached the Zentralfriedhof in late afternoon, the day's chilly wind once more giving way to sun breaking through the clouds. Brahms's inner circle of friends carried his coffin from the funeral carriage to the grave: Kalbeck, Simrock, Fellinger, Miller, Fuchs, Mandyczewski, Perger, Brüll, Door, Heuberger, Henschel. As Max Kalbeck sobbed noisily, Perger declaimed the final farewell: "Colleagues! It is our true duty to confirm the holy legacy of the Master. Let us solemnly vow in this hour, in this place, steadfastly to hold that legacy together, and struggle to bring it about as he conceived it. His works, now already the property of all art-loving humanity, must through our labor ever more penetrate to ears and hearts!"

Alice Barbi, his last muse, threw the first handful of earth into the grave. It lay in a place Brahms had once called a "sacred spot," and so his friends knew that was where he wanted to come to rest. The last Master of his line, he lies there in a circle of musicians gathered around a monument to Mozart—beside him Johann Strauss, Jr., at the head of the circle Beethoven and Schubert.

The words at the grave were spoken and forgotten. Brahms had already sung an unforgettable epitaph for himself, for his age, for his vision of music, and for the essential tragedy of humankind: *Even the beautiful must die!*

Epilogue and Provocation

THE DEATH OF BRAHMS was a watershed in Western musical history—not the end of Vienna's greatness, but the end of a school that had begun there with Haydn and Mozart, continued through Beethoven and Schubert, and ended with him. In the hundred years since, how has he fared? What has he meant?

As Brahms lay on his deathbed, Heinrich von Herzogenberg wrote Josef Joachim, "For thirty-five years I have asked myself with every note I composed: 'What will Brahms think of this?' . . . He was my ambition, my impetus, my courage."[1] Joachim, who had been touring in England when Brahms died, wrote a friend in Rome: "I often think sadly of the last pleasure it was in our power to give him. . . . I have never heard him express his gratitude so warmly as after listening to his G Major Quintet; he seemed almost satisfied with his work. We still have his works—as an individual I counted for little with him during the last years of his life."[2]

Along with the wave of laudatory obituaries and eulogies came others like the one by a critic of the *Fremden-Blatt*: "Against the symphonic world-ideas of Beethoven, Brahms's symphonies express only the private thoughts and private meanings of a clever man."[3] That charge would be echoed many times, because it was partly true. Thereby Brahms, whatever his popularity with legions of concertgoers, slipped into irrelevance in the scholarly and aesthetic dialogue. He would remain in that position for a century.

During that century the heritage of Brahms lay more in the sheer popularity of his music than in his influence on the polyphonic revolutions of Modernism. In his own time, besides his favored performers, who had been prominent in his camp except Hanslick the naysayer and a collection of composers like Fuchs and Röntgen and Herzogenberg—all competent and admirable, but in the end mediocre? (Dvořák being the shining exception to that rule.) As a bulwark against the New German/Wagnerian propaganda machine lay mainly Hanslick's little pamphlet *On Beauty in Music*, with its doctrine of absolute music that even Brahms could hardly swallow. Thus the futility of Perger's graveside vow to keep the legacy together in Brahms's own terms, and thus the seeming irrelevance of Brahms to the Modernist era.

By the turn of the last century before the millennium, Wagner's world-ideas were some of the most influential in the Western artistic milieu. In Austria and Germany the reactionary antisemitic nationalism that he helped inspire eventually culminated in violent and world-threatening forms. In the arts, the period called Modern became a vast, sprawling movement, different in every art, splintering into subdivisions from Primitivism to Futurism, Surrealism to Serialism (and including Modernists who claimed to despise Modernism). All the while a necessary underpinning for this Babel was the one Wagner and the New Germans proclaimed in the middle of the nineteenth century: the creator as high priest in the religion of art, not the entertainer of the public but a revolutionary leader to whom the masses owe understanding. For the duration of Modernism, even if the nature and extent of his victory is hard to pin down, Wagner had won the War of Romantics that raged between the two camps in the nineteenth century.

Early in this century, in the concert hall and opera house the competing camps receded into history. Now both Wagner and Brahms were counted among the gods. A Viennese silhouette-panorama made after Brahms's death shows Bruckner and Wagner at the head of the composers welcoming him into heaven. (If so, he might have put on his hat and struck out for hell.) Brahms, Wagner, and Bruckner were embraced by right and left, each in its own terms.

At the same time the terms of the relationship between artist and public had changed, and in Wagner's direction. For Brahms and his contemporaries, the middle-class audience had acted as a brake on the burgeoning Romantic imagination. Only at the end of his life did Brahms say he was writing entirely for himself. Until then he wrote for himself first, then for his friends, then for the bourgeois concertgoing public for whom people like Elisabet von Herzogenberg and Theodor Billroth stood as proxy. As Brahms said to Max Kalbeck, "If my music doesn't please people like Billroth, Hanslick, or you, then who is it supposed to please?"

Modernism, founded in some degree on the Wagnerian conception of the artist whose relation to the public is imperial, may be called *Romanticism without brakes*. In practice, during the twentieth century Wagner's conception of the artist was played out not at the head of, but in opposition to, the bourgeois public. In the nineteenth century that public had lavishly financed art and artists at the same time as its tastes grew steadily more conservative. The kind of audience for whom Brahms composed, while its general musical knowledge and sophistication declined after his death, maintained the pattern Brahms had helped create: by the later nineteenth century the concert hall existed primarily as a museum of the past. Yet in today's concert hall relatively few concertgoers can follow the course of any traditional musical form. The mode of listening that Brahms condemned Bruckner for fostering—wallowing without thought in a bath of sonority and emotion—is how audiences today largely listen to Bruckner symphonies, Bach fugues, Wagnerian opera, and Brahms.

Brahms prophesied this, but there was one more element of the decline that he experienced but whose threat he did not foresee—the phonograph. He may have hoped that recordings would spread classical music among the masses. So they did, but in the long run they also hastened the deterioration of the audience. In the Modern era the presence of easily available music on radio and television and discs, ubiquitous but rarely intensely listened to, only dilutes the kind of pleasure music lovers experienced in Brahms's day. In the era of electronic media, few people learn the musical literature in four-hand piano arrangements. In Brahms's time many learned it that way through their fingers, or sang in choirs, and waited eagerly to hear the rare performances of a familiar masterpiece. In other words, music was by and large available only to those who took pains, who went out of their way for it. Inevitably that made music more precious.

So because of intricate artistic and social developments including two World Wars, but also to a great extent because of new media, the devotion music enjoyed in the nineteenth century trickled away. It is unlikely to return. In the museums of modern concert halls and opera houses, Brahms piano trios, Bruckner symphonies, Wagnerian operas have melted together into the history of Western masterpieces, issued on little discs that all look the same, which pile up over the years in living rooms and their contents in an overcrowded collective memory. And as the educated audience for which Brahms composed faded, a prime goal of the Wagner/Liszt agenda—to keep the living composer in the center of musical life—broke down completely. The modern "standard repertoire" is not so far from the repertoire Brahms featured as director of the Gesellschaft der Musikfreunde in the 1870s.

Yet paradoxically, the attitude behind Brahms's conservatism, his knowledge of history and his awe before it, became another signature of Modernism. "Modern" music, Peter Burkholder has said, is "written by composers obsessed with the musical past and with their place in music history, who seek to emulate the music of those we call the 'classical masters.'"[4] The paradoxical ambition of most artistic revolutionaries in the twentieth century became this: to create museum pieces. Naturally, there came at the same time an avant-garde that attempted, without success, to raze the museums entirely.

AFTER BRAHMS, the next great names in the city would appear under the rubric of the Second Viennese School, with Gustav Mahler as patron, Arnold Schoenberg as headmaster. For another paradox, most of the revolutionary artists of Schoenberg's day in Vienna rose from the same liberal *Grossbürgertum*, still prosperous but essentially disenfranchised, that had formed Brahms's main public.

For the older generation of the *Grossbürgertum*, art had been an adornment of life and a sign of status. For the liberals' children, art was a way of life, in part because they had no effectual political power left, no other comparable field for their imaginations.[5] "The life of art," writes Carl Schorske, "became a substitute for the life of action. Indeed as civic action proved increasingly futile, art became almost a religion, the source of meaning and the food of the soul."[6] The innovations of Schoenberg and his followers, which were to set them unprecedentedly in opposition to the concert-going bourgeoisie—to the degree that they founded the "Society for Private Musical Performances" for invitees only—nonetheless presupposed the attitudes of that same class as to the significance of art. The bourgeois audience might not have liked what it heard from the radicals, but it still understood what was being done in music to be vitally important. Schoenberg and his followers were reviled, not ignored. (Was it only when Schoenberg came to the U.S. that he realized it was possible for important artists to be ignored?)

Almost from the moment Brahms died in April 1897, Vienna began to change, and with vertiginous speed. It is as if, with his accustomed skill in managing his career, Brahms had known precisely when to exit the scene. The very day he died, one-time fashionable historical painter Gustav Klimt led a group of students from the Künstlerhaus in the founding meeting of "The Secession," the spearhead of Modernism in

Vienna. Exactly one year after Brahms died, ground was broken for the revolutionary little exhibition hall named The House of the Secession. Its geometric shapes, severe white stucco walls, and bizarrely beautiful dome of gilded laurel leaves stand just off the Ringstrasse that the building rebukes, and across the way from the Karlskirche.

The architect of The House of the Secession, Joseph Maria Olbrich, conceived the building and its contents as a Wagnerian *Gesamtkunstwerk*, and wrote of it in visionary terms: "Subjectivity, my beauty, my building, as I had dreamed. . . . It was my noble right to show my own idea of beauty, to say that it has to be done with the heart, and that everything measured with the proportions of traditions and the traditional aesthetic teachers appears foolish and awkward."[7] Above the door of the museum is written the motto of the Secession movement: "To the Age Its Art, to Art Its Freedom." The freedom the building and its architect are talking about gave rise to the cryptic and elegant Viennese Jugendstil, the Freudian spectres of artistic Expressionism, and the tortured atonality of early Schoenberg and Webern. That freedom, in other words, was what Brahms called the end of art: when the laws of counterpoint, harmony, melody, and form that he called eternal no longer applied, and the insurrectionists took over the shop.

A few years after he died, Gustav Klimt, for an exhibition featuring Max Klinger's statue of a seated Beethoven, painted his Beethoven-frieze on the walls of the Secession. His spectral, shockingly carnal nudes float in a marvelous and macabre atmosphere of jewel-like textures. The panels illustrate Wagner's narrative interpretation of the Ninth Symphony, including "Weak Humanity" pleading with "The Well-Armed Strong Man" for salvation. (The Strong Man, here a knight in golden armor, Wagner surely intended as Germany in general, himself in particular. Klimt, however, gave the knight Mahler's features.) If Brahms's Fourth Symphony had been a "taking back" of Beethoven's "Ode to Joy," Klimt expressed that joy for a new and troubled time.

By the first decade of the new century in Vienna, Egon Schiele and Oskar Kokoschka were painting Expressionist canvases that wrenched forms and colors away from nature and the traditions of drawing. In architecture the post-Jugendstil elegance of Otto Wagner competed with the stripped-down, functionalist style of Adolf Loos. All these artists had in their own style fled from the crowded kitsch of the Ringstrasse and the Age of Makart, which was Brahms's age (even as his style remained his own).

On Good Friday of the April when Brahms died, Emperor Franz Josef finally conceded the inevitable and allowed Karl Lueger to take office as

Mayor of Vienna. It was the last nail in the coffin of liberal political power. Lueger and his Christian Socialists, with their blend of socialism and antisemitism, would remake Vienna in fateful ways.

In the April Brahms died, the Austrian Parliament passed the disastrous Bardeni Ordinance, which made the Czech language equal to German in communications among government departments. The German-speaking populace erupted in outrage. That autumn saw brawling in the streets and bedlam in Parliament. Shock waves spread through the tottering Empire. Parliamentary government, bastion of the liberals, sank into paralysis.

Two days after Brahms died, the Vienna Opera announced the appointment of Gustav Mahler as new Kapellmeister. After his debut in May, the *Deutsche Zeitung* commented that even if Mahler had gotten himself baptized in order to be accepted by the Opera, "That does not change the facts at all, that at this stage in one of the few non-Judaized artistic institutions in Vienna, from now on a Jew will be in a position to call the tune. The consequences will be inevitable: the Viennese public will not be held to blame for the proper response to this violation of its patent wishes."[8]

A number of well-educated, liberal Jews had signed on to the early nationalistic and even antisemitic manifestos, until they realized that the underlying agenda had to do not with culture but with blood and race, and so every Jew was tainted by birth. In 1896 Theodor Herzl, a journalist and an archetypal assimilated Viennese Jew, published his epochal Zionist manifesto *The Jewish State*, his answer to the threat gathering around the people he could no longer help belonging to. Vienna had become the territory that Karl Kraus called "The Proving-Ground for World Destruction," and that Adolf Hitler declared in *Mein Kampf* "the hardest but the most thorough school."[9]

During the preceding decades, which saw Vienna's (deceptive) golden years and a general peace and prosperity across Europe, Brahms had perfected an art evolving, fresh, utterly distinctive, in many ways prophetic, yet grounded in a conservative set of principles and techniques that he called eternal. For all his singularity, he stands as the model of a middle-class mainstream art at its most vital—and he is one of the last such figures. Malcolm MacDonald calls Brahms "Janus . . . , the spirit of beginnings and endings, who looks both ways at once, to the past and to the future."[10] Moreover, Brahms proved that the kind of historical eclecticism which compromised the extravagant agenda of the Ringstrasse could, with the addition of genius, courage, and ruthless persistence, achieve an extraordinary integrity. After Brahms's symphonies, in Vienna came those of Mahler, "Chief of the Insurrectionists": grandiose, defiant, often tormented and grotesque hymns to the inescapability of eclecticism, and the impossibility of integrity in the modern world. When Mahler's music finally triumphed some fifty years after he died, a precondition of that triumph was the collapse of the standards of craft and organic unity that Brahms had championed.

"Ours is a century of death," Leonard Bernstein said, "and Mahler is its spiritual prophet." In 1905 Hugo von Hoffmannsthal, in his teens a precocious creator of delicate and unworldly lyrics, later a dramatist and Richard Strauss's librettist, wrote a manifesto for Modernism, though he was probably speaking mainly for Vienna. He wrote, "The nature of our epoch is multiplicity and indeterminacy. It can rest only on *das Gleitende*, and is aware that what other generations believed to be firm is in fact *das Gleitende*." The word means "gliding," "slipping," "sliding," "shifting." The coming age, Hoffmannsthal wrote, can only be founded on the ultimate reality of the mutable and fragmentary: "Everything fell into parts, the parts again into more parts, and nothing allowed itself to be embraced by concepts anymore."[11] And to the intellectual and spiritual anxieties of *das Gleitende*, the twentieth century added the obdurate realities of world war and mass extermination.

The part of Modernism that flowed so powerfully from Vienna ranged from a fin-de-siècle irony to a sense of rootlessness and prophetic alarm, expressed unforgettably in the early atonal-Expressionist works of Schoenberg and Webern and the nightmare parables of Franz Kafka. From his psychiatric office in Vienna, Sigmund Freud created a picture of consciousness and will and civilization floating like a fragile crust on a sliding, slipping morass of primal drives and nursery tragicomedies. If once Galileo had knocked earth and humanity out of its central place in the cosmos, Freud threatened Enlightenment illusions of the triumph of order, reason, craft, and scientific progress. Surely the anguished and dissonant language of Expressionism, a movement that Schoenberg in his first fame embodied as both composer and painter, is a reflection of the fearful turmoil not only of fin-de-siècle Vienna, but of the Freudian unconscious—a territory that could have been imagined, perhaps, only in the social and spiritual chaos of Vienna in that era. That world, even as it overlapped Brahms's world, is a leap over an enormous divide away from the nineteenth-century rationalistic, humanistic, pre-Freudian skepticism that Brahms embodied.

In short, the catastrophes that Brahms and others prophesied came to pass, in and out of two world wars, in and out of art. After Austria touched off the first Great War in the wake of Sarajevo, the rehearsal for world destruction was over and the real thing took the stage. At its beginning, the house of cards called the Austrian Empire collapsed almost unnoticed and nearly unmourned.

Yet in music none of Brahms's desperate prophecies ("After me, music is done for!") quite came to pass. The music of the great masters that he loved did not die but prospered, even if more and more as exhibits in a museum. That museum's collection of masterpieces came above all from the work composed in Vienna during the 125 years before Brahms died—the most extraordinary concentration of genius in one medium in one place since the Florentine Renaissance. In the twentieth century, vital composers turned up across Europe and America in perhaps unprecedented numbers, but the divide between them and the bourgeois audience, and the time lag between the appearance of their work and public acceptance of it, yawned greater and greater. In the case of Schoenberg, Berg, Webern, and other historic figures, it is only as the millennium approaches that the audience has, possibly, begun to catch up.

THROUGH ALL OF IT, Brahms endured. He did not become what he had feared, a footnote in history like Cherubini. Peter Gay has noted the way in which Brahms, in his own time the "frigid intellectual," was transformed immediately after his death into the "sultry sentimentalist."[12] What other part could he play, alongside Schoenberg the terrifying, alongside Stravinsky the Primitivist in one incarnation, the chilly Neoclassic in another? Through the Modernist century Brahms's voice continued to sing in the museums of concert halls, and to win countless ovations.

At the same time he remained irrelevant to the historical dialogue, which Wagner had a large hand in laying out. In 1947 Arnold Schoenberg, who insisted he had learned the essentials of his craft from Brahms more than (as everyone assumed) from Wagner, set out to redeem his mentor with his article "Brahms the Progressive." In this and other writings Schoenberg explicated one of the essential things about Brahms: the depth and novelty of his motivic technique, which Schoenberg named "developing variation." That technique, with its corollaries—applied in the three-dimensional space that in Brahms unites the once-separate domains of melody, harmony, and form—is one of the seminal developments in all music, gold to the twelve-tonist and traditionalist alike. With the embrace of Schoenberg the most notorious of Modernists, Brahms apparently re-entered history.

Yet really not, because Schoenberg was in some degree wrong. He declared Brahms "progressive" mainly because of the more advanced bits and pieces of his language, the relatively rare pages when Brahms approached something like Schoenbergian harmonic freedom. Schoenberg was disposed to label as "progressive" anything that inspired his own work. Brahms was progressive, in short, because he inspired Schoenberg—just as Wagner had once declared Beethoven prophetic because he led to Wagner. At the same time, as Burkholder notes: in calling Brahms progressive, Schoenberg was also calling himself a traditionalist.

And so the label of progressive that Schoenberg put on Brahms, with whatever justification, would not stick. He did not succeed in making Brahms relevant to the aesthetic debates of the century, or to concertgoers' perceptions of Schoenberg. Dissonance and harmonic ambiguity do not, as Schoenberg presumed, define this century's tonal art. "Modernism in music," Peter Burkholder notes, "is not identical with progress in musical techniques." (He might have added: nor do musical techniques really "progress.") Rather Modernism—vast, complex, and self-contradictory as it may have been—was predicated on historical self-consciousness and on a particular sense of the artist as priest/revolutionary: the Wagnerian branch of Romanticism, without brakes. It is significant that for all his exalting of Brahms, after Schoenberg had created the twelve-tone technique he announced to his disciples in Messianic and high-Wagnerian terms: "I have invented a system that will insure the superiority of German music for a hundred years to come."

Contrary to what Schoenberg believed, the essential Brahms is the Janus-headed: Classical *and* Romantic, conservative *and* progressive, looking backward and forward at once. In the extraordinary power and integrity he achieved from that position, he is unique—which is to say, both singular and alone. In that position he remained standing to the side of Modernism as it played out its creative and destructive, magnificent and terrible course in all the arts, to the last decades of the twentieth century and Modernism's collapse in fragments, jumbled up with popular culture, in a climate of anarchy, rage, and paralysis of imagination.

Every creative era contains the seeds of its own destruction; each plays out its decadence in its own way. Modernism expired over the last decades of the twentieth century, lost in the wilderness it had thrashed into but turned out to be incapable of settling. In the process its supply line, the thread of Western artistic tradition, frayed and arguably snapped, leaving artists like so many explorers stranded in a wilderness of their own discovery. Today it appears that after the interregnum of postmodernism, Modernism gave way to chaos, to nothing: exactly what

Brahms feared, only taking a century—a dazzling, unprecedented, creative and destructive century—to run its course.

As that century reels to its close, it may be argued that Brahms has become more relevant to the future than he has been in a hundred years. As the Western world approaches the millennium, the great tradition on which he founded his personal and innovative art has faded, and likewise the sophisticated audience he composed for. The nineteenth-century cartoonist drew Hanslick the acolyte waving his censer at Brahms standing on a cracked pedestal. The pedestal is dust now, yet Brahms stands unbowed and unassailed. He is still vital, as is Wagner. One must add: Brahms lives on in something like his own terms, while Wagner, with his portentous sociopolitical baggage, must be reimagined and bent and constrained so we can bear to contemplate the extraordinary edifice of his art at all.

As long as the West wants to uphold the deepest, broadest, and finest part of its musical tradition, Brahms will be with us. For that long, we will know the Brahms Effect: music at once warmly, lyrically, Romantically expressive, and at the same time remote, Olympian. Only in a few moments does his work have that miraculous quality of Beethoven, the sense of an individual grasping our lapels and talking to us passionately and intimately, even if at times in a voice of thunder. (When Brahms reaches for a sense of Beethovenian heaven-storming, he is apt to get a little stiff, a little rhetorical.)

It is easier to talk about Beethoven's music, because of his quality of talking to us directly—as he did in life, his art speaks "dramatically," "angrily," "tenderly," with "naked anguish." Like the gods on Olympus, Brahms is fully and tenderly and lustily human yet unsearchable, in his art as in his life. After twenty-five years Clara Schumann declared him still a stranger, and she knew him better than anybody else. When we speak about Brahms's music, as when he did, most often we are forced to resort to abstractions: this theme, this rhythm, this design. Meanwhile, in contrast to Wagner and perhaps to Beethoven, Brahms was too realistic to imagine that music could save the world, no matter how much the world needed saving.

"It simply won't flow from my heart," Brahms confessed to Clara at the outset, about his composing. Surely in the end it did come from his heart, but because of who he was and where he came from and what was expected of him, his music had to take a circuitous route from his heart to the page. The reason he still reaches our hearts so persuasively is perhaps more than the warmth and lyricism and boldness, or the near-perfection of his craftsmanship. It is the underlying mystery of his voice, like that of his person. No one can say what lay behind the masks. His elusiveness of person and voice and "meaning" is close to the essential mystery of music itself. In that Brahms the "Beethovener" is nearer Mozart than Beethoven. Thus the familiar term: *absolute music*.

The musical progressives of his time, their ears and minds full of Wagner's epochal agenda for opera and art and humanity, condemned Brahms's art as "the private thoughts of a clever man," writing only for the private thoughts of his listeners. But after the betrayals of this century by one epochal agenda after another, the private thoughts of a private craftsman may be the best thing we have left.

As we approach the millennium, who better a model for the art of the next century than the survivor Brahms, and the inspiration of his craft? Not his fears of the end of art, not his conservatism, not his musical language, but his craft and his lonely courage, and the still enormous audience for classical music, an audience he has helped sustain.

Much has been lost since Brahms's time, but not everything. If we in the West do not have the nurturing milieu and the continuity of tradition Brahms relied on, we still have history and its gods and demigods. We have been enriched by Modernism's explorations and virtuosity of imagination, enriched by creative languages from the world over, the great universal chorus of human music. It is a chorus wild, confusing, dissonant, yet ultimately material to be shaped and made coherent and compelling by artists as individuals, working in their craft for individuals to hear.

For our time, a hundred years after Brahms left us, what better model than he? He gave us skills and inspirations: a private man speaking to each listener in our private selves, an eclectic of incomparable integrity. Perhaps beyond that we need only genius, a quality the fates have always parceled out in short, but steady, supply.

ON MARCH 31, 1913, Vienna heard a historic program at the Musikverein. It included Gustav Mahler's *Kindertotenlieder* (Songs on the Death of Children), Alban Berg's *Altenberg Lieder*, Six Pieces for Orchestra by Anton Webern, songs by Alexander von Zemlinsky, and Arnold Schoenberg's Chamber Symphony. The music competed with furious hissing and whistling from the audience, and also violent bravos and applause. Finally fistfights broke out around the Golden Hall, some patrons climbing over rows of seats to assault a stranger. Even after the police arrived, members of the audience stormed the stage, where the orchestra sat ashen with fear. Today all those larger works stand as masterpieces. (The uproar happened, after all, exactly because music was perceived to be of immense importance.)

If Brahms had lived to be seventy-nine, he would likely have been there in the middle of the fray. The year before, he could have heard one of the two seminal works in the Modernist musical canon, Schoenberg's *Pierrot Lunaire*. Had he survived that, in 1913 he could have experienced the other, Stravinsky's *Sacre du printemps*. Both were born accompanied by riot. The son of the Hamburg docks and protégé of Robert and Clara Schumann would not have been pleased by what he heard.

Instead, by 1913 Brahms was present in Vienna only in his music and in monuments. Opposite the Musikverein, on a spot that used to hold a bench where he would rest on the way home from too much wine, lies the city's primary memorial to him. Designed by Rudolf Weyr and erected in 1908, it stands as one of the last gasps of the style and spirit of the Ringstrasse. Brahms sits in the attitude of Michelangelo's *Moses*, and the Muse lies prostrate at his feet. She touches a silent lyre that she is clearly unsure will ever ring again. That Brahms hated representations of the Muse and her harp enough to cover up the one in his picture of Cherubini, did not deter Weyr's hoary iconography. In Hamburg, Max Klinger's Brahms Monument was installed in the Musikhalle: there he stands shrouded and ageless, imaginary figures gathered around his feet, a boy-cherub hanging suspended from his neck. Once more, in contrast to the solemn backward-looking icon of the Vienna monument, Klinger combined the "real" figure with the unruly shadows of imagination.

Today in Vienna the House of the Secession stands in its still-startling severity in that Baroque city, the little white building modeled on pagan temples yet entirely modern, beautiful and strange, its defiantly blank walls relieved by intertwining floral friezes at the corners. Floating atop the front door are three Jugendstil muses wearing necklaces of serpents biting their tails. From the roof the golden crown spreads like a magical tree, an echo from a different age of the nearby dome of the Karlskirche.

This year inside the Secession, the same art lovers and tourists who take in Klinger and Feuerbach and Makart and Brueghel elsewhere in the city, have a look at Klimt's Beethoven-Frieze—still shocking but tamed by time. In an exhibition room there is a forest of television sets on pedestals, each showing a video of a naked body-pierced skinhead jumping up and down and screaming. Now traffic flows around the museum, a bus stop faces it, pedestrians trudge past unheeding, tourists queue up. The House of the Secession has become, over time, a familiar icon, herald of a bygone artistic movement that still bears the paradoxical name of Modernism, and which Vienna helped shape as much as any city did.

And across the way from The House of the Secession lies its predecessor, Johann Fischer von Erlach's Karlskirche, High Baroque yet herald of Austro-German Romanticism and its yearning for the Unknowable, and the first thing Brahms saw from his window each morning for twenty-four years.

As of the end of the Romantic century, call those two splendid buildings the past and the future.

SOME TWO WEEKS BEFORE HE DIED, Brahms struggled out to the rehearsal of the Soldat-Röger Women's Quartet with Richard Mühlfeld. Despite his illness he still commanded enough of his old imperiousness to demand that they play Weber, not Brahms. Afterward the hostess offered to call a carriage for him. Complaining, "It's just around the corner!" Brahms insisted on walking home. He left leaning on Max Kalbeck.

As they slowly made their way, Kalbeck was shocked by the bony, almost fleshless arm draped in his. It was a heroic effort for the sick man, after all his years of hiking, to shuffle a few blocks. "This is the longest way I've made it since New Year's," Brahms sighed. Then in a whisper, "I tell you, it's wretched!" Kalbeck offered to find a carriage, but once more Brahms protested: "No, let me go! It's all right now." But then he stopped, groaning, and sank back against the wall of a house.

Leaning there, gathering his strength, with the Musikverein and all Vienna at his back, Brahms looked out across the plaza and said, "How beautiful the church is, just look! And right behind it used to stand the 'House of the Golden Moonlight' . . . of the Golden . . ." He faltered, losing his thought, then continued, "where Schubert used to have a drink and sing. Do you know anything in Germany like the Karlskirche with its two columns and green cupola?" Kalbeck spoke of Dresden: the Zwinger, the cathedral, the Japanese Palace.

"Ah, that's all really beautiful," Brahms said in wonder, "but it's still not the Karlskirche!"

Leaning on the wall, looking out at the cathedral, Brahms spoke of the Thirty Years War and the destruction it wrought on German culture. Yet eventually, for all its divisions of kingdoms and of spirit, that culture had created a dominion of imagination, filled with fairy tales and folk songs and sorcerers and Doppelgängers and magnificent music, all shaping a myth of another world more wondrous and eternal and perilous than this one—and named that world Romantic.

With Max Kalbeck watchfully alongside, Brahms began to shuffle forward, pausing every few steps to rest, and so made his way across the plaza, past the church, to Karlsgasse. At the corner his future biographer offered him his arm again. Brahms brushed it away. "I can make it up quite well by myself. You go right on now. I need to lie down. Well, *ade*."

Kalbeck understood. Brahms was afraid that if his young protégé accompanied him up to his rooms he would sit and visit, and the ailing man was embarrassed by his exhaustion. Trembling, Brahms turned away down the street. Kalbeck stood beside the church and watched him disappear alone, through the dark doorway.

Notes

The endnotes are in minimal form, usually consisting of an author's last name and the page(s) being cited from that author's book or article. The reader should consult the bibliography for full authors' names, titles, and publication data of the works. Where a given author has more than one work cited in the text, the endnotes include the (abbreviated) title. Many notes also contain textual discussion, and some are exclusively discussion.

CHAPTER ONE

1. Niemann 4.
2. May 50.
3. May 51, italics added (Brahms certainly meant it that way).
4. Kalbeck I, 4–5.
5. Dittrich 7.
6. Niemann 16.
7. Dittrich 7.
8. An old Hamburg musician told Schauffler (35) that Johann Jakob was known around town as "a block-head . . . a natural butt for all the boys." That is only the most blunt statement of the kind of thing everybody remembered about Johann Jakob.
9. Kalbeck IV, Appendix.
10. From Christiane Brahms's recollections, quoted in Geiringer *Brahms* 5.
11. Stephenson 12.
12. Kalbeck and Geiringer *(Brahms)* have Johann Jakob marrying in his town militia uniform, but Stephenson (17) doubts that, since Johann Jakob apparently did not join the militia band until 1835.
13. May 53.
14. Geiringer *Brahms* 9.
15. Stephenson 12.
16. May 57. May visited the Specksgang house while it still stood. It vanished along with most of old Hamburg during the bombings of World War II.
17. Keys 3.
18. Stephenson 23.
19. Kalbeck I, 6.

20. Stephenson 18.
21. Niemann 5.
22. Stephenson 21.
23. Dietrich/Widmann 188.
24. Kalbeck I, 14.
25. Waissenberger 117.
26. Gal 25.
27. MacDonald 6.
28. Specht 16.
29. MacDonald 7.
30. Kalbeck I, 23.
31. Jenner 193–4.
32. Stephenson entry on Elise.
33. Stephenson 51.
34. Keys 4.
35. May 72.
36. Kalbeck I, 25.
37. Niemann 21.
38. Niemann 21.
39. Niemann 21.
40. Niemann 19–20.
41. Kalbeck I, 34.
42. See Geiringer *Brahms* 18. He makes the point that Marxsen knew Chopin's work, was influenced by it, and could have shown (or played) his pupil some Chopin; but Geiringer mentions no other living composers. Brahms always claimed he knew nothing of Chopin until later, but his early E♭ Minor Scherzo suggests otherwise.
43. Niemann 21.
44. E. Schumann 153. Gal notes (104) "he often made similar remarks."
45. Schauffler 225–6. Schauffler's book is rambling and dicey, but this story, usually mentioned but handled gingerly by biographers, feels authentic. For one thing, it is only the most specific of several reports of Brahms talking about the dark aspects of his childhood—see Schumann and Gal above. For another:

there is no doubt of Brahms's lifelong weakness for prostitutes and his problematical relations with women in general. Finally: what else could it have been like, playing in cheap brothels?
46. Boyer 266.
47. Throughout his life, Brahms told a number of people about his time in the *Lokale*, but while he was no hypocrite condemning the prostitutes he visited, he was not so forthcoming about his adult sexual tastes and experiences. That's why I say he had something to hide.
48. Niemann 24.

CHAPTER TWO

1. May 72–80.
2. Geiringer *Brahms* 21.
3. Krebs *Schatzkästlein*.
4. Dahlhaus *Nineteenth Century* 1.
5. Quoted in Walzel 28.
6. Quoted in Strunk 3.
7. Strunk 6.
8. From an 1855 JB letter to Joachim quoted in Keys 5.
9. Krebs *Schatzkästlein*, respectively, entries #1, 2, 4. Hereafter in this chapter, quotations from the *Schatzkästlein* are cited in the text by entry number.
10. Krebs *Schatzkästlein* #6.
11. Krebs *Schatzkästlein* #24.
12. Krebs *Schatzkästlein* #30.
13. Krebs *Schatzkästlein* #36. I am rendering Novalis's neologism *verschwistert*, "sistered," as "coupled."
14. Krebs *Schatzkästlein* #39.
15. Dahlhaus 90–1. The article of 1813 is a combination and condensation of two earlier Hoffmann reviews, mainly the influential one of 1810 concerning Beethoven's Fifth. The

latter is both a technical analysis of the structure and a romantic evocation of the music; in one blow it gave the piece the almost mythical position it has retained ever since—a myth entirely in keeping with the force and character of the music.

16. The Hoffmann essay is in Strunk 35–41.

17. Kross "Brahms and Hoffmann" 194. This article first opened up this much-neglected aspect of Brahms studies with an examination of the "Certificate of Apprenticeship." I owe much to the article, but have taken my ideas in different directions.

18. Brahms biographers tend mainly to mention Kreisler in connection with *Kater Mürr*. Though Brahms liked that unfinished novel, other writings of the fictional Kreisler were clearly as important to him. *Kater Mürr* seems to take its basic idea from Tieck's *Puss in Boots*. The main character is Kapellmeister Kreisler's cat and "beloved pupil" Mürr, who writes his observations about life on the back of a sheaf of wastepaper. The reverse sides of the sheets actually contain fragments of Kapellmeister Kreisler's autobiography. When the printer unwittingly publishes both sides as if they were one manuscript, the result, in this berserk game of identities, is a book in which pages of Kreisler's (that is, in some degree, Hoffmann's) life story are interrupted by his own philosophical tomcat, who presumably is yet another avatar of Hoffmann himself. No wonder the writer was unable to get a handle on this incredible but ungovernable tale. (See Walzel 234.)

19. Translations from the preface to Kross "Brahms and Hoffmann."

20. Quoted in Charlton 127.

21. Quoted in Charlton 133.

22. Quoted in Kross "Brahms and Hoffmann" 197.

23. The unsuccessful beard is mentioned in an Elise Brahms letter of 6/11/1853 (Stephenson) to her brother. Schauffler's speculation that Brahms did not pass puberty at all until his twenties seems to me to be contradicted by that letter; surely Brahms was not so innocent as to try to grow a beard if he had no whiskers at all. The best guess is that at that point his beard was simply pale and skimpy, as is common with blonds. There remains the question of his abnormally high voice, which Brahms finally tried to lower artificially. In light of all that, my suspicion is that he reached puberty late in his teens, a highly problematical situation given his experiences in the *Lokale*, but maintained a childlike voice and appearance—an incomplete maturity that also goes hard on an adolescent.

24. Quoted in Charlton 130.

25. See Charlton 176 re Hoffmann and Gozzi.

26. Henschel 39.

27. May 82.

28. Niemann 25–6.

29. Watson 105–7.

30. Reich 127.

31. Niemann 25.

32. May 92.

33. May 90.

34. See Dahlhaus *Nineteenth-Century* 84: "In some of Beethoven's late works . . . the thematic structure is a mere facade: the actual musical idea . . . retreats into the interior of the music . . . as a subtheme."

35. Dahlhaus *Nineteenth-Century* 87.
36. Niemann 23.
37. Smyth 106.
38. Kalbeck I, 34. In that conversation Brahms also claimed to have learned nothing "from the thick books of Marx." Surely that is an exaggeration too. Marx, in the 1845 third volume of his *Lehre von der musikalischen Komposition*, bestowed the familiar name "sonata form" and elaborated the concept, principally in the works of Beethoven. (See Rosen *Sonata Forms* 3–4.)
39. MacDonald 60.
40. See MacDonald 61. Geiringer (*Brahms* 25) is dubious of the attribution of *Souvenir de la Russie* to Brahms.
41. Ostwald 232–3.
42. May 95.
43. Musgrave *Music* Chronology.
44. Hofmann.
45. Stephenson 23.
46. Kalbeck I, 69.
47. Mother to JB 5/23/1853, in Stephenson.

CHAPTER THREE

1. Niemann 167.
2. Niemann 29.
3. May 99.
4. May 98.
5. Bellmann 12.
6. See the 1879 Reményi interview in Kalbeck I, 65, in which Reményi claims that he had presented some of his own melodies as "national" songs, as many composers did in those days (including Brahms), and Brahms picked them up. It is exactly this practice that makes the whole question of "folk" music and poetry complex and deceptive. For

another example: Schubert's charming little lied "Heidenröslein" spread so widely in Germany that many came to think of it as a folk song. This is not to say that there is no such thing as folk music, only that identifying it is not a straightforward matter, and that the nationalistic exaltation of it was founded on sand from the beginning. Besides, authentic folk music is generally regional, geographical, and/or ethnic rather than national.
7. Kalbeck I, 72–3.
8. Hanslick *Criticisms* 78–81. In his 1861 review of Joachim's Vienna debut, Hanslick concludes that "[Josef] Hellmesberger's fine, stimulating naturalness would have played more directly to our hearts than Joachim's unbending, Roman earnestness." As usual, Hanslick preferred the known to the unfamiliar.
9. Walker 345.
10. May 107.
11. May 108–9.
12. May 108–9.
13. May 110.
14. Niemann 31.
15. Gal 33.
16. From Mason's recollection, quoted in May 110–11.
17. Charles Rosen's article "Influence: Plagiarism and Inspiration" details the connections of the Brahms E♭ Minor Scherzo to Chopin's in B♭, which seem too extensive to be coincidence. (Still, composers often hear a work and retain a surprising amount unconsciously, while forgetting they ever heard it.) Geiringer notes (*Brahms* 205) that the scherzo's main theme—which I nonetheless call the distinctive Brahmsian mi-

nor—is lifted from an overture by Heinrich Marschner.

18. Liszt was to take thematic manipulation at least one degree further than Brahms when he sometimes tilted a motive on end to create a harmony. This idea was of great importance to later generations including, of course, Schoenberg. It was easier for Liszt to use such techniques because he was more experimental than Brahms in harmony—and the more notes in chords, the more harmony and melody overlap. A complete diatonic ninth chord, after all, contains five of the seven notes in a key.

19. Gal 33.

20. Walker 230.

21. Brahms to Joachim, 6/29/1853, in *Brahms Briefwechsel* V, trans. in Geiringer *Brahms*.

22. Quoted in May 113.

23. Christiane Brahms to JB, 6/11/1853, in Stephenson, trans. in Geiringer *Brahms*.

24. Krebs *Schatzkästlein* #229 and #250.

25. Krebs *Schatzkästlein* #224.

26. Christiane Brahms to JB 7/10– 11/53, in Stephenson 44.

27. Christiane and Elise Brahms to JB, 7/23/1853, in Stephenson 44, trans. in Geiringer *Brahms*.

28. Quoted in Geiringer *Brahms* 33–4.

29. Letters from the Brahms family 7–8/1853, in Stephenson 46–7.

30. Christiane Brahms to JB 9/4/1853, in Stephenson 47.

31. Letters of September 1853, in Stephenson 48–9.

32. Niemann 38.

33. May 119.

CHAPTER FOUR

1. Reich 140.

2. May 121.

3. Burk 282.

4. Dietrich 3.

5. Burk 283.

6. Quoted in Burk 284.

7. Burk 284.

8. *Brahms Briefwechsel* V, 9/1853.

9. Litzmann *Life* 43.

10. Kalbeck I, 112.

11. May 126.

12. Storck R. *Schumann Letters* 10/8/1853.

13. May 123.

14. May 137.

15. Schumann to Joachim 10/13/1853, in Storck R. *Schumann Letters*.

16. Burk 286.

17. Dietrich/Widmann 2–7.

18. Niemann 39–41.

19. Ostwald *Schumann* 268.

20. Schumann to Joachim 10/13/1853, in Storck R. *Schumann Letters*.

21. Walker 341.

22. Ostwald *Schumann* 269–70.

23. *Schumann on Music* 28.

24. Trans. in May 131–2.

25. *Schumann on Music* 49.

26. See Ostwald *Schumann* 42. When he was a teenager especially, Schumann was connected with several young men and his diary mentions "pederasty" and "voluptuous night with Greek dreams." Schumann's homosexual episodes, fantasies, or whatever they amounted to, came at a point of great psychological stress for him, as well as of heavy drinking.

27. Walker 352n.

28. Niemann 46.

29. Litzmann *Briefe* 1.

30. Schauffler 45, which adds the original Plattdeutsch.
31. Litzmann *Briefe* 11/16/1853, trans. in May.
32. Quoted in May 135.
33. Quoted in May 140.
34. MacDonald 19.
35. Stephenson 55–7.
36. Grimm to Joachim 4/1854, in Bickley *Joachim Letters.*
37. Bickley *Joachim Letters* 36.
38. Schumann to Joachim 11/21/1853 and Joachim to Schumann 11/29/53, in Bickley *Joachim Letters.*
39. Joachim to von Arnim 11/27/1853, in Bickley *Joachim Letters.*
40. Kalbeck II, 435.
41. May 143–4.
42. Burk 290.
43. MacDonald 20.
44. Brahms to Joachim 12/7/1853, in *Brahms Briefwechsel* V, trans. in Niemann.
45. Burk 290.
46. Berlioz to Joachim 12/9/1853, in Bickley *Joachim Letters.*
47. Brahms to Joachim 12/10/1853, in *Brahms Briefwechsel* V.
48. MacDonald 20n.
49. May 147.
50. Brahms to R. Schumann 11/29/1853, in Litzmann *Briefe.*
51. Brahms to R. Schumann 12/1853, in Litzmann *Briefe.*
52. Frisch *Developing Variation* 36.
53. Musgrave *Music* 20.
54. Musgrave *Music* 21.
55. Bozarth "'Poetic' Andantes" 348.
56. Trans. in MacDonald 68.
57. Dietrich/Widmann 3.
58. Bozarth "'Poetic' Andantes" 373.
59. Niemann 55

60. Niemann 56.
61. May 160.
62. Quoted in May 161.
63. Niemann 57.
64. Burk 295.
65. Niemann 57.
66. Schumann to Joachim 2/6/1854, adapted from Bickley *Joachim Letters.*
67. Dietrich to Joachim 2/28/54, in Bickley *Joachim Letters.*

CHAPTER FIVE

1. Reich 140.
2. Ostwald *Schumann* 256.
3. Reich 138–9.
4. Reich 79–80.
5. Reich 25.
6. Reich 50–2.
7. Ostwald *Schumann* 36.
8. Ostwald *Schumann* 35–7.
9. Ostwald *Schumann* 61.
10. Ostwald *Schumann* 76.
11. Ostwald *Schumann* 77–8.
12. Among the theories trying to account for Schumann's mental condition the suspicion of syphilis has inevitably come up, since the disease was epidemic in the nineteenth century and afflicted many figures, including Schubert and Nietzsche. Psychiatrist Peter Ostwald convincingly refutes that theory in his biography. As Ostwald details, Schumann's mental problems appeared too early to be the product of syphilis, and in general his symptoms are not consistent with the disease. Ostwald concludes that we cannot say with any certainty what was the matter with Schumann, but it was probably a combination of a serious bipolar disorder with chronic physical illnesses, including an early case

of malaria and associated meningitis and cardiovascular problems (see Ostwald's *Schumann*, last chapter).

13. Ostwald *Schumann* 116.
14. Reich 84.
15. Article on R. Schumann in Grove's.
16. Reich 121–2.
17. Reich 155.
18. Reich 126.
19. Smyth 124.
20. Kalbeck 1, 113.
21. Litzmann *Life* 56–8.
22. Burk 299–301.
23. Marie Schumann in Reich 144.
24. It is not entirely clear how Brahms and Joachim first got the news about Schumann—it may have been from Dietrich's letter or from a Hanover newspaper.
25. Litzmann *Life* 60–1.
26. Litzmann *Life* 63.
27. Litzmann *Life* 63.
28. Litzmann *Life* 62.
29. Bickley *Joachim Letters* 3/6/ 1854.
30. Litzmann *Life* 67–8.
31. Litzmann *Life* 74.
32. Litzmann *Life* 69.
33. Reich 145.
34. Litzmann *Life* 71.
35. Reich 147.
36. Litzmann *Life* 71–2.
37. Stephenson 53–4.
38. Stephenson 55.
39. Niemann 62.
40. Neighbor "Opus Nines" 266–7.
41. Ostwald *Schumann* 77.
42. Litzmann *Life* 76.
43. Bickley *Joachim Letters* 6/9/ 1854.
44. Litzmann *Life* 63.
45. Quoted in Musgrave *Music* 29.
46. Horne 252. Brahms's proposed

collection of occasional pieces echoes Schumann's similar grab-bag *Bunte Blätter (Mottled Leaves)*. Sams ("Clara Themes" 433–4) finds suggestive connections in Brahms's B Major Trio to Schumann's *Genoveva* and general Clara-symbolism.

47. Keyes 18.
48. Holde 314.
49. Bickley *Joachim Letters* 7/27/ 1854.
50 Bickley *Joachim Letters* 9/12/ 1854.
51. Litzmann *Life* 65, 83.
52. Litzmann *Schumann/Brahms Letters* 8/15/1854.
53. May 171–2.
54. Litzmann *Schumann/Brahms Letters* 8/21/1854.
55. Litzmann *Schumann/Brahms Letters* 8/27/1854.
56. Burk 311.
57. Litzmann *Schumann/Brahms Letters* 9/14/1854.
58. Bickley *Joachim Letters* 9/17/ 1854.
59. Quoted in Burk 312.
60. Litzmann *Life* 87–8.
61. Litzmann *Life* 74.
62. Krebs *Schatzkästlein* #296.
63. Krebs *Schatzkästlein* #510.
64. Krebs *Schatzkästlein* #560.
65. Krebs *Schatzkästlein* #584–5.
66. Krebs *Schatzkästlein* 321.
67. Bozarth "Sprichworte" 17.
68. Bickley *Joachim Letters* 9/12/ 1854.
69. MacDonald 82.
70. Sams, "Clara Themes."
71. Rosen *Romantic Generation* 222–3.
72. Bozarth "Lieder ohne Worte" 378.
73. From Malcolm MacDonald's speculation in *Brahms* 86.

74. Litzmann *Schumann/Brahms Letters* 9/26/1854.
75. Litzmann *Life* 81.
76. Storck *R. Schumann Letters* 11/27/1854.

CHAPTER SIX

1. Reich 148–9.
2. Litzmann *Schumann/Brahms Letters* 8/27/1854.
3. Walker 343 and Litzmann *Life* 91.
4. Litzmann *Life* 91.
5. Litzmann *Brahms/Schumann Letters* 10/21/54.
6. Bickley *Joachim/Letters* 91.
7. Bickley *Joachim Letters* 91.
8. Bickley *Joachim Letters* 10/20/1854.
9. Schumann/Brahms *Letters* 10/21/1854 and end of Oct.
10. Stephenson 22.
11. Burk 315–17 and Litzmann *Life* 91–2.
12. Reich 149.
13. Stephenson 59.
14. Quoted in Keys 22.
15. Litzmann *Schumann/Brahms Letters* 11/30/1854.
16. Litzmann *Schumann/Brahms Letters* 12/15/1854.
17. Litzmann *Schumann/Brahms Letters* 12/15/1854.
18. Litzmann *Life* 98.
19. Litzmann *Life* 98.
20. Litzmann *Life* 99.
21. Litzmann *Schumann/Brahms Letters* 11/30/1854.
22. Bickley *Joachim Letters* 1/18/1855.
23. May 181–2.
24. Reynolds 5.
25. Litzmann *Life* 100n.

26. Litzmann *Schumann/Brahms Letters* 1/25/1855.
27. Litzmann *Schumann/Brahms Letters* 24n.
28. Suicide by starvation is the inevitably tentative but convincing diagnosis of psychiatrist Peter Ostwald, in *Schumann: The Inner Voices of a Musical Genius*. On a foundation of that conclusion I add my conjectures about what Brahms may have had to do with it.
29. Einstein 109.
30. That Clara Schumann could and eventually did take care of herself perfectly well does not apply in all this—she herself thought she needed a husband. In theory if not practice Clara conformed to the conventional wife's role of dependent and supporter of her husband.
31. Niemann 49.
32. Litzmann *Schumann/Brahms Letters* 3/20/1855.
33. Litzmann *Schumann/Brahms Letters* 2/3/1855.
34. Litzmann *Life* 102.
35. Burk 326.
36. Reynolds 5. With this letter Brahms enclosed a new musical idea that nearly a decade later would become the adagio theme of the G Major String Sextet.
37. Litzmann *Briefe* 3/3/1855.
38. MacDonald 225.
39. Brodbeck *Sprichworte*.
40. Litzmann *Life* 102–3.
41. Litzmann *Schumann/Brahms Letters* 2/23–4/1855.
42. Quoted in Ostwald *Schumann* 289.
43. Litzmann *Life* 107.
44. Litzmann *Life* 108.
45. The impression of Clara

Wieck/Schumann as a composer that one gains from her diary and from Nancy Reich's book is not of a woman whose creative side was thwarted. The men in Clara's life from her father to Schumann to Brahms encouraged her to compose, and she had the same distinguished publisher for her work that her husband did—Breitkopf & Härtel. Clara did seem daunted at the idea of being a female composer, in the sense that she felt if she were not first-rate at it she would let down her sex, perhaps adversely affecting future women composers. In any case, she declined to do anything less than first-rate. (Certainly her eventual decision to give up composing—if it was a conscious decision—was influenced by her being involved with two supremely gifted composers.) After her husband died Clara hardly wrote anything new, while her performing career skyrocketed. Everything suggests that Clara never felt as confident or happy in her composing as she did at the piano. As a result, she gravitated to what she knew she was good at and most loved, performing, and let go the thing she was not sure she was first-rate at or ever would be—composing. Her need to make a living for her family certainly reinforced that decision, but did not dictate it. With her genius and reputation it would certainly have been possible for Clara to find patrons and/or a second husband to provide for her and the children, and give her time to compose. There is no indication she ever considered that. In other words, Clara Schumann and Johannes Brahms made opposite career choices for similar reasons: going toward their main strength and greatest fulfilment. To say that Clara made the wrong choice is not only to second-guess a supreme artist and professional, but also to presume that pianists are inferior to composers—a dubious presumption.

46. Brodbeck "Brahms-Joachim Counterpoint Exchange" 69.

47. Litzmann *Life* 109.

48. Burk 325.

49. Litzmann *Life* 110.

50. May 190.

51. Bickley *Joachim Letters* 6/23 and 25/1855.

52. E. Schumann 4.

53. Litzmann *Schumann/Brahms Letters* 6/25/1855.

54. Litzmann *Life* 113.

55. Burk 330 and Kalbeck I, 250.

56. Litzmann *Life* 113–4.

57. Burk 331–2.

58. Litzmann *Life* 86.

59. Litzmann *Life* 115–6.

60. Litzmann *Schumann/Brahms Letters* 8/12/1855.

61. Litzmann *Schumann/Brahms Letters* 8/19/1855.

CHAPTER SEVEN

1. Litzmann *Schumann/Brahms Letters* 8/20/1855.

2. Besides the neo-Baroque A minor suite there were some pieces in B minor, perhaps toward a suite in that key.

3. Kalbeck I, 239–40.

4. Litzmann *Life* 78.

5. Specht 45.

6. Ostwald *Schumann* 291.

7. Litzmann *Life* 117.

8. Litzmann *Life* 120.

9. Litzmann *Schumann/Brahms Letters* 11/3/1855.

10. Brodbeck "Brahms-Joachim Counterpoint Exchange" 33.

11. Litzmann *Life* 120 and May 195.

12. May 195.

13. Litzmann *Schumann/Brahms Letters* 11/20/1855.

14. Litzmann *Schumann/Brahms Letters* 11/25/1855.

15. May 196.

16. Litzmann *Schumann/Brahms Letters* 12/4/1855.

17. Litzmann *Schumann/Brahms Letters* 12/4/1855.

18. Bickley *Joachim Letters* 12/9/1855.

19. Litzmann *Life* 123.

20. May 199–200.

21. Horne 269.

22. Litzmann *Life* 123.

23. Litzmann *Life* 126.

24. Kalbeck I, 255–6.

25. May 201.

26. Litzmann *Schumann/Brahms Letters* 1/15/1856.

27. Litzmann *Schumann/Brahms Letters* 1/15/1856.

28. Stephenson 65.

29. Litzmann *Schumann/Brahms Letters* 2/12/1856, quoted on 66n.

30. MacDonald 95–8 and Appendix. MacDonald is convinced the work is authentic, Geiringer doubtful.

31. Bickley *Joachim Letters* 2/26/1856.

32. Brodbeck "Brahms-Joachim Counterpoint Exchange" 34n.

33. The information in this section is largely based on the study by Brodbeck in "The Brahms-Joachim Counterpoint Exchange."

34. Joachim's complaint about the *Geistliches Lied* is a response to spots such as the first beat of measure 59, where a double suspension produces a startling superimposition of E♭, F, G, A♭, and on the second beat the soprano leaps to a sharp dissonance, producing a harmony of F, G, A♭.

35. See Brodbeck "Exchange" 73–6. Brodbeck also surmises that Brahms encoded his own name in the piece, and thereby "sought nothing less than to identify himself with the role of Clara's spouse"; but the encoding, if authentic at all, is obscure.

36. Ostwald *Schumann* 291–2. From the standard hospital procedures, Ostwald surmises that Schumann may have been tube-fed, but it was not enough to keep him alive.

37. Geiringer *Brahms* 49.

38. Litzmann *Schumann/Brahms Letters* 5/31/1856.

39. Litzmann *Schumann/Brahms Letters* 5/24/1856.

40. Litzmann *Schumann/Brahms Letters* 5/31/1856.

41. Litzmann *Schumann/Brahms Letters* 5/31/1856.

42. Litzmann *Life* 137.

43. Litzmann *Life* 138–9, Geiringer *Brahms* 349 (Brahms/Grimm letter).

44. Reich 151.

45. Litzmann *Life* 138–40 and May 213.

46. Bickley *Joachim Letters* 8/8/1856 and May 215.

47. Geiringer *Brahms* 50.

48. Kalbeck I, 285.

49. E. Schumann 154. It is usually presented in biographies that the trip to Switzerland was the deciding point, but I have noted that Brahms's letters imply he began pulling away well before then. It would be charac-

teristic of him to wax passionate when Schumann's prognosis was more hopeful, then to pull back when Schumann's decline meant Brahms would have to make good on his avowals of love. Clara was the first to experience that pattern of his, but not the last.

50. E. Schumann 154.
51. E. Schumann 154.
52. Burk 324.
53. Litzmann *Life* 145.
54. Litzmann *Life* 146.
55. Bickley *Joachim Letters* 10/6/1857.
56. E. Schumann 155.
57. Litzmann *Life* 147.

CHAPTER EIGHT

1. Litzmann *Life* 152.
2. Stephenson 70.
3. May 217. Though Clara Schumann spent her career playing her husband's A Minor Concerto, one of the most popular ever written, she always considered the later movements weak. She wrote Joachim of "how much it hurts to find a defect in one whom we love supremely. That will perhaps explain to you my tears when playing Robert's Concerto." She tried to convince Joachim to recompose the finale, but he declined. (Bickley *Joachim Letters* 154.)
4. Tovey *Concertos* 115.
5. S. Drinker 10–12.
6. Sisman 143n.
7. Litzmann *Schumann/Brahms Letters* 12/4/1856.
8. Reynolds 5.
9. The collection of notes in the introduction of the concerto's first movement imply E♭ major, but that never sounds like the tonic, which re-

mains obscure for some time even though the basses hold D as a pedal tone. In the recapitulation of the first movement the A♭ of the opening is redefined as G♯, as the chord superimposed on the D pedal becomes E major rather than B♭ major. The recap forms an interesting structural change on the original tritone with the bass; it is also tonally ambiguous, as in the introduction.

10. Most writers treat Beethoven's Ninth as a direct influence on the Brahms D Minor Concerto, but there is a caveat to that. According to the reminiscence of his friend Albert Dietrich, Brahms had three movements of the two-piano sonata, one of them eventually the concerto's first movement, sketched by March 9, 1854, less than two weeks after Schumann's suicide attempt. It was not until March 28 that Brahms first heard the Ninth live, with Grimm at a concert in Cologne. (Legend relates that he emerged saying, "I must write something like that!") The Cologne performance also came before Joachim gave Brahms the Liszt piano-duet arrangement of the Ninth. None of this says there was no influence of the Ninth on Brahms's concerto, only that the influence was less direct. Brahms had certainly gone over the Beethoven score in his studies, and several aspects of the concerto recall the Ninth—the key, the monumental scale, the expressive tone, even the initial dichotomy of D and B♭ (though that dichotomy is structurally more significant in Beethoven than in Brahms). Maybe the best way to think of it is that hearing the Ninth for the first time was an over-

whelming experience for Brahms because it connected so strongly with music he had already sketched out, and thereafter the Ninth became part of the creative ferment that produced the concerto out of the original two-piano piece.

11. The idea that the opening of the First Piano Concerto pictures Schumann's leap into the Rhine is the suggestion of biographer Max Kalbeck, which he said he got directly from Joachim. Geiringer rejects the idea, but most writers tentatively accept it. I accept it firmly for several reasons: the time it was composed, within days of the tragedy; that most of Brahms's music of that period had to do with Robert and Clara in symbolic terms; that he wrote another programmatic piece that year, the first of the Four Ballades; Joachim's testimony; and the dizzying, tragic tone of the opening itself. I don't particularly see, on the other hand, why we need to view the whole first movement as a programmatic description of events. It seems more likely that Schumann's disaster inspired the opening and its tragic tone, gentler contrasts to that came naturally into the movement, and from there on "abstract" formal principles and expressive contrast took precedence. At the same time, I'm convinced by Musgrave's refutation (in "Frei aber Froh: a Reconsideration") of Kalbeck's equally famous surmise that Brahms had a *frei aber froh* ("free but happy," F-A-F in pitches) motto to match Joachim's F-A-E / *frei aber einsam*. There is no convincing evidence that Brahms used F-A-F as a deliberate pattern with any consistency.

12. Gal 111.

13. MacDonald 101.

14. MacDonald 102.

15. Siegfried Kross ("Brahms and Hoffmann" 199–200) proposes a Kreisler connection for the Latin phrase noted in the second movement. All are speculations. Brahms here, as doubtless elsewhere, managed to insert a private reference in the score that, for a change, stayed private. For other speculations about Schumann connections in the second movement, see Reynolds.

16. Rosen "Plagiarism" 91.

17. Gal 115.

18. Kalbeck I, 292.

19. Litzmann *Life* 148.

20. Litzmann *Life* 150.

21. Bickley *Joachim Letters* 8/27/1857.

22. May 225.

23. Litzmann *Life* 152.

24. Litzmann *Schumann/Brahms Letters* 10/11/1857.

25. Bickley *Joachim Letters* 11/27/1857.

26. May 226.

27. MacDonald 50.

28. Hancock "Early Choral Music" 126.

29. Kalbeck I, 314.

30. Kalbeck I, 315.

31. Bickley *Joachim Letters* 1/3/1858.

32. May 232.

33. Stephenson 20. Kalbeck's listing of the family residences has them in Fuhlentwiete from 1859.

34. Litzmann *Schumann/Brahms Letters* 2/28/1858.

35. Bickley *Joachim Letters* 3/12/1858 and Christiane's report on Joachim in Stephenson 79–80.

36. Litzmann *Life* 159. In light of

Clara Schumann's and Theodor
Kirchner's later relationship, it is
striking that in this letter she goes
out of her way to talk about her affin-
ity for Brahms: "It was a special providence that let me find so true a
friend in that dark time, a friend
whom I admire as much as I am devoted to him." It is as if she was making certain that Kirchner knew the
extent of her connection to Brahms,
come what may.

37. Litzmann *Life* 159.
38. Litzmann *Schumann/Brahms Letters* 6/25/1858.
39. Ehrmann 66.
40. *Brahms Briefwechsel* IV, 50.
41. S. Drinker 13.
42. Geiringer *Brahms* 57.
43. Schauffler 138–9.
44. Schauffler 138.
45. Schauffler 226.
46. E. Schumann 4.
47. Geiringer *Brahms* 58.
48. MacDonald 51.
49. Burk 364.
50. S. Drinker 15.
51. *Brahms Briefwechsel* IV, 67.
52. *Brahms Briefwechsel* IV, 68.
53. Hancock "Early Choral Music" 126.
54. Keys 31. Likely Brahms is referring not to the original nonet
(there may also have been an octet
version) but to the small-orchestra
version of the D Major Serenade as
the "mongrel," and began working
on the full-orchestra arrangement
around this time. According to the
Hofmann *Zeittafel*, the full-orchestra
version was finished in February
1860. The fact that the later D Major
versions and the A Major Serenade
overlapped in composition makes for
confusion in the chronology.

55. Kalbeck I, 339.
56. Litzmann *Schumann/Brahms Letters* 11/8/1858.
57. Litzmann *Life* 165.
58. *Schumann/Brahms Letters* 12/20/1858. Clara is writing from Vienna.
59. Kalbeck I, 293.
60. Stephenson 83.
61. Jacobsen 43.
62. Bickley *Joachim Letters* 1/28/1859.
63. May 246.
64. May 247.
65. Bickley *Schumann/Brahms Letters* 8/5/1859.
66. Bickley *Schumann/Brahms Letters* 2/2/1859.
67. Dietrich/Widmann 117–18.
68. Schauffler 267–8.

CHAPTER NINE

1. Litzmann *Schumann/Brahms Letters* 3/26/1859.
2. Litzmann *Schumann/Brahms Letters* 3/29/1859.
3. Keys 35.
4. Litzmann *Schumann/Brahms Letters* 3/31/1859.
5. May 269.
6. S. Drinker 23.
7. S. Drinker 56–7.
8. S. Drinker 44.
9. Schauffler 270.
10. Geiringer *Brahms* 63.
11. Hancock "Early Choral Music" 126.
12. Litzmann *Schumann/Brahms Letters* 8/28/1859.
13. S. Drinker 23.
14. S. Drinker. Except where
otherwise noted, the information on the Hamburg Frauenchor
in this chapter comes from

S. Drinker, *Brahms and His Women's Choruses*, cited with page numbers in the text.

15. Litzmann *Schumann/Brahms Letters* 9/30/1859.
16. Keys 30.
17. Kalbeck I, 396–7.
18. Litzmann *Schumann/Brahms Letters* 11/9/1859.
19. S. Drinker (68) says "the public appearance of a Ladies' Choral Society was quite unusual" at that time, and Brahms's concerts with them were pioneering in that respect.
20. Bickley *Joachim Letters* 12/31/ 1859. The best guess is that Joachim is talking about the D Major, in its final version.
21. S. Drinker 49.
22. May 265–6.
23. Bickley *Joachim Letters* 191–2.
24. Trans. in May 269–70.
25. Gal 31.
26. Quoted in Weiss/Taruskin 380.
27. Walker 339.
28. Quoted in Weiss/Taruskin 382.
29. Quoted in Gal 34.
30. Walker 348.
31. Litzmann *Life* 178.
32. MacDonald 57.

CHAPTER TEN

1. Litzmann *Schumann/Brahms Letters* 4/26/1860.
2. Litzmann *Life* 181.
3. Drinker 51.
4. Laura Garbe was upset at this affectionate dig at her lateness until Clara pointed out that it would secure her a place in history (Drinker 56).
5. Litzmann *Schumann/Brahms Letters* 4/2/1860.

6. S. Drinker 60.
7. Litzmann *Schumann/Brahms Letters* 6/21/1860.
8. Kalbeck I, 414.
9. Kalbeck I, 132.
10. The measure grouping of the first four phrases in the B♭ Sextet is 2+2+1, then 3+1 before a series of two-bar phrases. Throughout the first movement, Brahms likewise plays off irregular against even groupings. The final rondo, which begins like the first movement with a lyric cello theme, seems almost teasingly stuck in two-bar units for some time—followed, naturally, by a surge of irregular phrasing and syncopation.
11. Translation from Braus 148. Braus also quotes another entry on form from the "Schatzkästlein": "I can neither sculpt nor tailor my work in compliance with the latest fashion: newness and originality happen of themselves, without my having to think about it." That may express Brahms's determination not to make a fetish of originality as the New Germans did, but we will see that over the years he consistently came up with fresh approaches to traditional formal patterns. Rather than always taking the words of the "Schatzkästlein" as his ultimate destination, it might be better to think of them as a youthful foundation that in some degree he grew beyond. True, the treatment of form in the first movement of the D Minor Piano Concerto is relatively free, far more so than the later B♭ Sextet; but that seems more a result of serendipity than planning—the movement was first drafted in a rush of emotion after Schumann's suicide attempt, and

probably despite much revision retained some of its initial improvisatory looseness. In contrast, Brahms's later games with sonata form are more purposeful and controlled.

13. Litzmann *Life* 188.

14. S. Drinker 67–8.

15. Litzmann *Life* 189.

16. Gal 232.

17. Litzmann *Life* 196.

18. Litzmann Schumann *Brahms Letters* 2/13/1861.

19. Reich 157.

20. Litzmann *Life* 244.

21. E. Schumann 72–3.

22. E. Schumann 87.

23. S. Drinker 69.

24. Keys 41.

25. S. Drinker 70.

26. Niemann 169.

27. Dietrich/Widmann 37–8. The toy soldiers are variously described as tin or lead. Brahms probably had both, grouped in collections.

28. Kalbeck I, 443.

29. May 284–5.

30. Rosen *Sonata Forms* 3.

31. Litzmann *Life* 200.

32. Litzmann *Schumann/Brahms Letters* 7/29/1861. Clara declared a variant (more or less inversion) of the second theme "too commonplace for Johannes Brahms." He left it there.

33. As testament of his admiration for "Brahms the Progressive" and in recognition of the orchestral scope of the G Minor, Schoenberg arranged the whole piano quartet for orchestra. In a number of Brahms's chamber pieces there is a sense that the music could work as well in another medium—just as in reality the F Minor Piano Quintet began as a string quintet and was made into a two-piano sonata before it found its final form.

34. Sisman 133.

35. Joachim said that ideas for the G Minor and A Major Piano quartets traced back to the same time as the unfinished C♯ Minor Piano Quartet—around 1855 (M. McCorkle 84.)

36. After the performance of the G Minor, Clara wrote in her journal: "The last movement took the audience by storm. The quartet only partially satisfies me, there is too little unity in the first movement, and the emotion in the adagio is too forced, without really carrying me away. But I love the allegretto . . . and the last movement" (Litzmann 200). Joachim wrote Brahms about the piece: "The *invention* in the first movement is not so pregnant as I am used to getting from you, but it's often quite wonderful what you make of the themes!"

37. Litzmann *Schumann/Brahms Letters* 10/1861

38. Litzmann *Life* 199. Around then Joachim tried to convince Clara to join him working at court in Hanover, but she declined in favor of performing.

39. Reich 209. Neither Reich nor MacDonald give details of Clara's only recently discovered affair. I have surmised its approximate dates from letters, etc.

40. Litzmann *Life* 375.

41. Litzmann *Life* 201.

42. Litzmann *Life* 202.

43. Dietrich 41.

44. Dietrich/Widmann 43–4.

45. Material on the articles is from Frisch "Brahms and Schubring." Here Schubring seems to define the main factions as the Mendelssohn camp and the New

Germans, with Brahms among the Schumannians in between. Excerpts from the articles are in Frisch *Brahms and His World.*

46. In a note to me, Ira Braus writes that the spread of development outside the development section was a common problem of post-1860 composers, "the price one pays for using developing variation technique in classical forms."

47. Keys 43.

48. Dietrich/Widmann 46–7.

49. Bickley *Joachim Letters* 283.

50. Litzmann *Life* 209.

51. Bickley *Joachim Letters* 262.

52. Litzmann *Life* 210–11.

53. May 300.

54. Dietrich/Widmann 51.

55. Stephenson 86–7.

56. Litzmann *Schumann/Brahms Letters* 11/3/1862.

57. Bickley *Joachim Letters* 288.

58. Stephenson 24.

59. Litzmann *Schumann/Brahms Letters* 11/18/1862. Paragraph breaks added. Brahms never blamed Stockhausen for taking the job. Still, for all his resentment Brahms eventually reconciled to some degree with Avé, who seems to have been a decent and likable sort.

CHAPTER ELEVEN

1. Kalbeck II, 10.

2. Schorske 25.

3. Schorske 36.

4. Schorske 45.

5. Morton 4.

6. During the war the Opera was largely destroyed. The current auditorium is a postwar design—one even more incongruous with the outside.

7. Schorske 4.

8. Blackbourne 9, 24.

9. I have deliberately left Brahms's mentor Robert Schumann out of this formula of influences, because while Schumann's influence was profound it was also subtle (for example, the interest in piano quartet as a medium, and in musical symbolism). Brahms can remind one of Handel, Bach, Beethoven, Schubert, Renaissance polyphony, folk song, and a number of other things; rarely do his harmonies and melodies remind us of Schumann.

10. Botstein "Time and Memory" 7.

11. Graf *Composer and Critic* 244.

12. Hanslick *Criticisms* 20–1.

13. Quoted in Gal 80.

14. Janik and Toulmin 103.

15. Watson 191.

16. Hanslick *Criticisms* 12.

17. Hanslick *Criticisms* 13.

18. Hanslick *Criticisms* 289.

CHAPTER TWELVE

1. MacDonald 232.

2. D. McCorkle *Haydn Variations* 22.

3. May 333 and Niemann 86.

4. Hanslick *Criticisms* 82–3.

5. Frisch *Developing Variation* 77.

6. Frisch *Developing Variation* 81.

7. Frisch *Developing Variation* 88–9.

8. The sketch is in Joseph.

9. Brahms's landlady in Mürrzuschlag recalled, "Er stellte sich zum Fenster Klavier, spielte ein paar Töne, ging in Zimmer auf und ab, summte einige Noten und markte sich davon Notizen." (Exhibition in the Mürzzuschag Brahms Museum)

10. See D. McCorkle "Five Fundamental Obstacles," which points out that later Brahms editors have not been impeccable either.

11. In fact, Bach made many revisions of his work, on strips of paper pinned to the scores. All that remains of most of these revisions are pinholes in the manuscripts.

12. Bickley *Joachim Letters* 283.

13. Quoted in Gal 39.

14. Walker 180.

15. Kalbeck II, 38.

16. Geiringer "Wagner and Brahms" 182–3.

17. Specht 151.

18. Heuberger 50.

19. Graf 185.

20. Trans. in Musgrave "Cultural World."

21. Gal 143.

22. C. Wagner II, 25.

23. C. Wagner 362–3.

24. C. Wagner 518.

25. Gutman 397.

26. Geiringer "Wagner and Brahms" 180.

27. Gal 39.

28. Geiringer "Wagner and Brahms" 182.

29. Kalbeck II, 44.

30. S. Drinker 80.

31. Geiringer *Brahms* 353.

32. May 339.

33. Bickley *Joachim Letters* 291.

34. Bickley *Joachim Letters* 295–6.

35. Stephenson 20.

36. From Dietrich 55 and Kalbeck II, 50.

37. M. McCorkle 203.

38. S. Drinker 72.

39. Litzmann *Life* 216.

40. May 344–5.

41. Hanslick "Memories" 171.

42. May 347–8.

43. May 348.

44. Specht 174. Hermann Levi, more and more taken by the Wagnerian siren song, surely had an ulterior motive in trying to drive a wedge between Brahms and Hanslick, but his words still ring true.

45. Dietrich/Widmann 57.

46. Holde 316–7.

47. Hancock "Early Choral Music" 130–31.

48. Specht 136.

49. Specht 135.

50. Litzmann *Schumann/Brahms Letters* 4/4/1864.

51. Kalbeck II, 113.

52. Litzmann *Schumann/Brahms Letters* 4/4/1864.

53. Schauffler 285n.

54. Barkan *Brahms/Billroth Letters* 29.

55. Sams *Brahms Songs* 5.

56. Sams *Brahms Songs* 5.

57. Janik/Toulmin 47.

58. Litzmann *Schumann/Brahms Letters* 7/19/1864. In fact, when she first met Brahms's parents a decade earlier, Clara had noted Johannes's preference for his father, though he was devoted to both parents. Probably in 1864 Clara was responding to his increased concern for his mother in her declining years. Johann Jakob, seventeen years younger than his wife, was still healthy and active.

59. *Brahms in Baden* 17.

60. E. Schumann 11–15.

61. E. Schumann 61.

62. E. Schumann 18.

63. E. Schumann 41–5.

64. From *Grove* s.v. Viardot-Garcia.

65. MacDonald 131.

66. *Brahms in Baden* 28.

67. Litzmann *Schumann/Brahms Letters* 11/3/1864.

68. Brody 25.

69. *Brahms Briefwechsel* XVIII, 65 n8.

70. E. Schumann 113.

71. Musgrave *Music.*

72. Kalbeck II, 154.

73. Geiringer *Brahms* 90.

74. *Brahms Briefwechsel* VII, 17.

75. *Brahms Briefwechsel* IV 113–14.

76. Gal 91.

CHAPTER THIRTEEN

1. Litzmann, *Schumann/Brahms Letters* 12/5/1864.

2. Litzmann, *Schumann/Brahms Letters* 12/5/1864.

3. Stephenson 104.

4. Geiringer *Brahms* 87. Geiringer notes that Brahms kept the letters he wrote his father but destroyed the ones to his mother.

5. Stephenson 106.

6. Stephenson 11–12, 107.

7. As Kalbeck details (II, 175), Florence May's melodramatic account of Christiane Brahms's death and funeral probably comes from the imagination of the Cossels' daughter. He also disputes the story, often quoted, that after the funeral Brahms cried, "I have no mother now, I must marry!"

8. Litzmann *Schumann/Brahms Letters* 2/8/1865.

9. *Brahms Briefwechsel* XVII, 41n.

10. Litzmann *Schumann/Brahms Letters* 2/10/1865.

11. Litzmann *Schumann/Brahms Letters* 2/8/1865.

12. Litzmann *Schumann/Brahms Letters* 3/23/1865.

13. Litzmann *Schumann/Brahms Letters* 3/6/1865.

14. Litzmann *Schumann/Brahms Letters* 4/24/1865. In this letter Brahms cites the wrong key for the "All flesh is grass" second movement.

15. *Brahms in Baden* 10.

16. What I mean by a composer *feeling* an instrument is an admittedly vague quality, but real all the same. It is a matter of the composer creating the illusion that exactly *this* instrument in *this* register is the inevitable vehicle of *those* notes, *that* gesture. Perhaps the supreme example of it is Mahler, who worked from daily experience as a conductor and had an uncanny intuitive connection with the orchestra. An audible demonstration is the difference between the original and reconstructed (expertly, from rough drafts) movements in Mahler's Tenth. When the symphony returns to Mahler's own scoring in the third movement, it is as if a light were switched on inside the music; suddenly every texture is lucid and every timbre wedded to every gesture. By no means does this imply that a piece can never be arranged for another medium. Stravinsky, another transcendent master of instrumentation, somehow made both the original *L'histoire du soldat* and his arrangement of parts of it for violin, clarinet, and piano sound inevitable for the medium at hand. Arguably, more often than with any other composer of his stature, Brahms's scoring lacks that sense of inevitability in chamber and orchestral

music. Thus his readiness to rearrange pieces for different media, beyond the usual pragmatic piano arrangements. This, however, is very different from saying, as many did in his own time and later, that Brahms "could not orchestrate." His scoring, manifestly uncertain in his early career, became more than merely competent in his maturity. As we will see, there are stunning and original moments in his scoring. To repeat a point made earlier: Brahms's scoring is not weak, but rather the *relatively* weak suit of an extraordinary technician.

17. MacDonald 175.

18. In a letter to Richard Heuberger, Brahms claimed a practical reason for the choice of natural horn: "If the performer is not obliged by the stopped notes to play softly, the piano and violin are not obliged to adapt themselves to him, and the tone is rough from the beginning." (Quoted in May 371–2.) Certainly the Trio presents balance problems, with the horn tending to dominate. It took some time to catch on, and only occasionally—including the Karlsruhe premiere with Brahms at the piano in December 1865—was it done on the natural instrument.

19. Litzmann 239.

20. Stephenson 115, trans. in Geiringer *Brahms.*

21. Specht 154.

22. Stephenson 115–6, trans. in Gal.

23. M. McCorkle 130.

24. Dietrich/Widmann 48.

25. Litzmann *Schumann/Brahms Letters* 12/3/1865.

26. Geiringer "Wagner and Brahms" 184–5.

27. Dietrich/Widmann 94.

28. Litzmann *Life* 242.

29. Bickley *Joachim Letters* 334–6.

30. Schauffler 132.

31. Litzmann 242.

32. Litzmann *Schumann/Brahms Letters* 1/24/1866.

33. Litzmann *Schumann/Brahms Letters* 2/4/1866.

34. Litzmann *Schumann/Brahms Letters* 12/30/1866.

35. Geiringer *Brahms* 94.

36. Barkan *Brahms/Billroth Letters* 6.

37. Gartenberg 153.

38. Stephenson 121.

39. Hanslick "Memories" 172.

40. Litzmann *Life* 246.

41. Litzmann *Life* 246n.

42. Geiringer *Brahms* 356.

43. Keys 55.

44. May 384–5.

45. Litzmann 247–8.

46. Litzmann *Schumann/Brahms Letters* 12/30/1866.

47. Litzmann *Life* 249.

48. May 386.

49. Litzmann *Schumann/Brahms Letters* 4/26/1867.

50. Gal 72. The "all-engendering love" that Levi proclaims as the indispensable moral and personal foundation for an artist hints at a reason for his future connection to Wagner, who proclaimed and at times marvelously evoked (not only in *Tristan,* but in the *Ring*) a world-encompassing vision of love. Part of the pathos of Levi's later idolization of Wagner is that he managed to convince himself of Wagner's personal goodness—a faith not only delusional but masochistic.

51. Litzmann *Life* 254.

52. Litzmann *Life* 256.

53. *Schumann/Brahms Letters* 11/
13/1867. (This letter is split between
Litzmann's *Life* and the *Letters*.)

54. May 390.

55. Stephenson 132.

56. Geiringer *Brahms* 97.

57. Gal 43.

58. From several letters, one of
them 12/7/1867 in Litzmann *Schu-
mann/ Brahms Letters.*

59. Keys 57.

60. Niemann 96.

61. May 396.

62. The manuscript of the *Requiem* reveals that the French horns
in the third movement fugue, which
with cavalier disregard for the en-
durance of the players' lips had originally been assigned the D for the
duration (though alternating—
Brahms did understand that horn
players have to breathe), were now
provided new figures with rests.
Meanwhile, the trombones and tuba
still alternate on one pitch for the
whole thirty-six measures, a stiff demand on any brass player, and one
saying much about Brahms's still
shaky understanding of orchestral instruments. On the evidence of his letter to Marxsen in the text, Brahms
appears to have worried that the sustained D would not have enough
weight without organ, which was
lacking in the old Gesellschaft hall,
so he awkwardly tried to build up the
sonority of the pedal tone in the low
brass. (In that Brahms was probably
thinking of another D pedal that
never got enough weight in his scoring—the one that begins the First Piano Concerto.) In all these
calculations and revisions he seems
never to have questioned the under-

lying problem, which I suggest is the
conception of the pedal D in the first
place.

63. Gal 187–8.

64. Gal 188.

65. There is a certain mystery
about Amalie Joachim's performance
of "I know that my Redeemer liveth,"
because she was a contralto and Handel's aria is written for soprano. Since
it seems certain that she sang the
Handel in the premiere, it either was
transposed or Amalie had a remarkable upper range for a contralto.
(The first possibility seems more
likely.)

66. *Brahms Briefwechsel* XVIII, 48–
9n.

67. May 406.

68. Litzmann *Schumann/Brahms
Letters* 2/2/1868. (Paragraph breaks
added.)

69. Litzmann *Schumann/Brahms
Letters* 3/19/1868.

70. Keys 57.

71. Litzmann *Schumann/Brahms
Letters* 9/4/1868.

72. Musgrave *Music* 103.

73. MacDonald 169, with further
commentary from Raphael Atlas—
MacDonald calls the form of the finale a sonata, Atlas a rondo.

74. Litzmann *Life* 258.

75. Litzmann *Life* 258.

76. Geiringer *Brahms* 99. Johann
Jakob was almost the only Hamburg
presence in the audience. Eduard
Marxsen was prevented from coming
by illness, and neither Avé-Lallemant
nor Brahms's other Hamburg acquaintances showed up. Their absence was noted and deplored.

77. MacDonald and Virginia
Hancock cite specific musical and
textual connections to Schütz in

MacDonald 196–7. For one, Schütz wrote a magnificent *German Requiem* of his own.

78. The leading theme of "Denn alles Fleisch," what I'm calling another version of the Brahmsian *Dies Irae*, was probably not in the original symphony sketch (which is lost), but added to the old idea.

79. Litzmann *Life* 258.

80. Dietrich 70–1.

81. Dahlhaus *Nineteenth-Century Music* 184. Dahlhaus complains that in the *Requiem* "a forlorn hope is made to substitute for faith."

82. M. McCorkle 171.

CHAPTER FOURTEEN

1. *Brahms Briefwechsel* III, 45.

2. Dietrich/Widmann 71–2.

3. Stark 147–8.

4. Litzmann *Schumann/Brahms Letters* 6/24/1868.

5. Litzmann *Schumann/Brahms Letters* 9/12/1868.

6. Litzmann *Schumann/Brahms Letters* 10/15/1868.

7. Litzmann *Life* 261.

8. *Brahms Briefwechsel* XVIII, 68.

9. These excerpts are from the Dover Score of the Songs, trans. anonymous.

10. Litzmann *Life* 368.

11. *Brahms Briefwechsel* X, 124.

12. Specht 236–7 and MacDonald 192–3.

13. *Brahms Briefwechsel* VII, 36. In the letter to Allgeyer on that page, Brahms astutely demolishes the idea that the *St. Luke Passion* is actually by J. S. Bach. He was one of the first to declare it a spurious attribution, and did it on purely musical grounds.

14. Geiringer *Brahms* 359.

15. Barkan *Brahms/Billroth Letters* 12.

16. Geiringer *Brahms* 102.

17. Stephenson 156–8.

18. Keys *Brahms* 63.

19. See Boyer.

20. MacDonald 186.

21. Stark 76.

22. The extent to which Brahms assembled his lieder opuses as a set and expected them to be presented that way is hard to pin down. Certainly they rarely have been.

23. Litzmann *Life* 266.

24. Brahms's famous letter to Fritz Simrock about the Rhapsody appears in Kalbeck II, 327–8, and Stephenson 145, each with a different date.

25. Kalbeck II, 299.

26. *Brahms Briefwechsel* IX, 82.

27. Schauffler 131.

28. E. Schumann 119.

29. The first sonority of the Alto Rhapsody is an augmented triad formed by a downbeat appoggiatura on the leading tone, with the third and fifth of the tonic triad added on the second beat: B♮-E♭-G, the B resolving up to C on the fourth beat. Brahms seems to have associated the augmented triad with a despairing tone; it figures prominently, for example, in the bleak song "Nicht mehr zu dir zu gehen." The unsettling effect in the beginning of the Rhapsody results from the *root* of the chord being displaced by an appoggiatura on the downbeat. Its resolution to C, on a weak beat, makes for a very shaky tonic triad, and the effect is amplified by the tremolo strings. The introduction engages in chromatic peregrinations without really establishing the tonic, and there is no strong dominant-tonic cadence anywhere in it.

30. Trans. Stanley Appelbaum, in the Dover score.

31. Garlington 528.

32. *Brahms Briefwechsel* IX, 85.

33. Dietrich/Widmann 74.

34. Kalbeck II, 330–1.

35. Kalbeck II, 333–4.

36. Litzmann *Life* 270. Ludwig's insanity seems to have been organic in cause, from a spinal disease (Mac-Donald 141n).

37. E. Schumann 65.

38. Stephenson 215.

39. Stephenson 187.

40. Litzmann *Schumann/Brahms Letters* 3/20/1870.

41. Geiringer *Brahms* 358.

42. Bickley *Joachim Letters* 390.

43. In Brahms's day the golden caryatids in the Musikverein held up the front of the balcony, so people in the parterre had to peer around them to the orchestra. Later they were moved back to the wall.

44. Litzmann *Schumann/Brahms Letters* 6/28/1870.

45. Geiringer *Brahms* 106.

46. Litzmann *Life* 274.

47. Litzmann *Life* 273.

48. Henschel 43.

49. Dietrich/Widmann 76.

50. May 448–9.

51. MacDonald 208.

52. Gal 188–9.

53. *Brahms Briefwechsel* IX, 143.

54. *Brahms Briefwechsel* IX, 103.

55. Trans. Stanley Appelbaum, in the Dover score.

56. Gal 194.

57. Tovey V, 229.

58. Schauffler 221.

CHAPTER FIFTEEN

1. *Brahms Briefwechsel* VII, 89.

2. Kalbeck II, 407.

3. Niemann 159–60.

4. Schauffler 85.

5. Schauffler 87–8.

6. May, "Personal Recollections" from *The Life of Brahms*.

7. Stephenson 190.

8. May 426.

9. *Brahms Briefwechsel* XVII, 77.

10. Litzmann *Schumann/Brahms Letters* Easter 1872.

11. *Brahms Briefwechsel* VII, 56.

12. Litzmann *Life* 291.

13. Barkan *Brahms/Billroth Letters* 17–18.

14. Litzmann *Life* 292.

15. Kalbeck II, 402.

16. Janik/Toulmin 34.

17. Kalbeck II, 418.

18. Specht 167.

19. Kalbeck II, 417.

20. Hancock "Early Choral Music" 126. Brahms's approach to Bach et al. is examined in this article, which includes reproductions of scores he has marked up with crescendos, etc.

21. The "where do you buy your music paper?" story also appears with victims other than Bruch, and with Bruch's Violin Concerto rather than *Odysseus*. It is entirely possible that Brahms used the put-down more than once—he was apt to repeat what he considered good lines. To his publisher Simrock, Brahms observed of his self-promoting friend, "Bruch is short-sighted, he sees only to the next laurel-wreath" (Ehrmann 70).

22. *Brahms Briefwechsel* VII, 128.

23. Litzmann *Schumann/Brahms Letters* 12/24/1872.

24. Keys 71.

25. Bickley *Joachim Letters* 398.

26. Bickley *Joachim Letters* 401–3.

27. Schauffler 157.

28. Bickley *Joachim Letters* 401.

29. Bickley *Joachim Letters* 405.

30. Bickley *Joachim Letters* 404–5.

31. Litzmann *Schumann/Brahms Letters* 4/22/1873.

32. Litzmann *Life* 300.

33. Litzmann *Life* 295.

34. D. McCorkle *Haydn Variations* 16.

35. The "Chorale St. Antoni" has been attributed to Haydn pupil Ignaz Pleyel, but that is also disputed. See D. McCorkle *Haydn Variations* 28–30n.

36. The discussion here comes largely from D. McCorkle *Haydn Variations;* other sources are cited. Why these sketches escaped destruction is a good question—it may have been an oversight, or Brahms may deliberately have left them to history as the sole extensive record of his working methods.

37. Geiringer *Brahms* 218.

38. D. McCorkle *Haydn Variations* 4–5.

39. As D. McCorkle details (58–9) Brahms went back and forth about how to replace the obsolete serpent horn that was the low voice in the original "Haydn" version of the theme. In the early 1870s the contrabassoon was in the middle of development between an obsolescent and modern version. Meanwhile, Brahms felt dubious about the tuba in general, especially tuba without the company of trombones. After much indecision he specified contrabassoon for the lowest wind part in hopes an adequate instrument would be developed soon—which it was.

40. In *The Music of Brahms*, Musgrave disputes a contention of Gei-

ringer's (*Brahms* 252) that the whole of the Haydn Variations exemplifies *durchbrochene Arbeit.* Clearly, though, several sections of the piece do show it. Historically, the climax of that fluid coloristic use of the orchestra came first with Mahler, who led directly to Schoenberg and Webern's concept of *Klangfarbenmelodie* (tone-color melody), in which changing instrumental colors washing through a single line are an essential feature of the composition. That in turn led to the "tone-color composition" of Stockhausen and other avant-gardists of the 1950s on.

41. Brahms said both quartets were "begun earlier" and "written for the second time" in summer 1873 (Frisch *Developing Variation* 109).

42. Krummacher 24.

43. Dahlhaus *Nineteenth-Century Music* 28.

44. MacDonald 209.

45. Schoenberg 402–3.

46. Keys *Chamber Music* 31.

47. Frisch *Developing Variation* 110–11.

48. Musgrave *Brahms* 115.

49. Krummacher 33.

CHAPTER SIXTEEN

1. D. McCorkle *Haydn Variations* 10.

2. Schorske 127.

3. Schorske 212.

4. Schorske 303.

5. M. McCorkle 208.

6. Barkan *Brahms/Billroth Letters* 22.

7. Kalbeck II, 479–80.

8. Litzmann *Life* 303.

9. Litzmann *Life* 301.

10. Litzmann *Life* 305.

11. Kalbeck III, 9.

12. Kalbeck *Brahms/Herzogenberg Letters* ix–x.

13. Litzmann *Schumann/Brahms Letters* 3/31/1874.

14. Geiringer *Brahms* 119.

15. Dietrich/Widmann 97. Brahms also recalled to Widmann that exchange with Götz, trying to justify himself. Götz died at age thirty-five.

16. Dietrich/Widmann 98.

17. Barkan *Brahms/Billroth Letters* 30.

18. The joining of old and new material in the C Minor Piano Quartet is so closely matched that scholars have never completely figured out the chronology. Musgrave (*Music* 117) surmises: first two movements in the mid-50s, second two later but hard to say when. Brahms apparently pulled the piece together during 1874–5.

19. Barkan *Brahms/Billroth Letters* 30n.

20. Holde 312.

21. Hanslick "Memories" 163–4.

22. Barkan *Brahms/Billroth Letters* 26–9.

23. May 456.

24. *Brahms Briefwechsel* VII, 178–9.

25. Schauffler 152.

26. Keys *Brahms* 77. That summer Levi also outraged Clara Schumann by claiming Wagner was a better musician than Gluck (Litzmann *Life* 313).

27. Gay 191.

28. Geiringer *Brahms* 120. He reports that Brahms began to grow his beard this summer, but other observers do not mention it until 1878.

29. Keys *Brahms* 78.

30. Litzmann *Life* 317.

31. Krummacher 33.

32. Musgrave "Cultural World" 8.

33. Specht 305.

34. Botstein "Brahms and Painting" 161.

35. Specht 304.

36. Geiringer "Wagner and Brahms" and Kalbeck III, 123–7.

37. Musgrave "Cultural World" 18.

38. Gutman 227.

39. Roses.

40. May 502.

41. Litzmann *Schumann/Brahms Letters* 6/1876.

42. Kalbeck *Brahms/Herzogenberg Letters* 4–7. For an examination of Brahms's comments on variation form in the letter, see Sisman.

43. Of course, when Brahms was composing the First Symphony Bruckner was already in his prime as a symphonist, but few took his work seriously in those years.

44. Kalbeck (III, 94) calls the opening chromatic fan the "fate-motive." Besides that, pounding timpani—especially the triplets—have an old connection with the theme of fate in Brahms's vocal music, from the *Begräbnisgesang* through the *Requiem* to the *Schicksalslied*.

45. Schubert 15.

46. Pascall "First Symphony." In the *Andante sostenuto* there are other references, some clear and some subtle, to the first-movement introduction, including the descending thirds of the winds at 12, the chromatic octaves at 53–5, 71–2, and 116–23. In general, all chromatic lines have a charged significance by this point.

47. Brinkmann 34.

48. Musgrave (*Music* 133–4) compares the chorale theme of the C Minor of course to the Beethoven's Ninth theme, but also to the folk song "Sandmännchen" (Sandman) that Brahms set for Clara's children, and to the opening theme of the B♭ Sextet finale.

49. Frisch, in *Symphonies* 61, presents the finale of the First as having no development, rather "a development/expansion within the recapitulation's transition."

50. Brinkmann 37–40. The thematic evolution is taken from Giselher Schubert.

51. Brinkmann (44–5) sees in the coda a symbolic resolution, calling the alpenhorn theme "nature" and the trombone chorale "religion." Thus, "The alpenhorn call and [trombone] chorale present an antithesis to the tragic note in the first movement and the introduction to the finale. Or to sum it up further: nature and religion intervene to resolve the dramatically sharpened conflict on a higher plane." This resolution he places in contrast to the similar one in Beethoven's Ninth: "It is no longer [Beethoven's] humanist fervor of freedom and brotherliness but nature and religion that resolve the issue for Brahms." I buy the "nature" side of that formulation more than the "religion," and add: the resolution to nature and perhaps religion may be true and intended, *if* the coda of the First Symphony is fully effective and purposeful. Hans Gal and Clara Schumann, however, questioned the effectiveness of the coda, saying that its material and tone seem unearned, not quite relevant. Gal (141): "The jubilation with which the movement comes to a close is the result of a self-delusion. One can sense in it more the desire to be joyful than real surrender to joy." He echoes Clara's demurral to Brahms (quoted in Gal 142): "To me its intensification [in the coda] seems to lie in external rather than internal emotion; it somehow does not organically evolve from the whole, but seems merely to have been added as a brilliant afterthought." I tend to agree with those sentiments (Brinkmann cites them as well), but once more add: if Brahms failed to achieve the ultimate apotheosis the coda called for, maybe it was because that was practically impossible. He planned a symphonic unfolding that intensifies between first movement and last—starting from a point of high intensity—and paid that off remarkably in the finale, at least until the coda. And after all, as Clara admitted, the coda is brilliant, even if it does not quite say what it proposes to. Brahms may have seized on the trombone chorale for the climax of the coda simply because it seemed to do the best job logically—but perhaps it doesn't succeed as well dramatically and expressively (a common complaint about Brahms).

52. Hanslick *Criticisms* 129–56.

53. Barkan *Brahms/Billroth Letters* 38–9.

54. Litzmann *Life* 312.

55. Litzmann *Life* 320.

56. Litzmann *Life* 319–20.

57. Schauffler 157.

58. May 492.

59. Barkan *Brahms/Billroth Letters* 40–1.

60. May 512.

61. Hanslick *Criticisms* 125–8.

62. Hanslick *Criticisms* 211.

63. Kalbeck *Brahms/Herzogenberg Letters* 8–9.
64. Litzmann *Life* 321–2.

CHAPTER SEVENTEEN

1. The narrative of Brahms's relationship with Henschel is based on Henschel's diary, *Personal Recollections of Johannes Brahms*. Some of the translations, punctuation, etc., of the standard English edition are updated.
2. *Brahms Briefwechsel* VIII, 122n.
3. Note from Ira Braus.
4. Gal 85–6.
5. Specht 164.
6. Kalbeck II, 110n.
7. Henschel 31–2.
8. Specht 182–6.
9. Kalbeck III, 2.
10. Geiringer *Brahms* 330.
11. Specht 199.
12. Kalbeck *Brahms/Herzogenberg Letters* 2/15/1877.
13. Smyth 79.
14. Smyth 88.
15. Geiringer *Brahms* 125–6.
16. Smyth 102–3.
17. Smyth 105.
18. Barkan *Brahms/Billroth Letters* 223n.
19. Smyth 101–2.
20. Smyth 90–1.
21. MacDonald 236.
22. Kalbeck *Brahms/Herzogenberg Letters* 11/25/1880.
23. Kalbeck *Brahms/Herzogenberg Letters* 8/2/1879.
24. Kalbeck *Brahms/Herzogenberg Letters* 3/10/1878.
25. Litzmann *Schumann/Brahms Letters* 4/24/1877.
26. Litzmann *Schumann/Brahms Letters* 5/2/1877.
27. Litzmann *Schumann/Brahms Letters* 6/6/1877.
28. Barkan *Brahms/Billroth Letters* 50n.
29. Kalbeck *Brahms/Herzogenberg Letters* 5/5/1877.
30. Kalbeck *Brahms/Herzogenberg Letters* 11/22/1877.
31. *Brahms Briefwechsel* X, 56–7.
32. Brinkmann 160, quoting Kalbeck.
33. This letter of Lachner's, which Brinkmann first published, appears to have been the starting point for his own meditation on the shadows in the Second, which he calls (79) "an emphatic questioning of the pastoral world, a firm denial of the possibility of pure serenity." The letter exchange is in Brinkmann 126–9.
34. Brinkmann 122–3.
35. May 528–9.
36. Dietrich/Widmann 106.
37. May 519.
38. Barkan *Brahms/Billroth Letters* 58.
39. Hanslick *Criticisms* 157–9.
40. Clapham 242.
41. Hanslick "Memories" 169–70.
42. Clapham 252.
43. Schauffler 99.
44. Schönzeler 66–7.
45. Clapham 243.
46. Smyth 79.
47. May 524.
48. *Brahms Briefwechsel* X, 73.
49. Geiringer *Brahms* 136.
50. Kalbeck III, 151–2, transl. in Schauffler.
51. Schwarz 513.
52. *Brahms Briefwechsel* VI, 147.
53. Musgrave *Music* 159.
54. Quoted in Schauffler 215.
55. Hanslick "Memories" 173–4.

56. Kalbeck III, 223.
57. May 537.
58. Kalbeck III, 223–4.
59. May 537.
60. Schwarz 508.
61. *Brahms Briefwechsel* XVIII, 139.
62. Keys *Brahms* 93.
63. Pulver 26.
64. Door 218 and Henschel 54.

CHAPTER EIGHTEEN

1. Litzmann *Life* 346.
2. Litzmann *Life* 337.
3. Litzmann *Life* 342.
4. Litzmann *Life* 350.
5. Litzmann *Life* 350.
6. Barkan *Brahms/Billroth Letters* 81.
7. Litzmann *Life* 349.
8. Stark 181.
9. Litzmann *Life* 351.
10. Heuberger 77–8.
11. Litzmann *Schumann/Brahms Letters* 9/1879.
12. Litzmann *Life* 352–3.
13. Kalbeck I, 298n.
14. Kalbeck *Brahms/Herzogenberg Letters* 105.
15. Barkan *Brahms/Billroth Letters* 92.
16. Kalbeck *Brahms/Herzogenberg Letters* 105.
17. Bickley *Joachim Letters* 421.
18. Holde 318.
19. Holde 319–20.
20. *Brahms Briefwechsel* X, 162.
21. Litzmann *Life* 355.
22. Barkan *Brahms/Billroth Letters* 94.
23. Ehrmann 68.
24. May 553.
25. Musgrave *Music* 218.

26. Niemann 128–9.
27. Schauffler 11.
28. Barkhan *Brahms/Billroth Letters* 105.
29. Kalbeck *Brahms/Herzogenberg Letters* 7/14/1880.
30. From the Stanley Appelbaum translation in the Dover score.
31. MacDonald 288. Several writers have seen a connection of *Nänie* also to composer and Brahms acquaintance Hermann Götz, who set the same text and died young in 1876.
32. Kalbeck III, 296.
33. Kalbeck *Brahms/Herzogenberg Letters* 7/7/1881.
34. Heuberger 147.
35. Barkan *Brahms/Billroth Letters* 75n.
36. Hanslick *Criticisms* 234.
37. F. Schumann 509.
38. Hanslick *Criticisms* 184.
39. Kalbeck III, 495.
40. Kalbeck III, 491.
41. Geiringer *Brahms* 150.
42. Geiringer *Brahms* 147–8.
43. Bozarth/Brady.
44. Tovey III, 120.
45. Musgrave *Music* 234. As Charles Rosen points out in "Plagiarism," just as the D Minor Concerto finale had been built on the model of the Beethoven Third Concerto, Brahms's B♭ has many Beethoven echoes, starting with the *Emperor*-like opening cadenza for the soloist.
46. Tovey III, 125.
47. Litzmann *Life* 362.
48. Kalbeck *Brahms/Herzogenberg Letters* 4/1882.
49. Kalbeck *Brahms/Herzogenberg Letters* 159n.
50. Brodbeck "New German School" 66.

51. Bickley *Joachim Letters* 415–16.

52. MacDonald 285.

53. Hanslick "Memories" 174.

54. Barkan *Brahms/Billroth Letters* 122–5.

55. Litzmann *Schumann/Brahms Letters* 8/23/1882.

56. *Brahms Briefwechsel* XI, 17.

57. Kalbeck *Brahms/Herzogenberg Letters* 181n.

58. Crankshaw 273.

59. Crankshaw 317.

CHAPTER NINETEEN

1. Kalbeck III, 377.

2. Litzmann *Life*, 370.

3. May 577.

4. Barkan *Brahms/Billroth Letters* 132.

5. Geiringer *Brahms* 151.

6. Kalbeck and others surmise that ideas for the Third Symphony went back some years, but there is no solid evidence for that (Brodbeck "New German School" 6n). Though it was likely working in his mind, the Third may essentially have been another one-summer job, like the Second. It is intriguing to speculate that Wagner's death may have galvanized it, but there is no evidence about that either.

7. David Brodbeck in "Brahms and the New German School" has examined the connection of the Third to Wagner. A few of his examples seem to me speculative. The ones in the text are perhaps speculative too, but are my own.

8. Brodbeck "New German School" 73.

9. Dahlhaus *Nineteenth-Century Music* 269.

10. Frisch 137.

11. Brinkmann 220.

12. Keys *Brahms* 113.

13. Langer 31–2.

14. Dahlhaus *Nineteenth-Century Music* 269.

15. Kalbeck *Brahms/Herzogenberg Letters* 190n.

16. Litzmann *Life* 371.

17. Litzmann *Schumann/Brahms Letters* 2/11/1884.

18. Litzmann *Schumann/Brahms Letters* 8/10/1882.

19. Holde 322–3.

20. Keys *Brahms* 116.

21. Geiringer *Brahms* 156.

22. Hanslick "Memories" 167–8.

23. Geiringer *Brahms* 156.

24. Kalbeck III, 438.

25. Kalbeck III, 440–1.

26. Litzmann *Life* 375.

27. Dietrich/Widmann 79–80.

28. Kalbeck *Brahms/Herzogenberg Letters* 12/29/1884.

29. Kalbeck *Brahms/Herzogenberg Letters* 215–16, n.d.

30. Litzmann *Life* 362.

31. Kalbeck *Brahms/Herzogenberg Letters* 1/12/1885, and Notley 109.

32. Gartenberg 178–9.

33. Morton 163.

34. Morton 18–19.

35. Morton 97–8.

36. Dahlhaus *Nineteenth-Century Music* 272.

37. Kalbeck III, 409.

38. Botstein "Time and Memory" 8.

39. Hanslick *Criticisms* 288–9.

40. Dahlhaus *Nineteenth-Century Music* 271.

41. Specht 262.

42. Notley 122; preceding paragraphs based on Notley.

43. Notley 110. She notes that many in Vienna, including the more liberal and assimilated Jews, were unsympathetic toward the strictly Orthodox Galician immigrants.
44. Kalbeck III, 158n.
45. Heuberger 30n.
46. Specht 288.
47. MacDonald 239n.
48. Gartenberg 183.
49. Morton 147.
50. Kalbeck III, 411n.
51. *Grove* (1954 ed.) IX, 333.
52. Geiringer *Brahms* 154–5.
53. Heuberger 41.
54. Gartenberg 188.
55. Ehrmann 75.
56. Zemlinsky/Weigl 206.
57. Heuberger 15.
58. Jenner 188.
59. Jenner passim.
60. Heuberger 15.
61. Heuberger 39.
62. Heuberger 132.
63. Heuberger 39.
64. Heuberger 50.
65. Helmholtz, 358.
66. Botstein "Time and Memory" 10–11.
67. Kalbeck *Brahms/Billroth Letters* 230n.
68. Kalbeck III, 538n.
69. Kalbeck III, 444.
70. Kalbeck *Brahms/Herzogenberg Letters* 5/21–2/1885.
71. Kalbeck *Brahms/Herzogenberg Letters* 8/29/1885.

CHAPTER TWENTY

1. Kalbeck *Brahms/Herzogenberg Letters* 9/8 and 9/31/1885.
2. Kalbeck III, 453–5.
3. Kalbeck *Brahms/Herzogenberg Letters* 10/10/1885.
4. Kalbeck *Brahms/Herzogenberg Letters* 252–63.
5. *Brahms Briefwechsel* XI, 103.
6. Litzmann *Schumann/Brahms Letters*, end of October 1885.
7. Kalbeck *Brahms/Herzogenberg Letters* 2/3/1886.
8. Litzmann *Schumann/Brahms Letters* 12/15/1885.
9. Litzmann *Life* 383.
10. Geiringer *Brahms* 159.
11. Specht 252–3.
12. Barkan *Brahms/Billroth Letters* 160–1.
13. Kalbeck III, 457.
14. Hanslick *Criticisms* 243–5.
15. Barkan *Brahms/Billroth Letters* 164–5.
16. The rejected four-bar introduction for the Fourth Symphony was mainly sustained wind chords in a iv $\frac{6}{4}$–i cadence.
17. MacDonald 312n.
18. Rosen *Sonata Forms* 327.
19. MacDonald 313.
20. Tovey I, 120.
21. MacDonald 309, translation slightly changed. Brahms's term for Bach's chaconne bass is *klotzig*, which MacDonald renders as "heavy." In fact, the closest translation might be "klutzy," but that Yiddishism seemed a stretch here, so I settled on "clunky."
22. Musgrave *Music* 225.
23. Musgrave *Music* 225.
24. Knapp 10.
25. Musgrave *Music* 226.
26. The tradition of ending a minor-key piece with a major chord (the raised note is called a "Picardy third") has a technical reason beyond an expressive one: the overtones of the fundamental note, especially no-

ticeable in a full organ chord, have a strong major third that can clash with the minor third in a prolonged triad. (Orchestral composers sometimes compensate for that acoustic dissonance by heavily doubling the minor third.) Still, nineteenth-century convention tended to think of the Picardy third more as an expressive device, a turn from "dark," "tragic," and the like, to "triumph," "optimism," and the like. Brahms, steeped in that tradition, was certainly thinking of it when he withheld the expected turn to major in the Fourth Symphony and in the F Minor Piano Quintet.

27. Quoted in Brinkmann 221.

28. Brinkmann 221–5.

29. Kalbeck *Brahms/Herzogenberg Letters* 12/2/1886.

30. Litzmann *Schumann/Brahms Letters* 107–8.

31. Litzmann *Life* 387.

32. Schonberg 235.

33. Schonberg 242.

34. Kalbeck IV, 1.

35. *Brahms Briefwechsel* XI, 120–1.

36. Niemann 119.

37. Dietrich/Widmann 133–4.

38. Dietrich/Widmann 131.

39. Dietrich/Widmann 122–3.

40. Schauffler 102.

41. Dietrich/Widmann 133.

42. Thatcher 8.

43. Thatcher 13–20.

44. Dietrich/Widmann 127.

45. Kalbeck III, 540–1.

46. Stark 326.

47. Musgrave *Music* 193.

48. Barkan *Brahms/Billroth Letters* 180.

49. The remarkable metrical structure of the C Minor Trio's slow movement makes one wonder if

Brahms had some experience with more authentic Hungarian folk music than what was usually played in Vienna cafés. Meanwhile, in the scherzo in several spots (such as measure 32) he uncharacteristically indulges in forbidden parallel fifths in the piano part, in a direct change from tonic to Neapolitan. In these and like ways Brahms seems to have loosened up in his old age. Maybe Bizet helped: in his notebook of parallel fifths, Brahms forgave all the ones he found in *Carmen*.

50. MacDonald 336.

51. Barkan *Brahms/Billroth Letters* 183n.

52. Kalbeck *Brahms/Herzogenberg Letters* 12/2/1886.

53. Kalbeck *Brahms/Herzogenberg Letters* 292n.

54. Heuberger 156.

55. *Brahms Briefwechsel* XI, 137.

56. Translations in Schauffler 195, 206–7.

57. Kalbeck *Brahms/Herzogenberg Letters* 310n and Keys *Brahms* 124.

58. Litzmann *Schumann/Brahms Letters* 5/1887.

59. Litzmann *Artist's Life* 390.

60. Hanslick "Memories" 164–5.

61. Litzmann *Life* 390.

62. Kalbeck IV, 49.

63. Litzmann *Schumann/Brahms Letters* 115–16.

64. Litzmann *Life* 393.

65. Litzmann *Schumann/Brahms Letters* 8/1887.

66. May 600.

67. Litzmann *Life* 394.

68. Barkan *Brahms/Billroth Letters* 189.

69. Litzmann *Schumann/Brahms Letters* 4/23/1889.

70. MacDonald 322.

CHAPTER TWENTY-ONE

1. Geiringer *Brahms* 164.
2. Geiringer *Brahms* 164.
3. Schauffler 123, translation revised.
4. Schauffler 154.
5. Shauffler 228–9.
6. Shauffler 141.
7. Henschel 56.
8. Morton 164.
9. Boyer 266.
10. Schauffler 258–9.
11. Schauffler 225–6.
12. Holde 288.
13. Graf *Legend* 99–100.
14. Schauffler 120–1.
15. Kalbeck IV, 118.
16. Specht 303.
17. Specht 76.
18. Litzmann *Schumann/Brahms Letters* 4/1888.
19. Geiringer *Brahms* 364–5.
20. Dietrich/Widmann 115.
21. Dietrich/Widmann 137.
22. Dietrich/Widmann 140–1.
23. Dietrich/Widmann 143.
24. Barkan *Brahms/Billroth Letters* 199.
25. Barkan *Brahms/Billroth Letters* 194–5.
26. Gal 81–2, transl. revised.
27. Hanslick "Memories" 178–9.
28. Litzmann *Schumann/Brahms Letters* 11/23/1888.
29. Litzmann *Schumann/Brahms Letters* 11/2/1889.
30. Litzmann *Life* 398.
31. Kalbeck *Brahms/Herzogenberg Letters* 345–64.
32. Brahms *Briefwechsel* VII, 265.
33. Morton 164.
34. Heuberger 40–1.
35. Heuberger 41.
36. Gal 128.
37. Hanslick "Brahms's Newest" 148–9.
38. Morton 181–2.
39. Litzmann *Life* 400.
40. *Brahms Briefwechsel* XI, 209, transl. in Morton.
41. Litzmann *Schumann/Brahms Letters* 3/19/1889.
42. Barkan *Brahms/Billroth Letters* 205.
43. *Brahms Briefwechsel* VIII, 97–8.
44. Litzmann *Schumann/Brahms Letters* 9/3/1889.
45. MacDonald 338.
46. Frish *Developing Variation* 62.
47. MacDonald 339.
48. Keys *Brahms* 130.
49. Kalbeck IV, 170.
50. Geiringer *Brahms* 140.
51. Geiringer *Brahms* 172.
52. May 617.
53. Hanslick "Memories" 171.
54. Specht 160.
55. Litzmann *Schumann/Brahms Letters* 7/1889.
56. Kalbeck *Brahms/Herzogenberg Letters* 294.
57. Litzmann *Schumann/Brahms Letters* 7/4/1889.
58. Litzmann *Schumann/Brahms Letters* 3/1889.
59. Schauffler 272–3.
60. May 617.
61. Musgrave *Music* 175.
62. Widmann 193.
63. Litzmann *Schumann/Brahms Letters* 5/16/1856.
64. Widmann 186.
65. Widmann 190.
66. Geiringer "Prickly Pet."
67. Gartenberg 181.
68. May 603–4. In the Brahms recollections of Sigismond Stojowski, he says Tchaikovsky told him he first met Brahms in Hamburg.

69. Gartenberg *Mahler* 98.
70. "Brahms on Record."
71. *Brahms Briefwechsel* VIII, 12.
72. May 621.

CHAPTER TWENTY-TWO

1. Heuberger 100.
2. Kalbeck IV, 208.
3. Kalbeck *Brahms/Herzogenberg Letters* 12/16/1890.
4. Kalbeck IV, 211.
5. Barkan *Brahms/Billroth Letters* 219.
6. Barkan *Brahms/Billroth Letters* 220.
7. Schauffler 147.
8. Heuberger 44.
9. Graf 102.
10. Graf 101–2.
11. Schauffler 274.
12. LaGrange 221.
13. Brodbeck "Mahler's Brahms."
14. Gartenberg *Mahler.*
15. Litzmann *Schumann/Brahms Letters* 12/25/1890.
16. Kalbeck IV, 226.
17. Litzmann *Schumann/Brahms Letters* 1/31/1891.
18. Litzmann *Schumann/Brahms Letters* 3/4/1891.
19. Dietrich/Widmann 198–9.
20. May 627.
21. Musgrave *Music* 250–1.
22. MacDonald 367.
23. MacDonald 362.
24. Litzmann *Schumann/Brahms Letters* 8/15/1891.
25. Litzmann *Schumann/Brahms Letters* 8/1891.
26. Litzmann *Schumann/Brahms Letters* 10/2/1891.
27. MacDonald 243.
28. Litzmann *Schumann/Brahms Letters* 201–4. In one letter Brahms

admits, "I know by experience that I am not a good editor."
29. Heuberger 49.
30. Kalbeck *Brahms/Herzogenberg Letters* 403.
31. Kalbeck IV, 266.
32. Heuberger 50–1.
33. *Brahms Briefwechsel* VII, 277n.
34. Geiringer "Brahms the Ambivalent" 2.
35. Litzmann *Schumann/Brahms Letters* 5/7/1892.
36. Kalbeck III, 250.
37. Kalbeck III, 247–8.
38. Keys *Brahms* 141.
39. Kalbeck IV, 315.
40. Litzmann *Schumann/Brahms Letters* 9/13/1892.
41. Litzmann *Schumann/Brahms Letters* 9/27/1892.
42. Litzmann *Schumann/Brahms Letters* 10/1892.
43. Litzmann *Schumann/Brahms Letters* 12/23/1892.
44. Litzmann *Life* 420.
45. Barkan *Brahms/Billroth Letters* 233.
46. Barkan *Brahms/Billroth Letters* 226.
47. Barkan *Brahms/Billroth Letters* 227n.
48. Barkan *Brahms/Billroth Letters* 229n.
49. Litzmann *Schumann/Brahms Letters* 5/10/1893.
50. Heuberger 61.
51. Litzmann *Schumann/Brahms Letters* 228–9.
52. Ira Braus feels that "the modulations in the C Minor String Quartet are more 'futuristic' than the 11ths and 13ths in the B Minor Intermezzo."
53. As has been pointed out by Peter Burkholder, Schoenberg was

overapt to present anything that led to his own music as "progressive," and in general applied that term to matters of motivic saturation, harmonic complexity, and the like. Brahms's rhythmic innovations, for example, he largely ignored. I suggest, though, that in proclaiming Brahms as his main inspiration, rather than Wagner as everyone assumed, Schoenberg deliberately obscured some of his debt to Wagner. Besides the obvious musical influences, one also finds in Schoenberg an echo of Wagner's messianic conception of the artist. Perhaps Schoenberg deliberately distanced himself from Wagner partly as a way of recognizing his genuine debt to Brahms; but surely he also did it partly, and understandably, because as a Jew Schoenberg was repulsed by Wagner's antisemitism. Schoenberg had converted to Christianity in the hostile atmosphere of 1890s Vienna; his reconversion to Judaism came before his epochal article "Brahms the Progressive." I am suggesting, in other words, that those two developments in Schoenberg's life were not entirely distinct, and not entirely aesthetic. Wagner could not be a father figure to Schoenberg; Brahms could.

54. Barkan *Brahms/Billroth Letters* 237–241. Composer Larry Moss first called my attention to this passage.

55. *Brahms Briefwechsel* III, 87.

56. Musgrave, "Cultural World" 11.

57. Dietrich/Widmann 201.

58. Botstein "Painting" 166.

59. Musgrave "Cultural World" 13.

60. Botstein "Painting" 165.

61. Botstein "Painting" 165.

62. Botstein "Painting" 163.

63. Botstein "Painting" 168.

64. Dietrich/Widmann 202.

65. Barkan *Brahms/Billroth Letters* 247–8.

66. Geiringer *Brahms* 187.

67. Geiringer *Brahms* 186.

68. Geiringer *Brahms* 187–8.

69. MacDonald 156.

70. Litzmann *Schumann/Brahms Letters* 7/1894.

71. Litzmann *Schumann/Brahms Letters* 8/1897.

72. Kalbeck IV, 348.

73. F. Schumann 507.

74. E. Schumann 166.

75. F. Schumann 507–10.

76. E. Schumann, 170.

77. F. Schumann 512–13.

78. Kalbeck IV, 400.

79. Heuberger 81–2.

CHAPTER TWENTY-THREE

1. Heuberger 83.

2. Specht 172.

3. Heuberger 85–6.

4. E. Schumann 172–3 and F. Schumann 515.

5. Heuberger 88.

6. MacDonald 412.

7. MacDonald 298.

8. Geiringer *Brahms* 178–9.

9. Specht 189–92.

10. Specht 191–2.

11. Bickley *Joachim Letters* 91.

12. Heuberger, 92.

13. Fellinger 50.

14. Heuberger 94–5.

15. Litzmann *Life* 436.

16. Heuberger 99.

17. Clapham 254.

18. Litzmann *Schumann/Brahms Letters* 4/1896.

19. Heuberger 103.

20. Litzmann *Schumann/Brahms Letters* 5/7/1896.

21. Heuberger 104.

22. Heuberger 104–5.

23. MacDonald 371.

24. MacDonald 417.

25. Litzmann *Life* 437–8.

26. Kalbeck IV, 435–6.

27. Specht 348–9.

28. Kaufmann 751.

29. *Brahms Briefwechsel* VII, 307–8.

30. Litzmann *Schumann/Brahms Letters* 7/7/1896.

31. Specht 353.

32. LaGrange 374.

33. Kalbeck IV, 464.

34. Niemann 152.

35. Dietrich/Widmann 208.

36. Heuberger 110.

37. Schauffler 292–3.

38. Dietrich/Widmann 209.

39. Biba "New Light."

40. Specht 352.

41. Barkan *Brahms/Billroth Letters* 251.

42. May 663.

43. Heuberger 121.

44. "Schatzkästlein" 640, 644, 645.

45. May 665.

46. Heuberger 123.

47. Specht 356.

48. MacDonald 195.

49. Kalbeck IV, 515–17.

50. Henschel 58–60.

EPILOGUE AND PROVOCATION

1. Gal 22.

2. Bickley *Joachim Letters* 458.

3. Notley 117n.

4. See Burkholder's "Viewpoint: Brahms and Twentieth-Century Classical Music," which has been a primary spur to my thinking. Our differences arise out of contrasting emphases on the question of what constitute the essential qualities of Modernism—and that is indeed a gigantic question, far from being resolved by scholarship or criticism.

5. Janik/Toulmin 45.

6. Schorske 8–9.

7. Latham 18.

8. McColl 102.

9. Janik/Toulmin 67.

10. MacDonald 417.

11. Schorske 19.

12. Gay 253.

Bibliography

Barkan, Hans, ed. and trans. *Johannes Brahms and Theodor Billroth: Letters from a Musical Friendship.* Norman: University of Oklahoma Press, 1957.

Becker, Heinz. Article on Brahms in *The New Grove Dictionary of Music and Musicians.*

Beller-McKenna, Daniel. "Reconsidering the Identity of an Orchestral Sketch by Brahms." *The Journal of Musicology* XIII/4, Fall 1995.

Bellman, Jonathan. *The Style Hongrois in the Music of Western Europe.* Boston: Northeastern University Press, 1993.

Biba, Otto. "New Light on the Brahms *Nachlass.*" In *Brahms 2: Biographical, Documentary and Analytical Studies,* edited by Michael Musgrave. Cambridge and New York: Cambridge University Press, 1987.

Bickley, Nora, ed. and trans. *Letters from and to Joseph Joachim.* London: Macmillan and Co., 1914.

Blom, Eric, ed. *Grove's Dictionary of Music and Musicians.* 10 vols. New York: St. Martin's Press, Inc., 1954.

Botstein, Leon. "Brahms and Nineteenth-Century Painting." *19th-Century Music* XIV/2, Fall 1990.

————"Time and Memory: Concert Life, Science, and Music in Brahms's Vienna." In *Brahms and His World,* edited by Walter Frisch. Princeton N.J.: Princeton University Press, 1990.

Boyer, Thomas. "Brahms as Count Peter of Provence: A Psychosexual Interpretation of the *Magelone* Poetry." *Musical Quarterly* 66/2, 1980.

Bozarth, George S. "Brahms's *Lieder Ohne Worte:* The 'Poetic' Andantes of the Piano Sonatas." In *Brahms Studies,* edited by George S. Bozarth. Oxford: Clarendon Press, 1990.

————, ed. *Brahms Studies: Analytical and Historical Perspectives.* Oxford: Clarendon Press, 1990.

————, ed. and trans. "Johannes Brahms's Collection of *Deutsche Sprichworte*

(German Proverbs)." In Brodbeck, *Brahms Studies*, vol. 1. Lincoln: University of Nebraska Press, 1994.

Bozarth, George S., and Stephen H. Brady. "The Pianos of Johannes Brahms." In *Brahms and His World*, edited by Walter Frisch. Princeton, N.J.: Princeton University Press, 1990.

Brahms, Johannes. *Johannes Brahms Briefwechsel*. 18 vols. Reprint of the 1902–22 Deutsche Brahms-Gesellschaft edition, plus new volumes. Tutzing: Hans Schneiger, 1974–94.

"Brahms on Record." *The American Brahms Society Newsletter* V/1, Spring 1987.

Braus, Ira. "Brahms's *Liebe und Frühling II*. Op. 3, No. 3: A New Path to the Artwork of the Future?" *19th-Century Music* X/2, Fall 1986.

Brinkmann, Reinhold. *Late Idyll: The Second Symphony of Johannes Brahms*. Cambridge and London: Harvard University Press, 1995.

Brodbeck, David. "The Brahms-Joachim Counterpoint Exchange; or, Robert, Clara, and 'the Best Harmony Between Jos. And Joh.'" In Brodbeck, *Brahms Studies*. vol. 1. Lincoln: University of Nebraska Press, 1994.

———. "Brahms, the Third Symphony, and the New German School." In *Brahms and His World*, edited by Walter Frisch. Princeton, N.J.: Princeton University Press, 1990.

———. "Mahler's Brahms." *The American Brahms Society Newsletter* X/2, Autumn 1992.

Brody, Elaine. "Operas in Search of Brahms." *Opera Quarterly* 3/4, 1985–6.

Burk, John N. *Clara Schumann: A Romantic Biography*. New York: Random House, 1940.

Burkholder, J. Peter. "Viewpoint: Brahms and Twentieth-Century Classical Music." *19th-Century Music* 8/1, Summer 1984.

Callomon, Fritz. "Some Unpublished Brahms Correspondence." *The Musical Quarterly*. 29/1, 1943.

Charlton, David, ed. *E. T. A. Hoffmann's Musical Writings*: Kreisleriana, The Poet and the Composer, *Music Criticism*. Cambridge and New York: Cambridge University Press, 1989.

Clapham, John. "Dvořák's Relations with Brahms and Hanslick." *The Musical Quarterly* 57/2, 1971.

Crankshaw, Edward. *The Fall of the House of Habsburg*. New York: Penguin Books, 1983.

Dahlhaus, Carl. *Between Romanticism and Modernism: Four Studies in the Music of the Later Nineteenth Century*. Translated by Mary Whittall. Berkeley and Los Angeles: University of California Press, 1980.

———. *The Idea of Absolute Music*. Translated by Roger Lustig. Chicago and London: University of Chicago Press, 1989.

———. *Nineteenth-Century Music*. Translated by J. Bradford Robinson. Berkeley and Los Angeles: University of California Press, 1989.

Dietrich, Albert, and J. V. Widmann. *Recollections of Johannes Brahms*. Translated by Dora E. Hecht. New York: Charles Scribner's Sons, 1899.

Dittrich, Marie-Agnes. *Musikstädte der Welt: Hamburg.* Laaber: Laaber-Verlag, 1990.

Door, Anton. "Persönliche Erinnerungen an Brahms." *Die Musik* 2/15, 1903.

Drinker, Henry S. *The Chamber Music of Johannes Brahms.* Philadelphia: Elkan-Vogel, 1932.

Drinker, Sophie. *Brahms and His Women's Choruses.* Publ. by author: Merion, Penn., 1952.

Ehrmann, Alfred von. "The 'Terrible' Brahms." *The Musical Quarterly* 23, 1937.

Einstein, Alfred. *Music in the Romantic Era.* New York: W. W. Norton and Co., 1947.

Epstein, David. "Brahms and the Mechanisms of Motion." In *Brahms Studies,* edited by George S. Bozarth. Oxford: Clarendon Press, 1990.

Fellinger, Imogen. "Brahms's 'Way': A Composer's Self-view." In *Brahms 2: Biographical, Documentary and Analytical Studies,* edited by Michael Musgrave. Cambridge and New York: Cambridge University Press, 1987.

Frisch, Walter. *Brahms: The Four Symphonies.* New York: Schirmer Books, 1996.

———. *Brahms and the Principle of Developing Variation.* 1984. Reprint. Berkeley and Los Angeles: University of California Press, 1990.

———. "Metrical Displacement in Brahms." In *Brahms Studies,* edited by George S. Bozarth. Oxford: Clarendon Press, 1990.

———, ed. *Brahms and His World.* Princeton, N.J.: Princeton University Press, 1990.

Gal, Hans. *Johannes Brahms: His Work and Personality.* Translated by Joseph Stein. New York: Alfred A. Knopf, 1963. Reprint. Westport, Conn.: Greenwood Press, 1977.

Garlington, Aubrey S., Jr. "*Harzreise als Herzreize:* Brahms's Alto Rhapsody." *The Musical Quarterly* 69/4, Fall 1983.

Gartenberg, Egon. *Mahler: The Man and His Music.* London: Cassell, 1978.

———. *Vienna: Its Musical Heritage.* University Park and London: Pennsylvania State University Press, 1968. (Called "Gartenberg" in notes.)

Gay, Peter. *Freud, Jews and Other Germans.* Oxford and New York: Oxford University Press, 1978.

Geiringer, Karl. "Wagner and Brahms, with Unpublished Letters." *The Musical Quarterly* 22/2, 1936.

———. "Brahms' Prickly Pet." *The Étude,* February 1941.

———. *Brahms: His Life and Work.* Reprint of the 1948 second edition, with supplements by author and wife. New York: Da Capo Press, 1981 and 1982.

———. "Brahms as a Musicologist." *The Musical Quarterly* LXIX/4, Fall 1983.

———. "Brahms the Ambivalent." In *Brahms Studies,* edited by George S. Bozarth. Oxford: Clarendon Press, 1990.

Glaser, Hermann, ed. *The German Mind of the 19th Century: A Literary & Historical Anthology.* New York: Continuum, 1981.

Goldman, Albert, and Evert Sprinchorn, eds. *Richard Wagner on Music & Drama.* Translated by H. Ashton Ellis. Lincoln and London: University of Nebraska Press, 1964. Reprint. Lincoln: Bison, 1992.

Graf, Max. *Legend of a Musical City.* New York: Philosophical Library, 1945.

———. *Composer and Critic: Two Hundred Years of Musical Criticism.* New York: W. W. Norton and Co., 1946.

Gutman, Robert W. *Richard Wagner: The Man, His Mind, and His Music.* San Diego and New York: Harcourt Brace Jovanovich, 1990.

Hancock, Virginia. *Brahms's Choral Compositions and His Library of Early Music.* Ann Arbor: UMI Research Press, 1983.

———. "Brahms's Performance of Early Choral Music." *19th-Century Music* VIII/2, Fall 1984.

Hanslick, Eduard. *Hanslick's Music Criticism.* Translated and edited by Henry Pleasants. New York: Penguin Books, 1963. Reprint. New York: Dover Publications, 1988.

———. "Brahms's Newest Instrumental Compositions." Translated by Susan Gillespie. In *Brahms and His World,* edited by Walter Frisch. Princeton, N.J.: Princeton University Press, 1990.

———. "Memories and Letters." Translated by Susan Gillespie. In *Brahms and His World,* edited by Walter Frisch. Princeton, N.J.: Princeton University Press, 1990.

Henschel, George. *Personal Recollections of Johannes Brahms: Some of His Letters to and Pages from a Journal Kept by George Henschel.* 1907 Reprint. Boston: Gorham Press, 1978.

Heuberger, Richard. *Erinnerungen an Johannes Brahms.* Tutzing: Hans Schneider, 1976.

Hofmann, Renate and Kurt. *Johannes Brahms: Zeittafel zu Leben und Werk.* Tutzing: Hans Schneider, 1993.

Holde, Arthur. "Suppressed Passages in the Brahms-Joachim Correspondence, Published for the First Time." *The Musical Quarterly* 45/3, 1959.

Horne, William. "Brahms's Düsseldorf Suite Study and His Intermezzo, Opus 116, No. 2." *The Musical Quarterly* 45/3, Spring 1989.

Hughes, Holly Elaine. *Richard Heuberger's* Erinnerungen an Johannes Brahms: *The Life, Work, and Times of Johannes Brahms as Revealed by a Contemporary.* M.A. thesis, Ball State University, 1987.

Huneker, James. *Mezzotints in Modern Music.* 2d ed. New York: Charles Scribner's Sons, 1989.

Jacobsen, Christiane. *Johannes Brahms: Leben und Werk.* Wiesbaden: Breitkopf & Härtel, 1983.

Jacobson, Bernard. *The Music of Johannes Brahms.* London: Tantivy Press, 1977.

Janik, Allan, and Stephen Toulmin. *Wittgenstein's Vienna.* New York and London: Touchstone Books, 1973.

Jenner, Gustav. "Johannes Brahms as Man, Teacher, and Artist." Translated by Susan Gillespie. In *Brahms and His World,* edited by Walter Frisch. Princeton, N.J.: Princeton University Press, 1990.

Johannes Brahms in Baden-Baden und Karlsruhe. Catalogue of an exhibition of the Badischen Landesbibliothek in Karlsruhe, 1983.

Joseph, Charles M. "Origins of Brahms's Structural Control." *College Music Symposium* 21/1, 1981.

Kalbeck, Max. *Johannes Brahms.* 1904–14. Reprint. 4 vols. Tutzing: Hans Schneider, 1976.

———, ed. *Johannes Brahms: The Herzogenberg Correspondence.* Translated by Hannah Bryant. 1909. Reprint. New York: Da Capo Press, 1987.

Kaufmann, Paul. "Brahms-Erinnerungen." *Die Musik* XXV/10, July 1933.

Keller, Will (commentary). *Hamburg in Frühen Photographhien 1848–1888.* Hamburg: Sammlung Bokelberg, n.d.

Keys, Ivor. *Brahms Chamber Music.* Seattle: University of Washington Press, 1974.

———. *Johannes Brahms.* Portland, Ore.,: Amadeus Press, 1989.

Kramer, Lawrence. *Music and Poetry: The Nineteenth Century and After.* Berkeley and Los Angeles: University of California Press, 1984.

Krebs, Carl, ed. *Des jungen Kreislers Schatzkästlein: Aussprüche von Dichtern, Philosophen und Künstlern, Zusammengetragen durch Johannes Brahms.* Berlin: Verlag der Deutsches Brahmsgesellschaft, 1909.

Kross, Siegfried. "Brahms and E. T. A. Hoffmann." *19th-Century Music* 4, 1982.

———. "Brahms the Symphonist." In *Brahms: Biographical, Documentary and Analytical Studies,* edited by Robert Pascall. Cambridge and New York: Cambridge University Press, 1983.

Krummacher, Friedhelm. "Reception and Analysis: On the Brahms Quartets, Op. 51, Nos. 1 and 2." *19th-Century Music* XVIII/1, Summer 1994.

LaGrange, Henry-Louis de. *Mahler,* vol. I. New York: Doubleday & Co., 1973.

Langer, Suzanne. *Feeling and Form.* New York: Charles Scribner's Sons, 1953.

Latham, Ian. *Joseph Maria Olbrich.* New York: Rizzoli, 1980.

Leyen, Rudolf von der. *Johannes Brahms als Mensch und Freund.* Düsseldorf and Leipzig: Verlag von Karl Robert Langewiesche, 1905.

Litzmann, Berthold. *Clara Schumann: An Artist's Life, Based on Material Found in Diaries and Letters.* Vol. II. Translated from the 5th ed. by Grace E. Hadow. New York: Vienna House, 1972.

———, ed. *Letters of Clara Schumann and Johannes Brahms, 1853–1896.* London, 1927. Reprint. Westport, Conn.: Hyperion Press, 1979.

———, ed. *Clara Schumann–Johannes Brahms: Briefe aus den Jahren 1853–1896.* 2 vols. Leipzig: Breitkopf & Härtel, 1927.

MacDonald, Malcolm. *Brahms.* New York: Schirmer Books, 1990.

Mason, Daniel Gregory. *The Chamber Music of Brahms.* New York: Macmillan, 1933.

May, Florence. *The Life of Johannes Brahms.* 2 vols. 1905. Reprint. Neptune City, N.J.: Paganiniana Publications, 1981.

McColl, Sandra. *Music Criticism in Vienna 1896–1897: Critically Moving Forms.* Oxford: Clarendon Press, 1996.

McCorkle, Donald M., ed. *Johannes Brahms: Variations on a Theme of Haydn.* Critical score. New York: W. W. Norton and Co., 1976.

McCorkle, Margit L. *Johannes Brahms: Thematisch-Bibliographisches Werkverzeichnis.* Munich: G. Henle Verlag, 1984.

————, with Donald M. McCorkle. "Five Fundamental Obstacles in Brahms Source Research." *Acta musicologiae* 48/2, 1976.

Morton, Frederic. *A Nervous Splendor: Vienna 1888/1889.* New York: Penguin Books, 1979.

Musgrave, Michael. "Brahms the Progressive: Another View." *The Musical Times,* May 1971.

————. "Brahms's First Symphony: Thematic Coherence and Its Secret Origin." *Music Analysis* 2/2, July 1983.

————. "The Cultural World of Brahms." In *Brahms: Biographical Documentary and Analytical Studies,* edited by Robert Pascall. Cambridge and New York: Cambridge University Press, 1983.

————. "Frei aber Froh: A Reconsideration." *19th-Century Music* 3/3, March 1980.

————. "Historical Influences in the Growth of Brahms's 'Requiem.'" *Music and Letters* 53/1, 1972.

————. *The Music of Brahms.* London and Boston: Routledge & Kegan Paul, 1985.

————, ed. *Brahms 2: Biographical, Documentary and Analytical Studies.* Cambridge and New York: Cambridge University Press, 1987.

Neighbor, Oliver. "Brahms and Schumann: Two Opus Nines and Beyond." *19th-Century Music* 7/84, April 1984.

Niemann, Walter. *Brahms.* Translated by Catherine Alison Phillips. New York: Tudor Publishing Company, 1945.

Notley, Margaret. "Brahms as Liberal: Genre, Style, and Politics in Late Nineteenth-Century Vienna." *19th-Century Music* XVII/2, Fall 1993.

Ostwald, Peter. *Schumann: The Inner Voices of a Musical Genius.* Boston: Northeastern University Press, 1985.

————. "Johannes Brahms, Solitary Altruist." In *Brahms and His World,* edited by Walter Frisch. Princeton, N.J.: Princeton University Press, 1990.

Pascall, Robert. "Brahms and Schubert." *The Musical Times* 116/1592, 1975.

————. "The Publication of Brahms's Third Symphony: A Crisis in Dissemination." In *Brahms Studies,* edited by George S. Bozarth. Oxford: Clarendon Press, 1990.

————. "Brahms's First Symphony Slow Movement." *The Musical Times.* October 1981.

————, ed. *Brahms: Biographical, Documentary and Analytical Studies.* Cambridge and New York: Cambridge University Press, 1983.

Pulver, Jeffrey. "Brahms and the Influence of Joachim." *The Musical Times* 1/1/1925.

Quigley, Thomas. *Johannes Brahms: An Annotated Bibliography of the Literature Through 1982.* Metuchen, N.J., and London: Scarecrow Press, 1990.

Reich, Nancy B. *Clara Schumann: The Artist and the Woman.* New York: Cornell University Press, 1985.

Reynolds, Christopher. "A Choral Symphony by Brahms?" *19th-Century Music* IX/1, 1985.

Rosen, Charles. "Influence: Plagiarism and Inspiration." *19th-Century Music* IV/2, 1980.

———. *Sonata Forms.* New York and London: W. W. Norton and Co., 1980.

———. *The Romantic Generation.* Cambridge: Harvard University Press, 1995.

Roses, Daniel F., M. D. "Brahms and Billroth." *Newsletter of the American Brahms Society* V/1, Spring 1987.

Sams, Eric. "Brahms and His Musical Love Letters." *Musical Times* 112, April 1971.

———. "Brahms and His Clara Themes." *Musical Times* 112, May 1971.

———. *Brahms Songs.* Seattle: University of Washington Press, 1972.

Schauffler, Robert Haven. *The Unknown Brahms: His Life, Character and Works; Based on New Material.* New York: Dodd, Mead and Company, 1933.

Schoenberg, Arnold. "Brahms the Progressive." In *Style and Idea: Selected Writings of Arnold Schoenberg,* edited by Leonard Stein, with translations by Leo Black. 1975. Rev. ed. Berkeley and Los Angeles: University of California Press, 1984.

Schonberg, Harold C. *The Great Pianists: From Mozart to the Present.* Rev. ed. New York: Simon and Schuster, 1987.

Schönzeler, Hans-Hubert. *Dvořák.* London and New York: Marion Boyars, 1984.

Schorske, Carl E. *Fin-de-siècle Vienna: Politics and Culture.* New York: Vintage Books, 1981.

Schubert, Giselher. "Themes and Double Themes: The Problem of the Symphonic in Brahms." *19th-Century Music* XVIII/1, Summer 1994.

Schumann, Eugenie. *The Schumanns and Johannes Brahms.* 1927. Reprint. Freeport, N.Y.: Books for Libraries Press, 1970.

Schumann, Ferdinand. "Brahms and Clara Schumann." *The Musical Quarterly* 2/4, October 1916.

Schumann, Robert. *Schumann on Music.* Translated and edited by Henry Pleasants. 1965. Revised. New York: Dover Publications, 1988.

Schwartz, Boris. "Joseph Joachim and the Genesis of Brahms's Violin Concerto." *The Musical Quarterly* 69/4, Fall 1983.

Sisman, Elaine R. "Brahms and Variation Canon." *19th-Century Music* XIV/2, Fall 1990.

Smyth, Ethel. *The Memoirs of Ethel Smyth.* Abridged and introduced by Ronald Crichton. New York: Viking, 1987.

Specht, Richard. *Johannes Brahms.* Translated by Eric Blom. London and Toronto: J. M. Dent and Sons, 1930.

Stark, Lucien. *A Guide to the Solo Songs of Johannes Brahms.* Bloomington and Indianapolis: Indiana University Press, 1995.

Stephenson, Kurt, ed. *Johannes Brahms in seiner Familie: Der Briefwechsel.* Hamburg: Dr. Ernst Hauswedell & Co., 1973.

Stojowski, Sigismond. "Recollections of Brahms." *The Musical Quarterly* 19/2, 1933.

Storck, Karl, ed. *The Letters of Robert Schumann*. Translated by Hannah Bryant. New York: E. P. Dutton and Co., 1907.

Strunk, Oliver. *Source Readings in Music History*. New York and London: W. W. Norton & Co., 1965.

Thatcher, David S. "Nietzsche and Brahms: A Forgotten Relationship." *Music and Letters* LIV/3, July 1973.

Tovey, Donald Francis. *Essays in Musical Analysis*. 6 vols. London and New York: Oxford University Press, 1948.

Wagner, Cosima. *Diaries*. Vol. II. New York and London: Harcourt Brace Jovanovich, 1977.

Waissenberger, Robert, ed. *Vienna in the Biedermeier Era*. New York: Mallard Press, 1986.

Walker, Alan. *Franz Liszt*. Vol. II, *The Weimar Years*. London and Boston: Faber and Faber, 1989.

Walzel, Oskar. *German Romanticism*. 1932. Reprint. New York: Frederick Unger Publishing Co., 1965.

Watson, Derek. *Richard Wagner: A Biography*. New York: Schirmer Books, 1979.

Weiss, Piero. *Letters of Composers Through Six Centuries*. Philadelphia and New York: Chilton Book Co., 1967.

———, and Richard Taruskin. *Music in the Western World: A History in Documents*. New York and London: Schirmer Books, 1984.

Zemlinsky, Alexander von, and Karl Weigl. "Brahms and the Newer Generation: Personal Reminiscences." In *Brahms and His World*, edited by Walter Frisch. Princeton, N.J.: Princeton University Press, 1990.

Index

Grateful acknowledgment is made to the following for permission to reprint previously published material:

DOVER PUBLICATIONS, INC.: Lyric excerpts from *Alto Rhapsody; Complete Songs for Solo Voice and Piano, Series I; Songs, Series II; Songs, Series III*, translated by Stanley Appelbaum; excerpts from *Hanslick's Music Criticisms* by Eduard Hanslick, translated and edited by Henry Pleasants (Dover Publications, Inc., Mineola, New York, 1988). Reprinted by permission of Dover Publications, Inc.

OXFORD UNIVERSITY PRESS: Excerpt from "Suppressed Passages in the Brahms-Joachim Correspondence Published for the First Time" by Arthur Holde (*The Musical Quarterly*, 45/3, 1959, pp. 318–320); excerpt from "Nietzsche and Brahms: A Forgotten Relationship" by David Thatcher (*Music and Letters*, LIV/3, July 1973). Reprinted by permission of Oxford University Press, Oxford, England.

UNIVERSITY OF OKLAHOMA PRESS: Excerpts from *Johannes Brahms and Theodor Billroth: Letters from a Musical Friendship* by Johannes Brahms, translated by Hans Barkan (University of Oklahoma Press, Norman, Oklahoma, 1957), copyright © 1957 by the University of Oklahoma Press. Reprinted by permission of the University of Oklahoma Press.

JAN SWAFFORD received degrees from Harvard and the Yale School of Music and is the author of *Charles Ives: A Life with Music*, which was a finalist for the 1996 National Book Critics Circle Award for biography, won the PEN/Winship Award, and was hailed by *Newsweek* as "one of the best biographies in recent memory." He is also the author of *The Vintage Guide to Classical Music* and a featured commentator on NPR's *Performance Today*. An award-winning composer whose work has been widely performed by ensembles here and abroad, he lives in eastern Massachusetts.

A NOTE ON THE TYPE

This book was set in Janson, a typeface long thought to have been made by the Dutchman Anton Janson, who was a practicing typefounder in Leipzig during the years 1668–1687. However, it has been conclusively demonstrated that these types are actually the work of Nicholas Kis (1650–1702), a Hungarian, who most probably learned his trade from the master Dutch typefounder Dirk Voskens. The type is an excellent example of the influential and sturdy Dutch types that prevailed in England up to the time William Caslon (1692–1766) developed his own incomparable designs from them.

Composed by NK Graphics, Keene, New Hampshire
Printed and bound by Quebecor Printing, Martinsburg, West Virginia
Designed by Robert C. Olsson